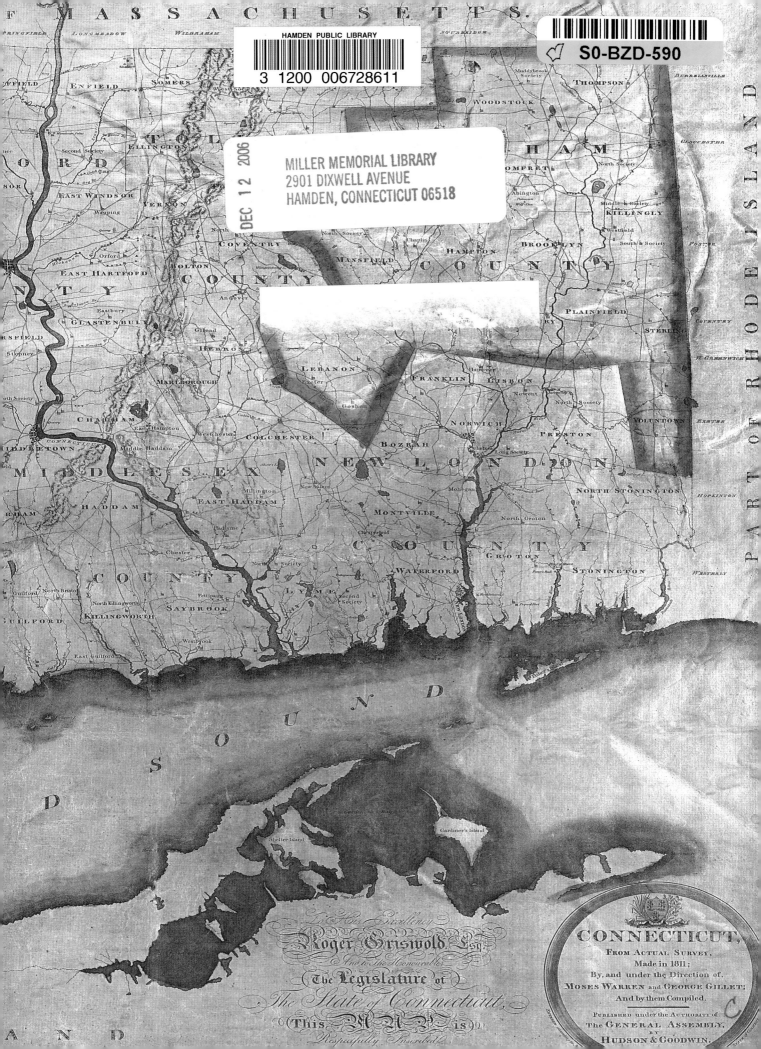

MASSACHUSETTS.

PART OF RHODE ISLAND

To His Excellency
Roger Griswold Esq.
And to The Honourable
The Legislature of
The State of Connecticut,
This MAP is
Respectfully Inscribed

CONNECTICUT,
FROM ACTUAL SURVEY,
Made in 1811;
By, and under the Direction of,
MOSES WARREN and GEORGE GILLET;
And by them Compiled.
PUBLISHED under the AUTHORITY of
The GENERAL ASSEMBLY,
BY
HUDSON & GOODWIN.

Voices of the New Republic
Connecticut Towns 1800-1832

Volume II: What We Think

The Connecticut Academy of Arts and Sciences
2001-2003 Officers

Voices of the New Republic

Connecticut Towns 1800-1832
Volume II: What We Think

Edited by Howard R. Lamar
Associate Editor Carolyn C. Cooper

Memoirs of the Connecticut Academy of Arts and Sciences
Volume XXVII
New Haven, Connecticut

First published in 2003 by the Academy, New Haven, Connecticut.
Printed and bound in the United States of America.

This book was typeset in Baskerville Old Face
Designed by Leslie Wilson, Inkmasters, West Haven, Connecticut
Printed by
Phoenix Color, Hagerstown, Maryland

The paper in this publication meets the minimum requirements of American National Standard for Information
Sciences—Permanence of Paper for Printed Library Materials ANSI Z39.48-1984

Voices of the New Republic : Connecticut towns, 1800-1832.
v. cm.—(Memoirs of the Connecticut Academy of Arts and Sciences ; v. 26-27)
Includes bibliographical references and indexes.
Contents: v. 1. What they said / edited by Christopher P. Bickford ;
associate editors, Carolyn C. Cooper and Sandra L. Rux—
v. 2. What we think / edited by Howard R. Lamar ;
associate editor, Carolyn C. Cooper.
ISBN 1-878508-24-5 (v. 1 : hardcover : alk. paper)
ISBN 1-878508-25-6 (v. 2 : hardcover : alk. paper)
1. Connecticut—History—1775-1865. 2. Connecticut—History,
Local. 3. Cities and towns—Connecticut—History—19th century.
4. Connecticut—Social life and customs—19th century. 5. City
and town life—Connecticut—History—19th century.
I. Bickford, Christopher P. II. Lamar, Howard Roberts. III. Series: Memoirs
of the Connecticut Academy of Arts & Sciences. v. 26-27.
Q11 .C85 vol. 26 etc. F99] 081 s—dc21 [974.6'03] 2003011446

Publications of the Connecticut Academy of Arts and Sciences
can be obtained directly from the
Academy, P.O. Box 208211, New Haven, Connecticut 06520-8211
caas@yale.edu

To the founders of the Connecticut Academy of Arts and Sciences
and to their collective vision of pursuing human happiness
through increasing knowledge.

Contents

To

Sir,

THE CONNECTICUT ACADEMY OF ARTS AND SCIENCES, defirous of contributing to the collection and propagation of ufeful knowledge, and of procuring the materials for a Statiftical Hiftory of Connecticut, requeft you to furnifh them with every fpecies of information which it may be in your power to obtain; relative to the Geography, Natural, Civil and Political Hiftory, Agriculture, Manufactures and Commerce of the State of Connecticut. Among the articles to which the Academy requeft your attention are the following:

1ft. The Hiftory of the fettlement of the Town or Society in which you refide—the fituation and extent of each—the number of focieties, fchool diftricts and fchool houfes in the Town—by what means the Lands were obtained from the Indians, whether by purchafe or conqueft.—The number of foreigners and of what country.

2d. The Indian names of places, mountains, rivers, lakes and ponds within the town; alfo any remarkable occurrences in the hiftory of the Indians, their cuftoms, mythology, battles, burying places, monuments, forts and any other traces of their fettlement—the tribe, to which they belong—their prefent number and fituation, as to fubfiftence, vices, &c.

3d. The face of the country, in regard to mountains, hills, vallies and plains, rocks, ftones, clay, fand, nature of the foil—curiofities natural and artificial, antiquities, monumental infcriptions elucidating points of hiftory.

4th. Rivers, ftreams, fprings (if remarkable) efpecially mineral and medicinal fprings; lakes and ponds, their fources and ufes as to mills, navigation and the production of fifh, or the watering of lands.—Cataracts or falls. Wells, their depth on different grounds.—Aqueducts or pipes for conveying water to families—the expence by the rod—plenty or fcarcity of water for domeftic ufes—change of quality within the prefent age—failure of ftreams in confequence of clearing the land,

increafe or decreafe of water in fprings and wells.—Accidents by damps or mephitic air in wells or other places, the time and other circumftances attending them.

5th. Mines and Minerals, efpecially thofe moft ufeful, as iron, copper, lead, filver, fulpher;—alfo, quarries of ftone, with the kind and quality of the ftone, and its diftance from navigable water.

6th. What was the natural or original growth of timber and wood, and what the variations in the fpecies on fucceffive cuttings—whether the timber is plenty or fcarce, increafing or decreafing, and the caufes;—the beft method of increafing the quantity—the beft time in the year for falling timber for durability and wood for fuel.—The fugar maple tree, and the quantity and quality of fugar made—improvements in making and refining it—the beft mode of procuring the fap without injuring the tree.—Quantity, quality and price of lumber of all kinds—diftance from navigable water.

7th. Fuel of all kinds, as wood, coal, peat, or turf—the quantity and quality—diftance

from navigable water—increafe or decreafe of fuel and price of the feveral kinds.

8th. Furnaces, forges and mills;—their fituation, conveniences and quantity of work performed. In particular a defcription of any curious machinery, by which the labor of man is abridged, and the operation of the mechanical powers fimplified and applied to ufeful purpofes.

9th. Agriculture; increafe or decreafe of the price of land, within the memory of the prefent generation—price of provifions and labor in the feveral occupations—the kinds of grain cultivated, quantity of each produced on an acre, and total quantity in a year—quantity of flour and kiln dried meal exported annually—quantity of hemp and flax raifed, and the beft mode of raifing, rotting and dreffing them—the quantity of flax and flaxfeed exported—quantity of land planted with potatoes, and fown with turnips, rotation of crops beft fuited to various foils—improvements by means of artificial graffes, improvements by draining and diking marfhes, meadows and ponds.

10th. Manures; the best for particular soils, and the best time and mode of applying them —as stable manure, lime, lime stone, shells, ashes, salt, compost, marl, swamp, creek and sea mud, plaister of paris, and sea weed,— the preparation best suited for particular crops —the best means of increasing manures—the effects of irrigation or watering lands.

11th. The best seed time and harvest time; —best time and modes of preparing lands for seeding, best modes of extirpating weeds and of preserving grains from insects. The effects of a change of seed.

12th. Mode of cultivation whether by oxen or horses—the expense, advantages and disadvantages of each—Number of teams—the number and kinds of waggons, carts, ploughs, harrows, drills, winnowing and threshing machines now in use—improvements in them both as to utility and cheapness. Fences; the materials and mode of erecting them, kinds most used—increase or decrease of timber for fencing—the best kinds of trees or shrubs for hedges, and the means of propagating them.

13th. Uncommon fruits and garden vegetables, native or imported—The soils on which particular fruits and vegetables best flourish, and the best modes of cultivating them—quantity of cider made annually— quantity exported—best mode of making, improving and preserving it; best mode of preserving apples and other fruits during the winter—improvements by ingrafting and innoculation—best time and mode of pruning —state of gardening.

14th. Number of tenants on leased lands; quantity of lands leased and the rent; the state of cultivation of leased lands compared with that in the hands of proprietors. Emigrations from the Town or Society. The number of persons convicted of capital crimes, and instances of suicide, within twenty years, or since the Town was settled, and whether committed by natives or foreigners. The time when pleasure carriages were first used.

15th. Number of sheep and swine, quantity of pork, beef, butter and cheese annually sent to market; the best mode of multiplying, improving, feeding and fattening sheep, swine,

neat cattle and horses; their diseases, description of them, and the best mode of preventing and curing them.

16th. Manufactures; distinguishing the kinds and quantity made in families and in manufactories; the market for them. The history of any useful manufacture including its increase and decline, and the causes.

17th. Breweries; time of their introduction—the kinds and quantity of beer made.

18th. Fisheries; the kinds, quantity and value of fish taken—best mode of curing them; the market. The years when shell and other fish have been unusually lean or sickly, and when they have declined, disappeared or perished, from causes known or unknown. The best modes of multiplying and preserving shell fish.

19th. Ship building; its increase or decline —harbors, depth of water, direction of the channels, obstruction, land marks and directions for entrance; the year when the first vessel was built, and the progress of trade. The means of facilitating transportation by land or water.

20th. Roads and Bridges; the present state of them, annual expence and mode of defraying it; description of bridges remarkable for elegance or utility: the best mode of securing bridges from the effects of frost, floods and sea worms; the kinds of timber not subject to be eaten by sea worms.

21st. Ferries; their situation, and whether public or private property—The places near them, where bridges may be erected, and probably made permanent.

22d. Wild animals, now or heretofore known; their increase or decrease, and from what causes—new species, migration and natural history of birds.

23d. Natural history of plants, their kinds, whether noxious or useful; new species, time of their introduction, their progress; effects of the barberry and other noxious plants, and the best modes of extirpating them.

24th. Places of public worship; their number, and the denomination to which they belong—the rise of congregations and various sects, the names of the successive clergymen, the time of their settlement and exit—

noticies of any eminent clergymen ; the salaries of clergymen and the funds by which religious worship is maintained.

25th. Academies and Schools ; in what manner supported ; number of winter and summer schools—the time they are kept in each year, whether by male or female instructors—number of scholars, salaries or wages of teachers ; kinds of knowledge taught ; improvements in the mode of instruction ; prices of board and expences of schooling.

26th. Poor ; their number, whether natives or foreigners ; their former occupations, the expence of maintaining them, the mode best calculated to unite humanity with œconomy in their support—the means by which they were reduced to want, or inability to labour.

27th. Free blacks ; their number, vices and modes of life, their industry and success in acquiring property ; whether those born free are more ingenious, industrious and virtuous, than those who were emancipated after arriving to adult years.

28th. Inns or Taverns—their number.

29th. Climate and Diseases ; variations in seasons and in diseasons from clearing lands, draining swamps and the like causes ; the diseases most prevalent in high and low situations, near streams of running water, or marsh and stagnant water, an the north and south sides of hills and mountains, and on different soils ; remarkable instances of diseases and mortality among animals of various kinds. Meteorological observations. Register of marriages, births and deaths, noting the sex, occupations, ages and diseases of those who die. Remarkable instances of longevity ; the local situation—the occupation and the habits of life of those who arrive to a great age, as also their temper, whether cheerful or melancholic, quiet or discontented.

30th. Remarkable seasons or occurrences in the natural world ; as tempest, rain, hail, snow, and inundations by which injury has been sustained, the time when they happened ; unusual insects, or usual insects in unusual numbers ; time of their appearance and disappearance, their generation and transformations ; injury sustained by them ; unusual death of

insects ; best modes of destroying noxious insects or preventing their ravages.

31st. Unsual failure of crops from causes known or unknown ; the years when it occurred, and the temperature of the seasons. An explication of the causes and phenomena of blast, mildew, rust, honey dew, bursting of vegetables, diseases and death of plants, trees or shrubs ; the times when they occured.

32d. Distinguished characters, who have been natives or residents in the town ; improvements in arts and sciences, and the authors of them ; inventors of curious machines ; vices, amusements, attention to civil and religious institutions ; remarkable instances of liberality, heroism or other virtue. Libraries ; when established and the number of volumes. Charitable institutions and endowments. Associations for the purpose of improvement or humanity. Benefactions to pious and charitable uses.

It is not expected, that in all the above mentioned articles information can be given by each or perhaps any gentleman to whom this letter is addressed ; but it is hoped and

believed that the magnitude of the object in view, will induce every one, to spare no pains in obtaining and communicating such information as shall be in his power. Should the exertion for this purpose be general and active, all the necessary information will probably be collected.

In Scotland, the first, and it is supposed, the only successful attempt of this nature, has been carried into complete execution, by a similar application to the clergymen, and a few other enlightened persons in that country.

It is rationally believed, that efforts equally-spirited and efficacious will be made in Connecticut ; should this be the case, our state will have the honor of leading in this important field of knowledge.

Every piece of information on the subject specified will contribute to the great object in view, and will be gratefully received by this Academy.

By order of the Academy,
SIMEON BALDWIN,
Recording Secretary.

New-Haven, March 19th, 1802.

THE *Connecticut Academy of Arts and Sicences,* again requeſt the attention of the friends of Science in this State, to the object of their Circular Letter of the 1ſt of January 1800, viz. The collection of materials for a Statiſtical Hiſtory of Connecticut.

While they acknowledge themſelves greatly indebted to thoſe gentlemen who have already favoured them with anſwers, for the valuable information contained in them, they earneſtly ſolicit the further attention of the public to the ſame objects.

From experiments which have been ſucceſsfully made in ſeveral Towns, they are perſuaded, that arragements may be formed, which will greatly facilitate the buſineſs, and contribute to render the anſwers comprehenſive and the information juſt. They therefore beg leave to recommend the following plan :

That ſuch gentlemen as are friendly to the deſign, whether heretofore particularly addreſſed or not ; hold ſtated meetings, within their reſpective Towns or Pariſhes.

That they diſtribute the ſeveral queſtions among the members, ſo as to divide the labor and confine the enquiries of each perſon to ſpecific objects.

That in their meetings they examine and digeſt the ſeveral anſwers, which they may receive ; and that after all the anſwers, which can be attained, ſhall have been received, ſuch of them as ſhall be approved, be drawn up in a regular manner, as conciſely as the ſubject will admit, and tranſmitted to the Academy.

The Academy beg leave further to obſerve, that, from the information they have gained on this ſubject, they have reaſon to believe, all the difficulties which have hitherto attended it, will vaniſh whenever ſuch ſocieties ſhall be univerſally formed. The pleaſure which thinking and inquiſitive men, will reciprocally communicate on topics ſo intereſting—the improvement which each will find in purſuing his own enquiries and in learning the reſult of the enquiries of others, and the habit of critical and extenſive reſearch neceſſarily created, will amply repay the trouble and inconvenience of the experiment.

The Academy alſo flatter themſelves, that a permanent and widely diffuſed ſpirit of inveſtigation, particularly reſpecting the vaſt field of uſeful knowledge opened to the intelligent mind, by the natural and ſocial ſtate of this Country, will be an honorable as well as uſeful effect of a general accordance with this propoſal.

By Order of the Academy,
STEPHEN TWINING, *Recording Secretary.*

The Controversial History of Connecticut

in the Early National Period, 1790-1830

Howard R. Lamar and Carolyn C. Cooper

The Connecticut Academy of Arts and Sciences (CAAS) decided in 1996 that as part of its bicentennial celebration it would publish in one volume all the responses that could be found to the survey of Connecticut towns it had initiated in 1800. The Academy also decided to obtain the views of an interdisciplinary panel of contemporary scholars on the significance of those responses. Individually, the essays these scholars have produced after studying the Town Reports offer surprising discoveries. Together, they offer a fresh and different picture of life between 1790 and 1830 from what we have learned in older, traditional histories of Connecticut.

Indeed, even these new scholars do not fully agree how to characterize that period of Connecticut history. Within living memory at that time, Connecticut citizens had gained political independence from the old world; were they now boldly shaping a new world, or did they resume the "steady habits" of their pre-Revolutionary forefathers? Were they quick or slow to adopt new methods in agriculture and industry? Were they helpful or mean to their poor, their ex-slaves, their remaining Native American neighbors? Were they observant or careless of their natural environment? Economically thriving or hard up? Healthy or sick? Law-abiding or criminal? Vigorous or lazy? Religious or irreligious? These, in fact, were some of the questions that the Connecticut Academy seemed to be aiming at in their questionnaire, or "Solicitation Letter" of 1800, and for which our essayists were now also seeking retrospective answers topic by topic, instead of town by town.

To address such questions, essayists have interpreted, to varying extent, not only what the available Town Reports said, but also, reading between the lines, the attitudes of the report writers. Stepping back still further, they have pondered the possible motives of the founding fathers of the Connecticut Academy, both in asking certain questions and more broadly, in initiating the survey at all. Was it simply, as their Solicitation Letter stated in 1800, because they were "desirous of contributing to the collection and propagation of useful

Timothy Dwight (1752-1817). President of the Connecticut Academy of Arts and Sciences 1799-1817; President of Yale College 1795-1817.

knowledge, and of procuring the materials for a Statistical History of Connecticut?" Christopher Bickford's introduction to the Town Reports in Volume I views the initial Statistical Accounts project as a very early social-scientific effort to provide information for enlightened governance of Connecticut, and presents evidence for considering charter member Noah Webster as the primary moving spirit behind it. Connecticut Academy correspondence with the federal government about the national census at that time strongly suggests the Academy wanted to set an example to the rest of the newly formed nation by expanding its scope of inquiry. (Fortunately for social science, the federal census-takers opted to keep a narrow scope in order to maximize response rate and consistency from census to census.)

In contrast, Richard Buel's essay in this volume argues that Academy president Timothy Dwight was the major shaper of the project. Conceding that the 21 founding members of the Academy shared "a common commitment to the revolutionary enterprise of indefinite improvement through the development and dissemination of knowledge," Buel says the real purpose of Dwight's survey was to create "a detailed description of Congregational Connecticut as an exemplary society." Dwight's motive, according to Buel, was that he felt the Revolution had caused a moral decline in American society and that State support of Congregationalism itself was being threatened by rival denominations in Connecticut: the Episcopalians, the Baptists, and the Methodists. Furthermore, Dwight felt Jefferson's election to the presidency in 1800 constituted a threat both to the Christian religion and to Federalist control of Connecticut government. No questions in the survey asked for election results, but Buel finds a bias in the response rate of the various towns according to their Federalist vote, and deems it not coincidental that the Town Reports' answers to the Academy's questions accord with Dwight's desire to show Connecticut to be a staunchly moral and Congregationalist state and therefore a model to the nation.

Ironically, Dwight was as enamored of agriculture as was Thomas Jefferson, the political figure he hated most. Like Dwight, Jefferson was proud of the new nation and assumed that its "sturdy yeomen" could create a great agricultural republic. And as Christopher Bickford has noted in his introduction to Volume I, Jefferson's famous *Notes on the State of Virginia*, first published in 1785, was in response to a set of assertions about America sent to him by the Comte de Buffon and constituted a precedent to the CAAS assumption that one "literary gentleman" per locality would suffice to speak for that town.

"Piety and patriotism ought to be united," noted an author of the Farmington Report, "& that government is best which is under the due influence of both." Similarly, Timothy Dwight and many other Connecticut citizens of his and preceding generations could not conceive of a society in which Christianity, and preferably Congregational Protestantism, was not paramount. Two essays in this volume shed light on the problematic condition at that time of the traditional close relationship between the Congregational church and Connecticut civil government. Largely unremarked by the Town Reports, that relationship was undergoing radical change, which became official in 1818 when tax support for the Congregational Church was abolished. David Kling, in "A View from Above: The Town Reports As Ecclesiastical History," explains that what led up to this abolition was in part an inherent "Puritan tension between tribalism and exclusivism, between a territorial church and a believer's church." This tension mutated into divisions between "strict congregationalists" and "Presbyterians," revivalist "new lights" and scholastic "old lights," which were further complicated by interfamily squabbles and a growing notion by ministers that their "calling" need not confine them to one parish until death. Other denominations—especially Methodists—grew while the Congregationalists splintered.

Like Buel, Kling considers the Reports biased, not politically but denominationally. They dwell on Congregational history and neglect Methodists, Episcopalians, and Baptists. Most of the Reports, after all, were written by Congregational ministers, who knew (and cared) less about the other denominations. He also points out the Reports' chronological bias: "Between 1800 and 1832, when the first and last Town Reports were issued, the religious landscape of Connecticut was turned topsy-turvy," from the bottom up. Since many of the reports were written at the beginning of that period, their writers had little inkling of what was happening, but even if they did, the survey questions elicited answers only "from the top down," giving us material in plenty for ecclesiastical history, but only hints of the period's full religious history.

Gretchen T. Buggeln's essay deals both literally and metaphorically with "The Religious Landscape" as shown in the responses to the survey's inquiry about "Places of public worship." This was a period in which many congregations perceived their old meetinghouses as too plain and undistinguished from ordinary buildings and replaced them with larger, handsome churches, with steeples and bells. Buggeln interprets this not merely as a sign of greater affluence but as a reflection of an inner change in religious attitude that for many individuals was also expressed in the more emotional affirmations of religious experience characterized by the Second Great Awakening of 1790-1830. More fervently than before, church buildings were felt to be reserved for the special event of worship and therefore should be especially beautiful. Such refined buildings also demonstrated to the post-Revolutionary world that their congregations had successfully survived that turmoil and were living as civilized Christian communities.

Another subject of debate between the new historians and earlier histories of Connecticut's late colonial and early national period has centered on the quality of the State's agriculture. Earlier historians have said Connecticut agriculture was primitive, non-progressive, and often more only for family or communal subsistence than for surplus and commercial profit, this despite the fact that during the American Revolution Connecticut was called the "Granary of the Continental Army." New essays here on particular aspects of Connecticut agriculture come close to destroying the older, more negative view.

Kathy J. Cooke, in her essay on "Art and Science in Crop and Livestock Improvement" as evidenced in the Town Reports, concludes that farmers were obsessed with finding ways to control wheat rust and the Hessian fly, with fertilizing the soil, and with breeding better livestock. Similarly, in his essay "Fertile Farms Among the Stones," Paul E. Waggoner emphasizes how hard farmers worked to make farming a success. Rather than being a simple, routine, unchanging life, Waggoner argues, it was a story of unending change, with which the farmers contended energetically. Holly Izard's informative overview of "The State of Connecticut Agriculture in 1800" comes to similar conclusions, noting that by the mid-eighteenth century, in response to expanding markets in the colonies and overseas, farmers began using more of their lands for grains and livestock. "Pork, beef, and dairy products became staple exports, as was amply evident in many Town Reports." Izard finds that there was a general optimism about the state of agriculture, so that "nearly everywhere farmers were improving their yields and increasing market activity."

Nothing demonstrates the trend toward commercialization and expansion of Connecticut agriculture more dramatically than the increase in dairy products for sale. In "Connecticut's Home Dairies c. 1800: 'Of Too Great Utility to be Passed over in Silence,'" Caroline F. Sloat finds that dairying towns like Goshen and Litchfield were shipping hundreds of thousands of pounds of cheese to New Haven and thence to southern states and the West Indian islands. Fresh butter went to New York City from Fairfield County, while New London was a major port for exporting pork, beef, horses, cheese, and other farm products.

In an important related essay, "With 'Unshaken Heroism and Fortitude': Connecticut Women's Life and Work Two Hundred Years Ago," Ruth Barnes Moynihan demonstrates that women were not only the chief makers of butter and cheese for sale, but that the income from these products probably amounted to half the value of all town exports. Moreover, women were also busy manufacturing woolen and linen cloth, much of which also went to market. Because the CAAS Solicitation Letter asked no questions about what women did, Moynihan's essay is especially revealing about the role of women in the economy, rearing children, teaching school, and providing nursing care and herbal medicine for illness.

The nursing role was particularly important during recurrent epidemics of disease, for the training and professionalization of doctors in Connecticut was just beginning, as Toby A. Appel explains in her essay "Disease and Medicine in Connecticut around 1800." The causes and transmissions of disease were not yet well understood, so prevention was difficult. For instance, a few towns answering the Academy's questions in Article 29 on "Climate and diseases" blamed mill ponds for "bad air" or miasma that made people sick, but had no notion that it was mosquitoes breeding in ponds that transmitted malaria and yellow fever. Ministers were often also physicians, and were in the best position to supply epidemiological information as well as to keep demographic records of births and deaths.

One of the survey's most intriguing "heads of inquiry," Article 27, sought information on free blacks in Connecticut: "their number, vices and modes of life; their industry and success in acquiring property..." Noah Webster appears to have been especially curious as to "whether those born free are more ingenious, industrious, and virtuous, than those who were emancipated after arriving to adult years." In his seminal essay, "'A Privilege and Elevation to Which We Look Forward with Pleasure': The Connecticut Academy of Arts and Sciences and Black Emancipation in Connecticut," Peter P. Hinks has noted that while Connecticut had 5,100 black slaves in the Colony in 1775, by 1806, twenty-two years after the Gradual Emancipation Act of 1784, 5,300 free blacks but also 1,000 black slaves lived in the state. He found that key organizers of the Connecticut slavery abolition movement in the 1790s were Timothy and Theodore Dwight, Noah Webster, Simeon Baldwin and others, many of whom were also founders of the Connecticut Academy. However, authors of the Town Reports who replied to this question were ambivalent in their responses to questions about the character of blacks; few deemed them "improved" by freedom. Tragically, the abolition movement faltered during the early 1800s, and members of the CAAS who had had high expectations for emancipation began to express support of the American Colonization Society, which formed to "return" blacks, even those born here, to Africa.

Most Town Reports used the past tense when addressing the question (under Article 2) of "the Indians...their present number and situation," saying either that they had disappeared or that only a few still lived on the margins of towns and villages. As Jill Martin demonstrates in her essay, "Invisible Indians: The Connecticut Academy Town Reports," that judgment of their demise was both premature and demeaning. Native Americans in Connecticut have not merely survived but have recently become nationally visible through their success in operating two highly successful casinos on the Mashentucket Pequot and Mohegan reservations.

One of the failings of the Town Reports was that because of the survey's strong emphasis on agriculture, they say little about the fact that Connecticut had always caught fish, built vessels, and carried on an extensive trade with the other states on the east coast and with the West Indies. Daniel Vickers, in writing his essay on Connecticut's "Fisheries," has noted that although cod, the great marketable fish on the northeastern Atlantic coast, were not to be found in Long Island Sound, Connecticut's residents did fish for shad, bass, alewives, and salmon that ascended the rivers every spring and summer. Meanwhile a less attractive but useful fish, the menhaden or "whitefish", which migrated through the waters of Long Island Sound in remarkable numbers, were harvested and used by Connecticut farmers as fertilizer. Shad were sold commercially, and with the growth of New York, offshore Connecticut fishermen began to supply that city with fresh cod, blackfish, bass, and lobster. Although Connecticut's participation in the rise of the whaling industry came later, by 1800 oystering had grown into an important part of the coastal economy of Connecticut, and grew greatly during the nineteenth century because of the New York market.

In writing about "Ships and Shipping in Connecticut, 1790-1811," William N. Peterson finds that seaborne commerce to the islands of the Caribbean as well as to sister states was the principal generator of maritime activity in Connecticut from 1790 to 1811. Supporting this trade was an active and growing shipbuilding industry as well as a nascent deep-sea fishing industry. Again, it must be noted that nearly all the Town Reports omitted answers about shipping, so we are dependent on outside sources of information. Peterson excites our imagination by listing the contents of the cargo manifest of one 43-ton schooner, the *Union*, bound from Fairfield to St. Eustatius in 1790, laden with Connecticut produce. The vessel carried beef, corn, oats, dried fish, pork, pickled fish, live hogs, horned cattle, horses, and rye flour. The *Union* returned in June with goods for Connecticut consumption: rum, brown sugar, coffee, salt, and one bale of cotton.

Besides the Caribbean market, New York City, as noted already, bought Connecticut products. In 1801, nearly 110 tons of cheese was shipped from New Haven alone to the City. Given such an expanding market, a new merchant class flourished. Their success was epitomized in the story of George and Nathaniel Griswold of Saybrook, who formed the well-known exporting and commission company, N.L. and G. Griswold, whose initials were often said to mean "No Loss and Great Gain." The rise in demand for Connecticut's farm products and increase in the fishing, shipping, and shipbuilding trade all undoubtedly led farmers to turn to grain, livestock, and dairy products that had high cash value and to think about distant markets.

As population grew and farmland didn't, it seems likely that some younger sons would go into shipping and merchandizing in preference to staying on the farm or emigrating westward. And although the industrialization of Connecticut would come after the War of 1812, residents were already engaged in quarrying, mining, ironmaking, and crafts in which they developed technological skills that presaged a dramatic industrial revolution.

Although the town reporters largely neglected the artisans that were already engaged in craft production of goods to sell, their important role has been brought to light by Edward S. Cooke, Jr. in his essay, "The Embedded Nature of Artisanal Activity in Connecticut, c. 1800." Cooke ascribes the small attention to craftsmen in the town reports to the fact that the Academy's survey did not ask about them, and in turn infers that the "learned men" leading the Academy valued artisanal activity below agricultural and manufactory production. In Cooke's view, then, both Jeffersonian agrarian values and Hamiltonian promotion of industrial change pushed the contribution of its skilled and productive craft workers below visibility. To overcome this invisibility, Cooke draws upon available tax assessment records for eighteen of the towns reporting by 1812, to flesh out a "landscape" of craft production in port towns, country centers and rural towns. He concludes that "The Academy and federal leaders'... focus on commercial activity and manufacturing investment foreshadows a drama that unfolded over the course of the nineteenth century: the decline in status of the craftsman from skilled contributor to a community's well-being to a mere mechanic."

Lest we assume that drama was already unfolding rapidly or evenly, Carolyn C. Cooper's essay, "Technology in Transition: Connecticut Industries 1800-1832," analyzes the Reports' evidence for new and old ways of producing things in households, mills, or factories, in order to assess the distance and pace of travel toward industrialization. She finds both medieval-style sawmills and lately-invented carding mills at waterpower sites on Connecticut streams, and that the pace was uneven between industries as Connecticut citizens tried out ways and places of producing textiles, flour, iron, shoes, oil, nails, timber, guns, tools, and alcoholic beverages. Some industries—such as textiles and shoes—were moving out of household production; others—such as iron and paper—had always been outside the home. Unlike England, where steam engines early and rapidly drew textile-making into crowded cities, Connecticut's abundant and dispersed small waterpower sites allowed pre-, proto-, semi-, and fully industrial workers to stay in the countryside.

Connecticut townspeople who engaged in crafts or industries, as well as Connecticut farmers going to market, literally traveled on an improving transportation infrastructure. Whereas early roads were torturous, making the arrival of "pleasure carriages" a rarity worth questioning in the Connecticut Academy's Solicitation Letter of 1800, a new taste for civic improvement and a shift from taxes to tolls helped create a useful network of passable roads in the next three decades. In his essay "Travel on Connecticut's Roads, Bridges, and Ferries, 1790-1830," Robert B. Gordon tells where and how the towns built them and paid for them.

Another alternative to farming was to go mining. No one struck gold in the mountainous Western Lands of Connecticut, and a "silver" mine turned out to be a scam. Nevertheless, hills were mined and quarried profitably for iron and stone, and the landscape changed accordingly. In "Mines, Minerals, Quarries, and Fuels: Connecticut, 1800-1832," Catherine and Brian Skinner outline the geological processes that had formed the several "terranes" of Connecticut, and the different rocks and minerals that the terranes yielded. Exploration and exploitation of the earth proceeded in ignorance of earth sciences, but geological and mineralogical research and teaching was beginning in the New Republic, and was conducted by

members of the Connecticut Academy, most notably by Benjamin Silliman. He helped Timothy Dwight answer the Academy's inquiry about "Mines and minerals...also quarries of stone..." (Article 5) when writing the New Haven Report.

As can easily be guessed, the farms, fisheries, mines, quarries, industries, and generally the inhabitation of Connecticut by more people affected their natural environment. The CAAS Solicitation Letter asked several questions bearing on environmental changes. One of these, Article 23, solicited information on "Wild animals, now or heretofore known; their increase or decrease, and from what causes." The answers were depressing. The Town Reports indicate the numbers of black bear, white-tailed deer, beaver, and wolves were all in sharp decline, and moose and the eastern mountain lion were virtually extinct, while passenger pigeons and wild turkeys soon would be gone, from loss of their forest habitat and from hunting. While town residents seemingly felt that the loss of the larger wild animals was a minor tragedy, they considered farms more important, and in any case big game was being replaced by a rise in small game. In their essay "Wild Animals in Connecticut's Changing Landscape," Harvey R. Smith and Timothy Clark provide a scientifically informed modern perspective on what happened to Connecticut's wild animals during the nineteenth century, but end on an optimistic note: "now, two hundred years later, many animal populations have been restored and people have developed new relationships with wild animals and natural habitats. Numerous laws at state and federal levels provide for the monitoring, management, and protection of a wide variety of species."

In his essay "Connecticut Woodlands," George McLean Milne explains the reasons Connecticut went from being almost completely forested when European colonists first arrived in the seventeenth century to mostly open land by the mid-nineteenth. Besides timber for construction and export, the settlers chopped down trees first simply to clear land for farming, and then continued in order to heat their homes with fuel wood. The shrinkage of woodlands was a concern of the Connecticut Academy survey. Article 6 asked not only about changes "in the species [of trees] on successive cuttings" of the "original growth of timber and wood" but also about the "quantity, quality and price of lumber"; Article 7 pressed for information on the quantity, quality, price, and distance from river transportation of fuel wood and its possible substitutes, coal and peat. The towns reported that wood was overwhelmingly the preferred fuel, and was increasing in price. The gradual introduction of shallower, more efficient fireplaces and even more efficient iron stoves helped slow the consumption of wood for fuel. But it was primarily the abandonment of farms in the late nineteenth century that allowed reforestation to take place and create our state forests today.

Botanist William A. Niering's essay makes "Some Botanical and Ecological Observations," pointing out the value of the Town Reports in testing hypotheses about tree and plant succession in Connecticut since colonization. The New Haven Town Report includes an extensive list of the trees and plants then growing there, which provides a botanical snapshot of that town c.

1811. Niering draws ecological observations from other town reports that also answered questions in Article 23 on "Natural history of plants; their kinds, whether noxious or useful; new species, time of their introduction, their progress."

The writers of Town Reports, then, were observant and curious about the natural world around them. In his essay "The Physical Environment of Connecticut Towns: Processes, Attitudes and Perceptions Then and Now," Robert M. Thorson dramatically captures the views of Connecticut citizens toward the natural environment and contrasts them with views today. Thorson's observations may have the most profound message of all for us today as we contemplate environmental policy for the twenty-first century. He cites a series of examples in which the report writers were able accurately to describe geological structure and phenomena—such as streambed changes or the Moodus noises—in their towns, before the teaching of geology was even begun in this country. Their direct observations as amateurs had a quality unknown in today's "laser-printed, electrically transmitted, remotely obtained data." He infers from what they wrote that they had a "sense of reasoned surrender to those things beyond human control" even while they were "busy regulating streams, draining swamps, shooting wildlife, and quarrying ledges." Thorson concludes that "environmental intimacy can still be achieved in our favorite places, but surrender cannot, for we now hold too much power over Nature," while "each of the forty-seven town reports—even when filtered over the gulf of two centuries—bespeaks a love of their state that few of us could capture today...These people were conversing with their environment, not just occupying it."

The "literary gentlemen" of the Connecticut Academy who asked questions about the towns of Connecticut in 1800 did not ask about political structure or processes. Probably they felt that was common knowledge already. Most historians of the early republic, however, have emphasized political history, and our essayists have referred to political events they deemed significant for explaining responses in the Town Reports. For instance, Richard Buel, as already mentioned, characterizes the launching of the Statistical Accounts as having occurred in the eye of a political storm between the Revolution and the War of 1812.

In the turmoil over Jefferson's Embargo of 1807 and the coming of the War of 1812, New England's economy was hard hit. Many Federalists in Connecticut and Massachusetts wanted to secede from the Union and were actually holding a convention in Hartford in 1814 to consider that possibility when peace was achieved by the Treaty of Ghent. In Connecticut the Federalist Party was repudiated, and by 1817 the Republicans had won control of the Connecticut Assembly. In 1818 Connecticut lawmakers drafted a new constitution in which there was a proviso disestablishing the Congregational Church. Perhaps fortunately for his own peace of mind, Timothy Dwight did not live to see that happen, for he died in 1817.

Even so, Dwight could have taken a wry comfort in the fact that the Second Great Awakening had drawn so many more people into church—albeit of other denominations—that Connecticut was now more devotedly Christian in character than it had been since the Revolution. He could also have found comfort in the fact that by writing about his own thirteen trips throughout New England and New York, he had gathered more information—enough for four volumes published posthumously in 1821-22—than the Connecticut Academy had been able to compile in response to its 1800 questionnaire.

A final commentary on the larger meaning of the town reports as interpreted by Christopher Collier in "The Ups and Downs of the Connecticut Town in the Pre-Industrial Era," and by Bruce C. Daniels in "The Remarkable Complexity of the Simple New England Town": in their heyday, the towns were vital little republics in which everyone seemed to play some role. In the lifetime of a single male resident he might well serve as a selectman or be sent to the Assembly or perform some other public service. In their town meetings every man had the right to speak, and church societies were run by laymen. There was a sense of independence from outside authority that was impressive, although Christopher Collier feels that must have contributed to a sense of isolation that could be stifling. Even so, they had a freedom that, among other things, led them to form new towns, join new religious societies, move to urban centers, to excel both in traditional crafts and in new industrial skills, and—to refuse to respond to the Connecticut Academy's questionnaire! As Bruce Daniels has written, "Connecticut towns were awash with the possibility of participatory political democracy." Indeed, he concluded that the town meeting was New England's primary contribution to American democracy.

It is our hope that the present two volumes of and on the Connecticut Town Reports—what they said and what we think—will stimulate enough interest and debate to lead to a new history of Connecticut in the early national period. As the essayists have noted, it will need to include: the history of Native- and Afro-Americans, the role of women, the Connecticut economy as it moved from agriculture into industrialization, a new appreciation of religious change from the bottom up, and a fuller understanding of the young state's ties to the rest of New England, New York City, southern states and the Caribbean. If *Voices of the New Republic* can stimulate curiosity and produce informed response, then the 200-year-old survey of the Connecticut Academy will not have been in vain, and the vital role of the New England town in the evolution of American democracy will be given a new visibility.

The Connecticut Academy:

A Child Born in the Eye of a Revolutionary Storm

Richard Buel

Americans expected independence to establish their cultural autonomy from Britain as well as to free them from the mother country's political, economic, and religious domination. The revolutionary era accordingly gave birth to a number of learned societies seeking to articulate a distinctive American culture. The Connecticut Academy of Arts and Sciences was not the first of these. Belatedly receiving its charter from the state legislature in 1799, it followed the American Philosophical Society, formally established in 1769, and the Boston-based American Academy of Arts and Sciences, founded in 1780. Ezra Stiles had dreamt of such a society as early as 1765 and had formally proposed that Connecticut charter a state academy when he assumed the presidency of Yale in 1780. At the time the government was overwhelmed with wartime problems. Stiles did manage to organize a group calling itself the "Connecticut Society of Arts and Sciences" which began meeting twice a year in conjunction with the convening of the legislature at Hartford and New Haven in 1786. Because of the state's political turmoil that accompanied the Revolution, however, Stiles' brainchild languished until a brief moment of calm at the turn of the century.[1]

Revolutionary Upheaval

Connecticut warmly embraced the continent's cause against Britain, and was never more than a step behind the region's leader, Massachusetts. In 1774 the colony rallied to Boston's support after Parliament closed the port; the General Assembly responded eagerly to the call for a continental congress; and Connecticut moved quickly to implement Congress's Continental Association and to enhance its military preparedness. When fighting eventually erupted in April 1775, the colony rose heroically to the military challenge. Men quickly filled Connecticut's quotas in the Continental Army during the first two years of the war. Their spirited support for the cause grew out of the difficulties they faced in providing for the rising generation. As the largest fully settled colony on the continent, people became a principal export after mid-century and bitter experience with British policy during and after the Seven Years War convinced both leaders and led alike that their best chance for the future lay in freedom from the mother country's control.[2]

Over the long haul, though, Connecticut's enthusiasm for the revolutionary struggle waned as the war inflicted immense hardships on the state. Connecticut had the unenviable distinction of being both strategically insignificant and dangerously vulnerable to British forces based on Long Island and at New York City. The enemy had no interest in holding any part of the state as

they held parts of New York and Rhode Island. Doing so would simply detract from achieving more significant objectives like seizing the Highlands of the Hudson or crippling the sea-borne commerce of southern New England. If the war had been a short one, strategic insignificance would have provided a cheap, relatively effective form of protection for the state's 120 miles of exposed seacoast. But the war dragged on for eight years during which time the British launched five major raids along the shoreline. Connecticut's Continental line stationed on the strategic Hudson was able to play a small role in responding to the Danbury raid in 1777. Otherwise the state was pretty much on its own when it came to defending itself.[3]

Major enemy assaults on Danbury, New Haven, Fairfield, Norwalk, and New London-Groton subjected the affected communities to great hardship. But in many ways the increasing pressure from loyalist raiders based on Long Island proved more difficult to cope with. Beginning in 1779 Connecticut's coast was ravished by waves of loyalist sponsored kidnappings launched from Long Island for the purposes of ransom, prisoner exchange, and demoralization of the coastal population. The burden of "defending" the state from this threat as well as larger military operations proved crushing because the task was essentially impossible. No matter what the size of the force the state deployed, the enemy always could find a point where they could strike with greater force. At the same time, if the state did not at least try to defend its people, it risked losing their loyalty.[4]

The requirements of domestic defense together with the burden of maintaining the state's line regiments in the Continental Army led to fiscal collapse. Connecticut raised much of its revenue by taxing polls and the increasing burden of taxes levied by the state and the towns inspired an accelerating emigration that sapped Connecticut's resources. Losses suffered directly from enemy raiding and indirectly from the depreciation of both the state and continental currencies compounded the problem and obstructed attempts to deal with growing tax delinquencies. When the war ended Connecticut lay in political as well as fiscal disarray.[5]

Those who had sponsored the Revolution in Connecticut emerged from the war with their authority severely compromised. That in turn limited their ability to respond to the difficult challenges that accompanied the peace. The revolutionary debt proved to be the most troublesome of Connecticut's postwar problems. In addition to a state debt, Connecticut was also responsible for a portion of the Confederation's or continent's debt, owed largely to the officers and men in Connecticut's continental regiments. Connecticut's neighbors enjoyed an overseas commerce that allowed them to raise revenue from an impost on imports. The importer customarily paid the duty at the point where the goods were landed and then recovered the tax in the price of the goods sold. Because those who chose not to purchase the imports did not have to pay the tax, an impost proved more politically acceptable in the difficult postwar period than taxes on assets like land, which one had to pay no matter what. Connecticut's dependence on its neighbors for most of its imports precluded raising much revenue from a state impost.

The only impost that might have benefited the state was a continental one, which also, incidentally, would have maximized the yields from this revenue source. Members of the state's council favored empowering the Confederation government to raise such revenue, but the measure was unpopular because it had become associated with "commutation." In response to the Continental officers' request, Congress had commuted the half-pay for life to which they were entitled to a lump sum amounting to full pay for five years. Since commutation accounted for much of the continental debt the states were being asked to shoulder in 1783, its sponsors mistakenly assumed adopting it would in turn compel the adoption of a continental impost as the most agreeable fiscal strategy for dealing with the burden of commutation. Instead, in Connecticut commutation led to a political insurgency that manifested itself in the Middletown Convention of 1783.

The Convention assembled ostensibly to protest commutation, but also to punish those in the council or "upper house" of the Connecticut State legislature who had endorsed a federal impost.[6] Connecticut was one of two states that had cast off British authority without changing any significant aspect of its colonial government. Under the charter of 1662 a new Lower House composed of representatives of the towns was elected every six months. Its popular character was balanced by an upper house selected in a manner designed to ensure a continuity that was lacking in the Lower House. Each September the freemen of the colony meeting in their respective towns to choose their representatives also nominated prominent figures for the council. The twenty who received the most nominations were then placed on a ballot for the freemen to choose from at their meetings the following April. This ballot listed the nominees in order of their seniority on the council rather than the number of nominations they had received and the April freemen's meetings acted on the nominations in that order. Every freeman was given twelve ballots to cast—one for each of the councilors to be elected. If one wished to vote for nominees at the bottom of the list, one had to withhold the requisite number of votes from nominees who were higher on the ballot. One also needed patience, since the selection of councilors was the last item on the agenda of the April freemen's meeting, and courage, since one's behavior would be noted by "the authority" supervising the meeting. Such procedures normally ensured the reelection of any sitting member of the council.[7]

Connecticut had earned the reputation for being a "land of steady habits" during the eighteenth century because of the permanency of its council. The Middletown Convention of 1783 sought to unseat offensive councilors through concerted action in the fall nomination meetings. Precedent of a sort existed for the attempt. In 1766 an enraged electorate acting under the guidance of a similar convention had turned out those councilors who had administered the Stamp Act oath to Governor Fitch. Though the Middletown Convention succeeded in eliminating six names from the ballot, when spring came all of the sitting councilors in the "upper house" managed to retain the places that custom entitled them to, and therefore their control over the state's government. Proponents of a federal impost thus won the battle in Connecticut, though they lost the war in the Confederation because of the continued opposition of states like Rhode Island. But the Convention had served notice to the state's elite that the bulk of the people were fed up and this limited the leadership's options in responding to other postwar problems.[8]

The populist insurgency of the Middletown Convention mirrored the intense localism of the state's political culture during the Confederation period. From the perspective of the localists most of the state's problems seemed to have originated beyond the state's borders. Had Connecticut concentrated on defending itself rather than dividing its military resources between local and continental commitments, much of the pain of the war could have been avoided. An unfavorable decision in 1782 by the Confederation government against the state's claims to western lands in Pennsylvania known as the Susquehanna lands also strengthened localist proclivities.

However, localism had little to contribute when it came to dealing with the state's postwar economic problems. Connecticut's economy continued to depend on the Caribbean trade, and the varying exclusions its entrepreneurs faced in the European-controlled West Indies limited its export markets. Restricted markets accentuated the severity of a postwar depression and limited the resources the state possessed to meet the demands made upon it. Though Connecticut discriminated against the federal creditors in its midst, it still failed fully to honor the claims of state creditors. Thus the entire war debt remained a liability rather than becoming the asset it might have been had the legislature been able to raise enough hard money to pay the going rate of interest on its nominal sum.

The state's revolutionary leaders remained on the defensive throughout the immediate postwar period. About the only resource at their disposal vis-a-vis their domestic critics was their superior cultural attainments. Some younger leaders known as the Connecticut or Hartford Wits—including in their ranks the recent Yale graduates, David Humphreys, Joel Barlow, Timothy Dwight, and John Trumbull (the author of *M'Fingal* and second cousin to the painter with the same name)—satirized their less sophisticated opponents in prose and verse. But this only diminished their adversaries' authority. It did not enable the Wits or their friends to take the initiative. The leadership knew after the Middletown Convention that on most matters they had to adjust to the expectations of the people, no matter how misguided, or cease to lead. They also realized that Connecticut's declining influence in the Confederation precluded seeking solutions to the state's problems on the national level.

Shays' Rebellion in 1786 eventually made the Confederation as a whole more receptive to strengthening the nation's central government. This was a debtor insurgency that shut down many of the county courts in neighboring Massachusetts against which the government had to deploy a sizable military force to reestablish its authority. But Connecticut's federalists—those favoring a stronger central government—contributed no more to the unfolding of that drama than a satirical poem entitled "The Anarchiad," a collaborative composition by four of the Wits.[9]

Nonetheless, Shays' Rebellion solved two problems for them. By persuading the second largest state in the Confederation that it could not master the problems left over from the Revolution on its own, it committed Massachusetts's leadership to strengthening Congress's powers and pushed leaders in other states to a similar conclusion. And by raising the specter of anarchy next door it tempered the localism that Connecticut's leadership had to contend with. As the prospect for strengthening the central government improved beyond the state's borders, Connecticut federalists acquired renewed authority. Though the state legislature waited until the last moment to appoint Roger Sherman, William Samuel Johnson, and Oliver Ellsworth to the Constitutional Convention in Philadelphia, its delegates played a crucial role in arranging the "Connecticut compromise." This compromise successfully accommodated the interests of the large and small states, ensuring that the Convention's handiwork would in turn be accepted by enough state ratifying conventions to implement the new government.[10]

Connecticut was appropriately rewarded for the statesmanship of its delegates and its enthusiastic endorsement of their handiwork by the success of the new government in dealing with the revolutionary debt. Besides relieving the states of the demands of the federal creditors, Alexander Hamilton's assumption as Secretary of the Treasury of a significant portion of the state debts relieved Connecticut taxpayers of an onerous burden. Hamilton's success in paying interest on the resulting consolidated federal debt with a federal impost converted it into an asset. Residents of the state that before had held almost worthless scrip now received regular interest payments in hard money. In addition, they could convert the principal of their debt into cash by selling their bonds at close to par. With their newfound resources they were admirably positioned to take advantage of other key developments outside Connecticut that promised to enhance the state's welfare.[11]

The wars accompanying the French Revolution that began in 1792 led to a revival of the state's economic ties with the West Indies. Though Britain seized vast quantities of American shipping at the end of 1793 in an effort to cut off France's Caribbean possessions, British military operations in the region subsequently created an expanded demand for North American provisions. Barreled salt meat that had been a state specialty since well before the Revolution now found a ready market.[12] In addition, the new federal Congress, with its principal fiscal problems behind it, proved more willing than the Continental Congress had been to honor Connecticut's claims in the west.

In 1785 the Continental Congress had pressed all the states claiming western lands to cede them so as to create a national public domain. Connecticut had responded in October 1786 by relinquishing most of her claims to western lands, which extended to the Mississippi, reserving only a strip of territory roughly 60 miles wide extending westward from the Pennsylvania border

for 120 miles. Congress's acceptance of the cession could be construed as an acceptance of the state's reservation. However, that in itself did not create a strong enough claim for settlers to rely on and the Assembly's initial efforts to sell the land came to naught. Indian resistance to European settlement north of the Ohio also obstructed effective occupation of the area.[13]

The institution of a new national government in 1789 might have further compromised the state's western claims. The Constitution vested unambiguous jurisdiction over the unsettled territories in Congress and Connecticut could no longer match the influence of states like New York and Pennsylvania that might have opposed her pretensions. Fortunately the new government did nothing to challenge the state's title and much to strengthen it. After a series of military disasters, Anthony Wayne finally succeeded in neutralizing the Ohio Indians at the Battle of Fallen Timbers in 1794. The following year the Connecticut legislature sold 3 million unsurveyed acres of its "Western Reserve" for $1.2 million to the Connecticut Land Company. Prior to this sale the General Assembly had set aside 500,000 acres of its claim as "firelands" to compensate those residents of the state's coast that had suffered as a consequence of enemy action during the war.[14]

The effective occupation of both tracts had to wait until the remaining Indian titles were extinguished, accurate surveys were completed, and both Congress and Ohio confirmed title. This consumed the better part of a decade. But by the middle of the 1790s relief was at least on the horizon. The state's expanding economy led to rising land values (noted in the vast majority of the replies to the Academy's town survey) and to a rash of bank foundings in all its major towns. Capital, hitherto in short supply, became relatively plentiful as was evident in the ability of the Connecticut Land Company to raise the required $1.2 million to consummate its deal with the legislature. All these developments made it easier to finance privately sponsored emigration to New York, Vermont, and New Hampshire. And after 1800 the Western Reserve provided homes for an increasing number of the emigrants that continued to stream from the state as well as some compensation for the families that had suffered most during the war.[15]

Continuing Foreign and Domestic Perils

Still, as the century came to a conclusion, the future remained clouded. Because the new federal government had proven to be an unqualified boon, Connecticut's leadership remained strongly Federalist. At the national level the party's leaders spent much of the decade fending off forceful challenges to United States neutrality from the rival European powers. As part of this effort, they had come to an accommodation with Great Britain in the Jay Treaty during 1794-1796. Relations with revolutionary France subsequently worsened to the point where by the beginning of 1798 swarms of French privateers were seizing American shipping on the high seas. Most Connecticut residents supported the central government's policy of waging a limited naval war against French armed vessels during 1798-1799. And Connecticut's economy continued to expand in this unpromising environment thanks to the willingness of the British navy to accept American vessels trading with the British islands into its convoys.[16]

However, the renewed prosperity of the state, based as it was on an informal commercial alliance with British interests, exacerbated another development that had been of concern to the state's leadership since before the Revolution. Beginning with the Great Awakening of the 1740s, Connecticut's Congregational establishment had met with increasing challenges from dissenters. The revival had led to a splintering of the Congregational churches and to the growth of competing sects. An increase of Anglican converts on the right of the Congregational establishment matched the proliferation of "strict" Congregational and Baptist secessions on the left. Its growing religious heterogeneity liberalized the colony's legal establishment to the extent of expanding formal toleration to include increasing numbers of dissenters. Anyone in principle could apply to the magistrate for a certificate that would exempt him from contributing to the support of the established Congregational church provided he could show that he was a member of and contributed to the support of an alternative church. But in fact the operation of the certificate law discriminated against all dissenting congregations that were not large enough to have a meetinghouse and a settled minister and thus reinforced the privileges enjoyed by the established Congregational Church.[17]

Despite its legal advantage, leading Congregationalists had felt their religious interests were in jeopardy on the eve of the Revolution. Financial resources available from England through the Society for the Propagation of the Gospel in Foreign Parts lowered the threshold necessary for establishing Anglican churches in the colony and tempted Congregationalists who found supporting their minister burdensome to transfer their allegiances. At the same time, the founding of a Baptist College in Providence and continued economic development of southern New England encouraged the proliferation of dissent on the left. Finally, the threat that Great Britain would establish an Anglican bishop with religious jurisdiction over all the American colonies seemed real enough in the context of the mother country's centralizing policies and the active pleas of some Anglican clergy in the colonies after 1760.[18]

If the civil leadership of Connecticut saw the Revolution as an opportunity to provide for the next generation, the Congregational clergy saw it as a chance to recover the high ground that had been lost since the Great Awakening. Consequently, a great many clergymen actively endorsed the movement, either by preaching sermons that supported revolutionary action or serving as chaplains in the Continental Army. Moral endorsement seemed appropriate in view of the widespread affirmations of civic and religious virtue that accompanied the beginning of the struggle. The clergy's providential view of the contest also led them to expect a short war. Their understanding of the moral dimensions of the controversy led them to conclude that if Americans repented and reformed, God would have no alternative to vindicating the colonists except repudiating the moral order of his Universe.[19]

The clergy had not bargained either on a prolonged struggle or on the decline in moral behavior that accompanied it. The moral decline manifested itself in a variety of ways. For instance, the militarization of society led to the increased use of profanity and to a rising incidence of armed robbery. Then the depreciation of paper currencies in the revolutionary economy spawned unscrupulous behavior in the marketplace. As the war dragged on, increasing numbers were guilty of either trading with the enemy or more actively assisting them. David Field writing many years later alluded to the "revolutionary war" as giving "a shock to the moral habits of the people, from which they have not yet wholly recovered."[20]

The established churches felt the effects of the moral decline accompanying the Revolution far more than did dissenting religious societies because of the role the Congregational clergy had played in leading the people to war. The established churches saw their congregations wither as a consequence of wartime demoralization. Many clergymen interpreted this as part of a general spread of infidelity exemplified by the rise of deism among the civil leadership of the Revolution by whom they felt betrayed. Peripheral sects—particularly Methodists, Baptists, and Universalists—fared far better, sweeping alienated believers from the established churches into their folds. The renewed prosperity of the 1790s further promoted dissent by making it easier for all who remained uninspired by a demoralized Congregational establishment to go their own way. Finally the Congregationalists suffered from the war's diversion of Yale's more talented graduates into civil rather than religious callings.[21]

In 1798 a crisis with France reunited the state's Congregational leadership with its civil leadership in a way reminiscent of the early phases of the Revolution. After Washington retired from the presidency in 1796, his successor, John Adams, faced escalating pressures from France over the Jay Treaty. These pressures seemed to be abetted by a domestic opposition, concentrated in the southern states and led by the nation's most prominent deist, Thomas Jefferson. Matters came to a head when it was learned early in the year that the three envoys Adams had sent to France to deal with the problems caused by the Jay Treaty had been treated in a humiliating way. The Directory demanded money and, when the envoys refused it, threatened to appeal over the government's head to what it arrogantly assumed were the superior loyalties of the American people to France and Jefferson. Though there was no danger that the American public would succumb to such bullying, the enormity of French behavior coupled with the success of French arms led some of the Congregational clergy, particularly Timothy Dwight, to see an unholy conspiracy of Jacobinism and atheism threatening the United States. Civil leaders like John Cotton Smith echoed the clerical leadership's new rhetoric. The willingness of civil leaders to join their religious counterparts in portraying the French threat as heralding the apocalypse helped overcome any lingering reluctance established clergymen entertained about reinvolving themselves in politics.[22]

The crisis quickly passed as the people rallied to the government and Congress launched a program designed to protect the national government against both internal and external enemies. As heartening as the government's success in defending its dignity on the high seas and in passing legislation like the Alien and Sedition Laws to muzzle the domestic opposition was the effect the quasi-war with France had on the Congressional elections of 1798. The sixth Congress, elected in the autumn of 1798, was thoroughly Federalist, offering security against French subversion in the future. Throughout most of 1799 the political and religious leadership of Connecticut enjoyed a sense of profound relief, particularly as Napoleon's waning military fortunes further diminished the threat that France would wield an undue influence in the new nation. As the end of the century approached, the threat of a violent apocalypse yielded to a prospect far more benign and hopeful.[23]

The Eye of the Storm

The project of establishing a Connecticut Academy of Arts and Sciences that had been simmering for more than a decade came to a head in the new environment of Federalist euphoria that characterized the last year of the century. Timothy Dwight, who had recently accepted the Presidency of Yale, was the leading force in bringing Stiles' original proposal to fruition. Though Dwight had been instrumental in drawing the established clergy back into politics, in March 1799 he transcended both politics and ideology in choosing twenty-one prominent New Haven residents to unite with him in the enterprise. Federalist political figures like David Daggett, James Hillhouse, Simeon Baldwin, and Elizur Goodrich joined religious leaders with whom Dwight was not entirely in agreement, such as James Dana and the Episcopalian Bela Hubbard, in signing the Academy's articles. The original membership also included prosperous businessmen such as Isaac Beers; Elias Shipman; Jeremiah Townsend; and Eneas Munson; a leading lawyer, Pierpont Edwards; the socially prominent Abraham Bishop; a Yale professor, Josiah Meigs; the inventor-industrialist Eli Whitney; and Noah Webster, at the time most famous for his readers and spellers. Several of these men, notably Edwards, Bishop, and Meigs, would soon become political opponents of Dwight, and Dwight already bore personal grudges against Dana and Webster. What united them at this point was a common commitment to the revolutionary enterprise of unlimited improvement through the development and dissemination of knowledge.[24]

The Academy's formal birth thus marked a high point of enlightenment optimism in the state. The expectations that accompanied its creation were all the more extravagant because of the uniqueness of the moment. To assuage fears that either Dwight or Yale would control the organization, the original signers were doubled to dilute the New Haven-centered character of the Academy when the charter was issued in October.[25] But Dwight remained the principal inspiration behind the new organization, serving as its first president until his death in 1817. And its first project, the town survey of 1800, reflected his guiding hand. Though ostensibly little more than an attempt to collect systematic factual information about the state's towns, the project was not quite as value neutral as it appears to be in retrospect.

Dwight hoped through the town survey to create a detailed description of Congregational Connecticut as an exemplary society. The Academy's project thus became part of his larger strategy for combating infidelity. Dwight had no illusions that Connecticut was either static or perfect. The whole project was rooted in requests for information about town histories. He was confident, however, that the survey would reveal an orderly connection with the past as well as improvement in the present. While Dwight labored successfully to stem the tide of deism among his students at Yale, he hoped the results of the survey would demonstrate to disbelieving empirics beyond the confines of his seminary that the traditional town-centered life of the state came as close as human society could, at least before the millennium, to what the creator had intended for the human race. The town survey was designed to speak to disbelievers in their own language.[26]

Ideological Confrontation

Dwight's expectations for the project assumed that there were enough Yale alumni of sympathetic orientation to bring the canvass quickly to fruition. Though Yale graduates composed most of the town replies, only 14 of an eventual total of 40 had been received before the euphoria that had accompanied the Academy's founding dissipated. Events beyond the control of anyone in Connecticut quickly frustrated the consummation of Dwight's plan.

During 1799 France had grown more conciliatory toward the United States. At the end of the year President Adams decided to seek an accommodation with the French Directory. His diplomatic initiative divided his own party and, together with the backlash from such measures as the Alien and Sedition Laws and a direct federal tax to pay for a provisional army, paved the way for Jefferson's election as third president of the Republic. Far from being the prelude to a millennium characterized by enlightenment and peace, the turn of the century ushered the Republicans into national power. Worse still, Jefferson's victory was seen as heralding the permanent displacement of the Federalists from the nation's government.[27]

The election of 1800 precipitated a fissure among the Academy's original members. Abraham Bishop seized on the occasion to launch a demagogic attack on the state's Federalist leadership in his *Connecticut Republicanism: An Oration of the Extent and Power of Political Delusion* (1800). Bishop was a member of Yale's most distinguished class in the eighteenth century, the class of 1778. He was also one of the richest men in Connecticut. Yet he had stooped to denounce the docility of the people in blindly following where the civil and established religious leadership led. His Federalist opponents suspected him of angling for the coveted office of collector of the port of New Haven that would be a patronage plum at the incoming president's disposal. They also knew that their hegemony over the state rested on a fragile foundation. If the stream of emigrants who each year moved west in search of new lives and homes instead remained in Connecticut, they would strengthen the ranks of the opposition that felt alienated from the Federalist order. The demagogic tone of Bishop's address inflamed Federalist ideological anxieties, derived from the French Revolution, of a violent and godless insurgency to which the events of 1792-1794 seemed to demonstrate all republics were vulnerable.[28]

Responding as much out of fear as out of frustration to their loss of control over the national government, New England Federalists after 1800 turned from focusing on a political program to pursuing an ideology. That is to say they abandoned addressing the concrete problems of the present, which they had been singularly successful at between 1787 and 1796, and instead concentrated on defending the values of an ideal past. Dwight and his collaborators in the town survey were in the forefront of this transition. They saw Connecticut's uniquely stable political and religious order as threatened about equally from within by civil and religious dissent and from without by France. Religious dissent continued to proliferate in the wake of the moral wreckage created by the Revolution while political dissent would be nourished by the federal patronage at Jefferson's disposal. Confirming their worst fears, a Republican opposition formed around newly appointed federal officeholders to openly contest the Federalists' control of the state in 1801.[29]

The opposition initially posed little threat to Connecticut's established order because the Episcopalians sided with the Congregationalists in resisting radical dissent and because of the procedures surrounding the selection of the upper house which had also been adapted to the selection of the state's Congressional delegation. Nonetheless, the Federalist majority in the Assembly took the precaution of strengthening their hold over the electoral system in 1801. The "Stand Up Law" of that year forced freemen nominating councilors to vote publicly for nominees rather than just writing names on a sheet of paper. This deprived dissidents of anonymity at the preliminary level of selection. The legislature also made it far more difficult for dissidents to become freemen by transferring the power to admit individuals to that status from the town selectmen to the local justices of the peace who were appointed by the Assembly.[30] Federal patronage was unlikely to counterbalance the effect of these measures, given Jefferson's commitment to minimal government.

The resources at the disposal of the Federalists in fact proved sufficient to turn back Republican challengers until 1817. Nonetheless the Republicans managed to score steady gains in the House up through 1807 as many of the larger, more dynamic towns, particularly in coastal Fairfield County, sent opposition delegates to the legislature. Most communities where dissidents were strong failed to reply to the Academy's survey either because the facts did not conform to what Dwight and his collaborators expected or because the clergymen to whom the queries had been sent were preoccupied with resisting such developments, or both. David Field, a sympathetic disciple of Dwight's project and the minister at Haddam, did eventually produce an account of Middletown which inadvertently revealed it to be a hotbed of industrial experimentation. But one senses he did so largely because Middletown could be made to take back seat to the majority of Federalist towns with which his survey of Middlesex County dealt.[31]

The growth of the Republican opposition was particularly disturbing to Dwight and his followers because it fed on the continued proliferation of religious dissent. Federalists should have been spared concern about falling behind their religious rivals because both benefited equally from the effects of the Second Great Awakening. The disadvantage Congregationalism had labored under during and beyond the Revolution began to ease after 1800. Whether the inspired young preachers Dwight succeeded in producing at Yale, or the example of the more radical sects, or some other cause influenced the established churches is impossible to say. What is clear is that the clerical leadership continued to run scared despite their success in mounting revivals. Increased piety was no longer enough. The Congregational clergy also sought to improve on the moment by mobilizing their congregations into a wide range of "missionary" activities that they used to expand their political as well as their religious influence.[32]

A similar insecurity characterized the behavior of the state's political leadership despite their continued control over the government. Federalist anxieties persisted because they saw themselves as contending not just with a domestic opposition but with hostile forces emanating ultimately from revolutionary France. If France had epitomized the dangers posed by Jacobinism and irreligion in the 1790s, during the first decade of the nineteenth century its evolution into a military dictatorship raised another frightening possibility to which Federalists feared all republics were vulnerable. While the Federalists dominated the national government they had controlled the American Republic's foreign policy. Now that Jefferson controlled the national government, Connecticut Federalists feared his alleged partiality for France. This led them to see the considerable achievements of Jefferson's first term, particularly the Louisiana Purchase, as a Napoleonic conquest that threatened the integrity of the republic.[33] Extreme versions of this warped perspective lay behind the secessionist plot of 1804 to save the original states of the Confederation from the nation's current "Jacobin" leadership. Several Connecticut Federalists participated in the conspiracy including James Hillhouse, one of the Academy's original members. They only avoided forfeiting their reputations at the time because Hamilton's death aborted the plan before it became public. They would be less fortunate a decade later.[34]

During Jefferson's second administration the European wars intensified, leading each of the belligerents to try to monopolize American trade at the expense of the other. Jefferson responded by eschewing another accommodation with Britain along the lines of the Jay Treaty. At the same time he distanced himself from France, at least to the extent of preventing the affront offered the flag by HMS *Leopard*, when it used force in 1807 to seize four alleged British deserters off the USS *Chesapeake*, from precipitating a war with Britain. Instead he recommended an embargo be laid on all American shipping so as to deprive both belligerents equally of the benefits of the nation's neutral commerce. The Republican leadership assumed that an American embargo would hurt the nation's European adversaries more than the United States because Europe imported essentials like food in exchange for manufactures that Americans could if necessary make for themselves. If the belligerents persisted in refusing the Republic justice on the high seas, the United States would still have the option of war after it had built up its military strength.[35]

The Embargo failed to elicit any support from New England's Federalists. The leadership saw it as a calculated attack on the region. Because the Embargo caused considerable economic distress, they had no difficulty in mobilizing public opinion against it and translating that sentiment into political action designed to stymie the measure's effectiveness. Resolutions passed in the principal seaport towns of New England condemning the constitutionality as well as the wisdom of the Embargo. These resolutions in turn encouraged violations to which the administration responded with ever more stringent enforcement measures. The state legislatures then passed resolutions condemning the constitutionality of Congress's response to the opposition the Federalists were orchestrating locally against the Embargo. When federal authorities in desperation tried to place local militias at the disposal of the officials charged with enforcing the Embargo, the Connecticut legislature met in special session to condemn and resist the effort.[36]

Federalist resistance to Republican policies came clothed in an ideology that reflected a lurid vision of world politics. Massachusetts took the lead in promoting these notions, but Connecticut was never far behind. According to Federalist ideologues, Napoleonic France presented such a serious threat to the survival of civilization as to justify any measure taken by Britain against her adversary, even when it conflicted with the interests of the United States. Thus New England Federalists were prepared to waive protests against the impressment of American seamen into the British navy. They also acquiesced in British attempts to control America's commerce, including the search and seizure of U.S. vessels for violating British commercial restrictions anywhere on the high seas, even as they cleared the American coast, instead of as they approached a blockaded port. Finally, they charged that Jefferson was covertly executing Napoleon's will rather than defending American interests. This accusation rested on the way the Embargo appeared to complement Napoleon's Continental system. Admittedly, the Administration's response to the belligerent powers was not entirely even-handed. However, Britain labored additionally under the burden of non-intercourse only because of her failure to give satisfaction for the *Chesapeake* incident.[37]

Eventually the Embargo was abandoned in 1809, but not for war. New England's opposition precluded that option. The only European power that the United States could realistically strike at was Britain and the resistance of New England's Federalists to restraints on their region's commerce with the former mother country suggested that war with Britain would lead to civil war.[38] Instead, non-intercourse with both belligerents took the Embargo's place. Beyond being ineffectual, non-intercourse directed at the belligerents alone favored Britain by making American exports available at neutral ports to which her command of the seas gave her unmatched access. Federalist spokesmen in Congress publicly rejoiced at the humiliations they had managed to impose on their Republican adversaries. They also repeatedly taunted the Republicans with their inability to secure national interests, though the Federalist opposition was clearly part of the reason for Republican failures.[39]

Party Before Nation

The period between 1807-1811 was hardly congenial to the consummation of the Town Reports project. Recording the prices of grain, wood, and livestock took second place to the larger issues of war and peace, not to mention the fate of civilization and the future of orthodox Christianity. Dwight realized by the end of the decade that the Academy's project was in trouble. Instead of abandoning it, though, he sought to reinvigorate it. In 1811 he published *A Statistical Account of the City of New Haven*[40] as a model for others to follow. This document of almost 35,000 words was a collaborative effort that addressed all the queries fully. But it was not likely to inspire emulation for several reasons.

Quite apart from the difficulty of finding volunteers to put together a text of that size, the queries had already become dated. They were structured in a way that minimized the significance of most of the economic changes transforming the state. The turnpike boom at the turn of the century was noted by many and the New Haven Report mentioned Whitney's invention of the cotton gin and use of interchangeable parts. But neither Dwight nor his fellow respondents showed much interest in the industrial revolution that was beginning around them. They also barely alluded to the political controversies rending the state or nation if they mentioned them at all. Thus the New Haven Report failed to note the burning of a sloop in New Haven harbor in March 1809. It had been seized by a United States vessel for violating the Embargo and was destroyed to deprive enforcement officials of some of their reward.[41]

The next decade would be even less kind to the Town Reports project. In the same year that Dwight published his canvass of New Haven, the Republicans resolved to threaten Britain with war if she did not cease violating the nation's commercial rights. The Republicans picked Britain not only because they could strike at her through Canada, but also because she posed a more dangerous threat to national interests than France did. Napoleon neither had the naval power after Trafalgar to do the Republic much damage nor a stake in the Western Hemisphere. Though the Federalists in the national government joined dissident Republicans in opposing the Madison administration's policy, a majority of the Republicans in Congress refused to be deterred. The threat of civil war remained, but a younger generation of Republican leaders had become conscious of another danger. If they allowed the Federalists to thwart their efforts to confront Britain, a new generation of Americans might be alienated from Republicanism, securing the political future to the Federalists. The situation required that the Republic's honor be vindicated against Britain whatever the cost.[42]

New England Federalists resisted the War of 1812 by every measure at their disposal short of civil war. In addition to public addresses by the region's governors and legislatures denouncing the war as unnecessary and impolitic, both Massachusetts and Connecticut refused to put their militias at the federal government's service. Additionally, Connecticut went to great lengths to obstruct enlistment in the federal army by harassing recruiters and drawing off potential recruits in rival volunteer corps for the defense of the state. Finally the state was deluged with a barrage of Federalist propaganda encouraging disloyal activities. Connecticut's people responded with behavior that ranged from trading with the enemy to, in the case of the notorious "blue lights," allegedly using lanterns to alert British naval vessels blockading Stephen Decatur's squadron at New London as to when he proposed to run the blockade.[43]

Federalist resistance culminated in the Hartford Convention of 1814. After meeting for several weeks at the end of the year in secret session, the Convention issued a set of resolutions calling for two sorts of changes. One demanded that all federal revenues in the region be turned over to state authorities so they could "defend" New England properly, as the Madison government had not. Sanctioning such an arrangement would have positioned the disaffected New England states to negotiate a separate peace with the enemy. After leveling this gun at the national government's head, the Hartford Convention demanded that the Republicans accept major modifications to the federal constitution that would give the New England minority more power in the nation's councils.[44]

For their behavior, which flirted with treason, the state's Federalist leadership paid a price. Not everyone approved of the Federalists' opposition to the administration's attempt to defend the nation's honor. Were they not making a mockery of the Revolution? Young people in particular rallied to the national standard when war was declared against Britain, some enlisting over the objections of regional and community leaders. In addition, cruising against British shipping proved to be lucrative and popular.[45]

The Federalists defended their behavior by arguing that the Republicans were destroying the nation by embarking on war with Britain. Either the Madison administration would ally itself again with France, in which case the republic would be transformed into a Napoleonic dictatorship, or a powerful British monarchy would crush the divided Republic. When the expected Franco-American alliance failed to materialize and Napoleon abdicated in 1814, they predicted Britain would quickly reduce the American republic to splinters. They saw themselves as standing apart from the catastrophe, positioning themselves to save what could be salvaged of a failed revolutionary experiment.[46]

While they followed dutifully in Massachusetts's footsteps on national matters, Connecticut Federalists prided themselves on maintaining the political purity of their state. Doing so, though, involved putting themselves out on an ideological limb. The Federalist vision of the world was either very right or very wrong. While Connecticut Federalists did everything they could to make their predictions self-fulfilling ones, their extremism discouraged opposition to their activities. As war loomed on the horizon, political resistance by Republicans fell off in Connecticut. The opposition experimented briefly with trying to build a parallel government in 1812, using committees similar to those that had put the Continental Association into effect at the beginning of the Revolution. However, the effort failed and the Federalists maintained an iron hold over the state's institutions throughout the war.[47]

Federalist political strength in Connecticut could sometimes infect local disputes with anti-nationalist significance. Take, for example, the General Assembly's failure to distribute according to a previously arranged formula the bonus money that it received for chartering the Episcopalian-backed Phoenix Bank in 1814. This has been credited with destroying the political alliance between Episcopalians and Federalists.[48] The betrayal involved more than reneging on a prior understanding, though. The Assembly withheld the portion due the Episcopalians because of war-related expenses facing the state. Everyone knew that the government needed the bonus money because the Federalist dominated state banks put redeeming their notes in specie ahead of financing the state's defense. They also knew that Connecticut's banks were strapped for specie because the Federalist banks of Massachusetts were tightening credit in the hope of frustrating the national government's attempt to borrow money in the emergency of 1814. The Federalists' willingness to put their interests ahead of the Episcopalians thus came to be seen as an extension of their determination to put their party ahead of the nation's survival.[49]

Federalist and Congregational Disestablishment

When the nation finally emerged from the war intact, the Federalists found themselves without a leg to stand on. Peace made them the laughing stock of the country. They had flirted with treason on the pretense that it was the only way to save the nation. Instead, the nation had survived despite their best efforts to destroy it.[50] Key figures like Oliver Wolcott, who two decades before as Secretary of the Treasury had been in the camp of the Federalist extremists, began to shed some of their ideological baggage at the beginning of the war. At its conclusion, Wolcott returned to the state from New York and positioned himself to lead Connecticut in a more accommodating direction. He accepted nomination as the symbolic leader of those who wished to revise the state constitution. After an unsuccessful attempt in 1816, he was elected governor in 1817. His political coalition then succeeded in changing the upper house enough to permit the calling of a constitutional convention in 1818. The new constitution provided for the disestablishment of the Congregational church, which had hitherto provided a sacred center around which the Federalists rallied, and an upper house of the legislature more responsive to the people's will and therefore more receptive to change. It received the endorsement of the state's voters and defined the institutions that permitted Connecticut subsequently to evolve into a modern democratic state.[51]

The collapse of the state's Federalist establishment coincided with the death of the Academy's founder and for all intents and purposes the end of the Town Reports project. However, Dwight did not die with the sense of complete defeat. Though he understood that the forces he opposed were triumphing, he could take solace in the knowledge that the Second Great Awakening had increasingly transformed Connecticut from a haven for infidelity into a rich garden of Christian commitment. If the heterodox benefited as much as the orthodox from the expansion of piety, Dwight's faith in God's providence continued to reassure him that all would eventually contribute to the anticipated millennium.[52] He also had the consolation of completing a version of the Academy's town survey on his own during Yale's summer vacations. Information collected by him over the years, appeared posthumously in four volumes as *Travels in New England and New York* in 1821-1822.[53] Not every Connecticut town was surveyed, but the material was at least assembled to make the political and religious statement Dwight had originally intended. It has also become a travel classic and was reprinted as recently as 1969. Finally his successors in the Academy have seen fit to bring his project to a new kind of completion two hundred years later. I suspect that would be the least of his consolations were he aware of it. But few in our state's and nation's history have been so honored.

A View from Above: The Town Reports as Ecclesiastical History

David W. Kling

Among the thirty-two topics or "Articles" listed by the Connecticut Academy of Arts and Sciences in its Town Reports solicitation letter of 1800, the subject of religion was directly addressed under one heading (Article 24: "places of public worship . . . congregations . . . clergymen . . ."), partially addressed under another (Article 1: "number of societies"), and potentially addressed under yet another (Article 32: "distinguished characters"). Given that only one of the thirty-two topics directly addressed religion, one might conclude that religious issues held marginal interest for the Academy's founding members. To be sure, the topic of religion was not foremost on the minds of those who framed the statistical inquiry nor was the subject of religion mentioned as part of the goal and mission of the Academy. In its act of incorporation, the Academy aimed "to promote, diffuse, and preserve the knowledge of those Arts and Sciences, which are the support of Agriculture, Manufactures and Commerce, and to advance the dignity, virtue and happiness of a people."[1] Nothing was said about promoting, diffusing, and preserving the knowledge of religion, and only by broadly construing the last phrase could one include religion as a subject to be examined by the Academy.

This is not to suggest that the topic (or the practice) of religion was unimportant to the members of the Academy or to the citizens of Connecticut. On the contrary, all of the contributors to the Town Reports were devoted church members (nearly all were Congregationalists), and the great majority held positions of leadership as deacons, elders or pastors. Moreover, at the time that the reports were written—and as is made clear in several Town Reports—Connecticut as well as the nation at large was in the throes of the Second Great Awakening, an upsurge of religious renewal, revival, and reform extending from about 1790 to 1835.[2] If one peruses the Town Reports and compares the space given to Article 24 relative to the other topics, it soon becomes apparent that religion was an important subject to the authors.

What then can be gleaned from these documents related to religious concerns? How should these documents be approached as historical sources? Of what value are they to a religious historian? Just as important as the information supplied is that which is missing, for often the history of a period—especially the one with which we are dealing—consists of those things omitted.[3] We thus begin with some observations pertinent to information that is absent or neglected in the Town Reports, then expand the discussion by examining the information contained therein.

Omissions and Limitations

To be sure, both individually and collectively the Town Reports are limited in their historical usefulness in several ways. First, the amount of information supplied by the respondents makes for a very uneven, piecemeal profile of religion in Connecticut. In some reports—those that are a mere four pages in length—all subjects, including religion, get a paragraph of attention. In longer reports, the subject of religion is given four or more pages. We should thus not expect to construct a consistent or comprehensive picture of Connecticut's religious situation from these idiosyncratic documents, or, apropos of the Town Reports project, provide a complete statistical town-by-town comparison of ecclesiastical life. Fortunately for historians, antiquarians, and genealogists of Connecticut, New England Congregationalists were particularly good record keepers—better than other religious bodies—so that the statistics provided in the Town Reports can be verified and supplemented by other records.[4] Moreover, manuscript sources (diaries, daybooks, correspondence, and sermons) and printed materials (histories, travel accounts, sermons, theological treatises, and periodicals) provide a rich deposit of other primary source material on religion in the colonial and early republic periods. The religious content in the Town Reports provides pieces of information that can be assembled into a larger framework when supplemented by other historical sources.

Second, the kind of information requested limits the scope of religious developments in Connecticut, and consequently the "big story" is missed. In keeping with the "statistical" history of Connecticut, Article 24 requests information on "Places of public worship; their number, and the denominations to which they belong—the rise of congregations and various sects, the names of the successive clergymen, the time of their settlement and exit—notices of any eminent clergymen; the salaries of the clergymen and the funds by which religious worship is maintained." Later, we will note the value of this statistical information to social historians, but here we note that Article 24 ignores many aspects of religious life, thought, and experience crucial to a more complete understanding of Connecticut's religious history. Between 1800 and 1832, when the first and last Town Reports were issued, the religious landscape of Connecticut was turned topsy-turvy. The Second Great Awakening, covering roughly this same period, not only added hundreds of converts to church membership rolls, but infused evangelical Christians with a vision to advance the kingdom of God across America, even throughout the world. Voluntary societies emerged to champion a myriad of religious and humanitarian causes: missions, Bible and tract distribution, ministerial education, Sunday schools, moral regulation (e.g., temperance and the elimination of Sabbath mail), and female-led charities.[5] Congregationalists and Presbyterians struck up a Plan of Union (1801) to facilitate the planting of Reformed churches in western settlements. State support for religion, which propped up the Congregational establishment, came to an official end in 1818, and all religious groups were placed on the same voluntary footing.[6] Finally, the stiff challenge to Congregational hegemony from Baptists and Methodists mirrored a nationwide upheaval that resulted in the numerical decline of Congregationalists and gains by Methodists such that by 1850 they had become the largest denomination in America.[7] All of these developments, with the exception of David D. Field's reports on revivals, went unmentioned in the Town Reports. In fairness to those submitting their reports in the early 1800s, the above-mentioned developments were either just underway or had not yet transpired. At best, the reporters had only an inkling of what was to come.

Third, an uneven response to the Academy's survey results in the under-representation of minority religious groups. While a good-sized fraction of the towns responded, the geographical distribution of the returns slights Episcopalians, Baptists, and Methodists. There are more returns from towns in the northern tier of counties (Windham, Tolland, Hartford), and especially Litchfield, which just so happened to have the highest concentration of Congregationalists, than from towns in the southern tier of counties (New London, New Haven, and Fairfield), with the exception of Middlesex. Since the geographical concentration of the religious minorities tended to be in the southern portion of the state, adjacent to the Long Island Sound, with pockets in Tolland and Windham counties, these groups were further marginalized by dint of the distribution of returns to the Academy's survey.[8]

Finally, these documents, as do all texts, reflect the views of those who wrote them. As noted, many of the authors were clergy and all were respected religious leaders within Congregational or Episcopal churches. All could be classified among the elite in Connecticut society. We thus get a picture of Connecticut ecclesiastical life considerably tilted in the direction of respectable, decorous, and established religion. One of the remarkable aspects to these documents is their lack of any mention of contemporary religious conflict among denominations (though there is discussion, as we will note later, of past conflict within local Congregational churches), or of the rising surge in popular religion. The authors convey the view that "a sovereign God is

in his heaven, and all is well with Connecticut." Congregationalists appear comfortably in control, while Methodists and Baptists number "few." Admittedly, in 1800, the Congregational church overwhelmed other religious bodies (with about 75 percent of the population), and a tax-supported establishment of religion remained in place until 1818. However, in 1790 there were over 100 dissenting religious bodies constituting about one-third of the total number, and Methodists had not yet established a single church in Connecticut![9] The Town Reports thus contribute a kind of public relations piece that enhances the somewhat misleading view that Connecticut was a land of steady Congregational habits.

The Town Reports as Ecclesiastical History

Despite these omissions and limitations, the Town Reports provide accurate and useful information. Taken together, they narrate the ecclesiastical history of Connecticut, covering the nearly two centuries from the establishment of the colony in 1636 to the last Town Report published in 1832. An ecclesiastical perspective denotes a certain approach toward religion. From the standpoint of those who framed the questions under Article 24 (and those who responded), religion is properly (or formally) expressed institutionally. Where does one find religion? In structures, be they organizational (groups, denominations, ministers), ideational (creeds, confessions, platforms), or physical (meetinghouses, churches).

This understanding of American religious history dominated the academic study of religion until the early 1970s. Though employing different methodologies and appealing to different professional audiences, both American historians and church historians wrote history "from the top down." They emphasized ideas and/or structures and depended upon elite ministerial sources to fashion their story. In sociological argot, this approach is known as the official model of religion. Viewed from an official perspective, religion is characterized by institutional differentiation. A worldview is standardized and expressed in articulated doctrine. Organizational structures are in place to maintain doctrinal and ritual conformity, to communicate teachings, and to support organizational programs. And religious roles are played by specialists such as clergy.

For over 175 years, Congregationalism reigned as the official or "established" religion in Connecticut. This church-state tradition exercised coercion: it required duties and obligations (such as a tax-supported clergy) enforced by the arm of state. The reason, not so clear to Americans today, was self-evident to Congregationalists in 1800. Religion had a vital place in the social order and by virtue of its ties to the state, was viewed as necessary for the well being of society. "Piety and patriotism ought to be united," noted one author in his report, "& that government is best which is under the due influence of both."[10] In addition, the church-state tradition was based upon the territorial parish: geographical boundaries (the town or "society") defined the space within which clergy exercised its authority. Over the years, this model was challenged both from within (e.g., by itinerant ministers in the 1740s who contested parish boundaries) and from without (e.g., by Baptists who championed a voluntary church freed from state support). Yet it remained intact until 1818.

We thus engage the Town Reports with the question, What do the reports tell us about the *ecclesiastical* history of Connecticut? Of course, this is not the only way to approach Connecticut's religious history. Since 1970 the New Social History has challenged the traditional paradigm and proposed writing history "from the bottom up," that is, from the perspective of ordinary men and women. In the mid-70s, the rise of women's studies recast the lead male actors in the script and gave women top billing. And in the 1990s, issues of race, class, and gender emerged as the predominant categories of historical research.[11] Where appropriate, we will refer to these newer approaches, but with the frank admission that we are severely limited in our comments by the contents of the Town Reports.

In our approach to the documents we generally follow a "text" and "context" approach. We note a pertinent text (or texts) from the reports, and then locate it within the broader context of Connecticut religious history, incorporating the contributions of recent scholarship. Our attempt is to tease out seven broad themes of Connecticut ecclesiastical history by presenting an informed commentary on the Town Reports.

(i) Worldview: "The Calvinist System"

> We have remarked that the first settlers, brought with them the Calvinist System of doctrines contained in the scriptures; they & their descendents have uncorruptedly adhered to the same principles down to the present time notwithstanding the variety of scenes, & trials they have passed thro . . . [12]

To the citizens of Connecticut, theology mattered. And to many, such as John Treadwell, it meant as much in 1810 as it did in the mid-1630s, when Thomas Hooker left Boston over a theological dispute, settled in Hartford, and founded the colony of Connecticut. Although the Town Reports offer but snippets of the theology and doctrine that informed the worldview of Connecticut's inhabitants, volumes have been written about this "Calvinist System of doctrines" brought by Puritans from old to New England. Here we offer a brief summary of the views that underlay the convictions and guided the people of seventeenth- and eighteenth-century Connecticut. To be sure, Calvinism underwent important changes, especially in the last half of the eighteenth century. It was challenged by Enlightenment thinkers, pilloried by Arminians and deists, ignored by the spiritually indifferent, and revised by its adherents. Nevertheless, it remained intact (in some cases, "uncorruptedly adhered to") as a dominant shaping force, permeating the hearts and minds of Connecticut's inhabitants up through the early national period.

With other Protestants, the Puritans and their progeny embraced the Reformation conviction of *sola scriptura*, the Bible alone as the only divine authority for faith and morals. However, their understanding of the Bible was filtered through John Calvin's *Institutes of the Christian Religion*, modified by "federal" or covenantal concepts, and further codified in the seventeenth century in the Westminster Confession of Faith (1647). These Calvinist or Reformed views characterized humans as utterly dependent upon the judgment and grace of a sovereign God. Whereas human depravity brought about alienation from God and the just deserts of hell, God in his own good pleasure predestined some individuals (the elect) to salvation and consigned the remainder (the reprobates) to everlasting punishment. Those saints "effectually called" by God and drawn by the Holy Spirit contributed nothing of their own merit or righteousness, but God alone, by the merits of Christ, imputed Christ's righteousness to them in the divine transaction of salvation. Once made righteous, the elect fulfilled the purposes for which they were created, namely, in the words of the Westminster Shorter Catechism, "to glorify God and enjoy him forever."

In addition, Calvinism in its Puritan strain was fastened to a philosophy of history known as covenant theology. Through a "voluntary condescension" God entered into covenantal relationships with his elect. While these covenants assumed several forms, the saving covenant of grace between the individual and God sustained all other covenants. According to the Old Testament pattern, which the Puritans adopted as a blueprint for their holy commonwealth, covenants extended to families, churches, and governments. Whereas the covenant of grace had a vertical dimension and affected one's eternal destiny, the other covenants had a horizontal dimension as they were necessary guides both to temporal human relationships and to sustain obedience to God's laws on this earth. In its civil form, then, covenant theology included all of society—saints and sinners alike.

To join in a covenantal relationship with a local church, that is, to become a church member, required a testimony to God's work of grace in an individual's life. For reasons that have never been fully known, the first Puritans in America restricted church membership to "visible saints." Although it was not necessary to point to the exact time and place of conversion (though many could), applicants for church membership were required to give a detailed account of their new found faith in Christ. At the same time, since God's original covenant with Abraham extended to his "seed," so too, according to Puritan theology, the covenant embraced one's physical descendents. By the same token, families, not individuals, constituted churches; children, by virtue of their parents' covenant, shared in a number of privileges of church membership. Baptism marked the entrance into the covenant, although the covenant was not fully secured until children (usually as young adults) gave a satisfactory testimony of their conversion. Living in a godly family and attending the preaching of the Word prepared one for salvation but by no means assured it. This mix of covenants and conversion created an inherent tension. On the one hand, covenantal notions intimated a certain tribalism or inclusiveness (all children of the covenant should become visible saints). On the other, a gathered church of visible saints suggested a minority people or exclusiveness (not all children of the covenant would become visible saints). As we will see, despite efforts to address this tension, it was never satisfactorily resolved.

(ii) Organizational Structures:
"They disclaimed independency"

It has been stated that the first churches of the county were congregational in their organization; but they disclaimed independency. They maintained mutual fellowship and assisted one another in cases of difficulty. The Cambridge Platform regulated their intercourse many years. But as that platform did not define accurately whence councils should be called in cases of difficulty, nor what number of ministers and churches should be requisite to constitute a council, and as some difficulties had arisen from want of a more explicit rule of procedure, the Saybrook Platform . . . was formed in 1708.[13]

The Cambridge and Saybrook Platforms

In his report on Middlesex County, David D. Field alludes to the formative documents that not only affirmed the Calvinist worldview but also regulated church governance. The Cambridge Platform (1648) defined the government of Congregationalism and so clarified the "New England Way."[14] In its essentials, the Platform outlined a church government whose power was centered in autonomous, covenanted, lay-ruled congregations. Individual churches were created by voluntary covenants and led by visible saints. The Platform designated that ministers alone had the authority to preach and administer the sacraments (baptism and communion). Lay "ruling elders" assisted the minister by screening new members, enforcing church discipline, and visiting the sick. They also, along with other ministers, ordained the minister. Other laymen served as deacons who administered church funds for communion and charitable purposes. While complete autonomy was given to the local church, "the communion of churches with one another" was encouraged, and as Field noted, practiced. According to congregational practice, councils and synods could recommend, advise, and admonish, but, unlike presbyterian governance, they had no binding judicial authority.

Despite such efforts to clarify the New England Way, the subsequent history of colonial New England religious life, especially in the Connecticut River Valley, was punctuated with strife over strict congregational versus presbyterian forms of governance. In the seventeenth century, Connecticut's controversy over presbyterianism culminated in the Toleration Act of 1669, which granted toleration to Presbyterians. By the early eighteenth century strict congregationalism prevailed in Massachusetts, where independent-minded clergy, a growing commercial elite, and the government (now controlled by the Crown) resisted efforts by a conservative party in Boston to strengthen the power of ecclesiastical councils. A considerably different mood prevailed in Connecticut. Both ministers and the General Court (still under its semi-independent charter and led by minister-turned-governor Gurden Saltonstall) favored closer relations among churches. Thus, a modified form of presbyterianism was introduced with the Saybrook Platform (1708). Formulated to address "defects of the discipline of the churches,"[15] as well as to arrest a perceived decline in lay piety, the Platform devised a unique "presbygational" polity by creating three forms of organization. First, it provided for county associations, composed exclusively of ministers, which licensed new ministers and dealt with issues of collective concern to clergy. Second, it created the colony-wide General Association, composed of delegates from county associations, which advised and oversaw ministers and churches. Though their duties were not explicitly defined, these two associations contributed to what David D. Hall has called a rising "sacerdotalism"—an attempt by the clergy to secure their status as professionals.[16] Third, the most explicit presbyterian feature of the Platform was its formation of all churches into county consociations of ministers and laymen whose decisions in local disputes were binding. In effect, the consociational structure transferred authority from the local congregation to an appeals court. Although the Platform was not acceptable to all churches, its prevalence made the distinction between Congregationalists of Connecticut and Presbyterians of the middle colonies largely geographical.[17] Despite a 1784 revision of Connecticut's statutes that legally repealed the Platform, presbyterian principles remained intact throughout most of Connecticut. We can now appreciate why numerous authors of the Town Reports designated Congregational churches as "Presbyterian."[18] Perhaps the boldest expression of presbyterian convictions was made by the Hartford North Association of ministers. In 1799, the association went so far as to repudiate the name of "Congregational churches" and to proclaim itself Presbyterian, noting that the "churches . . . of Connecticut at large, and in our district in particular, are not now, and never were, from the earliest period of our settlement, Congregational Churches."[19]

The Half-Way Covenant

When the evils of this covenant were exposed by President Edwards, Dr. Bellamy and others, and when ministers and churches came to examine it more thoroughly, one and another were disposed to reject it, or to lay it aside in practice, and it has now scarcely an advocate in Middlesex or in Connecticut.[20]

It was universally the practice for every adult person, to make a public profession of his faith in the gospel doctrines & every parent presented his children for Baptism. All in a sense were considered as members of the Church. The practice of owning the Covenant, as it was called, has been laid aside for about thirty years, which took place upon a more thorough attention to the Scriptures.[21]

We have noted the Puritan tension between tribalism and exclusivism, between a territorial church and a believer's church. This tension became particularly problematic as the colony's third generation came on the scene. Recall that the first generation of New England Puritans insisted on a church of the regenerate, of visible saints who gave credible testimony to the work of God's saving grace in their lives. Church membership qualified one's children for baptism and assured that those children would be raised under the watch, care, and scrutiny of the church. It was anticipated that as these children grew to maturity they too would undergo conversion, be admitted to the church, and hence guarantee the church's survival. But what if, as it so happened, that significant numbers of the second generation never experienced the requisite conversion experience, reached adulthood, married, and then had children? What was the spiritual status of their children? On one hand, a believer's church demanded that only those who experienced conversion would be admitted into the church; on the other hand, a territorial church demanded a close correlation between those residing in the parish and the parish's church members. If the former were enforced, church leaders feared that the church would become a tiny exclusive sect and the vision of a redeemed society would be lost. If the latter were enforced, the church would lose all tension with the world.

The Half-Way Covenant (a pejorative term not applied until the early nineteenth century) sought to address this problem. Meeting in Boston in 1662, a synod of eighty lay and clerical representatives ruled that the unregenerate married children of regenerate parents could present their infant children for baptism and thereby "own" the covenant. The terms of "full" church membership remained—one must give testimony to God's regenerating work. Now, however, an innovation was introduced whereby the "tribe" could remain intact. A special status was accorded those born of church members: they ranked a step below full church members but a rank above those who attended church but were neither converted nor the descendents of the converted. The terms of the Half-Way Covenant varied from church to church: generally, those who "owned" the covenant affirmed the doctrinal standards and agreed to submit to the watch and care of the church; but they could not receive communion or vote on church matters. In Connecticut, the legislature in 1669 left enforcement of the covenant in the hands of the local church. Some churches accepted it and even modified the terms of the covenant; many others rejected it.[22]

The Town Reports make two explicit references to the Half-Way Covenant, and in both the authors decry its practice, for they interpret its introduction as a clear sign of religious decline.[23] Beginning in the 1740s, Jonathan Edwards of Northampton, Massachusetts, and Joseph Bellamy, a student of Edwards and pastor at Bethlem, Connecticut, emerged as leaders of the so-called "New Light" (and later in the 1760s, "New Divinity") Calvinist party of Congregationalists in New England. Among other things, the New Lights favored the mass revivals of the Great Awakening, arguing that they manifested the work of God. Their "Old Light" Calvinist counterparts denied such claims and responded that wild-eyed lay people and itinerant preachers threatened the peace and stability of the church and established ministers. In addition, New Lights challenged the church-in-state ecclesiology and embraced "pure church" principles over against the terms of the Half-Way Covenant. Bellamy and his fellow "Edwardseans" (and John Treadwell of Farmington counted himself among their number) became the most vociferous defenders of pure church principles. Challenging their own congregations (Edwards was ousted for his intransigence) and waging a strategic pamphlet war, New Lights eventually won the day. According to the calculations of James Walsh, by 1800 the ratio of pure churches to open churches was four to one.[24]

(iii) Anti-Structure: "There began to be divisions"

As is evident by now, Connecticut ecclesiastical life was not always one of peace and harmony. The towns of provincial Massachusetts may have been the "peaceable kingdoms" as Michael Zuckerman described them in his book by that title,[25] but the same could not always be said of the churches of Connecticut. In *Valley of Discord*, a study of ecclesiastical life in the Connecticut River valley, Paul Lucas exposed the erroneous conception of cohesive, homogeneous, gathered churches insulated from internal bickering and intrachurch disagreements.[26] Competing visions of church and polity compounded disagreements within and between churches, and laity clashed with their pastor and among themselves over these issues.

The authors of the Town Reports document episodes of church dissension and division but with a notable emphasis upon the past tense. "We once had disputes, but now we've outgrown them," they seem to be saying. In several parishes, church unity and peace reportedly existed uninterruptedly from their founding to the present. At Ridgefield, "great harmony and peace has subsisted" between the pastor and his people; and in Tolland, "This Chh & Society have been happily united in religious Principles & Practices,—& in the congregational mode of Discipline."[27] The tranquility of the present was no doubt related to one of the unspoken goals of the Town Reports, namely, to applaud the virtues of Connecticut in 1800. But church divisiveness was not a thing of the past. In the late eighteenth century, a third generation of New Light Edwardseans, the New Divinity men, continued to press for pure church principles and to preach an unvarnished brand of Calvinist theology (the "hard doctrines" of predestination and limited atonement) that some parishioners found unpalatable. In addition, salary disputes between pastor and parishioners figured into the mix of contention. And behind these outward disputes were often personality conflicts, petty jealousies, and power struggles.[28] Of the nine episodes documented in the Town Reports, three are especially notable. They were well-known disputes and illustrate the kinds of contentions that wracked Connecticut ecclesiastical life between the first and second Great Awakenings.

Canterbury

> In December 28, 1744 the Revnd James Cogswell D.D. was ordained over [said churches] of the east society in Canterbury. P.S. Between the dismission of the Revnd Mr. Wadsworth in 1741 & Mr. Cogswell's settlement in 1744 the Great Reformation commenced. In this reformation an almost universal attention to religion was visible. Shortly after this happy period, there began to be divisions. These encreased until they threatened serious evils which were verified in the event. Dissentions arose to such a pitch that immediately upon Doct Cogswells being ordained part of sd society set up a meeting among themselves.
>
> N.B. Till this separation in 1744 Canterbury was in one society. These seperatists soon after the division ordained one Mr. Solomon Payne (a brother?) for their minister. After Mr. Payne's death, they ordained Mr. Joseph Marshall.[29]

Although the duration of the "Great Reformation" or Great Awakening in Connecticut was short-lived (1738, 1740-41), the results and ramifications of the revival shaped religious life for the remainder of the eighteenth century and well into the nineteenth. Under the bold, emotional preaching of itinerant revivalists such as George Whitefield, hundreds of colonists became convicted of sin and turned to (or renewed) the Christian faith. Few towns in Connecticut were untouched by the fires of revival. But while the Awakening brought spiritual healing to many, it ravaged the public order of New England, divided churches, weakened the authority of consociations over local churches, and unleashed a debate about the meaning of and means to conversion.

One of the churches so affected was Canterbury, one of sixty-three churches in Connecticut to embrace Separatist principles on either a permanent or temporary basis.[30] Separatists (also called "Strict Congregationalists") embraced spontaneous, fervent piety, revived the call for visible sainthood, and criticized the Standing Order clergy for its spiritually vacuous formalism to the point of attacking an "unconverted ministry." Moreover, they ignored the parish system, challenged the practice of supporting the clergy with public taxation, and believed that a "call" to preach rather than educational attainment defined a true minister of the gospel.[31] In response to their disruptions, Connecticut authorities passed laws against itinerating (1741) and generally harassed the Separatists out of existence. Within twenty years, Separatism died out, though a number of congregations moved into the Baptist orbit (see below, "The Rise of Various . . . Sects").

According to C.C. Goen, the frontier church of Canterbury in Windham County represented "the first instance in which an entire church became 'new-lighted' and withdrew from the communion of the established churches."[32] Between the dismissal of John Wadsworth in 1741 and ordination of James Cogswell in 1744, itinerant evangelists led by the brothers Elisha and Solomon Paine engineered the takeover of the church. The Saybrook Platform was rejected wholesale and the church voted for the Cambridge Platform (though they rejected the magistrate's power over the church) as its form of discipline. However, while the majority of the church joined the New Lights, a minority of the church, supported by the majority of the town, affirmed the Saybrook Platform and Old Light principles. Initially, both parties agreed on Cogswell as the prospective pastor, but when it became known that he supported the Saybrook Platform, favored the Half-Way Covenant, and ignored a public testimony of faith as a criterion for church admission, the New Lights withdrew and formed a Separatist Church. In 1746 Solomon Paine was ordained pastor over a church body 120 members strong. Following Paine's death in 1754, Joseph Marshall pastored the church from 1759 to 1768. No permanent minister was called after 1768, church membership declined, and the church eventually died out in 1831.

Wallingford

> In 1759 a number of families belonging to the First Society, who were opposed to the settlement of Reverend James Dana, withdrew, & obtained permission to worship by themselves—The Reverend Simon Waterman was ordained their pastor October 7th 1761 . . . These several events executed a division among the people; & were the cause of a state of discord and contention seldom exceeded in degree and duration in the history of small religious Societies—The neighboring Clergymen engaged warmly in the controversy, and the Churches assumed the character of "Churches militant," tho' not perhaps strictly in a scriptural sense—The details of this unhappy controversy would be tedious; and are not required either by the civil or religious interests of mankind.[33]

This controversy began a year earlier (1758) when the Reverend James Dana was called from Cambridge to Wallingford First Church. A vocal minority opposed him, contending he was a heretic, a covert Arminian who opposed the substance of Calvinist theology. A year of bitter controversy ensued over who had the authority to call the Reverend Dana. On one side, the New Haven Consociation, recently populated with an influx of young, New Lights pastors, sided with the minority and denied the legality of the call. On the other, the majority of the congregation denied the consociation's authority to tell it what to do and sided with an ordination council of local ministers stacked in Dana's favor. The council proceeded to ordain Dana despite the protestations of the consociation. Angered by this disregard for authority, the New Haven Consociation called upon New Light brethren in Hartford County to pronounce a sentence of non-communion with

Dana, his church, and members of the ordination council. When the New Lights declared Dana's opposition party the true First Church of Wallingford, Old Lights on the ordination council withdrew from the Consociation and declared their independence from any external ecclesiastical authority. In effect, the Old Lights, whose power base was eroding, turned the table as they increasingly decried the very consociations they had once used to their own advantage. A consociational structure designed to check heterodoxy and settle disputes in an orderly fashion now became identified by Old Lights with tyranny, slavery, the abuse of authority, and even the hierarchical Church of England.[34] When the Wallingford church declared its own independence and retained Dana as pastor, a Second Church of Wallingford was formed in 1759 and given formal recognition by the consociations of New Haven County and Hartford South. The Reverend Simon Waterman pastored the church until 1787, when the church was no longer able to support him. A year later, near extinction and the controversy but a memory, the church voted unanimously to rejoin First Church.[35]

Cornwall

> In the beginning of the year 1779 when the Continental Currency was greatly depreciated, & some persons in Town [were] some what Disaffected with the Revd. Mr. Gold, it was by some insisted on that Mr. Gold ought to continue to receive his Salary in that Currency at the Nominal sum, which he declined. But [he] made his Parishioners generous offers which were not accepted by them at that Time, they being much divided . . . Finally it was Voted [in town meeting] That they were Strict Congregationalists, and that they would set up the Congregational Worship in the Meeting House &c, &c, &c. . . And on Thanksgiving Day 1780 Mr. Gold's opponents early in the Day took Possession of the Meeting House & so obstinately defended the Pulpit against him & his Adherents that Mr. Gold did not perform Publick Worship on that Day . . . The next Court of Common Pleas in Litchfield County, The Honourable Andrew Adams, Esq . . . Filed an Information against those who took Possession . . . They were brought to Court, found Guilty by the Jury, & Fined. . . After which a large Number of the Inhabitants returned their Names as strict Congregationalists, Built a Meeting House &c, and continued to Assemble in the same.[36]

What is one to make of this convoluted but not all that unusual tale in the annals of Connecticut ecclesiastical history? As noted above, and as Stephen Foster has documented in detail, the case began over money but soon became a power struggle that ruptured First Church.[37] In 1779, the Reverend Hezekiah Gold, First Church's increasingly unpopular minister, demanded that his salary (now two years

in arrears due to the increasing burden of taxes and expenses of the American Revolution) be paid at full value rather than at the proposed face value in paper money. Already a man of means, Gold protested payment of his salary in paper money whose value was decreasing daily. The townspeople rejected Gold's demand and initiated proceedings to dismiss him. Amid this conflict, Gold favored one side in a dispute between two prominent Cornwall families. When the Litchfield Consociation, under the heavy hand of "Pope Joseph Bellamy," supported Gold, a majority of townspeople became disaffected, rejected the consociation's authority, and after a failed effort to seize the church building by force, they set up their own separate or "Strict Congregational" Church.

In 1781 this second Congregational church secured the services of the Reverend John Cornwall, a shoemaker turned minister. As typified many Connecticut ecclesiastical disputes, church members separated from non-member parish residents. In this case, the Separates attracted a majority of the town but a minority of the church members. No substantive theological issue was at stake, for both sides were in general agreement with Bellamy's New Divinity views or the "Edwardsean System." Rather, the conflict became—not unlike the conflict with Britain—one of popular self-determination versus the imposition of tyrannical (clerical) power. Several attempts were made to reunite the churches, and after both ministers left their churches between 1786 and 1788, reunification looked promising. By then, however, both churches had proceeded with new building plans in separate geographical locations that demarcated the Separates at the town's Center area from the adherents of First Church, now relocated a mile to the south. In 1804 the Assembly granted legal status to Second Church and in 1809 the church rejoined the Litchfield Consociation—nearly thirty years after its members had announced its withdrawal.

(iv) The Clergy:
"Highly and deservedly esteemed"

As we have observed, an ecclesiastical understanding of religion includes the notion that religion is embedded in formal structures, such as creeds or platforms. In addition, authority and leadership is often vested in a clerical body that facilitates human contact with the divine. Indeed, through sermons and officiating at sacramental occasions (baptism and communion), the Connecticut clergy fulfilled the basic duties of a Protestant minister, for it was primarily through these divinely ordained means that God's grace was communicated. Beyond these formal responsibilities, a minister was expected to faithfully serve his parishioners as a counselor, disciplinarian, and godly example. Article 24 on the Academy's roster of topics requested "the names of the successive clergymen, the time of their settlement and exit—notices of any eminent clergymen; the salaries of the clergymen." The heading broaches three aspects of clerical life that directly relate to the status and the perception of the Congregational clergy: tenure, salary, and reputation.

We are given a clue as to the nature of the ministry from statistics supplied regarding clerical tenure. Unlike today, where in Protestant churches the average tenure of a pastor in a single church is about seven years, throughout the seventeenth and most of the eighteenth centuries the ministerial office was conceived in terms of a lifelong tenure in a single parish. A minister's "calling" included not only the understanding that God had set him apart for the ministry, but also implied that within the divine economy, God assigned him to a particular place. "This conception of the sacred office as a calling," notes Donald Scott, "provided a powerful sanction against ambition and hence a powerful buttress to permanence."[38] An examination of the duration of clerical settlements as recorded in the Town Reports confirms this notion. For example, Ebenezer Kellogg in North Bolton, Nathan Strong in North Coventry, John Todd in Madison, and Samuel Hall in Cheshire served their congregations for fifty or more years, while nine pastors served a single church for at least forty years.

At the time that the Town Reports were being written, however, Connecticut was in the throes of a general transformation affecting Congregational clergy throughout New England.[39] Scholars have variously characterized this phenomenon as "from office to profession" or "from job-oriented to congregation-oriented."[40] The long-tenured "parson" of the mid-eighteenth century became, by the early decades of the nineteenth, a mobile professional. The mark of clerical success was measured less by the respect accorded him due to the office he filled, and more by his ability to arouse his congregation, make converts, and instill piety. By 1850, remarks Scott, "the clergy had become a 'profession' in the modern sense," wherein a pastor "now offered specialized services to a particular clientele," that is, to church members only.[41] Whereas a pastor's sphere of influence once extended to the whole community or parish, now it was restricted to his church members.

Several developments contributed to this transition from parson to pastor, from a permanent to a mobile ministry. First, unresolved conflicts abbreviated the tenure of an increasing number of ministers. The New Light-New Divinity rejection of the church-in-society model and insistence of a church comprised of saints exacerbated clergy-parish tensions, resulting in clerical dismissals and thus, an increased turnover rate. Moreover, both the libertarian ideology of the American Revolution and the general diffusion of knowledge among the laity combined to increase lack of deference toward authority that, in turn, further accelerated clergy-parish conflicts and eventual dismissals. Second, the changing status of the ministry itself contributed to a more mobile ministry. As new professional opportunities opened to clergy—such as becoming a college president, a seminary professor, or a benevolent society employee—they revised their notion of a sacred, life-long union with a congregation. Third, salary disputes, though probably more evident of the symptom than the cause of a mobile ministry, prompted clergy to explore alternative career options or to move to a parish offering a higher salary. Salary disputes had been a long-standing issue in Congregational life, but by the first half of the eighteenth

century, they represented the largest single cause of controversy within church life.[42] According to one study, 12 percent of the ministers in New England and northern Long Island were involved between 1680 and 1740 in serious financial disputes with their congregations, and 5 percent of them left their pulpits as a result.[43] Typically, however, contentions over salary alone were never sufficient grounds for severing the union between a pastor and his congregation. Only a gross flaw in the minister's character warranted dismissal, such as noted in the Town Report on Canterbury, where in 1741, the Reverend John Wadsworth was dismissed from First Church for unspecified misconduct.[44]

But in the revolutionary and post-revolutionary period salary disputes reached an impasse. Witness the case already noted of the Reverend Hezekiah Gold at Cornwall. On one hand, the traditional calling to the ministry presupposed a lifelong tenure with a single congregation; on the other hand, the post-revolutionary inflationary spiral pressured clergy into taking a market-oriented, supply-and-demand approach to their sacred vocation. We should note that a salary was not the only source of income for the clergy. Nearly all owned farms and profited from their yield; and even a few ministers became wealthy from real estate ventures. Viewed from the perspective of a Methodist itinerant, who was given an allowance of $80 per year in 1800, the Connecticut Congregational clergy were well off and ranked among the social elite.[45] But viewed from the perspective of a young Congregational minister entering the ranks of the profession, his salary was far from adequate. A "settlement"—somewhat like a signing bonus today—would offset a low salary during the first few years of a new ministry, but once it was spent, ministers began to feel the financial squeeze.

As a result of the failure of salaries to keep up with inflation, an increasing number of younger ministers were more likely to sever ties with their parish than were older clergy. Many had legitimate complaints, but for others, a salary dispute became reason enough, if not a pretext, for moving on to a more desirable position. For example, Ebenezer Porter supported a long-tenured ministry, but when the opportunity arose to take a more prestigious appointment at Andover Seminary, his low salary figured into his decision to leave Washington in 1811.[46] Porter also commented on the predicament of the Reverend Azel Backus, author of the Bethlem Town Report, and the pastor of the Congregational Church. Writing to a neighboring pastor, Porter noted that "Brother Backus is in trouble and talks plainly of being dismissed. . . . I do believe however, that the people, on reflection, cannot part with so worthy a minister at so cheap a rate."[47] Backus eventually left his church for the presidency of Hamilton College.

In addition to conflicts over low salaries, payment of salaries also figured into financial disputes between a minister and his parish. During the colonial and early national periods, many parishes set a fair salary, but then fell behind in payments to the point where ministers would sue for arrears. In other cases of conflict, those who held the church purse strings withheld a portion of the minister's salary.[48] In 1789, Ezra Stiles, Yale's president and an Old Light Calvinist, observed that Farmington

First Church "voted indeed a salary to Revd Mr. Olcott, but voted no collector" (i.e., no one to collect taxes for the pastor's salary) because of a longstanding dispute with the pastor.[49] Despite efforts by the Congregational clergy to set themselves apart from their parishioners (e.g., by eliminating laymen from ordination ceremonies, creating ministerial associations, and imposing discipline), they could only go so far, for their exalted status ultimately depended upon the support of the laity. Here again, the Connecticut Academy's Town Reports require a critical (and considerably wider) reading, for behind the matter-of-fact statements of clerical salaries one uncovers tales of conflict and ambition.

At the same time, these issues should not detract from the recognition of the Congregational clergy as men of stature and worthy of respect. Their knowledge (by virtue of their college education, typically at Yale), their power base (by virtue of their state support), and their spiritual standing (by virtue of their office) enabled the clergy to exert considerable influence. And, we might add, their reputation as godly men conferred upon them the high esteem of their constituents. In the Town Reports, there is, no doubt, something self-serving in ministers praising the reputation of fellow ministers, but in the main their estimations are accurate, though incomplete. Thus at Lebanon, Solomon Williams's reputation was so universally recognized that "His eminence as a man & a divine needs no comment from me."[50] At Guilford, Amos Fowler was "one of the meek & peaceable of the earth."[51] At Chatham, Dr. Cyprian Strong was "highly and deservedly esteemed for his good sense, his thorough acquaintance with theology, and his uniform and blameless conversation."[52] And at Killingworth, the Reverend Achilles Mansfield was "a gentleman distinguished for mild and pleasant manners, for uniformity and sweetness of disposition, and for the patient endurance of afflictions."[53]

The authors noted flaws of character or certain negative proclivities. The Reverend Daniel Brinsmade at Washington was "consciencious and inflexible, in his attachment to the doctrines of Christianity."[54] At East Haddam, the Reverend Timothy Symmes, struck by New Light doctrine, "pursued his work with misguided zeal,"[55] while at Guilford, Thomas Ruggles was a man "of considerable literary attainments, of sound judgment, & unimpeachable morals; but dull and unanimating as a preacher."[56] In his report on New Haven, Timothy Dwight characterized Chauncey Whittlesey as a minister held in "high respect,"[57] but neglected to mention the lack of respect given him during his days as a tutor at Yale College. In 1741 David Brainerd, a New Light student later enshrined by Jonathan Edwards for his missionary piety, made an offhanded private comment that tutor Whittelsey "had no more grace than the chair" he was leaning on. When President Clap got wind of this comment, he had Brainerd dismissed from Yale, and the episode soon became the cause celebre of New Light grievances.

In summary, the authors of the Town Reports portray the Congregational clergy as reputable men of the cloth, though by no means immune from criticism and controversy. Scholars debate the extent to which their status deteriorated as the eighteenth century progressed, but they agree that the clergy remained a powerful force in Connecticut's social structure and cultural life.[58]

(v) The Laity: "Happy revivals of religion"

Article 24 makes no mention of laity, and consequently, the Town Reports largely ignore these key constituents of religious life in Connecticut. There are, however, a couple of statistical clues that offer suggestive points of departure. One is the mention of religious revivals. The year a revival occurred is often accompanied by numbers of converts added to the church membership rolls. Some references are made to the Great Awakening, but more are made to the revivals associated with the Second Great Awakening. In Field's account of Madison, for example, religious awakenings are reported to have occurred in the autumn of 1801 and continued into the winter of 1802-03, when 80 were added to the church, "an unusual proportion of whom were heads of families."[59] Another revival occurred in 1805, principally among the youth; then in the autumn of 1809, 50-60 converted; another revival in 1820 garnered 100 converts; in 1826-27, 115 were admitted to the church; and finally in 1831, 83 were admitted.[60] Such statistics, supplemented with commentary ("heads of families," "youth") are the stuff by which social historians measure the extent (both geographic and demographic) and duration of the Awakening.[61] These statistical profiles (necessarily corroborated by more complete church records) provide social historians with raw data from which to gauge not only the decline and expansion of religion, but also to construct interpretations of religious change and continuity.

One of the more fascinating statistics supplied in the Town Reports is the number of females and males admitted to church membership. In his account of Washington in Litchfield County, James Morris noted that between 1742 and 1811, 154 males and 215 females joined the church. A higher rate of female admission occurred in the latter years, when between 1785 and 1811, 104 females joined compared to 66 males.[62] David Field, in his statistical account of Middlesex County, breaks down church membership numbers by sex for the year 1818. Of 2061 members of Congregational churches in Middlesex County, 1414 were female and 647 were male.[63] Questions arise. In what ways were females increasingly attracted to religion? What factors contributed to this increasing disparity to the point where females outnumbered males by a ratio of well over 2 to 1? This "feminization of religion" (as it is now commonly called) had been evident since the 1660s,[64] but as the statistics reveal, by the end of the eighteenth century and increasingly throughout the first decades of the nineteenth century, the disparity became even more pronounced.[65]

To account for this surge of female piety, scholars offer a variety of explanations. Some point out that religion was "the only game in town" for women seeking an outlet for public expression. Men had numerous options in social and political organizations and thus their religious commitment vied with and eventually lost out to these other options. Other scholars argue that the conventions of wifely submission in the marriage relationship had its analog in the spiritual relationship where regeneration necessitated submission to God. A theology of conversion thus augmented female cultural constraints and expectations, making women particularly susceptible to religion.[66] Whatever explanation is offered—and typically scholars point to not one but several—statistics such as those supplied in the Town Reports illustrate the data base used by historians to reconstruct the social structure of religious life in Connecticut.

(vi) Non-Congregational Bodies: "The Rise of Various . . . Sects"

At the beginning of this essay we observed that the Town Reports slighted non-Congregational religious groups, relegating them to the briefest of comments. To be fair to those who issued their reports in the year 1800, Congregationalism continued to dominate the religious landscape overwhelmingly, especially in those towns that responded to the Academy's statistical inquiry. According to Bruce Daniels' calculations, in 1790 there were a total of 307 societies in the state: 203 (two-thirds) were Congregationalist, followed by 58 Anglican, 30 Baptist, 14 Strict Congregationalist, and 2 Quaker.[67] In a state totaling about 240,00 inhabitants, 80 percent were legally classified as Congregationalist. The emphasis should be placed on legally, for perhaps only 25 percent of classified Congregationalists were actual full church members.

Accurate figures for dissenting bodies are hard to come by, but it is estimated that in 1800 Episcopalians numbered 1,500 communicants, Baptists 4,663, and Methodists 1,600. In 1820, these numbers had increased to 3,400 Episcopalian communicants, 7,500 Baptist, and perhaps as many as 10,000 Methodist.[68] In the next thirty years nothing less than a revolution in denominational affiliations occurred. By 1850, Baptist and Methodist adherents together outnumbered Congregationalists and had 298 churches (Baptists = 113, Methodists = 185) to the Congregationalists' 252.[69]

Among the major dissenting bodies in 1800, the Church of England was the oldest yet also the weakest. Connecticut's Puritans managed to keep the colony free of dissenters until the early eighteenth century, when Baptists in 1705 and Anglicans in 1707 established their first parishes. To add insult to Puritan injury, the Toleration Act of 1708 recognized their legal right to exist. Throughout the eighteenth century, the Church of England held a certain attraction for those seeking both to establish the church upon apostolic authority and to escape the persistent tensions within the Congregational church. In 1722, in a major coup for the Church (and a great scandal to the Puritans), Yale's Rector Timothy Cutler and tutors Samuel Johnson and Daniel Browne converted to Anglicanism.[70] This "great apostasy" or "grand defection" sent shock waves throughout New England and signaled the beginning of a respectable Anglican presence in Connecticut. With the coming of the American Revolution, however, the Church of England fell on hard times. Its formal ties to England and its members' presumed Loyalist sympathies discredited

the Church, and when its clergy fled the colony, the Church was left leaderless. Although the reorganization of the Anglican Church into the Protestant Episcopal Church lessened popular hostility and enabled the church to experience a slight rebound, in 1800 it had only 17 clergy in its 62 churches. David Field provided comparative figures for measuring Episcopal strength in Middlesex County in 1815. Out of 3,688 families, 2,330 (63 percent) were identified as Congregationalist and 421 (11 percent) as Episcopalian.[71] Statewide, Episcopalians comprised around 8 percent of the population in 1816.

If the Episcopal Church was a numerical "loser" in the wake of the American Revolution, Baptists and Methodists were the eventual "winners." The post-revolutionary democratic surge that affected economic opportunity and the structure of political authority also profoundly altered the religious life of the nation. Though given little attention in the Town Reports, the Methodists increasingly became a force with which to be reckoned. As we have noted, at the time the reports were written, Connecticut was on the cusp of religious upheaval, marked by the startling growth of the Methodists. No Methodist churches dotted the Connecticut landscape in 1790, but from that decade on, Methodist itinerants, including the Connecticut-born "Crazy" Lorenzo Dow crisscrossed the state, stirred up religious revival, and encountered hostility and even violence from Congregationalists and Baptists. The Town Reports are silent on tensions between religious groups and several even note amicable relations. The author of the Cornwall (Litchfield County) report observed that "there may be said in general to be a good Philanthropick, Neighbourly affection and mutual good offices of kindness between the Citizens of Different Denominations."[72] And yet Methodist itinerants dreaded the Litchfield circuit—a form of exile that tested the most devoted elder. While on a preaching tour in Litchfield County, Billy Hibbard reported having stones hurled at him and dogs loosed upon him.[73] Yet his dogged persistence paid dividends. By 1814 he could boast of 300 Methodist converts in his Litchfield circuit—the most homogeneous and staunchest of Congregational counties in the state.

The Town Reports offer no evidence that this kind of populist religious upsurge was in the making. That the Methodists had no "places of worship" (not until 1827 did Methodists build their first church west of the Connecticut River) or leading citizens as church members, consigned them to little more than passing notice in the reports. But in the years ahead, the fiery lay exhorter, the "love feasts," the camp meetings, and emotional religion attracted thousands of Methodist followers, many of whom defected from nominal Congregational allegiance. According to one study, in 1850 for every 134 Congregationalists per 1,000 population, there were 81 Methodists.[74] Such gains are particularly remarkable when one considers that sixty years earlier no Methodist group existed in Connecticut. Nationwide, trends accelerated at a faster pace than in Connecticut, where from 1776 to 1850, Methodists grew at an astronomical rate from a mere 2.5 percent to over 34 percent of all religious adherents. In that same period

Congregationalists fell precipitously from 20 percent of all religious adherents to 4 percent.[75]

Baptist gains were less remarkable than Methodist, but nonetheless significant. Statewide, the 59 churches and 4,600 members in 1800 increased to 83 churches and 9,200 members by 1830. As noted earlier, Baptists (inaccurately called "Anabaptists" in some of the Town Reports[76]) had an established presence in eastern Connecticut dating back to the Separates (Strict Congregationalists) of the Great Awakening who later joined the Baptist camp. Their democratic polity, itinerating practices, demands for a regenerate membership, and lack of a learned ministry enhanced their popular appeal. Strict Congregationalists were either absorbed by the Baptists or reunited with Congregational churches, so that at the time of disestablishment in 1818, only a handful of Strict Congregationalist churches remained.

(vii) Threats to Religion: "Infidelity"

> About the time that Paynes age of Reason came abroad, Infidelity presented itself to view . . . The horror of its features disgusted the people to such a degree that it has not as yet had one advocate in this town.[77]

Consult nearly any standard text on American religion and you will find reference to Thomas Paine's *Age of Reason* (1794) as an example of the attacks on revealed religion in post-revolutionary America. Two important books on Connecticut, Richard Purcell's *Connecticut in Transition: 1775-1818* (1918), and Charles Keller's *The Second Great Awakening in Connecticut* (1942) emphasized the theme of infidelity as a threat against which conservative Congregational clergy rallied to inaugurate the Second Great Awakening.[78] A subtext to this lamentation of spiritual waywardness was a growing awareness that Presbyterians (and Congregationalists) were losing out in the race for converts to the more aggressive Baptists and Methodists. Still, the alarm over the spread of a pernicious irreligion was real. Throughout the 1790s, the cries of infidelity and the decline of orthodox Christianity were heard on all denominational fronts. Evangelical leaders bemoaned the loss of religious fervor, the preoccupation with worldly concerns, and yes, the spread of infidelity. According to Martin Marty, infidelity took many forms, including "imported intrusions, British deism, French Enlightenment thought, German idealism, along with liberal theology, immorality, popular disaffection with the churches, and the formal indigenous attack on religion."[79] Infidelity thus became a code word describing either religious declension or opposition to orthodox Christianity.

In Samuel Goodrich's account, infidelity took the form of Paine's *Age of Reason*, an anti-clerical work that waged a frontal attack upon revealed religion, replacing it with a natural, deistic theology. Connecticut's leaders, including President Timothy Dwight of Yale, counterattacked, and in Dwight's case, he routed student "deistical societies" from the college after taking over the presidency in 1795. His well-known *Discourse on Some Events of the Last Century* (1801) represented a classic exposition of infidelity's history, tracing its origins to foreign godlessness imbibed by the likes of Tom Paine. In Dwight's view, such godlessness threatened not only orthodox religion, but also the very survival of the new nation, for only true religion provided the moral underpinnings upon which the republic was based.[80] Nations have come and gone, noted the Reverend Asahel Hooker of Goshen, because "they wanted that divine cement, the religion of Jesus, which united man to man, and men to God."[81] Curiously, apart from Samuel Goodrich's brief comment on Ridgefield's condemnation of infidelity, the Town Reports are silent on an issue that so inflamed the passions of Connecticut's Congregational clergy. Although infidelity had no takers in Ridgefield, and indeed was more a bogeyman than a real threat in Connecticut, its value as a rhetorical device roused Christians to spiritual action that in turn, contributed to the making of the Second Great Awakening.

Conclusion

By design, this essay has been more suggestive than definitive. I have approached the Town Reports from two perspectives—one descriptive, the other analytical. Given the kind of information requested in Article 24, I have used the documents to discuss themes in Connecticut's *ecclesiastical* history. And given the information supplied by the authors, I have used the documents to illustrate how students of history have analyzed such data to detect trends and offer explanations.

As commentaries on the contemporary state of religion in Connecticut, the Town Reports fall woefully short. As we have noted, they fail to capture what was probably the most lively and energetic period in the religious history of Connecticut. The terms used by historians to characterize the period from 1800 to 1832—"transition," "adjustment," "disestablishment," "voluntarism," "reaction," "revival," "awakening," and "reform"—were, with the exception of "revival," foreign to the authors of the Town Reports. We should not, however, be too quick to assign blame for these indiscretions, if they can even be called that. For one, the Town Reports were never intended to be more than *statistical* reports. For another, their authors did not have the benefit, as we do, of the long perspective. Put simply, they were not historians—nor were they asked to be. Rather, they were asked to record accurate information, akin to the task of an antiquarian. From that perspective the Town Reports must be judged, and indeed, we may judge them as useful, if fragmentary, guides to Connecticut's ecclesiastical history.

The Religious Landscape

Gretchen T. Buggeln

In article twenty-four of its solicitation letter of 1800, the Connecticut Academy asked respondents to note "Places of public worship; their number, and the denomination to which they belong—the rise of congregations and various sects, the names of the successive clergymen, the time of their settlement and exit—notices of any eminent clergymen; the salaries of the clergymen and the funds by which religious worship is maintained." Question twenty-four in effect asked the writers to record the state of religion in Connecticut. This question lies buried in a list that is largely directed towards natural history, manufactures, and the practical aspects of daily life. Yet the topic of religion received considerable attention from most of the respondents. In cryptic form, their Reports convey the contours of the religious landscape of early nineteenth-century Connecticut.

Why was religious life an important consideration for members of the Academy? By the time these Reports were written it was clear that Connecticut's religious atmosphere was changing dramatically. Old order Congregationalists (including most of the writers of these Reports) saw the writing on the wall; their privileged legal position was crumbling as dissenting groups gathered strength. The future would be one of multiple denominations and a new kind of competition for members and money. Yet dissent and even the ultimate disestablishment of religion altogether under the 1818 state constitution did not signal a decline in religious fervor in the state. In fact, the increasing variety of religious options was an outgrowth of strong religious sentiment.[1] The aim of Connecticut's concerned Protestants— such as members of the Academy and writers of the Reports— was to harness that new energy and diversity in ways that would assist their own social and political agendas. They believed that a Christian foundation and a virtuous citizenry were essential to the success of the new nation. These Town Reports consequently reveal a desire to see Connecticut society and landscape display an animated yet refined Christian character.

In answering questions about religion, the respondents came face to face with a problem that still plagues historians today: how do we measure the force and content of religious life? Do we read sermons? Do we count the people in the pews? Do we look at church growth? Religion is often a private, personal business. It is not easy to describe one's *own* religious experiences, let alone those of others. The Connecticut Academy asked its respondents to contribute "useful knowledge" to its "Statistical History." Without overtly demanding that its respondents be objective, they implied that this was to be a scientific record in the enlightenment spirit of the age. The respondents coped

with their task accordingly. Depth of emotion or commitment to a particular religious creed were not quantifiable, but one could objectively *count* things. The writers numbered the members of the different religious societies, recorded ministers' salaries, detailed church funds and budgets, counted meeting houses or steeples, and noted the number and location of graveyards. These numbers both reassured and concerned Connecticut's citizens; yes, religion was present, but couldn't it be much *more* present, and more powerfully so?

Another essay in this volume addresses the ecclesiastical history of Connecticut, the work of the ministry, and the composition of congregations. This essay will consider some of the more concrete aspects of Connecticut's religious life: money and buildings. First, we will examine the "the funds by which religious worship is maintained." Second, the essay will turn to "places of public worship, their number, and the denomination to which they belong." We will see how closely these two issues of financial stability and church buildings were intertwined, and how they became even more so in the new republic. Both financial resources and church buildings were quantifiable, important measures of the vitality of Christianity in Connecticut.

***

To understand the accounts of finances and buildings in these Town Reports, it is necessary to review the organizational history of religion in Connecticut. In the seventeenth century, the founding of a town was nearly identical to the founding of a religious society. Once a group of settlers had enough of a tax base to settle and support a minister, the ecclesiastical society incorporated. All voting members of the town were automatically members of the Congregational society, and were taxed accordingly. The society took care of the two main expenses facing congregations: they hired the minister and paid his salary, and they built and maintained the meetinghouse, a multifunctional building used for both sacred (church) and secular (town) business. It should be noted that the *church society* was a different organization, a subset of the ecclesiastical society made up of those who had experienced a conversion and "owned the covenant." The church society, while also a state-created corporation, dealt with spiritual, not financial matters. The intent behind this arrangement was that Congregationalism, the faith of the founders, would be integrated into the life of the colony and supported either by taxation or the revenue provided by the apportionment of town lands.

By the eighteenth century this neat arrangement was being constantly complicated by demographic changes and by the appearance of dissenting groups, particularly Anglicans and Baptists. A series of acts of the legislature increasingly gave dissenters their freedom and legal rights. For example, a 1727 act allowed Christian dissenters with proper certification to allocate their religious taxes to their own church societies, incorporated bodies which existed alongside the Congregational organizations. Further legislation, the Act of Toleration of 1784, legally recognized dissenting Christian societies and thus gave them all the powers granted to Congregational societies, including the power to raise taxes among their own members.[2] By 1790, there were 307 incorporated religious societies in Connecticut: 203 Congregational, 58 Anglican, 30 Baptist, 14 Strict Congregationalist, and two Quaker.[3] Methodists and, occasionally, Universalists, too, were increasingly making their presence felt, establishing congregations and building meetinghouses. Connecticut's older towns and counties, with a more diversified economy and social structure, tended to be the most religiously complex. New Haven or Middletown, for example, had a wider variety of congregations than did Chester or Durham.[4]

Much has been said about the strife within colonial churches and their tendency to splinter, and some of the Town Reports bear this out (see below). But these cases were the exception rather than the rule. Simple population dispersion and the consequent growth of new Congregational societies was the most common reason for the redistribution of taxes. These demographic changes, together with the right of dissenters to pay their taxes to their own denomination, meant financial trouble for the Congregationalists, whose tax base seemed to be constantly eroding. Members of all denominations knew by the time of these surveys that taxation was no longer the answer to their financial needs. Not only was the tax base shrinking, but the spirit of the age was one of voluntarism and free choice. What was once a legal obligation had become a matter of conscience. It became the burden of each congregation to secure its own financial stability.

As Congregationalism struggled with diversity and new financial concerns, the multipurpose Congregational meetinghouse was simultaneously losing its central place. Offshoot congregations and dissenting groups paid for and built their own places of worship, often with the expectation that they be used primarily if not solely for church business. At the same time, the construction and use of town houses drew away the former municipal functions of meetinghouses.[5] By 1800, a considerable variety of religious and civic buildings dotted the landscape—meetinghouses and churches, town houses, courthouses, almshouses, schoolhouses and academy buildings. These buildings shared the many functions originally united in the Puritan meetinghouse. As the bond between congregation and town (or church and state) dissolved, the meetinghouse lost its role as symbolic center of community life. On the other hand, a new breed of grand church buildings was linking religion with something that mattered just as much to Connecticut's citizens of the early republic: a Christian civility based in refined worship, a generous public spirit, good manners, and good taste.[6]

Although the degree of detail varies considerably among the responses to question twenty-four in the Town Reports, most writers included a brief account of the number of congregations and denominations, a list of church buildings, and sources of operating funds. John Cotton Smith's Report from Sharon, a rural community in Litchfield County, is typical:

> In the old society there are a Congregational and a Methodist Church and in Ellsworth one Congregational Church. There was formerly a handsome Episcopal church and a respectable congregation in the first society, but the former is now gone to decay and the latter dispersed, a few individuals only of that denomination remain. The Minister in the Society of Ellsworth receives a salary of ( ), raised from a permanent fund. In the First Society the salary of the Minister is $500, a small part of which is paid by a fund, the remainder by an annual sale of pews.[7]

Smith's account tells us the bare details of religious life in Sharon. What Smith and most of the other writers chose to include consisted primarily of what they would have already known. It is not at all surprising that Smith would have been aware of the number and state of religious buildings in his town. Nor is it unexpected that he would have known the financial affairs of his own First Congregational Society, where his father had been minister. He apparently was unsure of how much the Ellsworth Society's minister was paid, for he left that out of the Report.

Most Reports describe what was there at the time of writing; some also relate the histories and appearances of past buildings, or the manner in which a congregation had raised support through the years. The writer of the East Windsor Report, for example, in common fashion noted that the Congregational Society's "first temporary church" was erected in 1690, gave the dates of the second and third buildings, and mentioned that the latter had been "Paid for principally by the sale of tobacco."[8] Historical time was measured by the erection and decline of various religious structures and the tenures of past ministers. We can scan most of these Reports for ministers' names, the occasional mention of buildings, and a few numbers relating the size of congregations or the extent of their resources.

The Middlesex County statistical Report prepared by Haddam's Congregational minister David Field in 1818 is the most complete account of the state of religious affairs provided by these Town Reports. This Report goes well beyond the others in detail and demonstrates the writer's meticulous research in all the Middlesex County towns. Like most of the writers, Rev. Field was a clergyman with a vested interest in the ongoing health and wealth of the Christian church in Connecticut. It is no surprise, then, that religion plays a dominant role in his account of the public life of Middlesex County. With unusual precision, Field counted and briefly described religious buildings, detailed funds for the support of the ministry, listed ministers of the different denominations, and recorded the number of members of the various congregations.

Rev. Field was particularly thorough with his assessment of the financial situation of the many congregations in his county. He listed a variety of ways they managed the "support of the gospel": rents on land owned by the parish; money from the sale of such lands; legacies left by citizens who had died; "appropriation money" (government supplied funds), and money raised by subscription. The Hadlyme Congregational parish, for instance, had $340 from the sale of "parsonage lands" and an additional $48 from the "appropriation." The Pautapoug society, on the other hand, had a more complicated assortment of parsonage lands, a personal bequest, appropriation money, and a large subscription fund ($6,587) raised in 1817.[9] The church of Pautapoug additionally claimed three legacies.

Given that church finances are a relatively private and uninteresting business for most of us today, it is notable that the Academy asked about such things, and more notable still that the respondents answered that part of the query with such regularity. This was because the affairs of religious societies were a public matter. In becoming public corporations individually chartered by the legislature, religious societies traded some of their autonomy for legitimacy and stability.[10] Incorporation protected societies and their assets, but it also drew them into a system of state-chartered organizations—churches, turnpike companies, banks—that existed, implicitly, for the general good of the people of Connecticut. How they fared, then, was a matter of public concern. At the time of the survey, the present and future of financial support for Connecticut's churches was disturbingly uncertain. Church finances were an idiosyncratic and often complex arena of experimentation and change.

In addition to his statistical account, Rev. Field also wrote a narrative account of Middlesex County. This narrative illuminates the statistics of the other document and gives a more personal explanation for the state of affairs in Middlesex. Initially, the old system worked just fine. "The Congregational ministers of Middlesex," Field wrote, "have generally been supported by a tax laid on the lists of the inhabitants. While the people remained of one heart, and of one way to serve God, this method of support was attended with little difficulty, and excited little opposition." Competition, however, soon drew off funds from the Congregational society. "But as other denominations arose, it became somewhat embarrassed, and was made the subject of much complaint. The consequence is, that resort is had in many cases to other means of support." Some support came from land originally apportioned to the minister or the religious society: "lands reserved by the first settlers for the support of the ministry have, in some instances, become valuable, and by being rented or leased yield a considerable annual income." Other lucky societies received considerable bequests: "Several societies have received important legacies and donations" and "In other cases subscriptions have been set on foot for raising funds." Field does not conceal his sadness that the people of Middlesex were no longer "of one heart, and of one way to serve God." Yet religion was surviving, even thriving, in the county.[11]

Although Field's account of Middlesex is typical, there is no uniform way that these financial developments unfolded in Connecticut's parishes. Some places, like the Hanover Congregational parish, incorporated in 1761, for forty years relied solely on the interest from a fund of £1400 raised by subscription.[12] In Goshen as late as 1812 taxation was still the primary means of support: the minister's "annual salary of 600 dollars, which, together with other society expenses is defrayed by an annual tax on the society's list." Urban societies tended to be more innovative in their discovery and use of funding sources. For instance, Timothy Dwight recorded that in New Haven "each of the congregations in this town is possessed of a fund for the support of the Ministry. The fund of the First Society amounts to 11, 685 dollars and 10 cents; and consists of bank stock and money at interest." The newer, United Congregational Society also had a fund, but it was less than half that amount. The local Episcopal congregation, Trinity, had resources consisting of "lands in the city of New-Haven; the rents of which amount to 569 dollars and 75 cents, annually. They will soon produce more; as several of the leases will expire after a short time, and the rents will of course be raised."[13] In urban areas such as New Haven and Hartford, those responsible for society finances often took their cues from developments in the incipient banking and insurance sectors.

Most congregations, both urban and rural, had several options other than taxation or the rent or sale of church lands. Church "funds," mentioned so often in these Reports, were initially the most obvious solution to the growing problem. These were simply cash collections that were raised at one moment and added to or borrowed from over the years. After 1791, with the introduction of state and national banks to Connecticut, this money could be deposited at interest in one of these chartered organizations. The interest would then have been used to pay yearly expenses. Additions to funds could come from gifts or bequests, but more often the funds were established through subscription. "Subscription" referred to a capital campaign in which pledges were raised, usually to be collected over the next year. Subscriptions sometimes went to a general operating fund; at other times they were directed to a specific purpose, most commonly the construction of a new building. Religious societies joined canal builders, turnpike operators and all manner of public corporations in their use of the subscription paper. Pledges could prove difficult to collect, but most often those who signed the paper honored their commitments.

The "appropriation money" noted in the Middlesex account was another small source of cash that came along after most of the Town Reports were written. On several occasions the Connecticut state legislature made restricted funds available to ecclesiastical societies. For example, although the sale of lands in the Western Reserve was designed to benefit the schools, a 1795 act allowed individual districts, by a two-thirds majority vote, to use that money for the ministry.[14] The "appropriation money" referred to an act of the legislature passed in October 1816, which allocated a portion of the national refund of state war expenses to ecclesiastical societies "for the support of the Gospel": one third to the Congregationalists, one seventh to the Episcopalians, one eighth to the Baptists, one twelfth to the Methodists, and one seventh to Yale College. According to the Middlesex Report, this money has "generally been applied by them [the societies] to the increase of funds for maintaining religious institutions."[15] This act, sometimes called the Act for the Support of Literature and Religion, was more problematic than helpful, for the dispensation of funds required elaborate accounting, and the relative proportion of the denominations rapidly changed, quickly rendering the allocation unfair. Moreover, it was clearly in opposition to the new state constitution which mandated a separation of church and state matters.[16]

Lotteries were another means of raising support, although the Town Reports mention only one, the lottery which the legislature granted to the Episcopal Academy of Cheshire in 1802 for the purpose of raising $15,000.[17] Societies for a short time viewed lotteries as a means to relieve debt or pay for a meetinghouse. In 1803, for example, the four societies in Preston, Canterbury, Voluntown, and Winsted together asked the state to permit a $6000 lottery for "building and repairing the meetinghouses in those societies respectively."[18] Lotteries were commonly used to raise money for public works projects, and purchasers of lottery tickets appreciated their chance to gamble. But lotteries were fraught with problems—poor management, poor collection results, moral doubts. An 1834 law finally prohibited all lotteries in the state.[19]

Pew rents were ultimately the most important addition to this arsenal of fundraising techniques. Recall that in the Sharon Report dated 1807, John Cotton Smith made reference to the "annual sale of pews" in the First Society. The Society records reveal that this was quite a recent development. In October of that year the society voted that pews be rented to the highest bidder. This decision was a direct result of the realization that there was "a larger sum due from the society than will be convenient to raise by a direct tax." Furthermore, it was believed that "the present mode of occupying the Pews . . . is unequal & attended with great inconvenience."[20] The Sharon society was in need of a sum of money that exceeded the amount it could reasonably expect from a tax.

Although the record does not explain what that "present mode" of seating was, it was probably based on the colonial system of "doming" the pews in which a committee assigned seats to individual men and their families based on a ranking that took into account wealth, age, and position in the community.[21] This old mode of seat assignment, which reified social hierarchies, was out of step with the individualistic, market economy of the new century, and its old-fashioned seat assignments also neglected to market one of the best potential resources a congregation had—its pew space.

In a system of pew rental, members of the congregation paid a yearly fee for the use of a specific pew. While several pews were always reserved for the minister, widows and the aged, and strangers to the town, most members of the society paid for their seats. Pew rental was extremely effective because a congregation could annually determine its financial needs and charge accordingly for the pew space. Societies, such as the one in Sharon, recognized that this was a better means of extracting "a larger sum" from members. Although pew rentals are mentioned very little in these Reports, by 1830, most congregations in the state relied on them as a key component of their accounting.

Large, urban churches, seeking the means to pay for new buildings, tended to be the first to turn to pew rental. For some congregations, pew rental was an immediate success, its revenue covering the entire yearly budget. Soon after Trinity Episcopal Church in New Haven opened pew sales for its new Gothic church in 1815, a pleased building committee reported that, by renting out pews at from five to thirty dollars a year, it had raised a projected yearly income of $4,621.[22] This amount was nearly two thousand dollars over what the church thought it would need for the annual budget (including the minister's salary, building maintenance, and interest and principal payments on building debt). First Church in Hartford (built 1807) was not so lucky. The congregation made the mistake of initially selling its pews outright, raising about $28,000—$4,000 less than the cost of the new church—and leaving no means to generate additional annual income.[23] For decades, even after the congregation reclaimed many of the pews for annual rental, First Church struggled with chronic debt. Rural churches tended to be more tentative about adopting impersonal pew rental systems, although economic realities pushed them in that direction. Like any other asset, pew rental, wisely managed, could produce a substantial income.

Psychologically, pew rental was a more effective means of fundraising than simply asking for donations. Members of a congregation felt that they were getting something concrete for their money—the bigger the donation the better the pew space. At the time these Town Reports were written, it was becoming increasingly clear that carefully planned, voluntary giving was the wave of the future. Public support of religion was nothing to be taken for granted, and the leaders of Connecticut's churches had to adapt their financial strategies to this new reality.

Pew rental had an unintended side effect: it tied the well-being of a congregation directly to its church building. The amount and quality of pew space determined annual revenue for the congregation. Better pews in better churches drew more support. This may be one reason so many of Connecticut's congregations, at great expense, erected new buildings in the first decades of the nineteenth century. But there were other reasons as well: the dilapidated state of many pre-Revolutionary buildings; the competitive growth of new denominations and congregations as the result of both revival and demographic changes; and a widespread concern over what Connecticut *looked like*. In architecture one could see the manners and morals of a people. While the financial support of Connecticut's ministers was largely invisible to the outside observer, the quality and quantity of its religious structures was blatantly apparent. What would travelers see of religion when passing through Connecticut's cities and towns? How would that shape their impressions of Connecticut's moral character?

The writers of the Reports paid little attention to the specific qualities of ecclesiastical architecture; from the Reports alone we have little idea what these buildings looked like or how they functioned in Connecticut's towns. Yet the fact that the question was even asked, and the manner in which it was answered, reveals much about the surprising importance of religious buildings in Connecticut society. Religious buildings were the flagships of Christian society, the public markers of religious life. This is why, in Rev. Field's Middlesex account; he carefully noted not just the present buildings, but the ones they replaced. He noted as well the bare bones of what they looked like: their dimensions, and which among them had bell towers or spires. Other writers tend to mention just the dimensions of the building, the construction materials, and the date of erection. While these facts may seem rather dull and uninformative, they served one key purpose: they conveyed the relative amount of money that the congregation had been willing to give for its building. They were, in short, a measure of *investment and progress* in the realm of religion.

These Town Reports were written at a time when the religious architecture in the state was in most cases old and tired. This may be one reason the architecture is so infrequently described in detail: it was an embarrassment. Timothy Dwight, who wrote the New Haven Report, waxed eloquently about the new Grove Street burying ground,

"*South view of the churches in Durham. The church seen on the left is the new congregational church erected in 1835. The church seen standing in the street is the old congregational church...These churches are a fair specimen of the ancient and modern method of building houses of worship.*" John Warner Barber, Connecticut Historical Collections (New Haven, 1838), p. 523.

yet had only this to say about New Haven's five churches (three Congregational, one Episcopal, one college chapel) and other public buildings: "all of them decent, but none of them beautiful."[24] In 1815, when James Morris wrote his account of Litchfield County towns, Litchfield—a town often praised for its fine architecture—still retained the old, run-down, red meetinghouse of 1762.[25] Ten years later, in 1825, that building was still standing. The following year, a "Stranger in Litchfield" wrote to the *Litchfield County Post* that "Litchfield has long been considered one of the most beautiful Villages in New England." Yet there was a prominent scar on that image. Litchfield's ill-kempt, old-fashioned "meeting-house, standing conspicuously in the center of the village, 'like a city set on a hill,' unfortunately cannot be hid" the writer lamented. This "old, decayed, shabby building pains the eye of every stranger." Such an embarrassment was "a reproach to the taste, the opulence, and the good sense of a large and respectable society of worshipping christians."[26]

Litchfield's Congregationalists lagged behind many of Connecticut's congregations in the construction of a new church, but the story was a familiar one. The Middlesex Account of 1819 demonstrates the relative age of Congregational buildings in Connecticut. Only six of the eighteen Congregational meetinghouses in the county had been erected since 1790; ten of them were built prior to 1750. On the other hand, of the eighteen structures dissenters had built in the county, all but five had been erected since 1790. Some of these were, of course, the nondescript early barn-like buildings of Methodists and Baptists. Nonetheless, it was clear to Congregationalists that they needed to build anew: competition from other denominations encouraged it, successful fundraising depended on it, and "taste" and respectability demanded it. The Revolutionary era had not been one in which great attention was paid to religious architecture or one in which religious fervor was remarkable. In the new republic, however,

a great deal was at stake in the appearance of the religious landscape. The hope was that an observer in every corner of Connecticut would see what Benjamin Silliman saw when he looked down on Woodbury in 1820. "On reaching the top of a high hill, all of a sudden in a valley stretching North and South for a mile or two, Woodbury appears, with a handsome, well built street, and furnished with three churches, with spires,— two of them new and handsome."[27] Those "new and handsome" churches spoke volumes about the sturdy republican character of the town of Woodbury.

These Town Reports hint at but do not describe the major change in religious architecture sweeping the state; a change indicated by Silliman's use of the word "spire" to describe Woodbury's churches. This was not a simple rebuilding of structures in the old style, but a completely new approach to church buildings. Eighteenth-century Congregational meetinghouses were squarish buildings with an entrance on a long side, boxy pews facing several directions, a high pulpit, and occasionally an attached bell tower. In architectural design, new ecclesiastical buildings of Congregationalists looked more like the Anglican/Episcopal churches of the eighteenth-century. In fact, the white, steepled church on a hill, with pillars in front supporting a triangular pediment—the building we often think of as representing a "golden age" of colonial New England community life—is a product of this post-colonial era.

Historians have called this new architectural development, which was taking place among Congregational churches all over New England at this time, the "meetinghouse to church" transition.[28] The implication is more than simply one of a transformation in architectural design. "Meetinghouse" was a term meant to describe a multifunctional community building; "church" was a place reserved for the worship of God. In the period of these Reports the trend was towards a worship structure that served only spiritual purposes. In the eighteenth century, Anglican houses of worship had most always been

First Congregational Church, East Haddam (1791-1794). Attributed to Lavius Fillmore. J. Frederick Kelly, Early Connecticut Meetinghouses *(New York: Columbia University Press, 1948), Vol. 2, p. 118.*

referred to as "churches" to distinguish them from Congregational meetinghouses. But now Congregationalists were building churches as well. In these Town Reports and in other contemporary documents, however, this distinction is not clear. The term "meetinghouse" continues to be used interchangeably with "church" for Congregational buildings in period documents. In other words, the choice of word at this point is *not* a clue to architectural style. To know what the buildings looked like, we need to seek other documentation, and investigate the buildings which survive.

The reasons for this "meetinghouse to church" evolution are elusive. It was not simply a change in fashion, for the "church" form had been around for a long time in the guise of Anglican buildings. What made Congregationalists in Connecticut and the other northeastern states rebuild in this style? In part, they found that the new style answered a need for the public expression of refined Christian character, as noted above. The change was also a response to new theological and devotional imperatives. Revival did not just add numbers; it changed the character of worship. Worship became more emotional and sentimental, and the focus was on the preacher at the front of the church. New, elegant, neoclassical church buildings, with forward-facing pews, were

conducive to this kind of worship experience. These special buildings, set apart, marked the growing gulf between the rapidly moving world of work and money and the sphere of sentiment and contemplation.

There was also the influence of the Anglicans, who in 1789 reorganized into the Protestant Episcopal Church in America. Connecticut, particularly the southwestern and coastal portions of the state, had long been home to a considerable number of Anglicans, and the first American Bishop, Samuel Seabury, settled in New London. The pomp and dignity of the Anglican tradition, long a threat to the Puritan order, had emerged in post-Revolutionary Connecticut as something surprisingly appealing. The writers of these Town Reports discuss the fortunes of the Episcopalians in a tone subtly more accepting than that which they use to describe Methodists or, in some cases, Baptists. Part of this was no doubt due to their familiarity and, by the nineteenth century, their relative social prestige. For example, the Episcopal church in Middletown was built in 1752, apparently the same year the congregation formed. Four of the seven past ministers of that congregation had Yale degrees, and one was educated in Cambridge, England. That congregation in 1818 had the largest church fund in the county, owing to a $13,000 legacy coming to them from the estate of Captain Stephen Clay.[29]

Interior, First Congregational Church, East Haddam. The pews are not original. J. Frederick Kelly, Early Connecticut Meetinghouses *(New York: Columbia University Press, 1948), Vol. 2, p. 127.*

Other Town Reports also indicate a general acceptance of, and even admiration for, local Episcopalians. The writer of the New London Report (who may have been an Episcopalian) observed in 1811 that there was "a handsome & convenient church & a respectable congregation of the episcopal order" in his town.[30] Rev. Solomon Palmer, a Congregational minister in Cornwall who had been dismissed from his post about 1750 for becoming an Anglican, was nonetheless described by the writer of the Cornwall Report as "a gentleman of good Breeding, very social in Conversation, Generous in his House."[31] The Episcopal church served occasionally as an acceptable refuge for those disillusioned with Congregationalism.

An example of the complicated relationship between Episcopalians and Congregationalists and their church design is provided by the experience of the residents of East Haddam, in Middlesex County. East Haddam's Congregationalists and Episcopalians both built expensive new churches around 1792-1794. Not just the buildings, but the congregations themselves, were closely related. Disagreement over the proposed site for the new Congregational meetinghouse in 1791 actually led to a division in the society, and those who broke away formed St. Stephen's Episcopal society. (It is highly likely that the building project provided an occasion for a break that had been brewing for some time for other reasons.)

East Haddam's First Congregational Church (1791-1794) is probably early work of the builder Lavius Fillmore.[32] The church bears close resemblance to Joseph Brown's 1775 First Baptist Church in Providence, Rhode Island, and also to the Taunton (1792) and Pittsfield (1793) Massachusetts churches designed by Charles Bulfinch in 1789. The interior, with its octagonal dome within a cross, is related to the interior of Bulfinch's 1788 Hollis Street Church in Boston. Such similarities between buildings reflect the tendency of both

Interior of St. Stephen's Episcopal Church, looking forward. The gallery is only opposite the pulpit at the North end. Note the detail of the woodwork, the vaulted ceiling and the stove pipe behind the columns. The box pews are original.J. Frederick Kelly, Early Connecticut Meetinghouses *(New York: Columbia University Press, 1948), Vol. 2, p. 115.*

The entrance to St. Stephen's Episcopal Church, East Haddam, demolished 1921. This old photograph reveals the elegance of the original entrance and its similarity to that of the First Congregational Church. Note the round-topped second tier windows, a distinguishing feature of Episcopal churches. J. Frederick Kelly, Early Connecticut Meetinghouses *(New York: Columbia University Press, 1948), Vol. 2, p. 114.*

builders and building committees to borrow architectural ideas from existing or proposed buildings of their own or other denominations. Fillmore no doubt had a first-hand familiarity with the Providence church and with Bulfinch's innovative designs for Massachusetts's churches. This free borrowing accelerated and enhanced the development of a regional "churchly" style of rural Congregational and Episcopal buildings. And by 1797 a very similar building appeared as "Design for a Church" in the architect and builder Asher Benjamin's widely circulated *Country Builder's Assistant.*

In his narrative, Rev. Field called the East Haddam Congregational church "the present commodious and well-constructed edifice." This contrasts with his summary of Middlesex County religious structures as a whole: "generally convenient but plain structures."[33] Obviously this new building made an impression on the Reverend. He further explained that the church "was opened Thanksgiving Day, November 27, 1794. It is sixty-four feet long and forty-four broad, with a projection of eighteen feet by four, and cost about $6000."[34]

First Congregational Church in East Haddam still stands. The entrance to this building is through three doors in a pedimented portico (the "projection of eighteen feet by four") on the short side of the building. Interior seating consists of forward-facing pews on a main floor and a three-sided balcony, or "gallery." Large pillars with ornate capitals support the wide, plastered ceiling with a blue-painted, central octagon. One large Palladian window framed the original pulpit. An elaborate three-stage steeple crowns the exterior.

St. Stephen's Episcopal, also in East Haddam, was built on a rocky hilltop above the village. This building, called by Kelly "the finest Episcopal edifice then standing in the state of Connecticut," was demolished in 1921. Its white clapboard exterior was decorated with round-headed second story windows, a four-stage steeple, and a front entrance flanked by Roman Doric pilasters. One entered through a shallow vestibule to a sanctuary capped with a triple vaulted ceiling painted blue and supported by six square Roman Doric fluted columns. By Kelly's account, this was a truly remarkable, elegant building. The Episcopalians paid for their church by successive subscriptions and taxes as the construction progressed.[35] In his Middlesex County Report, Rev. Field described this building: the Episcopal "house of worship was erected in 1792, fifty-four feet long and thirty-seven broad, with an end gallery. It is well built, and standing on an eminence commands an extensive prospect."[36]

As this last citation suggests, the location of these buildings was a significant element of their presence. Traditionally meetinghouses had a central place, often on a rise where they could been seen from afar. Meetinghouses were reference points in the somewhat confusing geography of densely forested hills. That is why descriptions such as "crossing each other at the meeting house" or "within a few rods of the Meeting House" appear frequently in the Town Reports.[37] Having a centrally placed church or meetinghouse remained a mark of social acceptability in Connecticut's towns. It is no surprise that dissenting groups were often literally placed on the fringes of settlement. Levi Hart, Congregational minister and writer of the Preston Report, for instance, noted that "In the remote parts of the parishes" there were "very considerable numbers of Anabaptists and Methodists."[38] Those congregations, if they could not afford to build a permanent place of worship, met in schools or private homes, further signifying their marginality. As Hart recorded, in Preston they met "by themselves for social worship, on the Lords Day, & often have preachers of their respective Denominations. . . they have no houses built & appropriated for worship, but they occupy two large school houses for that end, in the bounds of the parish."[39]

A building signified permanence of place. This helps to explain why the writers of these Reports, mostly Congregationalists, were so attentive to the number and state of the structures erected by the newcomer dissenting groups. When Jesse Root wrote that in Coventry the Episcopalians, Baptists & Methodists "are so few that they have no place of public worship in the town," he conveyed the precarious position of those congregations.[40] Levi Hart seemed uneasy with the growth of dissenting groups in his town of Preston, as did many of these Congregational writers. "Sectaries of various description have arisen in the parish at different times," Hart wrote, "but they have not very materially affected the state of the society." Hart's own Congregationalists worshiped in "a

decent house for public worship of about forty four by sixty six" erected around 1770.[41] If the house was a metaphor for the congregation within, the Congregationalists most assuredly had the advantage over the Baptists and Methodists.

The erection of a place of worship was the clearest message that a new denomination could give regarding its stability, and a new building ensured the forward momentum of a congregation. Incoming denominations often bent over backwards to mark their presence on the landscape as quickly as possible. Because the Baptists of Wintonbury had by 1802 "increased in numbers," they "have since built a small meeting house."[42] The rush to build is also the reason many of these buildings were unfinished for so long. The Wintonbury (now Bloomfield) Congregational Society, incorporated in 1736, that same year voted "to build a church, which was afterwards erected, forty five feet in length, by thirty five in breadth, but never finished." That epithet, "never finished" can be applied to many of the buildings discussed in these Town Reports. Milton, in Litchfield County, had "two churches; one for Congregationalists, and one for Episcopalians; both unfinished."[43] By "unfinished" what was usually meant was that the church was usable but the steeple or the woodwork detail was incomplete.

In some communities, poorer congregations of different denominations were able to share a church building with relative goodwill between them. Sometimes, however, the ownership of the church erupted in a conflict that revealed underlying tensions. In Cornwall the Strict Congregationalists (New Lights) and the Congregationalists (Old Lights) fought just such a battle over possession of the meetinghouse. Old Lights preferred a rational, head-centered faith that emphasized moral living; New Lights, Congregationalists most influenced by eighteenth-century revivals, advocated a religion of the heart and stressed the necessity of an emotional conversion experience. While the distinction between the groups was on the surface theological, New Lights were often radicals who challenged the standing order. In Cornwall, the New Light members of the ecclesiastical society attacked their Old Light minister, Rev. Gold, and his right to control worship in the old church building. In 1780, in an obviously one-sided gathering of members, "Finally it was Voted That they were Strict Congregationalists, and that they would set up the Congregational Worship in the Meeting House." Soon after, the New Lights' "attempt to take Possession of the Meeting House was frustrated" but the perpetrators were not dissuaded. That Thanksgiving, Rev. Gold's "opponants early in the Day took Possession of the Meeting House & so obstinately defended the Pulpit against him & his Adherents that Mr. Gold did not perform Publick Worship on that Day." Mr. Gold, however, had many Old Light compatriots within the congregation, and they successfully wrested control back into their own hands. Those who had attempted to take over the house were reprimanded and later fined. "After which a large number of the Inhabitants returned their Names [registered on the tax list] as strict congregationalists, Built a Meeting House &c., and continued to Assemble in the same."[44] Contesting the ownership of the old meetinghouse, and eventually building its own new one, was the means by which this group of New Lights staked its claim in the community.

Accounts of controversy such as this were treated with a

light touch by the writers of the Reports, as if they were a thing of the past. They had come to terms with the fact that multiple Christian denominations would exist in their towns. So their aim shifted. It was no longer realistic or even possible to ensure dominance of their own denomination in ecclesiastical matters. They could, however, promote a social agenda that was based on a Christian moral program heavily dependent on a code of gentility. The enemy was no longer their fellow Christian of another denomination. The threat of intra- or interdenominational squabbles was nothing compared to the danger of a decline in appropriate religious sentiment altogether. The enemy was on the one hand the radical, overly enthusiastic, evangelical. On the other hand, the non-Christian or, worse, the dissipated heathen, threatened their vision of Connecticut. The hoped-for future was one in which different religious groups (all of them Christian) would coexist peacefully, sharing common goals for the betterment of society.

Question thirty-two of the Connecticut Academy's circular letter contained a clause about "attention to civil and religious institutions." Many of the writers of the Town Reports were sensitive to this trait as it was or was not demonstrated by their neighbors, primarily in their observance of the Sabbath. Between 1810 and 1830, Connecticut Sabbatarians conducted a wide-ranging campaign to restrict work, travel, and recreation on Sunday. The concerns of the Sabbatarians are reflected in these Town Reports. The writer from Goshen, a Congregational deacon, noted "the attention paid to religious institutions here is very considerable and encouraging. Our meetings on the sabbath," he recorded, "are pretty fully attended and we have long been accustomed to hear the truth impartially dispensed. Yet here, as in other places," he lamented, "persons are to be found who spend the sabbath at home and prefer the gratification of their slothful inclinations to the attainment and promotion of the better good." With regard to travel on the sabbath he commented "this is a growing evil; and its only remedy must be found in a revival of that morality which distinguished our forefathers; experience having long since proved that laws will ever be migratory which are not supported by the public opinion and morals."[45]

This was the crucial connection: observance of Christian practices led to the establishment of a moral society in its laws and the character of its citizens. The writer of the Farmington Report was sure of this relationship in describing the behavior of his neighbors. "Their attachment to civil institutions," he wrote, "arises primarily from the divinity of their religion, considering obedience to lawful human authority as obedience to God." "Piety of the heart," was a key component of "a useful public character."[46] Many of the writers betray concern that the state's increase in wealth and consequent luxury would lead its citizens down a path of vice and decay. It is important once again to remember that the writers of these Reports were social conservatives, wary of the changes coming to Connecticut with economic prosperity and demographic diversity. For them, public religion based on Protestant solidarity was the only way to ensure a prosperous, respectable future for Connecticut.

This desire for Protestant agreement is palpable in the Reports. In Ridgefield, the writer noticed happily, "there is and has been for a long time past the utmost harmony & friendship prevaling between the several denominations of christians here who frequently worship together and evince the efficacy of that spirit whose leading character is charity."[47] And in Cornwall "there may be said in general to be a good Philanthropick, Neighborly affection and mutual good offices of kindness between the Citizens of Different Denominations." At least this was true "where no publick Matter is in contemplation, or carrying on, which is Judged or apprehended to be in favour, or against, the Interest of either the first or 2nd Society who make the greater bulk of Inhabitants in this Town."[48] In other words, as long as the Congregationalists were relatively content, the scene was peaceable.

The material, public face of respectable Protestant solidarity desired by these writers was best expressed not in any of the accounts of church buildings, but in Timothy Dwight's detailed account of the new cemetery in New Haven. In 1811, New Haven had yet to replace its three eighteenth-century Congregational meetinghouses in the center of town. It had, however, embarked on a project that many claim to be the first rural cemetery designed and used in America. Dwight called this cemetery one of the "two interesting objects" in New Haven. He was taken with its geometric order, its wide alleys to permit the passage of carriages and funeral processions, and its tasteful monuments "almost universally of marble." Like the new "churchly" Congregational buildings, the cemetery was elegant and refined. The New Haven cemetery was a new sort of place, unlike the numerous, nondescript old burying grounds of Connecticut's towns. It was meant to incite sentimental feelings, to be a place for contemplation.[49]

Dwight found the New Haven Cemetery be a place that was religious yet tasteful. "An exquisite taste for propriety is discovered in every thing belonging to it," Dwight wrote. It exhibited "a regard for the dead, reverential, but not ostentatious," designed "to influence the feelings, and views, of succeeding generations." "No spot of ground, within my knowledge," Dwight declared, "is equally solemn and impressive." The cemetery was a meeting place for Christians of all denominations, and Dwight liked what it conveyed about New Haven. Religion there was "solemn and impressive" and displayed an "exquisite taste for propriety."

These are precisely the same descriptive terms that were being used by contemporaries to describe new church buildings. Here was a Christianity that was visible, socially acceptable, and impressive to both insiders and outsiders. If directed properly, Connecticut's Christians could both build and pay for that sort of a world in the new republic. Old meetinghouses would be replaced with stylish new churches. Citizens would persist in their churchgoing and church membership would increase. The public support of religion would be generous and consistent. And all eyes would see the visible proof that Connecticut was home to a virtuous, God-fearing people.

Art and Science in Crop and Livestock Improvement:

The Connecticut Towns Survey and Agricultural Change Around 1800

Kathy J. Cooke

Investigating the state of agriculture in Connecticut was clearly one of the best ways that the newly formed Connecticut Academy of Arts and Sciences could promote "useful knowledge." To that end, when the Academy in 1800 sent its Letter of Solicitation asking members of Connecticut towns to respond to a broad series of survey questions it included topics about agricultural practices and "improvements" in each town. The Academy thus foreshadowed the activities of the specific agricultural organizations that developed throughout the nineteenth century. Agriculture also bore a more specific relationship to the mission of the Academy itself, in that the Academy was and continues to be dedicated to the arts as well as the sciences.

The practice of agriculture is by many definitions an art, in particular because it consists of many techniques and traditions developed over time. However, even the most traditional farmer incorporates many elements of science, or techniques based on careful observation and even experiment, in his or her work. Thus, as the Connecticut Town Reports illustrate, for many farmers agriculture had elements of both art and science. This relationship can be seen most clearly through the attention paid to seeds and crops, to fertilizers for the land, and to livestock. The Reports also illustrate many avenues for research in general agricultural history of this period. Agricultural history draws on many of the other subdisciplines of history, including economic, social, and environmental history, and thus contributes to the larger historical enterprise as well. In particular, studying agriculture in Connecticut towns in the early nineteenth century contributes to a better understanding of the cultural values, social priorities, and commercial interests in the state, in New England, and in the country as a whole.

Agricultural Change and Improvement in Connecticut Towns

The Town Reports demonstrate different values with regard to agricultural improvement, change, production, and "progress." Many of the towns surveyed claimed explicitly and with pride, that agricultural activity was important and successful in their areas. In his Report on Franklin (1800), for instance, Samuel Nott stated simply that "Agriculture has greatly increased in 18 years," but said little more. Similarly, Chauncey Prindle of Watertown (1801) and Samuel Dunton of Willington (1805) noted that agriculture was "rapidly improving," but did not elaborate on that claim. Wallingford's (1811-12) reporter George W. Stanley acknowledged a state of

agriculture that was "not high, but improving," and Cheshire's (1803) John Foot claimed that "agriculture is improving" as well. Other towns commented less on the general quality of agriculture in the town, and emphasized instead the presence of good husbandry and farming techniques. According to David D. Field in 1819, Killingworth's land was, "by good husbandry," especially productive, and Durham's was a "good farming township." Most reporters found that the price and value of their land was increasing, implying that greater productivity was helping to drive up the price of cultivated land. On the other hand, Reports from townships such as Preston, evaluated by Levi Hart in 1801, demonstrated that productivity or improvement was not necessarily valued in all the towns—presumably current practice satisfied local needs for food and other goods.[1] Thus, the Connecticut Town Reports provide some interesting contrasts regarding agricultural practices and their perceived value. Three topics are considered below—seeds and crops, land quality and improvement, and livestock—and are followed by a case study that helps to draw more clearly the comparison between the tradition and change, or art and science, according to the values of the towns themselves.

Seeds, Crops, and Crop Rotation

Most towns expressed a strong commitment to the type of seed they used and the ways they collected it. For instance, Samuel Goodrich of Ridgefield (1800) emphasized the importance of bringing in seed from other areas, especially from the south. For him the specific goal was to find and use larger seed, which he and his colleagues expected to produce better crops. Others reflected the widely held conviction that the source of seed needed to be changed regularly—traditional agricultural lore suggested that seed collected from repeated crops on the same land would eventually wear out. The Canterbury (1801) Report, authored by Hezekiah Frost, noted that it was important to use new seed every few years at least, and East Windsor found it "profitable to exchange seed between meadow and upland."[2] However, not all of the Town Reports agreed. For instance, neither Eliphaz Alvord of Winchester (1813) nor Timothy Dwight of New Haven claimed special results from changing seed every few years.[3] Regarding the change of seed, however, students of the Connecticut towns survey need to exercise some caution when they interpret the language used by survey respondents. Authors vary with regard to what they mean by "changing seed." For some, the terms clearly did not mean varying the source of seed, but instead referred to rotating crops (discussed at greater length below). The purpose and expectations for these two practices were obviously very different.

Rotation practices varied widely as well. Farmers in the less venturesome towns of Winchester (1813) and New Haven (1811) reported no pattern for rotating crops.[4] Many other areas, by contrast, followed the practice and explained it in detail in the survey. Middlesex County followed corn with grain, oats, or flax, while Bolton planted wheat or rye, followed it with corn and potatoes, and then planted oats and flax. Field, the reporter for Middlesex County, claimed that rye and corn had been known to succeed for many subsequent years on the same land, but still chose to emphasize the important role that other crops, especially clover and timothy, could play in improving soil.[5] Other towns, including Canterbury and Washington, also highlighted rotation as an important means to good crop production. Franklin emphasized that it pursued the best methods with crops, but described no rotation procedures.[6]

In general, the towns planted the same types of crops, but with different goals and different levels of production. Rye, corn, oats, barley, buckwheat, flax, and grasses in general were clearly the preferred crops, while turnips and potatoes were grown somewhat less frequently. The authors generally acknowledged that different parts of the state, or what they frequently called the "country," allocated their land to crops in varying proportions. No knowledge of or interest in different crop varieties was exhibited in the Reports. Production per acre also varied widely. Middlesex County reported in 1819 that wheat production could be as high as 36 bushels per acre, rye up to 40, and corn up to 70 bushels per acre. The figures were essentially the same in Goshen, but the reporter there also noted that up to 60 bushels of oats had been raised per acre, and over 300 bushels of potatoes and 300 pounds of flax. Middlesex County and Goshen, however, demonstrated some of the highest yields in the state. Averages in Bolton, for instance, were substantially less, with wheat production of only 15 to 20 bushels per acre, and rye 7 to 12 bushels per acre.[7] These different levels of production stemmed from weather conditions, local practices, land quality and improvements, and the desire to have surplus crops for export. Some towns, like Union (1803) focused on trying to provide for its own consumption, while Ridgefield (1800) was happy to produce beyond its own needs. In Goshen, the farmers decided to emphasize dairy products rather than field crops.[8]

Wheat production is an interesting aspect of the history of agriculture in Connecticut. According to the Reports, late in the eighteenth century the area had experienced severe problems with the Hessian fly. This non-native pest, which probably was brought into the country only a few decades earlier, could devastate wheat crops and discouraged efforts to produce wheat. For instance, Canterbury marked 1788 as the beginning of infestations by the Hessian fly, and further claimed that since that year "wheat has been mostly destroyed by them." Lisbon referred to 1785 as about the time "the insect appeared," and remarked that since then "very little wheat is raised."[9] According to Franklin, the "Hession [sic] Fly . . . appeared 1785—and have continued more or less till the present time. They have almost prevented the raising of wheat in this Town."[10] However, agricultural historians and economists have explained the decrease in wheat production in New England in a different way. Claiming that soils found to the west, particularly in New York, were more suited for wheat farming, historians have argued that farmers were simply driven from the market by new producers from about 1800 to 1810.[11] The situation in Connecticut, however, suggests that the Hessian fly played a more important role than soil productivity. While soil productivity varied significantly from location to location in Connecticut, fertilizers and crop rotation often were implemented to maintain and improve the quality of the soil. Controlling the Hessian fly was more difficult, and the pest severely impacted crop yields, making it the likely culprit in decreased wheat production in the early nineteenth century.

Amending the Soil and Improving the Land

In Connecticut, levels of soil fertility upon settlement tended to be good. However, as one would expect, to maintain production for self-sufficiency or for export most farmers found it necessary to amend the soil. Ebenezer Kellogg of Bolton (1800) noted that the quality and quantity of crops were similar with both "new" and fertilized soil, demonstrating the fine quality of the land in general. The Report presented by Lewis M. Norton of Goshen (1812), however, suggested that efforts to maintain and even upgrade the soil were necessary for high production—in his town's experience the "extensive and valuable meadows...with the help of manure and in some parts, plaster of Paris, produces [sic] excellent crops of herds grass and red clover." This sort of interest in soil fertility was growing—as Azel Backus of Bethlem (1812) noted, "Manuring is an encreasing [sic] object of attention." Litchfield also reported that "more attention [was] being paid to manure, particularly to the use of plaster."[12] Some of the land improvement and maintenance was achieved through crop rotation, as mentioned above. However, frequent applications of fertilizers and other soil amendments also proved necessary. Thus, the Connecticut Towns survey asked specifically about manures used to maintain and upgrade the soil. Respondents interpreted this question broadly to include manure itself as well as other fertilizers and soil amendments: The descriptions of manuring practices thus discussed many items, including dung from a variety of livestock, plaster of paris (or gypsum), wood ashes, and whitefish.

Individual towns maintained different preferences according to the local art as well as land conditions. Nearly every locality that discussed fertilizers endorsed the use of livestock dung. Many ranked it the best form of manure for the local soil, and suggested that it would provide benefits to any soil. While some variations in methods of application and amount of rotting necessary did exist, for the most part the techniques advocated were very similar. The Stratfield Report explained that dung should be applied when the ground was being tilled, that it not be exposed to the sun, that the most useful and fertile contribution to soil was stable manure, and that ashes were second best. The author, Philo Shelton, also explained that plaster of paris was not useful for land near the shore.[13] The Middlesex County Report had similar findings, but also added that seaweed, rockweed, and marine shells could also be used to enrich the soil. Other, differently situated towns, including Sharon and Litchfield (1815) endorsed plaster of paris, or gypsum, as one of the most effective amendments for their areas. Cheshire also advocated "plaster" and ashes, noting that they were especially suited to drier soil.[14]

According to David Field, whitefish were introduced as manure in Middlesex County in 1801, and were an especially useful fertilizer for those near the shore. Timothy Dwight of New Haven (1811) described the process by which whitefish were used to enhance soil. Layers of whitefish were covered by layers of soil and left to rot. When the fish had decomposed completely, the manuring process was complete. According to Dwight, ten to twelve thousand fish were used per acre. Field explained that after amending the soil with whitefish "some of the finest fields of grain, corn and grass are annually presented on the margin of the Sound which exist in our country."[15]

Livestock Productivity and Breeding

For the most part livestock was not much emphasized in the Connecticut Town Reports, leading one to conclude that the land was mostly used for food crops, often for local consumption but also for export. Certainly, this must have been the case in some townships. Many towns, including those in Middlesex County (1819), found that the number of sheep and swine in the township was unknown, suggesting that maintaining livestock was not a central concern to the local inhabitants.[16] However, not all areas were so limited in their experience with livestock. Furthermore, during these early years in the nineteenth century it seems quite clear that many farmers were beginning a transition from the production of food crops to raising livestock.

The areas that did pursue the production of livestock quite aggressively used them for export or for the production of meat and wool. Middletown (1819), for instance, explained that livestock was an important export. Other towns counted the production of agricultural commodities derived from livestock. Thus, Goshen, while not emphasizing its cattle, did explain that cheese was its most important product. Pork and wool were also key commodities, noted most directly by Cheshire (1803). John Foot of Cheshire estimated the number of sheep in his township as "not large, say 3000 or 4000."[17] In this area, the towns emphasized the production of these commercial goods rather than their agricultural practices with the livestock that were required to generate them.

However, two categories of livestock—oxen and sheep—were discussed repeatedly. Oxen were universally described as the best animals for working fields. The Reports illustrate the controversy that continued to take place regarding the relative usefulness of horses and oxen. As the Sharon (1807) Report explained, where horses had replaced oxen the innovators

quickly realized that they had committed a serious error. This reporter noted that people kept horses only for amusement, and not for agriculture or warfare.[18] Cheshire (1803) also explained that oxen were used for fieldwork, and that horses more often pulled wagons; these sentiments were also reflected in Winchester (1813). Oxen had come to be preferred for the fields because, although they were slow, they were easier to care for, and, once spent for the purposes of fieldwork, they could be used for food.[19]

Information about breeds of animals also seemed to be spreading among the participants in the Connecticut Towns survey. Here the traditional art of appropriately using and caring for one's animals was modified by the new views about breeding animals in general that were gaining prominence at this time in the United States. For instance, Wallingford (1811-12) advocated the use of oxen in part because of the existing understanding about breeds and breeding of oxen. However, knowledge about breeds of sheep was becoming especially important, and sheep were generally counted among the livestock held and raised by farmers in the Connecticut towns. Most Reports said little more, except to give commercial figures about the value and quantity of wool produced. However, a few towns, including Sharon (1807) and Bethlem (1812) highlighted the importance of an increasingly popular breed, the Merino. Sharon simply referred to the introduction of a new breed. Azel Backus of Bethlem, however, showed greater awareness of breeding strategies by explaining that the "number of full blooded Merinos is not known, nor the 1/2 or 1/4 bloods."[20] The survey did not request such specific information; nonetheless, Backus responded by illustrating his knowledge of the growing popularity of Merinos, and of the importance of maintaining breeding lines and records. While this understanding was not widely illustrated among the towns, according to the survey responses, it is clear that the towns were beginning to develop a sense for alternative strategies in breeding.

Connecticut Case Studies: Art and Science

Regarding agriculture, Connecticut towns can be divided very roughly into two categories: towns that searched for and closely examined practices that questioned tradition—what one might call the "scientific" towns—and the conservative towns that valued the agricultural tradition and art that had developed over time. Canterbury and Farmington illustrate the former category, while New Haven and Winchester represent the latter.

The Canterbury (1801) Report depicts a town strongly motivated to question, and, when they found it useful, to change local agricultural practices. The farmers there, according to Hezekiah Frost, exhibited drive, initiative, and significant interest in experiment and observation. Frost was especially pleased with the "good farmers, who have tried many experiments upon flax."[21] Canterbury farmers also closely evaluated the value of plaster of paris as a soil amendment on town lands. Finding its effect temporary, they generally stopped using it. Frost also explained that farmers had recently begun a new practice that involved taking dirt from the highway and mixing it with barn manure to create a better fertilizer for corn. The portrayal by Frost, at least, shows Canterbury farmers to be enterprising men and women who not only reconsidered their practices on a regular basis, but also tried new approaches.

In his lengthy and detailed Report, John Treadwell of Farmington (date unknown) found similar traits among the current farmers of that town, although he was critical of earlier residents. In particular, he denounced the original Dutch settlers of the area who, he thought, found the soil rich early on and made no efforts to use soil amendments. Believing them to be "a people of not much enterprise," Treadwell explained that they instead "sat down contented with their old habits." Critical of these traditions, he went on to detail the different methods that had been tried to improve cultivation practices and upgrade the soil after what he saw as the travesty of the Dutch. Treadwell himself was particularly motivated by the desire to contribute to the improvement of agriculture in general. He believed that the agricultural advances in Farmington would prove advantageous not only to his local population but also to the entire country. Explaining that agriculture was "of great importance to the American nation and to almost all people living under the blessings of civil society," he argued that the manuring practices of Farmington should be shared to help improve the land of all those in similar conditions.[22] In particular, he noted that "Several of our best farmers have made experiments" with plaster of paris, but found it not useful. Using observation and experiment, the farmers were guided by their "own experience," and not by the traditions of agriculture alone.[23] In fact, Treadwell himself clearly disapproved of relying exclusively on traditional practice.

By contrast, the Report by town clerk Eliphaz Alvord of Winchester illustrated indifference to the farming methods in his town, and suggested that the farmers themselves chose to rely on tradition. In particular, his response indicated frustration or annoyance with the questions sent to him by the Academy, as well as a lack of pride, or perhaps simply a lack of bookkeeping talent, in the town. While the Academy no doubt asked the town clerks to complete a monumental task by presenting them with the lengthy surveys, Alvord made little effort to understand the nature of agriculture in Winchester. Certainly, he felt no drive to share information with the nation in the same way that Treadwell did. Thus, he found that the number of swine in the town was "unknown," the amount of pork sent to market was "inconsiderable," and that the beef produced for market could not "be correctly known." This approach also was evident in the description of specific practices, as the clerk found little commendable or unique about the agriculture in the town. Instead, he explained that agriculture in Winchester "is directed to most of the objects pursued in the husbandry of this part of the country."[24] Further, he was able to report little about usual seed times and preferences for rotation of crops. Certainly, Alvord knew little about his town and he did not try to learn more. However, it also seemed to be a place devoted to undistinguished traditions.

The New Haven (1811) Report was written by the much better informed Timothy Dwight, president of the Academy. He, like Alvord, found little unique about the agriculture of New Haven, thus indicated that it too was a place relying on traditional art in agriculture, and not scientifically oriented innovation. Interestingly, Dwight's Report contained wording exactly like that of Alvord—clearly Alvord was so little interested in the survey that at times he took the words directly from Dwight's Report, which had been distributed as a model for responding to the survey. Dwight's Report was far more detailed, and did demonstrate virtues in New Haven agriculture. These virtues rested primarily in the town's conservative and generally traditional practices in agriculture.

Of course, these characterizations are extreme, and cannot be used as universal categories to explain the visions of each town. Furthermore, the Town Reports were heavily influenced by the specific questions asked, by the individuals who responded to them, and by the previous Reports they may have seen. Thus, to expect uniformity in the level of response and consistent knowledge about the state of each town would be too much to ask. Nonetheless, the Reports do indicate some interesting patterns that bear further investigation. They also suggest some wider areas of study.

Implications for Further Study

In his recent review of agricultural history, James H. Shideler makes a convincing case for the breadth of study encompassed by agricultural history when he explains that it is "diffuse, discursive, and incoherent." Despite the varied adjectives, this description is meant to be positive and encouraging to agricultural historians. In a field that "has no discipline, no unique methodology," nothing is out of bounds or excluded from the study; no techniques or methods are inappropriate either. Through this field that has "no boundaries at all," and instead "merges insensibly into the totality of human experience," Shideler claims that historians experience the "wonderfully varied nature" of the agricultural past.[25] While Shideler's enthusiasm might be excessive, after studying the Connecticut Towns Reports a historian certainly does experience a sense of the wonderful variety and nearly endless possibilities for critical and creative inquiry in agricultural studies. Even more, however, the scholar can see the tremendous importance agriculture holds in American history more broadly, whether one thinks in economic, political, social, or intellectual terms. In what follows, I discuss some of the broader implications the Town Reports may have for historians and other scholars in a variety of fields. By no means is the following discussion comprehensive. Instead, the goal is to be suggestive and to encourage others to mine the riches that exist in these nineteenth-century survey responses and their commentary on agricultural and town life.

Understanding Agricultural Organizations

The Connecticut Academy of Arts and Sciences and its efforts to understand agriculture as one among its many survey topics help to uncover the role of amateur and professional societies throughout America's history. Other early scientific societies, like the American Philosophical Society, organized in 1743, and the American Academy of Arts and Sciences, organized in 1780, also included investigation of agricultural matters in their duties. Like the Connecticut Academy of Arts and Sciences, established in 1799, the interests of these societies were broad, and illustrated the general relevance that agricultural practice was understood to have on the development of arts and sciences in general.

Specialized agricultural societies also were organized early in American history, with the first appearing, according to Wayne Rasmussen, by 1781. Rasmussen also notes that the first society to publish its investigations was the Philadelphia Society for Promoting Agriculture, established in 1785, soon joined by the South Carolina Society for Promoting and Improving Agriculture and the Society of Maryland for the Encouragement and Improvement of Agriculture. Only a few more societies were formed before the early nineteenth century, when the number of agricultural societies began to increase rapidly.[26] While the Connecticut Town Reports do not uncover the existence of specific agricultural societies, they do illustrate the growing interest of some towns in sharing agricultural knowledge, and point to the development of agricultural societies that follows within the next few decades.

In other states, for instance, the past activities of agricultural societies are relatively accessible, and provide excellent opportunities for comparative study. As noted above, the breeding of sheep was just becoming a topic of discussion in some of the Connecticut towns. The Pennsylvania Agricultural Society in 1824 illustrates the extent of knowledge that developed over the next few decades. It emphasized the importance of choosing the proper "race" of cattle or sheep. In this context the Society claimed that inbreeding caused problems for breeders, problems like degeneration and the magnification of small defects. However, the authors also argued that inbreeding would also strengthen good traits, demonstrating some ambivalence. Thus, while the Society was critical of inbreeding, it certainly encouraged purifying breeds, and even allowed for very close breeding in order to speed breed improvement.[27] This growing knowledge in Philadelphia reflected the nascent but maturing considerations about full, 1/2, and 1/4 blooded Merino sheep mentioned in the Bethlem Report.

These concerns about breeding animals continued over the next several years and materialized in other agricultural societies in the mid-Atlantic and New England regions. Different breeding methods and theories certainly caused controversy among farmers and breeders. In the *Transactions of the Agricultural Societies in the State of Massachusetts for 1852,* numerous speakers addressed what they probably would have called the problem of crossbreeding and the solution of pure breeding. William S. King, Chairman of the committee on bulls for the Norfolk Society, ended a plea for wider use of pure-bred bulls with the observation "We are perfectly aware that it is an unpopular doctrine, and that we run counter to the prejudices of many excellent farmers and estimable men; but as our opinions have been carefully considered, and we believe them to be well founded, it would be cowardice to withhold them."[28] Farmers in Connecticut were about to begin this debate at the time of the survey.

At the same time, however, the Town Reports indicate a certain amount of democracy not necessarily evident in the work of other academies and societies. Before 1820, most agricultural organizations and breed associations in the United States were organized by and served the interests of wealthy and hobby-oriented farmers and breeders. These groups in particular focused upon intellectual and scientific evaluations of agriculture and animals, and intended to spread information about better breeding and farming techniques. In this way they were rather "bookish," and thus unappealing to traditional farmers who justifiably distrusted new techniques and ideas that, if they failed, could lead to disastrous yields. While the Connecticut Towns survey certainly had lofty and intellectual goals, through it the Academy also attempted to extend beyond the interests of the usual, elite agricultural organization. Thus, it recorded general practices and the art of agriculture along with the new or innovative methods of farmers who wanted to increase production and appeal to commercial markets.

Experiment and Tradition, Science and Art

The Connecticut Town Reports also illustrate some of the enduring questions that face agricultural historians and historians of science—the relationship between science and art. While some individual towns showed serious interest in new techniques and knowledge, and in using experimentation to verify and test ideas, other towns demonstrated strong commitment to tradition, and in some cases indifference or even hostility to new approaches in agriculture. Lewis Norton of Goshen illustrated a common attitude when he explained that "Of the chemical properties of [plaster of Paris] the farmer knows little; and, so long as he observes its beneficial influence on his crops, is content to leave to others to explain how these effects are produced."[29] As discussed above, New Haven and Winchester also demonstrated little interest in understanding or sharing their farming methods with others in the state.

However, many towns did emphasize the importance of understanding and sharing both traditional and new practices. Lisbon (Newent) and Canterbury especially highlighted the importance of appropriate farming practices, pointing out that the best production resulted from the devotion and knowledge of "good farmers." Cornwall went even further, explaining that the township's best farmers learned about better practices through experiment. Farmington made similar claims about the importance of experiment, explaining that the town was in its "infancy in discovering & applying the means of rendering the earth fruitful."[30] These attitudes, however, stand in sharp contrast to towns such as New Haven and Winchester, which had no special plan for rotation of crops and little desire to change or expand agriculture in their areas.

The Reports also supplement the claims made by historians about the state of agriculture and the state of science in New England during the nineteenth century. For instance, in

The Emergence of Agricultural Science Margaret Rossiter illustrates the increasing interest in science and new methods that took place in the nineteenth century, finding most of the change occurring in the mid- to late-nineteenth century. The Town Reports, however, indicate that curiosity about new methods and growing scientific innovation began quite early in some towns such as Farmington, while it lagged significantly in others. In this way, then, the survey of Connecticut towns conducted by the Academy illustrates growing devotion to science somewhat earlier than Rossiter claims, but also shows the resistance to change that one might expect among farmers, for whom change also tends to mean risk. In this way, the Reports show the complex relationship between the usually conservative art of agriculture and the often-aggressive science of agriculture.

Again, some specific examples from animal breeding help to clarify the point. Seth Sprague of Duxbury, Massachusetts, addressed the Massachusetts Board of Agriculture in the 1840s to explain the errors he had observed in cattle breeding in the United States. He claimed that "The course pursued since the first settlement of the country, has been directly calculated to deteriorate and run down the best cattle the world ever produced." By way of contrast, he argued that "The breeding of cattle has been reduced to a science in Great Britain. They produce cattle that do not vary in color and form, with as much certainty as any effect follows cause." Critical of what he believed were the unscientific and unthinking methods of the past, he argued that the problem was that "Our native cattle have been bred promiscuously together for more than two hundred years." Sprague advocated imitating the British, who were "breeding only from the best specimen of the same stock, and their more especial attention to the character of the males, has produced a purity of blood that produce offsprings of like form and general character."[31] This interest in purifying breeds had its roots in the work of English farmer Robert Bakewell (1725-1795), known to some as "the founder of animal breeding." Bakewell provided the model of one who was extremely committed to improving breed quality, so much so that "he even kept for future reference specimens of the bones or pickled joints of animals which he had bred and which he regarded as nearly ideal."[32] This devotion to critical inquiry into the validity of current practices and efforts to test and record important knowledge is evident in the Connecticut Town Reports, and helps to illustrate the roots of the claims made by Sprague and others in the mid-nineteenth century.

As the scientific leanings of some of the towns that responded to the survey suggest, Connecticut itself eventually became one of the foremost leaders applying the methods of science to agriculture in the United States. The first agricultural experiment station in the United States was established in Connecticut in 1875 at Wesleyan University.[33] Led by the efforts of Wilbur Atwater and supported by federal and state funding, experiment stations spread throughout the United States. The stations began their work by addressing a serious problem for Connecticut that could easily be addressed by science—fertilizer fraud. When it was first organized, the Connecticut station worked to uncover false claims about fertilizers, to develop standard and

proven methods to improve soil, and to warn farmers about fertilizer salesmen who were selling worthless or harmful products. Concerns about the quality and usefulness of fertilizer were well documented in the Town Reports, and help to explain this interest of the agricultural experiment station.

The Social Side of Agriculture

While in the nineteenth century farmers typically spent a great deal of time alone working their land, they also had a strong inclination to sociability. Although the Town Reports only briefly touch upon amusement and methods of entertainment, some hints are available regarding the importance of connections and conversations with other farmers. Levi Hart of Preston (1801) suggests the importance of these social connections from the perspective of agricultural change. In his Report he explained that Preston consisted of small-scattered country villages, and further claimed that such circumstances were not conducive to much agricultural improvement. In this way Preston also implied that sociability was necessary for progress in agriculture.[34]

Of course, in some cases, connections with other towns could have the effect of reinforcing one's commitment to traditional practices or to low expectations about the quality of agriculture in one's town. Many townships emphasized the similarity of their techniques to those of other towns, and thus chose not to elaborate on local farming practices. The decision not to say more suggested contentment with current practices with no thought to improve or change. Often this also indicated that the towns were happy to produce for their own consumption, and did not consider increasing production for export. Kent, for instance, noted that there was nothing especially unique or interesting about the town's methods of cultivation. New Haven explained that its agricultural practices reflected the methods used in most of the area. Winchester also explained that its agriculture was the same as that found in the surrounding area more generally.[35]

In their extensive lists of eminent persons, most towns did not include any references to farmers or agricultural leaders. A few exceptions did exist, however, primarily in the towns that demonstrated significant interest in changing agricultural practices and in increasing production. Middletown emphasized the importance of a minister named Huntington and his contributions to science. Killingworth also lauded one of its ministers, Jared Elliot, for his contributions to improving agriculture. Farmington was especially proud of its farming heritage, and seemed to equate strong leadership with agricultural acumen, explaining that its magistrates were always farmers.[36]

The dissemination of knowledge about Merino sheep especially suggests the importance of social events, in particular agricultural fairs. According to Rasmussen, agricultural interest in fairs can be traced "to the sheep shearings sponsored by George Washington Parke Custis on his Arlington, Virginia, farm from 1803 on, or to the fairs sponsored in Washington D.C., by the Columbian Agricultural Society beginning in 1809," but, he claimed, "the major impetus to purely agricultural fairs came from Elkanah Watson and his Berkshire Agricultural Society."[37] In 1807 Watson purchased a farm in Massachusetts as something of a retirement hobby. Seeking to enhance the quiet solitude of rural life he began buying unique breeding animals and organizing fairs and agricultural societies in order to make the animals more prominent and, presumably, more profitable. One of those purchases was a pair of Merino sheep, which he sought to publicize through an exhibition. The next winter he organized his local farmers into an agricultural society that would disseminate information about the Merino sheep, and the sheep themselves, "for the good of the whole."[38] While there is no mention of publicity for Merino sheep in the Reports from Connecticut towns, the emphasis on blood found in the Bethlem Report does suggest some knowledge of the growing popularity of the breed, and of the importance of pure-breeding. However, Watson's interest in improving pigs and cattle was not evident in the Connecticut Town Reports.[39]

These sorts of fairs did not figure specifically into the responses to the survey. Nonetheless, they were usually a function of agricultural societies and became an important avenue for the work of breed associations. They also illustrate the importance of social relationships to the practice of agriculture in the United States, something that is clearly evident in the Town Reports.

Class Relationships and Agricultural Success

Finally, the Connecticut Town Reports have some interesting implications for understanding the role of wealth and class among the people of Connecticut. Much that was written in the survey responses, for instance, reflected the status of the individual responding to the questions. Furthermore, even the local agricultural practices themselves depended on the wealth and status of the farmer. Thoughts on class were most evident in the Wallingford Report, which discussed the requirement to have an "estate" to be a "planter." Respondent George Stanley also emphasized equality in these rather vague terms: "A great degree of equality prevails among the citizens in their intercourse with each other, coinciding with the actual equality of property, education, & influence."[40] While he surely meant to de-emphasize class, his phrasing and claims demonstrated a definite interest in social stratification.

Of course, Stanley had some interest in distinguishing the young nation from England, where class relationships predominated. In her book, *The Animal Estate* Harriet Ritvo has claimed that livestock breeding in the eighteenth and early nineteenth century in England was extremely aristocratic, and that the breeding system helped to maintain and clarify class divisions. British breeders, she suggests, focused upon pedigree and fat animals not for profit, but for the pleasure and prestige that this expensive hobby could bring them. According to Ritvo, "In toasting their noble animals, the elite livestock fanciers were celebrating themselves."[41] Breeding was a pursuit generally too expensive for the common farmer, who neither could afford to maintain animals for several years and experiment with them, nor could afford the expense of fattening them to the extent that

the British livestock fanciers required. Although British breeders claimed patriotic intent, explaining that experimental breeders would develop superior strains that would then be adopted by ordinary farmers, their breeding did not directly lead to practical result. In fact, the girth bred and fed into the animals tended to prevent them from breeding either by preventing them from actually being able to stand, in some cases, or by robbing them of the vigor necessary for breeding. Cows were often rendered physically unable to reproduce. Thus, patriotic rhetoric aside, breeding and the breeding associations did not directly improve British agriculture, and in many cases the associations organized by the aristocrats became effective class barriers.

Certainly, Connecticut farmers and breeders were far less divided by the class issues raised by Ritvo. Also, breeders were not driven by the same standards as the British. While early American academies and agricultural societies did tend to be aristocratic in nature, and were based upon the organizational model of learned societies, as the Town Reports seem to suggest, American farmers associated with these groups also were more seriously inclined toward general improvement with the hopes of affecting agriculture throughout the country.[42] Rasmussen explained that "The early agricultural societies were made up of groups of men of all professions who could afford experimentation and who would seek out and adapt to American conditions the progress made in other countries."[43] The Philadelphia Society, in its charter, explicitly contrasted American methods of agriculture and efforts toward improvement with those undertaken in Europe. The Society itself was devoted to disseminating knowledge and techniques accumulated by members through "occasional communications of improved methods, and by honorary premiums given for experiments made." The Society anticipated success by addressing "a people sufficiently liberal to reject no practice they shall recommend, merely because it is new, or runs counter to former habits and prejudices."[44] Like the Philadelphia Society, through its survey the Connecticut Academy of Arts and Sciences hoped to spread knowledge and overcome traditional resistance and indifference to new, and perhaps improved, practices.

Conclusion

As suggested above, the agricultural topics addressed in the Connecticut Towns survey provide tremendous insights into agricultural understanding and practice during the era. Beyond the crop, land, and livestock concerns recounted, the Reports address methods of pest management, crop prices, and nature of the terrain, thus providing even more material for the scholar. Furthermore, these sources can contribute to a much broader understanding of the geological and human development of Connecticut, including the growth of local and state agricultural societies, different views of tradition and innovation, social relationships in rural and town life, and the relationship between agricultural practices and class differences. The topics are nearly endless, and open the door wide to furthering the art and science of scholarship.

Fertile Farms among the Stones

Paul E. Waggoner

A laborer in overalls stringing barbed wire around an overflow of cows at a country auction first connected *the times* to farming for me. Hammering a staple into a flimsy post, he hit his thumb and swore, "Damn Hoover." My dad explained how hard times that cut prices in half connected barbed wire and a swelling thumb to the President's name in 1932. Near 1800 the farmers who responded to the Academy's Solicitation Letter saw hard times, too. When hard times after the American Revolution cut prices to less than half, American Revolutionary veteran Daniel Shays led a farmers' rebellion in Massachusetts. When the Embargo stopped exports, farm prices fell nearly a quarter in 1808. And when the Napoleonic wars ended, the Panic of 1819 cut prices to half between 1817 and 1821.[1]

Among the Rocks Nature Threw up, Soil for Farmers

To ride out the hard and enjoy the good times between, Connecticut farmers had the endowment of land. Ezra Stiles's father described the endowment, such as it was, of his family farm in Cornwall,

"Nature exhausted all her Store
to throw up Rocks, but did no more."[2]

Two centuries later, geologists would conclude that a gigantic collision of plates had, in fact, thrown rocks together from 1000 to 3000 miles of proto-North-America, a carbonate bank, ocean sediments and an off-shore island to make Connecticut.[3] Stiles Senior's couplet had it right.

Fortunately, in the great crack between two of the colliding masses, sediment accumulated to form the fertile Connecticut valley. Making a farmer's contribution to the geology of the valley in 1802, Pliny Moody plowed up brownstone with unusual footprints. Intrigued by the first fossil evidence of a dinosaur in the New World but still practical, Moody made a doorstep of the stone.[4]

Erosion from adjacent hills or overflowing streams had enriched the low ground between hills or along the banks of streams, both in the Connecticut valley and elsewhere. Both Jared Eliot of Killingworth, the preeminent student of agriculture in the eighteenth century and Timothy Dwight, whose travel diaries described the state near 1800, called the low ground intervales or intervals, and every farmer treasured them. Eliot wrote that the first planters who settled by the large rivers and intervale lands found so much mowing without clearing forests that they improved only the best and nearest and let the rest lie.[5] Going north in 1795, working on his first *Travel*, Dwight entered the southern reach of the central valley at Northford as if he were entering Shangri-La. He wrote enthusiastically about "a rich loam spreading from Guilford on the Sound to ... West Springfield, an extent of 60 miles, comprehending a considerable part of the counties of New Haven, Middlesex and Hartford."[6]

Settlers also found fertile soil on the hills. Long after the massive plates collided to build Connecticut's foundation, glaciers scraped it and kindly receded thousands of years before settlers arrived. In such places as Goshen and Windham, glaciers left streamlined hills of clay, sand, pebbles and boulders that, when weathered for millennia and then cleared of forests, grew grass as lush as the intervales. The scatter of the good soils, however, exacted a price. John Treadwell of Farmington wrote, "The inhabitants have their home lots in the town plot, their lots, as usually happens, in various parts of the meadows, distant from a quarter of a mile to nearly three miles and their pastures for their cattle & horses in perhaps an opposite direction, & as far or farther distant. ... The time spent in taking their cows to pasture and fetching their teams in the morning and going to their fields in returning home, turning out their teams & fetching their cows at night ... is worse than lost."[7] Scatteration of the fertile soils made lots of trudging. Nevertheless, more than fertile intervales or hills, the rocks thrown together impress the visitor as they did Stiles Sr. Stone walls assembled by generations of farmers impart some of the impression.

Because visitors tend to travel west to east from New York to Boston, Providence and Cape Cod, Connecticut's north to south arrangement across their path adds further impression of Nature's store of rocks thrown together. The Housatonic, Connecticut and Thames rivers flow south. Along highways cut through solid stone, modern motorists see bald domes of rock. Traveling west to east long before Interstate 95 was blasted through stone, Dwight wrote about 1800, "From [Lyme] the ridges, which here in a continual succession extend themselves to the border of the Sound, render the traveling very disagreeable. They are steep, rough, covered with a cold and lean soil, unpleasant to the eye, and inhabited by farmers occupying houses and farms generally indicative of little prosperity."[8]

Fascinated by the patchwork of soils formed after the glacier passed, soil scientists of the U.S. Bureau of Soils surveyed the

Connecticut valley and Windham and New London counties during 1899-1912. During the 1920s, Marion Morgan of the Connecticut Agricultural Experiment Station in New Haven surveyed the entire state with detail suitable for discussion here.[9]

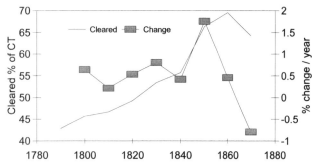

Fig. 1 *The percentage of Connecticut land cleared for farming, 1800-1870, and the average annual percent of change from 1790 onward. From David R. Foster, "Land-use History and Four Hundred Years of Vegetation Change in New England," in* Global Land Use Change. A Perspective from the Columbian Encounter, *B.L. Turner, A. Gomez Sal, F. Gonzalez Bernadaldez, and F. di Castri (Madrid, 1995), p. 269.*

After studying topography and vegetation and digging pits to study profiles, soil scientists name a soil type, often for a town such as Wethersfield. They then map the types, four of which exemplify the influence of soils on farming. The precious and productive Charlton loam on streamlined ridges in the western highlands and in the eastern highlands in Woodstock, Pomfret and Lebanon encouraged dairying. The red Wethersfield loam formed from the red sandstone of the central valley lay in varied but tillable terrain and encouraged diversified farms. The sandy Merrimac and related soils deposited in rich, tawny terraces with few stones near ancient lakes encouraged valuable crops of tobacco and potatoes, especially in the Connecticut valley. In some towns outside the valley, however, deposits of these soils produced fertile farms among the stones. For example, the first settlers of Guilford occupied what they grandly called the Great Plain. The Plain bracketed by tidal marsh is Merrimac fine sandy loam, a less sandy relative of the Merrimac sandy loam along the Connecticut river in Hartford county. Vegetables were grown on the Merrimac soil of Guilford's Great Plain as they were on the Merrimac of Hartford county. To the north of the Great Plain, however, four streamlined ridges were mapped as Charlton, and they encouraged orchards and dairying in Guilford just as the Charlton soils did in Woodstock, Pomfret and Lebanon.

Nature left Connecticut farmers fertile soil among the stones, even on the sides of Colts Foot Mountain in Cornwall where Nature exhausted her store of rocks on Stiles's farm. There lie "Luxuriant Meadows, good & feasible Plow Land which produces various kinds of Crops in abundance and very good grazing ground, A large part of which was in 1798 by the Assessors Appraised at 60 Dollars per Acre. ... [The produce enables] the Ladies who are generally Ambitious of not only appearing, but really of being, Neat, Agreeable & Elegant in their Persons and in the Deportments, to Deck

their Tables both for their Families and Friendly Visitants in an Elegant manner with Princely Fare of the most Nutricient and wholesome Viands."[10] Soils determined the sort of farms as exemplified by the ridges of Charlton soils that grew the grass to feed the cows to make the cheese that enriched Goshen.

Clearing Fields, Using the Wood and Growing Crops

In a favorite rural tale, a minister praises a farm that God and the farmer had made. The farmer replied, "You should have seen it when God had it alone." The first settlers praised land that Indians had cleared by fire. When they reached Litchfield county about 1720 "Many of the hills were nearly cleared of trees by fires, kindled [by Indians] for hunting."[11] Until 1740, Farmington farmers kept burning to encourage pasture. Then near 1800 after some 60 years without burning, the town reported a bonus of chestnut rails from the sprouts encouraged by first the burning and then its halt.[12]

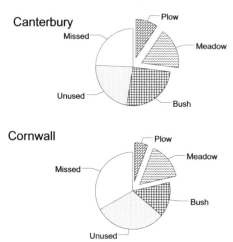

Fig. 2 *The proportions of land in 1798-1800 in Canterbury and Cornwall in five categories. Derived from the Canterbury and Cornwall 1801 Town Reports.*

Before crops could grow outside the clearings of the Indians and the meadows along water, trees and rocks had to be cleared—laboriously. In 1738 Cornwall required a settler to clear and fence six acres, about a half mile of fence, within two years.[13] Arriving in Guilford in the seventeenth century, the settlers spread slowly because "they did not understand the proper method of subduing forests. A law was early made that every planter should clear half an acre yearly. This they did ... by digging up the trees by the roots ... One of the first settlers at length cleared an acre in a different manner and astonished the people by gathering from it 20 bushels of wheat. From him the practice spread of clearing lands by cutting down the trees."[14] Technology encompasses electronics but also the ax.

Swing the ax the colonial farmers did (see Fig. 1). During the ninety years before 1790, they expanded cleared land about 1 percent per year. During the 1800-10 decade of the Embargo, they cleared little. In the decade after the Panic of

1819, they chopped faster. After the Panic of 1837, clearing accelerated to a peak in 1850 before clearings began shrinking.

Farmers cut trees for reasons other than cropland. The farmer burned wood for everyday activities, such as warming his own house, evaporating maple sap from his own trees and boiling water to scald his hog. "Open fire-places demanded constant replenishing during the winter and consequently the wood-pile formed an imposing eminence behind every farmhouse."[15] In 1708 the Town of Guilford promised the Reverend Jared Eliot 60 loads of firewood if he married, but in 1792 Hercules Weston received only 20 cords from the Ecclesiastical Society of Cornwall.[16] Extrapolating from the import of fuel wood in the New Haven Harbor, Dwight estimated that households in that city burned 10 cords; later foresters estimated that during 1800-1810 New England burned wood at the rate of 5 cords per capita.[17] Conservative estimates such as John O'Keefe's assume that a household of 6 persons burns 15 cords annually.[18] Presuming the wood lot yields 1 cord per acre, the family would need a 15-acre wood lot. J. Ritchie Garrison estimated that in the New England countryside settlement leveled off near 25 to 35 people or 4 to 6 households per square mile.[19] Sixty to 90 acres of the 640 in each square mile would have been needed to keep them in fuel. The 10 percent to 15 percent of the land needed for the farmsteads' fuel loomed large against the 30 percent of the land still not cleared in 1860.

During the winter when sleds traveled to town easily over the snow, a farmer could cut even more firewood. New Haven consumed 7,500 cords in a year, which it drew from itself, Guilford, Long Island and up the Housatonic.[20] The gradually increasing radius of 10 miles to supply New Haven in 1811 comes as no surprise. A demand for 7,500 cords would consume the annual growth on a half-forested semicircle 10 miles in radius.[21] From Guilford in 1832 much wood was "consumed by the inhabitants and much is carried to New York. The principal wood market is at the mouth of East river, at the wharf called Farmers' Wharf. There is another at East river Bridge."[22]

Wood sold so well that by 1806 East Windsor reported, "Within 20 years, the price of woodland has risen ten fold ... Meadow land has risen about three fold." Goshen reported that the profits from making maple sugar "are small, and the quantity of fuel required together with its scarcity, operates as a discouragement." In Wallingford despite stoves and improved fireplaces that economized on wood and despite abundant maples, the price of fuel rendered manufacturing sugar unprofitable.[23]

Near New York in Fairfield county, Dwight found fuel scarce. Concluding his *Travels*, he wrote that infertile soils of the U.S. "are less in their extent than the inhabitants will hereafter find to be necessary for furnishing them with timber and fuel."[24] Fortunately, efficiency, coal and oil sidetracked the onrushing desolation of Dwight's apocalypse.

The need for cropland and meadow, of course, also encouraged clearing. In 1798-1800 the tax lists of Cornwall in the west and Canterbury in the east showed how the farmers were using the land (see Fig. 2). The tax list missed nearly a

third of the land, and nearly as much was not enclosed. Fifteen percent (Cornwall) and 26 percent (Canterbury) were bush pasture. Another 16 to 17 percent were upland mowing and pasture, bog meadow and other land mowed. Finally, farmers

Fig. 3 *Farmington's wooden pole and rail fences with a detail of Colebrook's zigzag and stone fences. From John Warner Barber, Connecticut Historical Collections (New Haven, 1836), pp. 89 and 465.*

plowed 6 to 10 percent.[25]

Plowland, meadow and even bush pasture profited the farmer only when fenced to keep animals *out* of crops and *out* of meadow until harvest or mowing. And except for a few foraging pigs and cows, farmers must fence their animals *in* pastures. "Chiefly fence is made of Rails 12 feet long of Chestnut in general but some of Ash, Oak & other Timber laid up and locked together at the ends of the Rails which are laid on Stones or Billets of Wood at the ends of the Rails to keep them from the Ground. And to make Fence stand strong the length of the Rails are laid in a Zigzag form;" five or six rails were stacked up. Farmington's Report of the shilling and pence to erect and maintain a rod of fence for 50 years shows the advantage of wood about 1800.[26]

Post and rail	5 / 3
ZigZag, if timber is plenty	3 / 6
Stone, post and three rails where stone are plenty	3 / 3
Stone, post and two rails where stone are convenient	6 / 0
Stone wall where stone are good and plenty	13 / 2

When wood became scarce and expensive, stone replaced rails, and the stone survived for all to see. Although the rails decayed and disappeared, the stone wall persisted. However, John Warner Barber's drawing of Farmington in 1836 depicts farmers building rods and rods of inexpensive wooden posts and rails in that town but not one expensive stone wall (see Fig. 3). Barber's view of Colebrook, on the other hand, shows both a zigzag and a stone fence (see Fig. 3 insert). Keeping animals out and in required a pile of wood.[27]

How large a pile? For its zigs, zags and laps at two ends, let a 12-foot rail stretch 8 feet. Let Canterbury's 3,241 acres of plowland be divided into 324 square, 10-acre fields and its 11,051 acres of pasture comprise 276 square, 40-acre lots. If the fields do not adjoin and so share fences, Canterbury's fences would have stretched 440 miles. If the 12-foot rails were squares one half foot on each side, they would have consumed nearly 2 cubic feet of wood per foot along the fence and so 4 million cubic feet all together. In 1987, 1,325 cubic feet of timber stood on an average acre of Northeastern forests.[28] At that rate, farmers building Canterbury fences would have cut the timber from 3,000 acres or 12 percent of Canterbury's 40 square miles. If the fields adjoined, farmers could build fewer fences. Because many of the 1,325 cubic feet of trees on each acre would not make 12-foot rails, more than 3,000 acres would be searched for proper trees. Anyway one cuts it, however, fencing, like fuel, consumed a lot of wood. In 1812 the scarcity and expense of rails in Bethlem evoked a singularly good opinion of rock: "There are stones enough on the Surface of the Town to fence it into convenient lots."[29]

Isolation and Subsistence

In the 1920s, the Fisher Museum of Harvard Forest depicted the clearing and re-growth of New England forests in 3-dimensional dioramas. Even a 2-dimensional version, (as in Fig. 4) conveys the isolation of a farm and the loneliness of life on it as late as 1850. One can imagine the youthful extravagance of employing a fiddler for a full $1 so that young people could leave isolated farms to dance in Litchfield in 1748. However, it is more difficult to imagine that when the "instance of profusion took place, parents and old people exclaimed that they should be ruined by the extravagance of the youth."[30] One can also understand young men escaping dull and lonely chores on the farm of the diorama to follow the fife and drum of the Continental Army in 1776 or cheer the liberty tree of the Whiskey Rebels nearer 1800.[31] Although farmers were not completely separated from others if they knew of the dance, Continental Army and liberty tree, isolation must have been often felt.

Back on the farm and thrown largely onto their own resources, young people became subsistence farmers.[32] Until 1800 they subsisted on pea and bean porridge or broth from boiled salt meat mixed with meal and sometimes hasty pudding and milk—both morning and evening. The common bread of country people away from the coast was made of Indian cornmeal and rye flour. The farmer could have carried all his tools, except the cart and harrow, upon his back. His tools included a plow, a hoe, a pitchfork, a manure-fork and a shovel. The farmer made tools clumsily of wood, and he or the local blacksmith plated some with strips of sheet iron. A day's flailing yielded 4 to 6 bushels of wheat or 6 to 12 bushels of barley. Although Indian corn was sometimes flailed, high technology was scraping the grains from the cob across a spade. A craving for the stimulants from Connecticut's numerous distilleries arose in part from a coarse diet but "probably to a larger extent, from a desire to relieve at least temporarily the dreary monotony of village life."[33]

The subsistence farmers of the interior were distant from a market and thus from the money it would earn to buy better tools and improve their farms. About 1760 fetching wood three to five miles was a calamity that made "Fire Wood a heavy Article of Life."[34] Until a canal opened in 1807 in neighboring Massachusetts, an immense quantity of lumber was still useless because it lacked an easy passage to market.[35] Along the Connecticut River in New Hampshire in 1797, a road was so covered with stones that "in this spot no horse ever set his foot on the ground."[36] In Connecticut only 40 miles from Manhattan, Ridgefield in 1800 admitted "Potatoes are very much used and increased attempts are making to raise them for market but the distance from market is so great that it is not expected the practice will be general."[37] Although Connecticut had furnished enough food to the Revolutionary army to be called the Provision State, getting produce to market in 1800 was still arduous and thus costly for many farmers. With roads so bad that even 40 miles separated farmers from a market, improved husbandry and a surplus above subsistence brought a more abundant and cheerful life only if farmers endured a

Fig. 4 *A lonely New England farm, circa 1850. Diorama at the Fisher Museum of Harvard Forest in Petersham, Massachusetts.*

long haul to market. Examining the transformation of rural Massachusetts into a market economy between 1750 and 1850, Winifred Rothenberg found the median distance farmers hauled wagon loads in 1791-1805 was 20 miles, and they hauled loads as far as 150 miles.[38]

Connecticut cities that might have been markets disappointed farmers. A French visitor observed that produce from townspeoples' small farms made it impossible for farmers with a surplus of produce to sell it in New Haven.[39] As late as 1830 on his 160 acres within New Haven, William Kneeland Townsend wrote in his diary, "Sidney is thrashing oats. Julius and Daniel put rings in the Snouts of the 4 white Sows." His city bred pig (see Fig. 5) competed with rural bacon that might have found a market in New Haven.[40]

"The supplies of flesh and fish are ample, and of vegetables, sufficient for the demand of the inhabitants, most of whom are furnished from their own gardens."[41] A modern reader inundated by zucchini from neighbors' gardens understands how nearby gardens hinder sales of produce.

Farmers had to carry their surplus farther. Roads were first opened to pass from farm to farm and to the meetinghouse and store in the town center, however, not to a distant market. Cleared of rocks and most stumps, a narrow path carried packhorses and ox carts. In the middle of the eighteenth century, when the legislature ordered towns to build sections of a "state road" from Hartford toward Albany, the legislature failed to add the encouragement of money—with predictable results.[42] Speeding along the primitive roads with horse rather than oxen teams could be dangerous. In Madison in 1827, a horse capsized a wagon and fell dead. The driver also expired.[43]

Well into the nineteenth century, repairing the roads was a frolic to work off taxes. At the time appointed, "a motley assemblage gathers, of decrepit old men, each with a garden hoe on his shoulder; of pale, thin mechanics from their shoe shops, armed with worn-out shovels; half-grown boys sent by their mothers, who, perhaps, are widows; with perhaps the doctor, the lawyer, and even the minister, all of whom understand that working on the road does not mean hard labor, even for soft hands. ... The old men tell stories to an audience always ready to lean on their tools and listen. The youngsters amuse themselves by all sorts of practical jokes."[44] A relief from lonely chores but not much improvement of roads.

Even the subsistence farmers in the interior with their wooden tools had to trade something for the strips of sheet iron to plate their tools. They found ways, albeit ways to survive rather than prosper. During the fifty-three years from 1805-1858 farmer Charles Phelps of Hadley Massachusetts took one marketing trip into Connecticut, two to the states to the north and west, and one nearly to Boston along with his sixteen other trips to market.[45] One means of transporting farm produce on the roads repaired by the practical jokers was converting bulky grass and grain into cattle and then, as the reporter from Washington wrote in 1800, "Cattle are generally driven off on the leg."[46] But to what market? Dwight explained "The inland trade of [New Haven] consists of exchange of European, East Indian, and West Indian goods for cash and produce with the inhabitants of the interior."[47]

Although 40 miles kept interior Ridgefield's potatoes from New York City, about 1819 coastal Fairfield county had a fleet of twenty to thirty vessels regularly carrying grain, flour, beef, pork and potatoes to the City. The City held three times Boston's population and more than a third of Connecticut's total. Besides New York City, the American market was some 153 thousand including 114 thousand slaves, specializing in exportable rice and cotton along 250 miles of Carolina-Georgia coast, 800 miles from New England. Only farmers along the coast or behind New Haven and New London had access to this southern market, and the fact they exported to it at all showed their desperation for cash.[48]

Connecticut farmers found a better market in the West Indies. There 2 million specialized in sugar and lacked a backcountry to compete with what New England produced. New England did not export wheat because as Governor Sullivan of Massachusetts wrote President Jefferson in 1808, "The seaport towns are supported almost entirely by bread from the Southern and Middle States."[49] Rather, southern New England excelled in exporting "provisions": approximately half U.S. exports of salted beef and pork, butter, cheese and lard, potatoes and onions; a seventh of hams and bacon and almost all fresh meat and live stock came from Yankee farms. Bidwell figured southern New England's 1810 exports at 960 tons of butter, an estimated 486 tons of cheese, 850 tons of lard, 9.5 tons of hams and bacon, 75,000 barrels of beef and pork, 22,160 head of live stock and 48,000 poultry.[50] In 1801 Cornwall sent only 3 percent of its grain to market but fully 55 percent of its animal products.[51]

During the same era as Dwight lived in Connecticut, Johann Heinrich von Thünen[52] was analyzing his estates in northern Germany. When he published *The Isolated State* in 1826, he added accessibility to the well-known physical factors of soil and climate that determined a farmer's fate.

To remove distractions of other factors, von Thünen imagined a city at the center of a homogeneous region, much as we might conceive Connecticut. He assumed that farmers would maximize their incomes by considering yield, price and production expense, of course. He theorized they would also consider transport cost, the miles to market and the transportation rate and deterioration per mile. Farmers would then maximize income per acre using the following formula:

Income per acre = {Yield of tons per acre} *times*
{ (Value per ton) *minus* (Production expense per ton) *minus* (Transport and deterioration per ton per mile) *times* (Miles to city) }

The transport cost to the city market at the center of von Thünen's isolated state creates concentric zones. Nearest the market, gardening prevails but falls off in a short distance because fruit and vegetables deteriorate, and deterioration is part of transport rate. The low value of critical but bulky wood and hay restricts their production to the next zone. A dried crop containing many calories is worth many dollars per ton and doesn't deteriorate. Hence crops like grain or onions

Fig. 5
An urban, New Haven pig. From Doris B. Townshend, Journal of a Gentleman Farmer 1829-1832 *(East Haven, Connecticut, 1985), p. 85.*

Fig. 6 *Downtown Goshen in 1835. From John Warner Barber,* Connecticut Historical Collections *(New Haven, 1836), p. 468.*

grow in the third zone. Because cattle go to market on their own legs, the pastoral zone lies farthest from the city.

The gardens in and near New Haven illustrate von Thünen's first zone. The wood and hay from Wintonbury (Bloomfield) and Wallingford to fuel homes and horses in Hartford and New Haven demonstrate his second zone.[53] Selling wood to New York City made fuel scarce in Fairfield county and left few trees near the Academy at Greenfield Hill, also typifying the second zone.[54] Connecticut's analog of grain was onions that could be shipped dry with little deterioration; Wethersfield's onion fields demonstrate von Thünen's third zone. Guilford's Sachem's Head harbor illustrates the outer, pastoral zone; it was "a favorite place for the shipping of cattle for the West Indies before the Revolutionary War, driven hither not only from [Guilford] but from towns on the Connecticut River, particularly from Middletown."[55]

Beyond the obvious ways of raising yield per acre, bargaining for a higher value per ton and cutting production expenses, farmers tried other ways of coping with von Thünen's iron law. To lower transport rate per mile, towns tried to get roads on the cheap as turnpikes; and during 1803-1807 Connecticut chartered fully fifty companies. The turnpike companies laid out roads straighter than the old cart paths to lower cost of surface per mile between tolls, but the roads were steeper and merely built of the soil gathered along the way.[56] Although Goshen reported in 1812 that turnpikes changed ox carts to wagons and bragged of the new technology of an "ox scraper," the state of land transportation still impelled Dwight to exult, "Hardly any sight is more rare or more beautiful than the steamboats which move on the waters connected with New York."[57]

In addition to lowering the cost of a ton per mile, farmers could overcome von Thünen's law by raising the value per ton without waiting for town meeting or turnpike charter. Whiskey rebels in Pennsylvania raised the value of their corn per ton by distilling it into whiskey so valuable that packhorses could carry it economically. A Connecticut specialty was drying or

curing meat to make it lighter per dollar and lessen the deterioration per mile. In 1800 New London district helped pay for its imports of thousands of pounds of salt, coffee, sugar, and molasses plus 137 thousand gallons of spirits with 8 thousand barrels of beef, 3 thousand of pork and 2 thousand of fish.[58]

The quintessential Connecticut way to higher value per pound was transforming short-lived gallons of milk into long-lived pounds of cheese. "In cheese, moreover, an article was found for which the demand in the Southern states and in the West Indies was considerable. Cheese had enough value in proportion to its weight to bear the expense of transportation by land for some distance."[59] And, make cheese the Yankees did.

Of the estimated 486 tons of cheese that southern New England exported, Goshen provided nearly 200 tons and neighboring Norfolk, 100 tons.[60] Dwight enthused, "The wealth of Goshen is one proof of the superiority of grazing ground to that which is devoted to tillage. ... [It has] perhaps the best grazing ground in the state; and the inhabitants are probably more wealthy than any other collection of farmers in new England ... The quantity of cheese made by them annually is estimated at [200 tons] weight."[61]

When advised to move south for his health in 1792, Alexander Norton of Goshen took local cheese to sell. He continued in the business, and in 1810 his cousin Lewis Norton patented pineapple cheese, named for its peculiar shape. By the middle of the nineteenth century, Litchfield County was making nearly 1,500 tons of cheese annually.[62] John Barber's woodcut celebrated the town's source of wealth when he pictured cows in downtown Goshen (see Fig. 6).

When farmers converted milk to cheese, they lightened the load for market to one eighth and kept the other seven eighths to slop the hogs.[63] Exporting cheese instead of the milk to make it, the farmers of Goshen hauled about 200 rather than 1,600 tons, eliminating 1,400 tons from the haul by wagon to New Haven and then from the sea trip, chiefly to the southern states and West Indies.[64] Wherever the Connecticut Yankee went, he took his cheese hoop with him and made cheese. By 1820 the migrants made Connecticut's Western Reserve into "Cheesedom."[65]

Nothing, however, goes as smoothly as books tell. During the long waves of declining harvest of firewood, improving roads, lightening the load by making milk into cheese, and replacing ox carts with horse drawn wagons, the farmers rode wavelets. The happy increase in trade with the West Indies and other states was interrupted by the War of 1812, when depredations by British and then French almost stripped Bridgeport of foreign navigation. Nine ships, brigs and sloops were captured and upwards of seventy young men were lost.[66] The British blockaded Long Island Sound and attacked Stonington in 1815.[67] The boom in sheep ignited by David Humphreys[68] was promptly ended when the British flooded America with woolen goods after the War and drove wool prices down to one-sixth between 1814 and 1824.[69] As their carts and wagons bumped along the road, Connecticut farmers felt the separation from markets that Bidwell emphasized; and as prices in the market fluctuated, they felt the market economy that Rothenberg emphasized.

In the decades to come, canals, rails and steam ships would ease the trip to market. By 1832 Guilford would report that steamboats on the Sound made stage coaches on the Post Road unprofitable.[70] And most helpful of all, industrialization and growth of towns would create markets near Connecticut farmers. In the meantime, however, some farmers simply left.

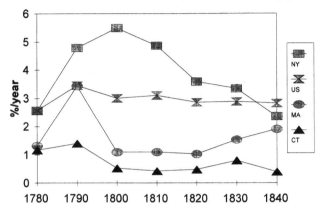

Fig. 7 *The slow change of Connecticut population versus faster change in Massachusetts, New York, and the nation, 1780-1840. Each point marks the average annual percentage change in population from ten years before. U.S. Bureau of the Census, Historical Statistics of the United States, Colonial Times to 1970 (Washington, D.C.: U.S. Government Printing Office, 1975), Series A 195 and Z 8.*

Emigration

In hard times, farmers do vote with their feet, seeking greener pastures. Connecticut's population grew more slowly than the nation and its New England neighbor, Massachusetts, and New York, as shown in Fig. 7.

Neighboring New York generally outgrew all. In a nation whose population doubled in a quarter century, Connecticut Yankees were increasing in number so slowly they would take near a full century to double, and compared to the rest of America they were shrinking. Even compared to itself in other periods, Connecticut's population grew remarkably slowly around 1800, as shown in Fig. 8.[71]

Paradoxically, Connecticut's slow-growing population was *rural* and *young*. It was 96 percent rural and surprisingly young (see Fig. 9). Figure 6 depicts cows in Goshen being driven by a child.

Nearly one in three was a child younger than five in 1800, compared to a scant one in fourteen in 1995. In 1800 Samuel Goodrich reported, "People here generally marry young and are very prolific; in 6 families a number of years since, all living in one neighborhood, there were 75 children."[72] In the state, only one person in six was 45 or older in 1800 whereas one of two was over 45 in 1995. In 1800, teeming farm children had to work to support the farm, and in 1995 the teeming population over 45 must work to support the still-older on Social Security.

The paradox of slow population growth despite an abundance of farm children is discussed below.[73]

The times were better in some American regions than in others. On the eve of the American Revolution, a free person in the Southern colonies had four times the wealth of a New Englander (see Fig. 10).[74]

Even without counting the value of slaves, Southerners and people from the Middle colonies were wealthier than Yankees. Farm prices, shown in Fig. 11, take the temperature of the times, as a thermometer might show our fever or chill.

The graph of farm prices in Fig. 11 begins with the hard times that accompanied and even prompted Shays's and the Whiskey Rebellion. European wars after the French Revolution lifted prices with an interruption by the Peace of Amiens. The Embargo of 1807 caused a depression, which the War of 1812 cured. Then speculation and overextended credit brought on the Panic of 1819. The Erie Canal exposed Connecticut farmers to western competition. After a banking recession in 1833-1834, a speculative boom in land, banking and transportation followed, only to be ended by the Panic of 1837.

Farmers rode a roller coaster. American exports dipped to a low in 1803 and plummeted during the Embargo and the War of 1812. Fig. 12 shows their low point that encouraged the Hartford Convention of 1814, "the foulest stain on [Connecticut's] escutcheon."[75]

Timothy Dwight in his *Travels* recorded the local symptom of New Haven exports, shown in Fig. 13.[76] The wonder is that the farmers survived the ride.

Evidence

The paradoxical combination of slow population growth and teeming children hints that many people left Connecticut. Testimonials from the rural towns poignantly confirm this fact.

Although Ridgefield sheltered a veteran so old that he had fought with Bonnie Prince Charles at Culloden, the town reported "In our revolution, many of the young people left the town and some of them now reside in the British domain;

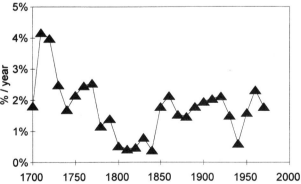

Fig. 8 *Average annual rate of population change in Connecticut, 1700-1970. Note the remarkably slow rate of change 1800 to 1840. U.S. Bureau of the Census, Historical Statistics of the United States, Colonial Times to 1970 (Washington, D.C.:U.S. Government Printing Office, 1975), Series A 195 and Z 8.*

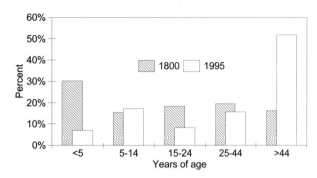

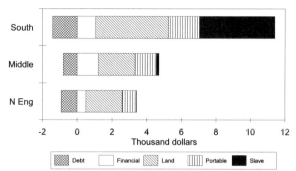

Fig. 9 *The frequencies of Connecticut people by age in 1800 and 1995.* U.S. Bureau of the Census, Historical Statistics of the United States, Colonial Times to 1970 (*Washington, D.C.: U.S. Printing Office, 1975), Series A 202-209 and U.S. Bureau of the Census, Statistical Abstract of the United States (Washington, D.C.: U.S.G.P.O., 1996), Tables 34 and 44.*

Fig. 10 *Private wealth per free person in the Southern, Middle and New England Colonies in 1774, expressed in 1990 dollars.* U.S. Bureau of the Census, Historical Statistics of the United States, Colonial Times to 1970 (*Washington, D.C.: U.S. Government Printing Office, 1975), Series Z 169-191. Portable wealth includes livestock, tools, crops, and consumer durables. 1990 dollars were converted by the author from 1973 dollars valued at $37.86 per 1774 pound sterling.*

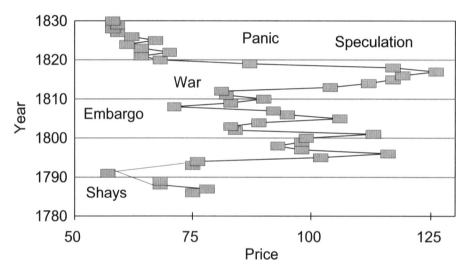

Fig. 11 *Indexes of wholesale agricultural prices in the United States, 1786-1830.* U.S. Bureau of the Census, Historical Statistics of the United States, Colonial Times to 1970 (*Washington, D.C., U.S. Government Printing Office, 1975), Series E 53. The index number of 100 equals the average 1910-1914 price of a basket of farm products, mainly in New York City*

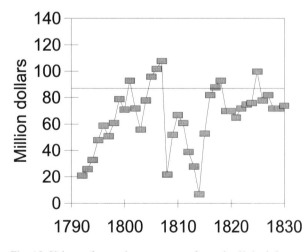

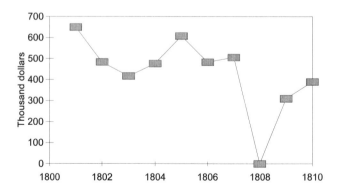

Fig. 12 *Values of water-borne exports from the United States, in millions of dollars, 1791-1830.* U.S. Bureau of the Census, Historical Statistics of the United States, Colonial Times to 1970 (*Washington, D.C., U.S. Government Printing Office, 1975), Series Q 521.*

Fig. 13 *Values of exports from New Haven, in thousands of dollars, 1801-1810, featuring the effect of the Embargo in 1808.* From Timothy Dwight, Travels in New England and New York, *edited by Barbara M. Solomon (Cambridge, Mass.: Harvard University Press, 1969), Vol. 1, p. 136.*

some returned and several are dead."[77] From Lebanon, "Emigration for more than 30 years has been so constant that it is judged that if all who have left the town who are still living and the descendants and the descendants of those who are dead were to return they would treble the number of inhabitants." [78]

> During the last forty years, the number of inhabitants has been nearly stationary [in Preston]. Beside the usual wastes of time and death the emigrations to new settlements have been numerous; for many years, the number of children in families is generally less than in the more early stages of society, the disproportion of the sexes occasioned by the loss of many young men in the revolutionary war, and since that time by the numerous removals of single men to the new settlements render it necessary that many females should go through life in a single state.[79]

Local statistics confirmed the testimonials. After its settlement, more moved out of the society of Judea within Washington town than lived in all Washington in 1810.[80]

Following Bidwell, one can estimate the number of migrants leaving as the difference between the 84 percent rise in the nation as a whole from 1790 to 1810 and the actual rise in six Connecticut counties.[81] For example if Litchfield's 1790 population of 39 thousand had increased by the national 84 percent, it would have been 71 thousand in 1810 rather than the 41 thousand it actually became. The difference between the hypothetical 71 thousand and actual 41 thousand yields the estimate that the shortfall due to emigration from Litchfield county during the twenty years numbered 30 thousand; fully 42 percent of those who would have been in the county were absent. Shortfalls ranged from 42 percent to 51 percent in three inland counties—Litchfield, Tolland and Windham. In the three counties of Fairfield, Hartford and New Haven that had an easier route to market on the Connecticut River or Long Island Sound shortfalls were somewhat lower: 35 percent to 39 percent.[82]

Emigration good or bad?

That emigration existed was clear, but whether it helped or harmed the state is uncertain. Dwight wrote, "At least three fifths of [the inhabitants of New York state] are of New England origin, and the number of these is rapidly increasing." He thought their loss was no great harm to Connecticut. He also found nothing to lament in Vermont gaining the settlers he called foresters, whose only business was

> To cut down trees, build log houses, lay open forested grounds to cultivation, and prepare the way for those who come after them....They are

too idle, too talkative, too prodigal and too shiftless to acquire either property or character....At the same time, they are usually possessed in their own view of uncommon wisdom.... Under the pressures of poverty and the fear of a jail [they] leave their native places and betake themselves to the wilderness.

Dwight concluded that liking a half lounging, half working life, the forester soon quits his clearing to girdle trees, hunt and saunter in another place. Federalist Dwight saw nothing bad that such men left Connecticut.[83]

When the Tolerationists and Republicans overturned the Connecticut Federalists, however, the new governor, Oliver Wolcott, told the legislature in 1817:

> An investigation of the causes which produce the numerous emigrations of our industrious and enterprising young men is by far the most important subject which can engage our attention....It is important to consider whether everything has been done which is practicable, to render the people contented, industrious, and frugal, and if causes are operating to reduce any class of citizens to a situation which leaves them no alternative but poverty or emigration, in that case to afford the most speedy relief.[84]

With Governor Wolcott, the people decided emigration was a symptom that all was not well among the largely rural Yankees.

Why Emigrate?

Elbowroom

In 2000 A.D., after a half century of flight to the suburbs for more room, an American will first think crowds and traffic jams provoke emigration. Since Connecticut people in 1800 suffered relative isolation at only fifty-two per square mile or 8 percent of the density in 1990, emigrants of 1800 certainly did not flee crowds.

Because Connecticut lived by farming in 1800, one might better ask if migrants fled because they lacked room for crops to feed themselves. At five persons per family, the rural population of 1800 formed about 50 thousand families or about a family per sixty acres. Because a bushel of grain contains about 100 thousand calories, a person eating the 3,000 per day ration of the Massachusetts militia in the eighteenth century would consume about twelve bushels in a year. So, if a farm family of five all ate like militia, they would need sixty bushels a year, the yield of six acres at a ten-bushel-per-acre rate for wheat or three acres at a higher twenty-bushel rate for corn.[85] Thus grain growing on only three to six of the sixty acres per family average would sustain them. Hunger did not drive the emigrants from Connecticut.

Depleted Resources

Near 2000 A.D. environmentalism has created an intellectual climate that inclines one to attribute the flight from Connecticut fields to their exploitation and depletion by five generations of European settlers. A similar intellectual climate prevailed in 1800. Reacting against mercantilism's claim that national strength rested on commerce and manufacturing, physiocrats of that time promoted land and agriculture as the source of wealth. As past physiocrats or present environmentalists, should one conclude that five generations of Connecticut farmers exhausted Nature's endowment of soils and forced them to flee in search of fresh soil to deplete?

Not according to Sharon's 1807 Report that soil "was formerly considered of little value, but with its present management it is productive of all sorts of grain, but chiefly of grass and pasturage and manifestly improved in strength and fertility by cultivation and judicious rotation of crops." Although one might question the reporter's attributing prosperity to using oxen rather than the horses Dutchmen favored in New York State, it is easy to believe his opinion that lime and legumes had improved the soils of Sharon. [86]

Swimming against the tide of opinion that Connecticut farmers had exhausted its soils, Michael Bell cites the high yields and modest use of fertilizer in Connecticut in the nineteenth century. [87] The Census of 1890 reported that Connecticut corn yielded 36 bushels per acre, equal to the yields in Ohio where so many Yankees had emigrated and considerably more than the 29 bushel average for all the states and territories.[88] One might conclude that Connecticut farmers had sorted the good from the bad soil by 1890 while the settlers of newer regions were still exploring which soils were best. But several generations onward when exploring farmers had had ample time to sort the soils in other regions, yields from Connecticut were still relatively high. In 1990 Connecticut soils yielded 19 tons of corn silage per acre, exceeding the Ohio average of 16 tons and the national of 14 tons.[89]

Piling on the fertilizer to restore depletion was not the cause of the relative fertility of Connecticut's long-farmed soils. In 1987 Connecticut farmers spent only 2.5 times as much per acre of cropland as the national average to produce 5.6 times the value of crop per acre.[90] The fertilizer bill did not indicate depleted soils.

Today a change in soil color at plow depth persists in some now-idle Connecticut valley soils, showing they were once tilled. Otherwise, however, the soils show little long-lasting modification by earlier farming.[91] This adds another argument against soil depletion driving farmers to emigrate.

Neither was a depletion of woodlots driving people away in 1800. The universally useful chestnut had sprouted and outgrown other trees when forest had been cut. The record it wrote with pollen in the soil showed its emergence was encouraged by the European settlement.[92] In 1812 in Kent "Wherever lands have been cut over within a few years past, the prevailing new growth is chestnut," and in Canterbury where oak had dominated the original forest, "We have much chestnut now." [93] Depleted resources did not drive out Connecticut Yankees.

The Stick of a Stringent Life

Although resources were not depleted, life on Connecticut farms was stringent—constricted, tight and short of money. Bidwell saw the nineteenth century beginning with a "period of self-sufficient economy, which had existed since the settlement of the country, reaching the highest point of its development at the beginning of the 19th century; a period in which the characteristic features of the rural economy were the absence of any market for farm produce and the consequent dependence of each town and, to a large extent of each household, even, on its own resources for the satisfaction of its wants.... For at least a generation [at the beginning of the nineteenth century], there had been practically no change in the manner of life of the inhabitants in most of the towns."[94] Bidwell discounted the theory that more and cheaper labor would ameliorate matters. He wrote that with little market "it would indeed have been poor economy to hire laborers to raise a surplus which could not be sold." Caught in the unremitting toil of subsistence by lack of a market "the farmer who had to be a handyman could not read and experiment to become a skillful farmer.... Because no division of labor existed except that between the sexes, the skill from repetition of identical processes was lacking."[95]

Decades later, Rothenberg argued, as I have cited above, that Bidwell overstated the absence of markets. True, valuable pineapples of cheese and barrels of salted meat were carried by carts and even ships as far as the West Indies even though growing potatoes in Ridgefield and hauling the bulky tubers forty miles to New York City was unprofitable. Flare-ups of price ignited in Europe and reaching American ports affected subsistence farmers in the interior only because they were connected to a market economy. But, they were connected at the end of long hauls by wagon and boat. They toiled on a treadmill described by Horace Bushnell.

> No mode of life was ever more expensive [than the self sufficient one]; it was life at the expense of labor too stringent to allow the highest culture and the most proper enjoyment. Even the dress of it was more expensive than we shall ever see again.[96]

Fig. 10 shows New England was not rich, at least compared to other regions in 1774. Yes, in 1800 provisions from Connecticut farmers were marketed as far as the West Indies. But making a barrel, salting fresh meat down in it and suffering a spread between producer and consumer to carry the barrel so far made a life sufficiently stringent, a stick sufficiently strong to prod a farmer who saw a carrot ahead.

The Carrot of Speculation

The pastor of Bethlem encouraged golden visions with a story of land bought from Indians: "A lot of 70 acres now worth 3000 dollars, was sold nearly one hundred years since to Col. Allen of Milford; for a *Jack-knife, a paper of pins, two quarts of molasses and a dozen of needles.*"[97]

Article 9 of the Academy's Solicitation Letter, the first agricultural question, asked about land price: Had it increased or decreased within the memory of the generation answering the question?[98] In 1803 Cheshire reported vaguely that the price of land is about "4 double," more than "provisions & labour about double."[99] Further inland and nine years later, Cornwall reported a doubling of land price in 40 years.[100] In East Windsor about the same time, "Within 20 years, the price of woodland has risen ten fold ... Meadow land has risen about three fold."[101] Prices could also fall, and Lewis Mills Norton of Goshen's cheese-making aristocracy complained, "The price of land [since about 1800] has decreased very considerably owing to the national embarrassments."[102] Nevertheless, the general message was "Speculation pays," frontier lands practically free of stones and cost were sure to appreciate, and they beckoned to the Connecticut farmer as a carrot beckons a rabbit.

A contemporary of the emigrants, Timothy Dwight, described the sticks and carrots:

> Those, who are first inclined to emigrate, are usually such as have met with difficulties at home. These are commonly joined by persons, who, having large families and small farms, are induced, for the sake of settling their children comfortably, to seek for new and cheaper lands. To both are always added the discontented, the enterprising, the ambitious, and the covetous. Many of the first, and some of all these classes, are found in every new American country, within ten years after its settlement has commenced. From this period, kindred, friendship, and former neighbourhood, prompt others to follow them. Others, still, are allured by the prospect of gain, presented in every new country to the sagacious, from the purchase and sale of new lands.[103]

Just as fife and drum enticed farm boys bored by chores into the Continental Army, the drumbeat of speculation as well as the other music Dwight described lured their sons into New York State, northern New England and the Western Reserve. Although the migrants would end further from markets than in Connecticut and have their hopes dashed by the Panic of 1819, the hope of buying land for little more than a jack knife then farming until its rising price made them wealthy, helped pulled them West and North (see Fig. 14).

Stirrings of Agricultural Science

Despite this setting of isolation, subsistence and emigration, a surprise was stirring—the beginnings of science to improve farming. If a large population pressing upon resources and demanding innovation causes invention, Connecticut was not ripe for science. If paving and companions evoke more invention than wilderness and solitude, Connecticut was a surprising place for science to stir.[104]

In addition, Connecticut seemed too conservative for innovative science. No less than President John Adams said, "The state of Connecticut has always been governed by an aristocracy, more decisively than the empire of Great Britain is. Half a dozen, or, at most a dozen families, have controlled that country when a colony, as well as since it has been a state."[105] An aristocrat, the very Pope of Federalism, was preparing a surprise.[106]

The Surprise at Yale

In her preface to Dwight's *Travels,* editor Barbara M. Solomon wrote that Dwight's greatest contribution to Yale's undergraduate curriculum was the appointment of Benjamin Silliman to teach chemistry, which in time encompassed the chemistry of how crops grow. Silliman's life before science intensifies one's surprise at his contribution. He joined the church during the Second Great Awakening when James Russell Lowell said, "Everybody was bent on reforming somebody or something." Further, Silliman was studying law rather than science when President Dwight sent him to Philadelphia, Princeton, and Europe to study science. Sparks of science at Yale surprised Joel Barlow, a former army chaplain and candidate for the ministry who met Silliman in London shortly after Austerlitz. Barlow was pleased but wrote, "He would have sent out a chemical apparatus and preparations had he not supposed that coming from him the college authorities would make a bonfire of them in the college yard."[107]

Indeed Silliman surprised Barlow and others. Far in advance of the rest of the country, Yale pioneered in chemistry, mineralogy, geology and scientific agriculture. Silliman's analysis of oily skimmings from Pennsylvania in the 1850s encouraged New Haven investors in the first petroleum well.[108] For agriculture, the Sillimans, Senior and Junior, nurtured in their laboratory the first agricultural experiment station in America, which opened in 1875.[109]

HARD TIMES IN OHIO

Fig. 14 *A satirical cartoon from 1819 of hope on the way to Ohio and defeat on the way back. From the collections of the American Antiquarian Society, Worcester, Massachusetts.*

Eliot of Killingworth

With the wisdom of hindsight, scientific agriculture in Connecticut seems less surprising. In all America during the eighteenth century, Jared Eliot of Killingworth was the preeminent student of agriculture. His *Essays Upon Field Husbandry in New England* during 1748-1762 valued trials and experiments over words because, "It being a good deal easier to write a book upon the known arts and sciences that shall be accepted and applauded, than to write upon husbandry so as not to be despised.... Our reasonings and speculations without experience are delusory and uncertain." Benjamin Franklin complimented Eliot with an order for 50 copies of his second essay. [110]

In 1747 Eliot scratched his head about a crop that would balance European imports as tobacco did for Virginia and rice for South Carolina. Unfortunately, only hemp and silk came to mind. He spent most of his ink, however, on the soil, its drainage, tillage and manuring. His concentration on soil and plant nutrients anticipated the revolution in agricultural science that Justus Liebig of Germany ignited in 1840 by his chemical analyses and Law of the Minimum.[111]

Pests

A half-century after Eliot, German soldiers carried the Hessian fly to Long Island during the Revolution, and the fly decimated wheat and focused minds on pests. In his *Travels*, Dwight recurs to another pest, wheat blast or rust, repeatedly and incriminated the barberry: "This bush is in New England generally believed to blast both wheat and rye. Its blossoms, which are very numerous and continue a considerable time, emit very copiously a pungent effluvium, believed to be acrimonious as to injure essentially both [grains]. ... A farmer on Long Island sowed a particular piece of ground with wheat every second year for near 20 years. On the southern limit of this field grew a single barberry bush. The southern winds prevailing at the season in which this bush was in bloom carried the effluvia, and afterwards the decayed blossoms, over a small breadth of this field to a considerable distance; and, wherever they fell, the wheat was blasted, while throughout the remainder of the field it was sound."[112] Struck by both the Hessian fly and rust, wheat dwindled in Connecticut.

Other pests provoked drastic remedies. "To kill Insects & Caterpillars from apple Trees various Expedients have been proposed ... as putting a Girdle with Tar around ye Tree, blowing off a Caterpillar's Nests with gunpowder, winding y^m off with a Stick or touching them with a Sponge conveying Spirits of Turpentine."[113] Exciting work!

Law of the Minimum for Soils

Rather than pests, however, Liebig, Silliman and the first American agricultural experiment station concentrated on soil. They were chemists. Briefly, Liebig's Law of the Minimum stated what now seems mere common sense: The minimum nutrient controls growth. Adding other nutrients won't help but adding some of the minimum one will. Liebig's 1840 book was so popular that a Harvard professor promptly issued two American editions. At Yale, however, Silliman published the first American review. Overflowing with enthusiasm, he wrote of Liebig's book, "Its acceptance as a standard is unavoidable, for following closely in the straight path of inductive philosophy, the conclusions which are drawn from its data are incontrovertible."[114]

The Law of the Minimum would eventually explain the mystery that puzzled the reporter from Farmington: "Thus sand may be manure for clay, & clay for sand: swamp mud & the earth which composes our plains may be manures to each other; and marl may be manure to most other soils."[115] The writer complained that much of the substance that goes under the name of plaster of Paris "is of no value & that which is genuine is of no use on many sorts of soil. ... Several of our best farmers have made experiments with it, but without any manner of discernible effect; our own experience, as far as it goes, is against it.... We are yet in our infancy in discovering & applying the means of rendering the earth fruitful."[116] Samuel W. Johnson, a student of both Liebig and Silliman, who campaigned for fertilizer analyses as well as science, could eventually solve the mystery of manures for Farmington.

In Dwight's era, however, Johnson's Connecticut Agricultural Experiment Station was still three-quarters of a century ahead, and its invention of hybrid corn over a century ahead. Farmers near 1800 simply relied on experience to justify their careful preservation of manure as when they accumulated everything possible, including earth, in a hog pen and found the urine of horses and cattle helped. With an attendant *fetor* recorded in Dwight's *Travels*, farmers along the shore would continue catching fat, oily white fish on the beaches for their astonishing effect, whether scattered at 10 to 12 thousand per acre or gathered in heaps, layered and covered with earth to compost. Because 200 thousand could be caught in a day with a single net, 10 thousand to the acre was not costly.[117]

Without understanding seed-borne viruses the Academy asked where farmers got their seed. Without understanding pest resistance, farmers changed from the best, white bald to yellow-bearded wheat to combat Hessian fly. And without understanding genetics they kept different plants far enough apart that "the farina of the blossoms shall not be mixed."[118] But the stirring of science would eventually bring understanding and practical results in train.

Relentless Change

The message here is "Because swift change isn't new, we learn it is relentless and should enjoy it."

The farmers of 1800 could compare their time with earlier ones and see change. The strips from home lots across meadows in Windsor continued to remind Connecticut farmers of 1800 of a far earlier arrangement of peasants' land in Europe. The Academy's respondents to the Solicitation Letter's 32 questions told stories of King Philip's War and Indian troubles that were fresh in the memories of their towns. When Eliot wrote in the sixth of his *Essays Upon Field Husbandry in New England* of a War and drafting 5,000 men in a year, he wrote of the French and Indian War of 1754-63 that would open land across the Appalachians to settlers from Connecticut.

The respondents to the Academy's Solicitation had seen change in their own time. The respondent in the town of Union was Revolutionary War Captain Solomon Wales. Respondent Samuel Dunton of Willington fought in Wadsworth's brigade in New York and White Plains. They had seen the colonies break from the mother country. They had seen the colonies change a confederation into the United States, add a unique Bill of Rights to the Constitution and begin adding new states. On the farm, blast and the Hessian fly had decimated wheat, and invasions and Embargo had interrupted the sale of their products.

In the Connecticut valley, John Wilson of Montague, Massachusetts invited relentless change. Unlike Henry Thoreau who withdrew to the solitude of Walden Pond in the middle of the nineteenth century, Wilson swapped farms, joined the militia and the social library, and married the daughter of a respected Deerfield family early in the century. He traveled to Canada on business and was captured. He served in the War of 1812, managed a printing business that failed in the Panic of 1819, served as a selectman, and designed a plow. He developed property in East Boston and recruited settlers for Texas. He suffered Merino madness and grew teasel, broom corn, tobacco and silkworms. He sought the "main chance."[119] Farmer Wilsons who enjoyed change outnumbered Transcendentalist Thoreaus who withdrew.

The changes that Dwight's generation *enjoyed* continued during the decades that followed. Canals and railroads that carried Connecticut goods to market and brought in competition rose and declined. Silk worms, broomcorn, and hemp had moments in the sun. Flax disappeared but is again promoted. Disease removed chestnut and elm, coal and oil displaced firewood and charcoal kilns disappeared from woodlots. Tobacco grew, went under shade, and faded; nurseries growing ornamental plants burgeoned; and tobacco re-emerged. Dairy farmers changed from cheese that was light to carry to fresh milk that tankers carried, and the cows' feed changed from English grass to hybrid corn.

Dwight's generation saw New York and the West Indies as the markets for farm produce. Reviewing the nineteenth century from the vantage point of 1916, Bidwell saw the greatest change ahead of them was where the markets were: "A great change was impending; soon the familiar, stereotyped ways of doing things, traditional habits of life and of thought were to suffer modification and in a few generations were to disappear almost entirely. The revolutionary force was to come from the rise of manufactures and the growth of a non-agricultural population in the inland towns."[120] Connecticut city folk would buy the milk and apples, smoke the cigars and set out the ornamental plants Connecticut farmers grew.

When the 75-year-old captain in the Revolution responded from Union to the Academy's questions, he complained woodchucks and squirrels destroyed his corn and grain. Natural history hasn't changed. But, Captain Wales also described his invention of a bin to keep the feed left by his hogs from "dishonest wagoners ... apt to take it for their horses."[121] Technology has changed. And more will come, relentlessly.

The State of Connecticut Agriculture in 1800

Holly V. Izard

Desirous of obtaining useful knowledge on this subject, the Connecticut Academy of Arts and Sciences queried the various towns on the following topics or articles:

9th. Agriculture; increase or decrease of the price of land, within the memory of the present generation; price of provisions and labor in the several occupations; the kinds of grain cultivated, quantity of each produced on an acre, and total quantity in a year; quantity of flour and kiln dried meal exported annually; quantity of hemp and flax raised, and the best mode of raising, rotting and dressing them; the quantity of flax and flaxseed exported; quantity of land planted with potatoes, and sown with turnips; rotation of crops best suited to various soils; improvements by means of artificial grasses; improvements by draining and diking marshes, meadows and ponds.

10th. Manures; the best for particular soils, and the best time and mode of applying them, as stable manure, lime, lime stone, shells, ashes, salt, compost, marl, swamp, creek and sea mud, plaister of paris, and sea weed; the preparation best suited for particular crops; the best means of increasing manures; the effects of irrigation or watering lands.

11th. The best seed time and harvest time; best time and modes of preparing lands for seeding, best modes of extirpating weeds and of preserving grains from insects; the effects of a change of seed.

12th. Mode of cultivation whether by oxen or horses; the expense, advantages and disadvantages of each; number of teams; the number and kinds of waggons, carts, ploughs, harrows, drills, winnowing and threshing machines now in use; improvements in them both as to utility and cheapness. Fences; the materials and mode of erecting them; kinds most used; increase or decrease of timber for fencing; the best kinds of trees or shrubs for hedges, and the means of propagating them.

13th. Uncommon fruits and garden vegetables, native or imported; the soils on which particular fruits and vegetables best flourish, and the best modes of cultivating them; quantity of cider made annually; quantity exported; best mode of making, improving and preserving it; best mode of preserving apples and other fruits during the winter; improvements by ingrafting and inoculation; best time and mode of pruning; state of gardening.

14th. Number of tenants on leased lands; quantity of lands leased and the rent; the state of cultivation of leased lands compared with that in the hands of proprietors. Emigrations from the Town or Society....

15th. Number of sheep and swine; quantity of pork, beef, butter and cheese annually sent to market; the best mode of multiplying, improving, feeding and fattening sheep, swine, neat cattle and horses; their diseases, descriptions of them, and the best mode of preventing and curing them.

The questionnaire in its entirety and as it regarded agriculture was exceedingly ambitious. Although the Academy urged respondents "to spare no pains in obtaining and communicating" the requested information, none thoroughly addressed all the queries and two-thirds of the towns did not respond at all (see Table I). Even Yale President Reverend Timothy Dwight, who was among those who initiated the project, grumbled at the weighty task of completing a survey.[1] He prefaced his own report on New Haven, filed in 1811, with the terse explanation: "The public will naturally ask why the answer has been so long delayed. The truth is, that every man, here, is closely engaged in his own business: and . . . no man of business is, ordinarily, willing to write on subjects, unconnected with his personal concerns." To emphasize his point, he noted "this account is drawn up in circumstances of extreme inconvenience."[2]

The Academy sent the questionnaire to ministers and men of letters, gentlemen whose primary "personal concern" was not agriculture.[3] Many completely ignored farming-related queries, preferring to focus on ecclesiastical concerns, historical and topographical topics, illustrious citizens, sensational occurrences, and cultural benchmarks. As a group they supplied far too little farming information to allow for quantitative or, for many areas of inquiry, even comparative analysis. While most addressed more general agricultural issues such as rising land values and shrinking timber supplies, only fifteen or roughly 40 percent provided any statistics on per-acre and annual yields, and just eleven supplied information on marketing (see Tables II-IV). Evaluation is also complicated by the varied dates of submission; most were written between 1800 and 1818, spanning nearly two decades of development and the War of 1812; two date to 1832, by which time industrialization had significantly transformed New England's economy. Still, the information supplied evokes an impression of the state of Connecticut agriculture and society at the opening of the nineteenth century.

The utility of the Town Reports is enhanced by Timothy Dwight's observations elsewhere on the state of society generally.[4] Between 1796 and 1811, he made thirteen journeys during which he recorded the physical, economic, political, cultural, and ecclesiastical landscape of the northeast.[5] His observations, published as *Travels in New England and New York*, include information on housing stock, improvements to the landscape (or lack thereof), farming practices, industries, and local populations.

In this essay, the information provided by Connecticut Town respondents on farming and related topics is considered in several contexts. First, it is compared to the current narrative of Connecticut history. Second, subjects that elicited common responses throughout the state are discussed. Lastly, production and marketing are addressed on a county-by-county basis. This summary report is a narrative on how the respondents perceived the state of agriculture and society in Connecticut around 1800; by nature of the Reports themselves, it is a subjective view. As folklorist Henry Glassie has eloquently explained, history resists neat categories of analysis; it resists completeness and even orderliness. This is especially true with reports such as these, wherein private citizens upon request presented their particular knowledge and understanding of their communities. They contain cultural commentaries as well as empirical findings. One respondent included a lengthy editorial about the erosion of traditional values. Some pondered the negative influences of the marketplace. Others used the Town Reports as a forum to comment upon lifeways of people not of English stock. Still others reflected upon simpler times. But that *is* history; it is lived and experienced by people who make of it what sense they can.[6] Objective quantified analysis of the state of Connecticut agriculture in 1800 is beyond the scope of the Town Reports.

I. Different Times, Different Perspectives

The Town Reports both confirm and in some ways challenge the conventional interpretation of Connecticut's agricultural history. Scholars generally have described the state as possessing "a paucity of fertile farmland."[7] While certainly this is accurate in comparison to other regions of the country today, early nineteenth-century inhabitants evaluated it differently. Timothy Dwight observed that the "surface" of the

state was "generally beautiful, and sometimes magnificent," its climate "somewhat milder than that of the other New England states, its soil strong and fertile." He believed, "No part of it can with propriety be called waste, and the lands incapable of convenient cultivation are fewer and smaller in extent than seems to demand."[8] Most respondents shared his opinion and also his optimism about the state's agricultural potential.

The trend universally outlined by scholars, from varied agricultural production for family consumption to specialized production for the market, is evident in the Town Reports. Towns that supplied details listed pork, beef, and dairy products as staple exports. But within this broad trend of specialization, Town Reports showed significant regional variations. Specialization did not occur in towns where soil was more suited to tillage than grazing or where agriculture was not the primary economic concern. Towns that listed significant exports of these staple commodities also exported a wide variety of other farm products, wood, and timber.

Even as historians pointed to marketplace specialization among eighteenth-century farmers, they generally argued, farmers did not husband the land well. Rather, farmers continued to practice extensive rather than intensive farming methods, and did not give adequate attention to agricultural improvements. As one historian stated, "agriculture was still in a primitive state" at the close of the eighteenth century, and "primitive agricultural methods coupled with low soil fertility resulted in unprofitable yields."[9] Only historians of the Connecticut River Valley have pointed to "improved and more intensive farming" among established farmers, undertaken as early as the 1750s as a strategy for economic security and advancement.[10] The Town Reports, on the other hand, indicate a nearly universal attention to agricultural improvement by 1800, even in the relatively new towns in the northwestern corner of the state.

The positive nature of responses may in part be due to the nature of the queries. In tenor, they were progressive, asking for details about the best mode of raising grains, crop rotations to replenish soil for the best yields, best times for planting and harvesting, most effective manures for fertilization, best means of fattening livestock, and more. But the fact that respondents who seriously addressed farming provided detailed information on these subjects indicates that Connecticut farmers were concerned with improvements long before the nineteenth-century "crisis" of the 1820s and 1830s, when cheaply produced western commodities began to flood New England markets. Their responses also indicate a fairly widespread and very early market orientation among the state's farmers, a pattern different from that of their northern neighbors in central Massachusetts.[11]

Scholars have noted high rates of emigration from the state beginning by the mid-eighteenth century. Some associated this phenomenon with the persistence of inefficient and unprofitable agricultural practices, others to the realities of land-tightness over time. Respondents were keenly aware of this constant outflow of people. Most linked it explicitly or implicitly to land scarcity in an agricultural-based economy, never to poor farming methods. Farmington lost 147 families between 1783 and 1802, "principally gone into the States of New York and Vermont, the some few to different parts of the North Western territory."[12] For Middlesex County, David Field observed in 1819 that "individuals and families have been almost perpetually removing from this county. They at first removed to the county of Litchfield in this State, and Berkshire in Massachusetts; then to New Hampshire and Vermont; in later years they have removed to New York, and to the Western States and Territories."[13] Goshen in Litchfield County replied similarly in 1812, explaining: "The emigrations from this town have been very numerous; chiefly first to the county of Berkshire, Massachusetts, then to Vermont, afterward to Bloomfield, New York, and to the town of Hudson, in the Connecticut western reserve.... It may be truly said that Goshen has contributed its full share to the peopling [of] the northern and western country."[14] The result for many towns was low population growth and relative economic stability. As Middletown reported: "The inhabitants of the southern, western, and northern parts of this town are very generally farmers, and as the lands in those parts have long been taken up for farms, the population has increased very little in many years.... Young, enterprising men, trained to husbandry, unable to get farms in their native town, have removed from time to time to other parts of the country."[15]

For New Haven, Timothy Dwight uniquely responded: "the great body of the emigrants are merchants, mechanics, or seamen; the principal part of whom remove to other commercial towns in the U[nited] States, and the rest to foreign countries, for the purpose of carrying on their respective occupations to greater advantage."[16] He also reported high rates of immigration, suggesting a whole town in motion, and continued population growth. "The places of these emigrants are continually supplied by immigration," he explained, "as is evident from the fact that; that, although new houses are annually erected here, every house is full; and many contain two or more families."[17]

Finally, while historians quite correctly point to the state's rapid industrialization beginning in the nineteenth century, the extent to which this process was underway the century before in many parts of the state may not be fully appreciated. All respondents who addressed queries about mills, forges, and manufactures listed the saw, carding, and gristmills necessary for life, and many noted the presence of other industries. For example, in the Middlesex County town of Haddam in 1819: "A scythe factory was improved some years ago on Pine Brook .... A gin distillery set up in Haddam Society in 1813 distills two hundred and fifty hogsheads of gin annually." In addition, he listed "one clothier's works, two carding machines, five grist mills, nine saw mills, seven tanneries, one gin distillery, two cider distilleries, one brick yard, and one machine for welding gun barrels."[18] Also, shipbuilding had been carried on there for one hundred years. Winchester's Winsted parish in Litchfield County similarly reported considerable non-agricultural pursuits. In 1813 there were "five iron works for making iron, in which there are thirteen fires or forges" and "six trip hammer shops," which were "kept in constant use in making axes, scythes, sleigh shoes,

drawing iron for wire, plating gun barrels." He also named "one establishment for manufacturing wire and "two infant factories for making cards," another for cutting nails, and a clothier's works. Finally, he noted "one establishment for making wooden clocks...in which three thousand clocks have been set in motion in the year past."[19] From other sources, we know that iron works also were operating in Salisbury, Sharon, Kent, Canaan, and Roxbury. Clock making flourished early in East Hartford, Norwich, and East Windsor, as well as Winchester. Chairmaking was a major and long-established industry in Wethersfield and Hartford. Shipbuilding was carried on in New London, Norwich, New Haven, Guilford, Branford, Stratford, Fairfield, Saybrook, Middletown, Essex, Middle Haddam, Glastonbury, Rocky Hill, Wethersfield, and Hartford. In port cities along major rivers and Long Island Sound, industry and commerce actually overshadowed agriculture in the eighteenth century.

II. Common Trends and Agricultural Practices Reported

Questions regarding farm tenancy, land prices, wood supplies, fencing, method of cultivation, and attention to manuring were most frequently and substantively addressed by respondents, whose answers indicate common trends and conditions throughout the state. Other topics, such as cost of labor and farm products, kinds of fruits and garden vegetables grown and methods of their cultivation, details of fattening livestock, methods of preserving grains from insects, enumeration of wagons and farm implements, attention paid to maple sugaring and cider making, were treated so irregularly as to make meaningful summaries impossible.

Farm Ownership, Tenancy

Respondents from all corners reported that the majority of farmers owned the land they tilled. Farmington in Hartford County reported in 1802: "We have few or no tenants on leased lands; there is not one farm in the town that is holden by a lease for years."[20] In Middlesex County generally, "we have very few tenants, and the land is rarely leased; the farmers being in most cases at once the owners and the cultivators of the soil."[21] In Wallingford, New Haven County, in 1811: "There is no leased land within the town."[22] The Windham County town of Lebanon reported in 1800: "There are but few farms rented," adding that "perhaps no town can be found where the lands are more equally distributed than this."[23] From the Tolland County town of Union, in 1803: "Our land is chiefly owned by the inhabitants and but few tenants."[24] The western towns of Bethlem and Goshen reported twelve and nineteen tenanted farms respectively in 1812.[25] However, most Litchfield County towns echoed Kent's spokesman, who stated in 1812: "the lands are generally owned by those who cultivate them."[26]

Most who reported tenanted land cast the situation in an unfavorable light. For example, the respondent for Preston in New London County answered in 1801: "The cultivation of leased land among us is, evidently, less favorable to the soil than that of the proprietor. Number of tenants, 64; number of acres of leased land 3,209."[27] The nearby town of Franklin similarly reported: "The number of tenants in the First Society is seven" in 1800. "Quantity of land improved by them 1,050 acres. The state of improvement about two-thirds as good as upon other farms."[28]

It appears that only the southeast corner of the state substantially differed from the consistently high rate of farm ownership reported. In his *Travels,* Timothy Dwight noted that in Groton there were more tenanted farms than the norm, and in the abutting town of Stonington he estimated that nearly fifty percent of the farms were rented in 1800. "A great part of these [tenants] are poor people from Rhode Island," he noted, "who make Stonington their halfway house in their progress towards new settlements."[29]

Price of Farm Land

Overwhelmingly, the Town Reports indicated significant increases in the price of land within the memory of the present generation, although actual values varied considerably (see Table II). The respondent for Windsor's Wintonbury parish (now Bloomfield) stated in 1802: "The price of land has greatly increased in the last twenty years. Common, good land averages from twenty-seven to thirty-four and forty dollars by the lot; the best mowing lands from sixty to eighty-four dollars per acre, and some lots higher, a small lot of woodland, a few years since, was sold for ninety dollars per acre."[30] David Field reported in 1819 that land in Middlesex County had "greatly increased in price" over the last several decades. "Good land near the river and Sound has sold some years past from fifty to one hundred dollars per acre, and in some instances for much more. On an average, it has not been sold much under a hundred dollars. Good land back [from navigable waters] varies in price according to its distance from market and other circumstances."[31] No dollar figures were provided in New Haven County Reports, but in Wallingford land values had increased "from 1 to 3; about 200 percent"; with timberland increased "from 1 to 10."[32] Samuel Goodrich, who replied in 1800 for the inland town of Ridgefield in Fairfield County, explained that "the price of land has gradually increased since the first improvement but is not so high as in the neighboring towns for the reasons that there are no gatherings of the people and our rivers are so small...that no water works can be carried on to profit on an extensive plan."[33] In Stratford's Stratfield parish, on the other hand, "the price of land near the harbour that is used for building is now [1800] about $1,000 per acre. Thirty years past it was about twenty or thirty. Land at a mile or two distance has risen in thirty years from twenty to forty or fifty dollars per acre."[34] In New London County, where Norwich was a thriving port of commerce, the adjacent towns of Franklin and Lisbon in 1800 reported respectively a one-third and two-fold increase in value, with wood lots more than doubled in market value. None of the New London county towns reported actual prices.[35] That same year, land in the nearby town of Lebanon sold for between $40 to $49 per acre.[36] In Union land had doubled in price in between 1783

and 1803, and wood land doubled in half that time, but values in this northern inland community were relatively very low. "Wood land that was sold fifty years ago for two dollars per acre will now sell for ten or twelve dollars."[37] Litchfield County respondents noted significant increases, from one hundred to three or four hundred percent. Elijah Allen of Cornwall included actual figures in his Report: "the common price of plow and pasture land per acre may be estimated at from $15 to $20 per acre, which is double what it sold for forty years ago."[38]

Wood Supplies

The Town Reports revealed a general concern about impending wood shortages in the early nineteenth century. David Field commented most extensively on the subject in his 1819 Middlesex County Report. He noted that "large and numerous tracts" were reserved for forests in the county, but acknowledged "it is, however, an alarming fact, that wood and timber are decreasing." The reasons he enumerated touch upon the down side of the drive for profits in the thriving world of the marketplace, a recurrent theme in the Town Reports. "They are cut down not only to supply our own inhabitants with fuel and fencing, and with materials for building houses and vessels, but immense quantities of wood are exported to New York and other parts of our country; the call for which has been increasing since the Revolutionary War."[39] In Farmington the price of wood had "considerably advanced," from $1.00 up to $1.50 per cord by 1802, "owing to a scarcity and consequent demand of that article in those towns bordering eastward on this and those lying on Connecticut River."[40] For New Haven residents, the price of wood for fuel in 1811, was "by the cord, hickory from seven to eight dollars; pine, three and a half dollars; other kinds of wood from five to six dollars."[41] The city imported one-third of its firewood from Long Island, Guilford, and towns bordering the Housatonic and Stratford Rivers. By 1812, wood was "scarce and decreasing" in New London "owing to the growth in this town, but more to the great demand for it in New York."[42]

While Reports most often cited market demand (and, by implication, profits) as the reason for this depletion, the comment made by the New London respondent, that "much of this scarcity might be attributed formerly to an improvident use of it when it was very cheap" resonated as well.[43] The Reverend Chauncey Prindle, who in 1801 replied for Watertown, chided local farmers. "The quality of fuel is good, but the quantity is scarce occasioned by the imprudence or rather oversight of the farmers in suffering too great a proportion of the land to be stripped of its timber to make room for the plow."[44]

Aside from urban areas, where Timothy Dwight's New Haven Report indicates it was substantially higher, in most locales wood sold for between one and two dollars per cord in the early decades of the nineteenth century.

Fencing

Town Reports revealed that farmers in all parts of the state employed the same fencing methods for their fields and pastures. The Farmington respondent described them in great detail.

> There are five kinds of fences used in this town, viz., post and rail fence. The posts are white oak & chestnut with five or six holes. The rails chestnut shaped at each end. The posts are set in the ground about eighteen inches and the rails put into the holes. The next is worm or crooked fence made out of large chestnut rails, the ends of the rails are placed on stones from nine to twelve inches thick laid on the ground. The ends of the rails crossing each other, there is generally five or six rails in each length. This fence when well made is more durable than the others. The next is stone wall in which there are placed posts with two or three rails. This is esteemed the best kind of fence and is generally made in the east and west parts of the town. The next is stone wall for which there is excellent stone in the west part of the town and in great quantities. The last, the least, and worst is bush fence made by loping young trees.[45]

Some respondents outlined a common evolution in fencing practices. Azel Backus of Bethlem reported: "Fence is generally of the Virginia construction with chestnut rails. But walls of stone with posts and two or three rails on the top are succeeding decayed fences of wood. Such walls unite in them both economy and security."[46] The Reverend Andrew Lee similarly reported that in the Hanover parish of Lisbon, New London County, "improved lands are fenced with stone walls and chestnut rails. The former increase," he noted, projecting that "by the next age they will probably be the only fence."[47] The respondent for Lisbon's Newent parish echoed this sentiment in 1801. "Where the materials are to be had, a low stone wall with two rails placed above in posts make an excellent fence.... This kind of fence is...coming much into use."[48] Throughout early nineteenth-century Connecticut, the favored method of fencing was stone walls topped with posts and rails. The Goshen respondent, housewright Lewis Mills Norton, provided detailed information on construction methods.

> A stone three or four feet long and of any convenient width or thickness is sunk level to the surface of the ground, and in a direction across the line of the fence. Upon this stone near one end of it the post is set, secured at the bottom by an iron dowel five or six inches long which should drive hard into both the stone and the post. An iron brace, about two and a half feet long, fastened in the stone and spiked upon the post, serves to make the fence steady and very strong. It is believed that in this mode, which is not very expensive, fences may be very durable....[49]

Methods of Cultivation

Connecticut farmers nearly universally preferred oxen over horses for cultivation. Farmington's respondent offered a very thorough explanation as to why, reiterated in abbreviated forms by nearly everyone who answered the question.

> Oxen will far exceed the horses both in strength and usefulness. Oxen are not liable to half the disorders or accidents, of course not so liable to die as horses. Oxen have the advantage of horses after they are past their prime for usefulness, their value not decreasing in half that proportion that horses do. The expenses of keeping two oxen through the year is not more than one horse. Oxen when so old as not to be profitable to keep for cultivation may be fatted so as to produce a profit to the owner. Horses in similar circumstances are good for nothing. Beef made from oxen is excellent for food and exportation, their hide, tallow, and even horns employ many useful and necessary manufactures, the manure of oxen is better than horses. In every view of the subject oxen are far preferable to horses.[50]

While most respondents stressed that oxen were best for plowing Connecticut's stony fields, both for steadiness and strength, a few western towns in Litchfield County reported a regional variant related to Dutch influences from New York. "Fifteen years ago there were not twenty ox teams in the town," John Cotton Smith of Sharon explained in 1807. The original settlers "had been educated to the use of oxen," but, he explained, they were "seduced by the example of their Dutch neighbors, with whom oxdriver was a term of reproach," and "very early discarded that valuable animal" in favor of the horse. He noted with obvious satisfaction, "experience at length demonstrated their error."[51] The use of horses persisted in some western Connecticut towns at the turn of the nineteenth century, though it certainly did not predominate.[52] In terms of maintenance costs, endurance, and residual value, oxen were far more practical.

Manuring

Manuring to increase soil fertility and crop yields was a topic of general interest in the various parts of the state, though the Town Reports indicate varying levels of attention and experimentation. It was one of the most frequently answered agricultural questions, implying a prevailing interest in improvement. Farmington, a town early involved in the marketplace, offered detailed information on more than a dozen applications or processes by which to enrich the soil, involving stable manures, ashes, brine, plaster of Paris, and the turning of grasses.[53] Most towns reported similarly, though less exhaustively. Even in the most recently settled part of the state, manuring was "an increasing attention" by the turn of the nineteenth century. Elijah Allen of Cornwall spoke for the county in stating: "Manure formerly was only taken from the stables, barn yards, [and] door yards...But in late years ashes are frequently used, especially for Indian corn, with good effect.... Plaister of Paris is fast coming into use in this as well as in other neighboring towns...and on dry land is found to be of great utility...."[54]

Coastal locales added to this general mix of manures the use of shells, seaweed, and white fish. Respondents for a number of maritime communities described the practice of applying white fish, no one more thoroughly than the Reverend David Field whose 1819 report on Middlesex County was written roughly twenty years after the introduction of this fertilizer. When these fish "visit the shores in immense numbers" in June and early July, he explained:

> They are carried as soon as taken and spread upon the land and plowed in, or are thrown into heaps, mixed and covered with earth or turf, and suffered to pulverize, and are then spread upon the ground, as suits the convenience and objects of farmers. In either mode, the effect on dry and poor land is wonderful...Under the influence of this manure, some of the finest fields of grain, corn, and grass are annually presented on the margin of the Sound which exist in our country....Eight thousand are requisite to dress an acre.[55]

Timothy Dwight, who similarly described their application and astonishing productivity added: "One very disagreeable circumstance attends this mode of husbandry. At the season when the whitefish are caught in the greatest quantities, an almost intolerable fetor fills the surrounding atmosphere; and, however use may have reconciled it to the senses of the inhabitants, it is extremely disgusting to the traveler."[56]

Seed and Harvest Times

While relatively few respondents elected to address the query on the best seed and harvest times, the few who provided information of substance suggest fairly uniform practices. In Lisbon's Newent parish, New London County, "by good farmers, spring wheat and rye are sown after the frost leaves the ground; flax the last week in April; Indian corn is put into the ground about 15th of May; potatoes about the same time.... Winter rye is sown at the close of August or beginning of September. Wheat was formerly sown at the same time, but now on account of the insect about the 15th of September."[57] David Field reported similarly for Middlesex County, where farmers began to sow rye in late August, that corn was planted in early-to-mid May, and that oats and flax were sown in the spring "so soon as the ground is in a condition to be plowed."[58] Elijah Allen stated that the "best" farmers in Cornwall "sow summer wheat, rye, flax, oats, and barley in the early spring...as soon as the land is dry enough to plow." He advised that, at least for western farmers, "Indian corn and potatoes should be planted by the 10th of May, beans later to prevent their

being injured by frost."[59] As in Lisbon, most farmers sowed winter wheat in mid-September. Many who addressed farming commented on the destruction of wheat crops by the Hessian fly in the 1770s and 1780s, and the constant difficulties of cultivating it since that time.

Regarding changing seed supply, David Field of Middlesex County mentioned that "a frequent change of the seed of grain and corn is generally supposed to be useful," but he personally doubted it had much effect.[60] Most who commented on this subject tended to share his opinion, though Hezekiah Frost of Canterbury believed "a change of seed has an excellent effect."[61] Washington's town clerk Daniel Brinsmade advised, "it is deemed very advantageous to procure seed from a distance."[62] The subject was not much addressed, intimating it may not have been of general interest.

III. Production and Marketing, A County-by-County Overview

Within a generally similar range of grains, grasses, livestock, and dairy products, Town Reports show variations relating to distance from markets, geographic location, and quality of soil. For the relatively few towns whose respondents provided statistical information, per-acre yields are presented in Table III, and quantities of beef, pork, butter, and cheese marketed annually are presented in Table IV. Although most respondents reported keen attention paid to agricultural improvements and marketplace involvement, for the most part they presented the information so imprecisely that it resists decoding. What follows are county-by-county sketches of regional economies that incorporate Timothy Dwight's observations from his *Travels*. In many ways accessible markets shaped the state of agriculture in any given locale: the potential of favorable returns in the marketplace provided the impetus for agricultural improvement; in turn, money earned in the marketplace enabled further improvement in farming methods *and* in family material well being. In this context, landscapes of orderly two-story houses in white clapboard or brick, nicely planted and fenced dooryards, and flourishing orchards and fields represent a community actively engaged in marketplace production (and consumption). Likewise, unkempt landscapes of unpainted "low" or one-story houses, rude dooryards, and ungentrified public spaces suggest limited attention to the marketplace and its potential financial rewards.[63] Descriptions of the architectural and artificial landscape provide a means of understanding the state of agriculture.

Hartford County

For Hartford County, the oldest settled region of the state, two towns and one parish submitted reports and they provided scant information (see Table I for responses by county). It is an expansive territory that embraces both sides of the Connecticut River and in 1800 included fifteen townships engaged in lively economic activity. Timothy Dwight's journal entries evoke an image of regional agricultural prosperity and commercial enterprise. Wethersfield's Rocky Hill parish, the gateway for the town's river trade, Reverend Dwight described as a "rich agricultural country" but also a place of "considerable commerce," where "the people are prosperous, the houses generally very good," and "everything which meets the eye wears the appearance of industry and prosperity." The town possessed excellent soil, expansive intervales [unwooded, low-lying land] "of the richest quality," and productive uplands, but, he reported, "for some reason or other, imperfectly known to me, Wethersfield has not kept pace with the general improvement of the country." At the same time, he mentioned that the export trade of onions, Wethersfield's specialty product, had declined.

The city of Hartford, where to Reverend Dwight's mind commerce "has always been considerable," contained many houses "handsomely built in the most modern style, and almost universally three stories." This thriving city was not, however, ideal for farming. It possessed some rich intervales and productive uplands for cultivation, but "a considerable part of this township is strongly impregnated with clay, and not infrequently is changed entirely into clay" and as a result, "gardens are made here with much difficulty." Windsor he found to be a place where "houses and husbandry are rather neat." In Suffield, to the north, he saw handsomely built houses lining the main road, painted white, and surrounded by lush vegetation and flourishing orchards. Like river towns generally, it possessed good soil and profited from easy market accessibility.[64] The Farmington Report included an equally pleasing description of white-painted houses in the village and handsome farmhouses beyond, as well as a wealth of detailed information on varieties of fruits and vegetables cultivated, but nothing on crop yields or marketing.[65] Farmington at the time included Avon, Burlington, and Plainville.

Windsor's west parish of Wintonbury (Bloomfield) and East Windsor (which included South Windsor) provided some information on cultivation in the county. In Bloomfield, where "there is little or no wasteland,...the soil, on the highest lands, admits of the cultivation of all kinds of grain, wheat, rye, Indian corn, barley, oats, buckwheat, etc."[66] Respondent William Miller named rye and Indian corn as the principal crops and estimated yields of 25 bushels per acre for wheat on new land, and from 30 to 40 bushels of Indian corn on old land well manured. Hay he knew was "a considerable article of produce," noting in his 1802 report that "about two hundred tons are annually sold, at Hartford market, at from ten to fifteen and eighteen dollars, according to the quality and the demand in [the] market." He also mentioned, "of late years the market has been rather dull and low," a price deflation caused by a significant increase in production due to manuring.[67]

In East Windsor, Indian corn, rye, wheat, oats, and barley were the grains chiefly raised. Respondent David McClure reported slightly lower yields per acre than in Bloomfield and estimated that 100,000 bushels of grain were raised annually. He also noted in his 1806 return that acreage formerly used for tobacco "at present gives place to the more profitable one of corn."[68] The Bloomfield respondent addressed marketing, stating that pork, beef, mutton, and cheese were not "large market articles," and explaining that "the vicinity of the market

makes butter the principal dairy article." This, he believed, was "to the great loss of some of the farmers," cheese production being more profitable. "Ready money, once a week," he admonished, "is a temptation which induces a market man to overlook his greater interest, in the well-managed but long-delayed cheese market."[69]

Interestingly, the Farmington respondent took the time to comment on the cultural ramifications of economic prosperity and market involvement.

> Till within about 40 years, a single retailer of imported goods with a small capital sufficed for the town. Of late years trade has greatly increased and greater capital is employed in it, than in any inland town in the State. That agriculture and commerce go hand in hand is true: but it is equally true that farmers never flourish in a populous settlement where the commercial character predominates. The reasons are obvious: commerce where it prevails creates riches, riches introduces a taste for luxury in building, dress, furniture, equipage and which agriculture can never support, the farmer is thrown into the shade. He feels himself degraded. The effect is not so visible in the householders whose habits were fixed before this change of manners took place; but it is extremely observable in the rising generation; young men of refinement are evidently ashamed of the manners, dress, and employment of their fathers.[70]

While not accurate in every detail, he highlighted a significant cultural and economic transformation that occurred unevenly throughout much of the northeast during the course of the eighteenth and nineteenth centuries. As economies diversified and market interaction intensified, a transformation of expectations occurred and New Englanders increasingly moved out of agriculture in search of more lucrative and genteel occupations. In the agricultural press, extolling farming as a noble profession and plain living as an honorable choice became recurrent and increasingly urgent themes, but it did not stem the tide.

Middlesex County

The Reverend David Field provided both a general overview for Middlesex County, a rather compact territory that lay on both sides of the lower Connecticut River, and an abundance of particulars pertaining to each of the towns in that county (for towns see Table I). His information only sketches production but mentions the same mix of grains, livestock, and dairying common throughout the state.

> Wheat was the principal crop in this county until the ravages of the Hessian fly about 1777, since which there has been but little raised.... Rye is

now sown abundantly and is of an excellent quality. More than forty bushels of this grain have been raised on an acre in Saybrook. Corn has ever been an important crop in Middlesex [County]. Seventy bushels have been raised on an acre.... Flax and oats are raised in large quantities in some parts of the county; potatoes abundantly more than they were thirty or forty years ago.[71]

As to marketing, he believed: "Very little grain and provisions are exported from Middlesex [County]; less, it is believed, than are imported." Also, "very little beef and pork are exported.... What is raised is almost entirely consumed in the county. The quantity of butter and cheese exported is not great."[72] Thriving marketing, he said, occurred *within* the county. Reverend Field noted that "a market opened for produce in 1743" in East Haddam, "since which most of the trade in the town has centered on this spot."[73] Its soil "is more suitable for grazing than for the culture of grain" and farmers there "derive considerable profits from their stock and dairies and from their wood and lumber."[74] Reverend Field described Durham as "a good farming township" where "the inhabitants are employed almost universally in the cultivation of the earth."[75] They formerly raised wheat, but now raise "good crops of rye, corn, oats, flax, etc." for the market.[76] Timothy Dwight evaluated Durham and neighboring towns as having "a rich loam" soil that was "almost universally fertile" and "happily fitted for every kind of cultivation and product." He also mentioned that it "has for many years been distinguished for a very fine breed of cattle."[77]

Middletown was a thriving place of commerce on the banks of the Connecticut River, the economic hub of the county in 1800. Reverend Field described the city as the principal place of business, where the dwelling houses, "299 in number, are very generally convenient, and some of them are elegant... constructed in most cases of wood...one, two, and three stories high, but vastly the greater portion of them are of the second description."[78] Here, and in county towns that border the river or the Sound, maritime concerns of shipbuilding and fishing were major components of local economies; in some places, the predominant focus.

New Haven County

Four Reports were submitted for the state's second oldest area of settlement, New Haven County: from Cheshire in 1803 (which included Prospect), Wallingford in 1811-1812 (which included Meriden), New Haven in 1811 (which included West Haven), and, belatedly, Guilford and its since hived-off town of Madison in 1832. While the inland towns of Wallingford and Cheshire reported limited attention to improvements, in the port city agriculture and commerce thrived. (The 1832 reports are too late for comparison.)[79]

The Reverend John Foot described Cheshire as "variegated with hillocks and valleys affording a fruitful soil, calculated to produce a greater variety of the necessaries of life."[80] He believed the town's "agriculture is improving,"

reporting that "about 20,000 bushels of corn, as much rye, and perhaps as many potatoes [are] produced annually; of wheat, very little." As far as products sent to market in the past, "the town has been noted for raising pork, but it has much declined since the practice of kiln drying corn meal.... This is not a dairy town, our land being better calculated for tillage than grazing."[81] Wallingford's Judge George Washington Stanley wrote "the state of agriculture is not high, but improving." He named rye, Indian corn, oats, buckwheat, flax, potatoes, and turnips, and "a very small proportion of wheat" as the usual crops. As to yields, "of rye on the plains, from 5 to 10; and on other lands from 8 to 20 bushels an acre usual crops; of Indian corn on good land, 30 bushels are considered a good crop." The soil varied from excellent to unproductive clay. Regarding marketing, he noted "the excess of pork, beef, butter, and cheese annually raised, beyond the consumption of the town ... is certainly not great.... The principal articles carried to market are hay, cornbrooms, flax and flaxseed, rye, corn, and cornmeal, oats, and potatoes." He explained that the distance to market rendered selling livestock unprofitable, noting that "prices are regulated by the prices in New Haven and Middletown" and the difference "seldom exceeds the expense of transportation." He also mentioned: "The vicinity of this town to New Haven, which affords a steady and profitable market for hay, and the comparative cheapness with which the crop may be raised and secured, are strong inducements to sell that article."[82]

In his New Haven Report, Timothy Dwight described the soil as "capable...of being rendered very productive by judicious cultivation," though on the whole it was of mediocre quality at best.[83] He named wheat, rye, maize, barley, oats, flax, and grass as the principal crops. "Wheat has yielded 40 bushels, rye 28, barley 45, maize 80, oats 60, flax 620 pounds, and grass 4 tons an acre," amounts considerably higher than most locales.[84] He provided very extensive information on goods shipped out of New Haven harbor for coastal and foreign trade, but did not itemize local products included in these shipments. New Haven was a bustling city in 1811, laid out in squares and thoroughly built up. "The whole number of houses," he explained, "is 750, of which 314 are built on the streets forming the [nine] squares. The stores, shops, barns, etc. are scarcely less numerous than the houses.... A few of the houses are of three stories; a moderate number of one; the rest, supposed to be more than 600, are of two."[85] In New Haven, farming was certainly not the primary economic activity.

Timothy Dwight provided a few details on other parts of this county. North Milford parish (Orange) possessed rich soil cultivated by plain but industrious farmers; Derby had mediocre soil but was a sprightly place of shipping and commerce; Oxford and Southbury possessed excellent soil. The coastal towns of East Haven and Branford possessed indifferent soil. In the former the houses "are generally good farmers' dwellings," but Branford in his opinion was "destitute of beauty. The situation is unpleasant, and the houses are chiefly ancient and ordinary.... The inhabitants are principally farmers," but "a considerable number of them are seamen, and are principally employed by the merchants of New

Haven."[86] In another entry, he likened Guilford to Branford in every respect.

Fairfield County

In this county, for which the Academy received only two responses, Timothy Dwight's *Travels* provided useful insight. Dwight described the surface this southwestern county as "very various" with a handsome plain bordering the Sound, and a hilly interior that is "in many places rough." The soil he believed to be "better than that of any other in the state, being generally rich and producing everything which the climate will permit"; the pastures and meadows "fine," and the crops of grain "abundant." He noted that "a few years since, more flax was raised here than in the whole of New England besides." In Greenwich, which contained the most fertile tract of its size in the state, he reported per acre yields of 40 bushels of wheat and 700 weight of flax.[87] The former is comparable to New Haven's optimum yield; the latter is higher than any figure given in the Town Reports. He described Fairfield "as the port of entry for the whole coast of Connecticut on the western side of the Housatonic." Its soil was "of the first quality," an observation he made of Stamford and Norwalk as well.[88]

The two Reports submitted for the County are a study of contrasts, Stratfield being a coastal parish engaged in trade and manufactures and Ridgefield being an inland farming town. In 1800 Samuel Goodrich reported that Ridgefield's fertile soil "produces good rye and Indian corn, a considerable more than for the consumption of the inhabitants; flax, large quantities of oats, buckwheat, beans, and peas.... The land is very good for grass."[89] As in the interior towns in New Haven County, "There are but few mechanics and manufacturers, traders, or men in the learned profession, in proportion to the number of people who follow agriculture and most of the inhabitants raise provision for their own consumption and some for exportation."[90] He estimated that from 2,000 to 4,000 bushels of turnips were "sacked" every year, and noted that "potatoes are very much used and increased attempts are making to raise them for market, but," he explained, "the distance to market is so great that it is not expected the practice will be general."[91] (Elsewhere he mentioned that the center of the town was about 14 miles from the landing at Norwalk.) Annual yields per acre ranged "from 10 to 30 bushels of rye, from 20 to 50 bushels of corn, from 20 to 50 bushels of oats, from 20 to 50 bushels of buckwheat, and from 100 to 500 or 600 wt. of flax per acre, varying in quality and quantity according to the strength of the soil and the seasons, difference of preparing the ground and manuring."[92] As to marketing, "there are from 150 to 200 barrels of pork annually carried out of the town and about as much beef." Also "from 150 to 300 firkins of butter," 9,000 pounds of cheese, and "about 100 head of fat cattle driven to market on their legs to New York." He noted that "the making of butter has much increased within 20 years, as it can now be carried fresh to New York market, the price is more than three times it then was."[93] (He and Bloomfield's William Miller differed as to the profitability of butter making!)

The Reverend Philo Shelton of Stratfield parish in Stratford outlined a rapid growth in population and commercial activity and a vigorous, outward-looking economy. "In the year 1783 the village [of Bridgeport, a borough within the parish] contained only eleven dwelling houses, two stores, two wharves, and four small vessels," he explained. But "from that period until the year 1793 the growth was rapid and a large trade to the West Indies and other States carried on from this port.... Notwithstanding the many misfortunes and disadvantages the port has sustained [largely from French incursions], the place has increased very considerably." By 1800 "within eighty rods of the bridge" in Bridgeport there were "fifty-five dwelling houses, seventeen stores for dry-goods, nine wharves each with a large granary and 15 sail of vessels."[94] Stratfield also enjoyed amenable conditions for farming. He described the "face of the parish" as possessing, on the south, "fine level tract, clear from stone; on the north a little more hilly and stony; the soil of a darkish loam, fertile for crops, especially for Indian corn, oats and flax, some wheat, rye, barley, potatoes, and onions" and for "a great variety of fruit, especially pears." He estimated yields of 20 to 40 bushels of Indian corn per acre, 8 to 20 of rye, 15 to 30 of oats, and 100 to 400 pounds of flax.[95] Reverend Shelton provided a comprehensive list of exports from the harbor, but did not include figures for locally produced exports.

Timothy Dwight, who passed through Stratfield in 1811, found the parish "extremely pleasant," and asserted "there is not in the state a prettier village than the borough of Bridgeport." In this part of Stratfield, he counted more than one hundred dwellings; nearly double the figure for 1800. While he thought none were "large or splendid, ... all of them, together with their appendages, leave upon the mind an impression of neatness and cheerfulness, not often found elsewhere." In this coastal borough he learned that "the inhabitants are almost all merchants and mechanics."[96] Reverend Dwight's journals provide no further information on this part of the state.

New London County

Like towns in the Connecticut River Valley, New London County towns enjoyed the advantage of navigable waters, making markets accessible. The Yantic, Shetucket, and Quinebaug Rivers come together in Norwich. The Thames River carries their waters from Norwich to the Sound. Timothy Dwight pointed out that there was a landing in Norwich, and the harbor at Groton and New London was "of great capacity and depth" where "vessels of almost any size find in it sufficient water and good anchoring ground."[97] Not surprisingly, fishing and commerce predominated in the harbor towns. Norwich was filled with places of business and trade, and crowded with five hundred dwellings, many of them in Reverend Dwight's estimation, "good, ancient houses, together with a number, not small, of those which are decayed." He explained in a 1790s journal entry that until the ravages by fire and French depredations on shipping, the people of Norwich were "distinguished beyond any other in the state for the variety and abundance of their manufactures, while at the same time they carried on a prosperous commerce." Despite those setbacks, commerce was "still considerable." While the Thames River and the abundance of men engaged in trade enhanced marketing opportunities for the region's farmers, the quality of much of the soil worked against them. Dwight described it as varied, some of it excellent but far more mediocre to poor.[98]

Three inland communities bordering Norwich and coursed through by rivers that flow together into the Thames submitted Reports to the Academy, which indicate their farmers cultivated the usual mix of grains, specialized in grazing and dairying, and clearly produced with their eye on the marketplace.[99] Preston (which included Griswold) supplied only a brief overview; reports for Franklin and Lisbon (which included Sprague) were more substantive.

The Reverend Samuel Nott reported in 1800 that Franklin's "agriculture is greatly increased in 18 years." He described the town as having an uneven surface with soil that is in some places "black and rich," and elsewhere "more sandy and gravelly," but good for tillage. Here "provisions of all kinds are raised," with average per acre yields of 10 bushels oats, 20 of corn, 12 of rye, 15 of wheat, 20 of barley, and 140 pounds of flax. He did not indicate the extent to which these products were marketed but noted: "Number of sheep sent to market in the town per annum about 1,000; pork 220,000 lbs, beef 220,000, butter 18,000; cheese 120,000."[100]

Lisbon's parish Reports of 1800 and 1801 reflected similar production. Timothy Dwight described it as "an excellent township, the soil being here, as in most of the region on the Quinebaug, the reddish loam...but less mixed with clay."[101] The Reverend Andrew Lee of Lisbon's Hanover parish noted that "the soil on the hills is a black deep mould" while "the valleys are of a lighter, warmer soil and more suitable for rye and Indian corn."[102] He boasted of increased yields and local attention to improved farming methods. "Indian corn is equal, if not superior, to former productions. Land properly prepared and cultivated yielding from twenty to forty bushels per acre and sometimes fifty." Also, "flax succeeds on the high lands, five hundred weight hath been raised on an acre, but two hundred is a middling crop," and "potatoes are raised in plenty. Manure of almost any kind put into the hill, answers a valuable purpose. One hundred bushels often grow on an acre and sometimes nearly 200."[103] The Newent parish respondent stated: "The most important crops of grain at present raised here are rye and Indian corn. The former is raised from 8 to 20 bushels on an acre...the latter is raised from 15 to 20 bushels to an acre."[104] As to marketing, he noted "there is of the former kind nearly twice as much raised as is consumed [in the parish], and a very considerable surplusage of the latter."[105] He named broom corn as another valuable market commodity. Andrew Lee reported: "The principal articles for sale in the town are butter, cheese, beef, pork, and cider. Oak and boards for building and some staves and hoops. Also mules and horses, especially the former. Sheep are also raised in considerable number."[106]

Windham and Tolland Counties

Windham and Tolland Counties, in the northeast corner of the state, are considered together in this essay because they are similar in soils and distance from markets, the substance of Reports for both is fairly slim, and Timothy Dwight did not provide amplifying information to flesh them out. Lebanon (which included Columbia), Pomfret, Canterbury, and Windham (which included Scotland) submitted reports for Windham County; North Bolton parish, Coventry, Willington, Union, and Tolland submitted reports for Tolland County. Generally, respondents delineated the common state agricultural base of grazing, dairying, and grains; attention to improvements; and production oriented to creating surpluses for the marketplace.

The undulating surface of the Windham County towns contained soil of uneven quality; some rocky, some good. Pomfret reported that "corn and rye are the main grains now raised here," as well as "considerable crops of flax," but little hemp or wheat.[107] Lebanon's Elkanah Tisdale listed Indian corn, rye, oats, but little hemp or wheat, and "flax is extremely uncertain."[108] Hezekiah Frost of Canterbury stressed the importance of grazing. He also noted that in the parish of Westminster there is, "some excellent mowing and many good orchards" and a "great growth of timber," and "corn and all kinds of English grain are raised with very little trouble."[109] As to marketing, "Our principal trade is at Norwich and New London. Considerable trade is carried on also with New York, Boston, and Providence. To Norwich is 12 miles. To Boston 80. To Providence 30."[110] In Lebanon, "of pork, 430 barrels; of beef, 657 barrels are annually put up for market. Of cheese, one of our traders has sent to market 20,000 pounds in a year. The whole annual amount of these articles exported is probably much more considerable."[111] Lebanon marketed at Norwich Port, some ten-to-twenty miles distant for its farmers, who transported their commodities principally by ox-drawn carts and sleds.

Tolland County towns generally reported land that was uneven and stony, with some "of a loomy soil," intermixed with gravel or sand.[112] North Bolton reported yields of wheat from 15 to 20 bushels per acre, and rye from 7 to 12.[113] Union reported "our land will not answer for Indian corn without manure, but put on a plenty of that will and it will produce 40 bushels to an acre in a good season."[114] As to marketing, he replied: "as our lands are good for mowing and pasture there is a considerable number of sheep and cattle fatted and sent to market, also of butter and cheese made for the market a considerable quantity."[115] North Bolton replied that "the butter and cheese carried to market annually is conjected to be about 2,000 wt of each, grains of all kinds (but principally rye) that is carried to market may be about 1,500 bushels....[and] pork...is supposed to be about 15,000 wt or 75 barrels."[116]

Litchfield County

The relatively high number of detailed responses from Litchfield County, the most recently settled part of the state, suggest an eagerness to be recognized by the rest of Connecticut. Ten towns—Bethlem, Cornwall, Goshen, Kent, Litchfield, Sharon, Norfolk, Washington, Watertown, and Winchester—submitted Reports between 1800 and 1815, outlining an agricultural economy based on grazing, dairying, and grains that was rapidly improving and focused on the marketplace. Elijah Allen of Cornwall explicitly made the connection between improved conditions and marketing. "The town did not for some years make but little progress in gaining wealth," he explained in his 1800-1801 return, but "the inhabitants at present are generally in good circumstances and many in a state of affluence, as must be seen by the preceding account of what is annually raised and how much is sent to market."[117] Lewis M. Norton of Goshen, in 1812 reported: "It will be readily seen that the great staple commodity here is cheese, and it is from this source chiefly that the inhabitants derive their wealth and prosperity."[118] While the Reports generally demonstrate this market specialization, Goshen's figure of 380,236 pounds marketed annually far exceeded any other locale. The shift to marketplace specialization in this county occurred within the memory of the present generation. According to John Cotton Smith, who replied for Sharon in 1807, "Since the introduction of the present system of husbandry, more than at any former period, the dairy and the culture of Indian corn, and as a natural and beneficial consequence of these, beef and pork, have engaged the attention of our agriculturalists."[119]

Litchfield County respondents commented on methods of marketing, which would have been common throughout the state's interior towns. In his Goshen Report, Lewis Mills Norton explained that "many wagons are employed in carrying the produce of this town to New Haven; from whence it is shipped, chiefly to the southern states and West India islands."[120] Typically, traders and marketmen gathered farm products from townsfolk and carted them to market. Export charts included in this report showed that Goshen served as a "sub-station" in trade for more remote locales; other towns conveyed their goods as far as Goshen, where they were loaded onto wagons destined for New Haven.[121] Some farmers carted their own goods directly to market, thereby avoiding the cost of middlemen.

The county's soil varied from excellent, capable of every cultivation, to marginal. Most of it was black or red loam, some was clay. In places of poorer soil quality, like Kent and Salisbury, iron works played a major role in local economies. Towns reported annual yields ranging from 12 to 30 bushels of wheat, 8 to 30 of rye, 15-50 of corn, 20 to 40 of oats, and from 50 to 300 pounds of flax. They annually marketed 400 to 600 barrels of beef, 250 to 500 barrels of pork, and widely varied quantities of butter and cheese. Some towns also sent considerable quantities of fatted cattle and grains to market.

Summary

The Reports submitted to the Academy by respondents from cities and towns throughout Connecticut reveal a general optimism about the state of agriculture: nearly everywhere farmers were improving their yields and increasing market activity. On the whole, respondents believed their towns' soils and dairies capable of good production. From the Reports and Timothy Dwight's observations, a picture emerges of a generally industrious population of farmers guiding ox-driven plows through stony but fertilized tillage land, building stone-and-rail fences around fields and pastures, judiciously clearing to avoid depletion of fuel resources, experimenting with new techniques to increase productivity, calculating market returns, and improving their standards of living.

The Town Reports beg for further study, on agriculture and every other topic addressed. To interpret the agricultural information more fully, population figures should be noted for responding towns, number of households, and their composition should be compiled from manuscript census schedules. Also, topographic maps and modern soil analysis should be checked against respondents' evaluations of terrain and fertility. Local histories should be mined, as should the vaults of town halls for tax lists and town meeting records to learn more about property values and local concerns. Deeds should be researched to determine average farm sizes, surviving schedules of the 1798 Federal Direct Tax should be matched with Town Reports to evaluate more fully housing stock and farm size.[122] Farm houses and barns still standing that pre-date the Reports should be recorded and documented, period landscape paintings of Connecticut towns, houses, and people should be studied for clues to material well-being and economic activity. The more complete Town Reports, when matched with an array of other sources, will be useful tools for analysis of agriculture and society in various towns or regions in the state. The fruitful end result of thorough individual- and community-based micro studies on this and every other topic covered in the Reports will be a truly comprehensive understanding of the state of Connecticut in 1800.

TABLE I

Respondents by County

County	Towns that responded (including names of towns hived off since 1800)	Percent of total towns in the county
Hartford	Wintonbury (Bloomfield), Farmington (inc. Avon, Plainville, Burlington), East Windsor (South Windsor)	3 of 15; 20%
Middlesex	Middletown (inc. Cromwell, Portland, Middlefield), Chatham (inc. Portland and East Hampton), Durham, Haddam, East Haddam, Killingworth (inc. Clinton), Saybrook (inc. Chester, Deep River, Essex, Westbrook)	7 of 7; 100%
New Haven	New Haven (inc. West Haven), Wallingford (inc. Meriden), Cheshire (inc. Prospect), Guilford (inc. Madison)	4 of 15; 27%
Fairfield	Ridgefield, Stratfield (Bridgeport)	2 of 14; 14%
New London	New London (inc. Waterford), Preston (inc. Griswold), Franklin, Lisbon (inc. Hanover [Sprague] and Newent parishes)	4 of 12; 33%
Windham	Windham (inc. Scotland), Lebanon (inc. Columbia), Canterbury, Pomfret (inc. Putnam)	4 of 14; 28%
Tolland	Coventry, North Bolton (Vernon), Tolland, Willington, Union	5 of 14; 36%
Litchfield	Litchfield, Goshen, Cornwall, Norfolk, Sharon, Winchester, Washington, Watertown, Kent, Bethlem	10 of 22; 41%

TABLE II

Land Values Reported by Respondents

County/Town	Descriptive phrases about land values	Dollar figures given for land values
Hartford County Wintonbury (Bloomfield) (1802)	greatly increased in the last 20 years	common good land, $27-$40 by the lot; best mowing lands, $60-$84 per acre; small lot of woodland, $90 per acre
East Windsor (1806)	--	--
Farmington (c. 1810)	--	--
Middlesex County County report (1819)	in last 20 years land values more than doubled; land near the River and Sound generally not much under $100 and some much more; good land back varies in price according to its distance from market and other circumstances	good land near the River and Sound, $50-$100 per acre; good land back in Durham and Middletown, $80 per acre
Chatham (including Portland and East Hampton, 1819)	in last 20 years more than doubled	see county figures
Durham (1819)	in last 20 years more than doubled	good land back, $80 per acre; see county figures
Haddam (1819)	in last 20 years more than doubled	good land for plowing and mowing near the river is from $100 to $250 per acre
East Haddam (1819)	in last 20 years more than doubled	see county figures
Killingworth (1819)	in last 20 years more than doubled	see county figures
Middletown (1819)	in last 20 years more than doubled	good land back, $80 per acre; see county figures
Saybrook (1819)	in last 20 years more than doubled	see county figures
New Haven County Cheshire (1803)	price of land is about four double	--
Guilford (1832)	--	--
Madison (1832)	--	--
New Haven (1811)	--	--
Wallingford (1811-1812)	price in present generation increased from 1 to 3, about 200%; wood and timber land from 1 to 10	--
Fairfield County Ridgefield (1800)	price gradually increased	--
Stratfield (1800)	land values dramatically increased	price of land near the harbor that is used for building, $1,000 per acre (was $20-$30, 30 years earlier; land at a mile distance up from $20 to $40 or $50 per acre in thirty years)
New London County Franklin (1800)	price of land has increased in present generation about one-third	--
Lisbon (Hanover) (1800)	in last 30 years, more than doubled	--
Lisbon (Newent) (1801)		--
New London (1812)	--	--
Preston (1801)	--	--

TABLE II

Land Values Reported by Respondents
(Continued)

County/Town	Descriptive phrases about land values	Dollar figures given for land values
Tolland County		
Coventry (1806)	–	–
North Bolton (Vernon, 1800)	–	–
Tolland (1804)	–	–
Willington (1805)	increase is from $2 to $10 per acre	–
Union (1803)	doubled in 20 years; woodlands doubled in 10	woodlands 1750, $2 per acre; 1800, $10 or $12 per acre
Windham County		
Canterbury (1801)	–	–
Lebanon (1800)	price of land is higher than formerly	lands have lately sold from $40 to $49 per acre; average value $16.11 per acre; average house is $297.60
Pomfret (1800)	–	–
Windham (1800)	–	–
Litchfield County		
Bethlem (1812)	land of all kinds has risen 100 percent within the present generation	–
Cornwall (1800-1801)	common price of plow land double what it sold for 40 years ago; (second voice) land values increased 100-150% in last 20 years	$60 to .25 per acre; common price of plow land $15-$20 per acre
Goshen (1812)	in 50 years increased from 1-3 or 4	–
Kent (1812)	in 20 years increased about 3 to 1	–
Litchfield County Report (1815)	values over 30 years up nearly 100%	–
Norfolk (in Litchfield County Report) (1815)	price of land in 50 years up 300-400%	–
Sharon (1807)	–	–
Washington (1800)	increased by 100% in last ten years	–
Watertown (1801)	in the last three-quarters of a century increased ten fold	–
Winchester-Winsted (1813)	–	–

TABLE III

Yields Per Acre Reported by Various Towns
(Figures are respondents' estimations, not official statistics)

County/ Town	Rye (bushels/ acre)	Corn (bushels/ acre)	Wheat (bushels/ acre)	Oats (bushels/ acre)	Potatoes (bushels/ acre)	Flax (lbs/ acre)
Hartford Wintonbury (Bloomfield) (1802)	-	30-40	25	-	-	-
EastWindsor (1806)	12	25-30	18	-	-	-
New Haven Wallingford (1811-1812)	5-10 (plains); 8-20 (other land)	30	-	-	-	-
New Haven (1811)	28 (highest)	80 (highest)	40 (highest)	60 (highest)	-	620 (highest)
Fairfield Ridgefield (1800)	10-30	20-50	-	20-50	-	200-600
Stratfield par. (1800)	8-20	20-40	-	15-30	-	100-400
New London Franklin (1800)	12	20	15	10	100	140
Lisbon (Hanover) (1800)	8-9	20-40	5	-	100-200	200
Lisbon (Newent) (1801)	8-20	15-20	-	-	100	-
Tolland North Bolton (1800)	7-12	12-25	15-20	-	-	-
Litchfield Bethlem (1812)	10-30	15-40	-	-	-	-
Cornwall (1800-1801)	8-12	25-30	12-20	20-30	150-200	200-250
Goshen (1812)	12-18	15-30	12-15	25-40	100-300	100-200
Washington (1800)	10-20	30-50	15-30	-	-	-
Windham Lebanon (1800)	15	20	little	20-40	abundance	50-300

TABLE IV

Beef, Pork, Butter, and Cheese Sent to Market by Various Towns*
(Figures are respondents' estimations, not official statistics)

County/Town	Beef	Pork	Butter	Cheese
Fairfield County Ridgefield (1800)	150-200 barrels (30,000-40,000 lbs)	150-200 barrels (30,000-40,000 lbs)	250-300 firkins (6,250-7,500 lbs)	9,000 lbs
New London Franklin (1800)	220,000 lbs	220,000 lbs	18,000 lbs	120,000 lbs
Tolland North Bolton (1801)	75 barrels (15,000 lbs)	–	2,000 lbs	2,000 lbs
Windham Lebanon (1801)	657 barrels (131,400 lbs)	430 barrels (86,000 lbs)	–	20,000 lbs* *(carried by one trader; not total for town)
Litchfield Bethlem (1812)	400 barrels (80,000 lbs)	250 barrels (50,000 lbs)	7,000 lbs	30,000 lbs
Cornwall (1800-1801)	94,540 lbs	59,380 lbs	9,998 lbs	53,880 lbs
Goshen (1812)	609 barrels (121,800 lbs)	171 barrels (34,200 lbs)	25,376 lbs	380,236 lbs
Norfolk (1815)	(sent livestock only)	100 barrels (20,000 lbs)	12,000 lbs	200,000 lbs
Washington (1800)	(sent livestock only)	400 barrels (80,000 lbs)	4,000 lbs	20,000 lbs
Watertown (1801)	100 barrels (20,000 lbs)	500 barrels (100,000 lbs)	150 firkins (3,750 lbs)	30,000 lbs
Winsted (1813)	–	–	–	25,000 lbs

*Herds of livestock were also driven to market for sale to farmers, butchers, and merchants involved in international trade; estimations of live animals sold annually are not included in the estimations provided.

Connecticut's Home Dairies, c. 1800:

"Of too great utility to be passed over in silence"

Caroline F. Sloat

15th. Number of sheep and swine; quantity of pork, beef, butter, and cheese annually sent to market; the best mode of multiplying, improving, feeding and fattening sheep, swine, neat cattle and horses; their diseases, description of them and the best mode of preventing and curing them.[1]

The intention of this ambitious multipart question was to probe the most significant aspect of human economic activity in Connecticut—farming. By 1800, agricultural work provided subsistence for household units and, to an increasing extent, yielded a surplus that could then be traded for the benefit of the household. Connecticut's communities and the economy and society of the state itself also benefited. Specific and direct information about agriculture around 1800 has been less forthcoming than that from the second quarter of the century leading up to the 1850 census, which provides quite specific data.[2] Thus, the existence of this earlier set of data for Connecticut offers an exciting opportunity to look closely at developments circa 1800 that would characterize northern agriculture and family life during the succeeding century.

The learned gentlemen of the Connecticut Academy must have hoped that answers to their questions about the agricultural sector would yield information about farming practice and what happened to the surplus production. They may even have had the intention of promulgating some success stories about improvements that resulted in surpluses. The responses, even when gaps for some sections of the state are supplemented with contemporary data, offer a useful glimpse of farm production around 1800. As this essay will show, the answers relating to dairying in the state reveal that changes and expansion of the economy were driven in part by household labor.

The majority of responses to this 15th article of the Academy's letter of solicitation focused on "the quantity of pork, beef, butter, and cheese annually sent to market." It is therefore possible to glimpse how surplus livestock—particularly, pigs and cows—and dairy products contributed to the statewide economy. Many of the respondents were able to provide numerical data that can be charted and analyzed. They reported how many live animals were marketed and how many pounds of meat were barreled and shipped. They offered some sense of the quantities of butter and cheese but very little information surrounding its production; these details can be filled in from contemporary sources.

This essay will look at the actual production data for towns clustered by county, then tie the information into regional patterns of trade. Because women made much, if not all, of the butter and cheese, the home dairy enabled them to perform a role in the household and regional economy. Connecticut's climate dictated the cycle of production: the butter making would take place in the spring and early fall; and cheese making in the summer. To support these activities, the farmer wishing to operate a home dairy needed to keep a supply of usable equipment on hand, including sufficient numbers of milk pans, butter churns, and cheese tubs as well as firkins and barrels in which to ship them. Demand for this equipment provided

Women milking a cow and churning butter. Illustration for the month of May. John Nathan Hutchins, Hutchins Improved: being an almanac and ephemeris...for the year of our Lord, 1761 (New York, 1760). Courtesy, American Antiquarian Society.

work for potters or tinsmiths and woodworkers in the weeks preceding production. Home dairies called on neighboring coopers for new or repaired containers, thereby helping to ensure that Connecticut's coopers had work virtually throughout the year.[3]

When more dairy products were made and preserved than the family could consume or barter for its own needs, the surplus found its way into the market economy. Although this would have been well understood at the time, the phrasing of article 15 did not generally invite a broader analysis by its respondents. It was the separate work of farm men and farm women taken together that resulted in a household surplus that could be used for trade. While some women had of necessity to engage in trade,[4] most households were headed by men, and while women performed the labor involved in dairy production, they did not ordinarily go into the marketplace. Neither did the women who made the dairy products negotiate prices or arrange for transportation. That bargaining and butchering, those cattle drives and coopering were part of a man's world. Finally, to provide a gendered dimension to the conclusions that can be drawn from the data, this essay will describe the work of the dairy from personal reminiscences and some prescriptive literature that was published just before the Academy took note of the new century by taking stock of Connecticut's resources.

The Data about Agricultural Production

The Respondents' Sources

This essay focuses on the reports of butter and cheese produced, without overlooking the stated value of the cattle and barreled meat, which offers a perspective on the worth of the dairy operations. Generating the data requested in article 15 was difficult because, as the respondents soon discovered, it had to be assembled from a variety of sources. While there were tax lists that might have been consulted, as several noted, neither sheep nor swine were included, so these were helpful only in providing numbers of cattle.[5] Although no public records were collected for meat and dairy products that were part of the inland domestic trade, such items were frequently used by farmers to pay their bills at the country stores. Two hundred years later, one might wonder why more respondents did not engage in conversations with local storekeepers, particularly when many of those charged with gathering the Academy's information were clergy. They were most likely to live in the centers of town near the stores that gathered local produce for sale. Using their account books, these storekeepers could have tallied the amount of butter and cheese that was credited to their customers' accounts. They could also have estimated how much was redistributed locally and how much they transported to their own wholesalers to pay debts that could be paid in country produce. But this information is not reflected in their reports.

Three of the Town Reports are based on public information. Timothy Dwight's somewhat grudging responses for New Haven in 1811, Philo Shelton's for Stratfield in 1800, and an anonymous c. 1812 report for New London, use custom house data and shipping reports for their respective towns. Taken together, these sources make a good case for the export of agricultural surplus. In 1806 the New Haven custom house books itemize nineteen products that were exported from New Haven, which "together with sundry small articles...all amounted to $466,367."[6] This figure did not satisfy Dwight because he knew that other vessels in the coastwise trade carried cargoes to New York that were exported from there and entered in that city's customs records. A second list "taken from the shipping books of those who are concerned in it, for the year 1801" amounted to fifty-eight items, in this case 219,702 pounds of cheese compared to the 18,693 pounds exported

directly from New Haven. The butter (828 firkins or 46,368 lb.) sent to New York compared to 67,648 pounds (1,268 firkins) exported directly from New Haven. Although Dwight's figures indicate the quantities exported, not their cash values, the cheese might represent a value of $19,786.79 and the butter a value of $17,102.40.[7]

Like the Academy of 1800, readers may well wonder where all this butter and cheese came from and how it got to the port of New Haven. Country traders and merchants in the trading ports linked rural agricultural surplus with city dwellers and customers abroad. The traders in the rural towns and countryside had to create a business relationship with farmers who had surplus products to trade. They could do so by stocking their stores with the goods, often imported, that local customers could buy and pay for with barter rather than cash—imported textiles and ceramics, shoes, farm tools, spices, and salt.

Article 5 of the Academy's letter, which asked about the distance from navigable water in conjunction with mines and minerals, and information about roads, including turnpikes, a new addition to the infrastructure, recognized the importance of transportation to economic success. Residents of regions whose economies lacked the mix of cattle, pasture, hay, and grains were consumers of New England's exports of butter and cheese. Answers to this question have been useful in interpreting the relationship between transportation and trade.

Of the more than forty extant Town Reports, nine lack a description of any kind of dairy activity—some because of their brevity and incompleteness, others because they focused on manufacturing. Of the remaining towns—eleven west of the Connecticut River and six on the east described production of butter and cheese. Although the quantities of both vary widely from town to town, several of the respondents' comments yield the clues from which one can assemble a more nuanced account.

Litchfield County

The Goshen reporter describes "the state of the export trade" the most fully of all the statements to the Academy. Merchants in that town were successful in trading with farm families from Goshen and neighboring Litchfield County towns, for that report offers separate lists based on the origin of the goods. "Exports *being the products of* the town of Goshen" were worth 77 percent of the grand total and exports "*from* the town of Goshen," presumably reflecting the traded produce of customers from adjoining towns, accounting for the remaining 23 percent. For the four products named in article 15, the total value of exports from Goshen was $64,731.88, of which cheese accounted for $49,010.33 (76 percent); compared with the quite similar 79 percent ($39,686.33) of the total exported ($50,470.73) by Goshen merchants. Not surprisingly, one "ripple effect" of exporting all of these goods in filled barrels, firkins, and boxes was that "many wagons are employed in carrying the produce of this town to New Haven; from whence it is shipped, chiefly to the southern states and West India islands."[8]

As the detail in the Goshen Report might suggest, data from Litchfield County provide the most complete picture of Connecticut dairying. Academy Reports for a cluster of nine contiguous towns indicate that much of Litchfield County's terrain was suitable for grazing, and that by 1800 farm dairies were becoming productive, significant, and visible elements of an active economy. In contrast, some midstate towns in Hartford, Middlesex, and parts of New Haven counties had already developed strong manufacturing bases. In the east, in Windham and New London counties, dairying was also part of a mixed but less robust agricultural economy.

It is evident that much of the prosperity of the Litchfield area could be attributed to agriculture, and in particular, its dairies. There is some suggestion that dairying on the scale being reported was a relatively recent development. Of Bethlem, we learn that farmers' "habits" with regard to the pork they had formerly raised for market were in transition by 1812 because of the cost of plowing and manual labor involved in raising the corn to fatten the pigs. "Some are convinced of their bad economy in this respect, and are turning their attention to dairies." Pride in the wealth derived from butter and cheese stands out in Goshen's Report.

The transformation that dairying effected becomes evident when observations made by Timothy Dwight during his statewide tour in 1798 are compared with his 1811 Academy report. Earlier Dwight had written, "The houses are good farmers' houses. There are a few in a superior style." Continuing with his comment on the large quantities of butter and cheese that were being exported, Dwight noted that Goshen was "perhaps the best grazing ground in the state; and the inhabitants are probably more wealthy than any other collection of farmers in New England. The quantity of cheese made by them annually is estimated at four hundred thousand pounds weight. Butter is also made in great quantities."[9] Their impact was apparently more evident on the landscape some fourteen years later. "The farmers here, having for the last 15 or 20 years turned their attention chiefly to the making of butter and cheese, have ceased to plough their lands as formerly. It will be readily seen that the great staple commodity here is cheese; and it is from this source chiefly that the inhabitants derive their wealth and prosperity."[10] In 1812 there were almost 1,800 cows yielding from 150 to 400 pounds of cheese (each) during the year. (Conservatively estimating an average yield of 225 pounds per cow, this would account for 495,000 pounds—a 20 percent increase over the two decades— which yielded more surplus for export.)

Cheese was the most significant of Goshen's exports, followed by beef, then butter, and pork. The butter exported was valued at only 10 percent of the value of the cheese, yet per pound it was worth nearly twice as much. The 588,124 pounds of cheese exported was valued at $49,010.33, and the 35,537 pounds of butter exported was worth $5,330. Other than describing how the exported cheeses were prepared by being painted with an annatto dye ("and it is not known that the taste of the cheese is affected by it"), the reporter declined to describe how the cheese and butter were made. "I will only observe that judgment, neatness, industry, and experience are indispensable requisites and that these are possessed in no inconsiderable degree by the females of Goshen."[11]

Like Goshen's, Norfolk's dairying reveals a recent change in agricultural emphasis. By 1815, "the soil being better suited to grass than tillage, the attention of the inhabitants has been turned principally to dairies."[12] The 1811 exports included 100 tons of cheese at $160 per ton, and six tons of butter at $320 per ton. Beef cattle (100 head at $20 average per head) and 100 barrels of pork at $12 per barrel rounded out the $21,120 realized from the sale of agricultural products. One hundred tons of cheese, accounting for 70 percent of the town's exports by value, far outranked the beef cattle, butter (six tons), and pork shipped. The sum of $21,120 was realized from the sale of agricultural products. As Norfolk was near the midpoint of the Greenwoods turnpike built to connect Hartford and Hudson, N.Y. in 1800, these products may have gone directly to New York State rather than shipping through New Haven.

Cornwall's respondent, like Goshen's, attributed much of the town's prosperity to its residents' industriousness in making goods at home for domestic consumption and export. Six domestic tasks were highlighted as "matters of too great utility to be passed over in silence." These were spinning woolen yarn for weaving and knitting into hosiery for their own use, preparation of flax to make linen and tow cloth "for our own use & for sale," and making butter and cheese. Through all this, "the industry and good economy both of the gentlemen and ladies are eminently conspicuous, both sexes having a sufficient stimulus to prompt them to these laudable pursuits." The questions prompted the Cornwall respondent—and this one alone in the entire Academy survey—to be discursive about domestic industry and the resultant benefits to both the household and the community. Through a family's "own industry," it could not only be "comfortably & decently fed & cloathed in winter & summer," but also have "a surplus to vend off for cash, cows, etc." The "industry" that made the difference was the work of women: "the greater proficiency they make with the distaff and the needle, the more cows they are likely to milk, & in consequence of that, the greater quantities of butter and cheese will be sent to market for cash."[13]

Cornwall's farmers were "so much in the habit of transporting their produce to market that it would be merely conjectural was any quantity named ... [of] pork, beef, butter, cheese, lard etc." In other words, some large-scale farmers dealt directly with distant markets; for others, "the merchants, who have five stores in town" performed this service for their customers. They "receive for their English and India goods and groceries ... butter [and] cheese ... which they send to market." Of butter, one of nine agricultural products, 9,998 pounds was shipped, worth approximately $1,549.69.[14] The amount of cheese exported was estimated at 53,880 pounds ($4,472); such economic rewards would make the formation of a trading habit worthwhile and contributed to the common good. It was spent on civic obligations such as "support of law, order, and good government and instruction in Church and State." Once these tax obligations had been satisfied and "the necessaries for family use" acquired, extra cash would permit more frivolous purchases for self-adornment. This local reporter described how members of these households might then satisfy their wishes for "the elegancies of superb dress...thereby, if possible to make their persons appear more elegant, amiable, and admirable."[15]

Another value of the products of domestic industry was that they could be used as cash to pay day labor. "Where farmers pay in grain, beef, pork, butter, and cheese, etc. as those articles were formerly sold at, they usually give 50 cents in summer, 42 cents in the spring & fall seasons and 34 cents in the winter."[16] Some of the tow cloth produced in Cornwall played a role in the expansion of its dairy trade because it was "carried by farmers into the State of New York & exchanged for cows & young cattle." Writing of Cornwall, it was acknowledged that inhabitants engaged in raising produce to send to market were "generally in good circumstances and many in a state of affluence."[17]

In the four remaining towns in Litchfield County for which there are Reports, more modest production and export of butter and cheese is described. Although dairying is not mentioned in the Kent Report, Washington (which had been part of Kent until 1782), in 1800 exported about ten tons of cheese annually and two tons of butter. Beef ($3.30 per hundredweight, "generally driven off on the leg") and pork (400 barrels at $16 per barrel) were also agricultural exports.[18] The reporter for Watertown (1801) described the average annual exports for fourteen agricultural products including 150 firkins of butter (8,400 lbs.; $1,302) and 30,000 pounds of cheese ($2,550). Reporting for Sharon in 1807, John Cotton Smith alluded to improvements in "exhausted lands" through the use of plaster as a soil amendment and the rotation of crops. Smith gave his impression in words, not figures, in response to Article 15. "To ascertain with precision the...productions of the earth and dairy...is attended with considerable difficulty," he wrote. "Since the introduction of the present system of husbandry, more than at any former period, the dairy and the culture of Indian corn, and as a natural and beneficial consequence of these, beef and pork, have engaged the attention of our agriculturalists."[19] This report is similar to that of Winchester (School Society) in 1813, where "many of the farmers keep dairies and therefore do not till as much land as farmers in parts where grain of all kinds is more plentifully produced. The quantity of butter sent to market from this town, although considerable, cannot with precision be known. It is believed the quantity of cheese is not less than 25,000 pounds [$2,075]." In neighboring Winsted, connected by the turnpike road to New Haven, the agricultural questions were left unanswered; however the responses to the industrial questions provided a description of iron work and forges, and wire, wool cards, and clocks made for export.[20] These non-agricultural households were far more likely to purchase farm products for their own consumption, than to produce surplus goods solely intended for export.

Fairfield County

Fairfield County is represented by only two of the Town Reports. Ridgefield's reporter in 1800 was its Congregational minister Samuel Goodrich, father and namesake of Peter

Parley, the prolific Connecticut author of the second quarter of the century. Goodrich estimated that "there may be from 250 to 300 firkins of butter [14,000 to 16,800 pounds worth from $2,100 to $2,520] and half the weight of cheese [est. 8,000 lbs., $680]." This represented a significant growth in volume, for as Goodrich observed, "the making of butter has much increased with twenty years; as it can now be carried fresh to New York market, the price is more than three times it then was."[21] Also behind the expanded herds of livestock and growth in milk production, in Goodrich's view, was the addition of turnips to the field crops grown in the community. He wrote (in a somewhat pastoral vein, perhaps) that "the old people love turnips ... and there are considerable quantities sacked every year from 2,000 to 4,000 bushels. They make good feed for sheep and cows that give milk."[22] Bridgeport (Stratfield) in 1800 was a rapidly growing town of "merchants and mechanics" based at the mouth of the Pequonnock River to take advantage of Long Island Sound for shipping, but, in comparison to New Haven's, the value of its shipments were modest: 92,582 pounds of cheese ($7,684.31) and 613 firkins, or 34,328 pounds of butter ($5,320.84).[23] Bridgeport's trade in 1798, Timothy Dwight wrote "is almost entirely carried on with New York or Boston." Dwight hints at what might have been written about by others in notes made in 1800 during his travels. "Fairfield is also the port of entry for the whole coast of Connecticut on the western side of the Housatonic. The coasting trade is of considerable importance, while that which is foreign is comparatively small."[24]

New Haven County

The reported position of dairy products in the economies of mid-state communities bordering the Connecticut River contrasts sharply with the information provided by the Litchfield County respondents. New Haven may have been a port through which the dairy products of this valley passed, but numbers are lacking and impressionistic accounts are often negative. In 1803 Cheshire's respondent noted that "this is not a dairy town; our land being better calculated for tillage than grazing."[25] Likewise in neighboring Wallingford in 1811-12 (the parish of Meriden, whose prosperity was derived from its successful tin plate manufacturing, had been incorporated in 1806, while the questionnaire was awaiting a response), its proximity to New Haven afforded a market for hay, corn, and potatoes with this convenience militating against raising cattle and setting aside fields for pastures. The "small proportion of pasture land reduces the quantity of butter and cheese & though the excess of pork, beef, butter & cheese annually raised, beyond the consumption of the town, cannot be ascertained, it is certainly not great.[26]

West of the Connecticut River, the reports for Madison and Guilford date from 1832, when David D. Field responded that the "inhabitants of Madison, like the inhabitants of Guilford, have very generally been farmers from the beginning." While not addressing Article 15 specifically, his report did comment about the soils in terms of their uses, For example, land in North Guilford that was "generally gravelly" and not good for growing the grains that were exported was reportedly "better adapted for grazing."[27] Did this mean that dairy cattle were pastured on it? If so, this is not mentioned.

Middlesex County

Of Middlesex, the county lying in the middle of the state between New Haven and Hartford counties, the general observation that it was not a net exporter of agricultural produce was borne out in the eight available reports. Bisected by the Connecticut River, the region's riverside wharves permitted the export of "lumber, wood, stone, fish, and whatever articles they have to spare." This might vary from one town to another and sometimes included dairy products. David D. Field's general observation was that "The quantity of butter and cheese exported is not great." The data for beef and pork suggest that Field took advantage of the only source of public information and checked with the inspectors of these products elected by the residents of each community. He was able to report that, "what is raised is almost entirely consumed in the county," and in "some years none has been inspected." Field generally ignores Article 15, but writes of East Haddam in response to the question about "the face of the country," that its terrain being "more suitable for grazing than for the culture of grain, the inhabitants are very generally farmers, and derive considerable profits from their stock and dairies and from their wood and lumber."[28]

Hartford County

Dwight describes the land in the valley south of Hartford as "rich agricultural country [that] carries on a considerable commerce."[29] There are three Town Reports for Hartford County: Bloomfield, known as Wintonbury in 1802; East Windsor, which includes what is now South Windsor; and Farmington which includes present-day Avon, Plainville, Newington, and part of West Hartford within its boundaries. Their trade was dominated by the Hartford market, which was close enough for many farmers to take their surplus directly there and resulted in different commercial patterns in which exports appear to play a lesser role. Dwight noted that while Hartford's location, particularly for inland trade, permitted "the commerce of this town [to become] considerable, yet, as it is not a port of entry, the amount cannot be ascertained. Its inland trade is, I suspect greater than that of New Haven."[30]

Farmington's "trade and commerce [were] flourishing," an adjective signifying that a large amount of cash was in circulation. This was a recent change, as "for several years after the close of the American War, a barter trade was carried on here. Money was extremely scarce[.] The farmer anticipated the products of his farm for goods consumed in his family. Now it is far otherwise, the merchant is neither the agent or factor in marketing the produce of the farmer. The latter transports and receives the full value of his produce in market and pays cash for the goods purchased at the merchants."[31] This would have made it difficult for the reporters to aggregate the items asked about in Article 15, and helps explain why no answer to this question was given in this report.

Close to Hartford, farm dairies in Bloomfield emphasized butter to the virtual exclusion of cheese. They could deliver fresh produce for immediate sale and use without the inevitable consequences of butter melting during a long journey in the heat of summer. "Pork, beef, mutton and cheese are not comparatively large market articles. The vicinity of the market [Hartford] makes butter the principal dairy article, to the great loss of some of the farmers, if they understood the more profitable way of making cheese. Ready money, once a week, is a temptation which induces a market man to overlook his greater interest in the well-managed but long-delayed cheese market."[32] Bloomfield was only seven miles from the center of Hartford, where demand existed for such "considerable market articles" as staved containers, cordwood, hay, grains, cider, cider brandy, and apples. East Windsor was a thriving town adjacent to the Connecticut River, which was then navigable at low water for loaded boats of fifty or sixty tons. There were fifty of these long boats owned in the town that navigated the river at least as far as Windsor, Vermont, some as far as Dartmouth College.[33] Describing his travels in the part of the Connecticut Valley surrounding Hartford, Dwight noted some of the same signs of growth and betterment that he had seen developing in end-of-the-century Litchfield County: "thrifty settlements," "well-built houses," and "an air of sprightliness and prosperity."[34]

Tolland County

The agricultural exports and what they represented for the economies of towns on the east side of the Connecticut River are not as well or enthusiastically reported to the Academy as elsewhere in the state. The mixed agriculture of the uplands and valleys of the northeastern part of the state elicits responses about pork, beef, butter, and cheese. Of the five reports for Tolland County, there is extensive commentary on two towns. North Bolton (which became Vernon), named dairying, spinning, and weaving as the domestic industries within the agricultural economy. From it, "the butter and cheese carried to market annually is conjectured to be...about 2,000 wt. of each; grains of all kinds (but principally rye) about 1,500 bush[e]ls. Pork that is marketed, yearly, is supposed to be about 15,000 wt. or 75 barrels. Of sheep's wool we have a sufficiency for home consumption & some to spare." The Reverend Ebenezer Kellogg, who responded promptly in 1800, described how he had derived these estimates. "'Tis difficult if not impossible for me to obtain exact information of these things; therefore with the aid of the opinions of some others of the Society I have stated as above."[35] The reporter for Union, who at age seventy-five had been engaged in agriculture for forty years, responded from a (male) farmer's perspective. He described the town's land as "rather sterile than fertile ... much better for mowing & feeding than tillage. ...As our lands are good for mowing and pasture there is a considerable number of sheep and cattle fat[t]ed & sent to market, also of butter & cheese made for the market a considerable quantity." He went into such detail about his own techniques for several areas of farming and gardening including the raising of swine for the market; one wishes for a similar description of dairying.[36]

It is possible that as his household had aged and diminished in size and strength, he had developed a specialty that he could manage without the extra hands that milking called for. These respondents' creative answers with numbers or descriptions can be appreciated in light of the absence of responses in the sketchy reports from Tolland County, although the land was observed to "yield good pasturage."[37] Not to be dismissed in this group of reports are instances of manufacturing—wool and silk in Mansfield, a cotton spinning mill in North Bolton/ Vernon and the iron ore in Union and Stafford that supported two furnaces principally for casting hollow ware.[38]

Windham County

When Dwight traveled through the northeasternmost towns of Connecticut, he noted his impressions of the Quinebaug Valley and the "beauty of its scenery." He remarked upon the groves of trees, orchards, and the "herds of cattle [that] are seen grazing the rich pastures, or quietly ruminating in the shade." Writing in 1800, having previously seen Goshen and Cornwall just as they, too, were beginning to develop their extensive farm dairy businesses, but before this air of prosperity had transformed their houses and public buildings, Dwight described the "pretty villages" with white-painted churches and "good farmers' dwellings" in Windham County. He observed that "The farmers throughout this tract are more generally wealthy than those of any other part of Connecticut. Their farms are chiefly devoted to grazing; and their dairies, it is believed, are superior to any others spreading over the same extent of country in the United States."[39] The description of Canterbury's Westminster Society confirms this description, noting that it "calculated very well for grazing" in contrast to the East Society, where corn was raised successfully, but land was not so good for grazing.[40] There are no reports for Woodstock, Killingly, and Brooklyn, and those of Pomfret and Windham say nothing on the subject. At the end of the century, the county historian offered hints about dairy activity in the region. In Quasset, one of Woodstock's villages, Thomas Bugbee, Jr., had established a pottery in 1793 where he and an assistant made and "sold all over Windham County" an assortment of redware including milk pans." The demand for milk-pans alone kept the kiln burning through the summer...turning out "perhaps two thousand milk-pans." These were the largest forms among the 5,000 pieces made in six reported summertime firings of the kiln.[41] In Woodstock, the first trade with Providence was by a "Butter-cart" which picked up small products from housewives in exchange for minor luxuries. Carts went all over the country picking up pork, beef, and ashes for potash, to be exchanged in Providence for molasses and rum.[42] Only Lebanon's report offers the kind of detail that suggests a longstanding pattern of agricultural surplus and export. "This town is better calculated for making beef, butter, & cheese than anything else, & this beginning to be more practised than formerly. Of pork 430 barrels, of beef 657 barrels are annually put up for market. Of cheese one of our traders has sent to market 20,000 pounds

in a year [$1,700]. The whole annual amount of these articles exported is probably much more considerable."[43]

Dwight described two farm dairies in Brooklyn, a town for which there is no Academy report. One wishes that there were, for Dwight wrote, "The cheese made in this region is not excelled by any on this side of the Atlantic, and not often by the best English cheese imported into this country." Ellen D. Larned, Windham County's historian, wrote of the town at the end of the century, "Brooklyn was much interested in agricultural affairs, and its dairies were reported as 'not exceeded in the State.'"[44] Larned confirmed what Dwight had written of the Putnam Farm. "The largest dairy within my knowledge is that of Major Daniel Putnam, son of the late Major General [Israel] Putnam, so distinguished in American history.... Mr. [Joseph] Matthewson, who received in Philadelphia a gold medal for producing in the market five hundred weight of cheese equal to the very best English cheese, according to a proposal published by the Society for the Encouragement of Arts and Agriculture in that city, is an inhabitant of Brooklyn, and may be considered justly as having materially improved the art of cheese making among his neighbors."[45] It does not seem coincidental then that with such quality and abundance to promote, the Windham County Agricultural Society was formed and established its annual fair.

Summarizing the situation in Windham County in 1800, without naming her sources, Larned describes a situation similar to that found in the Housatonic and Connecticut River watersheds. "Several business firms traded directly with the West India islands, owning their own vessels and buying up much surplus produce, whereby the farming interests of many towns had been greatly benefited. Towns with fewer farming facilities had turned attention to manufactures" of paper, potash, pottery ware, bricks, boots, shoes, hats and by the middle of the next decade, textiles. "Three shillings a day, paid in produce, was the common price for farm laborers, and a working woman would drudge through the week for two and sixpence. ... The poverty of the Notts of Ashford, who are reported to have worked their one cow upon the farm because they could not afford a horse or oxen, and lived chiefly upon brown bread and milk and bean-porridge, was not without its parallel in other households."[46] Meanwhile, the importance of the 1800 benchmark was underscored, for just over the eastern horizon in North Providence, Samuel Slater was experimenting with waterpowered cotton spinning that would come out to Windham County in the next decade, adding factories to the landscape that further expanded the economy from which some benefited more than others.

Farthest south in Windham County is Canterbury, and although its report does not directly answer the questions posed in Article 15, the town's proximity to several markets provided outlets for the products of its residents' industry and a source of its prosperity. "Our principal trade is at Norwich & New London. Considerable trade is carried on also with New York, Boston, & Providence. To Norwich is 12 miles. To Boston 80 to Providence 30."[47]

New London County

Among the Academy's documents is a manuscript "Schedule of Exports from & Imports into the District of New London,"[48] which constituted the easternmost coastal communities in the state—Stonington, Groton, New London, Waterford, and with the exception of a brief interlude around 1794 when it was part of Middletown district with other Connecticut River ports, Lyme. Covering the years from 1790 to 1811, this data sheet lists six "chief articles of export," horses, mules, horned cattle, barrels of beef, of pork and of fish, but does not include butter and cheese, which must have been among the lesser exports. The 163 vessels cleared for foreign ports in 1800 carried goods valued at $654,419. Even without the additional data for coastwise trade reported by Dwight for New Haven, the statistics for four of the towns in New London County indicate the draw of New London and its port. The mix of items named in the responses for Preston, Hanover, and Franklin suggest that dairy products might have been part of the cargo on the ships. The respondent for Preston reported the production and sale of 67,034 pounds ($5,698) of cheese and 11,119 pounds ($1,668) of butter, in addition to 162,166 pounds of pork and 73,032 of beef.[49] The description of the Hanover Society of Lisbon notes that "the principal articles of sale in the towns are butter, cheese, beef, pork and cider."[50] From Franklin 18,000 pounds of butter ($2,700) and 120,000 pounds of cheese ($10,200) were taken to market along with 1,000 sheep, 220,000 pounds of pork and 220,000 pounds of beef. In Canterbury and Franklin and likely other places too, these families were also making woolen and linen cloth, "but very little is made for market."[51]

Gendered Work Roles

Incomplete as they are, the Connecticut Academy's Town Reports managed to capture the evidence of a large amount of wealth created through the production of agricultural surplus. The Academy's Article 15 was written to probe for information about how cattle, sheep, and pigs were wealth-producing commodities. What is remarkable from these reports of dairy production is both how much butter and cheese were produced and how much of it was produced in the farm dairies of Connecticut's growing and maturing families.

Jackson Turner Main's study of the economy of colonial Connecticut, based on probate inventories of New Haven and Fairfield Counties, looks at much of the same land and livestock, confirming and further defining what was happening. Through his close study of data in the colonial probate records, Main discovered that within the range of farmers holding real property worth between £100 and £200 (mean of £170 and median of £195) those who added only a few livestock could increase their wealth substantially. "Of cattle, most owned at least six and over half had ten, enough to be called a herd and to produce a surplus." The median and mean numbers were both eleven.[52] Adding information about family size to his analysis of these expanding agricultural holdings, Main also noticed a high correlation between the addition of extra land and families with teenaged children.[53] When these households with an available work force added to their land, more livestock soon followed enabling the production of a surplus that could be sold.

While the livestock of these farmers did not double in proportion to their land, it did increase, showing that clear surplus over need, which enabled them to buy more comforts and more land. We are dealing now with some of the most prosperous farmers in colonial Connecticut. What, then, did the well-to-do farmers pasture on their land? Seventeen cattle, four horses, twenty-four sheep, and eight pigs.... A few individuals held much more than this. Herds of over fifty cattle occur. However, the majority of men did not deviate far from the median. Nearly half owned between ten and twenty cattle, at least at the date of the inventory. ...All of these figures are considerably in excess of family needs. Roughly, the typical farmer of this size owned, above the number needed for subsistence plus and so available for sale, eight cattle, three pigs, a couple of colts, and the wool from a dozen sheep.[54]

Thus it was possible to get ahead. By doing the extra work, both men and women could contribute to the extra income that was so apparent in the Connecticut countryside by about 1800.

With the few exceptions of the more garrulous respondents, the Town Reports do not reveal much about how this work was done. No late eighteenth-century Academy member apparently considered asking a woman to report about women's work. The results would surely have been different if they had. To ask about what this dairy production represented to those who were charged with the daily work; who did the work; what tools and equipment they used; and how they learned these skills, we must look to other sources. Some of the voices will be women's.

If, for instance, Hannah Heaton of North Haven (1721-94) had lived to respond, she might have noted the ways in which her domestic and agricultural work provided her with solitude and time for reflection on her relationship to God and the means to contribute to the wealth that she and her husband amassed. For Mrs. Heaton, the barn and the cow house were places that she would not be disturbed while reading her Bible and writing in her diary. "Milking was a good occasion for spiritual reflection, since tending three or four cows provided time for thoughts such as the following," her biographer notes. "'These light afflictions which/we/have but for a moment shall work for us a far more exceeding & eternal wait of glory.'" In the thirty-six years between her marriage to Theophilus Heaton in 1755 and his death in 1791, their real estate increased in acreage and value from £53/16/- to £533/5/7, their family grew, and their personal property including clothing, furniture and bedding, cows and sheep came to be valued at just under £100. This wealth enabled her to indulge her spendthrift younger son Calvin and also provided Hannah for the last few years of her life with a widow's third that included "three cows and seven sheep." Following a custom of the time, she "let out" this livestock for income presumably because she was too old to care for them and milk the cows.[55] That was work for a woman with a family as reminiscences reveal. Two reminiscences set the scene:

> In those summer days, mother and Aunt Sarah rose in the early dawn, and taking the well-scoured wooden pails from the bench by the back door, repaired to the cow yard behind the barn. We owned six cows, my grandmother four. Having milked the ten cows, the milk [sic] was strained, the fires built, and breakfast prepared. During breakfast the milk for the cheese was warming over the fire in the large brass kettle. The milk being from ten cows, my mother made cheese four days; Aunt Sarah having the milk the remainder of the week. In this way good-sized cheeses were obtained. The curd having been broken into the basket [an alternative method of straining the whey],... the house was righted. By the time this was done the curd was ready for the press. After dinner the cheeses were turned and rubbed. ...At sunset the cows came from the pasture. Milking finished and the milk strained, the day's labor was ended.[56]

Another reminiscence, again from a child's vantage point, describes the housework that included the dairying.

> During the summer, there was butter making, cheese making, spinning and weaving. After all the cows began to wean their calves and fill their udders with sweet milk made of June grass, cheese making commenced. We kept five cows and Grandfather Newell four, so we would join, we adding their milk to ours one day, and giving ours to them on alternate days. The milk from nine cows would make a cheese about eight inches in diameter and four inches high. I think Mother used to make ten or fifteen cheeses every year.[57]

But was the story really always this benign? Sally McMurry, who has painstakingly reconstructed cheese-making procedures in central New York State, suggests that as the nineteenth century progressed, the "informal and unsystematic" ways of the "early dairy era" were superseded by more structure and greater urgency. "Even the most careful cheese maker could not always prevent unwanted organisms or an incorrect guess from spoiling the cheese. Most of the problems did not become evident until after the cheese, innocent-appearing,

had sat curing for a while."[58] The record of the quest for a foolproof method of making and keeping cheeses that has survived in print suggests the subject of many a conversation in farm households around 1800.

Books of Instruction to Improve Connecticut Dairies

Two separate publications addressed to Connecticut's dairy producers appeared around the turn of the century, one preceding and the other just after 1800. *The Art of Cheesemaking Taught From Actual Experiments by which More and Better Cheese May Be Made From the Same Quantity of Milk*, which had appeared in Boston in 1797, was published the next year by John Byrne of Windham and T. Collier of Litchfield.[59] These booklets provided "Rules selected from the approved practice of distinguished dairy women—of dealers in Cheese—and writers on the subject, both in England and America." And, significantly, brought the directions for cheese making in a concise and printed fashion to Connecticut. "Butter Churns on a New Principle" was an illustrated article in the fourth monthly issue of the inaugural volume of *Connecticut Magazine* (published in Bridgeport in 1801).[60]

The pamphlets published by Byrne and Collier offered points to be observed for successful mastery of the art of cheese making. There were four critical elements to its successful preparation—milk, the curdling agent, the curd, and, finally, the cheese. Each of these stages required particular skills of observation and handling: correct temperature of the milk, a good quality rennet (called "runnet" in the 19th century descriptions) prepared from the skin of the calf's stomach ("maw-skin"), sufficient time allowed for the "gathering of the curd," its gentle handling when the enzymes had acted, and the proper care of the finished cheese.

It was assumed that the milk of twenty cows (ten for Collier) was being processed. In this context, the directions given in the first part of the rule for gauging the temperature of the milk becomes important. (If one's herd had fewer cows, it is likely that the dairy woman would obtain an equivalent amount of milk by combining fresh milk with that from the previous milkings. Under these circumstances part of the milk would already have cooled; in the summer the milk coming straight from the cow would have been too warm and would need to cool.) The author describes the correct temperature for the milk at the outset of cheese making in words rather than numerically as degrees on a thermometer. (This mode of instruction about temperature was a familiar one, for there was no way—other than experience—to know the temperature of the bake oven either.) To proceed successfully, the milk had to be cooler than when taken from the cow and, if necessary, warmed with care. Next, a quart of salt and a tea cup (3/4 cup modern measure) of rennet (a piece of the stomach of a calf providing enzymes) were to be stirred into the milk and allowed to rest from one-and-one-half to two hours. By then, the action of the enzymes would have formed a curd that would be sufficiently "solid" for cutting gently with a wooden knife into about ten divisions to separate the liquid whey and release pockets of air. As the whey rose to the surface, it could be carefully skimmed off with a flat ladle that could also be used to press gently on the slices of curd to remove all the liquid (slip) and be sure that only the solids remained in the tub. At this stage, salt was added and when sufficiently stirred in, the mixture transferred into the hoop lined with a cloth in the cheese press in preparation for pressing. After it was "put into the press ... no more is needful, except turning it several times in the first 48 hours while it is pressing. The finest, fattest and best Cheese is made in this way." After the cheese was removed from the press, it should be kept warm "till it has had a sweat, or 'has become pretty dry and stiffish.'" Acknowledging that this process was taking place in the house, the directions stated, "This can be done in a south-facing room or a room over the kitchen fire, and then afterwards, the cheese should be stored in "a cool shady room, or even a plaster floor," avoiding frost, and its maker should observe that it does not "heave" or "get puffy." Following the outline of the sequence of making cheese are several pages of tips, including a recipe for preparing rennet from a calf's stomach and preserving it. The sixth tip describes the use of annatto in the milk to color the cheese,[61] and although it is unlike the procedure that the Goshen reporter describes to color the outside of the cheese, it is possible that his was not an accurate account.

These pamphlets bear some resemblance to a 1796 reprint of a more extensive British treatise reprinted in Providence, Rhode Island. Josiah Twamley claimed that *Dairying Exemplified* was based on a thirty-year career in the English cheese trade and "frequent opportunities for consulting the best of Dairy-women in many counties, who I knew from experience know how to make good cheese."[62] The basic procedures about the temperature of the milk, the handling of the cheese curds and the cautions about slip, and the preparation of the "maw" to yield "runnet" were summarized in the American pamphlets. However, the considerably more detailed recommendations about the location and construction of the dairy and the more elaborate techniques set forth in this volume, "he hoped will be read by Dairy-women in general, who, if they pay due attention to it, cannot help receiving benefit from the advice it contains." Twamley's directions for making butter recommend setting milk for twelve hours in summer and twenty-four hours in winter to let the cream rise and then scalding the cream "till bubbles rise and the cream changes its colour." After standing for twelve hours more, it is ready to be skimmed and put into a tub or churn ("a cleanlier way") for beating or dashing until butter comes. "It should then be washed in many different waters, till it is perfectly cleansed from the butter-milk."[63]

In April 1801, around the time that the butter-making season began that spring, the editor of *Connecticut Magazine* offered his readers "a sketch of an improvement in the manner of working the Butter Churn." The assumptions on which it was based were "that the most butter is made in small quantities" by women and that "the vertical motion of the common churn is so intolerably fatiguing." The ingenious, but anonymous, mechanic took both the common churn and the barrel churn, which had enjoyed much less success, and fitted them to a stand and added a handle and a fly wheel, with the

result that the butter would come much faster. "We cannot but consider this application of the invention [the addition of a fly-wheel] as far the most valuable. Nor can we deny that we feel a considerable partiality for the good housewife's usual churn" in promoting the improved version.[64]

Fixing the directions for dairying in print in this way supplemented almanacs, previously the most accessible source. The conclusions of the anonymous pamphlets underscore their intended audience. "A good diary [*sic*] woman will soon

Amos Doolittle engraved this illustration, "Butter Churns on a New Principle" published in the first issue of The Connecticut Magazine *in April 1801. Courtesy, American Antiquarian Society.*

discover whether her present mode of cheesemaking is best— and time and observation will render her mistress of this important art to any agricultural country."[65] American cookery books published after 1800 begin to include concise directions for making cheese and butter, confirming that its production was, generally, in the woman's domain.[66] One cookbook advised on herd management recommending that the majority of the herd be bred to calve "at the end of March or beginning of April and one [cow] at the end of September; then the family will be supplied with milk in the winter."[67] The how-tos of butter and cheese production and the tools and containers used, are described in detail.[68] But although Twamley made quite specific references, neither of the Connecticut pamphlets offers any suggestions about a specific location for dairy work. Some contemporary reminiscences suggest that although a cool room with additional shelving was an important space, the need for fire meant that the kitchen hearth served for cooking and dairying. This domestic perspective appears in contrast to the description of practice in England. Twamley advised that "nothing is more commendable in Dairy-maids than cleanliness, nor will any thing cause them to be more esteemed; every one who perceives extreme neatness in a Dairy, cannot help wishing to purchase either Butter or Cheese from so clean and neat a place." The floor of the dairy should be "neatly paved with red brick, or smooth hard stone, and laid with a proper descent, so that no water may lodge; this pavement should be well washed in summer every day, and all the utensils belonging to the Dairy should be kept perfectly clean, nor should the churns ever be suffered to be scalded in the Dairy, as the steam that arises from hot water will injure the milk. Nor do I approve of Cheese being kept therein, or runnet for making Cheese, or having a cheese press fixed in a Dairy as the whey and curd will diffuse their accident throughout the room."[69] Although such dedicated space might not have existed in New England and the prescribed degree of care might not have been taken under the domestic roof, farmers who submitted their butter samples to agricultural society competitions, often described their cool, well ventilated cellars, some with stone or brick floors.[70]

But details like these were not sought by the Academy's questioners. They were involved in an economy that they took for granted, but that today's scholars are eager to reconstruct. Laurel Thatcher Ulrich, concluding a discussion and close investigation of women and textile work, called for "a more nuanced understanding of household production, a historiography that considers both its constraints and opportunities."[71] The Academy data for dairying suggest that this area of household production enriches and complicates the distinctive story of women's work in post-Revolutionary New England. The data also give credence to Timothy Dwight's enthusiasm for the increased prosperity that he observed on his Connecticut travels.

With "Unshaken Heroism and Fortitude:"

Connecticut Women's Life and Work Two Hundred Years Ago

Ruth Barnes Moynihan

No questions about women were put before the gentleman scholars and ministers who wrote their Town Reports for the Connecticut Academy of Arts and Sciences at the turn of the nineteenth century. In fact, like most scholars of their time and after, Academy members tended to presume women's lives and women's work had little to do with the important issues and histories of Connecticut towns. Many respondents, however, provided very specific information about women in their communities. Others wrote more obliquely, assuming the activity of women without naming them. A close look at all these Town Reports reveals the presence and significance of women in every aspect of community development, and a surprising amount of information about what they were doing.

Post-revolutionary Connecticut's agricultural economy and culture was poised at the edge of new industrial, commercial development, bringing changes that were to have a profound effect upon women as well as men. Business and industry were becoming separate enterprises rather than adjuncts of the farm economy, thus also separating the activities and production of the "domestic" home from the "public" workplace. There was a growing distinction between the poor and the well-to-do, between farming communities and prosperous urban commercial centers. As more and more emigrants left the state, women were increasingly separated from friends and relatives, including young men who were potential husbands. Even contemporaries noticed that the population's skewed sex ratio increased the likelihood of "spinsterhood." But greater educational opportunity, religious revivalism, and nascent "female charitable societies" were laying the foundation for women activists of the future.

In these narratives, dated variously from 1800 to 1819, and one in 1832, we can actually see the changes taking place. Though the writers still take the household economy—the small farmer with his wife and children—as the self-evident foundation of a stable community, and an egalitarian community as the norm of their societies, they often lament the erosion of these norms in recent decades. They also describe such innovations as academies for women or new textile mills, or Eli Whitney's cotton gin, which we now know, with the benefit of hindsight, to have been transforming elements in American history.

During the first two decades of the nineteenth century most Connecticut women still lived on farms, often quite isolated from one another. Lebanon, for example, in 1800, was typical of the circumstances in much of the state. Its population consisted of about 2,500 people scattered over a large rural countryside.

Farms averaged about 90 acres, though some included two or three hundred acres, and others were much smaller. There were five different churches, in different parts of town close to their members. Twenty-four school districts dotted the landscape, in addition to a "large brick school house" in what was known as "the 1st Society," the original church and town settlement to which scholars came "from the greater part of the States in the union." Roads were rough so there were "but few pleasure carriages," but many more than the two or three of pre-Revolutionary years.

Even though the town was so important that it had served as headquarters for the Revolutionary War army, and had produced such eminent citizens as Governor Jonathan Trumbull and his sons, it still had no business or industry except for its nine taverns. A few skilled craftsmen—"tanners, shoemakers, carpenters, house joiners, & blacksmiths scattered about the town"—traveled "from house to house ... except in the sumer, when they are generally employed at farming." They bartered their labor for wages or for goods, but the town's one attempt at "a manufactory of cotton cloth ... failed by reason of the high price of cotton & labour." In Lebanon as elsewhere, before Eli Whitney's cotton gin made southern cotton both plentiful and cheap, and northern factories both feasible and profitable:

> ...the manufacturing of cloth has been carried on
> in families for their own use principally, consisting
> of the coarser kinds of woolen & linen cloth,
> checked linen & woolen, some of which has been
> sent to the new settlements...the greater part of
> the cloth being wove by women in the families
> where the yarn is spun. [1]

Only a few "make weaving a constant business," and those few women probably bartered their labor just as the male craftsmen did.[2]

Lebanon's women, like farm women throughout the state, also made butter and cheese. Twenty thousand pounds of cheese per year went to market, but the whole amount exported was "probably much more considerable." This amounted to at least 40 pounds of cheese per household, in addition to what each family itself consumed. Farmers transported their "vendible produce" ten or twenty miles, mostly "on carts & sleds drawn by oxen." Of course, sales were registered to heads of households, not to women. But everyone took for granted that women's work was an integral income-enhancing part of the local economy.[3]

Cornwall's chronicler, Elijah Allen, was more specific about the value of women's production, especially in a barter economy:

> Manufacturing of Woollen Cloth & Hose, &c for our own consumption, and Linnen & Tow Cloth for our own use & for sale, as also the making of Butter and Cheese in this Town, are matters of too great Utility to be passed over in Silence.

There were five merchants in Cornwall who were paid "for their English & India goods & Groceries" not only in meat and grain but also in "Butter, Cheese, ...Tow Cloth, &c. which they send to Market." Other farmers themselves exchanged "Tow Cloth" in New York "for cows and young cattle." [4]

What this meant, Allen continued, was that both men and women were stimulated to productive pursuits, and elegance was the result of hard work, not leisure. A Lady knew that:

> Riches are increased by her good Conduct in the Family and...they and their Descendants are in this way rising to Reputability and Fame.... [She was] excited with alacrity to take the Distaff in her Hand in the Winter & Spring, & to Teach her Daughter by her example as well as her precept, That Gold, Pearls, Silk and Embroidery are the Fruits of Industry.

He continued in one breathless sentence to tie together women's work, tax payments, good government, and elegance of dress—the harder a woman worked the more elegant she could be:

> The greater proficiency they make with the Distaff and the Needle, the more Cows they are likely to Milk, & in consequence of that, the greater Quantities of Butter and Cheese will be sent to Market for Cash to enable them to pay their Taxes for the support of Law, Order and good Government and Instruction in Church and State, and that the Remainder...will be prudently laid out in purchasing other acquisitions to increase their Wealth, and in the Necessaries for Family Use & in the Elegancies of Superb Dress to Enrobe them with, and thereby, if possible, to make their persons appear more Elegant, Amiable and Admirable. [5]

In Cornwall, all textiles were made at home, from locally grown wool and flax, at least "4500 Yards of Woollen Cloth and 21,000 Yards of Linnen Cloth," annually. Women in Bethlem were working 80 looms that produced 15,600 yards of cloth in 1810. They also knitted 2,350 pair of stockings. There were only 414 women over the age of ten, 315 over sixteen; we can calculate that the latter made 49.5 yards of cloth each (if they shared looms), whereas the women altogether averaged 5.68 pairs

of long socks. [6] (In actuality, older women probably did much more of the knitting than younger ones.)

Wallingford women in 1812 were producing 36,459 yards of linen and cotton cloth, valued in those times at $12,396.06, plus 12,153 yards of woolen cloth worth $9,114.75, on 145 looms used in families. This amounted to 41 percent of the value of manufactures in that town, which already had several other industries, including a tin ware factory. Wallingford also had six carding machines, which eased women's work by preparing 18,000 lbs. of wool before it could be spun. Winchester (Winsted) was experimenting with "two infant factories for making cards:"

> The teeth are wholly set by children, and if the business should be continued, may prove an incentive to industry, at a period of life, when their hands cannot be usefully occupied in ordinary pursuits. [7]

Thus children (but generally not the daughters of the well-to-do), who would formerly have helped their mothers to prepare the wool at home, were becoming paid laborers. A class differential had been introduced into ordinary women's work.

Similarly, in Sharon, in 1807, "Woolen manufacture has hitherto been principally confined to private families and to the common cloths." But Merino sheep had just been introduced from which "excellent specimens of cloth" had been "fabricated by *individuals*" [italics mine] causing hope "that this valuable manufacture will soon be attempted upon an enlarged scale." [8] As was true of many other "manufactories," once women's work became sufficiently profitable it was very likely to be co-opted by a male-managed factory where needy women received wages—and owner-organizers the profits.

The first stages of such industrialization, a "putting out system," can be seen at a Farmington linen factory. The owner would "purchas the flax [and] let it out to spinners who return him the yarn." He then dyed the yarn in his own shop or let it out again to be bleached and returned, then delivered it "out to women weavers chiefly" who returned him the cloth. He paid the women "in European goods," not cash, and thus produced "about 15000 yards of cloth in a year." [9] The efficiencies of organized large-scale production were achieved at the cost of the independence and self-sufficiency of individual women. And the owner even took credit for making the cloth.

Writing in 1800, Lisbon's chronicler wrote of the "husbandmen, who manufacture the greater part of their common clothing," while Ridgefield's "people generally manufactor their wollen and linnen cloaths in their own families, using all their wool and most of their flax." Aaron Putnam said of Pomfret, "People, here, in general, make their own wearing apparell." The reporters' words hide the *women* who made that apparel. True, a farmer might make leather boots and shoes, and maybe even a coat or pants, out of the hide from one of his cattle. But women made everything else, spinning linen thread from the "considerable crops of Flax" they grew in the town, spinning yarn out of wool from a few sheep, weaving the two together to make a rough "linsey-woolsey" homespun, and sewing that cloth into shirts and skirts and children's clothes and blankets.[10]

There was, in fact, in 1800, a new "cotton factory for the spinning & twisting of cotton yarn built by & the property of a Mr. Warburton, a few years since from England," in the northern part of Bolton (which became the town of Vernon). It was reported to be "of considerable business & increasing," and was probably the first cotton manufacturing establishment in the state.[11]

By the second decade of the century many more such mills were built throughout the state—wherever there was water power, sufficient access to a trade route, willing labor, *and* enough available cotton. Women themselves began to appreciate and buy the attractive new textiles—the beginning of the end for homespun linsey-woolsey. In that respect, it was Eli Whitney's invention of the cotton gin which made such factories possible; by significantly increasing the production of southern cotton, cotton cloth could be made more cheaply in the north.[12]

It should be noted that Pomfret's Aaron Putnam mentioned a unique labor-saving device for women: "Mr. Weld's (Braintree) Lavator; a few Instances of which are among us, & it is reckon'd much relieving women, in ye toilsome Labour of washing of Clothes." This is without doubt one of the earliest washing machines in America. Doing the laundry was a heavy, time-consuming task, and it was to become even more so during the nineteenth century with rising standards of cleanliness and clothing variety. As the woman's rights movement later developed, activists frequently complained that doing laundry should not even be women's work because it involved such heavy lifting—of multiple pails of water, and of water-laden work clothes. But early nineteenth century women were losing rather than gaining the economic wherewithal to make Mr. Weld's machine successful by buying it (and hired help was cheaper); it took another sixty years before any similar device came widely to market.[13]

Besides making cloth, women were large-scale producers of butter and cheese. In the prosperous town of Goshen, cheese was the "great staple commodity," and the chief source of local "wealth and prosperity." Lewis Norton specified that cheese-making required "judgment, neatness, industry and experience" and these were "possessed in no inconsiderable degree by the females in Goshen." The town produced 380,236 pounds of cheese, worth $39,686.33 in those days, and, as an important market town to New York State, actually exported 588,124 pounds, worth $49,010.33 during the year 1811. This amounted to 93 percent of the value of local products and 76 percent of total products exported from the town of Goshen in 1811. In addition, the town produced 25,376 pounds of butter, worth $3,956.40—another 9 percent of local produce, and it exported 35,537 pounds, worth $5,330.55 or 8 percent of the total exports. The only other exports were barrels of beef and pork, and these too probably involved a significant input of women's labor, in cooperation with the men who slaughtered the animals.[14]

Goshen was not unique in its butter and cheese production. Watertown's 1,622 inhabitants in 1800 averaged annual exports of 30,000 pounds of cheese and 150 firkins of butter. (Each firkin weighed 56 pounds.) Franklin marketed 18,000 lbs. of butter and 120,000 lbs. of cheese. In 1811, Norfolk marketed "100 tons of cheese at $160 per ton" plus "6 tons of butter, at $320." The seaport of Stratfield (now Bridgeport) exported 613 firkins of butter and 92,582 lbs. of cheese, along with 4,634 lbs. of feathers, 33,733 yards of tow cloth, and 1155 firkins of lard, among other things, in 1799. These were undoubtedly from many towns in the hinterland, but the labor they represent is significant—especially those feathers![15]

Only Goshen's historian, however, gave clear and unequivocal credit to the women producers. He pointed out that there were about 1,800 cows in his town (among 240 families), and each cow's milk could make "from 150 to 400 pounds" of cheese. Butter required hand-churning, while cheese required careful preparation in a controlled environment over a period of months, an art best explained by women themselves, he said. In fact, Norton had reason to know the details of cheese production, because his own relative, Abraham Norton, had recently "invented a mode of pressing cheese . . . called an increasing press." (One may wonder if his wife cooperated; perhaps it was even her idea. But, even so, the patent would have been in his name, as head of the household. Law prohibited married women, unlike adult single women or widows, from personal ownership of property.) The device gradually increased pressure on the cheese as it ripened, making the process easier and more efficient. Thus, in Goshen, says Norton, "The farmers here, having for the last 15 or 20 years turned their attention chiefly to the making of butter and cheese, have ceased to plough their lands as formerly" and now had to import wheat and rye to meet their needs.[16]

In another 1812 report, Bethlem normally exported 7,000 pounds of butter and 30,000 pounds of cheese per year, though it had a population of only 1,118 people in 173 families in 1810. Some women in Bethlem evidently spent time instead on making straw hats and bonnets to export from a local "manufactory"—150 hats in 1810 to be exact. And this was in addition to the weaving and knitting mentioned above.[17]

Ridgefield housewives, in 1800, produced for export "from 250 to 300 firkins of butter and half the weight of Cheese.— (9,000)." Butter making, said Samuel Goodrich, had become more profitable since the Revolution because it could be "carried fresh to New York" and be sold for three times more than twenty years earlier. The list of exports from New Haven in the coasting trade of 1801 includes large figures for women's home produce: 219,702 lbs. of cheese, 828 firkins of butter, 14,129 yards of tow cloth, 6,982 lbs. of tallow, and 33 yards of flannel, not to speak of whatever part they had in the production of candles, grains, meats, fruits and vegetables.[18]

Aside from the production of cloth, clothing, butter, and cheese, women frequently helped in their husband's taverns—of which there were many in almost every town. In New London, a busy seaport with many transients, they kept boarding houses. And in prosperous Middletown, three milliners' shops, probably run by women seamstresses, were established by 1819.[19]

Women everywhere were also responsible for family vegetable and herb gardens, the latter for medicine as well as food. These were not small. In fact, they often filled half or whole acres of land, tended mainly by mothers and their daughters. Saving and exchanging seeds each fall, planting, harvesting, and preparing the produce, or preserving it for winter by means of drying, pickling, or making jams and jellies—all this was women's time-consuming, skillful work. Knowledge of medicinal herbs and their preparation was also part of the job.[20]

Farmington's Treadwell gave a long list of typical garden vegetables, including several varieties of most of them. He also listed flowers, many with medicinal purposes. Cornwall's reporter rhapsodized at length about the "sundry Ladies of elegant Taste [who] have superadded to the Useful Store of Succulent and Cullinary Fruits, Foliage and Roots cultivated in their Gardens, many knots and Beds of Suparlatively Beautiful and Aromatick Flowers," whose spectators were "unsensibly led to Esteem and Venerate the good Judgement and Refined Taste" of the ladies who "planted and reared the Garden to such a State of Peerless Beauty." Ridgefield's Goodrich spoke more prosaically of "plenty of squashes, cucummbers, musmellens, water mellens . . . . beets, carrots, parsnips, cabbages, lettuce & radishes." New Haven's Timothy Dwight, president of Yale, affirmed that "The city of New-Haven contains, probably, as many good kitchen gardens as any town in the state: and all, or nearly all the objects of horticulture, within the state, may be found here." He provided a long list, noting the number of varieties of each, which even included "Tomatos, or Love Apples" (not found in Farmington, and then only recently discovered to be edible).[21]

In almost every town, both men and women tended fruit trees of all sorts, while cider-making from apples was an essential process everywhere. Fermented hard cider was ubiquitous; no temperance movement yet existed to oppose alcoholic beverages. But Goshen's Lewis Norton did comment about the excessive and "unnecessary use of spirituous liquors." He deplored the fact that the current generation "seem unable to perform the most trifling business of life without the help of artificial stimulus," and then detailed Goshen's "distilled spirits" consumption in 1811. It included rum, gin, French brandy, and cider brandy to the amount of 24 gallons or $25 a year per family.[22]

The corn, wheat, rye, and oats that men grew in the fields was either exported or ground into whole-grain flour at numerous gristmills located on nearby streams in almost every town. Mills relieved women from grinding grain at home, but only occasionally produced "refined flour" for fancy baking. Thus women were not expected to produce the complicated meals, cakes and pastry which would later become symbols of female domesticity. The only cookbook a few ladies might have owned was published in Hartford in 1796 and devoted mainly to pies, puddings, and the dressing of turkeys, turtles, and calves' heads.[23]

Many women thrived on the farming life. In Lebanon, "one woman, a farmers wife, in the habit of industry, lately died at the age of 101; there is one woman of like habits now living between 95 & 96 yr old." Garden lovers of any generation can identify with the "old lady" from Canterbury "who always in spring summer & autumn spent her time in cultivating her garden. She lived to see 98 years . . . . She was naturally weakly, but seemed to draw her life from the earth & plants."[24] Throughout the state, statistics showed that if women lived beyond the childbearing years (as many did not), they often achieved a healthy and active old age.

But child rearing and family health care were heavy burdens on these hard-working farmers' wives. Population figures in all the Town Reports show prolific birth rates, frequent epidemics of illness and fatalities, and a great loss of life among small children. For example, one can deduce several things from the figures for the County of Litchfield in August 1800. Almost 33 percent of the males were under ten years old, and 31 percent of the females; it was a very youthful population. If one considers the proportion of population aged twenty-six and under, the figure is 65 percent (not including the 656 "other free persons" of color and 47 slaves). Certainly this indicates that mothers had many children to care for. Only 14 percent of the population were over 45.[25]

Similarly, figures for New Haven in 1787 show 614 families in 466 houses with an average of five people per family. The death rate is more revealing: between 1763 and 1786, 23 percent of the deaths were of children under 2 years old, plus 7 born dead; 34 percent of deaths were children under five. The population doubled about every twenty-five years. East Windsor's reporter wrote that "By natural increase, the inhabitants doubled their number in periods of about 21 years" up to 1775, and he pointed out that less than half were aged above 20 (1350) and more than half below 20 (1614).[26]

Housing figures show that it was quite common for families to share a house, especially in more rural areas. Sometimes parents added an "ell" to accommodate a newly married son or daughter, or siblings might share a house until one of them was able to move to another farm. In Guilford there were 438 families occupying 401 houses, while Madison had 353 families in 290 houses. Cornwall's 1,561 people in 272 families, plus "30 Blacks including Indians," lived in 215 houses. This was an average of 5.74 people per family, plus servants. Ridgefield's correspondent described what was true of most other towns as well:

> People here generally marry young and are very prolific; in 6 families, a number of years since, all living in one neighborhood, there were 75 Children [12.5 per family]. The number of births greatly excede the number of deaths; there may have been 4000 since the settlement of the town [in 1714].[27]

Diseases, however, took their toll on almost every family. Women, as primary caregivers, had to both provide for the sick and contain their grief over suffering and death. Half of all those who died between 1772 and 1812 in the South-Farms section of Litchfield were under ten years old, even though the township "has been noted for being remarkably healthy." A terrible epidemic of dysentery swept the town in 1776-77, the same one remarked upon in numerous other Town Reports. Two hundred people died locally, plus thirty young Litchfield soldiers imprisoned in New York by the British.[28]

Nothing was yet known of the germ theory of disease. People recognized contagion from person to person in some cases, but could only speculate about the reasons for other illness. Thus epidemics of typhus, dysentery, and various kinds of fever often invaded particular neighborhoods and mystified those who sought to explain them. In Union, "a number of women were met on a special ocation & water was taken from a well that had been covered with a flat stone for a year or more & every one that drinked of it was took sick & puked to such a degree that they had to send for a physician." And "a ruged hearty man of about eighty" cleaned stagnant water out of a ditch in his meadow and "was struck with a mortification which soon ended his days."[29]

In Wintonbury (now Bloomfield), William F. Miller perceived an inexplicable connection between a swampy brook on the west side of town and the "slow fever and the dysentry" among "the inhabitants lying on the road running parallel with this stream, in some particular seasons." In the dysentery epidemic of 1775, the majority of deaths occurred on that street, in thirty out of its thirty-three houses. It happened again "in the fall of AD 1795." Considering that outhouses were often located where drainage might occur into local streams, and that manure from farm animals accumulated in every farmyard, often close to the family's well, and was later spread on the fields as rich fertilizer, it is not surprising that fevers were so common. Wintonbury's Miller reported that "the most prevalent diseases are the pleurisy, consumption, dropsy, slow or long fever, bilious and nervous fevers, dysentry and hoarse canker" and that in the ten years from 1792 to 1801, forty-eight out of 163 deaths had been "under two years of age, 22 from two to twenty years of age."[30]

Timothy Dwight methodically listed the dates of various epidemics in New Haven, including something called "Angina maligna" which was prevalent in 1736, 1742, 1773 and 1774 and always "extensively fatal." "In 1794," he said, "about 750 persons were affected by it, of whom 52 died." Dysentery frequently ravished the town in the autumn. Various "inflammatory fevers" often took many people at a time, while a 1794 yellow fever epidemic killed 64 out of the 160 ill. Typhus epidemics occurred often after 1805, while nine epidemics each of measles and influenza occurred between 1739 and 1802. In addition, the "most common" chronic diseases were "Dyspepsia, consumptions [lung disease], and affections of the liver."[31]

When an epidemic struck, women nursed neighbors and friends as well as their own families. In Middle Haddam in 1761:

> ...a large miry marsh...overflowed. The water became so putrid...it produced a sickness among the inhabitants for a mile or more about it...called, from its origin, *the pond fever*. Of this some died, and the inhabitants of the town were so alarmed that the authorities were under the necessity of pressing individuals [meaning women] to go and take care of the sick."[32]

Epidemics of yellow fever occurred in numerous seaport towns during the 1790s, as they did in New York and Philadelphia. In New London 100 died in 1798. David Field specified that it had been brought in 1796 "from the West Indies to Knowles's Landing," on the Connecticut River, where it killed eight people. Typhus fever had been "most malignant" in several Middlesex County towns, while "consumption is thought to be more common with us now than formerly."[33]

Mothers everywhere contended with what Pomfret's narrator called "the camp Distemper, & the Throat distemper, by this last, many of our Children & youth, have been taken away." This was probably diphtheria, like the "hoarse canker" above—in which the victim's throat became increasingly blocked until he or she choked to death. Mothers must have been devastated by such suffering, which frequently took several children at a time. In Lisbon, 38 percent of the deaths occurred among children under five. Most of the children "died of the obstructions common to infants, which have often occasioned convulsions," though two "died of rattles & several of...dysentary." Of the other fatal diseases which Lisbon's Andrew Lee cited, consumption took 46, dysentery 19, fevers 18, palsey 11, and smallpox 10. (Palsey was a frequent complication of liver disease.) There were also five accidents, including someone who died horribly of lock-jaw (tetanus poisoning) after stepping on a nail.[34]

Farmington's John Treadwell described a spotted fever epidemic, of which the victims were "more commonly, & more fatally, young women & little children, [and] women after parturition." It occurred from March 1808 to May 1809, claiming numerous deaths every month—95 out of 700 altogether: "The scene was awful, no tongue can tell the distress of the inhabitants, the well were hardly sufficient to take care of the sick, who from the nature of the disease required unremitted attendance, no help could be obtained from abroad, thro' fear of the dreadful malady." Treadwell's defensive explanation of the healing method—large doses of brandy, suggest to a modern reader that the "clamour" against such treatment may well have been justified. (Goshen lost only eight out of "two or three hundred" with spotted fever in the same year. Farmington's death rate was almost 14 percent versus Goshen's approximately 3 percent.) "The notion that the use of brandy carried off many by actual intoxication was idle, &, what is worse, pernicious," declared Treadwell.[35]

Probably some of the accusations, which Treadwell called "loud & senseless," came from women midwives and healers. In wealthier communities, their practice of traditional non-invasive medicine was being replaced by the theoretical, "educated" methods of elite male physicians, who often made things worse rather than better. In this case, Treadwell praises Doctors Eli Todd and Solomon Everest. Women's voices can be heard only between the lines.[36]

While progress brought changes in medical practice, it also brought change in people's social lives. Wallingford's George Stanley thought that "a great degree of equality prevails among the citizens" in comparison to "the state of manners previous to the Revolution, when the wealthy and influential families ...found an order of self-created nobility," though he deplored relaxed morals and "diminished respect for government." Like many other respondents, he noted "Amusements ... sought by the youth of both sexes, & by the females of mature years, in small & social afternoon & evening parties." But he huffily regretted their "frivolous & uninstructive" conversations.[37]

Canterbury had a similar clash of generations. Hezekiah Frost observed that many of the young who doubted "the truth of revelation, even sport with it where they durst" were those whose parents were "over noisy & zealous in religious worship, obstinatelly opposed to allmost every puerile amusement virtuous or vicious." Some church people had wanted a covenant "never to let their children dance or their houses be used for dancing. A prohibition but moderately attended to by any of them," he said. Farmington's Treadwell was convinced that the increase of consumptive disease in his town, especially among young girls "passing from childhood to puberty," was caused by "dancing assemblies protracted to one or two o'clock in the night, and the habit of undressing in public in the true Parisian mode"—certainly not the behavior of simple farmers' daughters.[38]

In prosperous enclaves like Farmington, Litchfield, Middletown, or New Haven, some luxury had begun to overwhelm the old simplicity. According to John Treadwell, Farmington's central settlement was more compact than most, which encouraged the "prevalence of a commercial spirit" detrimental to farmers. "Commerce where it prevails creates riches, riches introduce a taste for luxury in building, dress, furniture, equipage & which agriculture can never support; the farmer is thrown into the shade," jealous of "the powdered beau rowling in his carriage with horses richly caparisoned."[39]

Treadwell had just given a precisely detailed description (every costume designer should read it) of all the clothing—mostly home-made out of homespun cloth, which had once been part of men's "simple apparel, suited to their moderate circumstances & agricultural state." He noted that up until 30 years ago, women had dressed equally simply:

> They wore homemade drugget, crape plaincloth and camblet gowns in the winter and the exterior of the under-dress was a garment lined and quilted extending from the waist to the feet, their shoes were high heeled made of tanned calf skin & in some instances of cloth, in the summer they wore striped linnen and callico gowns, cloth shoes & linnen under dress; & every young lady when she had attained her stature was furnished with a silk gown and skirt if her parents were able, or she could purchase them by dint of labour; their head dress has always occupied a great share of their attention while in youth.... the elderly women have worn ch[eck] holland aprons to meeting on the Sabbath and those in early life, & of the best fashion were accustomed to ware them in their formal visits.[40]

"The same simplicity has been conspicuous in their diet, their houses & their furniture," Treadwell continued. They had no pleasure carriages or sleighs; instead women rode horseback "mounted on a pillion" behind a man to attend worship or "in short excursions ... & even to this day, this practice is not wholly laid aside." Farmington's "simplicity" would have been luxury to many a farmer's wife 100 years earlier in Madison, for example, where "the families settled at Hammonnasset, attended public worship for some time at Guilford; & women, it is said, often walked thither, 8 or 9 miles, on the sabbath."[41]

Farmington's growing luxury, where once "a single retailer of imported goods with a small capital sufficed for the town," was proved by the change in women's behavior:

> The young ladies are changing their spinning wheels for forte pianos, & forming their manners at the dancing school, rather than in the school of industry; of course the people are laying aside their plain apparrel manufactured in their houses, & clothing themselves with European & India fabrics; labour is growing into disrepute.... The present time marks a revolution of taste & of manners of immense import to society.[42]

In Ridgefield, "amusements commonly in vogue are Ball, Chess, Coits & dancing," except for "robbing orchards and gardens in the season of fruit . . . and other indulgence of fleshly appetites." But Litchfield, like Farmington, had become more sophisticated. Among the early settlers:

> ...amusements were of the athletic kind. When young people of both sexes assembled together for amusement, they employed themselves principally in dancing, while one of the company sung. The first use of the violin in this town for a dance, was in the year 1748. The whole expense...did not exceed one dollar; out of which the fiddler was paid...parents and old people exclaimed, that they should be ruined by the extravagance of the youth. [But] in the year 1798, a ball, with the customary entertainment and variety of music, cost about $160, and nothing was said about it.[43]

Another entirely different "amusement" had come upon the scene in towns all over Connecticut in the early nineteenth century. Emotional revival movements, a "second great awakening" as it was later called, swept through the churches and led to large numbers of conversions, especially among women. Town after town reported this (partly because ministers were writing the reports), and gave the years and numbers of converts. The statistics of Middlesex County's church membership reveal a preponderance of women members which had become typical of many towns; out of 2,061 members, 1,414 were women, only 647 men. It was the beginning of a process later dubbed "the feminization of religion" in America.[44]

Like the separation between public business and domestic hearths, the churches would increasingly represent the "spiritual" over against the secular in society. It became women's work to care about people's souls, about the poor and afflicted and neglected; men's work was to get ahead in the world, build bridges and businesses, make money, manage politics.

One fruit of the revivals was that women established charitable associations in almost every sizable town. They are reported from Haddam, East Haddam, Saybrook, Goshen, Norfolk, Middletown, New Haven and elsewhere. Middletown's first was "the Female Charitable Society, formed in 1809, whose special design [was] to provide for the education of the children of the poor, and to furnish clothing to the destitute." It was incorporated and "possessed $1,100 in bank stock," a considerable sum which also represented considerable power. A "Female Benevolent Society" was formed in 1816 to help educate "indigent pious young men for the ministry," and a "Middletown Sunday School society," formed in 1818, taught both religion and "the rudiments of learning" in three Sunday schools, including "one composed of blacks."[45]

Connecticut's African-Americans avidly sought such education in their own church groups as well, and then organized their own activist associations (though none were noted in the Town Reports). Middletown's Nancy Scott Beman (born ca. 1790), daughter of a well-known black minister, in 1834 founded Connecticut's Colored Female Anti-Slavery Society, the second women's abolition society in the United States. The first black woman abolitionist lecturer in America got her start in the Colored Congregational Church of Hartford. Maria Miller Stewart (born in 1803) moved to Boston and raised the eyebrows of male African-Americans by lecturing publicly in 1832-33. She opposed the colonization movement (to end slavery by sending blacks back to Africa) and called for black women to do the same as white women—organize themselves for education and action.[46]

New Haven had three Female charitable societies by 1811. Members paid "a cent a week" to join, and each society "has set up, and maintained for several years, a charity school for the education of poor female children." The two Presbyterian societies had established "a school for the education of black female children." They had also "distributed...clothes and other necessaries to the women and children in poor families."[47]

At a time when many towns were noting an increase in the number of poor, women were taking over a function that had once belonged to the whole community. They were also learning to function in organizations, in quasi-political fashion. And they were developing a concern for local blacks that would soon develop into an active anti-slavery movement throughout New England. By the 1830s women's organizations were primary supporters of abolitionist speakers and anti-slavery petitions. They also promoted libraries and education and women's rights. But they started small and with great piety. In Coventry, for example, Mrs. Sarah Hales left a donation in her will to establish a library for young clergymen. And in Goshen, "The only institution for a charitable purpose here is the female cent society," founded in 1808 with about 100 members, who each paid 50 cents per year to help educate "pious young men as candidates for the ministry."[48]

Farmers had big families, and land was limited for succeeding generations, especially since, as the Reports show, land prices were increasing in every Connecticut town. Furthermore, new lands to the westward, in New York State and the Ohio Valley, had opened to settlement following the Revolution. Emigration became a factor in every community, and almost every family. In Middlefield, in 1819, David Field noted that "Young enterprising men, trained to husbandry, unable to get farms in their native town, have removed from time to time to other parts of the country." As Lebanon's Elkanah Tisdale colorfully put it: "Emigration for more than 30 years has been so constant that it is judged that if all who have left the town who are still living & their descendants & the descendant[s] of those who are dead were to return they would treble the no. of inhabitants." Wallingford's George Washington Stanley (who eventually himself moved to Cleveland, Ohio) reported that in the 30 years before 1770 the number of emigrants equaled the number of inhabitants of the town and "since that time, the emigrations have at least equalled the natural encrease of population."[49]

Emigration's effect on women was multifaceted. Inevitably, some young women were left stranded in regard to marriage prospects. Preston's Levi Hart noted in 1801, "the disproportion of the Sexes, occasioned by the loss of many young men in the revolutionary war, & since that time by the numerous removals of single men to the new settlements render it necessary that many females should go through life in a single state."[50]

More and more "spinsters" had to find occupation and meaning for their lives in someone else's household rather than their own, for neither law nor custom allowed any woman to be on her own unless she were a widow, or the heir of a deceased father. Meanwhile, sisters or cousins or best friends might be among the emigrants. Several related families often emigrated together, leaving an inevitable void in the hearts of those left behind.

Time and again, local narrators name the emigrant families, and specify the destinations. For example, in the eastern Connecticut town of Franklin, there had been an out-migration of "about 60 families & about 50 young men" by 1800, while the emigration of young men from Pomfret to new lands meant "its much more difficult getting Help now than formerly." In Cheshire, "in the year 1774, 100 persons removed out of the town of all ages." Canterbury's "great" emigrations had been principally "to Vermont." Durham's population had little increase in population for many years because "individuals and families have removed almost perpetually to other places." Some had gone to Granville, Massachusetts in 1750, to Sandersfield in 1765, to West Stockbridge in 1786, to Durham, N.Y. in 1788, to Whitestown, N.Y. in 1796, and most recently "to New Connecticut" (the western reserve in northern Ohio). Other Middlesex County emigrants went first to Litchfield, then western Massachusetts, then New Hampshire and Vermont, and most recently, "to New York, and to the Western States and Territories." From East Windsor, "about 20 families migrate annually, principally into the State of New York; some to NW Connecticut."[51]

The conditions faced by such emigrants to western New York or northern New England replicated those of their parents or grandparents on the farms of Connecticut. Sharon, like many other towns in northwestern Connecticut, was originally founded by settlers from other Connecticut towns, especially eastern

Connecticut, when the state lands were auctioned off in the mid-eighteenth century. Sixty families from Lebanon and Colchester settled there just before the extraordinarily cold and snowy winter of 1740-41. Their sufferings were great, as were those of neighboring Cornwall's new residents, especially because of lack of food, which had to be brought in from as far as 60 miles away. Of these intrepid families, "Zephaniah Hough's Wife was the first Inhabitant who Died in Cornwall in the summer 1740." Three other women gave birth in March, May, and October of 1740, so they were pregnant when they moved into the wilderness, and new mothers during the terrible next winter. Women who moved and women who stayed behind, in any year of emigration, were well aware of the dangers and griefs being faced by relatives and friends. Their lives were neither secure nor easy.[52]

But optimism prevailed and gave Connecticut women far-flung connections to the nation's development, best expressed perhaps by Farmington's reporter. He specified that 147 families had emigrated "between August 1783 and March 1802." He estimated "five to a familly, will make the whole number 735," besides about 40 more "young unmarried persons of both sexes." According to the Report, they had gone "into the States of New York and Vermont, the some few to different parts of the North Western teritory. —It is hoped and believed that these emigrants had generally formed so strong a predelicton for the customs, habits, and manners of their parent town and state, that they will be eminently instrumental in training up a race of citizens friendly to morals, order, and good government."[53]

Education was increasingly important for women expected to carry such heavy responsibilities. With greater separation of home and workplace, women took on more intensive child-rearing functions; boys who would grow up to be voters required intelligent, informed mothers, it was said. After the Revolution, both men and women began to insist on expanded schooling for women, beyond the rudimentary reading, writing and arithmetic taught in local one-room schools in every New England town.[54]

Of course, women were already teachers in many of those schools. Bright girls had always continued to read and study informally, and teaching was one of the few jobs that a woman could hold without losing her dignity.[55] Every town in the state listed its numbers of schools and pupils in local districts. Almost without exception, men taught the winter sessions and women the summer. This meant that men taught the older boys and some girls, while younger children attended in the summer when their older siblings had to work. Women were paid less than half of what men earned—a factor which would, later in the century, provide the rationale for turning most of the teaching profession over to women.

Middlesex County numbered 112 district schools, all one-room except for one in Saybrook and two in Middletown that had two rooms each. In 1815, the pupils numbered 5,983, "instructed by men in the winter season. . . generally by women in the summer; by both from six to ten and eleven months annually." The number of pupils in each schoolroom varied from 20 to 90, though all of them did not attend all the time. The men were paid "ten to twenty dollars per month," the women "from seventy-five cents to one and two dollars per week." In

addition to reading, writing, and arithmetic, men sometimes taught "grammar, geography, and ... other branches of science." Though it used to be difficult to obtain enough books, now "the only serious difficulty in the way of obtaining qualified instructors lies in the unwillingness of districts to give the requisite wages." There were, in addition, some "subscription schools," taught in people's homes, while "the clergy also instruct youth in the branches commonly taught in academies."[56]

The same conditions were found throughout the state, the only differences being the pay. In Wallingford's nine district schools, winter male instructors were paid "15 to 18 dollars pr month including board," while female instructors got "One dollar pr week exclusive of their board." In Goshen teachers received "from 1.25 to 1.50 cents a week in summer, and from 9 to 14 dollars a month in winter." But in Union "There is about 4 months schooling in winter & 3 in summer...& about 200 scholler in winter & 100 in summer & the wages of male teachers from 9 to 12 dollars per month & for female teachers in summer from 4 to 6." In Winchester, five schools served 150 scholars during the winter term from "November...'til March or April." Summer schools "begin in May & continue 'til September or October." Male teachers were paid "from twelve to fifteen dollars per month and his board, and a female from one Dollar to one dollar and fifty cents and her board per week." Winter instructors were obliged to have "a certificate under our law, approving him to teach" and to have "good moral character" and knowledge skills. There was also "one other school for small children, independent of the district schools, in which from fifteen to twenty are usually convened ...kept by an instructress...in a part of a dwelling house...for several years." This was because of "the largeness of the districts, which renders some neighbourhoods too remote from the District school house, for small children to attend."[57]

Cornwall's Elijah Allen wrote warmly of "The Ladies'... good proficiency in Literature, some of whom have Taught Schools in this Town to the satisfaction of their constituents and...have Received the Plaudit and Thanks of the Visiting Committee and other good Judges." There were eight school districts, with schools "kept by Teachers competently Learned and of good Morals." Men were paid "15 to 20 Dollars per Month in the Winter Season; & in the Summer Season when the School is Taught by a well instructed Young Lady, the expence is commonly about 8 Dollars per Month."[58]

Farmington had only three school districts, but John Treadwell claimed a "discernible superiority" in the middle district school which was taught by a man both winter and summer. He detailed the instruction, noting especially that the school committee had "discontinued all attempts at public speaking in declamations, dialogues, & theatrical representations, as not suited to the years of the scholars... to raise them in their own views into men & women before their time, & like hot-beds to force a premature growth for ignorance & folly to stare at. They have preferred the useful to the ornamental," and methods had changed from the rote and "monotonies" of the past.[59]

Aside from the district schools, there were Academies in many towns. Most had been established to prepare boys who would go on to college and the ministry. Despite its rural location, Lebanon in 1800 had "a large brick school house in which...a school has been constantly kept many years (say 70 or 80) by instructors well skilled in the learned languages, & where scholars have been taught from the greater part of the States in the union."[60]

But more and more girls were getting advanced education, either in their own towns or by boarding out in order to attend an academy further away. Although there were no academies at all in Middlesex County, nearby New Haven more than made up the difference. There, in addition to the fifteen public and six private elementary schools enumerated in 1801, and Hopkins Grammar School (an academy for boys which had been endowed by the first governor of Connecticut), there were two secondary schools, the Union School founded in 1801 and the New Township Academy founded in 1809. Each had "two departments, one for males, the other for females." A new female academy "established by the Rev. Mr. Herrick," said Timothy Dwight, was "one of the best schools of this nature in the United States." Its instruction was "calculated to expand the mind, and amend the heart, with sound wisdom," so that girls could be "withdrawn from that frivolity, and those trifles, which unhappily are too often made significant parts of female education." These "young females" were "habitually allured to sober thought, useful knowledge, and the best principles." None of them were eligible to attend New Haven's Yale College, of course, but at least they were getting an intellectual foundation that would qualify them to be worthy wives of professional men.[61]

New Haven's teachers were paid much better than others. Men got $25 a month, while women were paid by the week and by the number of scholars, at 8 1/2 cents each. But, in contrast to other towns, seventeen out of the twenty-one city schools were taught by women regardless of the season. In New London a "great publick school, the grammar school, & female academy are kept through the year" half of them staffed by "female instructors." Boarding students paid from $1.50 to $3 per week.[62]

Winchester was proud of its "Proprietors school house" separate from the district schools, which had "two schools, one for young misses, who are taught the rudiments of literature by a female, and one for pupils of both sexes" with a male teacher who "taught the Latin & Greek languages, Arithmetic, Surveying, when required, Geography, Rhetoric and English grammer." Wallingford opened Union Academy in 1809, with a "convenient & handsome building" erected in 1810. With "one male instructor who employs a female assistant" the school had seventy-five to one hundred pupils who were taught "Reading, writing & common Needlework @ 21 Cents pr week—Arithmetic English grammar & Geography @ 25 Cents—Composition the higher branches of needlework, Drawing, Painting, Latin & Greek languages, Logic & Moral philosophy at 33 1/2 Cents," according to the school's advertisement. Students paid board of $1.50 per week. Cornwall's Academy, held in the South Meeting House since 1797 "with excellent good Collegian Instructors," taught "Reading, Writing, Arithmetick, Surveying, Navigation, English Grammar, Geography, History and the Learned Languages." The school included both "Young Gentlemen" who "paid $1.17 per Week for Board...and Ladies one Dollar each week for Board." They also paid fees for each subject studied.[63]

One of the earliest academies for women in Connecticut, and in the United States, was the Litchfield Ladies' Academy, founded by Miss Pierce in 1792. James Morris said in 1815, that it "has very justly merited, and acquired, a distinguished reputation." This was the school attended by Catharine Beecher and her sister, Harriet—both later to become famous throughout the country, Catharine as an educator and Harriet Beecher Stowe as a writer. Like Tapping Reeve's nearby Law School, it drew students from all over the country, many of whom became prominent citizens. There was also an Academy founded in 1790 for both sexes in the South Farms section of Litchfield, which sent "more than 60" of its students on to Yale and other colleges. "It was originally instituted for the purpose of improving the manners and morals of youths, and of attracting their attention from frivolity and dissipation."[64]

There were other informal institutions of learning for women in Connecticut, though rarely were they considered significant by men. The "amusements" of "females of mature years" in their afternoon gatherings, which Wallingford's correspondent considered "frivolous & uninstructive," included sewing circles and study groups where women discussed current events, child-rearing methods, history and theology. Such groups had origins in the Revolutionary era when women organized spinning bees and carried out boycotts of British tea and textiles.[65]

A ladies group in Hartford, calling itself "The Oeconomical Association," started with 100 members and expanded to "a majority of other ladies," as reported by the Hartford Courant on November 6, 1786. They launched a boycott of "ornaments and superfluities" and called for "strict attention to domestic economy and frugality" as "a duty they owe their country" while the nation was developing its new policies. Their statement, reprinted in the American Museum, or Repository, a national magazine, was influential far beyond Connecticut.[66]

Women certainly read many other writings in that magazine, as well as in The Lady's Magazine and Repository of Entertaining Knowledge, whose first issue in 1792 featured an engraving about women's rights. That magazine also serialized Mary Wollstonecraft's Vindication of the Rights of Women. We know that at least one Connecticut woman read and discussed Wollstonecraft's ideas with energy because her copy of the book, with expressive marginal comments, is in the Connecticut Historical Society Library. The poems of Connecticut's first published woman writer, Martha Brewster of Lebanon, as early as 1757 told women to value "increase in Learning" and "delight in Reading." Essays about women's rights, like those of Judith Sargent Murray in Massachusetts Magazine, circulated widely among Connecticut women readers, echoed, for example, by the letter of "Female Advocate" in an 1801 New Haven newspaper. She argued that it was insulting to value women only for their "beauty and gaity" rather than for their learning and skills.[67]

Nor was it only city women who sought self-recognition and self-improvement. As early as 1790, thirty-nine women of the Chelsea Congregational Church in Norwich established a "sisterly covenant" for prayer meetings and then expanded into a Ladies' Literary Society for "promoting useful Knowledge among our Sex." Within a few years they concluded that "We I mean females are of importance in the scale of beings—let us then enquire what we can do toward securing those rights & priviledges we have so nobly gained."[68]

But none of these endeavors are mentioned in the Town Reports. Nor are there even many women mentioned by name. Some authors singled out certain ministers' wives, but only a few women rated more than passing remarks. Those few, however, are representative of many others in Connecticut's history.

Two of the women mentioned were Indians. Levi Clark provided a copy of the original deed of sale for Haddam township in 1662, signed by five Indians, of whom two were women: "Sepunnomoe Subscribes in the behalfe of her and her child," and "Towkishke...in behalfe of her selfe and children." Both drew their own very distinctive "markes" as signatures. These women each received ten coats in exchange, as did two of the men. Perhaps they were acting under duress; Chief Uncas also signed and may have insisted that they follow his lead. Or perhaps it seemed a good deal at the time, because the Indians had kept "free Liberty to hunt and fish and our other Royalty in the aforesaid land." In reality, of course, they were signing away their old way of life for an entirely new culture that had no room for them.[69]

Another woman mentioned, and one who also lost her freedom, lived in Durham. One can only guess at the transformations in her life, and what kind of physical and psychological strength enabled her to live to "the age of 113 years, or, as some supposed, 118. She was grown up before she was brought from Africa, and was a slave in this country ninety-five years."[70]

Here and there in the Town Reports are a very few women who committed suicide or infanticide or went out of their minds over the previous 200 years. Destitute widows sometimes ended up in a poorhouse or as dependents upon others who were paid by the town to take them in. But one "state pauper" who lived in Goshen had a unique story. She was described as: "a woman who was in early life taken by the Indians and condemned to die; but, possessing in an eminent degree the art of tormenting, the Indians resolved to release her, (to use their own words) 'that she might plague white folks.'"[71] How this woman was able to torment even her Indian captors in order to get her own way tantalizes the imagination.

In East Windsor, David McClure respectfully cited the ten daughters of the town's first minister, Timothy Edwards. Long before the Revolution, or the establishment of female academies, they and their mother, Esther Stoddard Edwards, had "a great reputation, in their day, for good sense, virtue and female accomplishments." Their house "was the seat of religion and urbanity, of 'white robed innocence' and the graces. Young ladies from abroad resorted thither, to be instructed in the useful and ornamental accomplishments of the sex." It was an early, informal, female academy or women's study group, which apparently also had a profound effect on the development of their only brother, the renowned theologian and educator Jonathan Edwards. The meetings included readings from the Bible and other books, commentary from Esther Edwards herself, and a decidedly un-frivolous discussion among the women of all ages who regularly attended.[72]

Ultimately, one must note a housewife from Cornwall whose experience was typical of many among Connecticut's "founding mothers." Elijah Allen's flowery rhetoric about male superiority and protection serves only to highlight the difference between women's actual behavior and male assumptions about them at the beginning of the nineteenth century:

> A Mrs. Griffis, Wife of Mr. Thomas Griffis, went to a den of these Poisonous Reptiles [Rattlesnakes] not far from their House sundry Times and, with an Unshaken and firm display of Heroism and Fortitude uncommon to the Tender and Amiable Diffedence, which so highly Recommends the Fair Sex to the Protecting Care and Complaisant Friendship and Regard of all Gentlemen of Really Magnanimous and good deportment, and at the Mouth of the Den and near thereto Attacked and killed large Numbers of Rattle-Snakes without being bitten by them.[73]

Women like Mrs. Griffis did whatever had to be done, with or without the "protecting care" of gentlemen friends.

In summary, in Connecticut two hundred years ago, more and more women were getting an academy education, fitting them to become intellectual equals of men, though this was still justified only in terms of supporting future husbands and sons as voters and citizens. In cities and larger towns, increasing wealth was making it possible for some women to have leisure for balls, piano lessons, pleasure carriages, and other "frivolous" pursuits. But women were also asserting their own equality, forming charitable aid societies, and participating in a religious revival movement that would gradually "feminize" American Protestantism and lay the foundations of major reform movements.

At the dawn of Connecticut's industrial age women were producing half of the value of all exports and at least half of every family's subsistence, mainly by making cloth and clothing and through vegetable, butter and cheese production. Other women were beginning to lose their home-based economic independence by working for wages in male-owned mills, though it would take another generation for this to be a significant part of the Connecticut scene. Women were providing a major portion of early education to all children, for which they were generally paid only half the salary of men teachers. Women were also providing most of the medical care for a variety of illnesses and not-infrequent epidemics, plus carrying the emotional burden of losing almost half their children as babies or small children. Their many other offspring were major actors in America's westward expansion, thus contributing widely to national development.

Whether or not nineteenth century scholars recognized the significance of women in their society, women themselves knew what they could do, and did it. American history is the richer because they did.

Disease and Medicine in Connecticut Around 1800

Toby A. Appel

The Academy's Query About Disease

In 1799, Noah Webster, Connecticut lexicographer and founding member of the Connecticut Academy of Arts and Sciences, published in Hartford *A Brief History of Epidemic and Pestilential Diseases.* In two lengthy volumes, Webster surveyed epidemics from the Bible to 1799 as well as available mortality data in order to demonstrate that pestilences such as the bubonic plague in Europe and the yellow fever in the United States were not "contagious" and "imported" but rather originated from environmental changes in the atmosphere.[1]

The issue of whether certain epidemic diseases were contagious was heatedly debated in the eighteenth century. This was especially so in the case of the yellow fever that attacked port cities in the northeast in the 1790s including New Haven and New London. The model of a "contagious" disease was smallpox, a disease that clearly spread directly from person to person and might even be communicated by inanimate objects, although what actually was communicated was unknown. Webster wrote:

> That quality of a disease which communicates it
> from a sick to a well person, on simply inhaling
> the breath or effluvia from the person of the
> diseased, at any time and in any place, may be
> called *specific contagion.* Such is the contagion
> of the small-pox and the measles, which are
> therefore called contagious diseases.[2]

Contagious diseases could be imported. That is, someone afflicted with the disease could enter a town by sea or land and start an epidemic. The appropriate response to an imported, contagious disease was to enact legislation to quarantine ships, bar newcomers to town, and isolate the sick. Such measures, which severely hampered commerce, were highly controversial.

Since bacteria, viruses, disease vectors such as rats and mosquitoes, and the role played by human carriers were not understood, other diseases presented a much more confusing picture. Plague and yellow fever did not seem to spread directly from one person to another. As Webster pointed out, caretakers of disease victims often did not themselves succumb to the disease. These diseases were moreover associated with certain seasons of the year. Everyone knew the yellow fever epidemic would subside after the first frost. Some physicians agreed with Webster that yellow fever was "domestic," while others were equally certain that yellow fever was imported. Eneas Munson, a prominent New Haven physician, and his

son Elijah, reporting on the New Haven epidemic of 1794 in response to an earlier request by Webster for data on yellow fever, argued that yellow fever was an imported contagion because it always arose in seaport towns near wharves, docks, and warehouses, but never inland.[3] If diseases such as yellow fever were of domestic origin, the appropriate response, in Webster's view, was to improve personal hygiene and enact laws to ameliorate environmental dangers:

> If they can be convinced of this, that sources of
> disease and death may be found among
> themselves created by their own negligence, it is
> a great point gained; for until they learn this they
> will never attend to the means of preserving life
> and health. They will still wallow in filth, croud
> their cities with low dirty houses and narrow
> streets; neglect the use of bathing and washing;
> and live like savages, devouring, in hot seasons,
> undue quantities of animal food at their tables,
> and reeling home after midnight debauches.[4]

The polarized and highly politicized debates throughout the Northeast over the origin of the yellow fever and the proper measures to prevent and treat it, led Webster, a strong nationalist and humanitarian, to enter the fray. Though not a physician, Webster felt he could contribute because resolving the issue depended more on historical analysis than on medical skill.[5] For an earlier book on yellow fever, he had sent in 1795 a circular letter to physicians in New York, Boston, Philadelphia, Norfolk, and New Haven, as well as elsewhere, to seek more recent data.[6] A few years later, in 1798, he sent another circular letter to ministers in Connecticut towns asking for statistical data on "the arts, agriculture, manufactures, and improvements of every kind," including:

> State of health—climate and diseases—Bills of
> mortality, comprehending the ages and diseases,
> when it can be done—The years when
> remarkable sickness has prevailed, and diseases
> —Instances of longevity[7]

Webster's treatise was the most comprehensive and boldest of a number of efforts by physicians and laymen in the eighteenth century to investigate disease and climate by means of statistics. For a definitive understanding of the issues raised in his volumes, Webster realized that a great deal more statistical information was needed. He believed that the fledgling scientific and medical societies in the nation could assist in obtaining those data.[8] As a founding member of the Connecticut Academy of Arts and Sciences, Webster no doubt had a hand in drawing up the questionnaire to be sent to ministers or officials in Connecticut towns. In the Academy's questionnaire, Webster's earlier queries about health and disease were greatly amplified. Thus, the first part of the question concerning disease in relation to the environment was worded:

> 29th [Article]. Climate and Diseases; variations in seasons and in diseases from clearing lands, draining swamps and the like causes; the diseases most prevalent in high and low situations, near streams of running water, or marsh and stagnant water, on the north and south sides of hills and mountains, and on different soils.

In his *Brief History*, Webster contended that pestilences arrived in constellations, presaged by unusual natural occurrences such as severe climate changes or deaths of large numbers of animals or insects. His subtitle proclaimed that his chronology of epidemics would be examined in the context of "the Principal Phenomena of the Physical World, Which Precede and Accompany Them." Thus, in accord with Webster's interests, the next part of the Academy's 29th Article asked for "remarkable instances of diseases and mortality among animals of various kinds." The following two Articles, 30 and 31, inquired about "remarkable seasons or occurrences in the natural world; as tempest, rain, hail, snow, and inundations by which injury has been sustained, the time when they happened; unusual insects, or usual insects in unusual numbers; time of their appearance and disappearance; ...unusual death of insects....unusual failure of crops from causes known or unknown, and the years when it occurred, and the temperature of the seasons..." It was important to collect such environmental facts because abrupt changes in the natural order, according to Webster and many others, could correlate with or serve as portents of periods of pestilence.

Which individuals succumbed to disease, Webster and others believed, was affected by a combination of environment and of the person's temperament and lifestyle. Thus, the Academy also sought data concerning mortality, which might shed light not only on the origin of epidemics but also on the habits of those most susceptible and those most resistant to disease. The remainder of Article 29 asked for "Register of marriages, births and deaths, noting the sex, occupations, ages and diseases of those who die. Remarkable instances of longevity; the local situation—the occupation and habits of life of those who arrive at great age, as also their temper, whether cheerful or melancholic, quiet or discontented."[9] Needless to say, this tall order for numerical data could not be met; the information was simply unavailable. Respondents could supply only a partial and very general reply to the queries.

Epidemic Diseases in Connecticut

The recipients of the Academy's Solicitation letter were primarily ministers, not physicians. Only one part of a single Town Report (Goshen) was written by a physician, Elisha North. But ministers were, in fact, the best placed individuals to respond to the questions asked. As educated men, they were quite knowledgeable about the overall state of health in their congregations and communities. There was much less distinction in the eighteenth century than there was to be later between lay and medical knowledge. Ministers were familiar with some of the same medical books as physicians (authorities such as William Cullen in Edinburgh or Benjamin Rush in Philadelphia or the first medical journal in the United States, the *Medical Repository*, begun in New York in 1797) as well as the wealth of popular medical literature that circulated in the new nation. Ministers, rather than physicians or town officials, were most likely to keep records of the health of their communities (see below).

As boosters for the towns, ministers and other authors of Town Reports were unlikely to claim their town was other than healthy. "Healthy," for the respondents to the question, had a specific meaning. If no diseases were always associated with the town, then, despite the ravages of epidemics from time to time, a town might be declared healthy. Most people believed that high and dry places with good air circulation were healthier than low, marshy areas with still air and water. The author of the Tolland Report wrote, for example, "The air is healthful,—the Land being mostly *high*, & free from stagnant water—excepting a marshy spot, not far from the Centre of the Town." All respondents agreed that swamps were unhealthy, although their association with disease-bearing mosquitoes was not suspected. In several of the Town Reports, respondents told stories of dramatic improvements in health when marshy areas were drained or flooded.[10]

Most of the authors of the Town Reports recalled the various epidemics of infectious disease that wreaked havoc in Connecticut towns in the eighteenth century and created sharp peaks in the town's annual death tolls. At an earlier era, in the first part of the eighteenth century, New England ministers were likely to view the onset of epidemics as a portent from the Creator that the town's population was ignoring their spiritual duties. In the Bethlem (Bethlehem) Town Report, the current minister, Azel Backus, inserted a description of earlier epidemics by the town's founding minister, Joseph Bellamy. Bellamy accounted for an epidemic of typhoid fever in 1750 in religious terms: "In the spring, the anger of the Lord began to burn hot against this people for all their abominations, and he sent a destroying angel among them, who slew about 30 of them and filled the place with the greatest distress. A long slow nervous fever, very malignant spread and prevailed 4 or 5 months."[11] By the time of the writing of the Town Reports, ministers viewed epidemics as predominantly natural occurrences, not as direct results of sinfulness. Ministers, physicians, and learned men in general sought to classify and understand them but had little control over most of them.

Interpreting the various pestilences described in the Town Reports is problematic for it is often difficult to translate eighteenth-century disease terms into twentieth-century equivalents. Eighteenth-century diseases were named according to observable symptoms, not according to bacterial or viral causes or the underlying pathology. "Fever" and "convulsions" were diseases in themselves, rather than symptoms that might be associated with a number of current disease entities. On one hand, many names for what is now considered the same disease appear in the reports, while on the other, the designations do not distinguish between currently accepted diseases. Typhus and typhoid fever were not differentiated, nor were diphtheria, scarlet fever and scarlatina. To complicate matters further, eighteenth-century physicians and laypersons generally believed that diseases were not distinct entities, but instead that they shaded or transmuted into one another according to the season of the year, topography and climate, and the presence of other diseases. Each region of the country was said to have different forms and patterns of diseases.[12]

The accounts of epidemic diseases in the Town Reports go back to roughly 1725, within the memory of living townspeople. At the time of the Town Reports, the native American populations in Connecticut had long since been decimated by disease, especially smallpox. Since that occurred before the personal memory of the respondents, they had little to say of it.[13] Several of the major scourges of the eighteenth century and first decade of the nineteenth century will be discussed here.

Diphtheria, scarlet fever, and scarlatina were recurrent diseases of children that eighteenth-century physicians could not clearly distinguish. They are

Noah Webster (1753-1843), Connecticut lexicographer and founding member of the Connecticut Academy of Arts and Sciences, published A Brief History of Epidemic and Pestilential Diseases *in 1799.*

described under many names in the Town Reports including throat distemper, cynanche maligna, angina maligna, infantile cynanche trachealis, canker, cankerous sore throat, and rattles. The most devastating epidemic in Connecticut, diagnosed in retrospect as diphtheria, took place in 1736, and was mentioned in the Farmington and New Haven Reports. It has been estimated that 1,000 residents of Connecticut, almost all young children, died. The Bethlem, Guilford and New Haven Reports note a severe epidemic of what was probably scarlet fever in 1793-1794. Timothy Dwight reported that some 700 people were infected in New Haven in 1794, of which 52 died.[14]

Smallpox, understood by everyone to be contagious, was a frequent visitor that especially attacked children. The Wallingford Report noted an epidemic as far back as 1732 in which there were 124 cases and 17 deaths.[15] Smallpox was one of the few epidemic diseases for which a method of control existed. It was known that once a person had smallpox, he/she was immune to further attacks. Variolation or inoculation,

a procedure for securing immunity adapted from Asian folk practice, was introduced into America during the Boston smallpox epidemic in 1721. It consisted of inserting a small amount of smallpox matter from a pustule of a smallpox victim under the skin of a person who had not yet had smallpox. If all went well, the person would have a very mild case and henceforth acquire immunity from the scourge. However, the procedure could sometimes confer a fatal case of smallpox or other infection found in the septic inoculated matter. Moreover, the newly inoculated person could spread malignant smallpox to others.[16] The state and the individual towns therefore attempted to regulate inoculation, including banning the practice outright. By the 1780s, a number of physicians had obtained permission from their towns to set up inoculation hospitals, or pesthouses, on the edge of town where those who were inoculated would remain until they could no longer communicate the disease.[17] Inoculation became quite popular among those who could afford it, but it remained a dangerous procedure. Samuel Goodrich wrote in the Ridgefield Town Report, "the smallpox has become familiar and has in a great measure lost its terrors since the practice of inoculation which has been generally adopted by allmost all the inhabitants; 3 or 400 have had it in a season, out of which number from 1 to 2 have died."[18] The Reverend David Dudley Field, author of the Guilford Report, recalled, "In 1795, nine died of the small pox taken in the natural way from persons who had left the pesthouse in Haddam imperfectly cleaned."[19]

In 1800, vaccination, the discovery of English physician Edward Jenner in 1798, began to replace inoculation in Connecticut. Patients were vaccinated with matter from pustules of those infected with cowpox, a disease of cattle that could be communicated to humans. Cowpox or kinepox vaccination, Jenner discovered, produced a relatively harmless reaction and conferred immunity to smallpox with the advantage that those vaccinated could not infect others with smallpox. Although not the first to vaccinate in Connecticut, Dr. Elisha North, who wrote part of the Goshen Town Report, became the state's most vocal advocate of the new procedure. Despite vaccination's obvious significance, there is no reference to it in the Town Reports, except for North's claim of having found a case of natural cowpox in Connecticut and thus a fresh source for vaccine. "A man by the name of Ives, who was an inhabitant of this town, is probably the first person *ever known* to have the casual cow pox within the United States," North wrote.[20] For most of the nineteenth century vaccine matter was transmitted "arm to arm." That is, the vaccine matter was obtained not from a cow, but taken from a ripe pustule of a recently vaccinated person. Although large numbers of Connecticut residents were vaccinated — Dr. Samuel Cooley, for example, claimed that he had vaccinated some 1,600 persons in the New London area between 1801 and April 1803[21] — vaccination in the nineteenth century was neither universally accepted nor safe, and thus smallpox remained a health problem in Connecticut.

Typhoid fever, a water-borne disease, appeared in many of the Town Reports, under the names typhus (typhoid fever was not yet distinguished from typhus), long fever, slow fever, nervous fever, and possibly, putrid fever. The Farmington Report noted a severe epidemic around 1730 of "a fever often attended with putrid simptoms & delirium, commonly called the long fever; it was protracted from twenty to sixty days before it made a crisis. This fever prevailed here, at that period, three autumns successively, and many fell prey to it, & those who did not, held their lives in long suspense, & recovered by slow degrees." The Bethlem, Lebanon, and Litchfield County Town Reports noted epidemics in the 1750s. In the first parish of Washington in Litchfield County in 1753, for example, "a putrid fever prevailed in this parish, of which about 30 persons died in the space of six months." New Haven reported an epidemic in 1805 and Elisha North noted recurrences in Goshen in 1798, 1805, and 1808. North believed typhus to be of imported origin and "evidently contagious." In particular, he attributed the 1798 epidemic to a person coming to town from New York. "The disease spread from this person until 20 were infected, of whom five died."[22]

Dysentery, or inflammation of the intestine producing severe diarrhea, was a serious and recurring problem frequently mentioned in the Reports. Like typhoid fever, it could be communicated through contaminated water or food. It visited Connecticut towns a number of years, but was particularly severe and widespread just before and during the early years of the Revolutionary War, according to the Town Reports. Two hundred residents of Litchfield died of it in 1776-1777, "the greatest mortality ever known" in the town, although about thirty of this number actually died in New York as prisoners of war. Farmington reported a death toll of sixty-one in the first parish in 1776, a large proportion of it due to the dysentery. Dysentery was regarded as a seasonal disease, referred to by Timothy Dwight as "the most prevalent autumnal disease." Three Town Reports — Lisbon (Hanover), New Haven, and Wintonbury (Bloomfield)—noted another serious epidemic of dysentery in 1795.[23]

Malaria, now attributed to a plasmodium transmitted by the bite of the Anopheles mosquito, was associated in the eighteenth century with low, marshy areas, and known to be seasonal. It was called the (burning) ague, or remittent or intermittent fever. Andrew Lee of the Hanover parish of Lisbon recalled an epidemic in about 1725 that "broke out in the South part of the town, near a large pond, which had been damed, (I suppose with a view to help in distroying the trees & bushes) & spread for five or six miles around—It proved very mortal carrying off one third part of the adult inhabitants—It was thought to be highly contagious—After the pond was drained the disorder ceased." [24] Elkanah Tisdale noted in the Lebanon

Report, "Formerly intermittent fevers were more frequent than since the clearing of the land & draining of the swamps. About the year 1753, intermittents & the burning ague were very prevalent; but not mortal. The principal dependance for cure was on bark."[25] The "bark"— also called Jesuits, Peruvian, or chincona bark, later discovered to contain quinine, was one of the few effective remedies in the arsenal of the eighteenth-century physician. Although valuable for treatment of malaria, it was also used for a host of other illnesses with less certain results.

In comparison to the thousands of yellow fever deaths in Philadelphia and New York in the 1790s, Connecticut's yellow fever epidemics were modest, but they were terrifying nonetheless. Residents and their physicians fled seaport homes for the interior of the state, quarantines of people and ships were instituted, and public health measures were hastily enacted. The port cities of New Haven and New London suffered the greatest losses. Of 160 stricken in New Haven from June to November 1794, there were 64 deaths. Elijah Munson, New Haven physician, and son of Eneas Munson, who published an account of the epidemic, was convinced yellow fever in the United States has "always been imported from abroad." "No person had the Yellow Fever," he claimed, "unless in consequence of attending the sick, or of being exposed by nurses, infected houses, clothing, or furniture."[26] In New London in 1798, more than 100 succumbed, according to the unnamed New London respondent. Two-thirds of the inhabitants including four of New London's seven practitioners were said to have fled the city, and two more were themselves confined with the yellow fever, leaving the young Dr. Samuel H.P. Lee to care for the victims. In contrast to the Munsons, the New London Report author declared: "The prevailing opinion is that its origin was domestick." Two other contemporary accounts of the New London epidemic, by the Reverend Henry Channing and Dr. Thomas Coit, agreed. The fact that the epidemic began near the docks and that nearly all of the approximately 246 cases could be traced to this area, suggested not contagion, but rather that decaying matter, perhaps a large quantity of dried fish known to be present, was the cause.[27]

"Spotted fever," now thought to be epidemic spinal meningitis, was the most recent new pestilence to appear in the Town Reports. A fearsome disease with a rapid course and a high mortality, spotted fever first arrived in Connecticut in 1807-1808. John Treadwell, in the Farmington Town Report, included an extended discussion of the epidemic, which affected some 700 people in the town and led to some seventy deaths: "The scene was awful, no tongue can tell the distress of the inhabitants, the well were hardly sufficient to take care of the sick, who from the nature of the disease required unremitted attendance, no help could be obtained from abroad, thro' fear of the dreadful malady; the panic was so widely extended that for many months the roads were unoccupied; but here & there a solitary traveller to be seen with handkerchief at the nose, flying as for life to avoid the contagion."[28] Physician Elisha North reported between 200-300 cases in Goshen in 1808-1809, but only eight deaths. He believed the disease not to be contagious. North's 1811 monograph, *A Treatise on a Malignant Epidemic Commonly called Spotted Fever; Interspersed with Remarks on the Nature of Fever in General, &c.*, mentioned in the Goshen Report, was the first ever written on spinal meningitis, and one of the earliest American monographs on any disease.[29]

Other epidemic scourges of eighteenth-century Connecticut found in the Town Reports include measles, which was considered contagious but not often fatal; pleurisy and pneumonia, which were hard to distinguish; influenza; and worm infestation, affecting predominantly children.[30]

One recurring generalization appearing in the Town Reports was that the nature of diseases had changed in recent years from a preponderance of "inflammatory" diseases to more "bilious," typhus, or "putrid" diseases. As John Treadwell, author of the Farmington Report, put it: "The great variation which is remarkable, in the period mentioned [1729-ca. 1812], is the decrease of diseases highly inflammatory & the increase of such as are occasioned by the disordered state of the bile. The inquisitive will probably look for the causes of this in the variation of climate & habits of living." Medical authors attempted to classify diseases in a hierarchical system similar to that of Linnaeus for plants and animals. A popular classification of "fevers" divided them into "inflammatory fevers" such as pneumonia, in which the pulse was strong, and "typhus," in which the pulse was weaker and the patient more debilitated. The "typhus" class included typhoid fever, yellow fever, and spotted fever, among others, that is, the most recent epidemic diseases.[31]

Ministers as Collectors of Vital Data

Azel Backus, Congregational minister of Bethlem, reported that soon after his ordination in 1791, his friend, Wethersfield physician Elihu Hubbard Smith asked him to "keep a particular record of the sex, age, and disease of all who would die in my parish." Smith, who moved to New York in 1793, planned to use the data in an article in the *Medical Repository*, of which he was one of the founding editors.[32] Although records of births and deaths were by law to be collected by the town clerks in Connecticut, in practice, ministers, officiating at baptisms, weddings, and funerals, and having an overview of the inhabitants of their congregation (Society), if not of the entire town, were better placed to act as record keepers.[33] In the eighteenth century, a number of Connecticut ministers began to collect mortality data in a deliberate effort to study disease more scientifically. In 1797 Backus reported in *Medical Repository* a plan whereby the Congregational ministers of Connecticut in General Assembly, had agreed to "keep an accurate bill of mortality [a record of deaths], beginning January 1st, 1798, in their respective parishes and towns, comprehending age and disease." He explained, "This can be done with little trouble by our profession, and as it is understood that we keep a bill not only for our particular people, but of those of different denominations that happen to fall within our local precincts, it probably will be quite accurate."[34] However good the intention, this ambitious plan

to obtain annual mortality data for the entire state did not materialize.

Various types of numerical data related to health and disease appeared in the Town Reports. Since there was no standard for collecting the data, information cannot be readily compared from town to town. The first type of data was a census of the population at a given time, undertaken irregularly, and more likely by town officials for tax purposes than by ministers. In some cases the only information in the Town Reports was a simple population figure. For Bethlem, however, the population of 1,133 in 1800 (omitting the one slave for whom no age information is given) was broken down into sex and age brackets, from which one can gain a sense of the youthfulness of the population. The youngest category, under 10, accounted for 29.8 percent of the population, while the oldest category, over 45, accounted for only 15.9 percent.[35] The New Haven census for 1797, "made by a number of gentlemen in the city," was finely broken down by single year of age for ages 1 to 90. According to these data, 29.5 percent of the population of 3,347 were under 10, while only 11.0 percent were over 45.[36] The most elaborate census in the Town Reports was that for Litchfield County in 1800, which included a breakdown by sex and age categories for free white males and females for each town, covering a total of 40,511 individuals. Using these data, we find 31.9 percent of the population under 10 and 14.4 percent in the oldest bracket, 45 and over.[37]

The other major category of data in the Town Reports was a record of deaths over a period of time. Sometimes the minister provided simply the total number of deaths for a period of years, typically coinciding with the years of his ministry. If the data were aggregated over time periods, they might be called a "bill of mortality." Such bills of mortality had long been kept on an irregular basis in Great Britain, originally begun in order to compare normal years and plague years.[38] John Burgis, for example, kept bills of mortality for Guilford from 1746 to 1799, covering 2,024 deaths. The average number of deaths per year over this period was calculated at 38, but in 1769 and 1770, years of a dysentery epidemic, the death toll reached 70 per year, while in 1751, the year of an unknown "awful epidemic," the number soared to 110.[39] For the next period, 1799 to the end of 1832, Deacon Abraham Chittenden of Guilford kept a bill of mortality covering 895 deaths or an average of 27 a year. The Reverend David Dudley Field, author of the Guilford Report, divided deaths per year by an estimated average population of 1,850 to obtain a crude death rate of nearly one in 69.[40] Comparisons between towns were very rough, for they did not take into account their different age structure and population movements in and out of the town, but they are evidence of a real desire to obtain some sort of standard measure of healthiness. Azel Backus of Bethlem also provided the number of deaths by year, a figure that varied from 8 to 28 with an average of 15 for the period 1792-1811.[41]

In addition to mortality by period of time, a minister might add a sex and/or age breakdown of the deaths. The age categories differed from town to town. Of the 455 persons who died from 1753 to 1812 in the South-Farms parish of Litchfield, half (227) were under 10 years of age.[42] Similarly, Ammi R. Robbins, minister of Norfolk, reported that of the 760 deaths exclusive of the Revolutionary War from his ordination in 1761 to 1811, "more than half died in infancy."[43] In Wintonbury (Bloomfield), 29.4 percent of the deaths from 1792 to 1801 were children under two, and 37.7 percent of the deaths in the Hanover parish of Lisbon between 1768 to 1800 were under 5.[44] Timothy Dwight presented deaths by age for the First Society (parish) of New Haven from 1763 to 1786, and then for all the religious congregations in the city by year from 1797 to 1801. For the earlier period, stillborn and infants under the age of two accounted for 24.3 percent and children under ten accounted for 41.1 percent of deaths.[45] Much better mortality statistics were reported for the Judea parish of Washington. Of 148 deaths between 1796 and the end of 1811, 75 died under the age of 40 and 73 died over the age of 40.[46] It is very likely that the data were not collected in the same way for each area and are not truly comparable. However, even these limited data underscore the tremendous mortality of newborns and children and, as a corollary, the considerable improvement in life expectancy after early childhood.

Finally, a few enlightened ministers toward the end of the century attempted to keep a record over time of causes of death. Given the limitations of diagnosis around 1800, this was extremely difficult to do. Even with using such catch-all categories as "fever" and "old age & debility," respondents who collected such data were unable to assign a cause to about one-third of the deaths. Data of this type are found for Bethlem for 1791-1811, Judea, the first parish of Washington, for 1796-1811, and Lisbon (Hanover) from 1768 to 1800. Azel Backus of Bethlem provided the most elaborate data, arranged in a table, broken down by disease and by year.[47]

These data provide insight into life-threatening diseases in Connecticut other than epidemics of infectious diseases. In particular, we see that consumption, roughly equivalent to tuberculosis of the lungs, was already a major killer around 1800. It accounted for 9.5 percent of deaths in Bethlem, 12.2 percent of the deaths for the Judea parish of Washington, and 20.6 percent of the deaths in Lisbon (Hanover). Timothy Dwight reported that consumption accounted for about one-ninth of the 329 deaths in the First Society (parish) of New Haven from 1770 to 1786.[48] Tuberculosis would become even more deadly in the nineteenth century. Because it killed slowly, tuberculosis was generally regarded as due to heredity or to lifestyle rather than a contagious disease. John Treadwell of Farmington, for example, attributed "casual consumptions" of "young girls when passing from childhood to puberty" to "dancing assemblies protracted to one or two o'clock in the night, and the habit of undressing in public in the true Parisian mode."[49] One popular form of therapy, mentioned in the Farmington Report, was travel to a warmer climate. The previous minister, Joseph Washburn, "having rapidly declined with a pulmonary consumption brought on him as was supposed by his intense labours in the service of his people & being advised by his physicians to take a journey to the southward for the benefit of a milder air during the then

approaching winter," died at sea on the way to Charleston in 1805.[50]

Cancer, insofar as it was (or could be) diagnosed, was a relatively minor cause of death. Heart disease was not understood as such, but one may suppose that some of the deaths from "apoplexy," "palsy," and "dropsy" (fluid accumulation in the chest), were due to heart disease and stroke. "Cholera morbus," listed among causes of death, was a diarrheal disease of infants ("cholera infantum") and not the Asiatic cholera that first appeared in the United States in 1832.

The Academy's Solicitation letter did not ask about mental disease. Although some deaths were attributed to insanity, mental illness appears in the Town Reports primarily in answer to the queries concerning the number of suicides and care of the poor. Mental illness served as a common explanation for why certain people took their life or were reduced to destitution and dependence upon the town's charity.[51] Most of those suffering from mental disease in 1800 were still cared for by their families. But within a few decades, care of the insane would become a medical issue and a social responsibility.[52]

While, as a result of high infant mortality, the average age of death was much lower than in the twentieth century, potential longevity was roughly the same as today. Every respondent could identify townspeople in their eighties and nineties and ten Town Reports pointed to someone in their town who had lived to a hundred or more. The oldest was a woman in Milton who had died in 1803 having reached the age of 105.[53] Respondents wanted to confirm the generally held belief that those who lived to advanced ages had lived temperate, industrious lives, though this was not always the case. The writer of the Ridgefield Report, for example, had to admit that a man who lived to 102 "was temperate in his diet but animated in his passions."[54]

Although one can calculate the average age of death in these samples—a figure under 40—in the absence of information on the ages of the living population over time, no meaningful calculations of life expectancy were yet possible. We know from the Town Reports that the populations of the towns were constantly changing as the result of many young adults emigrating to newer settlements. Reliable vital statistics were not available in Connecticut until at least the mid-nineteenth century.

Therapeutics in the Town Reports

Since the Academy's Solicitation letter did not inquire about the best modes of treatment, a question better suited to physicians than ministers, medical therapy was mentioned mainly in passing in the Town Reports. Most people still held the traditional belief that disease affected the body by bringing about a general imbalance of bodily fluids or humors. The four humors of antiquity were blood, phlegm, yellow bile, and black bile, corresponding to combinations of the four qualities, hot and cold and wet and dry. In the eighteenth-century influential physicians in Edinburgh had suggested instead that disease was due to disturbances of the solids of the body — an excess or deficiency in the irritability of the blood vessels or nerves. According to any of these theories, however, disease was a holistic phenomenon, varying by the individual patient afflicted. A number of common remedies were intended to readjust the body's balance by evacuating body fluids. Bloodletting was one form of evacuative therapy. Other types of evacuative medicaments included cathartics or purges, emetics, diaretics, and sudorifics. The goal of medicine, understood by both physicians and patients, was to control the secretions. Insofar as the remedies had predictable and highly visible effects, they "worked." Some diseases, such as spotted fever, were thought to be primarily debilitating, and remedies were instead designed to shore up the system. Among these types of stimulating remedies were the bark, alcoholic beverages, laudanum or opium and other narcotics, astringents, and tonics.[55] In the main discussion of therapy in the Connecticut Town Reports, that of recommended therapy for spotted fever in the Farmington Report, the author, John Treadwell, followed the general prescription of Elisha North to avoid bloodletting and purging and rely primarily on a regimen of supplying external warmth, teas, alcoholic beverages, bark, opium, camphor, and ether to keep up the patient's strength.[56]

Most people in the eighteenth and nineteenth century dosed themselves without calling a physician at all. Many of the traditional remedies were herbal and could be grown in kitchen gardens. Dr. Eli Ives, who taught the first course of materia medica (pharmacy) at the Medical Institution of Yale College, provided in the New Haven Report an inventory of all the plants grown in New Haven County, including many for medicinal purposes.[57] Other remedies were made of imported plant materials such as the bark, or of minerals and chemicals. Calomel, for example, an oft-prescribed purge, contained mercury. One study of the practice of New England doctors found that about 40 percent of the ingredients used by physicians were imported.[58] Physicians and patients could obtain these remedies through apothecaries, who typically sold both native and imported drugs as well as so-called patent medicines in their shops (see below).

Article 4 of the Academy's Solicitation letter asks about rivers and streams, including medicinal springs. Several respondents mentioned the existence of mineral springs in their locality that were primarily used to treat chronic diseases such as eye and skin disorders, and rheumatism. In some cases the mineral content had been determined, but for the most part, the springs were not commercially developed and known only to locals. The most famous spring in Connecticut, Stafford Springs in Tolland County, though not mentioned in the Town Reports, had acquired a reputation as a mecca for health seekers since the 1760s. The spring was managed by the minister/physician Rev. John Willard. By 1810, under the care of his son, Dr. Samuel Willard, who had built a hotel and other tourist amenities, it had reached its height of popularity as a celebrated health spa.[59] Though Stafford Springs quickly declined after 1810, springs in general became more important in the nineteenth century with the growth of the medical sect known as hydrotherapy.

Physicians and Other Healers in Connecticut

The period covered by the Town Reports was a critical one in the institutional development of Connecticut medicine. Between 1790 and 1830, Connecticut acquired a state medical society, medical societies for all eight counties, a medical school, and a hospital. Since the Academy's questionnaire inquired about diseases rather than about healers, little of this transformation of the medical profession appears in the Town Reports.

Like other states in the Union, Connecticut had a variety of practitioners of the healing arts. The physicians in 1800 are relatively easy to identify. Other healers are much harder to find in the printed record and, if found at all, it will likely be through personal papers and court records. Through the eighteenth century, anyone could practice medicine and be called a doctor. There was no state legislation regulating medical training or medical practice. For most, medicine was a part-time profession and not the sole means of making a living. In the eighteenth century, Connecticut was home to several prominent minister/physicians. The best known was Jared Eliot, an early Yale graduate, who was a well-respected minister and at the same time a highly regarded physician who trained many of the next generation of Connecticut physicians including his son-in-law, Benjamin Gale. Timothy Collins, the first minister of Litchfield, mentioned in the Town Report, also served in dual capacity as a healer of both bodies and souls.[60] Ministers knew the members of their congregation intimately and it was natural that when they visited ailing members of their congregation to attend to their spiritual needs, they also sometimes attended to their physical needs, especially at a time when there were fewer physicians. By 1800, however, the minister/physician was largely displaced by the physician trained by apprenticeship.[61]

Professional aspirations of American physicians derived from those of Great Britain, but with significant North American modifications. In England, there was a theoretical difference among the functions of physicians, apothecaries, and surgeons. Physicians, who were university trained, examined and prescribed but performed no surgery and sold no drugs. Apothecaries filled prescriptions and compounded and sold drugs. Surgeons limited their activity to surgery, most of it minor operations, since there were as yet no anesthetics or means to control infection. Even in Britain, these functions had over time become blurred. Apothecaries and surgeons were on the way to becoming general practitioners, though lower in rank than physicians. In the United States, there was little division of labor. Physicians typically compounded and carried with them their own drugs and performed minor surgery. A few Town Reports mention surgeons and apothecary shops. For example, Timothy Dwight noted that New Haven had nine physicians, one surgeon, and ten apothecary stores.[62] Those few who called themselves surgeons specialized in surgical operations, but most physicians also performed surgery. Apothecaries in America were mostly shopkeepers and importers of drugs and patent medicines. These latter were proprietary or brand name medicaments whose formula was secret; they were usually not patented since the patent would have to disclose the ingredients. In 1800, most patent medicines were imported from Great Britain, but Americans, including Connecticut physicians, had begun to produce their own brand-name remedies with the usual very broad claims. The 1790s saw Dr. Samuel Lee, Jr. of Windham's Bilious Pills; Dr. Samuel H. P. Lee's New London Bilious Pills; Dr. Mark Newell of Southington's Jaundice Pills; David Harris of New London's Genuine Bilious Pills; and Dr. Cooley's Vegetable Elixir and Dr. Cooley's Genuine Anti-Pestilential, Attenuating and Restorative Pills, both produced by Dr. Samuel Cooley of Bolton. The various "bilious pills" were claimed to be effective against yellow fever as well as a host of other ailments.[63] Physicians' organizations strongly opposed the marketing of such "nostrums."

Women's role in healing is noticeably absent from the Town Reports and from published records in general. Since most medical care was of the do-it-yourself variety that took place within families, women were the first line of defense against illness. They kept watch over the sick in their homes and the homes of their neighbors, and prepared remedies from the family's kitchen garden and collection of dried herbs. Newspapers were full of health information and of recipes for curing various ailments. Popular medical works circulated widely. British works for the public such as William Buchan's *Domestic Medicine*, John Wesley's *Primitive Physick*, and *Aristotle's Master Piece* (which provided popular information on reproduction) were published in numerous American editions. Buchan, in particular, appeared in several Connecticut editions.[64] Earlier in the century, some women in Connecticut had earned reputations as healers and may have received payment for their services. By 1800, however, female healers were much rarer in New England, marginalized by the growth and organization of the medical profession in the state. Yet, in rural Maine from 1785 to 1812, Martha Ballard, who is known only through her diary, served as a general herbal practitioner as well as a widely respected midwife.[65] In 1800, midwives were still in practice in Connecticut, although some male physicians had begun to take over normal births. Some midwives, such as Rebecca Rogers Hobart of Branford and Philena Smith Hickox who practiced in Chester and Waterbury, left record books listing the dates of the children they delivered, and, in the case of Rogers, counts by year and career. Rogers claimed to have attended 1319 births before 1800.[66] In addition to serving as midwives, women throughout the period, served as unskilled but paid nurses, tending to the sick in their homes.[67]

Connecticut physicians, unlike those in Great Britain, were very unlikely to have medical degrees. The leading practitioners in eighteenth-century Connecticut were apprenticed-trained in medicine. That is, a would-be practitioner would study with and become an assistant of a practicing physician for three years or so, often living in his home. There were no medical schools in the colonies before 1765 when the College of Philadelphia (later the University of Pennsylvania) was founded. It was followed by King's College in New York in 1767 and the Harvard Medical School in 1782. While some Philadelphia physicians like John Morgan, William Shippen, and Benjamin Rush traveled abroad for medical training and returned with an M.D. from one of the Scottish universities, none of the prominent Connecticut physicians were so educated. Although some physicians, such as Elihu Hubbard Smith or Elisha North, attended courses of Benjamin Rush and others in Philadelphia, they did not stay long enough to complete the requirements for an M.D. When the Connecticut Medical Society was formed in 1792, none of the original officers had medical degrees. Though lacking formal academic medical education, many of the leaders in Connecticut medicine were graduates of Yale College. Over 250 graduates of Yale College in the eighteenth century were known to have practiced medicine at some point in their careers, most of them in Connecticut.[68] The number of physicians and hence, the competition for patients, seems to have greatly increased in the later part of the century. Though we still know little about them in Connecticut beyond the complaints of the more elite physicians, self-trained "doctors" and folk healers also offered medical assistance to the public.

Beginning in the 1760s, Connecticut physicians tried to join together to obtain legislation to limit medical practice through licensing. In this effort Connecticut physicians paralleled those in Massachusetts, creating first various short-lived local societies, followed by a permanent local society, a state society, a medical school, and a hospital. Although Massachusetts physicians were able to establish a state society in 1781, a decade earlier than in Connecticut, the Massachusetts Medical Society was more limited in membership until 1804 and dominated by Boston until mid-century, whereas the Connecticut Medical Society was statewide and inclusive from the outset. Because it was so inclusive, a much larger percentage of Connecticut physicians belonged to the state society in the early nineteenth century than did physicians in neighboring states.[69]

In 1763, an association of physicians in Norwich unsuccessfully petitioned the colonial legislature to establish a society to license physicians. There followed a society of physicians in Litchfield in 1767 and another society founded in 1779, centered in Sharon, which adopted the pretentious name, First Medical Society in the Thirteen United States since their Independence.[70]

Early petitions to the legislature, such as that from the Norwich physicians in 1763, emphasized the need to protect the public and the reputation of the "proffession" from the "Quack or Emperical Pretender."[71] These efforts failed, presumably because the legislators distrusted a self-perpetuating monopoly that would limit public choice. The founding of the New Haven County Medical Society in 1784 and its publication of *Cases and Observations* in 1788, the first published transactions by a medical society in United States, set the stage for a series of renewed attempts at obtaining legislation for a state society.[72] To succeed, the physicians had to scale back their goals. The preamble to the legislation of 1792 did not mention quacks at all; the purpose of the organization was education of the members. The preamble read simply: "Whereas well regulated medical societies have been found to contribute to the diffusion of true science, and particularly the knowledge of the healing art; Therefore..." The legislation provided for the establishment of county medical societies for each of the eight counties in Connecticut, and a state organization, the Connecticut Medical Society, to be administered by fellows elected by each of the county societies and officers chosen by the fellows. Members of the county societies were to be automatically members of the state society. The Connecticut Medical Society was awarded the right to examine and license new physicians entering practice and presenting themselves, but nothing in the original legislation limited practice to those licensed. By its enacting legislation, the Society was also empowered to award honorary degrees. By that means, prominent physicians such as Leverett Hubbard, Eneas Munson, North, and others, were able to append M.D. to their names.[73]

Forty-seven physicians were listed as incorporators in the legislation of 1792. By 1793, after the county societies had formed, whose members became the initial members of the state Society, there were 309 members. Connecticut, with a population of 237,946 according to the U.S. census of 1790, was well provided with physicians, about one member of the Society per 760 persons. Nearly every town had at least one practitioner. In New London County, for example, there were 43 founding members of the Connecticut Medical Society, located in Bozrah, Colchester, Groton, Franklin, Lisbon, Lyme, Montville, New London, Norwich, Preston, and Stonington.[74]

By 1800, the Society had enacted preconditions for

Yale's Medical School was located in this building at the corner of Prospect and Grove Streets from 1813 until 1860. The wings were added after 1860.

taking the licensing examination. A candidate must be 21 years of age, of good reputation, and have studied either three years with a preceptor, or, if a college graduate, two years. To be licensed, the candidate would have to demonstrate "A general knowledge of Natural Philosophy, Chemistry and Botany, and a thorough knowledge of Materia Medica, Pharmacy, Anatomy and Physiology, Theory and practice of Physic and Surgery." That year the Society obtained an amendment to its charter stating that all those newly entering practice after 1800 would be required to obtain a license from "some medical society or college of physicians" or have no recourse to state laws for collection of fees.[75]

Physicians had formed the Connecticut Medical Society in part to combat competition from ill-trained pretenders outside its ranks. However, having no control over such competitors, the Society devoted its attention to policing the ethical behavior of its own members. In 1793 it enacted a rule "that it shall be highly disreputable for any member to assume or hold the knowledge of any nostrum, or palm any medicine or composition on the people as a secret." But the lure of money from selling proprietary devices and medicines led several early members to ignore the injunction. Elisha Perkins of Windham County, an original incorporator and one of the first fellows of the Society, had the dubious distinction of obtaining the first U.S. patent for a medical device in 1797. He acquired widespread fame in America and in England for his metallic tractors, known as Perkins' tractors, consisting of small two metal rods, made of different alloys, rounded at one end and pointed at the other. When the tractors were drawn over the skin, they supposedly extracted noxious electrical fluids from the body. At first Perkins claimed the tractors provided an effective treatment of gout, pleurisy, and rheumatism, but soon he began to advertise their use also in treating yellow fever. The fellows of the Connecticut Society declared in May 1796 "that they consider all such practices as barefaced imposition, disgraceful to the Faculty, and delusive to the ignorant," and called upon Perkins to account for his conduct. When Perkins failed to respond, the following year, in May 1797, the fellows passed a resolution expelling him.[76] In 1805, Samuel H.P. Lee narrowly avoided expulsion for selling a nostrum, by revealing under oath before a justice of the peace the ingredients of his New London Bilious Pills. When he subsequently suggested in advertisements that in his complying with the Society's by-laws, the Society had sanctioned his pills, the Society published a statement in the newspapers that declared that the pills were in many cases "inefficacious" and "injurious."[77]

The formation of the Connecticut Medical Society helped to bring to fruition the vision already advanced by President Ezra Stiles of Yale as far back as 1777 that Yale would eventually establish medical instruction. When the Corporation began to plan a medical school in earnest in 1807, it invited the Connecticut Medical Society to collaborate. Joint committees of Yale and the Society approved the project and obtained a charter from the State in 1810. When Timothy Dwight wrote the New Haven Report in 1811 the school was in the process of organization:

> A Medical Institution is established in this Seminary; but has not begun its operations. It is to consist of three Professorships, besides that

of Chemistry; one, of the Materia Medica; one of Anatomy and Surgery; and one of the Theory and Practice of Physic.[78]

At the time the school opened in 1813, the four professors were Benjamin Silliman, Eneas Munson, Jonathan Knight, and Nathan Smith. Munson's position was largely honorific, since he was quite elderly and unable to teach. The courses in pediatrics and materia medica were taught by a fifth professor, Eli Ives. Except for Smith, who had been invited to Yale from New Hampshire where he had founded the Dartmouth Medical School, all were graduates of Yale College who had not earned medical degrees. By the terms of this unusual collaboration, the Medical Society participated in the naming of professors and in the examining of students and granting of degrees. At the same time, the Medical Society raised its requirements for licensure to include a year's course in a medical school.[79] A large portion of Yale's new physicians in the nineteenth century were from Connecticut and settled there to practice. In Connecticut, the Medical Institution of Yale College and the Society worked together, avoiding the early friction that developed between the Harvard Medical School and the Massachusetts Medical Society.[80] The Society's relation to the Medical School also ensured, that unlike most other states, including Massachusetts, where competing schools were easily founded, Connecticut would have only one medical school throughout the nineteenth century.

In 1800, there were as yet no permanent hospitals in Connecticut (there had been temporary smallpox inoculation and quarantine hospitals). There was only a handful in the United States, the earliest and most prominent being the Philadelphia Hospital. The tendency, in evidence in the Town Reports, to concentrate the town's poor in alms houses rather than homes of members of the community, provided one form of public institution in which physicians could gain professional experience. Since many of the poor cared for by the town were unable to work because they suffered from physical or mental illnesses, the town hired physicians and nurses to care for them. Hospitals were founded as charitable institutions to provide a better environment than the alms house for treating the "worthy poor" who were unable to be cared

for at home. The general hospital was much better adapted than the alms house to the professional agenda of nineteenth-century physicians.[81]

A major stimulus for the creation of hospitals was the need for patients to aid in training medical students. The physicians who were named to attend at hospitals were typically unpaid, but the appointments carried with them prestige and the opportunity to be accompanied in rounds by students. In Massachusetts professors at the Harvard Medical School were instrumental in founding Massachusetts General Hospital, which opened in 1821. In Connecticut, the state medical society helped to plan the state's first hospital, the State Hospital, later known as the New Haven Hospital, founded in 1826 and opened in 1833, and the five faculty members of the fledgling Medical Institution of Yale College, were among it incorporators. From its beginning, Connecticut's first hospital provided a locus for training of Yale medical students. A committee of the Connecticut Medical Society was also instrumental in creating the State's first mental asylum, the Connecticut Retreat for the Insane (now Institute of Living) in Hartford, opened in 1824, under the direction of Dr. Eli Todd of Farmington.[82]

Whenever physicians were mentioned in the Town Reports, they were treated with respect and deference. This is not surprising since the leading physicians formed part of the same elite of learned men as the ministers and town officials who responded to the Academy's questionnaire. By the time of the last of the Town Reports in 1832, Connecticut physicians had completed a major period of organizational development, resulting in a series of interconnected institutions for creating standards for entry into the profession, training new entrants into the profession, overseeing professional ethics, protecting medical interests at the state level, and creating new institutions for patient care. Although they would soon be challenged by the arrival of medical sectarians such as the botanical healers and the homeopaths, and by the influx of graduates of proliferating medical schools in other states, Connecticut's physicians had achieved a remarkable professional solidarity in the decades around 1800.

"A privilege and elevation to which we look forward with pleasure:"

The Connecticut Academy of Arts and Sciences

and Black Emancipation in Connecticut

Peter P. Hinks

In 1800, just a few months after its chartering by the state legislature, the Connecticut Academy of Arts and Sciences (CAAS) circulated a lengthy questionnaire to the young state's numerous towns, seeking information on a host of matters pertaining to the life and history of the localities. The questionnaire comprised thirty-two Articles or topics but the vast majority of them addressed matters "relative to the Geography, Natural, Civil and Political History, Agriculture, Manufactures and Commerce of the State of Connecticut." The replies were intended to afford a vast panorama of the life and ways of Connecticut's peoples and land and to testify to the purposive and moral busyness of the inhabitants and the reasons for their solid and deserved prosperity. The first statewide undertaking of the fledgling CAAS, nothing could have better fulfilled than this questionnaire the Academy's recently articulated objective "to promote, diffuse & preserve the knowledge of those Arts & Sciences, which are the support of Agriculture, Manufactures & Commerce, & to advance the dignity, virtue & happiness of a people."[1]

Article #27 of the questionnaire provided a perhaps less conspicuous dimension to this panorama of enterprise, improvement, and prosperity but one that was nevertheless integral "to advance the dignity, virtue & happiness of a people" for it addressed the solemn subject of freedom. It sought information on "Free blacks; their number, vices and modes of life, their industry and success in acquiring property; whether those born free are more ingenious, industrious and virtuous, than those who were emancipated after arriving to adult years."[2] Enslavement of Africans in Connecticut had existed throughout the state's colonial history, peaking in 1775 when the colony had almost 5,100 black slaves, second by only a few hundred to Massachusetts, which had the most of any colony in New England. Yet in the latter quarter of the eighteenth century, acts facilitating the manumission and emancipation of the state's slaves were passed by the assembly and the number of free blacks steadily grew in the state, especially after the passage of a gradual emancipation act in 1784. By 1800 as Article #27 was being posed and 1,000 blacks continued to be enslaved in the state, free blacks numbered over 5,300 and it was this class of individuals about which the query was directed. For the leaders of the CAAS, emancipation was a dramatic moment in the state's commitment to advancing freedom and to renovating a despised and degraded race. Thus, they likely intended Article #27 to celebrate as much as to investigate. Yet as the responses were returned over the ensuing years, they could only have disappointed the CAAS leaders, for they increasingly told a tale of the freedmen's poverty and failure to improve and uplift themselves. This essay explores the historical background to these reports, the Town Reports themselves, and the reinforcement they offered to fateful changes in racial thinking in the state by the early 1820s.

Stirrings of Abolition

By the late eighteenth century, much excitement existed in the United States—especially in the North but also in the Upper South—among a stratum of the educated elite of lawyers, clerics, doctors, academics, merchants, and others for the possibility of ending slavery in the whole of the nation in a manner similar to the way in which it was currently being ended in the North.[3] Members of the Federalist party were the ones most associated with this movement and their adherents almost exclusively peopled the numerous state abolition societies that arose especially after 1790. That year in Connecticut, the state's first abolition society was organized and cumbersomely entitled The Connecticut Society for the Promotion of Freedom and the Relief of Persons Unlawfully Holden in Bondage. It was led by such Federalist luminaries as Timothy and Theodore Dwight, Noah Webster, Simeon Baldwin, Levi Hart, Zephaniah Swift, Elizur Goodrich, and James Dana. Over the ensuing decade as gradual emancipation was unfolding in the state, the Connecticut Society aggressively assisted a number of blacks unlawfully held in bondage by initiating freedom suits on their behalf and sought to return those removed illegally from the state by owners seeking to sell them elsewhere. Members of the society were also some of the most dedicated combatants in 1793 and 1794 for legislation fully abolishing slavery in the state. While the measure ultimately failed and slavery would not be completely banned in the state until 1848, they contributed significantly to the fact that over 80 percent of the state's blacks were free by 1800.

In the 1790s, the members of the Connecticut Society shared with most of the constituents of abolition societies in other states the conviction that nationwide emancipation over the coming years was all but inevitable. In 1791, the Reverend Jonathan Edwards, Jr. declared that "if we judge of the future by the past, within fifty years of this, it will be as shameful for a man to hold a Negro slave, as to be guilty of common robbery or theft."[4] The next year, Simeon Baldwin proclaimed that "Calm reflection will in the end convince the world that the whole system of African slavery is unjust in its nature—impolitic in its principles, & in its consequences ruinous to industry and enterprise—The world is now almost ripe for abolishing the trade, and the revolution of a few more years more will root out slavery itself."[5] Moreover most of these abolitionists believed the significance of racial distinctions was declining in the nation and blacks were clearly moving toward becoming citizens. In 1792, the American Convention of Abolition Societies, with which Connecticut was closely affiliated, and which was *the* representative body for all state abolition societies, then declared that "[we must] prepare [the emancipated slaves] for becoming good citizens of the United States, a privilege and elevation to which we look forward with pleasure, and which we believe can be best merited by habits of industry and virtue."[6] These opinions were voiced by shrewd men of the world whose very conservatism inclined them not to be carried away with visions of rapid and profound social change; yet they were truly in awe of emancipation's progress and readily projected slavery's imminent collapse throughout the nation.

Emancipation and assimilation, however, were to occur through a controlled and measured process. The same men who advocated emancipation also deeply feared any sign in the United States of the bloody tumult and terror that characterized the successful slave revolt in St. Domingue in the 1790s as well as the possibility that the untutored and irresponsible slaves might fall prey to the demagogic manipulations of their then bitter political opponents, the Jeffersonian Republicans.[7] Realistic fears or not (and most likely they were not), the Federalist abolitionists wanted to manage closely this social transformation and—as they indicated in a pronouncement in the *Connecticut Journal* in 1796—to supervise the moral elevation of the emancipated to education, worship, industry, temperance, and self-regulation. This rearing would check their impulse to turbulence and irresponsibility, while cementing their allegiance to the Federalists civically and electorally as they acquired more of the rights and duties of citizenship. Connecticut's emancipated and their offspring would be reformed to recognize their interests in preserving the current political and social dominance of the Federalists or—as they were often called—the Standing Order.

In service to understanding more fully this process and gaining control over it, the Connecticut Academy posed query (Article) #27. It is no surprise that the Academy was explicitly interested in the process of emancipation since all the members of the aforementioned Connecticut Society were also key members and founders of the Connecticut Academy. This statewide effort to gather information on the current condition of African Americans and on the course of emancipation was not unique at the end of the eighteenth century. In part the questionnaire as a whole reflected an Enlightenment-era rationalism and scientism to which the Academy and other similar state societies were dedicated. They sought to gather as much information as they could regarding the material and social life of the state and thereby gain a greater control over the direction and well-being of the polity. But Article #27 embodied an even more specific objective. The mounting excitement in the Atlantic world for democratic experiments and for assertions of universal equality coupled with unprecedented levels of slave assertiveness and rebelliousness had led many progressive thinkers to weigh the possibilities of freeing the hundreds of thousands of slaves in South America, the Caribbean, and the United States and to inquire into the social impact of taking such a radical step. Many also sought to determine through these investigations whether blacks were ready to accept the responsibilities of freedom after having been enslaved in many cases for generations. Although not conducted in the form of a circulated questionnaire, Thomas Jefferson made such inquiries in 1784 in Queries 14 and 18 of his famous *Notes on the State of Virginia*. While acknowledging in #18 the risk the nation ran of incurring God's wrath if it continued to enslave Africans, in #14 Jefferson nevertheless hypothesized their innate biological and intellectual inferiority to white Euro-Americans to explain why they must be maintained in slavery so long as they continued in the country. But in service to establishing this supposed inferiority more firmly, Jefferson called for a scientific inquiry into the character and causes of human racial diversity.

> The opinion, that they are inferior in the faculties of reason and imagination, must be hazarded with great diffidence. To justify a general conclusion, requires many observations, even where the subject may be submitted to the Anatomical knife, to Optical glasses, to analysis by fire, or by solvents...To our reproach it must be said, that though for a century and a half we have had under our eyes the races of black and of red men, they have never yet been viewed by us as subjects of natural history.[8] Until such a systematic investigation had been concluded, Jefferson advanced "it therefore as a suspicion only, that the blacks...are inferior to the whites in the endowments both of body and mind."[9]

Jeremy Belknap of Massachusetts and the Virginia jurist, St. George Tucker, pursued an investigation in 1795 more similar to that in Connecticut when Tucker had a questionnaire circulated to various town notables in the Bay State seeking a wide variety of information on the history of slavery in the state and the results of emancipation there.[10] Tucker in large part made these inquiries because he himself had been wrestling with what to do with the institution in his own state. Recognizing that state legislation during the Revolution had allowed for the private manumission of slaves, he anticipated that the state might now be receptive to passing a general emancipation. With that prospect in mind, he turned to the Reverend Dr. Belknap.

> [H]aving observed, with much pleasure, that slavery has been wholly exterminated from the Massachusetts; and being impressed with an idea, that it once had existence there, I have cherished a hope that we may, from the example of our sister state, learn what methods are most likely to succeed in removing the same evil from among ourselves. With this view, I have taken the liberty to enclose a few queries, which, if your leisure will permit you to answer, you will confer on me a favour, which I shall always consider as an obligation.[11]

Numerous responses to the questions flowed in to Belknap over the coming months and were subsequently forwarded to Tucker. The letters illuminated the process of emancipation enormously for a man who had never visited the state, and they (along with a letter from CAAS's Zephaniah Swift) provided vital evidence for Tucker's *A Dissertation on Slavery*, one of the most important antislavery essays from the early national era.[12] These queries, together with their replies, then were no desultory exercises in information gathering but rather played a dynamic role in the articulation of antislavery in the late eighteenth-century Atlantic world. These antislavery advocates believed they were in the midst of a momentous change in human history and that the world was watching New England and the North.

Yet as the Academy's Solicitation letter was being circulated to Connecticut town fathers—many of whom were themselves members of the CAAS—and while visions of emancipation and racial inclusion remained alive nationally, doubts about the capacities of newly freed blacks to use their freedom responsibly were creeping more and more into the consciousness of whites in the state who had hoped for black improvement and inclusion. The various responses to Article #27 indeed would chronicle this infiltration of racial doubt far more than they would celebrate the accomplishments of emancipation. They thus help to illuminate this fateful transformation of Connecticut's Federalist elite between 1800 and 1820 from some of the nation's most dedicated supporters of black freedom and inclusion to some of the most vocal proponents of black containment and removal from the country.

Slavery in Connecticut

Slavery and Africans came to the colony very slowly in the seventeenth century.[13] By 1680, William Leete, the Governor of the colony, wrote to the British Committee for Trade and Foreign Plantations that African slaves were "not above 30, as we judge, in the Colony" and "there comes sometimes 3 or 4 [blacks] in a year from Barbadoes."[14] But slavery would steadily extend its presence by the early decades of the eighteenth century as the British Board of Trade ended the Royal African Company's monopoly on the African slave trade and opened it to private merchants while placing mounting pressure on their North American colonies to increase their supply of laborers by purchasing Africans. Accurate figures for the number of slaves in Connecticut in the early part of the eighteenth century do not yet exist but by the 1710s their presence was clearly growing and they probably numbered at least a few hundred.[15] By no later than 1708, scattered laws were being written to regulate this new stratum of population. One acknowledged that "negro and molatto servants or slaves are become numerous in some parts of this Colonie, and are very apt to be turbulent."[16] A response to a Board of Trade query in 1730 placed the black population at about 700 while another respondent in 1749 reckoned the colony now had "1000 blacks, and they are greatly increased within the ten years last past."[17] Indeed the figure for 1749 was likely understated for "a more careful and particular enquiry" conducted for the colony in 1756 placed the black population

at 3,019 or more likely 3,587.[18] A further "careful enquiry" in 1761 illustrated the dramatic influx of Africans into Connecticut by pegging their population then at 4,590.[19] The number of blacks in the colony would peak at 5,083 just before the outbreak of the Revolution in 1774, when they would comprise almost 3 percent of the total population.[20] After entering the eighteenth century as a colony which was near exclusively white, Connecticut approached the Revolution inhabited by well over 5,000 blacks. While still a relatively small minority, their labor and skill nevertheless had helped fuel the colony's dramatic growth in wealth over the previous seventy-five years.[21] Moreover their enslavement and distinctive racial difference would also pose serious problems for many whites in the state far exceeding their seeming insignificance in numbers.

Slavery in Connecticut had a dispersed character which in fact led many in the state to be exposed to people of African descent and to the institution of slavery even if they were not slave owners themselves. While the largest concentrations of slaves by the mid-eighteenth century was in such commercial towns as New London, Fairfield, Hartford, Stratford, Groton, and Stonington, where perhaps a third or so of the colony's slaves were held, a remarkable distribution of the slaves throughout Connecticut's numerous small rural towns and settlements distinguished it from colonies such as Massachusetts and New Hampshire where the slaves were overwhelmingly concentrated in the key coastal ports.[22] Godfrey Malbone of Rhode Island was said to have had upwards of sixty slaves on a large estate he owned in Brooklyn, Connecticut and William Browne of Salem, Massachusetts about the same number on his huge holdings in Lyme. But such holdings were extremely exceptional in Connecticut where the vast majority of slaves were owned in very small lots—usually not exceeding two or three per slave holder. This also contributed to their broad distribution throughout the colony.[23] One recent work on New England slavery has estimated that there were actually enough African Americans in Connecticut for one out of every four families potentially to have a slave and these small levels of individual ownership could well make it possible.[24]

Slavery in Connecticut thus was an unusually intimate institution, breeding a remarkable degree of familiarity between owner and enslaved. The whole of the slave's life was centered around the household of his or her owner. Training and directives for work issued daily directly from the owner who well might be working alongside the slave. Slaves in the colony commonly took their meals with the family, received religious instruction and prayed with them, slept in a corner of the house, and relaxed with the family around the hearth in the evening. Even marriage for the slaves did not relieve them of this proximity to their owners for betrothal no more entitled them to leave the house and establish their own family than would have the impulse to leave on their own.[25] While life for the more populous blacks in the colony's ports and leading towns would provide limited opportunities for more community life such as the annual ritual of electing a Black Governor,[26] the dominance of their owner's household in their lives was sustained there as well and little chance afforded to build any social infrastructure beyond informal ties among individuals.

Nowhere would the opportunity for some autonomous community and cultural life be provided blacks in Connecticut such as slaves had in the Chesapeake and the Carolina lowcountry on isolated outland tobacco farms and huge rice plantations, where large numbers of Africans and African Americans lived and labored in the midst of only a handful of white overseers.

Slavery in Connecticut and New England has traditionally been characterized as familial and gently paternalistic in part because of the small numbers held within households.[27] However, the fact that individual black identity and life in Connecticut was seemingly so subsumed within the family in which one was simultaneously a member and a dependent alien deeply reinforced white doubts about the ability of African Americans to support themselves as independent freemen. Indeed this doubt prior to 1770 was near axiomatic. Brutally capturing this sensibility as late as 1774 was one correspondent to the *Connecticut Journal* who wrote God had given Adam dominion over all of the animals of the earth and "the beasts of Ethiopia," among whom were included "the Negroes of Africa." He continued:

> I beg therefore you would mention this in your paper, to silence those writers who insist upon the Africans belonging to the same species of men with the white people, and who will not allow that God formed them in common with horses, oxen, dogs, &c. for the white people alone, to be used by them either for pleasure or to labour with other *beasts* in the culture of tobacco, indigo, rice, and sugar.[28]

The Roots of Antislavery in Connecticut

In Massachusetts, Samuel Sewall published his famous antislavery tract, *The Selling of Joseph*, in 1700 and the Nantucket Quaker, Elihu Coleman, his *Testimony...* in 1733, but prior to the mid-1760s, opposition to slavery had virtually no voice in Connecticut.[29] Whites in Connecticut appear to have embraced slavery with little reflection, accepting it as one of several labor options available to them. The opening to one of the earliest laws in the colony pertaining to slavery (1690) suggests a simple unthinking exercise of an option: "Whereas many persons of this Colony doe for their necessary use purchase negroe servants..." and then immediately turns to discuss the regulation of runaways.[30] No special slave code was ever written in Connecticut extensively defining and regulating them. Laws were written in an *ad hoc* manner as problems arose from a growing population. None seemed prompted to devise statements defending or explaining the institution, for the vast majority of whites accepted the inferiority of blacks and the consequent propriety and even beneficence of their enslavement.

That is until no later than 1767. In December of that year, a lengthy front-page essay by the anonymous "Phileleutheros" broke the long silence with a vehement antislavery essay in the weekly *Connecticut Journal*. Why was the author opposed to "this horrible, barbarous custom"? Because "mankind are born free and liberty is a common gift all receive from God

himself [and it is thus wrong to] enslave a part of their fellow mortals, merely because they are black; for there seems to me to be no natural or divine right to it." Moreover "Phileleutheros" fretted: "How can we expect our endeavors at the court of Great-Britain should be bless'd, when we are acting a more cruel part with our neighbours, the blacks?" Slavery was an offense to God, it was cruel and unnatural, and for Americans, hypocritical. Although countered one week later by the pro-slavery "Philonous," the appearance of both works bespoke the colony's rising disquiet and uncertainty over slavery.[31]

What was a smattering in 1768 became by 1773 a flurry. In October of that year commenced a series of lengthy attacks on slavery in the *Connecticut Journal*, authored under the pseudonyms of first "Antidoulios" and later "Philander," that would continue into 1774. These essays were in fact written collaboratively by Jonathan Edwards, Jr., the son of the great Northampton theologian, and another arch-Calvinist associate, Ebenezer Baldwin. In New England, Edwards along with Rhode Island's Samuel Hopkins would be one of the great clerical antislavery voices during and after the Revolution. His importance for Connecticut was particularly salient because he would be a founder of the state's antislavery society in 1790 and his pronouncements in the 1770s would largely presage those of the Society in the early 1790s.

Edwards and Baldwin amplified on the arguments of "Phileleutheros" while particularly arraying their enormous Biblical erudition to undermine the use of Scripture by their opponents to sanction slavery through the story of Ham, the Israelites in Canaan, and the edicts of Paul. They also challenged the common argument that Africans brought to America were captives from just wars in their own land and thus were legitimately enslaved in America. Relying on the political philosophy of John Locke, they reckoned that few of those Africans transported to America had justly surrendered their liberty and that certainly none of their offspring in the colonies had been deprived fairly of the natural liberty adhering to them. Thus they constructed a devastating attack on the justification of slavery, the likes of which the colony had never before seen and which signaled a mounting antislavery conviction among some of the elite of the colony's clerics.

Although abolition was still decades away, 1774 nevertheless closed on a favorable advance as the General Assembly voted to prohibit any further importations of Africans into the Colony. This ended the growth of the colony's previously expanding black population and raised new questions about what was to be their place in Connecticut as it moved closer to breaking free of Great Britain, evinced by a notice from Danbury "that something further might be done for the relief of such as are *now* in a state of slavery in the colonies, and such as may hereafter be born of parents in that unhappy condition."[32]

Less than a year later, Levi Hart, a key Connecticut Congregational minister and friend of both Edwards and Hopkins, proposed just such a plan. His brief treatise "Some Thoughts on the Subject of Freeing the Negro Slaves in the Colony of Connecticut" would enormously advance planning for emancipation in the state.[33] Not only did "Thoughts" boldly condemn slavery and the slave trade but it also directly addressed the issue of individual black character and what to expect of it once emancipated. Hart argued that blacks could and would improve themselves once removed from slavery, given an appropriate mix of time, public and private assistance, and real opportunity. Hart who would later be one of the founders of the Connecticut Society, knew full well that such an expectation ran contrary to the outlook of virtually every white member of Connecticut, that all of them were convinced that:

> The Negroes have not sufficient discretion to conduct their own affairs & provide for themselves, & that many of them are addicted to stealing, & other enormities *Now* & would probably be much more so if they were not under the care & government of masters who restrain them—that if they were free, they would find means to perpetrate so many horrid crimes in stealing & house-breaking if not robbing and murdering that private property would, by no means, be safe, & an irreparable injury be hereby done to the public.[34]

To the above charges, Hart replied:

> ...that there is no apparent want of capacity in the Negros in general to conduct their own affairs & provide for themselves, but what is the natural consequence of the Servile state they are in, & the treatment they receive. —Our national pride leads us to imagine them, by nature, much inferior to ourselves in intellectual powers; but this ungenerous self-applauding preference, doth not appear to be supported by fact, when proper allowance is supposed for the difference of education & condition in our favor.... [A] state of abject Slavery breaks the spirits & benumbs the powers of the human mind.[35]

"Thoughts" revealed the degree to which assumptions of black inferiority and unfitness for freedom were beginning to be challenged at least within Connecticut's educated elite as the Revolution burst out. Hart had no question but what emancipation was not only economically and socially feasible for Connecticut but that "we are bound by that great law of reason & religion" absolutely to implement it, regardless of feasibility.

But a distinguishing conservatism informed his plans. Hart proposed a careful program of emancipation that would both slowly release blacks from bondage after they reached a delayed age of majority while thriftily compensating owners for any earnings and investment they may have lost as a result of their slaves being released between the age of 25 and 37 when they were assumed to be at the peak of their productivity. Emancipation was not to happen for all immediately; rather it would occur over the space of numerous years, slowly but steadily increasing the number of free blacks in Connecticut

society who would hopefully have begun to be prepared for the duties of freedom while under the tutelage of their owners as well as supervised by an appointed white guardian during the very first years after their release. Stern punishment was also provided for the errant. Thus white fears about the governability and assimilability of free blacks were supposed addressed. Social disruption was believed avoidable:

> One great, & perhaps the greatest cause of the imprudence & misconduct of free Negros, & from whence we should have the most to fear, is the sudden, very great change in their condition, from a state of absolute slavery to the same extensive freedom with englishmen. Sudden and great changes, especially from a low, to a comparatively high state, are always dangerous to the morals of persons whether white or black—provision is made to obviate this difficulty in the second article by proposing a gradual change from absolute slavery.[36]

The key to Hart's vision was to argue and plan for an expanding black freedom while maintaining a temporary white control over the course of that expansion. Emancipation was not to disrupt Connecticut society nor unbalance in any way the rule of the state's traditional elite. Indeed emancipation was intended to reinforce their rule. In no way did Hart's vision of emancipation sanction blacks seizing freedom independent of white consent and close supervision. Emancipation was to be wholly white-initiated and controlled. Yet over the coming years, he assumed, they would become more independent of white control, acquire an ever greater freedom that would enable them to "be members of the community, & have a common interest with others in the support of good order & preservation [of] private property."[37] But currently slavery had left them nothing other than benighted, savage, larcenous—thoroughly unable to direct their lives purposively and morally on their own. Any independent freedom seeking by them now would invariably decline into a dangerous social anarchy.

Hart's proposal was never promulgated. The state actually took its first very tentative step toward emancipation by passing a law in 1777 which facilitated the manumission of those adults determined able to care for themselves. The law was enacted especially to benefit those male slaves who volunteered to serve or entered as a substitute for their owner in Connecticut regiments of the Continental Army. Gradual emancipation such as that envisioned by Levi Hart had to wait until after the end of the Revolution in 1784 when the first measures were passed which required the freeing of African Americans born after 1 March 1784 when they reached the age of 25 in the case of men and at the age of 21 for women. Although it made no provisions for compensating owners, the measure was in fact very much in the spirit of Levi Hart's proposal: it required young African Americans to remain with and labor for their former owners until their age of majority and the total slave population would be freed only very gradually over a number of years.

By 1800, the numerous representatives from the

Connecticut Society for the Promotion of Freedom who formed the core of the founders of the Connecticut Academy were in agreement about the essentials of black emancipation in the state: abolition was a good; blacks should be protected in their freedom; they were susceptible to dramatic improvement under regular moral and religious instruction; blacks could be made good citizens of the United States and the white reformers desired this.[38] Christianity, free and independent labor, and property ownership—these would be the ingredients of this progressive reformation of African Americans. While advance was by no means certain, in 1800 most members of the Academy had high hopes for black improvement and national inclusion, "a privilege and elevation to which we look forward with pleasure."[39] As Noah Webster echoed Levi Hart in 1793 with the assertion that "slavery benumbs the faculties of the mind, and renders men unfit to plan and direct the cultivation of a farm," the Academy's confident hope in 1800 was that, under the virtuous and bracing influence of freedom, this earlier unavoidable degradation of the human spirit was now being reversed and emancipated African Americans and those born free after 1784 would evince economic advance and moral improvement.[40] Thus Article #27 sought to determine to what degree these forces were operative on Connecticut black society by the turn of the century and what changes they had wrought. We can only imagine that the numerous antislavery figures in the Academy eagerly awaited the responses to this question.

Yet for these conservative abolitionists, blacks remained a people still very dependent, although revealing signs of wanting more independence but *with the assistance of caring, responsible whites.* All of them held in common an understanding of slave character: they were by definition degraded, devoid of responsible will, ignorant, and villainous. As Webster observed in 1793 in his seminal "The Effects of Slavery on Morals and Industry," the slave had "never had any will of his own" and was perfectly "subject to perpetual compulsion" from his or her master.[41] Of course this characterization is wrong: slaves were of value precisely because of their capacity to act independently of supervision, to solve problems on their own, and to act responsibly. Numerous examples of such agency and responsibility abounded from the era of the Revolution onward when slaves in Connecticut petitioned for their freedom, were manumitted for fighting in militias or, more commonly, seized freedom extra-legally by running away. Most recently, the narrative of the life of the Connecticut slave, Venture Smith, of whom all of these abolitionists would have been aware, established the tenacious dedication of African Americans to a responsible liberty despite enormous countervailing obstacles.[42]

Nevertheless this understanding of the effects of enslavement on individual character and on a culture—regardless of whether it was of African or European descent—pervaded the thinking of conservative abolitionists in the late eighteenth century.[43] The slave could not help but succumb to indolence, profligacy, and the wiles of demagogues. Freedom without a simultaneous commitment to uplift the ex-slaves and supervise them would prove worse for all than leaving them in slavery. And the members of the Connecticut Society were intent on directing that uplift.[44] The principal proponents of abolition in the North—a powerful stratum of the white elite who in Connecticut were responsible for authoring the town questionnaire—did in fact evince real hope that a wholly free and racially inclusive society could be forged in the North and possibly—if done correctly and very carefully and slowly—in the South as well.[45] But this conviction was grounded in their confidence that they wielded a near perfect domination over blacks, that blacks were willing to submit to their guidance, and that they could transform popular white antipathy toward blacks into a racial benevolence even though they recognized the deeply-rooted nature of those racial prejudices. As Henry Channing of the Connecticut Society wrote to Simeon Baldwin in 1790, "[our work] would diffuse thro the State much thinking & useful information and raise the feelings of many, who do not yet feel as they ought, upon the Subject."[46]

Emancipation in Connecticut and the Town Reports

Thus while in part describing accurately the conditions under which some of the state's African Americans lived, the Town Reports often illuminated the racial preconceptions and expectations of the observers as much, if not better, than they did the true state of Connecticut's African Americans. The respondents sought evidence to confirm their belief that the blacks once freed would become oriented toward achieving independent agency and to using their freedom responsibly by attending church, behaving with the proper decorum when in public, maintaining stable employment and families, avoiding all "low vices," and striving to accumulate property and secure the regard of the worthies of local society. In short, that they would follow the Connecticut Society's mandate to them in 1796 to "act worthily of the rank you have acquired as Freemen, and thereby to do credit to yourselves, and to justify the friends and advocates of your color in the eyes of the world."[47]

Yet the respondents commonly evaluated the state's blacks with little understanding for the complexities of the difficulties they confronted or with the willingness either to credit them for those advances attained or—perhaps most importantly—the willingness to wait patiently for evidence of these hard-won changes after generations of subjugation and racial disdain. Lacking literacy and the capital for land purchases while confronted with enduring white prejudices against their assimilation into local life; the newly emancipated confronted daunting challenges. This essay will perforce be focused on those white responses and their broader meaning rather than on an effort to characterize free black life in Connecticut in the late eighteenth and early nineteenth centuries and to determine the accuracy of the white responses.

Unfortunately the vast majority of the Town Reports give little or no substantive commentary on free blacks or slaves. Many towns that received the questionnaire from the Connecticut Academy did not respond to it. Of the 100 or more towns solicited, the Academy received replies from 44 towns. Of those 44 towns, only 24 included any reference to blacks, many with just a fleeting mention of their local population or that there were simply "No free blacks or Indians in town."[48] Of these 24 replies, only 17 directly addressed Article #27 and its concern to determine the degree and quality of changes in black character as African Americans moved from slavery to freedom. Finally only 10 of these can be said to respond to the question with any substance beyond, for example, the very brief—yet nevertheless worthwhile—observation from Willington: "free blacks old and young about 15 Generally industrious & quiet but acquire little or no property."[49] The absence of blacks from approximately half of the Reports attests to their scarcity in many towns in Connecticut, a fact partly due to increased mobility among the freed blacks by 1800 and a consequent movement out of rural areas. Their absence or the mere fleeting reference to them in the Reports also reveals their marginalization in those towns where they lived and the incidentalness with which they were viewed by the numerous commentators. Yet unfortunately and for reasons uncertain large towns such as Hartford, Stonington, and Groton, which all had significant black populations, did not submit reports and thus we are deprived of valuable information. The 25 percent or so of Reports with substantive commentary on local blacks nevertheless afford us invaluable insight into the lives of African Americans in turn-of-the-century Connecticut and perhaps even more so into the minds of the white elite cautiously observing and measuring them. It is also important to remember that documentary material directly treating black life in New England in the late eighteenth century and early nineteenth is unfortunately quite sparse and thus what the Town Reports yield is from that perspective actually quite extensive and rich.

The Reports revealed some hopeful developments but even more information, which might discourage the readers at the Academy. In Pomfret in 1800, the author observed that there were "very few (if any) negroes" but those residing there were free and "in general, pretty industrious." Winchester, responding late in 1813 to the queries, remarked that the town had few blacks, only "two or three families . . . and those not numerous." With a backhanded compliment, the author stated that he knew of none who were "addicted to any uncommon vices" and even "was informed" that some had read the Bibles he distributed in each of their households. Yet, he could not comment on "their ingenuity & industry previous to emancipation" because they were not resident in the town while slaves. Ridgefield in 1800 was even more affirmative. There, the eight blacks, who were mostly female and due to be free in a few years, were not only *not* "remarkably vicious" but were indeed "well educated and are no ways deficient in genius." The author also briefly recounted the story of a local "freeborn negro man" from the time of the Revolution who was married, a member of the church, and acquired property "by his own industry" and went to his grave worth £500. However the racially uplifting tone of the tale was sundered by the fact that his "adopted son a free molatto" squandered the whole of it in ten years.[50]

Significantly New London, Connecticut's leading port, offered the most encouraging appraisal of local blacks, differing distinctively from the vast majority of the Reports. The author proclaimed the vices of blacks "are fewer than those of the whites, in the same grades of society" and added that the "proportion [of blacks] married, & having families, much the same." The same proportions held true with religion and virtue, where there existed "as many professors of religion, & as many of exemplary life & conversation among the blacks, as among the whites." Likewise with blacks' industriousness. However, in concert with virtually all the other Reports noting it, the New London commentator once again acknowledged that in the critical area of property acquisition, blacks seem "to fall short." Nevertheless this report shone as the most optimistic submitted about black capacities and prospects.[51]

The counterweight of the skeptical, however, was onerous. Again and again towns referred to free blacks' supposed predilection to dissipation and idleness. Those giving little information at all often asserted this sole characterization. In 1803 Cheshire observed that the six to eight black families living there were "noted for very great want of economy" while the 30 or so free blacks in East Windsor in 1806 were "generally, not provident, fond of amusements and strong drink." Those whose responses regarding blacks were more extensive concluded likewise. Lebanon in 1800 reaffirmed that "they are generally more inclined to dissipation than industry" and Lisbon reiterated the same year that they are "troublesome members of society, being idle & thievish." Sharon found them in 1807 "indolent and thoughtless they make no calculation for the future." In 1811, Timothy Dwight of New Haven replied disdainfully: "Their vices are of all the kinds [called] '*low vice*.'" Farmington perhaps best summarized the baleful situation of free blacks in turn-of-the-century Connecticut: "Their ingenuity we have not had a specimen of & their virtues if any they have are a tallent hid in the earth." The motivation to improvement and virtue often appeared absent, even among those deemed otherwise inoffensive. This could only raise doubts among the readers of the free blacks' willingness to seize the opportunities for responsibility and advance with which their new-won freedom supposedly provided them.[52]

Moreover, whether or not the Report was largely favorable, virtually all authors commenting on the acquisition of property remarked that free blacks, with the exception of a few individuals, failed in this area. Farmington recorded that free blacks have had "no success in acquiring property" and Sharon that "not one is possessed of any real property." These findings were largely echoed by all other towns commenting on it including Lebanon, Cheshire, New Haven, New London, Willington, and Winchester. This failure could only be interpreted as significant, for the dutifulness and virtuousness apparently fostered by the desire to acquire and even more so by the actual ownership of property was assigned a central role in the reformation of black character. In the New Haven Report, Timothy Dwight acknowledged that "almost all, who acquire an attachment to property, appear to assume better principles; or at least better practices. Several of the men have in this manner become good members of society." If the free black population evinced little sign of the desire to possess property, let alone actually own it, that finding could only be damning, for without these attributes—

the *sine qua non* of black reconstruction according to key antislavery members of the Connecticut Academy—favorable black change simply could not occur and the prospects for the inclusion of African Americans could only dim.[53]

Unfortunately these were not the only findings—or even the most serious—raising grave doubts about the course of blacks' character under freedom. If Zephaniah Swift and Noah Webster were looking for clear-cut support for their theories that those born into quasi-freedom after 1784 or those removed from the degradations of slavery at an early enough age would evince a far greater capacity to improve themselves than would those who had lived under slavery well into their adult years and then been manumitted, they would find little comfort in the Town Reports. The mere commentaries cited above suggest doubts about such projections. But some towns specifically addressed Article #27's interest in "whether those born free are more ingenious, industrious and virtuous, than those who were emancipated after arriving to adult years." Sharon was blunt: "[there does not] seem any essential difference in the habits of those manumitted and these born free." Despite its relatively optimistic appraisal of black capacities and prospects, New London still observed little difference between those born free and those formerly enslaved: "The superiority of the natives, born free, over the emancipated, if it exists at all, is not very striking, perhaps all the difference may be imputed to different education." Stratfield added forebodingly that the roughly twenty free blacks in town in 1800 were "in low circumstances, not so profitable to themselves or Society as when slaves; as to improvements not very ambitious."[54]

The reporter from Lebanon amplified upon this notion that slavery actually benefited blacks, instructing them in industry and even virtue: "Those born free are not more industrious &c. than those who obtained freedom at abt. 30 years of age; the latter having acquired the habits of industry at a time of life when men of all classes and descriptions are most prone to amusements."[55] Not only were those born free not better in character than those raised in slavery, but indeed slavery for blacks had proven a much better environment for acquiring "the habits of industry" than evidently freedom had. Given the widespread assessment that blacks endowed with freedom were dissolute and idle, the implication of both the Stratfield and Lebanon Reports is that blacks under slavery were not only more productive and better regulated, they were better educated and prepared for freedom. This turns Webster's understanding of the impact of slavery on character on its head: far from being an inherently degrading experience, it was a benevolent if firm schoolhouse, to paraphrase Ulrich Bonnell Phillips, rearing the slaves up to industry and inner regulation.[56]

The Lebanon quote even implies that through their enslavement blacks received a benefit that "men of all classes and descriptions"—presumably referring to whites—did not gain by being removed from those "amusements" at precisely the time in a male life they prove so tempting. This is not to say that the author believes young white men might profit as well from the useful discipline of slavery! But the statement clearly asserts that for blacks—perhaps because of a deep-set belief that those of African descent had a uniquely and particularly strong predisposition toward dissolution and savagery—slavery actually shaped character in positive, fruitful ways, allowing young black men in particular to gain greater control over this likely predisposition. It is important to recognize that this provocative statement from Lebanon does not explicitly condemn blacks becoming free, although the author provides a grim picture of how free blacks use their liberty. However it does illustrate that as Connecticut emancipation, around which so many hopes adhered in the 1780s and '90s, was steadily being extended, some of those commenting on this great humanitarian event were coming quite paradoxically to weigh the real possibility that enslavement for blacks may have been and indeed might continue to be a real good. Such surprising reversals potentially held enormous implications for a young nation still grappling over whither it would go with African Americans and slavery. And certainly it raised grave doubts about the validity of the frankly optimistic environmentalism of Webster and Swift.

Indeed this selfsame environmentalism seems applied— whether deliberately or not is unknown—by Wallingford's reporter to trump that very hopefulness for improvement and inclusion embodied in Webster. Writing significantly in 1812 after emancipation had been underway for some time, George Stanley of Wallingford, a local Judge of Probate Court, discerned that blacks "hold in society that rank to which their unfortunate situation among white men, their superiors in numbers, education, & property; rather than the appointment of their Creator, or the benevolent wishes of the philanthropist, seems to have confined their race."[57] Notably this rank has not been fixed by divine mandate so is therefore not ineluctable. Nor is it susceptible to the idle visions of how humanitarian reformers wish human society to be ordered—among whom perhaps Stanley included the Noah Webster and Zephaniah Swift of their 1790s works. Rather it is the tough result of the interaction of individual capacities and power in the context of Connecticut over the past near two hundred years. It is unavoidably the result of environment. The author does not make clear whether that superiority is due to the inherent greater capacities of whites or is due simply to the fact that whites were enabled to progress far more than blacks while the latter were enslaved. Perhaps it is a bit of both. Yet, regardless of causation, the fact remains that blacks, according to Stanley, were at the bottom of society where they were likely to remain "confined" as a result of whatever conditions allowed whites to gain such an apparently irremediable superiority over them.

And this characterization of the world confronting the emancipated black was in fact far more accurate than the environment projected by Webster and Swift. They imagined the young adult free black would readily be able to assume the opportunities freedom provided, unhindered by the enduring prejudices and antipathies of whites or the legacy of deprivations and demoralization adhering to African Americans whether born free or enslaved. In the world of Judge Stanley the social environment operated much more so as to frustrate any noble black promptings to economic, moral, and civic improvement—promptings, which, while maybe infrequent, he does not altogether dismiss as impossible. This is a significantly different understanding of the world confronting free blacks than the dominant view advanced by the antislavery elite in the 1790s. This was the outlook that flowed directly into the conclusion that striving blacks had no choice but to remove themselves from this world and that proper white society had no choice but to refuse to include the remaining dissolute blacks into their society. This of course was the ideological animus of the American Colonization Society.

Although the New London Report was written about 1812, Stanley's from Wallingford and Dwight's from New Haven—both of which were among the most substantial reports collected— were issued in 1811 or 1812 and suggest a trend toward increasingly negative conclusions about black prospects. Timothy Dwight's was particularly grim as we have already noted and a sermon he gave just a year earlier resonated with similar doubts. Dwight also merits closer attention because he was such a central member of the Academy and his opinions carried such weight within the organization. In *The Charitable Blessed*, preached in New Haven in August 1810, Dwight's evaluation of the current situation of blacks was anything but upbeat:

> [T]hese people...are, generally, neither able, nor inclined, to make their freedom a blessing to themselves. When they first became free, they are turned out into the world, in circumstances, fitted to make them only nuisances to society. They have no property; nor any skill to acquire it. Nor have they, in the proper sense, generally any industry. They have indeed been used to labor; but it was under the controul, and for the benefit, of others. The hatred of labour, in this situation becomes habit; not the labour itself. They have no economy; and waste, of course, much of what they earn. They have little knowledge either of morals or religion. They are left, therefore, as miserable victims to sloth, prodigality, poverty, ignorance, and vice.[58]

Moreover, Dwight continued, black people will communicate all of these propensities to their children who will decline even further "until they have reached the lowest point of degradation both in ignorance and vice; and will become blots and burdens upon society." However, remaining the good environmentalist, Dwight concluded for both parents and children: "Who in such circumstances would not be vicious?"

Yet he offered a foreboding characterization: "They have the usual appetites and passions of man; and love to eat and drink, to wear finery, and to riot in amusements, just as we do; but are unfurnished with those restraints on those propensities, with which a merciful God has furnished us."[59] On the one hand, this is an assertion of equivalence between black and white with regard to animal appetites and capacity for profligacy. Yet there is an equally striking absence of blacks from those furnished by "a merciful God" with the devices for overcoming these dangerous impulses. Is this to suggest that the capacity for self-regulation was not bestowed upon them? It is ambiguous and Dwight does not assert their lacking it, but they certainly are also not included among those possessing such capacity and

that is significant in even hinting at some innate, insurmountable moral difference between the two races. A statement a page later seems to resolve the confusion. Dwight argues that blacks are not becoming social encumbrances "because they are weaker, or worse, by nature, than we are; but because they are destitute of the advantages, which, under God, raise us above their miserable level."[60] Presumably "advantages" here refers to the social conditions such as schools, stable families, civic institutions, Protestant worship, free labor and property ownership, all of which promote a vigorous and responsible citizenry and all of which local free blacks were destitute. But Dwight explicitly did not attribute their weaknesses to "nature." Yet once again he hints at the probability that whites have been endowed with capacities allowed to advance "under God" so immeasurably beyond the attainment of blacks that they render *de facto* the superiority of whites absolute—if not innate. This racializing of difference, however tentative, is particularly significant issuing from a traditional Calvinist such as Dwight, for it was by way of this theological mainstream in New England of which he was a vital part that the essential unity of black and white through God's singular act of creation was traditionally asserted.

Dwight argued that if blacks are ever to have even the pretense of approximating the levels of whites' self-regulation and accomplishments, whites must immediately offer blacks broad-based charitable assistance to uplift them. They cannot do it alone, but remain absolutely dependent on responsible whites. "To give them liberty, and stop here, is to entail upon them a curse. We are bound to give them, also, knowledge, industry, economy, good habits, moral and religious instruction, and all the means of eternal life...The performance of this duty will make them blessings, the neglect of it will make them curses, to society."[61]

While the clarion to white charity is meritorious and such extensive assistance to the freed people would be essential, in fact very little would be forthcoming from Dwight or from any of Connecticut's other abolitionists who had spoken so often and so eloquently about the centrality of racial benevolence. At the same time the force of popular prejudice and of economic privation continued to impede any black initiative. Indeed the total absence of any form of state assistance to the freed people or of only the most random or sparse voluntary aid from individuals and organizations distinguishes the emancipation in the North from that in the South where—however finally limited—the Freedmen's Bureau, Land Commissions such as existed in South Carolina, and innumerable teachers and missionaries affiliated with the American Missionary Association provided at least a modicum of useful transitional help to the hundreds of thousands of Southern freed people. No such services would be available to those in the North and their absence would contribute to the grim conclusions reached by white observers about African Americans in the early nineteenth century. Failing this assistance, blacks in New Haven revealed, to Dwight, no prospects for progress amid much for profligacy.

The impress of a profound black dependence pervades *The Charitable Blessed*, and Dwight's New Haven Report of a year later seemed only to confirm that it persisted and grew. These were a people deemed hopeless without extensive benevolent white intervention, a people who by the very definition applied to slavery by Dwight, Webster, Swift, and others had known only degradation and submission in slavery and had no capacity to understand what the virtues and responsibilities of freedom were. Their freedom, Dwight declared, was bestowed upon them by whites: "Under the influence of overwhelming conviction, we have made the descendants of these abused people [i.e., the original Africans] free."[62] Moreover blacks now were perceived as equally dependent upon whites to make them capable of freedom, an endeavor requiring great and deliberate exertion from whites if that dependence was ever to be extirpated. It could not have escaped the astute eye of Timothy Dwight that assistance on that scale was not and likely would not be forthcoming, despite the evident intention of *The Charitable Blessed* to rally such assistance. And precisely because the enormity of black problems would require such an unlikely level of charity, blacks were consequently always poised on the very edge of the precipice of abandonment either to a permanently inferior status or to a demand that they be removed. As town after town reported little improvement if not outright decline and that little difference was discerned between those born in slavery and those not, blacks drew that much closer to the edge. Rather than being represented as steadily if slowly evolving free agents, the contrary condition of blacks as essential dependents sharpened and extended. Not long after Dwight finished his report, white Connecticut in fact was giving clear signs of initiating that abandonment. In 1814 the Connecticut State Legislature passed a law denying the vote to all African Americans and this disfranchisement[63] was cemented through its incorporation into the new state constitution of 1818. By the latter year, the former friends of the emancipated offered no opposition whatsoever to this devastating measure.[64]

The abandonment of the cause of black uplift and inclusion by those white men most involved in promoting it since the 1790s became explicit as some of the most important members of the Connecticut Society for the Promotion of Freedom who were also original members of the CAAS threw their support by 1820 to the organization calling for the voluntary removal of free blacks to Africa, the American Colonization Society (ACS). Created in late 1816 under the immediate inspiration of the New Jersey minister, Robert Finley, the ACS coalesced the mounting frustrations and anxieties of the white elite in the North and Upper South with the growing number of free blacks who they increasingly concluded were "an idle, worthless, and thievish race" and who faced a barrier between themselves and free whites "which [they] can never hope to transcend."[65] Thus the best plan for America and the most benevolent for free blacks was to encourage them to emigrate to some land where, with the assistance of the ACS, they might better be able to develop and exercise the real gifts with which God endowed them.

By the late 1810s, the ACS found a number of prominent recruits in Connecticut.[66] Jeremiah Day, elected to membership in the CAAS before 1810 (and later succeeding Dwight as President of the Academy), was also an active member of the Connecticut Society, but nevertheless by 1820 had become one of four vice-presidents of the auxiliary of the American Colonization Society in New Haven. Aeneas Munson, one of the founding associates in the CAAS, had earlier been a prominent member of the Connecticut Society, yet in 1820 was designated a manager in the ACS auxiliary. David Daggett, an original member of the CAAS, by 1820 had become a vice-president of the auxiliary even though in 1792 and 1793 he had, as a key representative of the Connecticut Society, doggedly pursued and litigated against individuals in Cheshire, Durham, Wethersfield, and elsewhere who continued to hold in slavery individuals who had been freed through deed or through the Gradual Emancipation Act of 1784.[67] Indeed another principal actor with Daggett in these actions was Simeon Baldwin, who by 1820 had become no less than the president of the auxiliary. This transformation to colonizationist is perhaps illuminated most tellingly in Baldwin who in 1792 had spoken glowingly of fellow members of the Connecticut Society serving diligently as blacks' "guardians and protectors" while they acquired the skills that might allow them to "become the expert fellow citizens of a free people." By 1820, however, Baldwin was one of the state's leaders in promoting the very same people's removal.

The rise of the colonizationist movement in the United States testified to the widespread collapse of inclusionist hopes among leading white clerics, professionals, and academics in the North who had been some of the most important purveyors of this vision at least through the early years of the nineteenth century. This was certainly the case in Connecticut. What were tentative suspicions and doubts in the Town Reports had by 1823 hardened into axioms. The Reverend Leonard Bacon, newly appointed Pastor of New Haven's First Church, its leading Congregational parish, and the inheritor from the deceased Timothy Dwight of local leadership of conservative benevolence toward blacks, effectively articulated this critical transition by the mid-1820s. Couched in humanitarian terms, Bacon's plea highlighted the degradation of blacks in New Haven and beyond which currently seemed ineradicable:

> [W]hen you look over this city, what do you find to be the actual state and character of its coloured population? How many of the privileges which belong to other classes of society do they enjoy? How much of the happiness in which you are now rejoicing is theirs? How many of the motives, which are urging you to honest industry or to honourable enterprise, are operating upon them? Who among them ever aspires to wealth or office, or ever dreams of intellectual pursuits or intellectual enjoyment? In short, are they not, in the estimation of the community and in their own consciousness, aliens and outcasts in the midst of the people?[68]

Although in the form of questions, Bacon's words nevertheless clearly asserted an essential exclusion of blacks from the responsible world of citizenry and ownership. Two years earlier in a review of early annual reports from the ACS written for *The Christian Spectator*, Bacon was more pointed:

> Are there not thousands of blacks in New England? And do they add anything to the good order and happiness of society? Or rather are they not, and must they not continue to be, as a body, ignorant and vicious, adding more to the poor rates of the parishes in which they reside, than they do to the income of the government?[69]

In effect, Bacon wrote his own town reports and reinforced the findings of Wallingford in 1811-1812 and of Timothy Dwight in 1811. Only now their nature was no longer in doubt: "There are in the United States 238,000 blacks denominated free, but whose freedom confers on them . . . no privilege but the privilege of being more vicious and miserable than slaves can be. Their condition . . . may be repeated in two words—irremediable degradation."[70] No longer is there an inquiry regarding the relative station and character of slave and free black in Connecticut and the nation. It is self-evident that the mass of free blacks is in fact far more degraded and of far less value than slaves. It is significant that these conclusions were reached by Bacon for he unlike most colonizationists continued to believe that some efforts must be made to ameliorate the great problems and poverty confronting blacks in America and that some free blacks in the country revealed a striking capacity for enterprise, self-regulation and self-improvement, and civic responsibility. He also observed that some uplift of industry and racial integrity would redound to those blacks remaining in the United States from the inevitable successes realized by their more courageous and visionary black brethren in their African colony. Yet Bacon made clear that the highest form that uplift could take domestically would be to impel those "thousands of young men of color to seek a home on the . . . shores of Africa" as well.[71]

Bacon is definitive regarding the ultimate ineffectualness of directing the mass of benevolent efforts domestically to resolve the nation's racial crisis.

> What other scheme [than colonization], then, for the improvement of the blacks, is there before the public? What other efforts are we exhorted to make? What other projects do we hear of? There are a few Sunday schools established for their benefit in our large towns; and in some of our cities the Africans have churches of their own, and tolerably well qualified ministers of their own....But efforts of this kind, taken by themselves, hardly amount to anything; they do not in the least affect the essence of the evil.[72]

Significantly Bacon then turned to extend this conclusion of futility to the very embodiment of this energetic optimism for black advance and inclusion at the turn of the century. "The same remark will apply with at least equal force to the projects of "the American Convention for promoting the Abolition of Slavery, and improving the condition of the African race...." With this judgment, Bacon dismissed outright most of the basic racial preconceptions and hopes embraced by all of the state abolition societies—including Connecticut—who comprised the American Convention and even in an attenuating form by Timothy Dwight in the early 1810s. While agreeing with them that blacks held the capacity to improve themselves, he firmly rejected the argument that vigorous white efforts would lead to substantive improvement for them anywhere in the United States. Here they will only remain degraded and "dangerous to the community, and this danger ought to be removed. . . . If then there is any hope of extensive good for these two millions of beings, it must be found in the plans proposed by the American Colonization Society."[73] The abandonment of hopes here for any form of black assimilation is near complete. As Bacon stated bluntly: "[Y]ou cannot bleach him into the enjoyment of freedom."[74] He thus reflected the re-direction of elite white benevolence by the early 1820s away from domestic endeavors striving for some form of racial inclusivity and instead toward a distant, foreign site which would enable racial separation and an eventual removal of all blacks from America. This was a broad and pragmatic realism that refused to chase further the chimeras of the American Convention of Abolition Societies. Bacon predicted that those most benevolent toward blacks would recognize that true amelioration for blacks would be focused on the African settlement, not on futile gestures here.

Bacon's cordoning off of African Americans and encouraging their removal also reflected an important shift between the 1790s and the 1820s in the relationship of leading Connecticut Congregationalists to blacks. Virtually all of the members of the Connecticut Society who were also members of the CAAS were Congregationalists of one form or another, ranging from New Divinity figures such as Levi Hart and Jonathan Edwards, Jr. to moderate Old Lights such as James Dana, Simeon Baldwin, and Theodore Dwight. Despite their doctrinal disputes—some of which, such as that over the source of evil, could be quite pitched—all of these men in the 1790s were largely in agreement that all humans were united by their innate depravity and their inability to do anything to effect their salvation and this concurrence could help to forge racial union. Thirty years later, however, as Congregationalism came under increased pressure to spur revivalism and compete with other denominations for adherents, the ruling divines became increasingly comfortable with according some role to human agency in the process of conversion, and with believing that one might choose or not to open one's heart to the offer of God's grace. One might then be blamed for a failure to experience regeneration, especially as the image of God was softened in the early nineteenth century and a benevolent deity was recognized as potentially extending grace to all who open themselves to it.

This theological shift could have significant implications for blacks, especially as their former paternalistic supporters simultaneously underwent this shift and confronted the apparent intractability of black "problems" and failure to improve. As Bacon—an eminent representative of these changes—so clearly emphasized, blacks as a whole failed to choose to advance themselves, a failure which well might be fundamentally a failure to accept God's grace and which in turn could cause or foster the other problems. The efficacy of human choice played a much greater role in the explanation of blacks' current condition than it did in the late eighteenth century. By the 1820s it had become much easier to isolate, marginalize, and quarantine free blacks based on their supposed failure of volition and motivation. While this process was a complicated one drawing on a variety of political, social, and economic changes, doctrinal trends in Congregationalism informed it importantly, all the more so because religious leaders in New Haven and elsewhere in the state were so prominent in current movements addressing racial issues.[75]

The Connecticut Town Reports were critical in redirecting white elite thinking about the character of and prospects for free blacks. Initiated in the midst of the real hopes by the authors of the CAAS inquiry for steady and substantial improvement in the physical and moral condition of the state's black population, in the end the Town Reports seemed only to have strengthened into conviction the persisting suspicion that blacks would be profligate with their freedom, that their dependence on whites would prove permanent rather than transitory, and that they would encumber rather than uplift society. Nothing pointed more clearly to the colonizationist reformulation of conservative white benevolence than did the Wallingford Town Report of 1812 which asserted that "they hold in society that rank to which their unfortunate situation among white men, their superiors in numbers, education, & property...seems to have confined their race."[76] The fact of emancipation in the North and the existence of blacks there by the early nineteenth century in a world largely free of slaves provided the first opportunity in the United States to evaluate what happened to blacks in America when they existed outside of slavery. Such an evaluation could not be made among the free blacks of the South—even in Virginia where the nation's largest numbers of free blacks lived—because they were always mingled with a far larger population of slaves. If free blacks in the North faltered—if they were determined not to show signs of improvement—then it became harder to argue that their "degradation" and failures of enterprise were "owing to the

degrading state of slavery."[77] It could in fact become easier to blame these failures on innate character and biological differences such as Thomas Jefferson hypothesized in 1784.

While hinting at it, Bacon and other white colonizationists still did not rely on such essentialist categorization of the races such as would become more common after 1830.[78] They continued to look to the social environment of the North to explain why black advance had failed to occur more substantially after emancipation *and* why African Americans were fully capable of that advance in an environment free of the deep impediments the American one posed. Indeed sensitivity to the impact and obdurateness of discrimination and racism as important environmental factors affecting black station and advance was much greater in the 1820s than in the 1790s when paternalist hopes were relatively high for transforming such white prejudice. Only now this persisting environmentalism was brought full force to justify black removal. Moreover white prejudice in the 1820s was increasingly upheld as reflecting the not-unreasonable anxieties about the capacity of blacks to incline toward a dangerous depravity and fear that freedom for them—and for the local community—could prove more of a curse than a blessing.

Perhaps this shift reflected a recurring tendency in American racial politics, one we witnessed as well in the 1970s: a reaction against blacks once reformers were brought to face directly the complexity and perdurability of racial dissonance in the nation and how difficult it would be to alter. While the American Convention of Abolition Societies in the 1790s would especially require that reformers must be dedicated to seeking broad-based public and private support and instruction for freed blacks, in fact little was produced, certainly in Connecticut where the will to such assistance largely seems not to have existed. The thousands of freed blacks in the state would require far more than one simple transformative gesture by reformers and state legislatures. Yet these conservative reformers—deeply concerned as they were not to distress social order—together with popular thinking on the very limited sphere of governmental action, virtually made impossible the more radical approaches needed to address the profound problems that entrenched racial inequality and slavery posed in early nineteenth-century America.

Invisible Indians: The Connecticut Academy Town Reports

Jill E. Martin

Introduction

The Connecticut Academy of Arts and Sciences asked towns in the early nineteenth century to answer a series of questions about life in their towns. Two sets of questions related to Indians. The first set asked how the lands of the town were obtained—whether from Indians, and if so, whether by purchase or conquest. The second set asked about Indian place names, "also any remarkable occurrences in the history of the Indians, their customs, mythology, battles, burying places, monuments, forts and any other traces of their settlement," the tribe, and "their present number and situation, as to subsistence, vices, &c."[1]

The questions themselves reveal a lot about the state of Indian affairs in Connecticut at that time. Most of the questions address Indians in relation to the past. Asking how the land was acquired is asking about an historical event, in some towns, almost 200 years in the past. Asking if there are "any traces of their settlement" implies that the questioner believes the Indians are mostly gone. Questions about the Indian customs and mythology would be better asked of Indians, rather than town fathers. There are negative implications in the questions, from a twentieth-century viewpoint. The question regarding Indians' present situation implies that Indians would be subsisting outside of the dominant, white economy, rather than integrated into the life of the town, and that Indians would be known for their vices, rather than their virtues.

Responses to these questions are the main references to Indians in the Town Reports. Occasionally, Indians were also mentioned in response to questions dealing with suicides, or murders, which took place within the past twenty years from the time of the report. Farmington, Litchfield, Middlesex, Saybrook, New Haven, and New London all mention murders committed by Indians in the town.[2] Indians are also mentioned occasionally in regard to agricultural methods adopted from them. Bethlem, Bolton, Farmington, Kent and Litchfield all mention the Indian practice of burning the woods, " to procure feed for their game or other purposes."[3] The practice was continued by early English settlers.

But the overriding sense one receives, when reading the Town Reports, is that Indians existed in the past. And those in the present are on the periphery of the town reporter's vision. Yet there were Indians in Connecticut at this time, whose descendants are living in Connecticut today. Colin Calloway, in his introductory essay in *After King Philip's War: Presence and Persistence in Indian New England* comments "that invisibility, like beauty, is in the eye of the beholder, that Indians have been here all along and that any portrait of New England's past that omits Indians through the eighteenth, nineteenth and early twentieth century is an incomplete sketch."[4] This essay will attempt to show why the town reporters viewed Indians as a historical fact, and will complete the sketch with Indians.

Land Purchases

Land was always important to the English colonists. Land was scarce in England, which looked abroad to expand its land holdings, and obtain raw goods for import. The colonists therefore valued land as a commodity. In many early colonies, owning land was a prerequisite to voting and having a say in the running of the community. Having land meant one could support a family. In America, there was no system of titles or primogeniture where land was passed only to the oldest son. Land was so readily available it could be bought cheaply. And then the land could be improved by the colonists, thus increasing its value.

Most towns received their land by purchase from the Indians. Individuals were appointed on behalf of the town to negotiate and buy land from the Indians. Often these individuals were from some larger nearby community, which was splitting off to form a smaller, new town, or, as in the case of Haddam, by an appointment from the general court or colony of Connecticut. The town reporter in Sharon, settled in 1738, noted that the Indians opposed the settlers. "The settlers contented themselves with titles purchased of the Colonial Government and the government it is feared was too regardless in this instance of the justice due to the original lords of the soil."[5] Some of the English settlers had royal charters or patents, which gave them rights to the land.

Early European explorers claimed right to the land under a right of discovery. As to other European nations, the country that first landed or explored the land owned it, so long as there were no Christians living on the land. If there were only "infidels" and "heathens," the land belonged to the discovering nation. The European right of discovery was accepted as a legal doctrine by the "civilized" nations of the world, and they were the only ones who mattered to each other. But having a royal charter wasn't much help when faced with the realities of the New World. It might mean something to the French or the Dutch, but would have no import with the Indians. So land was purchased from the Indians. This European right of discovery was considered by the United States Supreme Court in 1823, during the time many of the town reporters were writing.

In *Johnson v. McIntosh*, the Supreme Court, in an opinion written by Chief Justice John Marshall, upheld the right of discovery.[6] The United States, through the Treaty of Paris, had all the rights that England had as the discovering country. This included all rights to the land within its boundaries, except for the Indian right to occupancy. The Indians had the right of occupancy to the land as long as they occupied the land, or until it was purchased or conquered by the government. Chief Justice John Marshall wrote, "Although we do not mean to engage in the defence of those principles which Europeans have applied to Indian title, they may, we think, find some excuse, if not justification, in the character and habits of the people whose rights were wrested from them."[7] Marshall finds this justification in the fact that " the tribes of Indians inhabiting this country were fierce savages, whose occupation was war, and whose subsistence was drawn chiefly from the forest. To leave them in possession of their country was to leave the country a wilderness."[8] So it was legal and moral for the United States to hold the title, and take the land from the Indians. The town reporters knew the Indians were savages; it was confirmed by the Supreme Court.

Many scholars argue that Marshall had no choice but to uphold the right of discovery; to do otherwise would have affected over 200 years worth of land title, and brought into question almost all of the land ownership in the United States. Less than ten years later, Marshall's doubts about the right of discovery were raised in *Worcester v. Georgia*.[9] While acknowledging that the Court needed to look at and support the present day reality of Indian/Anglo-American relations, he commented on the right of discovery. "It is difficult to comprehend the proposition, that the inhabitants of either quarter of the globe could have rightful original claims of dominion over the inhabitants of the other, or over the lands they occupied; or that the discovery of either by the other should give the discoverer rights in the country discovered, which annulled the pre-existing rights of its ancient possessors."[10] Marshall's doubts did not affect the national attitude towards Indians. And it did not affect the title to lands in Connecticut.

Deeds for the purchase of land from Indians are described in the Town Reports and the purchase price always seems modest. Bethlem reports that "the price given to the Indians is not known but supposed to be triffling." In Haddam, four of the signatories for the Indians each received 10 coats, while the Middlesex County Report notes the purchase price as thirty coats, "which may have been worth one hundred dollars." New Haven and the surrounding towns were purchased from two Indians, Momauguin, sachem of Quinnipiack, and Montowese, sachem of Mattabeseck, in two transactions in 1638. The price paid to Momauguin was 12 coats of English cloth, 12 alchemy spoons, 12 hatchets, 12 hoes, two dozen knives, 12 porringers, and four cases of French knives and scissors. Preston was purchased from Oanoco, son of Uncas, and sachem of the Mohegan Indians, for "fifty pounds, in four equal, annual payments, to be made by them, to him, provisions or other goods at current prices." Most of the town

of Guilford was purchased for 12 each of coats, fathoms of wampum, plates, shoes, hatchets, stockings, hoes, kettles, knives, hats, porringers, spoons, and two English coats.[11] One could argue that the Indians negotiated with the English settlers and received what they considered a good price. The metal tools and implements, and the manufactured goods were not items the Indians could produce themselves. Certainly in the early purchases, the Indians outnumbered the English, and could have refused to sell land, or exacted a higher price. But the Indians' concept of land ownership and land usage was different from the English concept.

In many of the deeds conveying land, the Indians retained to themselves the right to hunt and fish on the ceded land. The Town Reports of East Windsor, Farmington, Guilford, Haddam, Middlesex, Killingworth, New Haven all mention the inclusion of such a provision.[12] The Indians considered that the English would use the land as they did. The majority of Indians in Connecticut migrated seasonally, traveling between one, two or three sites. They were hunters, and gatherers, with some agricultural and fishing sites, and they expected the English to behave the same. They used what they caught, and grew what they needed. William Cronon, in *Changes in the Land*, discusses how many Indian people viewed ownership of the land. "What the Indians owned—or more precisely, what their village gave them claim to—was not the land but the things that were on the land during the various seasons of the year. It was a conception of property shared by many of the hunter-gatherers and agricultural peoples of the world, but radically different from that of the invading Europeans."[13] It was the right to use the land held in common by the tribe.

The English saw land used only for hunting and fishing as vacant and unoccupied, and therefore "unused." Allowing the Indians the right to continue to hunt and fish on the land did not mean maintaining the land in its then form. The English would develop the land—build homes, clear fields, grow crops on the land, and the Indians would be allowed to hunt and fish until they interfered with the English growth. The Indians did not expect the fast growth of English settlements, the cutting down of the forest, the thinning of game and fish. By maintaining the right to hunt and fish, and travel across the land, they most likely believed that the land would still be available for the means for which they "used" it, and did not expect the land to be so changed as to be unusable for their needs. "Indians were unable to comprehend the European pattern of land ownership because none of their existence corresponded to anything like it. They considered land to be part of their sacred universe, an aspect of the divine order of things, held in trust for posterity. For someone to have the selfish audacity to insist on restricting part of the soil for his exclusive control was beyond their comprehension."[14]

Many towns reported that the land was purchased from Uncas, sachem of the Mohegans, or his sons Owanaco (Oanoco) and Joshua. These included purchases in Canterbury, part of Guilford, Lebanon, Killingworth, Saybrook, Pomfret, Preston, and Windham.[15] The deeds from

"John Underhill, an English army captain, along with Captain John Mason, led the attack on the Pequots fort at Mystic in 1637. This engraved diagram of the fort, which was originally part of Newes from America published in London in 1638, is the only representation of the event by an eyewitness." Quoted from the Mashantucket Pequot Museum and Research Center, Archives and Special Collections, MSS 52, Bibliography of Pequot Materials.

Uncas, and his sons cover a large area of land, because he claimed all the Pequot land, besides Mohegan land, as the spoils of war.

The Pequots were the strongest tribe in Connecticut, with their main location along the Pequot, now Thames, River. They had overpowered the tribes as far west as New Haven, and as far east as the Narragansetts in Rhode Island. The English believed themselves threatened by the strength of the Pequots, who controlled trade and land. A series of small skirmishes between the English and the Pequots occurred. In 1637, a murder committed on an English trader by an Indian from another tribe provoked the English. The alleged murderer escaped to Pequot land and the English wrath turned against the Pequots. The Saybrook Report gives details of the attacks on the settlers by the Pequots, though there is no mention of any attacks by the English against the Indians. "By these repeated murders and injuries the inhabitants of Connecticut Colony were greatly alarmed, not only for the safety of their friends at Saybrook, but for the safety of themselves and families. They saw nothing before them but destruction, unless the rage and power of the Pequots could be broken. The General Court, therefore, being summoned together on the 1st of May, came to the resolution of waging immediate war with that perfidious and cruel nation."[16] The Connecticut colonists assembled an army of 90 men, and were joined by Uncas, sachem of the Mohegans, and 70 of his men. The Mohegans were a group of Pequots who had broken away from the main tribe, and were willing to fight their former tribe. Uncas may have hoped to revenge himself against the Pequot leadership, and used the English to assist him.

The English, led by Captain John Mason, sailed past the Pequot fort, leaving the Pequots to believe they were not attacking, and went to the Narragansetts in Rhode Island. Mason asked the Narragansetts for permission to cross their territory and strike the Pequots from the land. The Narragansetts were enemies of the Pequots, and were willing to allow this to help defeat their enemy. Some Narragansett Indians joined the colonists, but may not have taken part in any of the fighting. The Pequot fort was a palisaded village, with many dwellings inside. The colonists surprised the fort at daybreak, at a time when most of the warriors were away, and killed between 600-700 men, women and children, burning down the village. The colonists and Mohegans lost two soldiers. The Town Report of Saybrook includes this narrative.[17]

The Pequots who escaped spread out throughout Connecticut, seeking refuge in other tribes. The town of Guilford includes a report of an incident that took place after the Pequot battle, which resulted in the naming of Sachem's Head.[18] A Pequot sachem, fleeing westward, was pursued and fatally shot by Uncas. Uncas then cut off the sachem's head and stuck it in the fork of an oak tree, where it remained for years. The town of Saybrook includes an account of the same event.[19] Middletown reports that Sowheag, the great sachem of the Mattabesett (Mattabeseck) Indians, who had given land to the settlers, aided the Pequots during the Pequot War.[20]

The Pequot War affected the ownership of land. The war was officially ended with the Tripartite Treaty, also known as the Treaty of Hartford, signed by the colonists, the Mohegans and the Narragansetts. There was to be permanent peace between the Narragansetts and the Mohegans. If there was any quarrel between the two tribes, it would be settled by the Connecticut authorities. The Pequot survivors were forbidden to reorganize and live together as a tribe. The surviving Pequots were divided among the tribes who had sided with the colonists. The Pequot land was to be the property of the colonists by right of conquest.[21]

Uncas however, claimed much of the conquered Pequot territory as his, by virtue of his descent from the sachems of the Pequots, and as a right of conquest. The colonists allowed him to make these claims. Uncas was seen by the colonists as a strong ally, and the colonists still needed Indian allies. Uncas was willing to work with the English to make himself and his tribe more powerful. Uncas was willing to sell this Pequot land to settlers because it was not land his tribe used to maintain their lifestyle. Only one town claimed land by conquest—New London, near where the Pequot stronghold was located. The Report notes "it being also the only place which the english in these parts have possessed by conquest, & that upon a very just war, upon that great & warlike people, the Pequots."[22]

The Tripartite Treaty changed the balance of power among the Indians and the colonists. The most powerful tribe was destroyed, and was never to reorganize. Two other tribes, the Mohegans and the Narragansetts, had agreed to let the

Engraving of an Algonquian village street, showing a well-established agricultural and hunting village. From Theodor de Bry, Grand Voyages (Franckfort am Mayn: Matthier Merian, 1624). Mashantucket Pequot Museum and Research Center, Archives and Special Collections, MSS115.

sachems reveals the change in the power structure. The Indians, by conquest and agreement, had allowed the English to take power over them.

Invisible Indians

In many of the Town Reports, Indians are not even mentioned. And when they are mentioned, it is usually in an historical context, telling about when the town was founded, and all mention of Indians is in the past.

In some towns, it is stated that there are no Indians. East Windsor reports that of the descendants of the Indians who sold the town land, "None of them now exist." In Haddam, there was " but one Indian family." There was only one family in Cornwall, "five in number." In Kent, there were 40 Indians, because there had been a reservation set up for the Schaghticoke. The reporter from Lisbon (Newent) comments that "Indians may still be seen passing and repassing, vending articles of their own manufacturing and performing their kind of labor where any wish to employ them," but he notes that "they have as a settlement or village been wholly extinct." The Middlesex town reporter notes that "the last remnant of the Indians left the country half a century ago, and no certain information is possessed of their present situation and character, nor even of their existence." New Haven reports that "The Quinnipiacks have long since been extinct." In Pomfret, "there are but very few Indians." Preston lists eleven Indians, while Ridgefield recognizes one, Lisbon (Hanover) four, Stratfield twelve, and Union, Washington, and Willington, none.[24]

Yet we in the twentieth century know that there are five state recognized tribes

colonists settle their disputes — let the colonists have a hand in the internal conduct of their own affairs. The Town Report of East Windsor includes a report of the General Court of Hartford in 1656, which ordered two sachems, of the Mohegans and the Podunks, to come before the court to settle differences over the murder of a Mohegan sachem.[23] The Court could not get the Indians to resolve their differences, but made it clear that no injury should come to the English. While "the solemn arbitration of the English, on the disputes of the Indians, as now mentioned, prov[ed] ineffectual," the fact that the Court could summon Indian

in Connecticut— the Mashantucket Pequot, the Mohegan, the Paucatuck (Eastern) Pequot, the Golden Hill Paugussett and the Schaghticoke. Two of these tribes, the Mashantucket Pequot and the Mohegan, are also federally recognized, and the other three tribes are seeking federal recognition. Part of the process of achieving federal recognition is showing or proving that the tribe has existed as a political and cultural entity since European contact. So the question we must ask ourselves is how could we have Indians at the end of the twentieth century, with few to no Indians noted at the beginning of the nineteenth century? Where were these Indians, and why were they invisible?

In his book, *History of the Indians of Connecticut from the Earliest Known Period to 1850,* published in 1850, John DeForest comments that the Indians are in a "steady and apparently irremediable decline."[25] But he has no problem accepting the decline of the Indians, and in ways even celebrating it. What would happen if the Indians still lived in Connecticut? He writes,

> Tracks of wild beast would be found where now extends the solid pavement trodden by thousands of human feet; the savage bear would be seen coming out of his hollow tree, where now crowds of intelligent youth are emerging from the seats of learning; the screams of the wild cat, or the panther, would be heard where now resounds the busy hum of machinery, or the sweet melody of sacred music; the land, which is now as the garden of Eden, would then be a desolate wilderness.[26]

While DeForest is writing a few decades after the Town Reports were sent into the Connecticut Academy, he was expressing the ideas of most of the American citizens, and also the earlier English colonists. Replacing the uncivilized Indians with the civilized, Christianized English was considered a positive outcome of colonization.

So DeForest was correct when he stated, "Neither in Connecticut, therefore, nor in any other civilized community, need we expect to hear an outcry of grief at the fact, that a state of society, such as we have described, has been supplanted by one such as we now see flourishing around us."[27] He admitted, however, that "we may drop a tear over the grave of the race which has perished, and regret that civilization and Christianity have ever accomplished so little for its amelioration."[28] The town reporters obviously agreed.

Where did the Indians go? The native population certainly decreased substantially with English settlement. The first reason was epidemics. Small pox and other illnesses decimated Indians who had not built up immunities as the English had done. In an essay on the Pequots, William Starna writes that "a conservative estimate of disease mortality, based upon comparative data, is set at 55 percent. Others have provided estimates ranging up to 95 percent."[29] Looking specifically at the Pequots, he notes that there were about 13,000 Pequots before contact with Europeans. "After contact and the effects of European diseases, but before the Pequot War of 1637, their population had been reduced to some three thousand individuals, indicating a mortality rate of 77 percent. Following the War, this number was further diminished to one thousand."[30] While the Pequot tribe was the most affected by the

Pequot War, the decrease in the tribe before the war due to disease is likely to have occurred within the other tribes in Connecticut also. None of them had resistance to European diseases. Even those who survived the epidemics were affected by them. Social, political, and religious structures of Indian villages would be altered drastically when a large percentage of the village died. "Villages which had lost their sachems and whose population had declined twentyfold were often no longer viable entities; surviving Indians were forced to move to new villages and create new political alignments."[31]

A second cause of mortality was war. There were two major Indian-English wars in the seventeenth century which involved the settlements. The Pequot War, described above, killed 600 Pequots in one day. The survivors of the tribe were scattered, and by the terms of the Tripartite Treaty, were forbidden to reorganize and live together as a tribe. The surviving Pequots were divided among the tribes who had sided with the colonists. The tribe not only lost 600 people in a single day, but it also was no longer allowed to exist as a tribal entity. Individual Indians are not as easily noticeable by the town reporters as tribes would have been. Additionally, individual Indians would have a harder time surviving without the support of the tribe.

The second Indian-English conflict, noted in some of the Town Reports, is King Philip's War (1675-76). The sachem Metacom of the Wampanoags, known to the English as King Philip, tried to unite the Indians residing in Massachusetts, Rhode Island and Connecticut, in a series of attacks against English settlements. There were many "causes" of the war. The settlements were taking over the Indians' land base, thereby affecting their political, economic and social systems. The English imposed their laws and courts on the Indians. The Indians viewed this as a war of resistance, and many settlements were attacked and burned. While many

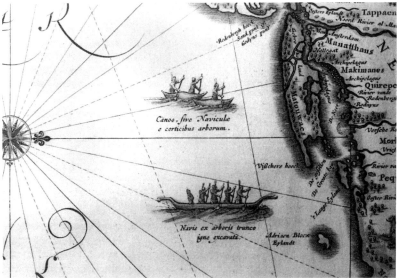

Depiction of Native Americans in canoes along the Connecticut coastline, from Blaeu's map of New England. William Janszoon Blaeu, Nova Belgica et Anglia Nova, Netherlands, ca. 1635. Mashantucket Pequot Museum and Research Center, Archives and Special Collections, MSS 26.

Connecticut tribes were not involved, and wished to stay friendly with the English, the English were fearful of all Indians.[32] DeForest writes, "The Pequots, like the Mohegans, throughout the whole contest continued faithful to the English. The other tribes of Connecticut mostly remained neutral, except that a few of the Nipmucks of Windham County joined Philip, and also the Podunks of East Windsor and East Hartford."[33]

The town of Guilford voted to fortify two houses during the war, and "to bear in common all damage done by the enemy."[34] Some Guilford residents served in this war, and were later rewarded with land. Wallingford also had two houses fortified, and required "that every man should bring his arms and ammunition compleat on the sabbath day and that Watch and Ward be kept by the whole town in rotation, day and night till further orders."[35] The Town Report from East Windsor mentions the case of a local Windsor Indian, Toto, who helped save the town of Springfield from King Philip's army. Toto heard that Philip intended to burn Springfield and kill all its inhabitants. He ran to Springfield and back in one night, and warned the English settlers there. The reporter noted, "As Indian ingratitude is proverbial, it is pleasing to find an exception, and to record the gratitude and friendly attachment of an individual."[36] The United Colonies provided for an army, which eventually defeated the Indians. Philip himself was shot, beheaded, and quartered. His head was taken to Plymouth, "and set on spike, visible to passersby for decades."[37] Casualties were high for both the colonists and the Indians. One author put Indian casualties at 5,000.[38]

Indian survivors were captured and put into the slave trade. Captured Indians were sold as servants to colonists, or sent as slaves to the West Indies. In *The Name of War: King Philip's War and the Origins of American Identity,* Jill Lepore writes that the colonists tried to distinguish the proper punishment for the Indians. "Slavery was considered to be just this kind of a compassionate compromise: notorious Indians, like Philip himself, were executed; harmless enemies, mainly women and young children, were forced into servitude for a period of years; and those who were neither notorious enough to be hanged or harmless enough to remain in New England were routinely sold into foreign slavery."[39] While it is known that King Philip's nine-year old son was shipped off into foreign slavery, it is unclear how many Indians were actually sold. Lepore refers to "hundreds" of Indians.[40] Knowing that they might be sold into slavery made many Indians flee the area. "Surviving members of the Wampanoag, Narragansett, Nipmuck and Pocumtuck tribes either submitted in abject surrender or fled to the relative safety of New York and Canada."[41] These all caused a reduction in the number of Indians in Connecticut. After King Philip's War, the balance of power had completely shifted from the Indians to the settlers.

A third reason for the decline in the number of Indians was the encroachment of English settlements and the loss of tribal land. In *Puritans, Indians, and Manifest Destiny*, the authors note, "in a way that few colonial Europeans could understand, the land *was* Indian culture: it provided Native Americans with their sense of a fixed place in the order of the world, with their religious observances, and with their lasting faith in the importance of the struggling but united community."[42] When the English arrived, and the Indians sold the land to them, the Indians expected to be able to maintain their existing lifestyle. They retained rights to hunt and fish over ceded land in most of the deeds. But the English concept of land ownership was different. English land was plowed up, and fenced. Forests were cleared, and streams dammed. It was difficult for the Indians to maintain their way of life. Game disappeared when the forest was cleared. Fish disappeared when the streams were dammed. Natural plants used for subsistence disappeared when fields were plowed. The growth of English settlements limited the amount of land that the Indians could use for subsistence living, and altered the availability of resources needed to sustain their tribal communities.

Besides the right of discovery, another legal concept of land ownership followed by the English was the doctrine of *vacuum domicilium.*[43] Under this concept, one could claim untilled or vacant land. Since much Indian land was used for hunting, gathering, berry-picking and fishing, and was, to the English, vacant and unused, the English could claim rights to the land. So, even where the Indians had a piece of land, recognized by the English as their own, it didn't mean that the Indians were free to use that land as they wished. Colonists would run their cattle in lands owned but not "used" by the Indians. Even in land "used" by the Indians, such as plowed fields, the Colonists would treat the land as they wished. In some cases, the Colonists would allow their cattle to run free in the Indians' unfenced cornfields, destroying their crops. If Indians did fence their fields, the fences would be torn down. Indians had a hard time getting the colony to enforce its own laws.

Indians would also be brought into court for various misdemeanors, and fined by the colonial courts. As they had no money to pay fines, their land was often taken and sold to pay off the fines.[44] Without land, the Indians had a difficult time surviving.

Many of the Indian tribes complained to the colony/state. Connecticut would set up a commission to investigate, and often found that the land had been surveyed wrong originally. In other cases, the commission would suggest that the Indians couldn't use their land as they wished because it was surrounded by white settlement, and exchange pieces of land with the Indians, giving land that was further from white settlement, and not already developed by whites, generally because it was of poor quality. But the English continued to expand and want the land owned by the Indians. So the Indians lost much land, and without a land base, it was almost impossible to maintain a tribal lifestyle.

Mary Guillette, in a series of reports prepared in 1979 for the Connecticut Indian Affairs Council, explains how land was taken from the Mashantucket (Western) Pequots:

> Typically, an Englishman would settle on a piece
> of reservation land and fence off a lot, claiming
> it as his on a variety of grounds, the most

common ground being that the Indians were not "using" all the land so they did not need it all. The Pequots, having neither the power nor the means to oust the trespassers, would then petition the Connecticut authorities to right the wrong. Connecticut, stuck in the middle between its Indian wards and land-hungry colonists, would avoid making a decision in the case as long as possible, appointing committee after committee, sometimes for several years (while encroachments were occurring constantly). In the end, the colony usually chose to avoid a confrontation with the colonists and upheld the English claims. This was often accomplished by a reexamination and survey of the reservation lands, ostensibly to determine if encroachments had been made by whites. Their surveys nearly always revealed that there had been no encroachment, but that the previous boundaries had been inaccurate.[45]

She continues:

> The public records are full of cases like this, especially in the 18th century when encroachments on Mashantucket lands were at their highest point. This is not to imply that the General Court always beat around the bush when reviewing Mashantucket land disputes; it sometimes settled cases firmly. However, the outcome nearly always favored the English, immediately or in the long run. That is, if the English claimants did not win the case, they simply ignored the decision and the colony did not move to enforce it.[46]

Early on in the colonies, laws were passed preventing individuals from acquiring land from the Indians. This right was retained by the colony, and then the state.[47] And the first Congress of the new United States passed the first of a series of Trade and Intercourse Acts, which required that only the Federal government could enter agreements with the tribes.[48] But land depredations continued, both by the settlers themselves and by the colony/state. This is the basis for many of the twentieth century land claims of New England Indians. Sales made to the state or settlers after the passage of the Trade and Intercourse Act were improper, as not approved by the Federal Government. So the Indians claim that the sale was void and that they still own the land.

Connecticut set up some reservations for different tribes. The Kent Town Report talks of the reserved land for the Schaghticokes:

> At the time the general assembly sold the lands on the West side of the Ousatonic, they reserved for the use of the Indians the tract on which they were settled, containing about one thousand

acres. Of this tract about 100 acres was of very productive soil. Where any portion of the industry remained among the Indians they were enabled to raise a sufficiency of corn for their own consumption and lived in a state removed from want. But a habit of extreme idleness and intoxication has long prevailed among them, and almost without exception their lands have remained uncultivated. In the year 1804 the legislature directed that 600 acres of the tract be sold, and the interest of the avails to be annually appropriated to the charges of such of the tribe as from sickness and age were in necessitous circumstance.[49]

This was a common occurrence. When reservations were established, the state appointed white overseers to handle the affairs of the Indians. The overseers often ran up debt on behalf of the Indians, and then would petition the state to sell some of the land to cover the debt. The reporter in Stratfield notes that the twelve remaining Indians, living on twenty acres of land, are living hand to mouth. "They have a guardian appointed by the General Assembly who takes care of their land, the avails of which are not sufficient to satisfy him. Fifty pounds worth of land was sold last Nov. to answer his demand."[50] Less land meant both less income, and less ability to make a living. It was a vicious circle for the Indians. Segal and Stineback note, "As long as the land remained in the possession of the tribe, the individual Indian could retain the essence of his culture, though disease, war, liquor, and slavery might take their toll."[51]

Many had to leave the land because it was not able to support them. Indians entered into trades, and worked for white farmers as laborers. Many went to sea, as whalers, which meant they had to leave their family and tribe behind. Tribal connections were being broken. It was harder for the town reporter to see individual Indians, who might be living in European style houses, and wearing European/American style clothing, than if the Indian were living in a tribal community. "Nineteenth-century Anglo-American misperceptions of native identity reinforced the disappearance template. When Indians moved off reservation lands, and adopted Anglo-American dress, dwellings, and lifestyles, their Indian-ness disappeared."[52]

In "They Were Here All Along," the authors researched New England town records, narratives, account books, and government records to find Indians in the nineteenth century. They noted:

> This proved a difficult task: nineteenth century public records often exclude or obscure the presence of Native Americans. Indian births, marriages, and deaths were only occasionally recorded by New England's town clerks. Until 1850, native households that paid taxes were enumerated on the federal census schedule for "free negroes"(1790-1820) or "free colored people" (1830 and 1840), as there was no specific

schedule for them. Indians who exercised a right to tax exemption were excluded from the census. Such practices tended to confirm the thesis of the vanished Indian.[53]

As the Indians became increasingly integrated into the wider colonial community, through intermarriage and adoption of English lifestyles, they no longer were considered Indians. Lepore writes that Ezra Stiles visited Hassanemesit (sic) in 1760 and found no male Indians. "Because there was considerable intermarriage between Indians and free blacks, some Algonquians passed as white and some were considered black. Stiles would not have counted these people as 'Indian,' even if they themselves did."[54] So the town reporters responding to the Connecticut Academy's questions would not have found Indians in public records. And if they looked around, they may not have seen the Indians who had adopted and adapted to Anglo-American lifestyles.

Colin Calloway notes that for a historian today to "find" the Indian in the eighteenth and nineteenth century one must do a lot of searching for individuals, rather than tribal communities. "It requires gaining familiarity with the names of Indian families in particular communities, piecing together people's lives from the scattered occasions when those individuals appear in the records, tracing lineages and connecting family histories; it demands painstaking detective work, shifting to other sources when one set of records has played out, and poring over reels of microfilm for hours to find one brief reference that might later provide a small piece in a larger but always incomplete puzzle."[55] The authors of "They Were Here All Along" have done this type of painstaking research. It is an area in which more research can be done.

Indian Vices

The Connecticut Academy specifically asked the towns to comment on the Indians' vices. This was a negative view of Indians, held in common by most, if not all, of English/American citizens. Indians were unChristianized, and uncivilized. The Town Reports most often refer to Indians as vile, wild, intemperate, drunken, idle, degraded, unfaithful, lazy and debased. Lisbon (Newent) noted that Indians are "generally intemperate, unfaithful and seem willing to live in a most debased condition both with respect to knowledge and the comforts of life." Lisbon (Hanover) remarked that "they are idle and intemperate." The reporter in Farmington notes a natural occurrence called Round Hill, which some imagined might have been constructed by the Indians, "but it is clear that this must be visionary, as their power could never be equal to such a work, and if it were, there (sic) aversion to labour & impatience of fatigue would never permit them to exert it." Kent reports that "The constant and universal habit of drunkenness among them has degraded them to a station but little superior to the beasts."[56]

The prevailing thought was that Indians were on a lower level of civilization than the whites. They could be trained and taught the white man's ways, and could eventually attain a higher

Modern representation of a seventeenth century Northeast Woodlands adult male, wearing clothing typical of Algonquians in New England. Tara Prindle, Northeast Woodlands Man (Connecticut, 1993). Mashantucket Pequot Museum and Research Center, Archives and Special Collections, MSS 35.

level of civilization. But few seemed willing to learn. The Town Report in Guilford, in the section of the notable persons in town, mentions two ministers who went to preach the gospel among the Indians.[57] Haddam also mentions a minister who preached to Indians in New York and Pennsylvania.[58] And there were converts, including those referred to as the Praying Indians. But it has also been pointed out that the English, among all the European countries settling in the New World, spent the least time, money, and support for missionary work among the Indians.[59]

The early English settlers in New England were Puritans. The Puritans' view of Indians was based on their religious beliefs. Moral, self-righteous and unbending, they had left England because they could not tolerate compromise of their beliefs and conduct. They viewed the wilderness as the land of Satan, and the Indians as instruments sent by God to demonstrate that they were the chosen people. The Indians "were primarily the villains in a sacred drama, counterpart of the heathen tribes that Joshua conquered, children of the Devil who tempted Christ in the desert, forerunners of the legion of darkness that would gather at Gog and Magog for a last furious but futile battle against the elect."[60] With such strong feelings, the Puritans could see nothing good at all in the Indians. Representatives of the devil himself, they must be converted, and if they refused to accept Puritan teachings as the truth, they could be destroyed. It is not difficult to imagine that Puritans would enumerate the vices of the Indians, and see no virtues. This same narrow view of Indians was still evident in the Town Reports.

Alcohol was a problem in the Indian communities. DeForest lists alcoholism as a cause of population loss among the Indians. "Now too, ardent spirits, which at first had been scarce and dear even among the whites, became more plentiful and found their way to the lips of the Indians. Intemperance is destructive of the happiness of the civilized communities, but it is destructive of the lives of the savage ones."[61]

It would have been an interesting comparison if the Connecticut Academy had asked the town reporters to expound upon the vices found within the white community. The only vice referred to was laziness, where the towns refer to those who need public support. But most of those needing public support were old, infirm, widowed, or orphaned. It makes one wonder whether the writers of the Connecticut Academy's solicitation letter of 1800 thought that certain Indian vices were genetic, or limited to a Native population.

Conclusion

History is written by the victors. The English were the victors over the Indians, not just in conquest by war, but in subjecting the Indians to English culture, law, societal structures, dress, and land-use patterns. We hear and read the English side of all events. Lepore notes in *The Name of War* that following King Philip's War, colonists wrote many accounts in order to draw boundary lines between themselves and the Indians. She writes, "more than four hundred letters written during the war survive in New England archives alone, along with more than thirty editions of twenty different printed accounts. In

letters, diaries, and chronicles, Englishmen and -women in New England expressed their agonies, mourned their losses, and most of all, defended their conduct."[62] The Indian version is generally not heard. Lepore comments, "It was not until the Pequot William Apess in 1836 that a New England Indian writer would emerge to write the history of King Philip's War."[63]

The town reporters, answering the questions posed by the Connecticut Academy, were interested in writing of the present and the future, and less so about the past. To them, Indians were the past, and while interesting historically, had no real impact on the reporters' lives, or the life of the town. The reporters gave a quick response to those questions about Indians, and then moved on to the positive, exciting issues the town was facing—agriculture, industry and growth. More discussion appears in the Town Reports on manure than on Indians. The Reports reflect what was most important to an educated person at the beginning of the nineteenth century. This knowledge, collected and shared by the Connecticut Academy, could have a positive effect on the future of the town and the state.

Indians represented a dying race. The settlers did not view this end of the Indians as sad, or something to try to prevent. It was the inevitable result of a savage people coming into contact with a superior and civilized race. It was destiny. DeForest refers to the remaining Indians as "mere fragments, [who] still cling, like ghosts, around their ancient habitations,"[64] and as "half withered leaves [who] may sometimes be seen clinging to the upper branches of a blighted and dying tree."[65] The East Windsor Report includes this account of the "last" Indian:

> The rapid diminution and final extinction of numerous tribes of Indians in New England, is a subject of wonder, and perhaps unparalled in the annals of mankind. The Podunk nation, as before observed, were numerous, at the first coming of the English. They did not emigrate; but unaccountably disappeared with the game of the woods. The final extinction of the Tribe, as information received from aged people, many years ago, was as follows. The last man of the Tribe, whose name was Coggery, and who lived in a wigwam in a swamp, not far from the place of the church in the First Society, in a fit of intoxication, murdered the *last* Indian woman, and then put an end to his life by stabbing himself."[66]

This paragraph sums up many of the views of Indians at the time of the Town Reports. They are in the past, as this comes from reports of aged people many years ago. The Indian is living in a swamp, a very uncivilized place to live, is drunk, and takes both his life and that of another. For the whites, there is nothing of the Indians worth saving.

The town reporters reflected the national attitude towards Indians during this period. National Indian policy in the early 1800s focused on the removal of Indians from their homelands.

The United States would exchange the land of Indians in the east for a permanent territory west of the Mississippi River. The idea was first considered by George Washington, but first discussed nationally during the presidency of Thomas Jefferson, after the purchase of the Louisiana Territory made the idea possible.[67] The Removal Act was finally passed by Congress and signed by President Andrew Jackson in 1830.[68] While calling for the voluntary removal of tribes, the actual implementation did not give the tribes any choice. Francis Paul Prucha writes that "behind the removal policy was the desire of eastern whites for Indian lands and the wish of eastern states to be disencumbered of the embarrassment of individual groups of aboriginals within their boundaries."[69] It was easier to remove the Indians from contact with Anglo-Americans than to have to deal with them.

Indians tribes held an odd legal status at this time. While they were not foreign nations, they were not Americans either. Individual Indians were not and could not be citizens, even if they followed Anglo-American ways of living, and could read and write English.[70] The United States Supreme Court, in *Cherokee Nation v. Georgia*, in 1831, determined that the tribes were "domestic, dependent nations."[71] The Indians are "in a state of pupilage. Their relation to the United states resembles that of a ward to his guardian."[72] They were uncivilized children, and the United States government knew what was best for them. But unlike children, Americans preferred that they not be seen or heard.

Even if unseen and unheard, the Indians did not disappear. They were there, just out of the narrow vision of the town reporters. And we know that because their descendants are with us today. Much has changed since the town reporters responded to the Connecticut Academy. Indians in Connecticut have made themselves heard and have asserted their tribal identity and tribal sovereignty. The two federally recognized tribes have had land settlements with the federal government, and assert sovereignty over their own land and reservations. They have reestablished systems of governance, and judicial systems. They have recognized the need to be politically active and to assert their rights.

Anglo-American historians are now using native sources to write about the interaction of Indian and white cultures. And the tribes will be involved in writing their own history now, from a native perspective. Should the Connecticut Academy submit the same survey questions to towns today, the responses received would reflect a growing and dynamic Indian culture in Connecticut.

Fisheries

Daniel Vickers

The logic that governs the relationship between maritime communities and the waters they frequent is difficult to fathom. What drew the whalemen of Nantucket to the South Pacific? What connected Salem to Sumatra? What caused Marblehead to become the largest fishing port in the American colonies? Some seaports such as Halifax seem destined for a greatness they might never achieve, while others like Boston exceed what anyone would have predicted. Seaports do carry, of course, certain marks. They are supposed to have decent anchorages—though Nantucket harbor is plagued by sandbars and Marblehead lies open to the sea. They should serve productive hinterlands—though none of the seaports of New England was particularly blessed in that respect. Government initiatives can favor one location over the next, though not if nature and the marketplace prove unwilling. The good fortune of having been settled first can also be advantageous—although Philadelphia grew into the largest seaport in colonial North America in spite of being settled after Boston, New York, Charleston, Newport, and Quebec. In short, one can list the factors that contribute to a maritime tradition easily enough, but knowing how to weigh these factors comparatively is another matter. The history and geography of fishing communities should be easier to sort out, since the fishing grounds they exploited were geographic givens. Yet, even in pre-industrial times fishermen, whalemen, and sealers were remarkably peripatetic. They could work around home or they could chase their prey hundreds, even thousands, of miles across the oceans, and they could change their seafaring habits in remarkably short order. Some ports adopted fisheries while others dropped them—often in the span of a decade or two. In 1850, hundreds of vessels from New London, Connecticut, which had been the most minor of fishing ports in colonial times, were catching shad in the Thames River, drawing seines for menhaden in Long Island Sound, fishing for cod on Georges Banks, hunting elephant seals in the South Indian Ocean, and following the right whale into the North Pacific. The same year, the fishing fleet of Marblehead, Massachusetts—once the largest in the New World—was in free fall, destined to disappear entirely within a few decades. In short, the pattern and history of fishing effort is as complex as that of any other branch of the maritime economy.

Connecticut has always had fisheries, though their story is little known and poorly integrated into the wider history of the region.[1] This is understandable during the colonial and early national period, when local involvement in fishing was, indeed, slight. Yet, even during the nineteenth century, when Connecticut acquired prominent whaling and sealing industries as well as a range of different saltwater fisheries, these activities appear in the historical record, if at all, in ways that seem marginal to the major themes of the day. The question of why these maritime industries were so slow to develop in the early history of Connecticut and so quick to take off subsequently is a problem of some import to the history of this coast. It is one, moreover, that the Town Reports that accompany this volume can help to answer. Solicited by the Connecticut Academy of Arts and Sciences between 1800 and 1820, they catch these new fishing industries during the period in which they were launched. With their help the historian can identify some of the forces that were driving them forward.

Although Connecticut possesses more than 150 miles of coastline, most of it faces on Long Island Sound, which is from the fisherman's standpoint more like a massive bay. The waters are shallow, protected, and variable in temperature, and there are no banks directly offshore. Seasonally, fish used to enter and leave the Sound—often in great numbers—with the rising and falling temperatures, but nowhere within it did there exist massive stocks equivalent to those of the great fishing grounds that sit on the continental shelf to the north and east. It was there, on Georges Banks, the many Nova Scotia banks, the banks of Labrador, and the Grand Banks of Newfoundland, as well as in the Gulf of Maine and the Gulf of St. Lawrence that cod, mackerel, halibut, hake, and pollock—the major commercial species that New Englanders have historically pursued—were to be found in greatest abundance. Above all, it was there that one sailed in search of cod. For centuries the size and number of these fish commended them to the fisherman; their firm and agreeable flesh always agreed with consumers; and their amenability to drying and salting made them easy to preserve in the preindustrial age. Indeed, before the coming of the railroad and possibility of moving quantities of fresh fish swiftly to market, commercial fishing in the Northwest Atlantic depended overwhelmingly on this one species.[2] Few professional fishermen chose to locate themselves beyond reach of the cod's natural range, and so few of them ever settled in Connecticut.

If Connecticut did possess any commercial sea fisheries during the colonial period, the fact has entirely escaped historians.[3] The records of New Haven Colony, which extend to its annexation by Connecticut in 1665, contain no reference to any sea fisheries, and the Connecticut authorities dealt with the industry only twice during the whole colonial period.[4] In May 1687, the legislature passed an Act for the Assizing of

Cask and Preventing Deceit in the Packing of Fish that established rules for the barrelling of "green, dry salted or pickled fish." The following month it passed a further Act to Regulate the Fish Trade and Fishermen, which addressed the problem of "salt burnt and dry fish" by establishing cullers to sort fish by quality and tried to conserve mackerel stocks by forbidding their capture before the summer months.[5] These two acts may have constituted an attempt to regulate existing fishing activities, but if so the industry was a tiny one, too small to have generated exportable surpluses. The customs records of Barbados—the principal overseas destination for all New England shipping during the seventeenth century—describe in detail dozens of cargoes that arrived from New London, New Haven, and Milford during the 1680s, and although barrelled meat, grain, ale, flannel cloth, and horses figure prominently in these lists, fish are entirely absent. Possibly there were traders in Connecticut exporting fish through Boston or Salem, and it is conceivable that some high quality merchantable cod was being shipped to Spain.[6] The Barbados trade is, however, an excellent litmus test. All New England ports with known local fisheries did send fish to Barbados, so the total absence of shipments from Connecticut is telling.[7]

Yet, it would be wrong to think that colonists in this part of the world did not fish at all. During the seventeenth century, throughout New England, millions of shad, bass, alewives, and salmon ascended the rivers every spring and summer to spawn, and the settlers in Connecticut, as everywhere else, took time off from their farm labors to take part in this freshwater harvest. In 1647, New Haven Colony passed an order, which probably just confirmed existing practice, allowing inhabitants to set up new weirs in the rivers and harbors of the colony, provided that they did not interfere with existing weirs or with coastal and river shipping.[8] Beginning in 1685, Connecticut colony began to grant exclusive fishing rights on certain prime pieces of frontage along the Connecticut River—perhaps to encourage the development of local fisheries, but more probably to try and forestall competition over these sites between individual fishermen.[9] After 1715, all people constructing weirs that obstructed "the natural or usual course and passage of fish . . . in spring or proper seasons of the year" on a number of important rivers were required to obtain licences from their county court.[10] As the eighteenth century proceeded and the population of the colony rose, however, fishing efforts intensified and the stocks of fish in all of these rivers began to shrink. By 1766, the legislature observed that licensed fishermen had "almost wholly stopt and obstructed the natural course of the fish" and had "greatly destroyed the common priveledge and benefit" of these fisheries, and accordingly repealed tax licensing provisions of the 1715 Act.[11] The demand for fish, however, could not be decreed away and throughout the last decade of the colonial period much of the legislature's business was taken up with the intricacies of adjudicating disputes over fishing rights on an individual basis.[12]

Shad was the most prolific species in the rivers of southern New England, and the regulatory legislation mainly pertained to the fishery that revolved around their annual spawning run

in May. During this month, the waters were alive in fish—so much that boatmen claimed that in going about their business, they could not keep their oars out of the shad that swam below. Close to Long Island Sound, farmers constructed stone weirs by the riverside, and twice a day during the season they would empty them with the help of a horsecart. Further upstream they used scoop-nets and haul seines wherever the shad were prone to gather, but especially in the pools below waterfalls. Immediately after they were caught, the fish were dressed, salted, and barrelled, for they spoiled rapidly in the sun and bruised easily if carried any considerable distance.[13]

This was not a subsistence fishery. Boats, seines, barrels, and salt were a considerable investment, and at the height of the season, an ambitious fisherman hoped to net several hundred fish in a day—at a penny apiece worth £1 or more together. An account for the operation of a single seine in Hadley, Massachusetts, in 1766 recorded revenues of £23 and expenses of £14—no small sum for a business that would have lasted a few months at the most. Account books from the same region record the sale of shad to local farmers in lots ranging from thirty to a hundred fish, and it is hard to imagine that their Connecticut cousins were not in the same game. Boston merchants of the 1730s advertised Connecticut shad, and as late as 1815, the price of this commodity was quoted in New York's *Price Current*. Shad may have been considered a poor man's food—indicative of one's inability to afford salt pork—but it clearly found customers.[14]

In light of this evidence, the claim that fish were caught mainly for home consumption and that communities of farmers treated river fisheries as a common resource to be husbanded for the public good seems implausible at best. Perishable foods that present themselves in great abundance for short periods of the year lend themselves to commercial exploitation, and although none of these freshwater species were commonly exported overseas, they seem to have commanded a regional market of some size. Connecticut farmers interested in feeding their families and earning a profit were preying on shad and salmon to damaging effect long before the coming of the factory and the milldam destroyed the river habitats for good. The persistent attempts of the colonial government to regulate these fisheries testify mainly to the pressure that fish stocks were already under during the eighteenth century, and the colony's admission in 1766 that the system of regulation had failed suggests that this pressure was unsustainable.

The Town Reports, composed at the beginning of the nineteenth century, were unanimous that the fisheries had been in decline for some years. By 1808, Levi Clarke of Haddam could claim that the salmon fishery in the Connecticut River was "now at an end," and the same year, David McClure of East Windsor noted that the abundance of shad and alewives was also diminishing. Timothy Dwight of New Haven observed in 1811 that in the Quinnipiac River, shad could still "be taken in considerable numbers, when the season is favourable," but that they were formerly much more numerous. So commercially valuable had the fishery been, he remembered, that the competition over fishing spots had at one time prompted "a considerable number of law suits." In 1819, a report from Middletown remarked that the Connecticut River "used to abound . . . with salmon, shad, bass, alewives, pike, carp, perch, etc.," but that "for several years the quantity of fish . . . [had] very considerably decreased."[15] By this date, locks and dams were contributing to the destruction of fish stocks in the river systems of Southern New England, as Timothy Dwight among others recognized.[16] But as the evidence from the colonial records demonstrates, the problem predated the construction of these river barriers. Industrial capitalism may bear most of the responsibility for the destruction of fish stocks—in Connecticut as everywhere else in the modern world—but to absolve these ambitious farmer-fishermen from blame, simply because they lacked the technical means to drain the rivers of fish is probably wrong.[17]

The truly devastating blow to all of the fish populations of the northwest Atlantic and eastern North America over the past two hundred years has been, not the degradation of their marine and riverine environments, but rather the creation of gigantic domestic markets for fish and fish products. There was considerable demand for American fish in colonial times, but it was located overseas, and it was largely restricted to one easily preserved species—cod. The economic development of the United States in the late eighteenth and early nineteenth centuries, however, created large seaports with sizeable populations hungry for any kind of fresh, palatable food. The largest of these was New York, and its proximity transformed Connecticut's fisheries during the early national period. At the end of the colonial period, New York was only a small provincial seaport with a population of less than 25,000. Doubtless, the local population consumed some fish but probably no more than could be furnished by fishermen who lived around Manhattan, at the eastern end of Long Island, or on the New Jersey shore. If New Yorkers searched farther afield for fish during the colonial period, the fact seems not to have entered the historical record.[18] By 1800, however, the city's population had soared to 60,000, and by 1820 to 123,000. These numbers overwhelmed the stock of local provisions, and word spread up and down the coast of the booming seaport's nearly insatiable markets.

With this commercial opportunity in mind, the residents of coastal Connecticut turned their attention for the first time to the prosecution of the sea fisheries. Many species that had never been thought of any value, since they could not easily be preserved, were now every bit as marketable as cod. Nearly virgin stocks of bass, bluefish, flounders, tautogs, eels, weakfish, scup, and swordfish swarmed over the banks and ledges off the southern coast of New England, and as the eighteenth century wound to a close, they too became the object of a commercial fishery. Some of these could be found along the Connecticut shore, but by far the better grounds were to the east off Rhode Island and Massachusetts or on the continental shelf off the southern coast of Long Island. Accordingly, the towns that took up this business were those at the eastern end of the Sound, closest to the open sea, and none of them was more important than New London.

Although a port of some note since the seventeenth century, New London possessed no sea fishery of importance in colonial times. It did stand within striking distance of some tolerable cod grounds, but as long as farming, foreign trade, and the artisanal crafts connected to both could absorb most of the local population, few men took up the ocean fisheries as a commercial profession. Since the sea was a common property resource, fishing industries usually served as an employer of last resort for poor families, and these were comparatively few in number during the first century of settlement.[19] After 1750, however, the number of propertyless, underemployed young men in Connecticut began to grow. At first, most of these probably found work around home, but some of them went to sea—in the West Indies trade or in the whaling industry of southeastern Massachusetts.[20] Then, when fishing became a commercial possibility at the end of the century, many residents of New London and neighboring communities took it up.[21]

By the outbreak of war in 1812, New London had acquired a fleet of sixty sloops, almost all engaged in supplying the New York market with fresh cod, tautogs, bass, and lobsters. The author of the New London Town Report took the time to describe these vessels in some detail:

> The vessels thus employed are denominated smacks, from the [sic] having a birth [sic] in the hold to contain the fish caught & to receive & discharge continually the seawater, which preserves the fish alive & in as fine condition, for many days, as when first taken. It is even practicable to improve their condition, by giving them more to subsist on than they would ordinarily find in the sea.[22]

Although fishing smacks had been in use in Europe since the 1500s, they were never employed during the colonial period in Connecticut or anywhere else in New England. The urban markets of that period had been satisfied by local fishermen who worked in skiffs or shallops and carried their catch to town every day or so. However, the larger cities of the nineteenth century—and New York above all—consumed more fish than could be fetched in small boats of this nature. The sloop-rigged smacks of New London were designed to reach richer banks offshore, catch large quantities of fish, yet return with their hauls alive in the hold. Although they were sluggish and not particularly seaworthy, the fish they landed fresh commanded prices that made up for these shortcomings.

With its fine harbor and central location between the major fishing banks to the east and New York City to the west, New London was admirably situated for the fresh fishery. Already in 1800, it possessed an excellent fish market of its own and supplied what Timothy Dwight termed "a considerable part of the fish sold in New York . . . from the waters in its neighborhood."[23] Later in the nineteenth century, when Georges Banks became the principal grounds for the pursuit of cold-water species such as halibut and cod, New London vessels often worked there as well. Before 1820, however, Georges was considered too dangerous to fish, on account of its shallow depth and the strength of the tides that swept across it. Yet, even the waters around the eastern end of Long Island seem to have been enough to launch New London on a path that would make it, through most of the nineteenth century, the major fishing port of southern New England.[24]

A second market-driven innovation of the early national period was the development of the oyster fishery. Oysters were once plentiful along the entire Atlantic coastline south of Cape Cod. Wherever the water was warm enough to encourage spawning, the bottom firm enough that they would not be smothered by shifting sand or mud, and the location protected enough that the shells would not be crushed in the surf, oyster beds abounded. Although the colonists probably enjoyed them for an occasional meal, there is no evidence of any great commercial demand for these shellfish before late in the eighteenth century. Still, a hint of rising interest was reflected in a colony order of 1766, allowing New Haven, Fairfield, and other towns with oyster or clam beds to regulate these two fisheries and prohibit residents from gathering them in "improper seasons." Resembling as it does the attempts to control Connecticut's commercial river fisheries, this legislation implies that the oyster and clam beds already were being worked for profit. At the beginning of the next century, Timothy Dwight writing in the New Haven Town Report of 1811, remembered that "formerly the harbor of New-Haven furnished oysters in great quantities and of a very fine flavour," but where these or any other oysters were sold during this early period is anyone's guess.[25]

By 1800, however, oystering had grown into an important part of the coastal economy of western Connecticut. Dwight described the beds of the Quinnipiack estuary in 1811 as a considerable local resource. Privately owned and cultivated by families that lived along the waterside, they were raked regularly through most of the year to produce between 400,000-500,000 bushels annually. Some of this harvest made it no farther than the New Haven market, but most proprietors turned over the bulk of their catch to their wives and daughters who shucked them, and packed them in kegs for shipment "during the cold season over large tracts in Connecticut, New-York, Massachusetts, Vermont and New Hampshire."[26] Dwight did not mention New York City in particular, but the seaport had been consuming oysters since colonial times and was now growing rapidly into the largest market in America. An anonymous author put it later in the century: "Oysters pickled, stewed, baked, roasted, fried, and scalloped; oysters made into soups, patties, and puddings; oysters with condiments and without condiments; oysters for breakfast, dinner, and supper; oysters without stint or limit, fresh as the pure air, and almost as abundant, are daily offered to the palates of the Manhattanese."[27]

The limits to which the natural oyster beds of coastal Connecticut could be pushed, however, were quickly reached and beginning to decline, even in Dwight's time.[28] By the 1820s, proprietors recognized the need to replace their diminishing stocks and began sending schooners to fetch oysters from Chesapeake Bay. Originally, these imports were sold directly upon arrival, but in time the proprietors took to transplanting the shellfish into their own beds along the New England coast. After being cast from dories evenly about the grounds, the newcomers were left to fatten for several months and then harvested and sent to market. Later in the century, oyster-cultivators would supplement these with immature native oysters dredged from the natural beds on the reefs offshore and then scattered over new beds leased from the towns in the estuaries of the Connecticut coast. Although in Dwight's time, the progressive intensification of this fishery was still in its infancy, the process had nevertheless begun and the demand that powered it was already in place.[29]

Less appealing to the palate than the oyster, but just as important to the Connecticut economy of the nineteenth century was the menhaden or "whitefish."[30] This was "a kind of herring, remarkably fat, and too bony to be eaten," that at one time migrated through the waters of Long Island Sound in remarkable numbers and every summer visited the shores by the millions. During the colonial period, they were largely ignored, but early in the nineteenth century, agricultural improvers began to recommend them as a fertilizer for depleted soil. Fish had always been used in this way, and this particular species was a known resource, but several Town Reports agree that it was between 1799 and 1802, that the menhaden boom began.[31]

The enthusiasm with which farmers adopted this practice was startling. Initially, of course, it was popular because it seemed to work. Ten to twelve thousand fish spread across and ploughed into an acre of land, wrote Timothy Dwight, were an "excellent dressing; and in many places esteemed superior to every other."[32] As he put it, "they appear to suit most soils and almost every kind of vegetation." The Madison Town Report advised in the same spirit that "they are best on low, cold, dead grounds, & are thought to have an influence in saving grain from being winter-killed."[33] In Middlesex County, their "effect on dry and poor land is wonderful," still another reporter commented. "Under the influence of this manure, some of the finest fields of grain, corn, and grass are annually presented on the margin of the Sound which exist in our country."[34] Here then for tired and exhausted soils was a miracle cure–cheap at "a dollar a thousand" and free for those with the time and energy to gather the fish themselves. The "intolerable fetor" menhaden generated when fermenting in the sun made a considerable impression upon Dwight, but the farmers themselves, "by the force of habit and the prospect of gain," seemed hardly to notice it.[35] With market opportunities for agricultural produce blossoming around them and with growing competition from newer lands to the west, they were plainly seduced by what seemed like a quick fix to the general problem of declining fertility.

Menhaden were caught in enormous seines–up to a mile in length–set around these shoals by teams of boats and then drawn into shore using capstans. On Long Island (and probably along the coast of Connecticut as well), it was said that during this period most farmers owned a right in a seine, and part of their yearly business was to go (or send a hand) fishing during the season. As fishermen, they operated in sizeable companies—of as many as sixteen men and four boats together—and the scale of their operations was not small. A single, successful draw could take two days to set, haul, and empty, and the yield often amounted to 100,000 fish—fifty tons in total and worth about $100, the equivalent of a summer's wages for a farm hand.[36]

Over time, however, unprocessed fish proved to be a poor fertilizer, drenching the ground in oil, "parching it and making it unfit for tilling."[37] Yet, this same oil also rendered menhaden the perfect fish for industrializing New England, and as the century progressed, the demand for it grew. Although not of a high grade, menhaden oil was cheap, and almost any other greasy substance—from tallow to whale oil—could be cut with it and sold for greater profit without much loss in quality. Tanneries, which were critical to New England's boot and shoe industry, made particular use of this product. Once the oil had been boiled and squeezed out of the menhaden, moreover, the remainder, called "scrap," could be sold as fertilizer without any of the whole fish's deleterious side-effects.[38] So profitable was this fishery and so intensively was it worked by these farmer-fishermen that by the decades following the Civil War, the menhaden stocks in the coastal waters around Connecticut had much diminished. For the remainder of the nineteenth century, powered by sail and then by steam, commercial fleets based in towns around the Thames estuary and also around Milford continued to chase this prolific and profitable fish farther off at sea. Finally, during the first half of the twentieth century, possibly in search of lower labor costs, better access to the remaining healthy stocks, or driven away by local communities anxious to rid themselves of the noxious factories, the menhaden fishery shifted southward to New Jersey, the Chesapeake region, and the southern states.[39]

Two other important elements in the maritime economy of nineteenth-century Connecticut, although the period of their development followed that of the Town Reports, were the seal and whale fisheries. Neither of these had been practiced in Connecticut to any extent before the American Revolution. The rural economy of the colony had more than enough to offer in the way of gainful work, and the carrying trade to the West Indies was the most profitable maritime enterprise around. After the Revolution, however, the West Indian trade was complicated by the poor relations that prevailed between the United States and Great Britain. At the same time, however, the reports of extraordinary herds of fur seals to be found on the islands of the South Atlantic, Pacific, and Indian Oceans combined with the discovery of insatiable markets for fur in China to waken New Englanders' interests in sealing. Although the Town Reports make no mention of this fact, one important center of interest in this new industry was the Connecticut shore, especially the community of Stonington. Between 1795 and 1825, sealers from this port sailed around the southern hemisphere, from South Georgia to New Zealand, calling in at a host of remote, forbidding islands, clubbing and skinning hundreds of thousands of seals every year for export to Asia. Within thirty years, the herds had been thinned almost to extinction—certainly past the point of commercial profitability—and the industry dwindled away.[40]

Connecticut was also a late entrant in the whale fishery. Southern New England had always been the American center of this industry, which was born on Long Island in the seventeenth century, developed on Nantucket during the eighteenth century, and dominated by New Bedford in the nineteenth century. To the end of the colonial period, anyone from Connecticut interested in shipping himself on a whaling voyage generally travelled to Massachusetts, and even as late as the War of 1812, the state's whaling fleet numbered only a handful of vessels.[41] Indeed, whaling, like sealing, made no impression whatsoever on the authors of the Town Reports. About 1820, however, the whaling business began to boom, largely in response to industrialization and its demand for lubricants and illuminants. Mystic and Stonington acquired small whaling fleets, and New London rose to become by 1850 the second largest whaling port in New England. During the 1840s and 1850s, anywhere between sixty and eighty vessels from this port were combing the oceans of the world for whale oil. Indeed, whaling was for some time the major industry in town. By the later nineteenth century, however, the whale population of the world had been greatly thinned, and after the Civil War, the New London fleet fell into decline. By 1890 there remained of it only one schooner, the *Era*, chasing bowheads in the Canadian Arctic.[42] Whaling lasted longer than sealing, but neither whales nor seals possessed reproductive capacities that were capable of keeping up with the carnage inflicted upon them during the nineteenth century.

In sum, it was only during the nineteenth century that Connecticut ever possessed a significant interest in the fisheries. During the eighteenth century, the colonists lacked a sufficient market for the species they could profitably pursue, and by the twentieth century, local fishermen had helped to push most of those species to the brink of commercial extinction.[43] What powered this process was plainly the creation of a national market in fish and fish products that Connecticut helped to service through its connections to New York. Soaring population, improved means of landward transport, and the requirements of industrialization meant that fish, shellfish, oil, whalebone, fur, and fertilizer were now in demand as never before. Still, it is instructive to note that the river fisheries, which predated the industrial revolution, were also commercial, predatory, and destructive. Certain species amenable to aquaculture, such as the oyster, have managed to survive this human onslaught, and others, such as the menhaden, were prolific enough to withstand it for a very long time. Yet, on balance, it is difficult to believe that since the arrival of the European settlers in the seventeenth century, Connecticut has ever practiced sustainable wild fisheries.

Ships and Shipping in Connecticut 1790-1811

William N. Peterson

Seaborne commerce to the islands of the Caribbean as well as to sister states on the Atlantic coast was the principal generator of maritime activity in Connecticut from 1790 until 1811. Supporting these trades was an active and growing shipbuilding industry as well as a nascent deep-sea fishery, all of which combined to create important economic dependencies that would influence the state throughout the nineteenth century and beyond.

While numerous factors contributed to Connecticut's shipping and shipbuilding successes from 1790 until 1811, it was the West Indies trade which proved to be the most beneficial. For Connecticut, this trade had been particularly important, dating back to the early eighteenth century. It remained so until just before the conflict that all but brought the lucrative business to an end—the War of 1812. The last few decades of this era also coincided with eager attempts by the newly-independent United States to establish itself commercially in the roiling maritime world of the tumultuous Napoleonic age. The economic and military competition among the principal European powers of the day would have profound maritime consequences for Connecticut. Interestingly, this was also the period when most of the Town Reports were written for the Connecticut Academy of Arts and Sciences.

The Town Reports devote a great deal of space to the various agricultural commodities produced in their localities. Although this is an obvious point, it is also an important one because agriculture was the basis for Connecticut shipping and shipbuilding activities during this period. Historian Richard J. Purcell, writing in 1918, noted that in post-revolutionary Connecticut "Men were convinced that the state's future wealth lay bound up in shipping, the sister industry of agriculture."[1] Nevertheless, few of the Town Reports give a great deal of attention to maritime activities, not even those towns such as Haddam that had access to navigable waterways. A number of important maritime towns such as Hartford and Stonington responded in a cursory way to the questionnaire, or not at all. One of the notable exceptions is the report from New London.

The "Schedule of Exports from and Imports into the District of New London" appended to the New London narrative, written in long hand by an unidentified contributor, is particularly instructive as it shows the various quantities and values of imports and exports from 1790 to 1811. While it illustrates the significance of agriculture to the towns encompassing the New London customs district, it also represents, to a large degree, the extent and type of maritime activity taking place elsewhere in Connecticut. For example, similar growth in shipping can be seen in Fairfield, Connecticut. Licenses for vessels in that southwestern district increased from 50 in 1794 to 112 in 1807.[2] Although cattle and horses seem to have been a less important export from the Fairfield area than they were from New Haven, Middletown and New London, the production of potatoes, corn, onions, flour and meal, flax, feathers and quills proved equally profitable exports.[3] The cargo manifest of the 43-ton[4] schooner *Union* sailing from Fairfield to St. Eustatius in 1790 gives an idea of western Connecticut agricultural activity. Sailing in March of that year under Captain Naphthalie Raymond, this vessel carried 74 barrels of beef, 514 bushels of corn, 319 bushels of oats, 7 barrels of dried fish, 10 barrels of pork, 4 barrels of pickled fish, 24 live hogs, 12 horned cattle, 2 horses, and 5 barrels of rye flour. *Union* returned in mid-June 1790 with 2,207 gallons of rum, 3,217 pounds of brown sugar, 174 pounds of coffee, 297 bushels of salt, and 1 bale of cotton.[5] To some degree or other almost all of Connecticut's towns, from Stamford to Stonington on Long Island Sound and from Hartford to Saybrook on the Connecticut River, were profitably engaged in this trade.

Significantly, in 1795 all of the Connecticut River towns that had been a part of the New London customs district were consolidated into a new district centered at Middletown, thus complicating the statistics. In fact, by 1800 the commerce reported from the Middletown district was greater than the combined districts at Fairfield (Bridgeport), New Haven and New London. For example, while New London issued registers for 55 new vessels in 1800 the Middletown district issued 114 registers.[6] The towns on the Connecticut River had long been engaged in the West Indies trade, going back at least to 1666 when the ketch *Diligent* (built in New London by John Coit) sailed from Essex for Barbados under Captain John Chester of Wethersfield. Rocky Hill [Stepney], Connecticut was a typical upper-river port active in the trade. The Grimes family of that locale was particularly prominent, and it was said that "the West Indies was the Grimes family burial ground."[7]

The importance of the West Indies trade to southern New England cannot be ignored, for it was this particular commerce which accounted for much of the region's overall mercantile prosperity during the Town Report period and the century before. New England farms, fishing grounds and forests all produced commodities that found ready markets in the Caribbean.[8] Prior to the American Revolution the West Indies trade of Connecticut and other American colonies operated within the broader European mercantile system.

Each nation traded solely with its own colonies under strict sets of laws and navigation acts. Thus the American colonies traded with such British possessions as Barbados, Antigua, Jamaica, St. Christopher (St. Kitts), St. Eustatius, Montserrat, Dominique, and St. Lucia. That these and other islands changed hands periodically as a result of military action or treaties accounts for some of the variations in the stated destinations of Connecticut vessels as they were reported in the published marine lists of the period before the American Revolution. Following the Revolution the French islands of St. Martin, Guadaloupe and Martinique become more common destinations for Connecticut vessels. Some trade was also allowed outside the mercantile system but only for special "enumerated articles" desired by one party or the other. Enumerated articles were colonial products that could be sold to foreign buyers but only if the commodity first was transshipped through the mother country. Although this mercantile system was essentially closed to outsiders, many American merchants and ship owners, including those from Connecticut, were able to prosper within it. Specific American ports or regions often specialized in certain exports to the islands. Marblehead and Salem, Massachusetts, for example, provided vast quantities of fish while Newport, Rhode Island, sent finished products like furniture and spermaceti candles. Philadelphia exchanged its abundant corn and flour while Charleston, South Carolina, produced marketable quantities of rice.[9] Connecticut ports in contrast specialized in exporting livestock and "country produce."[10]

Agriculture's importance to both the West Indian plantation and Connecticut maritime economies at the time of the Town Reports was only a continuance of a long historical reliance between the Caribbean and southern New England. Since the first quarter of the eighteenth century, Connecticut farmers had been producing marketable quantities of agricultural produce for shipment to the larger towns and cities in the region. Some produce had even been exported to Barbados prior to 1700.[11] In the eighteenth century the West Indies trade had become significant enough that merchants along the Connecticut and Thames rivers began to construct numerous wharves and warehouses to support the activity. These structures, which were specifically built to accommodate the storage of molasses and rum, became landmarks of the built environment. Often imposing in size for their day many of these storehouses were constructed from brick and stone. Clearly, it was an era of general prosperity for Connecticut's maritime-dependent merchants.

As we have seen, this was also a time when American vessels, as a part of the British mercantile empire, could still freely engage in trade with the islands controlled and protected by Great Britain. The Revolution and its aftermath changed all of this, and American diplomats would later spend decades trying to reopen the carrying trade to the British-held West Indian islands, with little success.[12] Nevertheless, as neutral traders in a turbulent time, Connecticut's merchants and their vessels began to find alternative markets in the Caribbean and elsewhere.

The American Revolution had brought trade within the British mercantile system to an all-but-total halt, resulting in attempts to establish new commercial connections elsewhere around the globe. The well-known voyage of the New Haven ship *Neptune* in 1796 was among the earliest attempts to open Chinese ports to American trade. Most attempts to break into markets in Cork and Dublin, Liverpool and London, Amsterdam, Calcutta, as well as China, were not particularly successful or long lasting.

In his seminal work *The Rise of New York Port*, maritime historian Robert Albion noted the growing commercial dominance of New York City as the chief entrepot of the nation in the early nineteenth century. This was due, in large measure, to the participation of Connecticut merchants whose maritime enterprise flourished during our period. Albion noted that Connecticut towns derived a good portion of their income from supplying "cattle and dairy products which they gathered from the back country."[13] These products were primarily sold to buyers in the West Indies or, with increasing frequency, to merchants in New York City. An example from the reports is New Haven, which in 1801 sent 219,702 pounds of cheese to the growing metropolis. The return cargoes of Caribbean molasses, sugar and rum went directly back to Connecticut towns or to New York's growing markets.[14] In addition, a modest trade also developed with some middle Atlantic ports in the United States.

New England merchants had long been involved in New York's maritime-based economy. This link extended all the way back to Isaac Atherton of Plymouth Colony, who in the mid-1600s established a commerce with both New Amsterdam, as New York was called when it was a Dutch colony, and the New Haven Colony. Albion also noted that the prominent involvement of Connecticut-based entrepreneurs was not surprising since the Connecticut Yankee was already well known for his trading proclivities. Around 1800 "talent poured in from all parts of the state, Stonington being particularly prominent for its sea captains and Stamford for its shipbuilders, while potential merchant princes came from all parts of the state."[15] Among the first of New York's leading post-Revolutionary merchant houses was that established in 1794 by George Griswold of Saybrook. His brother Nathaniel joined him within a few years, and together they formed the well-known exporting and commission company N.L. & G. Griswold, whose initials were often cited as "No Loss & Great Gain" for the brother's uncanny business acumen and occasional good luck. The Griswolds were primarily engaged as East India merchants and were so well known that "everybody of any consequence knew where such a prominent concern could be found."[16] Joseph Howland, of Norwich, along with his sons Gardiner Green Howland and Samuel Shaw Howland, were the progenitors of another successful maritime firm, G.G. & S. Howland, which rose to prominence in New York. Later Nutmeggers, Anson G. Phelps and William E. Dodge formed Phelps, Dodge & Co., a leading importer of metals. Charles Morgan of Killingworth became a ship chandler and fruit importer[17] while Samuel Russell of

Middletown founded Russell & Co., which was among the earliest firms that attempted to open China to American commerce.[18] These men and numerous others would have profound influence on the growing maritime trade of New York, and in consequence would also bring both direct and indirect economic benefits for their native state. As their need for vessels grew these "merchant princes" often turned to Connecticut shipbuilders and investors with whom they were already familiar, thus multiplying the state's effect on the New York market.

Connecticut during the early National period, as the Town Reports clearly acknowledge, was still largely an agricultural state specializing in animal husbandry. The chief varieties of livestock exported were horses, hogs, mules and "horned cattle." In fact, at this time Connecticut was among the nation's principal producers of livestock. "Farmers need never fear having too much cattle for the constant export of...livestock of all kinds, to the West Indies...will never fail them."[19] Likewise, commodities such as barreled beef and pork, a natural adjunct to the livestock trade, are also listed as important associated exports (see "Schedule of Exports..." in the New London Report in Volume I).

By the mid-eighteenth century, the typical West Indian plantation operation had evolved into a dependence upon single-crop agriculture. Sugar plantations were the most numerous while others focused on growing coffee, indigo, tobacco or spices. This single-crop dependency followed a general pattern of the period. Their American plantation counterparts, during this same period, focused on the production of tobacco and rice, and were just starting to discover a growing market for cotton that would have profound consequences.[20]

In the seventeenth and eighteenth centuries, planters in the West Indies had increasingly become the importers of these Connecticut animals and animal products. Sugar planters had become especially dependent upon the Connecticut-bred horses, cattle and mules. They were valued because, except for some of the larger islands like Jamaica, the "Sugar Islands" were not particularly suitable for producing and sustaining reserves of livestock. Indeed, plantation work, which was known to be extremely hard on the African slaves who provided the human labor that was essential to its success, was equally brutal for the imported beasts of burden. And, for a time, both man and beast were considered replaceable and expendable. Prior to the abolition of the slave trade in 1808, at times it was actually cheaper to replace slaves than it was to husband them as resources. Likewise, it was cheaper to import fresh new animals than it was to try and nurse along the older livestock. These Connecticut-bred animals hauled endless bundles of raw sugar cane from fields to the mills, provided the motive power to grind the cane and hauled the processed sugar and molasses to the ports for shipping. The animals were also valued for the manure they produced, which was used to fertilize the cane fields. Interestingly, while the cattle did provide food for the slaves and servants, the planters preferred barreled pork and beef shipped from New England. This accounts for the large

quantity of this product mentioned in the New London Report.

Storms and adverse weather conditions were also an ever-present danger adding to the mariner's risks. Most of the vessels involved in this trade from Connecticut prior to 1800 were relatively small sloops, schooners and brigs, although a few larger ships were built or purchased as well. The larger animals that they carried as cargo were tethered under awning-covered stalls on deck, which frequently made the vessels top heavy. In rough seas this could mean disaster. "Known as 'Horse Jockeys,' these ships were strong and heavily built. They were dull sailers, with low decks and very high waist ... and were generally excellent sea boats."[21] They made two and very occasionally three voyages a year, avoiding the hurricane season if they could. In 1784 the brig *Zephyr* of New London made a voyage to Jamaica and back again in thirty-seven days. The brig *Milley* from that same place under Captain Samuel Stillman made three voyages in one year to Jamaica carrying a total of 122 horses.[22] Some vessels were obviously well suited for the trade such as the 118-ton brigantine *William*, which was advertised as having "...a famous deck for stock."[23] Nevertheless, as one wag noted, whether the vessel was designed for the trade or not it still resulted in combining the "worst features of both a sea voyage and a barn yard."[24] Large animals were particularly unsuitable for vessels. Aside from the obvious inconveniences, the animals required large amounts of fresh water and hay as well as other maintenance.

While the loss of important cargo was to be avoided it nevertheless was not infrequently reported in newspaper accounts of the time that a vessel had lost its live cargo or was forced to jettison the hapless animals in order to save itself. The sloop *Orange*, arriving in 1784 at Stonington reported that on her outward voyage she had lost her entire cargo of horses overboard in a November gale.[25] The schooner *Federal George* under Captain Edward Merrill of New London was completely wrecked off Jamaica in 1800. Although the crew was saved, the vessel and cargo were a total loss.[26] That same year the brig *William* under Captain Samuel Freeman "foundered at sea....Her stock was swept overboard; she was dismasted; lost her rudder, and in this situation the crew remained ten days, when they were taken off by a Spanish vessel and carried to the South American coast, one man only being lost..."[27] Weather of a different sort in mid-January of 1791 caused more than thirty vessels bound for the West Indies to be locked in the ice in the Connecticut River "very likely to remain there till next April."[28] The schooner *Harriet* reported in 1801 that it arrived at Demerara after 76 days at sea with "her stock all died on deck, except one ox."[29] The brig *Godfrey & Mary* hardly made it out of the Thames River in 1811 with a load of oxen when she was saved from foundering through the efforts of launches sent from the frigates *Constitution* and *President* which happened to be stationed there in order, ironically, to enforce trade restrictions.[30] These and other mishaps such as masts shivered by lightning and crew members lost to fever and accident were all frequently reported. In 1805 at least twelve seamen from New London alone were lost.

Frances Manwaring Caulkins, in her *History of Norwich*, gives an excellent idea of the importance of West Indies commerce to that small city at the head of the Thames River. Norwich was a part of the New London customs district, and Miss Caulkins recalled that Norwich and its sister city New London were connected through a number of mercantile partnerships. The cargoes of incoming vessels were frequently distributed among the merchants of both towns. "The West India trade was an alluring path of adventure. The horses, cattle and alimentary produce of a thriving back country converged at Norwich and sought a market abroad....It was prosecuted with vigor, and was rich in its returns."[31] Livestock was the principal export from Norwich but it was very unusual for horses and cattle to be loaded at that port. Rather, they were driven to New London to be taken on board just prior to departure. This avoided the trip down river where the stock would otherwise have to be off loaded again to await the loading of additional cargo, a task that could sometimes take days or weeks.

"We are struck with astonishment," Miss Caulkins continued, "at the quantity of live-stock carried even by the smaller vessels, or sloops, popularly called horse-jockeys, in these voyages."[32] Among the soon to be famous Connecticut captains was Isaac Hull, of Derby, who was later to command the frigate *Constitution* in the coming war with Great Britain. Hull had previously been master of the 124-ton brig *Liffey* out of New London and the 178-ton brig *Nancy* from Norwich. In 1796 he sailed from New London to the West Indies in the ship *Minerva* during which voyage he carried a deck load of 98 oxen and 100 hogs.[33] This many animals was unusual. Generally, 30 to 55 seem to be the average number, since most voyages were undertaken by much smaller vessels than the 189 ton *Minerva*. Captain Hull, for all his later glory on the USS *Constitution*, had frequent bad luck as a merchant captain. While his first voyage in the *Minerva* seems to have been moderately successful, a year later, in 1797, during the Quasi-War with France the ship was captured by the French schooner *Bayonaise* and condemned as a prize at Guadaloupe. Both vessel and cargo were a total financial loss.[34]

Another, perhaps more typical, voyage might be that of the ship *Josephus* under Captain Elisha Huntington, of Norwich, which left New London for Demerara, September 12, 1789. Her cargo consisted of "62 horses and mules, a few cows, a yoke of oxen, and a dozen sheep and swine." *Josephus* also carried "4500 bunches of onions, 18 hogsheads of potatoes, 86 boxes of cheese, 18 firkins of butter, nearly 80 [hogsheads] of beef and pork, 30 kegs of crackers, 34 barrels of bread, and 30 barrels of flour. She had a large amount of brick and lumber, planks, clapboards, [barrel] staves, joints, and spars; 115 water hogsheads; a lot of parlor furniture, such as mahogany tables, green chairs and sofas, and a few saddles and bridles."[35] The mixed nature of the cargo is indicative of the merchants' attempts to avoid flooding one market with a single commodity, which would serve to reduce prices.[36] The great quantities of wood products listed for this cargo also indicated another marketable resource that was abundant in Connecticut.

Miss Caulkins also reported 7,403 horses, mules and cattle exported in the year 1791, while the "Schedule of Exports from and Imports into the District of New London," which appears in the New London Town Report lists 6,520 animals.[37] This suggests discrepancies but still gives a good indication of the overall importance of the commerce. Although numbers of animals and the quantities of agricultural produce fluctuate enormously after 1790, the total value of the exports steadily increased from $471,786 to $818,637 by 1807, the first year of the embargo. New London was not alone in this maritime success. In towns on the Connecticut River, as well as along the Connecticut shore, the wharves and warehouses that had proliferated prior to the Revolution were reinvigorated with activity. At Black Rock, a section of Fairfield, "the bustle along the harbor continued as ship after ship came into port, bringing molasses and rum from the West Indies..."[38] Timothy Dwight, President of Yale College, also noted that "not withstanding the excellence of the harbor and the convenience which it furnishes for commerce, Black Rock has long been neglected... business is now commencing... with a fair promise of success."[39] Although Black Rock soon was overshadowed by rivals Bridgeport and Southport, it did for a time enjoy some success in the trade, particularly in the decade just after the Revolution. Likewise in Groton, which at that time included parts of Ledyard and Mystic, men like Jonathan Barber, who became one of the "'largest buyers of farmers products and dealers in farmers supplies on the Thames River, and carried on a considerable trade with the West Indies..." found renewed prosperity.[40] We can infer from this passage and other sources, that farm implements also became exportable commodities for Connecticut.

Although New England vessels were frequently engaged in the slave trade before its abolition in 1808 there is little evidence that Connecticut merchants were more than occasionally involved in the direct sale of slaves to or from the West Indies. Merchants in Newport and Providence, Rhode Island, seem to have been much more actively engaged in this increasingly controversial business. "Negroes" sometimes are listed on import manifests of Connecticut-bound vessels, but the numbers could not be large. Only 6,000 blacks lived in Connecticut in the years just prior to the American Revolution.[41] Many of these people were "free" blacks and most, whether slave or free, were in domestic service of one kind or other rather than agricultural work. More typical, in Connecticut, was the importation of rum, molasses, sugar, salt, tropical fruits (such as oranges and limes), as well as plaster and "old iron."[42] The West Indies trade out of Connecticut has also often been linked to the so-called triangular trade, but more often than not Connecticut vessels traded specifically with the West Indies, and then carried the imports directly back to Connecticut. New York, of course, was also an obvious natural market for these products, and the greatest number of ships entering Boston harbor back in 1773, for example, hailed from Connecticut.[43] Undoubtedly some of these point-to-point voyages were part of the triangular trade as so-called, "broken voyages." This practice allowed the importation of West Indian goods that were then off loaded to "Americanize" the cargo, which was then reloaded and shipped as commodities originating in North America with the customs duties often rebated. The Connecticut-West Indies leg was usually a defined voyage only indirectly connected to the other two legs.

The Napoleonic era, which coincided with the period when America was first establishing its own commercial identity, also ushered in a time of continuous turmoil between the leading European powers, particularly Britain, France, Spain and the Netherlands, all of which had colonies and other economic interests in the Caribbean. The possibility of great profits for successful neutral traders lured American vessels in astonishing numbers.[44] Even the British West Indian ports that had remained closed to most American-owned vessels after the War for Independence often lifted their restrictions or looked the other way to allow for the importation of badly needed products during this turbulent time. The ever present danger of seizure or detention of vessel and/or cargo was a constant concern, and the most vexing aspect of this was created by the quirky, on-again off-again, importation enactments imposed by European powers and their local administrators. These temporary and often arbitrary rules would prohibit trading in certain commodities at different times and at different ports. American vessels were "subject to all the degrees of molestation, from simple detention and abusive words, through plundering, capturing, libeling, adjudication and condemnation, to entire loss of vessel and cargo, and often impressment of the crew."[45] In spite of the obvious risks Connecticut merchants found such trade opportunities, as the numbers of vessels engaged suggests, still appealing.

A typical marine list reported in a New London newspaper, posted on January 29, 1806, prior to the American embargo, mentions seven vessels clearing the port with destinations listed as Martinique, Tobago, Barbados and Surinam (trade with ports on the northern coast of South America was an associated business).[46] Other destinations were often simply noted as "the West Indies."[47] Edward Hallam & Co. of New London advertised in June of 1806 that they had "just received an offer for sale, very low, for cash or credit - 10 hhds [hogsheads] molasses, 35 hhds Montserrat rum, 14 hhds Dominco [Dominique] rum, 2000 bushels of Turk's Island salt." The advertisement concluded by stating that freight of 40 horses was sought "on deck of the schooner *Marcus*, and two or three hundred barrels, on board to any Windward Island."[48] New London's maritime success was not unique in Connecticut. Vessels entering other Connecticut ports reached an all time high during the period prior to the 1807 embargo, a trend that was also reflected elsewhere in New England.[49]

The West Indies trade was a boon to Connecticut shippers and merchants until 1807, the year that the first of the American-imposed embargoes and non-intercourse acts against Britain and France went into effect. Intermittently, and only by special permit, very limited legal trade continued until the War of 1812. These acts and the war itself essentially closed the lucrative business that had sustained so many Connecticut families and merchant enterprises, thus creating economic hardship for farmers, shipbuilders and storekeepers alike. While some of these people found employment and

financial reward in maritime privateering, this risky investment was not sustainable over the long term and only somewhat ameliorated the economic situation during the conflict.[50] Nonetheless, many felt that while the war lasted, the hazards of privateering were not much worse than the general risks of the trade in peace time.

An example of the effect of the first embargo and the long standing uncertainties inherent in the West Indies trade can be seen in the published saga of the New London schooner *Windham* under Captain John McCarty (sometimes reported as McGouty). Captain McCarty had long been engaged in the trade and was a well regarded master of West Indian vessels. He had previously commanded the sloop *Orange*, the schooners *Ariel*, *George*, *Phebe*, *Richard* and the brig *Dove*, all sailing from Norwich or New London. McCarty wrote:

> The *Windham* left the 1st of December [1806] for Surinam/Demerara, Trinidad and St. Martins [St. Martin]. Arriving in Surinam, 30 days, all well, found the market very bad, was not allowed to land any salted provisions, or take away any produce but rum and molasses, and that very high. Left that port, and tried the markets down to Demerara, and found the same order from England relative to the American trade. Sold part of the stock at Berbece [Berbice] and the remainder at Demerara then went to Trinidad, and at last got permission to land all provisions, to a good market: but the government proclamation, granting this permission, was limited to the 20th of April. The *Windham* stopped at the island of St. Martins (sic) in order to sell some candles; the inhabitants were much in need of them, but could pay in nothing but produce. When the order prohibiting American vessels from landing salted provisions or taking away coffee or sugar, came out from England, there were a number of vessels in the river of Berbice, which had entered and received permits from the government to land their cargoes and to load coffee and sugar. The masters and supercargoes of these vessels thinking themselves safe, sold their cargoes and some partly loaded, when the government took their permits from them and ordered them to unload. A petition and remonstrance was presented to no effect; they were obliged to take out the cargoes, land them on shore, and put them on board English vessels. The reason assigned to this injustice was that the American government had curtailed the English trade to America.

Captain McCarty also added as an aside that "in March the coast of Demerara was infested by French and Spanish robbers, from the [Spanish] Main to leeward; they take many American vessels under pretense that they have English property on board; and a vessel may well be condemned as carried up the Oronoke [Orinoco] River and cleared."[51]

In spite of the specific prohibition against the trade, after 1807 attempts were made to circumvent the restrictions because the chance of success and huge profits was much too alluring. A July 27, 1808, newspaper report mentions a "sloop with 500 barrels of flour was brought into this port [New London] on Friday last, by the Revenue Cutter *Revenge*, of New York, for attempting to evade the embargo laws. She has no name on her stern and no papers. A brig taken in the Sound by the same schooner, under suspicious circumstances, is carried into Stonington."[52]

With the 1807 embargo the West Indies trade in Connecticut declined precipitously, but a concurrent increase in trade with southern and middle Atlantic ports can also be noticed. The American coastal trade had begun to take on an importance to Connecticut merchants and its relative safety and predictability was alluring. "Just received..." advertised merchant Daniel Thatcher of New London, in November of 1808, "Richmond flour!"[53] Trade with Norfolk, Richmond, Baltimore, Wilmington, Charleston and Savannah are all mentioned in newspaper advertisements with much more frequency following 1807. Always innovative and looking for new commercial ventures for their vessels, which were often built to carry animals, New London merchants sought new opportunities. The brig *Godfrey & Mary*, for example, was among the first vessels to import Spanish Merino sheep to the United States, arriving from the Iberian Peninsula in September of 1811 with several pair. The Merino sheep was long sought after in America for its long and superior fleece and with these early imports and others Connecticut farmers came to play a prominent role in the breed's introduction to American agriculture.[54]

In March 1810 the *Connecticut Gazette* excitedly exclaimed, "Embargo Off!" A cautious trade was again reestablished with the West Indies, although fundamentally no changes in policies had occurred. Arbitrary revocations of licenses continued, as did the irksome practice of impressing American seamen into the British navy. The Non-Intercourse Act of 1811 once again stymied trade to the West Indies, and the start of the war itself in June of 1812 brought commerce of all types to a "ruinous" halt. While numerous attempts were made to slip through the maritime British blockade of the Connecticut coast, most were unsuccessful. Many merchants simply laid up their vessels for the duration in as safe a place as they could find. The Schooner *Mary*, for example, was even scuttled in the Pawcatuck River and only raised after the cessation of hostilities.[55]

In retrospect, the years from 1784 to 1807 had been, with some exceptions, extremely prosperous ones for Connecticut shippers, all of whom were loath to see anything happen that might upset the delicate and tenuous balance of circumstances that permitted the trade to thrive. It is for this reason that the various embargoes and the War of 1812 itself were generally unpopular in Federalist Connecticut and were the cause for much vocal and editorial discussion. Unhappiness with the war eventually led to the Hartford Convention of New England states in December of 1814. Some delegates even toyed with the idea of secession from the union. The war's end a few weeks later brought all such ideas to an end.

The *New London Gazette* on February 8, 1815, heralded the news of peace, a sentiment echoed by the *General Shipping and Commercial List* of New York which proclaimed the return of prosperity and the restoration of commerce.[56] It was hoped that trade with foreign ports, and particularly the European colonial holdings in the West Indies, would return to the halcyon days of the previous decades. This was not to be. The end of the Napoleonic Wars meant that the European mercantile rivalries that had heretofore characterized the maritime world were greatly reduced or eliminated. Great Britain had maintained its dominance of the world's oceans and finally with the passage of restrictive Navigation Acts closed all of its colonial ports in the Western Hemisphere to American vessels in 1826.[57]

Fishing

After the American Revolution, Connecticut's fishing industry, perhaps partly spurred by federal bounties, began to be a more important part of the maritime economy of the state, and Connecticut shipbuilders were active in supplying vessels for this enterprise. This was especially true for ports on Long Island Sound east of the Connecticut River. Fish such as cod, sea bass, blackfish and lobster were the principal catches, and were generally transported to local and New York markets. The Town Report from New London specifically mentions that sixty fishing vessels were home ported in the district at that time.[58] The sloop *Rambler*, launched at Mystic in 1792 by Edward Packer, and the *Revenge*, launched in the same place in 1795, for example, were specifically listed in the cod fishery during our period. Most of these fishing vessels were sloop or schooner smacks, which were designed to carry fresh fish. The term smack indicated that the vessel had a "live well" in its hold. In other words, the hull of the vessel incorporated a large watertight box or compartment through which holes were drilled to allow for the free flow of fresh seawater. This allowed the freshly caught fish to be kept alive and even fattened by feeding until their arrival at markets from New York to Rhode Island.

It was probably during this early period that the evolution of a distinctive type of fishing vessel called the "Connecticut Smack" began. The construction of fishing vessels in Connecticut prior to 1815 was modest in scale by the standards of the generation to follow, but it did contribute to the overall shipbuilding activity then taking place. By the mid nineteenth century the Connecticut smack had evolved into a well known and frequently imitated type. Construction of these vessels was centered in eastern Connecticut, at places such at Noank, Mystic, New London, and Waterford, which came to specialize in them. They were not only designed for use in local southern New England waters but were frequently seen off the coasts of South Carolina, Georgia, and Florida as well as the Bahamas, and even in Cuban waters.

This so called "Southern" or "winter fishery," so named for the time of year it took place, came to be increasingly important to southeastern Connecticut fishermen, particularly as the nineteenth century progressed. Red Snapper, grouper and other food fish common to southern waters were caught by these Connecticut vessels and brought into markets at Savannah, Charleston, Havana, and in the Bahamas.[59] Although this fishery did not begin in earnest until after 1815, as early as 1798 the smack *Rover* was mentioned as returning from a five-month cruise to southern waters where "they caught fish which they sold in the Charleston market, to the amount of 3000 dollars."[60] Key West, Florida, in fact, came to be the southern home for many of these vessels and their crews after 1818.

These men, primarily from southeastern Connecticut, not only fished out of Key West but were among the first to settle on the island where they also became involved in "wrecking." The coral reef that runs from the Miami area to the Dry Tortugas was especially treacherous for the unwary, and vessels that navigated along this increasingly busy seaway did so at their peril. Although this salvage activity has often been associated with illegal wrecking, the fact of the matter is, so many vessels were caught up on the reef all on their own, it was unnecessary to lure them ashore. When vessels went aground, as they did frequently, salvaging them and their cargoes was profitably rewarded in the admiralty courts, and much of this wealth found its way back to Connecticut where it was often reinvested into shipbuilding.

Secondary ports within the New London custom district, such as those located in East Lyme (Niantic), Waterford and Stonington, also became more active in the various deep sea fisheries. In 1804, a New London newspaper reported that "a company is about forming in Stonington, for the purpose of pursuing the fisheries, upon an extensive scale...."[61] By the early 1820s Connecticut vessels extended their voyages to the fishing banks off the Massachusetts coast and as far away as Newfoundland and Labrador.[62] New London, in addition to its growing fishing fleet, also established a fledgling whaling industry that was eventually to develop into the city's most important "fishery" by mid century. The sloop *Rising Sun* set sail on a hunt for the leviathan in May of 1784, although vessels did not regularly begin to trickle out to sea in pursuit of whales until 1802.[63] Reporting on the successful whaling voyage of the ship *Dauphin* in 1806, the editor of the *Connecticut Gazette* newspaper concluded, with perhaps little knowledge of the realities, that "the fisheries are, at once, a safe and secure nursery for seamen, and an unfailing source of wealth to the enterprising and industrious...."[64]

Shipbuilding

Another essential maritime activity important to Connecticut at this time, which has already been mentioned, was shipbuilding. Indeed, shipbuilding was in many respects the supporting basis for all the maritime activity reported by the various towns. Fishing and maritime commerce could not develop without vessels. The sound of the shipwrights' saw and adz and the ring of the caulker's mallet had long echoed along Connecticut's shores. As early as the mid-seventeenth century, Wethersfield and New Haven were launching vessels.

In 1680 Joseph Wells of Stonington contracted to build (on the Pawcatuck River) "one good ship or vessel..." for a New London merchant.[65] Hugh Mould and John Coit were also active in the same business at New London in the 1650s. These early enterprises and others began an important Connecticut industry that by the mid-eighteenth century witnessed no fewer than twenty simultaneously active shipyards throughout the state. By the time of the Town Reports, there were close to that many in operation just within the New London customs district.

The early nineteenth-century West Indies and coastal trades, as well as the state's newly energized fishing industry, reinvigorated shipbuilding and positioned Connecticut's shipyards for entry into a broader national market for vessels. Within a generation Connecticut ships and shipbuilders became well known in the important commercial centers of New York, Philadelphia and New Orleans and were even specifically sought by some merchants during the mid-nineteenth century. This great maritime age of sail saw the construction of scores of Connecticut-built cotton packets and clipper ships as well as steamships, many of which became well-known fixtures along the wharves and docks of the nation's principal seaports. This reputation for building good ships dating back to the eighteenth century was clearly maintained in the period of the Town Reports.

By 1800 shipyards along the Connecticut River had become the most important in the state. That year alone more than 13,000 tons of shipping slid down the scores of ship-ways along the river.[66] This activity ranged geographically from East Windsor, near the Massachusetts border, to the mouth of the river at Saybrook. By later standards these operations were small. In fact, the shipyards of this period seldom boasted more than two launching ways. A typical Connecticut River shipyard during this time would normally be composed of a single launching way and a mold loft building where full-scale construction molds (or "moulds") were created from half-hull models or drawn plans. These early shipyards also contained a saw pit or two where the often massive timbers used in construction were cut to the specifications indicated by the plans. The vessels, mainly sloops, schooners and brigs, were seldom larger than 250 registered tons. Also of interest among statistics in the New London Report is the fact that while the value of the exports climbed during the 1790-1807 period the number of vessels engaged in trade decreased. Some 238 vessels cleared for foreign ports in 1791 as compared with 142 in 1806; which indicates that the size of vessels was increasing during the period, allowing more cargo to be carried by fewer vessels. According to a notation on the Schedule of Exports in that report, the average tonnage rose from 85 tons in 1790 to 125 tons in 1811. A typical Connecticut clipper ship fifty years later, by contrast, ranged between 800 to 1500 tons.

Shipbuilding on the Connecticut River can be no better represented than by the shipyards of Middlesex County which included Essex ("Pautapoug"), Chatham, Haddam, Middle Haddam and other river towns with active shipyards. In 1815, the first full year of peace following the War of 1812, Middlesex county launched forty-nine vessels including eight ships, eleven brigs, thirteen schooners and seventeen sloops totaling a respectable 7,503 tons of shipping.[67] The Report from Haddam, for example, stated that in 1808 that town had an "abundance of excellent timber for shipbuilding...but the fatal word 'Embargo' unnerves the arm of the axemen..." It goes on to state that "there are five Building-yards, at which until the Era of Disaster a great number of vessels have been erected with profit to the builder, & general advantage to the town and the country."[68] At Middletown itself shipbuilding was centered at the north end of the settlement which during this period was known as "Upper Houses," and later would become the town of Cromwell. The Middlesex County Report[69] suggests the industry may have started as early as the 1720s. At "Upper Houses" shipbuilding had certainly been established since at least 1759, but it was the trade to the West Indies that gave it new life. In 1792 Abijah Savage purchased a yard and began to launch a number of ships and brigs on a regular basis until 1815. Robert Decker, in his history of Cromwell, shows that the 269-ton ship *Huldah*, which was built for Captain Nathan Sage in 1795, was paid for with "money, flour, West Indian Goods and tea."[70] Other builders during this period were Thomas Belcher, Isaac Webber, Captain Luther Smith, Joseph Belden and Jared Post.   Shipyards also sprang up at East Haddam, Glastonbury, Hartford, Chester, Lyme, Deep River, Portland, Wethersfield and elsewhere. At Essex at least four shipyards were operating in the early nineteenth century.

In the New London customs district shipyards were also abundant. They were located along the Thames River at Norwich, Montville, Gales Ferry, Groton and New London, as well as along the Sound at Waterford and Niantic. Further to the east, shipyards also were active on the Pawcatuck River and at Stonington Borough. But it was on the banks of the Mystic River that the New London County shipbuilding industry was centered.

Following the American Revolution two shipyards were reenergized at the head of the Mystic River, at what is now Old Mystic. One of these was operated by Christopher Leeds and the other by Silas Burrows. A third shipyard run by Benjamin Morrell began operations at "the narrows" opposite the present Elm Grove Cemetery, and a fourth was active in what is today Mystic, operated by Eldredge Packer.[71] One yard at Mystic launched three vessels in 1806, which represented a sizable output for the period. Similar activity was also beginning at the mouth of the river at Noank where James Latham and John Palmer each began building vessels. Both of their families would continue as shipbuilders throughout the nineteenth century.[72]

It is clear that a fundamentally significant maritime activity underpinned Connecticut's economy in the early nineteenth century. It is an activity that has been overshadowed by the state's vibrant and diverse mid-nineteenth century industrial story and deserves much more attention than it has heretofore received from chroniclers of the Connecticut experience.

The Embedded Nature of Artisanal Activity in Connecticut, ca. 1800

Edward S. Cooke, Jr.

While the learned men who comprised the leadership of the Connecticut Academy of Arts and Sciences earnestly sought to gather data on the state's "Agriculture, Manufactures, and Commerce" in order to "advance the dignity, virtue, and happiness" of its citizens, they apparently had little interest in craft work.[1] If one looks only at the contents of the Town Reports, the fit of artisanal activity within Connecticut's mixed agricultural, manufacturing, or commercial economies seems unclear or even negligible. There is little mention of the blacksmiths, joiners, or shoemakers who worked in each town, or the coopers, saddlers, tailors, hatters, potters, pewterers or silversmiths who worked in many of the towns. However, the questions posed to the various towns and the responses sent back to the Academy do offer valuable insights into the period's perspective on craft work. The following study draws from the Town Reports, but links the narrative information with other documentary and material sources to tease out the fit of crafts within the economy of Connecticut in the early national period and to explain the invisibility of artisanal activity to the gentlemen of the Academy of Arts and Sciences.

Period Distinctions

The key to understanding the place of crafts is to recognize the distinction that the state's leaders made between different modes of making a living. Close reading of the Town Reports reveals that a certain hierarchy existed in the minds of the Academy's founders and the respondents who compiled the reports. Throughout the endeavor agriculture was given top billing. As the Farmington Report stated, it was "of great importance to the American nation and to almost all people living under the blessings of civil society."[2] The Reports all provided very detailed information on types and prices of land, fertilizing techniques, yield of the land, etc. The universality of detailed knowledge about farming is readily evident in both the series of question pertaining to it (Articles 9-13) and in the data found throughout the Reports.

The correspondents provided less detail about mills and manufactories, for which there were merely two questions, Articles 8 and 16. Most Reports mentioned or enumerated the various essential saw, grist, and tanning mills used to process agricultural products into materials used by craftsmen and commented upon the fermentation of fruits such as apples and pears. While the number included in the Reports seems incomplete when compared with the sites shown on period maps of Connecticut, the evidence of the Reports and maps together demonstrates that the leaders held a greater interest in the processing of natural resources and agricultural products than in the application of technology or workmanship to transform the materials into household goods.[3]

In terms of multi-step fabrication, the correspondents paid particular attention to cotton or wool manufactories. Among the essential criteria were the size of operation (number of employees or amount of investment) or extent of market. For example the returns specifically cited Eli Whitney's New Haven factory for the production of cotton gins that permitted 60 million pounds of cotton to be cleaned per year and his factory for military muskets. Samuel Goodrich wrote that two shoe manufactories in Ridgefield took in materials from New York and then exported about 5,000 pairs abroad. The Middletown reporter celebrated the steampower, 80 employees, and $70,000 annual gross of the Middletown Manufacturing Company; and the 100 employees at the Starr Sword Factory. In certain towns such as Farmington and East Windsor woolen and linen cloth was "made in families," but in these cases the correspondents made note because the export market for these cloths began to exceed the local market. Similarly the writers noted that in 1832 many Guilford and Madison families made shoes for a Southern market. The Academy and its circle of respondents recognized the growing importance of manufacturing in a new national economy and valued mechanical invention as a noble pursuit, but knowledge of and involvement in manufacturing was not widespread. As a result mills and manufactures lagged behind agriculture in terms of prestige.[4]

Even lower in the occupational hierarchy was craft work—the fabrication of useful or common articles in a small shop.[5] Such endeavors, often organized by household and pursued part-time or seasonally within the agricultural calendar, seemed to exist below the scrutiny of the Connecticut Academy's gentlemen who privileged mechanical genius and technological applications that would bring profits to investors. For example, the Bolton reporter raved about the "uncommon mechanical genius" of a Mr. Warburton, the English immigrant who had set up a cotton factory, but did not make reference to the skilled Windsor chairmaker Erastus Dewey, who had worked briefly for Lemuel Adams, Hartford's leading cabinetmaker, before returning to Bolton. The Farmington Report praised Stephen Brownson, "a man of enterprizing & adventurous disposition" who learned about weaving and dying but then hired "foreigners, that were skilful in the art of weaving & dying" to do the actual work, as well as Asa Andrews, who used his "ingenuity & close application to the business" to

Chest of drawers, Ebenezer Williams, East Windsor, Connecticut, 1803. Cherry, white pine; H: 34 in., W: 44 1/8 in., D: 18 1/2 in. Connecticut Historical Society, Hartford.

organize an effective outwork system for the japanning or decorative painting of tinned sheet iron. The most esteemed mechanic was one who used knowledge of the trade and organizational skills to escape the drudgery of work in the shop and to coordinate the skillful work of others. The Farmington reporter did provide a general list of the trades in the town, but neglected to mention by name the successful cabinetmaker Luther Seymour, the silversmith/engraver Martin Bull, or the silversmith/clockmaker Lewis Curtis.[6]

Also revealing is that many craftsmen regarded as leaders in their craft by twentieth-century decorative arts scholars are also noticeably absent from the Town Reports. The prolific gravestone carvers Thomas Gold and David Ritter of New Haven are only statistical numbers, the two unnamed stonecarvers, even though both had regional reputations as the most fashionable and prolific carvers in the area. Signed examples of Gold's and Ritter's works can be found throughout southern coastal Connecticut. In East Windsor, there is no mention of the cabinetmakers Eliphalet Chapin or Ebenezer Williams or the influential clockmaker/engraver/silversmith Daniel Burnap even though their reputations extended throughout and even beyond the Hartford County area. Products from these shops reveal considerable skill and command of fashion. Chapin and Burnap had gained such expertise from masters outside the region—the former had worked for several years in Philadelphia, and the latter had apprenticed with Thomas Harland, the British trained clockmaker who worked in Norwich. Chapin's shop made furniture for many of the leading merchants in northern Hartford County and also served as the training school for many of the cabinetmakers who then moved to Hartford at the end of the century and dominated the trade in that town. These craftsmen included Aaron Chapin and Aaron Colton. Burnap ran the largest clockmaking shop in the Connecticut Valley at the turn of the century—more than a fifth of surviving clocks from this region were made in his shop—and trained Eli

Terry, whose wooden clocks dominated the New England market in the early nineteenth century.[7]

Similarly the pewterer William Danforth is not mentioned in the Middletown Report even though the Danforths and their relatives the Boardmans together were arguably the largest producers of pewter in America. Using molds to cast multiples of their sturdy reliable product and spreading production throughout a series of family-run shops along the Connecticut River from Middletown to Hartford, the Danforths sold their wares throughout New England and sent peddlers to the coastal South as well. In the Lisbon Report, neither the Tracy family of Windsor chairmakers nor the gravestone carver John Walden appear. Each of these shops made large quantities of goods for local and regional markets and even provided goods for such leading families as the Trumbulls or Leffingwells, but the Academy officers and their peers did not consider them equal to cloth and arms production.[8]

The Landscape of Craft in Connecticut ca. 1800

Only a few of the Academy's respondents discussed artisanal activities in their town or compiled a list of craftsmen. Among these exceptions are Elkanah Tisdale's report on Lebanon in 1800 and Lewis Norton's on Goshen in 1812. Both agents had familiarity with craft work—the former's father was a tanner, and the latter was a builder and related to other joiners and builders in town—and thus had insights into its mysteries, practices, and importance. After discussing how cloth was woven within family homes primarily for local consumption, Tisdale wrote that "there are tanners, shoemakers, carpenters, house joiners, & blacksmiths scattered about town, so many of the latter as to do the necessary work of horseshoeing, ox shoeing, sharpening plow irons & making axes & scythes for the inhabitants. A considerable part of the shoemaking

Chiming tall case clock, clockworks by Daniel Burnap, East Windsor, Connecticut, 1780-1800. Cherry, white pine, brass, steel, glass; H: 92 in., W: 20 in., D: 10 1/2 in. Connecticut Historical Society, Hartford.

Bow-back Windsor armchair, Ebenezer Tracy, Lisbon, Connecticut, 1785-1800. Maple, ash, hickory, chestnut; H: 38 5/8 in., W: 20 7/8 in., D: 17 1/2 in. Yale University Art Gallery, Mabel Brady Garvan Collection, 1930.

is done in families by men who go from house to house for that purpose, except in summer, when they are generally employed at farming ... ." Norton reported that "the domestic manufactures of this town differ little from those of most in the inland towns of this state." He described a fledgling woolen mill, but then listed 7 tanners, 6 coopers, 5 blacksmiths, 5 joiners, 2 potters, 1 cabinetmaker, 1 forge, 1 carding machine, and 1 wool manufacturer in that town of 240 families.[9]

Ascertaining the actual number and varieties of craftsmen active in Connecticut at the end of the eighteenth century is a difficult task. There are no town directories, and legal documents such as probate records, wills, or land deeds rarely provided the occupations of their subjects. As a result scholars have only been able to infer trades by examining tool ownership in probate inventories or compiling lists derived from account book references on a town-by-town or county basis. Decorative arts scholars and antiquarians have compiled lists of craftsmen who made buildings, furniture, silver, clocks, ceramics, or gravestones, but these lists tend to focus on master craftsmen and also exclude shoemakers, blacksmiths, tailors, saddlers, coopers, and similar trades. As a result there is no comprehensive study of Connecticut craftsmen from this time period, only broad generalizations. Many historians have assumed that all the Connecticut towns had a basic complement of craftsmen that supported the relative self-sufficiency of that community.[10]

However, the Town Reports, when linked with tax lists and assessments of master craftsmen or shop owners in those towns, shed light upon the scope of craft activity in those towns as well as patterns of that activity on a state-wide level. Together the sources suggest a topography of artisanal work in Connecticut.[11] The correlation of these two sources addresses the question of typicality and apportioning of craft activities within Connecticut towns at the turn of the nineteenth century—what were the usual categories of craftsmen, what was the proportion of artisans to the overall population, and what were the variations by town or region. What becomes clear from an examination of the tax lists and Town Reports is that the only truly universal

craftsmen were the joiners/carpenters, blacksmiths, and shoemakers. Numbers of master craftsmen had less to do with population than with the nature of the local economy and availability of materials. The fact that a town had 400 mature males did not necessarily mean that a certain number of each type of artisans worked in that town to support a relative self-sufficiency within that community. Instead there were considerable variations between towns based on a variety of factors including type of land, natural resources, location and time of settlement, social structure, and the influence of a prominent craftsman such as Daniel Burnap. In short, craft work was an inextricable part of a town's and region's mixed agricultural economy.

Of the thirty towns that submitted reports to the Academy by the end of 1812, tax information for eighteen was analyzed (see Table 1). Among these towns there is considerable variation in population size, location, and age. The towns could be broken down into three different types: port towns, country centers, and rural towns.[12] The two port towns—New Haven and New London—reveal a balance of merchandising and production. The number of merchants and shopkeepers greatly exceeded those of any other town studied, but there was also considerable variety of processing operations. The expected ancillary trades of shipping such as blockmaking and ropemaking appear only in these towns, but several other crafts reveal a certain specialization within these towns. The great quantity of woodworkers reflects the reliance on wood as a building material for dwellings, docks, warehouses, and ship interiors, while the number of tailors, shoemakers, and hatmakers suggests that artisans in these towns used raw materials gathered from the neighboring rural communities to make products for export. Other shops such as bakers and barbers

Gravestone of Nicholas Justin of South Canterbury, Connecticut, carved by John Walden, Lisbon, Connecticut, 1804. Granite schist. Photograph by Dr. Ernest Caulfield; print from the Dan and Jessie Lie Farber Collection at Yale University.

provided specific products and services that indicate a certain specialization of tasks within the port towns; in country towns, bread was baked within the household and haircuts were given within the home as needed. The presence of attorneys to draw up legal documents and interpret the law, printers to issue newspapers and broadsides, and silversmiths to make holloware and sugar tongs as well as spoons also distinguished the complexity of the economy and craft structure in these towns.[13]

Certain inland towns, by virtue of their early founding within that region or central location, became country centers for surrounding villages. Within these two towns— East Windsor and Farmington—there was considerable variation in craft activity. The rich alluvial soils of East Windsor ensured a prosperous grain economy dominated by a class of wealthy farmers and controlled by powerful merchants who shipped the grain down the Connecticut River. This upper stratum, in turn, supported a great number and variety of craftsmen from the middle of the eighteenth century to the turn of the nineteenth. The great number of woodworkers, blacksmiths, and shoemakers suggests a strong local and regional market for their works. The presence of a gunsmith and clockmaker further reinforces the artisanal importance of this town, which supplied craftsmen and products to Hartford and throughout the Connecticut River Valley. The widespread availability of red sandstone also permitted the Drake and Lathrop families to make and engrave tombstones that were sold throughout the valley.[14]

The large town of Farmington also supported a variety of craftsmen. In his Town Report, John Treadwell noted the recent transformation from an agricultural community to one in which "agriculture & commerce go hand in hand." Just before the Revolution three or four shopkeepers in Farmington had invested $8,000-10,000 in trade, but by 1800 commercial activity had quickened so that nine large shops worked with $125,000 in capital. Treadwell commented that the new commercial energy of the past thirty years had created "riches," which in turn "introduces a taste for luxury in building, dress, furniture, equipage … ." Contrasting the previous generation of laboring farmers dressed in homespun and covered in sweat and dust with the rising generation who sought to be lawyers, physicians, or some other sort of professional and who eagerly purchased "European & India fabrics," Treadwell believed that "the present time marks a revolution of taste & of manners of immense import to society." The fecundity of the land and the industriousness of its farmers and artisans had encouraged the entrepreneurial spirit of the new professionals. The distribution of master craftsmen in Farmington supports Treadwell's comments: Martin Bull and Lewis Curtis made silver objects that defined and articulated genteel behavior; Luther Seymour built fashionable homes with academically inspired details; Asa Andrews, one of three tinners in town, had a brick shop and used an outwork system to produce more than 10,000 articles of japanned ware annually; and the three hatmakers Corral Case, James Hunt, and the partnership of Norris and William Stanley annually made about 2,500 hats that were sold to merchants and shopkeepers throughout the region.[15]

In country centers, shopkeepers directed their town's involvement in the external market and catered to an eager, fashion-conscious clientele who sought to solidify their social position through the ownership, use, and display of household goods. The interest in material possessions supported ambitious artisans who intensified their work rhythms to reach a broader market, and yet also undercut the smaller, part-time maker of household goods who had to compete with the wave of imported goods made increasingly available through better distribution systems. Only those small shops engaged in maintenance activities or in direct conversion of local raw materials seemed secure in the country centers.[16]

The rural towns ranged considerably in population and age, from the old and populous community of Wallingford to the small, relatively recently established towns of Cornwall and Goshen. Yet the varied artisanal composition of these towns underscores the importance of local context. The two most populous towns, Wallingford and Lebanon, had fewer master craftsmen than many smaller towns. Wallingford's economy in the late eighteenth century was linked closely to the poor quality of the land and the town's proximity to New Haven. Farmers cut hay and wood to send to the densely populated port town where people with little land used the former to feed horses and the latter as building material or fuel. Some of the carpenters and joiners in town even hewed and framed building members before shipping them to New Haven. The high cost of fattening stock precluded much exportation of meat, but the local animals were prized for their skins, which were tanned and cut for either local shoemakers or those in New Haven.[17]

The town of Lebanon, another town characterized by hilly terrain, lacked depth in its artisanal composition. Considering the high population, there were few shops in town and most of these were valued at the minimum of $17. The small number of woodworkers, shoemakers, and clothiers suggests that the local shops processed locally available materials that had been procured by individual families. Furthermore, Elkanah Tisdale's report hints that many of the craftsmen were engaged primarily in maintenance activities rather than full-scale production for local and regional markets. Perhaps the town's proximity to Norwich, the center of manufacturing in Connecticut, had stifled a broad-based artisanal community. Another important influence upon the local economic choices was the legacy of the town's most famous inhabitant, Governor John Trumbull (1710-1785). In the 1750s and 1760s, Trumbull amassed his wealth and power by raising stock to export as salted meat through Norwich. The success of his ventures and the continued power of his descendants in the Lebanon area directly shaped the economic life of the community, one that focused almost exclusively on meat for export. Unlike Woodbury and other communities whose economies relied on animal husbandry, there were no large number of coopers building barrels and casks for meat and dairy products and no cordwainers making use of the leather for shoes.[18]

Among the less populous or less centrally located rural towns there was no certain formula for the artisanal population. Small towns such as Canterbury, Pomfret, and Tolland in the eastern part of the state and Goshen in the northwest supported a silversmith who produced spoons primarily, and coopers were active in only about one-third of the towns even though barrels, hogsheads, and firkins were essential storage containers, especially for meat and dairy products. The small hill town of Ridgefield in the southwest section listed seven blacksmiths and five clothiers but only a single hatmaker even though neighboring Danbury was the center of hat production in the state. In Preston, just to the east of Norwich, twelve shopkeepers set up shop to distribute goods acquired through Norwich manufactures and merchants. Unlike Lebanon, Preston's economy did include a number of successful local craftsmen such as the silversmiths John Avery and Daniel Billings and the joiners Joel Hyde and John Wheeler Geer. In Preston the growing shortage of wood and emphasis on commercial animal husbandry—beef and dairy products for export—exerted a substantial effect upon the composition of craftsmen. Three shoemakers and four saddlers comprised more than half of the craftsmen with faculties—the period term for equipped shops. Shoemakers and saddlers were also relatively plentiful in Tolland, suggesting that in both towns the large supply of animals provided a ready selection of material and the nearby market towns of Norwich and Hartford provided a clientele for shoes and saddles. Tolland's assessment reveal that several families used craft careers to keep sons in town. The Holbrook and Howard family each had a tanner and a shoemaker; the Scott family included two joiners and one shoemaker; and the Eaton family listed a tailor and a blacksmith.[19]

In the northwestern corner of the state, settled only beginning in the 1740s, the towns of Cornwall and Goshen revealed complex economies. In Cornwall, proximity to the prominent iron works of Salisbury and the presence of three forges contributed to the livelihood of ten blacksmiths, who specialized in bar iron, nail rods, and nails that they made for a local market and for export. Joiners and carpenters also worked for local and external markets: " ... some of the Carpenters & Joiners go out of the Town to Build Houses & Barns, &c. Cabinet Work is also made for those who belong to other Towns in the Vicinity of Cornwal, by Workmen in this Town, as well as for our own Inhabitants." As in Tolland, several families seem to have crossed trade boundaries in this town that boasted a buoyant mixed agricultural economy founded on grains, animals, and craft work—the Wilcox family included a bloomer and a blacksmith, while the Clark family included a blacksmith, weaver, and mason. In Goshen the land was best suited to grazing and animal husbandry, and the location on the New Haven-Albany post road made commercial enterprise relatively easy. A silversmith provided simple spoons and other small items; four shoemakers provided shoes for the town and for export; and two potters, Jesse Wadhams and Harvey Brooks, made utilitarian earthenware in Goshen. The bulk of their ware was either dairy pans and platters or simple drinking vessels, and the extent of their market reached to Woodbury, Bethlem, Cornwall, Kent, and Salisbury in Connecticut and extended to Holbrook, New York, and Sheffield, Massachusetts.[20]

In these rural towns, decentralized shops in which part-time craft work was spread among many inhabitants and integrated with the local seasonal rhythms helped to balance the population and resources. This type of artisanal activity prevented the glut of makers that might have accompanied full-time activity, provided products and services that bound the inhabitants together as a community, and fostered flexible technologies and progressive skills that allowed the craftsmen to adapt to changing market conditions.[21]

Interpretation

The considerable number of craftsmen revealed in the tax lists and their integral fit within their local economies raises questions about the Academy gentlemen's silence on craft work. Why did they overlook the value of the craft sector for the towns' economies? What was the basis of their hierarchical view? A broader examination of the political economy of the early national period and social attitudes reveals that the Connecticut leaders' selective vision was rooted in agricultural reform, economic theories of the time, and misguided perceptions about domestic-based craft.[22]

The range of questions relating to agriculture reveal the Academy's leaders to be upper-class reformers who sought to overturn what they viewed as old, inefficient farming practices. Linking strategies that emphasized family subsistence to poor crops and a worrisome outmigration of Connecticut families, the reformers instead favored new breeds, improved crops, enriched soil, and a market orientation. Agriculture had historically been important to Connecticut's economy, but the leaders in the early national period emphasized that careful cultivation and maintenance of lands would ensure prosperity, self-sufficiency, and good citizenship. Knowledge of the arts of agriculture and animal husbandry would be a pillar of the new republican government. The French traveler Jean Pierre Brissot de Warville articulated this physiocratical vision well in 1788 when he commented about Connecticut:

> Here nature and art have displayed all their treasures; it is indeed the paradise of the United States. ... This state owes all its advantages to its geographical situation. It is a fertile plain enclosed between two mountains which make difficult communication by land with the neighboring states and hence provide security and protection. It is watered by the superb Connecticut River, which flows into the sea and provides a safe and easy passage to navigation throughout its length. Agriculture being the basis of the state's prosperity, wealth is more equally distributed; there is more equality, less poverty, more simplicity, more virtue, more of what constitutes republicanism.[23]

The reformers who sought to transform traditional agriculture seem to have associated part-time craft work within the agricultural calendar with the old ways. Their silence on craft activity reflected their desire to replace the older mode of production with new improved and market-oriented modes.

Just as the reformers sought to improve agricultural practice, so they argued for the improvement of production. Dominant among these economic views was the program of Alexander Hamilton, the Secretary of the Treasury, who argued for the development of American manufactures in order to develop a balanced national economy. Hamilton believed it essential that the newly independent, agricultural, undeveloped country quickly develop a manufacturing capability to complement its farm production, thereby ensuring sound credit, new possibilities for investment, greater economic opportunities, and a national market for the products of American farmers. The result would be national power and prestige in which profits would remain in America. To hasten the development of American manufactures, Hamilton articulated a plan that placed protective duties on imported finished goods, removed duties on imported raw materials, encouraged American businesses to import machinery or pirate technological secrets, argued for the substitution of machinery for manual labor, and encouraged expanding manufactures to exploit the benefits of the division of labor. Implicit within Hamilton's agenda was a dismissal of small shop work dependent upon the skilled workmanship and flexible production of the individual artisan. With a concerted focus upon new machinery, the division of labor in centralized facilities, and the construction of large new factories often of brick or stone, the low-technologies of craft work scattered throughout the domestic arena slipped below scrutiny.[24]

The invisibility of useful craft was also reinforced as certain merchant artisans began to expand their production in the new national markets facilitated by a federal currency and transportation network. These artisans focused upon the organization of work and viewed themselves as members of a professional class. The elevation of the merchant artisan to manufacturer and its attendant status within the Hamiltonian world left little prestige or power for the producing artisan. The tension between manufacturer and craftsman in Connecticut first flared up in the Artisan Protest of 1792. At that time a coalition of craftsmen petitioned against the state's taxation system. Two issues formed the heart of this protest: the faculty assessment and the subsidization of manufactures. Tax assessors were instructed to add a certain faculty assessment to the total for any person who ran a shop engaged in "any Mechanical Art or Mystery." Rather than taxing individual skills, even those of journeymen or pieceworkers, the faculty assessment targeted the masters of active artisanal shops. The assessment of a faculty, or shop, was at least £5 ($17), but could be higher. Artisans considered this assessment unfair because it gave the assessor arbitrary power to define who was an artisan and to determine how profitable each shop was. Furthermore the tax particularly burdened the young artisans just mastering their skills and establishing their own shops. Walter Brewster, a shoemaker from Canterbury who wrote under the name "Mechanick," argued that "To tax a man for his skills, is taxing the genius of the people; it is taxing enterprise and industry." What made the artisans even angrier was the preference extended to manufactories at the same time. To encourage large cloth, iron, or similar industries, the state had extended tax exemptions and subsidies to certain establishments.[25]

The biased view toward crafts continued even through the 1820 Census of Manufactures. Secretary of State John Quincy Adams instructed his marshals not to include "household manufactures" who make "works of handicraft." After several marshals found this directive unclear, Adams sent out "elucidations," in which he reiterated that the purpose of the census was to identify those people whose primary occupation was manufacturing and not to document those of the "mechanical professions or handicrafts." Location of work in a large, centralized factory apart from the domestic realm seemed to have been the key, not skill or product. Robert Fairchild, the marshal for Connecticut, revealed such a point of view in the notes he added to his assistants' responses. For the statistical abstract and final printed digest, he eliminated

the "small establishments as are common to most of the towns in Connecticut," including cabinetmakers, hatmakers, blacksmiths, coopers, and shoemakers. In his notes on Berlin, he was even more explicit: "Many of the manufactures herein stated are of minor importance & such as are common to most of the towns in Connecticut & have not generally been noticed by my assistants in their returns, but still may be of use to show the nature & course of business & industry in this state."[26]

However, the task of gathering information on the raw materials, employees, machinery, expenditures, and production of the numerous small shops proved impossible. The embedded nature of skilled preindustrial craft work within a specific technical, social, and economic network made it difficult to extract quantifiable information. Many of the Connecticut artisans worked in small and flexible spaces, often within the home or adjacent to it; made use of fairly low technology characterized by human powered tools that could be used in a variety of ways; relied on internalized skill, the workmanship of habit, and the occasional use of jigs to ensure consistent and efficient work; interspersed craft work with other domestic and economic activities according to the season; produced predominantly for a local market; and exchanged goods and services with their local community.[27]

The difficulty of acquiring accurate financial information is clear in the 1820 Census lists compiled by John Langdon, a marshal's assistant who sought to document every person who earned some portion of their livelihood from craft work in Lincoln County, Maine. This unusual response to the federal instructions demonstrates the poor fit between the type and purpose of the questions and the actual ways in which craftsmen practiced their trade. The questions for the 1820 Census favored the large-scale operation that purchased stock with notes or bills of credit, paid wages to its employees, sold their product for cash, and kept financial accounts that permitted easy annual summaries. The local craftsmen worked in a very different manner with running accounts that extended over years. Rather than relying on currency, they exchanged goods or services to acquire materials, hire assistants, and sell products, and kept track of these exchanges in a ledger book, with credits and debits assigned to each person. Seasonal activity and the varying costs of each trade also made it difficult to compile comparable information for all crafts. Many of the artisans worked at their craft for a portion of the year or hired young assistants for the busy season only. Several types of trades (for example, clothiers, tanners, and blacksmiths) required extensive raw materials and stock, while others (especially joiners, cabinetmakers, and silversmiths) expended more on labor than on stock.[28]

Further compounding the difficulties of the reporters for both the Town Reports and the 1820 Census was the dynamic nature of production and consumption during this time. This period witnessed an intensification of small shop craft activity as some part-time craftsmen devoted increasing amounts of time to non-agricultural work and as more people purchased goods for their homes. The constantly shifting arena of markets—local production, local bespoke, export production—

seen in the weavers of East Windsor or the woodworkers of Cornwall—made it difficult to anticipate work and develop a business plan. The accounts of the time period and Census responses indicate that few craftsmen had control over their activities; most seemed to respond to the demands of the moment, remaining vulnerable to poor harvests that constricted demand, competition from floods of imported wares that were often lower in price, or recruitment difficulties when young help sought other opportunities in the professions or in another town.[29]

The Academy and federal leaders' desire to transform craft work, their lack of familiarity with the flexible nature of small shop work, and their focus on commercial activity and manufacturing investment foreshadows a drama that unfolded over the course of the nineteenth century: the decline in status of the craftsman from skilled contributor to a community's well-being to a mere mechanic whose identity was submerged below his employers and whose skills were concealed by machinery. As Connecticut's service economy began to emerge in the early national period, the new professional class who provided the bulk of the Town Reports foregrounded consumption, marketing, and sales and backgrounded the human side of production. Unable to measure the importance of skill and incapable of recognizing the way in which craft work fit the varied mixed agricultural economies of the state, they became puzzled by and distanced from the benches of the craft shop and instead focused upon the shelves of the shopkeeper. Such a perspective continues to the present, as few people today understand the subtleties involved in craft work or the meaning of workmanship.[30]

Looking back at the past from the vantage point of the forty-hour work week, the separation of work and leisure, and an abstraction of production in a post-industrial economy, many people cannot comprehend the manner in which craft work was formerly inextricably connected to other aspects of the preindustrial economy. They cannot understand how someone could work accurately and efficiently without machinery, how a part-time artisan could be fully-skilled, or how makers could combine craft work with other agricultural and domestic duties. Nor do these contemporary professionals understand the true role of skill and workmanship in today's economy. Like the members of the Academy, they are removed from the thought and action of an artisan and consequently do not "see" craft work, whether that of blacksmith/car mechanics in a rural setting or studio craftspersons who sell their work in a gallery.

EDWARD S. COOKE, JR.

TABLE I

Faculty Assessments by Town – 1798

Towns	Sq. miles[1]	Polls 21-70	Merchants	Attorneys	Physicians	Tavernkeepers	Joiners/Carpenters[2]	Blacksmiths	Silversmiths	Shoemakers/Tanners[2]	Tailors/Clothiers[3]	Hatters	Saddlers	Others
New Haven	110.8	550	31	8[4]	6	15	13	4	3	11	5	4	2	2 bakers, 1 barber, 1 ropemaker, 1 printer, 1 brass founder, 1 blockmaker
Lebanon	77.9	534	6		4	9	7	4		6	3	2	1	
New London	90.5	509	39	3	5	12	8	4	1	17	6	2	1	6 bakers, 3 barbers, 3 butchers, 2 ropemakers, 1 printer, 1 blockmaker
East Windsor	55.3	476	8	1	4	7	12	7		13	2	1	2	4 stone engravers, 3 coopers, 1 gunsmith, 1 clockmaker
Wallingford	105.5	473	7	2	5	5	8	5		10	3	1	1	
Farmington	224.1	459	8	2		14	10	11	2	8	3	3		3 tinners, 2 coopers
Preston	68.9	438	12		2	13	1	2		3			4	
Chesire	41.6	308	7	2	2	4	13	8	1	12		1	2	3 coopers, 1 wheelwright
Canterbury	46.7	284	5		1	3	1	2		3	1			4 coopers
Coventry	38.6	282	4		3	6	7	9		5			3	1 cooper
Ridgefield	57.7	276	4		2	5	4	7	1	4	5	1	1	
Tolland	40.4	267	3		1	5	4	2		5	2	1	2	2 saddletree makers
Pomfret	53.1	265	7		3	5	3	4	1	5	2			
Washington	38.7	263	3	2	1	5	5	3		3	1			1 cooper, 1 bloomer
Watertown	64.2	252	3	1	2	2	6	5		5	4	2		
Cornwall	46.8	238	4		2	7	5	10			8	1	1	4 bloomers, 2 coopers
Bolton	36.8	228	4		4	6	4	4		2	2	1	1	1 wheelwright
Goshen	45.6	220	3		2	8	6	2	1	4			1	

Source: Connecticut Assessments, 1797-1798 (Connecticut Historical Society).

[1] The figure for the square mileage is derived from Bruce Daniels, *The Connecticut Town: Growth and Development, 1635-1790* (Middletown, CT: Weslyan University Press, 1979), pp. 181-85.

[2] I have lumped joiners with carpenters and shoemakers with tanners because many of the tax assessments did.

[3] I grouped clothiers and tailors together because both trades focused on post-weaving processes--clothiers fulled, dyed, and dressed cloth; and tailors cut and sewed finished cloth. The faculty assessment for either was usually low, about $17.

[4] New Haven also listed 34 dealers, who were probably shopkeeprs or merchants.

Technology in Transition:

Connecticut Industries 1800-1832

Carolyn C. Cooper

Farming technology was familiar to most of Connecticut's citizens in 1800, and continued to be so well beyond 1832—indeed, into the twentieth century. Yet by 1850, the state was also a major producer of guns, clocks, tools, machines, and other necessities of an industrializing society. Connecticut became renowned for the inventiveness of its urban-centered "ingenious Yankees." It hummed with the new industrial technology of its day.[1]

What can the Connecticut Town Reports tell us about this transition? Technologies—information, skills, and equipment—that were reported present in the responding towns between 1800 and 1832 can give us hints about the locations and pace of the beginnings of industrialization in the new republic. In most respects the prevailing technologies would have been familiar to a visitor from medieval Europe. Yet some industries were starting to move out of households and into specialized workplaces, using new technology. From today's perspective, the pace of change that people in those towns were experiencing may seem very slow, but it was the beginning of what would later be called an industrial "revolution."

The Town Reports can inform us about this process if we keep in mind a few precautions: first, the Reports themselves account for somewhat less than half of the towns and parishes in Connecticut at that time. The responding towns have a good geographic spread, but do not include the important and populous towns of Hartford and Norwich. So we should generalize only cautiously about Connecticut industries as a whole. Further, since the reports span two or three decades, it may be misleading to compare conditions between towns reporting at widely different times.

The Connecticut Academy's Solicitation Letter in 1800 asked about industrial establishments.[2] The town reporters usually counted them but did not consistently mention their size or output, although their number alone is not a precise measure of importance of an industry. Also, the reporters had differing interests and capabilities, resulting in differing blanks of information. By consulting other contemporary sources of information about industries we shall address the question of what the reports left out. Finally, some "industrial" activities of today, such as shoe making and cloth making, took place in households instead of mills or factories. We are able to discuss them, however, because such domestic industry produced goods that reporters did count.

In discussing industries described in the Town Reports, we should recognize that our language is necessarily anachronistic. "Manufacture" at that time took place "in families" as well as "in manufactories" or "factories," and did not necessarily imply powered machine work. "Industry" was an admirable personal characteristic rather than a category of economic activities. "Technology" would hardly be a familiar word to writers of the Town Reports. Our descriptions of what was occurring in the past, like those of any visitors to a different land, would strike the natives as strange.

By the time the Connecticut Academy inquired in 1800 into such matters, the former colonists had built their material world both by technology transfer and by innovation. They had brought familiar ways of making and doing things from England; they adopted and adapted unfamiliar ways from other European immigrants to America and from Native Americans; and they were inventing new ones. This essay discusses the natural resources involved, the power source, and the machine technology and inventions applied to the industries most often mentioned in the Town Reports.

The Importance of Waterpower

The first colonists had arrived in New England with expectations formed by their experience with established farms and towns of late sixteenth- and early seventeenth-century England. Wood was scarce where they had come from; here they found cold winters, no coal to burn, and too many trees and rocks. First settling on what grasslands they could find for their cattle, they soon set about converting forests to fields by chopping down trees and grubbing out rocks. Native Americans taught them how to defoliate trees and plant corn and beans among them. The forest proved to be both a challenge and a valuable resource, supplying timber to build and furnish houses, and firewood to heat them. New England's other plentiful gift was the many streams rushing down hills. The water was fresh and clean to drink and could be harnessed to do work. The settlers were few and needed the extra "hands" supplied by waterpower.

Harnessing water for power was itself an old technology. For nearly two millennia people in the Old World had been building water wheels to make use of running and falling water.[3] By 1800, water-powered mills for several uses were commonplace in Connecticut towns, as in the rest of New England. Town respondents almost always mentioned rivers, streams, and their mill sites. Those present in 1811 are shown on the Warren and Gillet map of 1812, reproduced on the endpapers of this book.

Mill sites varied in height of fall and flow of water available. Millwrights tried with varying success to tailor each mill to its surrounding terrain. Each waterpower system needed a dam to store a higher "head" of water in a pond upstream from the mill, also channels and gates to guide water to the millwheel and back down into the stream.[4] Within the mill building, cams, gears, belts, pulleys, levers, and cranks variously conveyed, speeded, redirected, or changed the rotary motion of the wheel and its shaft into the needed motions of machinery for grinding, crushing, squeezing, blowing, pumping, sawing, cutting, hammering, or other work.

Usual accounts of industrialization emphasize the use of coal for fuel and steam for power, because that was the path that industrialization took in England. In fact, however, waterpower prevailed in England many decades after an effective steam engine was invented in the late eighteenth century. It prevailed much longer in America, especially in New England, which had so much waterpower that it did not need steam engines in order to undertake industrialization.[5]

Where the terrain allowed, the owner of a new mill or factory in early nineteenth-century America could choose either the initially high cost of building a waterpower system, followed by virtually free energy except for maintenance, or the usually lower expense of installing a steam engine, followed by the constant expense of supplying cordwood or coal to fuel the boiler. For decades the choice was usually for waterpower, even though steam engines could be located wherever convenient and functioned regardless of seasons when streams dried up, flooded, or iced over. Federal reports in 1838 and 1840 indicate that steam engines accounted for 10 to 15 percent of the power used in U.S. manufacturing at that time. Only by 1870 did the use of steam power in U.S. manufacturing slightly outweigh (52%) that of waterpower (48%).[6]

In 1838 only 47 (not quite 3%) of the 1616 stationary steam engines in the United States were operating in Connecticut. From 1800 to 1832 only one of the Connecticut Town Reports mentioned a steam engine, adding that "the consumption of fuel was a serious drawback upon the profits."[7] We may assume that where other industrial sites mentioned in the Town Reports required more than man- or animal power, they were powered by water.[8]

Some industrial sites, such as tanneries and grain distilleries, needed water for processing but not for power. Paper mills and fulling mills required both waterpower and process water. Table I gives a "statistical account" of both kinds of site.[9] Although they were smaller than nowadays, the water exiting downstream from tanneries, distilleries, fulling mills, and paper mills must have been less palatable for drinking than water that had provided only power. Yet the Town Reports do not mention this particular environmental concern about mills. Bethlem complained instead that mills diverted water from use for irrigating fields, while Farmington and Lisbon (Hanover) observed that swampy areas created by dams seemed to cause "fever and ague."[10] Otherwise, however, report writers seem to have regarded the existence of mills as a good thing.[11]

In view of precautions mentioned above, what information can we derive from the numbers in Table I? We notice first that these towns had many more gristmills and sawmills than other industrial sites. Fulling mills, tanneries, and iron works were next most frequently present, fulling mills far outnumbering mills for carding or spinning, which were also engaged in cloth production. Distilleries also outnumbered carding and spinning mills. Finally, oil mills and paper mills were least prominent on the landscape and in Table I.

The Town Reports enumerate these various uses of water and waterpower but only occasionally describe them. We turn to other sources of information in order to understand what they did and how they related to one another.[12] Except for the carding and spinning mills, the technologies for these types of industrial site already existed in medieval Europe.

The Primacy of Gristmills

When water wheels were devised more than two thousand years ago, their first use was to power gristmills for grinding grain into meal for porridge and flour for bread. They came to be regarded a necessity. When European colonists settled in America, their towns frequently offered a free grant of property—a mill "privilege"—to a miller establishing a gristmill. The millers learned to grind maize, the American grain, in the same mills as wheat, rye, or other grains transplanted from Europe. In New England their tolls, fixed by custom or ordinance, were usually one-sixteenth of the wheat and one-twelfth of the "Indian corn."[13] Despite such fees, farmers in outlying areas would haul grain long distances to the mill rather than grind it at home by hand. For instance, Wallingford reported that when closer gristmills suspended operation "In dry seasons grist is frequently carried a distance of 20 miles to the mills on the [East] river."[14] The towns mentioning gristmills in reports to the Academy had an average of four each. Gristmills were also a place for distant neighbors to exchange news and socialize while their grain was grinding.

Nearly all of the more than 144 gristmills enumerated in the Connecticut Town Reports operated about the same way as they had done in Europe for centuries. Water powered the grindstones, but a miller needed helpers to haul, shovel, rake, and pour grain, meal and flour in and out of containers to clean, grind, cool, and sift it. However, a new and laborsaving kind of mill had originated in Delaware in the 1780s, and was being adopted at Cornwall, Connecticut, in 1801. After reporting that there were six corn mills in town, Elijah Allen later noticed a novelty at one of them:

> Since forwarding an Account to yourself as Secretary of the Academy of Arts and Sciences I have been at Mr. Philo Swift's Corn Mill on Ousetonack River in this Town and find that a Machine is fixed to carry the Meal in Tin Buckets fixed on a Leather Strap to the Hopper which conveys it into the Bolt which is turned by the same Water Wheel which sets the whole Machinery of that Run of Stones agoing. The

TABLE I

Number of Mills and Other Industrial Sites Mentioned in Connecticut Town Reports

Town	Year	Saw Mill	Grist Mill	Fulling Mill	Iron Works	Tannery	Distillery	Spinning Mill	Carding Mill	Oil Mill	Paper Mill
Bethlem	1812	4	1	2		3	8^	-1			
Bolton (N.)	1800	6	5	1			4^	1		1	
Canterbury	1801	10	9	2			1				
Chatham	1819	3	2	1		2	1^	1			
Cheshire	1803						1~				
Cornwall	1800-01	7	6	3	3	1					
Cornwall	1812	sev.	3	sev.	2		1~		1	2	
Coventry	1809	sev.	sev.	sev.					sev.		1
Durham	1819	4	2	2		6					
E. Haddam	1819	10	3	1	1	7		3		-1	
E. Windsor	1806	8	6				6^		1	1	
Farmington	c.1810	8	7	3		4					
Franklin	1800	7	3	2-3							
Goshen	1812	9	3	1	2	1#	0	1	1		
Guilford	1832	4	3	1		4				1	
Haddam	1819	8	5	2	-1	7	3^		2		
Kent	1812				6						
Killingworth	1819	2	4	1	-1	1		1			
Lebanon	1800	8	11	5		1#		-1			
Litchfield	1815	18	5	6	6	5+		1	2	1	1
Madison	1832	2	1		-1	2					
Middletown	1819	5	5	4	1	4	1^	4		1	1
Milton	1815	5	2						1		
New Haven	1811		3	3	1	1#		1			2
New London	1812		1					-1			
Norfolk	1815					2		1			
Pomfret	1800	1	1								
Preston	1801	4	9	2	2					1	
Ridgefield	1800	sev.	5	2	sev.	1					
Saybrook	1819	1	2	1	3	0					
Sharon	1807	11	7	3	3		4		2		
Stratfield	1800		3			2					
Tolland	1804	5	4	2							
Union	1803	7	1	1	1						
Wallingford	1811	5	5	2		6	5		6		
Washington	1800	6	5	2	4						
Washington	1815	5	4	2	6				2		
Watertown	1801	5	3							1	1
Willington	1805	6	6								
Winchester	1813	1					1~				
Winsted	1813	4			13	3					
Wintonbury	1802	1	1	1			2~				
SITES PRESENT		193+	147+	60+	57+	61+	38	14	19+	9	6
REPORTS	42	36	37	29	20	19	14	12	10	9	5

The SITES PRESENT row shows totals of industrial sites present at the times of the reports.
The REPORTS row shows totals of towns and parishes reporting present and past industrial sites.
sev. or + indicates an unspecified number more than one, e.g. several.
-   a minus sign indicates an establishment reported as no longer existing.
\#   indicates a tannery inferred from the mention of tanners.
^   includes distillery with drinkable product other than apple brandy.
~   includes distillery inferred from the mention of drinkable distilled product.

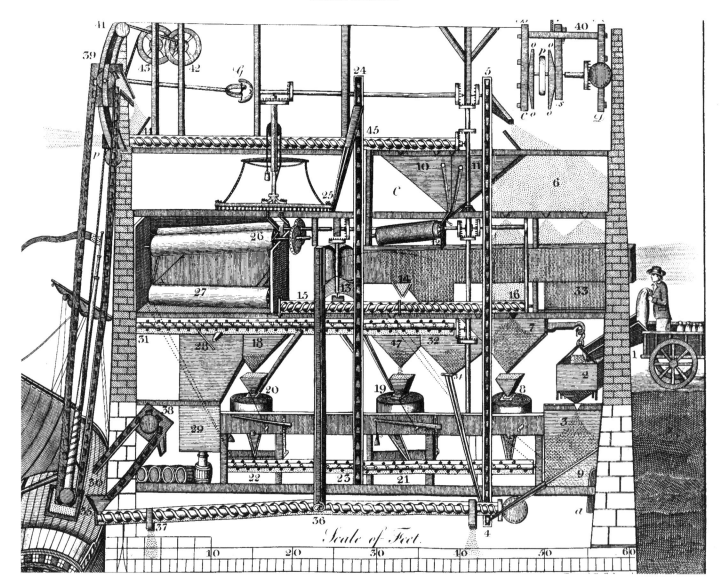

Fig. 1: **Oliver Evans' patent gristmill**
Evans connected new and already known devices in inventing his powered flow production system. Arriving by cart at right or ship at left, the grain progressed through the mill on variable paths for cleaning, grinding into meal or flour, cooling, and sifting before pouring into barrels at lower left. Key: endless-screw "conveyers" 15-16, 44-45, 37-4; endless-belt "elevators" with sheet-iron buckets 4-5, 23-24, 30-38 or -39), millstones 8, 19, 20; rotating rake "hopper boy" 25; cylindrical rotating screen 12; rotating sifting "bolters" 26, 27. Oliver Evans, The Young Mill-Wright and Miller's Guide, 13th ed. (Philadelphia: Lea & Blanchard, 1850) pp. 216-218, Plate VIII.

other run of Stones is constructed to be fixed in the same manner; but the Buckets and other Apparatus for Bolting is not procured as yet.[15]

This type of gristmill was invented and vigorously promoted by millwright Oliver Evans of Newport, Delaware from 1783, patented by Congress in December 1790, and is regarded as the first American example of modern, automated flow production.[16] As pictured in Figure 1, it used gravity, belts of small buckets, and Archimedean screws for continuously moving the grain and meal and eventual flour up and down and sideways through the mill. Evans' labor-saving mill ostensibly required no human effort except to set it in motion,

pour sackfuls of grain into it at one end, and regulate the flow of flour into barrels at the other.

At first reviled by millers as "rattletrap," Oliver Evans' invention became standard equipment of large-scale "merchant" mills all over the expanding nation, including Philo Smith's in Cornwall. Farmington reported a similar gristmilling innovation, identifying two of its seven gristmills as built according to "Macoomb's patent." Farmington's mills "in the aggregate" ground about 45,000 bushels of different kinds of grain annually. At a total of 18,000 bushels per annum, Franklin's three non-patent gristmills ground only somewhat more slowly.[17]

When western flour became inexpensively available in the East, especially after the Erie Canal opened in 1825 and railroads ran westward in the 1830s and 1840s, Connecticut farmers began shifting into dairy farming and out of grain production (except for cattle feed). Most local gristmills fell into disuse before the twentieth century.

The Prevalence of Sawmills

The "up and down" variety of sawmill originated on the European Continent in the late middle ages,[18] came to America in the 1630s, and stayed essentially the same throughout the period of the Connecticut Town Reports.[19] Its mechanism

John Winthrop Jr. built a sawmill in New London in 1652, for which skilled ironworker Joseph Jenks sent him saw blades he was making at the Saugus ironworks in Massachusetts.[22] In England, sawmills had not yet replaced pairs of sawyers working in sawpits, but in New England sawmills became at least as common as gristmills and frequently shared waterpower sites with them (see Fig. 2).

The Connecticut Town Reports of 1800-1832 mention over 190 sawmills in 36 towns, ranging in number from one to eighteen per town, with an average of five or six.[23] They sawed, as in Farmington, "timber of our own forests into plank, board, scantling, & slitwork of every description."[24] Boards ranged in

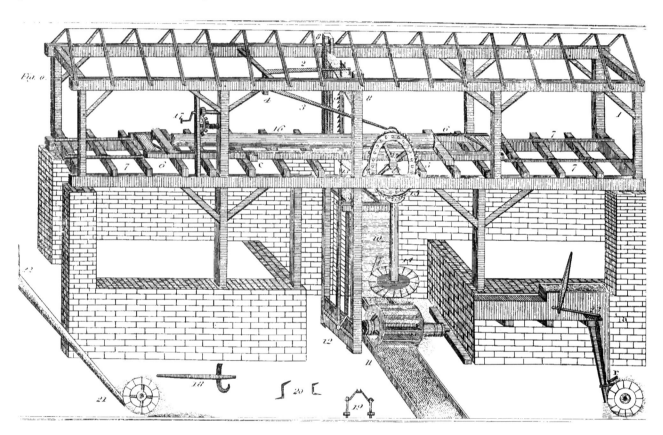

Fig. 2: **Water-powered up-and-down sawmill**
Oliver Evans wrote "The mechanism of a complete saw-mill is such as to produce the following effects; namely:—1. To move the saw up and down, with a sufficient motion and power. 2. To move the log to meet the saw. 3. To stop of itself when within 3 inches of being through the log. 4. To draw the carriage with the log back, by the power of the water, so that the log may be ready to enter again." The sawmill depicted here ran by two water wheels—a vertical "flutter wheel" for sawing and a horizontal "tub wheel" for drawing back. After each downward stroke of the saw, the carriage, controlled by the ratchet wheel, carried the log forward for the next stroke, about 120 times a minute. At the end of the cut, the carriage reversed direction and the sawyer shifted the log sideways for the next cut. Oliver Evans, The Young Mill-Wright and Miller's Guide, 13th ed. (Philadelphia: Lea & Blanchard, 1850) pp. 342-45, PlateXXIII.

imitated pitsawyers pulling a saw up and down, but also pushed the log forward to meet the saw at every stroke, and near the end drew the log back to begin the next cut. The first American sawmills were aimed at exporting timber to England.[20] Colonists, however, needed boards and planks at home as well. A water-powered seventeenth-century sawmill was capable of producing 500 to 1,000 feet of white pine boards a day, many more boards than sawyers could cut with a two-man pitsaw.[21] In Connecticut

price from $6.00 to $50.00 per thousand feet, depending on quality and the type of wood.[25] Today, visitors to the town of Ledyard in Connecticut can see such an up and down saw mill demonstrated seasonally.[26] A few circular saws, much faster in operation than the straight saws, arrived in the United States between 1790 and 1814 and came into greater use from the 1820s onward. Band saws, invented in England in 1808, first became practicable in the 1860s, when steel-making technology was capable of producing a band of steel that was uniform, flexible, and durable enough not to break frequently in use.[27] By the late nineteenth century up-and-down sawmills had given way in most places to circular and band saws.[28]

As discussed in other essays in this volume, the period of the Town Reports was one of deforestation in Connecticut, primarily because of the demand for firewood. Later in the nineteenth century New England's sawmills dwindled in number as forests in the South, Midwest, and eventually the Pacific Northwest began supplying most of the wooden building materials even in New England, by way of expanding rail transportation. Into the twentieth century, however, Connecticut's forests supplied charcoal fuel for making and shaping iron. The fuel both for smelting and for forging iron was charcoal, obtained by charring wood from nearby forests in earth-covered mounds called "pits." Charcoal burned hotter than wood, and contained fewer impurities than a "stone"-coal fire.[29] Ironmasters maintained the supply by staggering cutting from one woodlot to the next, coppicing trees to harvest when they were the right size for charcoaling, and letting the woodlot regrow.[30]

The Multi-faceted Iron Industry

As shown in Table I, 57 iron-working sites were reported to the Connecticut Academy, predominantly in towns of Litchfield County, which was a major producer of iron in the early American republic. These sites were bloomeries, fineries, slitting and rolling mills, triphammer shops, and naileries. Blast furnaces were present in Connecticut, but absent from the Town Reports, as explained below.

Connecticut iron makers were producing two kinds of iron—wrought iron and cast iron—suitable for different purposes. Bloomeries and fineries produced wrought iron; blast furnaces produced cast iron.[31] Iron ore manipulated skillfully in a bloomery fire did not melt, but consolidated into a spongy mass or "bloom" of iron. The bloomer would remove this from the fire, further consolidate and shape it while hot under a water-powered hammer and possibly also run it through a water-powered rolling mill into convenient wrought iron rods, bars, or plates. Blacksmiths would later make these into useful objects, by reheating and hammering them into different shapes and welding them together.

In the higher heat of a blast furnace, by contrast, iron melted from the ore and periodically flowed in liquid form into sand molds to make such things as kettles, firebacks, or simple "pigs." (See Fig. 3.) Such cast iron objects were hard and strong, but brittle and not weldable. However, iron pigs could not only be remelted at a foundry to make other cast iron objects; at a finery forge they could also be remelted under a strong air blast that removed carbon and silicon, and hammered to produce wrought iron.

Producing a ton of pig iron in an early blast furnace required about 265 bushels of charcoal, three tons of ore, and two tons of flux such as limestone.[32] Waterpower worked large bellows that pumped air into the fire, sometimes for a year at a time before the furnace needed repair and went "out

of blast." Such an installation required a large team of workers and much capital to be successful. In mid-seventeenth century, Massachusetts Bay colonists had sent John Winthrop Jr. to England to find investors for an iron works. The one they built at Saugus, Massachusetts included a blast furnace, a finery, and a rolling and slitting mill to shape bars and rods. It operated from 1646 for only several years before financial failure and its last recorded blast was in 1668.[33] Winthrop started another large-scale iron works in about 1660 in New Haven Colony; it survived until about 1680 before going into debt and closing.[34]

Most iron-making in seventeenth-century America was less ambitious and more successful, using bloomery forges to satisfy local needs for wrought iron. Bloomeries were smaller than blast furnaces, operated at lower temperatures, and could be more quickly shut down and restarted. In the early eighteenth century, ironmasters who acquired enough capital began again to build blast furnaces and finery forges for larger-scale production. In Connecticut, New Haven and Hartford investors backed the beginning of an iron industry in the northwest hills bordering New York and Massachusetts.[35] Pioneers moving into this area began bloomeries in the towns of Litchfield, New Milford, Lime Rock, and Canaan in the 1730s, followed by others who drew on the convenient juxtaposition there of ore deposits, abundant wood for charcoaling, and streams for waterpower. Ethan Allen (later of Revolutionary War fame) and two partners established a blast furnace at Lakeville in the town of Salisbury in 1762. Under different management, it produced cannons during the American Revolution. By mid-century Americans had been supplying enough pig and wrought iron to England to provoke trade restrictions, another irritant to the colonists. By 1775, when the Revolution began, the American colonies were the third largest producer of iron in the world.[36]

By 1800 Litchfield County ironmasters were working fifty bloomery and finery forges and three rolling and slitting mills to produce wrought iron in the shape of bars, gunbarrel plates, and nail rods. For several crucial decades, Salisbury bar iron turned out to be consistently uniform, posing few problems for shaping, cutting and drilling by machine.[37] As such it was particularly suitable for the needs of the infant industries of machine-tool makers and users then getting under way in New England. For instance, when Eli Whitney was setting up his musket manufactory in Hamden in 1798, iron-makers Forbes & Adam of Salisbury supplied him with trip-hammer heads and other ready-made millwork, then went on to ship him rolled bars of "best bloomed iron" of specific widths for making gun barrels and other gun parts.[38] This benefit to the making and using of machines was the primary contribution of the Connecticut iron industry to the state's and the nation's industrial "revolution."

The Town Reports mention blast furnaces only indirectly, for they were located in towns that either did not submit reports (Salisbury) or submitted them before their blast furnaces were built (Sharon and Kent). The Lakeville blast furnace had undergone many changes in ownership since 1762 but remained in operation until 1832. The next oldest blast furnace,

Fig. 3: *Typical charcoal-fired blast furnace*
This cut-away view shows the "casting bridge" over which workmen continually brought baskets and barrows of ore, flux, and charcoal to keep the furnace going. Counter-weighted water-powered bellows "blasted" air into the fire. Liquid slag floating above the molten iron was tapped off from time to time into a puddle shown tended by a worker. At the left, workers are preparing "pig" beds in the sand. When the iron master judged sufficient iron to be ready in the bottom of the furnace, he made an opening through which the iron flowed into the pig molds. National Park Service, Hopewell Furnace (Washington D.C.: U.S. Department of the Interior, 1983), p. 10.

completed at nearby Mount Riga in 1810, stayed in business until 1856. It produced pig iron that became bar iron at its associated finery forge and went to the national armories at Springfield, Massachusetts, and at Harpers Ferry, Virginia. Nine blast furnaces were producing cast and pig iron by 1830 in the Salisbury district of Litchfield County. By 1860 eighteen blast furnaces had been built there, some had closed, and ten were still in operation.[39]

Connecticut blast furnaces sometimes served their own associated iron works, but also typically sold pig iron to independent finery forges. The Town Reports from Litchfield County mention the presence of forges, but do not consistently identify which forges were bloomeries, smelting wrought iron from ore, and which were fineries, converting pig iron into wrought iron. The mention of ore supply in the reports from Chatham, Sharon, and Kent indicates that their forges were bloomeries.[40] Each of Kent's six forges made 30 to 40 tons of wrought iron annually, which "when delivered at the Slitting Mills in Canaan and Washington has generally been worth

$100 a ton." Together they were earning $20,000 to $30,000 annually.[41] In 1800 Washington's three forges were making about sixty tons of iron annually; in 1815 Washington's "four bloomers" in a list of occupations indicate that its two "forges for iron" were bloomeries.[42]

In contrast, Winsted's finery forges made wrought iron from pig iron. Of all the reports, Winsted's description in 1813 of different components of the Salisbury district iron industry is by far the most complete:

> In this part of the town of Winchester are Five Iron works for making Iron, in which are thirteen fires or forges—No oar is used at the works; The distance of the oar bed is so great, that the business is more advantageously carried on by working the pig Iron only, which is brought from the furnace at Salisbury, a distance of twenty three miles... The contracts the last year for the supply of the works amounted to Five hundred

Tons.—It is found that Three tons of Pig Iron, will produce about two Tons of wrought Iron, [so] of course the yearly amount of Iron here made cannot greatly differ from Three hundred and thirty four Tons.

The report continues with an account of sizeable establishments for reheating wrought iron in yet a third kind of "forge" in order to hammer it into useful shapes:

Here are also six trip hammer shops, in which are contained fifteen fires or forges—These are kept in constant use, in making axes, scythes, sleigh shoes, drawing Iron for wire, plating Gun Barrells, together with such other employ as the exigincies of the vicinity require.[43]

Nailmaking Innovation

On a small scale, blacksmiths traditionally hammered out nails one at a time from nail rod. Eight of the Town Reports, however, mention production of nails on a larger scale in a factory or manufactory, or with machines to help make them.[44] The technique of making tacks by shearing pointed slivers at an angle from the end of a strip of rolled iron was a recent and distinctly American invention. Jeremiah Wilkinson of Cumberland, R.I. made tacks that way around 1775; other inventors applied it to nail-making in the 1790s.[45] "Cutting nails" implies some such machine, such as the one "for cuting Shingle Nails" in Cornwall. Said to produce 100,000 nails annually, it had been sold by 1800 for £8 and moved to Sharon, which reported a "very considerable establishment" for "manufacture of nails" in 1807. New Haven's nail "manufactory" in 1811 was explicitly for "cut nails," implying machine production, as did Winsted's "one factory for cutting nails employing twelve workmen" in 1813.[46]

More ambiguously, in Litchfield County in 1815, Litchfield and Washington each reported a nail "manufactory," while in Middlesex County East Haddam and Middletown each listed a nail "factory" in 1819.[47] And without the machine it had sent to Sharon, Cornwall in 1800 reported that "from 3 to 4 Tons of Nail Rods are Wrought into Nails" annually.[48]

Machine-cut nail production in the United States soared for several decades, along with demand for new houses by westward-trekking Americans. From the 1870s, newly invented wire nails, also machine-made, rapidly superseded cut nails for most purposes.[49]

Steelmaking Attempts

Iron-smelting in Connecticut ceased in 1923, when the last blast furnace closed in East Canaan. Fineries and bloomeries disappeared everywhere, for in the latter half of the nineteenth century processes were invented for producing steel so cheaply that in the twentieth century it replaced wrought iron for all purposes it formerly served.[50] Before then, steel was expensive.

Steel was the more or less intentional result of ancient smiths' repeated heating of wrought iron in a charcoal fire, hammering it on the anvil, and quenching it in liquid potions. From the seventeenth century in England, steel could be made in larger quantities by the "cementation" or "blister" process. To make blister steel, bars of wrought iron were packed with layers of powdered charcoal into stone or refractory brick chests that were baked at red heat in a special-purpose furnace for several days. A small quantity of carbon partly permeated the bars, whose surfaces blistered.[51]

Making steel this way is mentioned obliquely in one Town Report, that of Saybrook in 1819:

A quarry of steatite or soapstone exists in Pautapoug...Thirty or forty years since it was procured by the owners of a furnace in Killingworth, for the purpose of making an oven for baking steel.[52]

The furnace owners may have included Aaron Eliot, who built a cementation furnace as well as a bloomery forge on the Killingworth farm of his father, the Reverend Jared Eliot. Jared used the bloomery to make a 50-pound bar of "excellent Iron" from 83 pounds of magnetite beach sand, and "In his son's steel-furnace, above mentioned, a portion of the bar was converted into good steel." The Killingworth Town Report mentions Jared's experiment with "black sand," for which he had in 1764 been "honored with a medal by the society instituted in London for the encouragement of arts, manufactures, and commerce." But it doesn't mention Aaron's steel-making experiments, which other sources say continued until 1785.[53]

From the 1740s English steel-makers had learned to melt blister steel in closed crucibles so that its carbon blended evenly; however, attempts in America to produce this higher-quality "crucible steel" succeeded only after the period of the Town Reports.[54] Crucible steel was imported from England for making springs for firearms and clocks and sharp edges for axes and scythes, as well as cutters for an increasing variety of machine tools, as discussed in the section below on arms-making and the "American system" of manufactures.

The importation of Bessemer steel-making technology from England in the 1860s (most effectively by Alexander Lyman Holley, a native of Lakeville, Connecticut) made steel cheap and gradually drove bloomeries, fineries, and wrought iron out of existence.[55] Blast furnaces near coal fields in Pennsylvania, Ohio, and elsewhere began feeding pig iron to the steel mills that sprang up around them. Ironmaking on an expanding scale for the needs of the growing and increasingly integrated nation took place where coal-fired steam engines pumped air through larger coke-fueled blast furnaces.[56]

Blast furnaces in the Salisbury iron district, however, remained small and continued to use charcoal fuel into the twentieth century to make cast iron products such as railroad car wheels, having gained a reputation for high quality. The environmental effects of using charcoal for fuel were drastic but reversible. Hillsides denuded of trees in the district became woodlots for charcoal production. Ironmasters bought large acreages of woodland and learned to plan for sustainable supplies of charcoal. They did not greatly enlarge their works at their stream-side sites. Today the wooden buildings of blast-furnace sites in the Salisbury district have moldered away, leaving those gothic-arched stone furnace stacks that survive as picturesque ruins.[57] Former woodlots have grown into state forests.[58]

Tanneries and Shoemaking

The Connecticut Academy did not ask about tanneries; nevertheless, nearly half of the Town Reports list a total of more than 61 tanneries, indicating their importance among industrial sites at that time (see Table I). Tanners moved hides from vat to vat of successively stronger tannic solutions (see Fig. 4). In the last stages of this slow process, the hides lay flat in a vat, layered with crushed oak or hemlock bark. It took many months to complete the tanning. Sumac was also a rich source of tannin, used chiefly for treating skins other than cowhides.[59]

Nineteen Connecticut towns reported or implied the presence of one to seven tanneries each, of different

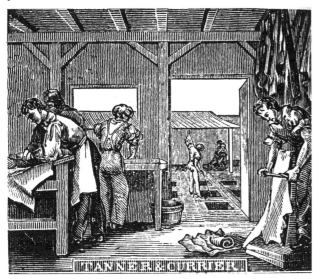

Fig. 4: *Tanner and currier*
Both the tanner, working with thick cowhides and the currier, working with the thinner skins of calves and other animals, had to scrape all hair and flesh off before putting them in vats of astringent tanning "ooze" of gradually increasing strength. After twelve to sixteen months for hides or two to six months for skins, the tanned leather was compacted and smoothed by beaters or rollers. Edward Hazen, The Panorama of Professions and Trades: or Every Man's Book *(Philadelphia: Uriah Hunt, 1837) p. 67.*

sizes. Ridgefield boasted of "a good Tan works...in which about 50 Vats are ocupied" although "it has however been the custom for almost all of the farmers to tan their own leather." The town of Litchfield noted "5 large tanneries, besides sundry others on a small scale." Cornwall had a barkmill to supply its tannery with tanbark, so did New Haven. Four towns reported output, ranging from an annual average of 115 to 600 hides and 40 to 1,000 skins per tannery. Only Wallingford reported prices: $3.00 for a hide and $2.50 for a calfskin.[60]

Some of the leather from all these tanneries went out of the state: records for the port of New Haven showed 17,696 lbs of "soal leather" headed "wholly, or almost wholly, to New York" in 1801 and 20,298 lbs. of leather shipped in 1806. Port

towns of New London and Stratfield did not mention shipping of leather, even though Stratfield's two "manufactories of leather" had produced 1,050 hides and 700 calfskins in 1799. Instead, Stratfield shipped 2,791 pairs of shoes that year.[61] Although these shoes were not necessarily made of leather tanned in Stratfield, shoe production was one of the more obvious local uses of leather. Nine of the eleven towns that mention shoemaking also mention tanners or tanneries.[62] Other leather products mentioned in Town Reports were saddles, harness, gloves, and bellows.[63]

From studies primarily about Massachusetts, we know that shoemaking was not yet mechanized during the period of the Connecticut Town Reports.[64] Shoemakers used hand tools to cut out pieces of leather, shape them over wooden shoe lasts and sew them together.[65] Eleven towns reported shoes produced, shoemakers, shoemakers' shops, shoe manufactories, or shoe stores; the varied terminology suggests a variety of locales and modes of shoemaking co-existed in this period in Connecticut.

First, it is probable that shoemaking was one of the jobs done on farms in the wintertime by and for family members themselves. Itinerant shoemaking also took place "in families," for instance in Lebanon, by "men who go from house to house for that purpose, except in the sumer, when they are generally employed at farming." Second, specialized shoemakers' shops in urban areas made "bespoke" shoes for customers who came in to be fitted. New Haven's thirty "shoe and boot makers" probably operated in this way.[66]

Third, with the development of a "putting out" system, the urban shoemaker shops, or indeed the farmers' families, could receive materials from a middleman entrepreneur. Working with standardized shoe lasts of different sizes, they returned ready-made shoes to be shipped for strangers' feet in distant markets. A shoemaker and a son or other male helper typically worked on soling shoes in small "ten-footer" shops, while the wife and daughters sewed uppers inside the adjacent house. For instance, Guilford had eight and Madison four shoemakers' shops of some kind in 1832: "For many years shoes were manufactured far beyond the wants of the people. Large quantities were sent to the Southern States for market."[67]

Finally, some entrepreneurs undertook larger "manufactories," such as the two in Ridgefield that together "will probably send abroad 5,000 pair of shoes and boots." These likely employed men to cut leather for uppers and soles and to fasten the soles onto uppers sewn by women working in households elsewhere. Ridgefield had two sizeable tanneries, "but the materials they [the shoe manufactories] work are chiefly from New York or abroad."[68] The products of such manufactories probably reached consumers by way of "shoe stores," of which Middletown had three and New Haven six, "where ready made work is constantly kept for sale."[69]

Mechanized shoe factories eventually took over the industry later in the nineteenth century, with inventions elsewhere in New England of machines for different steps in shoemaking. These promoted the growth of larger-scale factories and the specialization of shoemaking in towns such as Lynn and Haverhill in Massachusetts.[70]

Cider Mills and Distilleries

The Connecticut Academy's Solicitation Letter of 1800 asked (in Article 17) about breweries. Town respondents reported much less about breweries, which were evidently non-existent at the time, than about distilleries, of which there were many—38 in the 13 towns reporting any.

New Haven (1811), New London (1812), and Middletown (1819) each reported that a brewery had in recent years been started and discontinued.[71] In 1801 New Haven had shipped 1,200 gallons of ale, primarily to New York. But in Ridgefield Samuel Goodrich wrote in 1800 that even the former practice of "making small beer for family use is almost entirely neglected."[72]

People in Connecticut apparently preferred cider to beer. A question about apples and cider under Article 13 inspired several detailed disquisitions in Town Reports on how to make cider, cask it, and keep the casks from going musty. It is clear from the Litchfield, New Haven, New London, and Union accounts that unlike the usual American sweet "cider" nowadays, this was a fermented alcoholic beverage, as it remains today in England.[73]

Cider-making, implicitly, took place on the farms where the apples were grown. From Canterbury Hezekiah Frost wrote that "This town abounds with good orchards from which our farmers frequently make from one to 200 barrels of cyder." Farm cider mills could be horse- and man-powered, but the Sharon reporter also describes a water-powered mill in the main village, by which "ninety three barrels of cider have been made...in one day," more than twice the usual forty barrels a day. He "doubted whether such a rapid mode of extracting the juice is to be preferred" by "all those who intend their cider for the table" and pointed out that a distillery near by "generally receives the cider made in this mill."[74]

Of the 38 distilleries listed in Table I, 28 were for converting cider into apple brandy. Eight towns mentioned cider-making without reporting distillation of alcoholic spirits, but reports more often associated the two processes, and towns reporting distilleries also reported higher cider production.[75] In Bethlem Azel Backus reported an estimated production of 7,315 barrels of cider in years when the apple trees bore well. He also implied that its seven cider distilleries produced 10,000 gallons of "spirit" that if exported at 50 cents each would bring in $5,000 to the town. But, Backus lamented, "the worse than waste of home consumption reduces the neat profits to half that sum."[76] In Wallingford the price of a gallon of spirits made from "Cyder" was also 50 cents; its five distilleries earned $3,750 from 7,500 gallons produced. Prices in Canterbury, Sharon, and Bolton ranged from 50 cents to $1.50.[77]

Cider was popular, but distillation yielded a drink that was not only more potent but also higher in value and therefore more economical to ship: a barrel of apple brandy would be worth about 15 barrels of apple cider.[78] Stratfield shipped out 815 barrels of cider in 1799 along with 237 barrels of "cider spirits." New Haven, with "comparatively small" local production of cider, exported only 36 barrels of it to New York in 1801, along with 3,894 gallons (equalling 123 barrels) of cider brandy.[79]

Table I notes that some stills made gin or rum instead of apple brandy.[80] Such stills required a supply of good water to mix with the grain, potatoes, or molasses that was their raw material. In Bethlem, potatoes ground "fine like apples," fermented "as beer," and then distilled, yielded a "liquor" that after aging was judged by "devotees of ardent spirit" to be "preferable to Holland Gin."[81] When fermented and distilled, rye or corn mash also yielded "gin," as in North Bolton, where in addition to three cider brandy stills, a fourth still made 3,117 gallons of "gin from rye" in 1800.[82] Some, at least, reached New York by way of New Haven, which shipped 6,321 gallons of "Country gin" in 1801. In contrast, New London imported large quantities of molasses from the West Indies, on which rum distilleries relied for their raw material.[83] Middletown's rum distillery, established in 1791, was in 1819 producing 600 hogsheads (37,800 gallons) of rum annually, while the rum distillery in Chatham, dating from 1785, was producing half that amount.[84]

The Embargo of 1807 and War of 1812 probably encouraged establishment of more distilleries in Connecticut for brandy, gin, and rum to make up for any fall-off of imports from abroad.[85] While the 1800 Cornwall Report did not mention distilling, in 1812 the Cornwall reporter boasted "Cider is made in sufficient quantities and much is distilled—no grain of Consequence is tortured in this way—or lost to the World by distilling."[86]

Although one purveyor in Hartford in 1809 offered "50 STILLS containing from 3 to 800 gallons, with worms complete," we can only guess that most of Connecticut's stills were, like three-quarters of the nation's 37,880 stills counted in 1816, less than 100 gallons in capacity.[87] Only one town's report tells a still's capacity: in 1814 Haddam's gin distillery was "calculated" to make 90 gallons in 24 hours from 30 bushels of rye and corn.[88]

Compared to the number of stills in the entire country, the 38 counted and implied by these Town Reports would not seem to have loomed large nationally. Yet they were very important to Connecticut. According to the Connecticut *Gazetteer* by Pease and Niles in 1819,

> Of the various manufactures of the State, those
> of domestic spirits, consisting principally of gin
> and cider brandy, claim the first rank as articles
> of exportation, and for their aggregate value.[89]

With respect to "grain distilleries," Pease and Niles expansively identify Hartford County as the county in which "this manufacture is pursued to greater extent...and with more practical knowledge and experience...than in any other in the United States."[90] Comparison of the Town Reports, most of which were written between 1800 and 1813, with the 1819 Pease and Niles' *Gazetteer* suggests a growth in numbers of distilleries and an increase in the proportion of non-cider distilleries.[91]

Was drinking becoming a problem? Pease and Niles devote half a page to debate on "the general policy and influence of this manufacture, in a pecuniary, moral, and social point of view."[92] Perhaps surprisingly, almost none of the Town Report authors make judgments. The Goshen reporter, however, more than compensates for the others' silence on "the unnecessary use of spirituous liquors." He notes first that "the quantity of cider made does not much exceed the home consumption," that "It is not known that there was ever a distillery of any kind in this town," and that "A drunkard is seldom seen." He has nevertheless calculated that the average family in Goshen consumed 24 gallons of distilled spirits per year, at a cost of $25. This very much exceeded the amount it spent on government, education, roads, and religion. Exclaiming "'O Shame where is thy blush!'" he seems to presage the temperance movement in looking forward to

> the time as not far distant when not only the swords and spears shall be beat into ploughshares and pruning hooks, but the copper of which our stills are composed will be converted to the more useful purposes of commerce and domestic use.[93]

With or without an onset of temperance, distilling did lose its economic preeminence among Connecticut industries. Others came to the fore, including the textile industry. The Town Reports show its mechanization was just getting underway.

Textile Production in Family and Factory

Overall, changes in textile technology were of immense significance to the economy of the new republic and to the promotion of technological change in other industries. The traditional way of describing the beginnings of textile mechanization is overly dramatic: the household spinner of "the golden age of homespun," who has been producing cloth with which to clothe her family, relegates her spinning wheel and loom to the attic and sends her daughters off to slave at machines in the new textile mill. The Town Reports show a much more complex and gradual process.

A double shift was taking place from home production of linen cloth into machine production of cotton cloth. But at first only cotton spinning was mechanized in mills, while cotton weaving still took place on hand looms, either in those mills or by outworkers at home. Woolen cloth production was slower to mechanize, first with machine carding, and only later with machine spinning, and still later with power looms to replace handlooms. The Town Reports provide a window onto the first of these transitions.

Table I, above, distinguishes among three machine processes in making cloth—spinning, carding, and fulling.[94] Town reporters listed these processes separately but left weaving almost completely unmentioned. This suggests an uneven pace of mechanizing these textile processes. To provide a closer look, Table II focuses on those towns reporting cloth production in families as well as textile processes at industrial sites, and distinguishes between wool and cotton mills combined

under "spinning" in Table I.[95] In this table, handloom weaving is implicit in "families" and possible in "wool mill" and "cotton mill," whose output might be either yarn or cloth. As discussed below, a "flax mill" probably engaged only in fiber preparation.

Household Cloth Production

Fourteen towns explicitly remarked on household production of fabrics, but the existence of over sixty fulling mills in 29 towns implies that home production was widespread in other towns, too. How did this cloth production take place "in families"? At a minimum, the families would need to prepare fibers for spinning, then spin them into yarn, then weave them into cloth (see Fig. 5).

In fiber preparation, family members would wash and

Fig. 5: *Cloth manufacture "in families"*
This picture shows the old way of carding wool with hand cards, spinning with a wool wheel, and weaving with a handloom. Connecticut families manufacturing cloth made use of these implements, but ten towns reported more than nineteen carding mills that were making it easier for them, while nine towns reported 14 spinning mills, half of them for wool. Edward Hazen, The Panorama of Professions and Trades: or Every Man's Book *(Philadelphia: Uriah Hunt, 1837) p. 42.*

dry sheep's wool and align its fibers with hand-wielded wire-toothed paddles called "cards." They would soak flax stems until they partially rotted, break off the brittle outer layers in "flax brakes," then soften the inner fibers by "scutching" and align them by drawing them through increasingly finer sets of iron teeth called "hackles" or "hetchels."[96] Children could card wool, but preparing flax took grown-up expertise.

Households usually had two types of spinning wheel, one for wool and one for flax. With the wool wheel, the spinster drew a small roll of fiber out into an arms-length of yarn as it twisted, then guided the yarn onto the spindle. The linen wheel twisted and wound the yarn simultaneously while the spinster fed flax fibers into its hollow spindle. Women and girls were the "spinsters" of the household.

The wooden loom for weaving was several feet long, wide, and high, in which the warp yarns stretched between two beams

TABLE II
Family Cloth Production and Textile Processing Sites Mentioned in Connecticut Town Reports

Town	Year	Families	Fulling Mill	Carding Mill	Clothiers	Flax Mill	Wool Mill	Cotton Mill
Bethlem	1812	X	2			1		-1
Bolton (N.)	1800		1					1
Canterbury	1801	X	2					
Chatham	1819		1				1	
Cornwall	1800	X	3					
Cornwall	1812		several	1				
Coventry	1809		several	several	several			
Durham	1819		2					
E. Haddam	1819		1		1		1	2
E. Windsor	1806	X		1				
Farmington	c.1810	X	3		3			
Franklin	1800	X	2-3					
Goshen	1812	X	1	1	4	1	1	
Guilford	1832		1		3			
Haddam	1819		2	2	1			
Killingworth	1819		1				1	
Lebanon	1800	X	5					-1
Litchfield	1815		6	2				1
Middletown	1819	X	4		1		2	2
Milton	1815			1				
New Haven	1811		3					1
New London	1812					-1#		
Norfolk	1815						1	
Pomfret	1800				1			
Preston	1801	X	2					
Ridgefield	1800	X	2					
Saybrook	1819		1					
Sharon	1807	X	3	2				
Tolland	1804		2					
Union	1803		1					
Wallingford	1811		2	6				
Washington	1800		2					
Washington	1815		2	2		1		
Watertown	1801	X						
Willington	1805	X						
Wintonbury	1802		1					
SITES PRESENT		Many	60+	19+	15+	3	7	7

The SITES PRESENT row shows totals of industrial sites present at the times of the reports.

The REPORTS row shows totals of towns and parishes reporting present and past industrial sites.

\#   indicates former duck manufactory; other flax mills were probably for preparing fiber

-    minus sign indicates former industrial site

X   indicates cloth production in households

were wound forward intermittently when the cloth lengthened as the shuttle carrying weft yarn wove back and forth between the warp yarns. An uninterrupted weaver could make about a yard of fabric an hour, depending on the strength and thickness of the yarn and the weave pattern desired.[97] Men as well as women wove on hand looms, especially in larger towns, where weaving became a full-time occupation for some. Providence, Rhode Island, for instance, had weavers who were already organized into traditional ranks of masters, journeymen, and apprentices when they contracted to weave cotton cloth for

Almy & Brown, owners of the new cotton-spinning mill there in the 1790s. Those weavers also served "the community at large...to produce fabrics for home use out of native-grown flax and wool."[98]

The reports only tell us the number of looms in a town, and never the number of spinning wheels.[99] This suggests that census-takers or report writers tended to perceive looms but not spinning wheels as different from ordinary household equipment. Indeed, there were many fewer looms than families reported per town; for instance, only one for every two or three families in Bethlem.[100] Unfortunately, only two other Town Reports—from Wallingford and Washington—mention looms, but they too reported many fewer looms (145 and 50, respectively) than the likely number of households.[101] The view that each family completely made its own cloth does not tally well with the reported number of looms.[102]

The ratio of looms to households in Bethlem, Wallingford, and Washington suggests that weaving was a specialty of some households. On the other hand, Lebanon reported "There are but few who make weaving a constant business; the greater part of the cloth being wove by women in the families where the yarn is spun."[103] Some reports list occupations, but "weaver" appears on none of these lists, indicating perhaps that women who wove, even for more than their own families, did not count as having an occupation.

Two manufactories in Bethlem were producing "Dutch spinning wheels," probably for export as well as use within the town. Bethlem's families produced 15,600 yards of cloth in 1810, presumably using its 80 hand looms to do so, and "dressed" 4,000 yards, probably at its two fulling mills.[104] The report is not explicit whether the 15,600 yards included or excluded what they used themselves, but at nearly 14 yards for every man, woman and child counted in the census of Bethlem that year (1,118), it seems likely they sold at least some of it out of town.[105]

That year (1810) Wallingford (population 2,325) was producing 36,459 yards of linen/cotton cloth (more than 15 ½ yards per capita) and 12,153 yards of woolen cloth (5 yards per capita), using 145 looms "in families." The weavers of the linen/cotton cloth probably obtained cotton yarn (for weft) from spinning mills elsewhere, while the linen yarn (for warp) was probably homespun.[106] Despite Washington's 50 looms reported in 1810, neither the 1800 nor the 1815 report for Washington (population 1,575) mentioned cloth produced.

Of the fourteen towns reporting household production of cloth, nine mentioned linen, usually along with wool. Cornwall in 1800, for instance, was producing an estimated 21,000 yards of linen per annum, which amounts to 13 yards per person, or about 78 yards per family. Figures of this size, far more than their production (4,500 yards) of woolen cloth, strongly suggest production for market.[107]

Marketing Cloth

The Town Reports show that home-produced cloth found three different paths to market: direct, indirect through local merchants, and (in Farmington at least) through a putting-out arrangement, as explained below. Although some reports give annual production figures or estimates, only a few mention prices. For instance, Cornwall's farm families were selling "good Tow cloth" (coarse linen) at 34 cents per yard to local merchants (five stores) in exchange for "English and India goods and groceries." The farmers themselves also took the cloth into nearby New York and exchanged it for cows and calves. East Windsor reported that tow cloth and woolen flannels were "manufactured in families, and some of it sent by the merchants to Albany and the northward." Watertown reported an average annual export of 12,000 yards of tow cloth.[108]

Besides the overland trading routes into New York state, merchants sent cloth to Connecticut ports. Ridgefield reported production of a heavy flaxen fabric: "A large quantity of Ducking (not for sails but for the southern market), perhaps 3,000 yards at 1/ per yard is annually made and sold."[109] Stratfield shipped out 33,733 yards of tow cloth in 1799 and New Haven shipped three bolts of duck and 14,129 yards of tow cloth in 1801.[110]

A Putting-out System for Linen

Farmington "familys" were producing checked and striped linen "chiefly for family consumption," which together with woolen flannel accounted for an estimated 10,000 yards.[111] But in addition some was explicitly produced for "export." Although Farmington store-keeper and dyer Stephen Brownson had acquired a "shop & tools for cotten" as well as linen, he had "found that the linen is the most profitable," and was running a linen "manufactory" with a classic putting-out system, as in England. The Farmington reporter describes it in enthusiastic detail, which suggests that it was unknown to him elsewhere:[112]

> His method of carrying on that business is to purchas the flax let it out to spinners who return him the yarn, then the yarn after it is dyed & bleachd, the former is done in his own shop the latter is also let out to women & after bleaching returnd to him again, then is delivered out to women weavers chiefly & returnd to him in the cloth. The pay in each process is made in European goods in thus pursuing the business he is able now to make about 15000 yards of cloth in a year.

These 15,000 yards Brownson "sold to the merchants & retailers in this & the neighboring states."[113] Presumably he used the proceeds to buy the "European goods" with which he "paid" the Farmington women who spun, bleached, and wove the cloth. He likely credited their accounts at his store with a value for their labor, from which they "paid" for the goods. Cash was rarely needed to settle accounts.

Apparently Brownson was successful in organizing linen cloth production in Farmington households for the market, even though household production of linen was generally beginning to decline in the new republic. As factory-produced cotton fabric from England was dropping in price and rising in quality it was simply replacing linen for most purposes. In Ridgefield in 1800, for instance, already "The great quantity of Cotton cloaths as muslins &c imported and sold at a low price, has a tendancy to discourage the makeing of linnen cloath—tho many make linnen & exchange with the shop keepers for cotton stocking."[114]

Fulling Mills for Wool

Brownson dyed linen yarn before putting it out to weavers. Woolen cloth could be dyed "in the wool," in the yarn, or after weaving. It was not very thick as woven; for use in warm winter clothing it required fulling, which cleaned it and felted together the woven fibers. To full a cloth at home, one trampled it underfoot in a tubful of wet soapy cloth for hours or days. This disagreeable, time-consuming task was the first of the textile processes mechanized in medieval Europe, and was also promptly mechanized in New England colonies (see Fig. 6). Massachusetts acquired four fulling mills near Boston between 1643 and 1662, while colonists in Connecticut established its first four fulling mills in East Hartford (1686), New London (1693), Stamford (1700), and Guilford (1707).[115] As Tables I and II show, 29 Connecticut towns alone had more than 60 fulling mills by 1800-1832.

Clothiers

Brownson's system for producing linen resembled that of "clothiers" in England, who in sequence "put out" and "took in" wool or cotton fibers, yarn, and cloth. Eight Connecticut Town Reports do mention clothiers, clothier's works or clothier's mills, but what little is said of them suggests they were engaged in the final portion of woolen cloth processing—fulling

Fig. 6: **Fulling mill**
Fulling mills like this one were for many centuries an important adjunct to home manufacture of woolens in Europe and America. They saved immense amounts of tedious labor in cleaning and thickening the woven cloth. Here, tappets protruding from the shaft of an overshot water wheel raise ponderous wooden-headed mallets—two are shown—and let them fall into a stock, to beat and turn wet cloth and cleansing substances. The handles are eight feet long and pass through the heads, which are four feet long and shaped so as to turn the bundle of cloth over and over in the stock. Oliver Evans, The Young Mill-Wright and Miller's Guide, *13th ed. (Philadelphia: Lea & Blanchard, 1850) pp. 348-49, Plate XXIV.*

and dressing—instead of putting out fibers to be spun and yarn to be woven. Guilford's report, conveying more than other reports about what clothiers did, mentioned three clothier's works; saying one of them was

the first, & for several years the only one in Connecticut...[Its site was] granted to Samuel Johnson in 1707. The most that this could do was to full the cloth sent to it, a large portion of which was worn without sheering or pressing. Cloth dressing at this establishment has been carried on by the family of Samuel Johnson until the present time.[116]

Dressing—raising and shearing the nap on woolen cloth—was time consuming and required highly specialized skills when performed by hand, so it is possible the clothiers had napping and shearing machines, of which several were recently patented.[117] Pressing, either of woolen or of linen cloth, was simply accomplished by folding it carefully, with interleafs of pasteboard or wood, into vertical stacks that were compressed in a large screw press.

In short, the clothiers' works or mills mentioned in the Town Reports were less likely to organize production as Brownson did than to provide services to families producing cloth. They might, however, constitute a node of activity around which a full-fledged woolen mill could later be built. Conversely, a full-fledged woolen mill could also provide such service to home producers, as did the one in Chatham, where the report in 1819 commented "The quantity of cloth wholly manufactured here has not been great; considerable has been fulled and dressed for customers."[118]

Carding Mills for Wool

Like fulling mills and clothier's works, carding mills supplied a water-powered service for the production of homespun and home-woven woolen cloth. Except for Goshen, towns reporting woolen mills did not report carding machines, and towns reporting carding machines did not report woolen mills. The over nineteen water-powered carding machines shown in Tables I and II presumably operated independently. At that time, carding machines far outnumbered woolen mills both in the United States generally and in Connecticut.[119] Since wool was grown on local sheep and already used in home production, while cotton was imported from the South, mechanization of carding had a different effect on these two textile industries in New England. Cotton-carding machines went into textile mills; some wool-carding machines did too, but most of them operated independently.

Carding machine technology was recent. It had been developed in England in the 1730s-1760s and arrived in America in 1793 with brothers John and Arthur Scholfield from Yorkshire, England, who first settled north of Boston. Several years later they moved to Connecticut and Berkshire County, Massachusetts, where they made and used carding machines.[120] Carding machine technology spread rapidly: the 1810 census reported 1,776 of them in operation in the United States.[121]

Instead of wielding hand-held cards, the spinner's children could now take large baskets of wool to the carding mill, where it would swiftly pass between successive counter-rotating wire-studded cylinders (see Fig. 7).[122] They could bring it back carded into batting for quilts or into strips, which would speed the spinning into yarn. According to wool industry historian Arthur Cole, the carding machine "imparted an added virility to the household production...[which] was enabled to compete to better advantage with the rising factory production."[123]

Textile Technology Transfer

Factory production of wool met stiffer competition from household production than cotton factories did, but both faced strongest competition from high-quality, low-cost imported English textiles. Between 1733 and 1785 a series of famous inventions in England had mechanized carding, spinning, and weaving. These were John Kay's "flying shuttle," Thomas Wyatt and Lewis Paul's spinning and carding machines, Samuel Hargreaves's spinning "jenny," Richard Arkwright's carding machine and spinning "throstle" or "water frame," Samuel Crompton's spinning "mule," and Edmund Cartwright's power loom. Powered successively by horse, water, and steam, and coupled with changes in iron making and -working technology, they had set off the world's first "industrial revolution." Farm laborers' families crowded into mill towns to operate these textile machines, in turn spurring invention and production of machines to make these and other machines.

American colonists had heard about these developments but had to fight a political revolution before they could begin to emulate them. Thomas Jefferson's early qualms about deleterious social effects of industrialization were countered by Alexander Hamilton's arguments in favor of economic independence for the new republic. Early efforts by American mechanics after the Revolution to build textile machines, made on the basis of hear-say instead of know-how, were unsatisfactory. Technology transfer frequently requires personal, face-to-face instruction—know-how plus show-how.

Alexander Hamilton's Society for the Establishment of Useful Manufactures, among other agencies, offered incentives for English emigrants skilled in the new textile technologies to bring them to the new republic in spite of British laws forbidding such emigration.[124] The immigrant who receives most historical credit for doing so was Samuel Slater, who in 1790 set up four Arkwright-type machines for carding, roving, and spinning cotton in a water-powered clothier's shop at Pawtucket, Rhode Island.[125] Eight or nine children "manned" the machines, including a ten-year-old brother of Slater's new bride, Hannah Wilkinson. After moving in 1793 into a factory built for the purpose, the Slater mill expanded in machinery and output, and was employing more than 100 people by 1800.[126]

Cotton Mills

When Yale graduate Eli Whitney patented an improved cotton gin in 1793, the supply of southern American cotton quickly increased dramatically, not only to England but also to New England, stimulating construction of more mills for spinning. Slater-type cotton spinning mills, sometimes with associated handloom weavers, spread in Rhode Island, Massachusetts, and Connecticut.[127] Samuel Slater and his

Fig. 7: *Early nineteenth-century carding machine*
Loose wool placed on an endless belt at the end of the machine fed into the series of smaller cylinders, closely studded with wire teeth, that rotated in the opposite direction against the teeth of the central main cylinder, alternately carding the wool and moving it from one pair to the next over the main cylinder. It could card the wool into batting for a quilt or into strips for "roving" to be spun into yarn. As was usual, this wooden-framed, water-powered carding machine at Old Sturbridge Village in Massachusetts operates independently from a woolen mill, and still occasionally services household textile manufacture. Courtesy Old Sturbridge Village, photo by Robert B. Gordon.

relatives owned or managed many of them. For instance, Slater's brother-in-law Smith Wilkinson, who had been part of the initial workforce at Pawtucket, became manager and co-owner of the cotton mill built at Pomfret, Connecticut in 1806. The 1800 report to the Connecticut Academy from Pomfret of course does not mention Smith Wilkinson's arrival in 1806, and remarks instead "People, here, in general, make ye own wearing apparell." On the site Wilkinson purchased were "a Grist mill, a saw mill & a clothier's mill, standing together."[128]

According to the census of manufactures taken in 1810, Pomfret's was one of "altogether fifteen [cotton] mills erected before the year 1808" in the United States, totalling "at that time about eight thousand spindles."[129] The Embargo against English imports beginning in 1807 spurred this nascent cotton industry so effectively that by the end of 1809 it had nearly quadrupled in size: sixty-two cotton mills were in operation in the United States, working 31,000 spindles. Four of these mills were reported to be in Connecticut: in Pomfret, Stirling, New Haven, and Derby.[130]

Cotton yarn production in Connecticut developed very rapidly during the War of 1812. By 1819, Pease and Niles reported 67 cotton factories in Connecticut.[131] Although not nearly comprehensive on the subject, the Town Reports spanning the years 1800 to 1819 give some information about nine cotton factories, manufactories, or mills present or past at their time of writing and indicated in Table II.[132] Their machines were almost certainly solely for producing yarn, not cloth, for power looms did not begin weaving in American mills until Francis Lowell set up his integrated cotton mill in Waltham, Massachusetts in 1814. Until then, handloom weavers—mostly "outworking"—made the cloth.

The North Bolton Report (1800) waxes enthusiastic about one of the mills that the 1810 census missed, the "cotton factory for the spinning & twisting of cotton yarn built by & ye property of a Mr. Warburton, a few years since from England, who is of uncommon mechanical genius. This factory is now of considerable business & increasing."[133] In 1808 and 1814 Middletown acquired "two cotton factories, standing near each other, on a small stream." In 1819 they were running 630 spindles total, with room for expansion, while East Haddam had two cotton factories, the smaller with 500 spindles, the larger with 1,500-2,000 spindles. The New Haven Report (1811) tersely acknowledges "one cotton manufactory, containing all the usual machinery for spinning and twisting cotton." The Litchfield Town Report (1815) merely lists one cotton "manufactory." [134]

Spindles were the unit of measurement for cotton mills. Looms—surely hand-operated if present at all all—were unmentioned. Elsewhere in Connecticut, for instance, in 1811 Timothy Dwight observed on one of his travels that Humphreysville's cotton manufactory was housed "in a building about one hundred feet long, thirty-six wide, and of four stories, capable of containing two thousand spindles with all their necessary apparatus."[135]

Not all adoptions of the new textile technology had been successful, however. Lebanon reported already in 1800 that a former "manufactory of cotton cloth" had "failed by reason of the high price of cotton & labour." Similarly, in Bethlem in 1812 Azel Backus remembered a "Manufactory of Cotton...which was one of the earliest in the State," whose proprietor had "on account of the difficulty of procuring workmen, and the high price of labor" sold off the machinery to the cotton manufactory in Humphreysville.[136]

Woolen Mills

Humphreysville's woolen mill was better known than its cotton mill. Col. David Humphreys, former Revolutionary War hero and United States ambassador to Spain and Portugal, had not only imported Spanish Merino sheep to Derby, Connecticut in 1802, but also set up a woolen mill there in 1806. He employed orphan boys from New York City and built housing for them and other workers in the eponymous Humphreysville factory village, later named Seymour. In 1808 Thomas Jefferson, having heard that Col. Humphreys' woolen fabric was "the best fine cloth made in the United States," paid $24.75 for five and one-half yards, and had it made into a coat.[137] Jefferson's purchase was a minor act of Hamiltonian encouragement for infant industries, following his Embargo in 1807 on imports, which had a major effect. By 1811 Humphreys' mill employed as many as 150 persons in its four-story building, which was equipped with "a picker, four carding machines, two jennies, a billy of forty spindles, four broad and eight narrow looms, two newly invented shearing machines, and four fulling mills, besides eighteen stocking frames."[138]

American woolen factories had, however, already made a hesitant start in Connecticut two decades earlier. Established in 1788 with an initial capital of £1250 from courageous investors, and subsidized by a state bounty of a penny per pound of wool spun by June 1789, the Hartford Woolen Manufactory was an object of patriotic pride. At first its equipment consisted of little more than handlooms and a fulling mill, while it put out wool to be spun "by the country people," but by 1795 it included two water-powered carding machines, a spinning jenny, a twisting machine, and eight looms. Despite commendation as a "precious embryo" by Alexander Hamilton and a visit and purchase of cloth by George Washington, its goods competed poorly against imported woolens from England and vigorous household production as discussed above. It wound down over the years 1795-97.[139]

Hartford's woolen mill seems not to have stimulated emulation elsewhere in Connecticut, but Col. Humphreys' may have. In 1807 John Cotton Smith wrote about Sharon,

> from the attention now paid to the propagation of the Merino Sheep, and from the excellent specimens of cloth already fabricated by individuals from that specie of wool, a well grounded hope is entertained that this valuable manufacture will soon be attempted upon an enlarged scale.[140]

Perhaps the infusion of good wool genes into Connecticut sheep from David Humphreys' imported Merinos helped raise the quality of wool available; certainly Jefferson's Embargo and the War of 1812 encouraged the establishment of woolen mills as well as the production of woolen cloth "in families."

Secretary of the Treasury Albert Gallatin reported in 1810 "there are yet but few establishments for the manufacture of woollen cloths"—fourteen nationwide. Humphreysville's was the only one listed for Connecticut.[141] Yet by 1819 Pease and Niles's *Gazetteer* reported "66 woolen factories" in Connecticut. Since half of the Town Reports were written earlier than the 1807 Embargo, textile mills established between 1807 and 1819 are underrepresented.[142] Of the seven woolen mills mentioned in the Connecticut Town Reports, none predated Goshen's "one small establishment for manufacturing wool, which employs 12 hands and 120 spindles," built c. 1810. The Goshen reporter apologized in 1812, "its profits as might have been expected have as yet been small; owing to the inexperience of the workmen, and all the other difficulties incident to the infancy of manufactures." Also in Litchfield County, Norfolk's reporter wrote in 1815 "There is a woollen manufactory in this town, which, with its appendages, employs from 10 to 15 work men." [143]

The other five wool factories mentioned in the Town Reports were in Middlesex County and ranged in size. One established in 1810 in Middletown employed "from sixty to eighty hands" and was powered from mid-June 1811 by one of Oliver Evans' celebrated 24-horsepower high-pressure steam engines.[144] Some hands were apparently weavers, for "forty yards of fine cloth were sometimes manufactured in a day, and $70,000 worth in a year."[145] Oliver Evans wrote in 1812 that his steam engine, "the property of the Middletown Woollen Manufacturing Company," was "driving all the machinery for carding, spinning, reeling, weaving, washing, fulling, dyeing, shearing, dressing, and finishing" and also that the steam "warms the house, heats water, &c." The superintendent wrote to Evans that the engine "requires about 96 feet of oak wood, or three-fourths of a cord, to work 12 hours with our present machinery."[146]

Despite the expense of fuel for the steam engine, the manufactory apparently prospered during the War of 1812 until there was a "sudden fall [in price] of goods, upon the late peace with Great Britain, since which it has not been much improved." Middletown's other woolen mill, "erected...in 1814 on Pameacha River" housed its machinery "in a fine brick building 64x34 feet, three stories. Here 25,000 pounds of Merino wool are annually manufactured into blue broadcloths. The coloring is done wholly in the wool. The number of hands usually employed is forty," including, implicitly, both weavers and operatives of spinning machines.[147]

A somewhat larger building at Lord's Mills on the Salmon River in East Haddam not only housed the 500-spindle cotton factory mentioned above, which by 1819 was employing 15 hands, but also "machinery for the manufacture of woolen cloths," employing 20 hands and consuming 16,000 pounds of wool a year. Built in 1814, it had burned down and been rebuilt in brick.[148] A smaller woolen factory dating from 1814 in North Killingworth was consuming 6,000 pounds of wool a year, while from 1811 the woolen factory in Chatham, as mentioned above, "fulled and dressed" more home produced cloth than it "wholly manufactured."[149]

As with the cotton factories, the Town Reports do not give detailed information about machinery in the woolen mills they mention. With the exception of the steam-powered one in Middletown, we can guess that like the one at Humphreysville, these woolen mills did contain waterpowered machines for fulling and for carding, but probably left spinning and weaving hand-powered. Arkwright-type water frames worked for spinning cotton, but not for wool. In 1811 William Humphreys of Connecticut patented a water-powered machine for spinning wool, but there is no record of its use. Spinners in wool factories more likely used hand-powered spinning jennies.[150] Their replacement by powered "spinning jacks" began perhaps in 1802, but did not fully get under way until the 1820s or become standard until 1840s.[151]

It is also unlikely that the Connecticut towns' woolen mills contained many power looms, for the earliest ones (from 1815) operated too harshly for woolen yarn. By using linen or cotton for strong warp threads, however, manufacturers found they could use wool for the weft to produce a less expensive hybrid called "satinet" on power looms, so "by the 1830s many American mills were equipped with power looms." For pure wool and fancier weaves, handlooms continued to be necessary until the introduction in the 1840s of power looms invented at Lowell, Massachusetts by William Crompton, another recent immigrant from England.[152]

Flax Mills

Relative to wool, conversion of flax to cloth was a difficult, labor-intensive process, better done by specialists, yet in America commonly performed by farm families, as discussed above. In Ireland, water-powered "scutching" mills, with wooden rollers and rotating blades to break the stems and separate the fibers of flax, were common by 1820 and a few were attempted in the United States.[153] Three "flax dressing mills" mentioned in the Connecticut Town Reports for Bethlem, Goshen, and Washington may have been of this sort.[154] Flax spinning machines introduced from Europe in the 1820s were used in mills in mid-Atlantic states, and several successful linen manufacturing companies operated in Massachusetts from 1835 onward. For most purposes, however, machine-made cotton textiles made linens a comparative luxury.

Raising flax for seed to export to Ireland had become more profitable than growing, harvesting, processing, and making cloth of it.[155] Besides the hand-produced duck and tow cloth mentioned above, in 1801 the port of New Haven already was shipping out 11,146 pounds of flax and 6,372 bushels of flax seed, while Stratfield in 1799 had shipped 129,789 pounds of flax and 6,338 bushels of flax seed.[156] Flax farmers in Connecticut were also able to take flax seed to oil mills for conversion to linseed oil, as discussed below.

Summing Up

With historical hindsight, we know that all stages of textile production—especially cotton textile production—in antebellum America were successfully mechanized and integrated into factories within a generation after the period of the Town Reports. These reports draw attention to the relatively undocumented transition between total home (or "hand") production and total factory (or "machine") production.

Having teased out from the Town Reports a sketch of the co-existence of domestic and factory textile production for "the market," we have also noted that the pre-industrial "putting out system," by which clothiers had linked the market with domestic production in England, does not seem to have operated here, with the exception of Stephen Brownson's linen "manufactory" in Farmington. The link seems instead to have been the local storekeepers, who accepted home-produced woolens and linens from farm families, along with agricultural produce, in exchange for store credit or imported goods.

Household production of textiles for market, separate from that organized by specific manufactories, should be discernible in general storekeepers' account books as well as these Town Reports.[157] Showing a more direct relationship between "family" workers and "the market" for their goods, such production is rather different from the "outwork" indicated in records of early textile factories.[158] It deserves more study for the sake of better understanding of America's transition from "the golden age of homespun" to "industrialization."

Paper Mills

Unlike textiles, paper for the market was never made "in families"; it was always made in mills. The mills, however, at first included many operations by hand that became mechanized only after the period of the Town Reports, five of which mention the presence of paper mills (see Table I).

Paper made from rags or hemp beaten to a cellulose pulp originated in China, began to replace vellum and parchment for manuscripts in medieval Europe, and reached England around the turn of the sixteenth century. In 1690, the first paper mill in America was built on Wissahickon Creek near Philadelphia. New England's first paper mill was established in 1728 on the Neponset river near Boston.[159] Connecticut's earliest was erected in Norwich in 1768.[160] By 1797 there were sixteen paper mills in Connecticut.[161]

The national census of 1810 counted 202 paper mills in the new republic, producing 425,521 reams of paper valued at $1,689,718.[162] Of the six Connecticut paper mills listed in Table I, Middletown's is the only one described even briefly in its Town Report (1819):

> The paper mill was built in 1793, employs from nine to twelve hands, and manufactures from 1,200 to 1,600 reams of writing, printing, and wrapping paper, together with considerable quantities of bonnet, press, and sheathing paper.[163]

The New Haven Report barely mentions its two paper mills and gives no indication where the 2,476 reams of paper—wrapping, printing, and writing—were made that were shipped out of New Haven "wholly, or almost wholly, to New York" in 1801.[164]

To supplement such minimal mention of paper mills, Judith McGaw's thoroughgoing study of nineteenth-century paper mills in Berkshire County, Massachusetts informs our guesses as to how these mills worked in Connecticut.[165] Rags were the raw material. The "Hollander," also called washing, breaking or beating engine, performed the only mechanized part of the process, macerating and beating the rags into pulp.[166]

The way to form a sheet of paper was to dip a wire-bottomed mold into a vat of pulp, and shake it gently side-to-side and front-to-back while water drained out. "Vat men" dipped the molds and shook them, "couchers" made stacks of sheets of moist paper interleaved with felts. Many hands together turned the screw of the paper press to squeeze water from the stacks of paper and felt. "Layboys" separated them after pressing, and "loftmen" hung the paper up to dry.

At the beginning of the process, women sorted rags, removing buttons etc., and cut them up. At the end, they inspected, sorted, and counted the finished sheets of paper into reams. Women constituted about half of the labor force, and earned by this important but relatively light and unskilled work about a fifth to a quarter of the mills' wages.[167] Men performed the heavy labor of beating the dust out of the rags and powering the press, and the relatively skilled tasks of

Fig. 8: *Sixteenth-century oil mill. The three main operations in making vegetable oil of various kinds are here shown performed by a horse-powered edge runner to crush the seeds, a woman to cook the resulting meal, and a man-powered screw press to squeeze oil from a cake of meal. Oil mills mentioned in the Connecticut Town Reports used waterpower for crushing seeds and pressing the meal. Jost Amman and Hans Sachs, Ständebuch (Frankfurt a/M: Georg Raben, 1568), p. 101. Reprint Inselbücherei 133, (Leipzig: Insel Verlag, c. 1934).*

dipping and shaking the molds, and of stacking, separating, and hanging up the fragile sheets of paper.

Further mechanization was on its way, but had not yet reached the mills of the Connecticut Town Reports. The "cylinder" machine and the "Fourdrinier" machine both made a continuous instead of discontinuous process out of the tasks of the vat men, couchers, loftmen and press, and produced long rolls of paper instead of sheets. Berkshire County papermills began installing cylinder machines in 1827.[168] The first Fourdrinier machine built in the United States was constructed in South Windham, Connecticut, and put into operation in May, 1829 at Norwich Falls, Connecticut.[169] Both kinds of machine quickly superseded hand methods. By 1845 only two mills in the country were still making paper "by hand."[170]

Shortage of rags was a chronic problem. Housewives were urged to bring rags to their local storekeeper for credit, who sold them to the paper mills. They were an item of longer-range, even international, trade: 81 sacks of rags were shipped from Stratfield in 1799; two and a half tons from New Haven in 1801.[171] Mechanization of papermaking expanded the scale of the industry and increased the demand for rags. Attempts to substitute straw, rope, and exotic foreign fibers proved unsatisfactory. From the 1850s experimentation settled on grinding up wood to obtain cellulose pulp, and ground wood remains today the predominant ingredient for paper.

Oil Mills

Flax was harvested not only to make linen from its straw, but also to press oil from its seeds. As Table I indicates, eight towns reported the presence of oil mills; in East Haddam a former oil mill site now contained textile mills. North Bolton's reporter was the only one who specified a "linseed-oil mill," but we shall assume the others predominantly if not solely produced linseed oil. It has had many industrial uses—in making paints, varnishes, linoleum, patent leather, printers' ink, soap, waterproofing for carriage tops and "oil silks," among others—and is even recently purveyed as a health food.[172]

Flax was grown in all the American colonies, especially plentifully in the river-bottom land of the Connecticut Valley. In the mid-eighteenth century the seed itself was a considerable item of export, particularly to Ireland, as mentioned above.[173] In 1718 an oil mill was established in New Haven, followed by one in Derby.[174] In 1810 there were 283 linseed-oil mills reported in the 14 states; 24 of them were in Connecticut, counting some at least of the nine reported to the Connecticut Academy between 1800 and 1819.[175]

The Town Reports say nothing about their oil mills except that they existed at the time of the report, or had previously existed. To describe them even sketchily requires some guesswork based on descriptions of oil mills elsewhere. The common operations in these descriptions are crushing the seed into meal, possibly cooking the meal to increase the flow of oil, and then pressing it.[176] The left-over cake of meal could be run through the mill a time or two more for further extraction before selling it as cattle feed or fertilizer.

The best description is in Carter Litchfield's carefully informed study of documents for the late eighteenth-century oil mill in Bethlehem, Pennsylvania. It used cam-lifted stampers for both crushing and pressing. Two men could process ten bushels (about 560 pounds) of flaxseed a day, to produce 14 to 17½ gallons of linseed oil. The mill ran seasonally from mid-autumn through the winter and spring.[177]

Did all oil mills work the same way? A less documented account suggests alternatively that instead of stampers, "from a very early date, oil has been extracted from the seed of the flax by means of hand-screw presses," similar to cider presses (see Fig. 8). It also says such presses were superseded early in the nineteenth century by hydraulic presses.[178] In nineteenth-century America flax continued to be grown commercially for its seed long after its use for linen dwindled. The plant thrived best where it had not been planted before, and was recognized as a particularly good "first crop" for westward-trekking pioneers.

Over time technological changes squeezed more oil from the seed. The 1810 average national output was 1.9 gallons of linseed oil per bushel of flaxseed, from which modern mills c. 1909 produced 2.5 gallons.[179] The oil-cake byproduct continued to be valued for cattle feed and fertilizer, but flax straw was considered useless, and even burned in the fields, until new uses were found for it in the twentieth century—particularly in production of fine paper for bibles and cigarettes.[180]

Ingenious Yankees

The Connecticut Academy solicited information on "improvements in arts and sciences and the authors of them" and "inventors of curious machines."[181] Responses to this query were few, but include two that serve to illustrate the ways in which "Yankee ingenuity" not only stimulated but also integrated technological change among different industries.[182] Both inventions were for production rather than consumption.

Ebenezer Chittenden

The New Haven report of 1811 mentions that "Mr. Ebenezer Chittenden, of this town, is the inventor of the first machine, in this country, perhaps in the world, for bending and cutting card teeth with a single movement." The Guilford report informs us that Ebenezer Chittenden (1726-1812), who "possessed a great mechanical genius," was born in East Guilford (Madison).[183] He settled in New Haven and invented his card-tooth machine sometime before the Revolution. John Warner Barber described Chittenden as "of an open and communicative disposition" of which "some person" took advantage, "obtained a knowledge of his invention, went to England and took out a patent, claiming himself to have been the original inventor."[184]

Around 1800, according to another source, "But two machines...were as yet known; one [presumably Chittenden's] for cutting and bending the wire into staples, and another for piercing the sheets of leather with holes, into which the staples were placed, one by one, with the hand."[185] These two machines seem to have been the basis for an "infant" card industry in 1812 in the village of Winsted, whose anonymous reporter wrote:

> We have also one establishment for manufactoring wire, in which wire has been reduced to No. 28. and is found to possess the requisites necessary for Card teeth, in a degree equal, if not superior to that which is imported for that purpose.—In this shop about Eight tons of iron have been made [into wire] for the year past and nine workmen have ordinarially been employed.[186]

This wire supplied Winsted's

> two infant factories for making cards. They are of so recent establishment, that the introduction may yet be considered in the light of experiment, and what degree of permanency they may hereafter acquire may be considered uncertain.

The cards are said to be well made and approved by those who have used them. The teeth are wholly set by children, and if the business should be continued, may prove an incentive to industry, at a period of life, when their hands cannot be usefully occupied in ordinary pursuits.[187]

Meanwhile, in New York City, a highly-capitalized company was putting into operation the machinery that New Englander Amos Whittemore patented in 1797 in America and thereafter in England, for production of "cotton and wool cards." Whittemore's machine not only cut and bent the wire into staples, but also pierced holes in the leather, stuck the staples through, and gave them the final bend necessary for acting as card teeth. Carding machines required wider and longer strips of wire-toothed leather card clothing than did hand cards. Children's hands, "their tiny fingers rapidly placing staple after staple into its appropriate place," were no longer needed for this task.[188]

Eli Whitney

Timothy Dwight's New Haven report of 1811 also praised Eli Whitney (1765-1825), a Massachusetts farm boy who remained handy with tools despite his Yale education. Soon after graduation in 1792 he had invented and patented a new type of machine or "[en]gin[e]" for removing the tenacious green seeds of short-staple cotton grown in upland Georgia. In New Haven he set up a cotton gin manufactory, which he proceeded to "systematise and arrange...in a proper manner" while instructing "a number of workmen and apprentices...in working Wood and Metals."[189]

Making the cotton gins required metal- and wood-working skills that could be applied elsewhere as well—perhaps most obviously in building a carding mill or other textile machines, but also in building carriages (soon to become a thriving industry in New Haven) or other wood-and-metal products. When the costs of patent litigation drove Whitney's cotton gin enterprise deeply into debt, he appealed successfully to the United States government in 1798 for a contract to make military muskets. He said he wished "to keep employ'd" the men and boys he had trained to make cotton gins, by undertaking to manufacture "ten or Fifteen Thousand Stand of Arms," another metal-and-wood product.[190] Whitney audaciously asked for and received the largest contract despite his lack of previous experience making guns.

In the factory he built at a disused gristmill site just north of New Haven, Whitney organized his work force of about forty men into unusual specialties. Lacking experienced gunsmiths, he trained his workers to file metal according to "patterns" (filing jigs) that he designed. They produced the different gunlock parts that Timothy Dwight said were "so exactly alike...that they may be transferred from one lock and adjusted to another, without any material alteration." Whitney also trained them to use what Dwight described as "machinery, put in motion by water, and remarkably well adapted to the

end...for hammering, cutting, turning, perforating, grinding, polishing, &c."[191] Dwight's rather vague description remains one of the very few primary accounts available of the factory's operations.

Armsmaking and the American System of Manufactures

Other Town Reports also mention manufacture in Middletown and Farmington of muskets, pistols, rifles, and swords, and in Haddam a machine for welding gun barrels, "connected with the gun factory at New Haven."[192] The earlier mentioned superior quality of Connecticut iron at that time was vital for their successful manufacture of Connecticut arms. Like Whitney, his contemporaries in Middletown—Nathan Starr, Simeon North, and Robert Johnson—got underway as arms makers with governmental contracts. Besides firearms, Starr and North manufactured scythes at various times in their careers, a process easily adapted to making bayonets and swords.[193] According to the Middlesex County Report, North's 55 to 70 workmen were producing 8,000-10,000 pistols in a year, while Johnson's 25-35 employees turned out 1,000 to 1,200 "rifles," and Starr's workers made about 5,000 swords.[194] Simeon North's factory a decade later went into production of breech-loading muskets designed by John Hall, whose parts were interchangeable with those Hall was making at Harper's Ferry.[195]

*Fig. 9: **Oldest extant milling machine, c. 1827.***
This bench-top machine was used to shape lock parts for flintlock muskets at the Whitney Armory, reducing the need for filing them. Now missing, a sliding platform holding a workpiece advanced beneath a toothed cutter rotating on the right end of the spindle. At the end of a cut, a latch disengaged the worm gear, stopping the motion. Unshown here, a cutter with a flat profile would cut a flat surface; a curved cutter profile produced a curved surface. After serving into the 1850s, during which more sophisticated milling machines were developed, this one was preserved from the scrap heap by Armory workmen. Photo courtesy New Haven Colony Historical Society.

Historians of technology deem such contract arms factories and the federal armory in Springfield to have been where the characteristically "American" system of manufactures was first developed.[196] As at Whitney's armory, the system involved division and specialization of hand-tool labor, and also mechanization, first of heavy tasks and later of precise and specialized tasks, in shaping iron, steel, and wood into parts of firearms. The aim, promulgated by the Ordnance Department in 1815, was to make the parts sufficiently uniform to be assembled, instead of individually fitted, into a whole weapon. "The advantages, in actual service, resulting from this unusual degree of uniformity," Dwight remarked in his New Haven report, "are too obvious to need explanation."[197]

Despite Timothy Dwight's assessment of Whitney's lock parts, neither Whitney nor his contemporaries reached the goal of interchangeability for standard-issue military muskets within his lifetime.[198] A later generation of arms makers made this achievement toward the end of the 1840s. The method of interchangeable parts spread gradually into the manufacture of other consumer hardware, including those later invented, such as sewing machines and typewriters, and in the early twentieth century, automobiles.

Use of this method promoted the development and spread of machine tools to make special-purpose machines to be arranged in the sequence of operations for producing standardized parts of a given object. Early "American system" factories and textile mills made their own machinery; some of them went on to make machinery for other factories, thus beginning the machine tool industry.[199] Arms makers, trained in early factories to excel in use of filing jigs and such machines as Dwight had seen at Whitney's armory, moved about, not only among arms factories, but among machine shops generally as these developed in other industries.[200]

From this sort of personal technological diffusion emerged a new machine tool invented at Simeon North's armory, and presumably in use there and at Robert Johnson's factory just about the time of the Middletown Report.[201] Versions of this new American invention, the milling machine, were used by John Hall at Harper's Ferry in the 1820s and by Whitney's successors at his armory. Figure 9 shows the oldest extant milling machine, which was used at the Whitney Armory after his death, and is now preserved at the New Haven Colony Historical Society.[202] A later model produced in the 1850s by the George S. Lincoln Co. in Hartford and named "the Lincoln miller" became the hallmark not just of firearms factories, but of "American system" factories generally, in which special-purpose machines were arranged according to the sequence of production.[203]

The Saybrook Town Report shows that in 1819 a sequence of water-powered specialized machines in a factory in Chester was already turning out large numbers of standardized tools for boring holes in wood:

> L' Hommedieu's factory was erected in 1811, for making patent double podded gimlets. In this, machinery is used for cutting steel plates

(A)   Pod Auger

(B)   Spiral Auger

*Fig. 10: **Augers***
The auger, like the smaller gimlet, had a sharp edge that would cut a hole when twisted into wood. Carpenters, coopers, bridge builders, shipwrights, wheelwrights and others used augers of various sorts to bore holes for fastening timbers by wooden pegs or "treenails," putting hubs on axles, tapping wine out of barrels, or making wooden pipes for water supply. In time, "pod" augers were superseded by "single twist" or "spiral" augers, as were patented by Ezra L'Hommedieu. (A) and (B) show a pod auger bit and a spiral auger bit, respectively. Drawing by Robert B. Gordon.

into pieces of proper size and length for gimlets, for double stamping and rounding them, smoothing the shank and bowls, forming the screw, and for turning and perforating the handles. Twenty men have been sometimes employed, and more than $10,000 worth of gimlets manufactured in a year. In 1815, the owners procured machinery for making patent single twist augurs, and since that time have directed their attention principally to this branch of manufacture. Within about twelve months they have made more than 8,000 for the navy of the United States and some for individuals.[204]

According to Chester local history, brothers Ezra and Joshua L'Hommedieu moved from Norwich to Chester "about 1812" and built a factory on the south bank of the Pattaconk River for the manufacture of double-podded gimlets and single-twist ship augers (see Fig. 10).[205]

The Saybrook Town Report emphasizes that the gimlets and augers produced there were patented. From 1809 to 1838, in fact, Ezra L'Hommedieu obtained five patents for gimlets and augers.[206]

Federal patents gave some protection to inventors of new technologies and their financial backers: a patent holder had the right to sue anyone who copied the patented device without paying royalties. From an average of 77 a year in 1790-1811, the number of American patents granted soared to an average of 540 patents a year in 1820-1840.[207] During this period Connecticut spawned a higher proportion of patents relative to its population than did other states.

The end of the War of 1812 in 1815 and resumption of trade with England was a shock to the increasingly interacting infant industries, large and small, that the war had fostered. Some (like L'Hommedieu's) survived and others (like Winsted's card factories) didn't. But the skills gained and technologies learned were not lost; they were available when the economy came out of the depression that followed 1816, "the year without a summer," and the business "panic" of 1819.

Conclusion

The Town Reports mention other mills and manufactories in fewer numbers than those included in Table I—mills for grinding bark for dyeing or tanning, a snuff mill, gunpowder mills, a scythe factory, tinsmiths, brass foundries, a pewter button factory, a japanning shop, ropewalks, block makers, carriage makers, spinning wheel manufactories, wagon manufactories, a clock factory, broom makers, comb factories, and hat manufactories. Some of these, especially brass, tin, and pewter works and clock, carriage, and hat factories, became important industries later in the nineteenth century. Future readers of the Connecticut Town Reports can use them in research on these industries.

What have we learned from this study of the Town Reports concerning the "industries" listed in Table I? They have supplied a view of transition from medieval European technology to American industrialization that in hindsight seems uneven—not quite underway in some instances and comparatively far progressed in others—but proceeding in ways that were different in many respects from European ways, not least in its usage of waterpower at many scattered small sites, financed and managed by local entrepreneurs.

One senses from the reports that the persons experiencing and undertaking new technologies were generally confident that the changes were desirable, but would not be devastated if they failed to work. A tentative tone about the card-making "experiment" in Winsted or "the well-founded hope" of expanded wool production in Sharon reflects neither a negative assessment of a new technology, nor wishful thinking, but a realistic recognition that failure was possible. Yet ways of organizing how to make things were fluid; a different arrangement might succeed better, and could be tried. A family farming its own land—a diversified occupation in itself though rarely a highly lucrative one—was the fall-back position that sustained flexibility. Manufacturing something either in household or in factory was frequently a part-time or temporary venture, from which family members could shift to a different product or retire to full-time farming without risking severe hardship. The Town Reports show practically no tenant farming and very few people on poor relief.[208] In contrast, English farm laborers who moved to steam-powered mill towns had much less recourse to resume farm work.

Connecticut youngsters on farms gained experience in trying new ways of doing things that stood them in good stead when they ventured into "manufactures." Such a farm was that of Solomon Wales, who was almost 75 years old in 1803, when he wrote the Town Report for Union. Although he had married twice and fathered six children, he was farming with "no help but a boy of eight years old." He had been a Captain in the Revolutionary War, and at various times town clerk, selectman, and representative to the Connecticut General Assembly. In his Town Report he exuberantly shared with readers his ways of threshing grain, making cider, grinding clover seed, tapping maple trees for sugar, fertilizing and irrigating his garden, poisoning crows, and feeding hogs with a trough of his own design that kept the poultry out and the hogs peaceable "till fit to kill."[209] No peasant he, but a vigorous exemplar of a culture in which creating and shrewdly assessing new technologies thrived. And his eight-year-old helper was learning.

Travel on Connecticut's Roads, Bridges, and Ferries, 1790-1830

Robert B. Gordon

When the Connecticut Academy began its survey of the state's towns, most people still had to use roads, bridges, and ferries inherited from colonial times. Through the seventeenth century people in Connecticut journeyed between towns infrequently. When they did travel, they preferred to use waterways whenever possible since on the land they had only winding trails that often followed animal tracks or Indian routes. Settlers built their first roads in the new towns to reach their fields and the meetinghouse, where they spent most of every Sunday.[1] Next they extended these roads to the grist, saw, and fulling mills that processed the products of their fields, woodlands, and pastures. Since many other tasks demanded their attention, the best they could do was to limit road building to cutting trees while leaving the stumps in place, and moving aside the largest rocks. Horses could avoid the stumps, and few people had wheeled vehicles in the seventeenth century. To get across a bog or swamp, the road builders put down brush, or sometimes logs to make a corduroy road. By 1673 a traveler could follow a trail from New York to Boston crossing Connecticut by way of New Haven and Hartford, or, after 1684, along the shoreline.[2]

Colonial settlers forded streams on foot or, if the stream were deep and swift, used a "horse-tail" ferry.[3] Townspeople built their first bridges in the simplest possible way by placing tree trunks, sometimes with the top flattened, over a stream.[4] In Guilford, residents built their twelve-foot-wide bridge over the East River in 1648 with hewn trees supported by a central pier, and covered with brush and split timber. They raised the money for the bridge by subscription.[5]

The members of Connecticut's legislature considered roads a common good and a community responsibility. They expected the men of every family (the minister excepted) to contribute to their construction and maintenance. As early as 1641 New Haven followed established English practice by appointing citizens to supervise the town's roads, ferries, and other community services. New Haven historian Rollin Osterweis noted how this practice made citizens who were not among the governing elite active participants in the management of the community.[6]

In 1643 the General Assembly attempted to put some order into the early efforts at transportation planning by requiring towns to appoint surveyors of roads; Guilford got around to appointing its surveyors three years later.[7] The surveyors were to call out all able-bodied men for two days work a year. They were to make and mend both local roads and the King's highways, the routes that were supposed to interconnect the towns. In 1650 the legislature increased the call to two or more days per year, as needed to get the work done, and added a fine of 2/6 for those who failed to appear. In 1674 it defined those required to work as all men aged sixteen to sixty.[8]

The colonial surveyors typically accomplished little coordination of their efforts, either within town or between towns. As late as 1678 the inadequately planned road system in Guilford still left some farmers' fields totally shut in by the property of others. To remedy this a town meeting that year appointed a panel of citizens to draw a map that would show how to improve the layout of its roads.[9]

Colonists' need to reach their fields, the meetinghouse, and the local mills determined the layout of roads and bridges in many of the state's towns. Additionally, settlers in Connecticut's northwestern and northeastern counties needed roads to the port towns, such as New Haven or Norwich, as soon as they had products to export. New Haven merchants began shipping livestock to Caribbean buyers shortly after 1700, and soon added a vigorous coastal trade with Boston to their port's activities, drawing products from the inland towns.[10] By the 1730s, adventurers in iron in the northwest had added a new demand for improved roads. In Salisbury, Canaan, and Kent they had to haul iron ore from mines to the sites of bloomery forges and blast furnaces, which they could not place near the mines because of their need for water power to run their blowing engines and forge hammers.[11] In the mid-eighteenth century Connecticut farmers and merchants had ox and horse carts in general use for moving goods. By 1760 farmers were petitioning the legislature for better roads and the removal of fences that obstructed travel. Individuals had virtually no vehicles for personal travel, and generally went on journeys on horseback.[12]

Despite its citizens' continuing agitation for improvements, colonial Connecticut remained notorious for its bad roads. It had accomplished little in road and bridge construction through the eighteenth century compared to most of the other colonies of British North America. Citizens began shirking the road surveyors' calls, and with the colonial economy thriving, preferred paying the 2/6 fine to doing a day's work. In 1739 the legislature raised the fine to 6s, in 1746 to 8s, and in 1748 to 20s, which proved enough to discourage non-appearance at road-work days.[13]

Although the legislature appointed committees to lay out inter-town roads, it appropriated no money to make or repair them. Towns regularly ignored the legislature's demands that they make or mend roads. The Greenwoods road that took travelers from Hartford toward Albany was "in great want of amendment" by 1766, just two years after completion.[14] The main King's Highway through Connecticut "was an insult to its proud title," and wheeled vehicles could not pass over parts of the road from New Haven to New York. Despite the General Assembly's good intentions, problems persisted well into the eighteenth century like those encountered by travelers passing through Willimantic: on leaving town eastbound on the King's Highway they came to a dead end at the Plainfield town line.[15] To get travellers over its rivers, the colony had nothing like Hale's 1760 bridge across the Connecticut River at Bellows Falls, Vermont, or Sewell's 270-foot long bridge built in 1761 over the York River in Maine.[16]

By the 1770s, New Englanders began to think of the calling-out system of road work as oppressive and an unfair burden on the poorer members of the community. Towns began to petition the General Assembly for the right to tax residents for road maintenance. The legislature began granting these petitions, starting with Norwich's in 1774. However, taxation soon became a sensitive issue so that most towns were unwilling to raise taxes enough to make decent roads. Nevertheless, town taxes remained the principal support for road construction and maintenance through 1795.[17]

Roads and the Town Reports

People often carried on trade by barter through colonial times and the first years of the republic because of scarcity of money. While a few individuals managed to accumulate some wealth in the West Indies trade, entrepreneurs had no banks from which to borrow, and lacked capital for industrial ventures. The period described in the Town Reports (generally 1790 to 1830) began with a growth of trade that brought prosperity and created the capital that enterprising Yankees such as Simeon North and David Humphreys used to launch manufacturing of textile, wood, and metal products in Connecticut. Alexander Hamilton's 1791 financial plan coupled with the outbreak of war in Europe led Connecticut citizens to increase their exports. Difficulty in obtaining imported goods kept money at home that would otherwise have gone overseas, and aided local entrepreneurs undertaking manufactures. Many individuals now prospered through trade with the West Indies. By 1818 ten Connecticut banks gave entrepreneurs access to capital.[18] While eighteenth-century export of farm products to other colonies and the West Indies had required roads to the port towns, the general increase of commerce and the beginnings of manufactures in the 1790s called for better communications throughout the state. In the period covered by the Academy's Town Reports, Connecticut made great strides in improving its internal communications, leaving it ready for a new venture into railroads after 1830.

The authors of nearly all the Town Reports believed (probably accurately) that most roads were either generally bad until 1790 or, as in Lebanon, "still very rough."[19] David D. Field reported in 1819 that until recently water routes had so sufficed for travel within Middlesex county that residents saw little need to improve their roads, which he described as badly

made over rough and uneven ground.[20] (Middlesex County residents could get along with fewer roads because most of their towns had frontage on the coast of Long Island Sound or along the shore of the Connecticut River.) Several Report authors described the poor quality of roads off the main routes as a serious problem while others, generally writing later, commented on the great improvement in roads they had seen recently. In Lebanon, the roads remained very rough despite the imposition of a tax to pay for repairs. The correspondent for Farmington was exceptional in his claim that its roads were good enough for pleasure carriages before 1755.[21] Also unusual was the 1788 decision by residents of East Windsor to sell off all but a five-rod strip of a right-of-way twenty rods wide which had been laid out by colonial settlers from the Connecticut River to the east side of town.[22] Farmington sold off parts of the town highways not needed by the public for notes to support its schools.[23]

Some of the Report writers listed needs for roads that had existed since colonial times, such as reaching mills and markets. Thus Canterbury farmers travelled to the town's twenty-one mills, and sent their products to market in Norwich and New London. The wealthier farmers in Cornwall took their own produce to Derby or the Hudson River ports. Lewis Norton reported that Goshen's farmers hauled the 380,236 pounds of cheese they exported a year to one of the port towns, using roads such as those to Derby, New Haven, or Bridgeport.[24] Several reports mention the increasing scarcity of fuel wood. This meant that residents had to haul fuel from woodlots more distant than they were used to using, and needed better local roads. Farmers hauled firewood to ports such as the one in Guilford for export to New York and other cities. Cattle walked to market urged along by drovers as mentioned in the Cornwall report.[25]

Through colonial times, oxen pulled farmer's plows in the fields and their carts to the mill or market. The reports for Cornwall (1801) and Goshen (1812) described how improved roads let farmers replace their ox carts with faster, horse-drawn wagons for trips to market. Sleighs remained the best way to travel or move goods in winter. Cornwall had eighty-two carts, twenty-six wagons, and a hundred twenty-one sleighs in 1801. The farmers of the northwest were more forward in making the change to horses than those in the northeast. According to the reporters for Lebanon (1800) and Lisbon (1800), farmers in these towns still preferred their ox carts, and used few horses, perhaps because they had not adequately improved their roads.[26] Connecticut farmers did not commonly use four-wheel wagons until 1800; they were still a novelty in Windham in 1809.[27] People in the coastal towns used coastal vessels whenever possible if they had to travel or ship goods.[28]

The higher speed horses could attain came at a price. In his Madison report, David D. Field tells how on November 9, 1827, the horse pulling the Reverend John Ely's wagon near the end of the Durham & Madison Turnpike suddenly dashed forward "with the greatest fury," turned, and capsized the wagon, throwing the driver upon the ground. Ely, carried to a neighboring house, lay helpless and speechless until he died.[29]

Oxen, though slow, were more reliable.

The increased pace of commerce during the period of the Town Reports also meant that people wanted faster, more reliable mail service. Mail delivery by post rider in British

Fig. 1. *John W. Barber's drawing shows the the multiple-span, trestle bridge supported by four piers that crossed the Housatonic River to connect Derby, on the east bank, with Huntington, on the west bank. From John Warner Barber,* Connecticut Historical Collections *(New Haven: Durrie, Peck and Barber, 1838) p. 197.*

North America began between New York and Boston in 1673 by way of New Haven, Hartford, and Springfield, the original Post Road route. Benjamin Franklin improved the organization of the service by having milestones placed along the route in 1751.[30] Post riders also used a middle route from New Haven passing through Coventry and Pomfret. In 1784 the postal service moved mail from New Haven to New York City twice a week, and once to Boston by the northern Post Road.[31] In 1794 the postal authorities added the route along the shore line (today US Highway 1) to the mail route from Georgia to Maine. In Middlesex county, additional post roads radiated from Middletown to New London in 1800, to Saybrook in 1802, to Windham in 1814, and to Colchester and to Killingworth in 1817.[32] Similar developments probably took place in the other counties, although not remarked upon in any of the Town Reports. Stagecoaches plied the lower Post Road route from 1794 carrying mail and passengers until steamboats took away much of their trade, rendering the line unprofitable in 1832. Service was resumed in 1837 and continued until construction of the Shore Line Railroad. Stages had been running from New Haven to Hartford since 1785.[33]

Methods of road construction failed to attract the attention of any of the Town Report writers. The town supervisors probably simply continued to use the traditional techniques of colonial times until some of the turnpike companies began to set a higher standard for road building at the end of the eighteenth century.

Bridges

A dense network of streams with a reliable flow all year, offering abundant waterpower sites for mills and factories, was one of Connecticut's most valuable natural resources through the nineteenth century. However, numerous rivers meant that towns had to build a lot of bridges.

In 1789 Christopher Colles published a series of route maps for roads in the eastern states based on surveys he carried out with the aid of his perambulator. This device measured distances by counting the revolutions of the wheel of known diameter. Each map, drawn to scale, showed the crossroads, dwellings, smithies, taverns, and waterways the traveler would encounter. Parts of the routes Colles mapped from New York City to Stratford and from Stratford to Albany passed through Connecticut. Along this stretch of 65 miles of road there were fords at two tiny streams, and a larger ford over the Mill River in Southport. All other crossings were bridged.[34]

Throughout the period covered by the Town Reports, artisans met most of the state's need for bridges with traditional, colonial techniques.[35] Towns owned and maintained bridges. Occasionally an individual would build a bridge to sell to his town for cash or for remission of taxes. Gifts from townspeople financed the first bridge in New Milford, built in 1736. The town rebuilt it in 1741, and collected tolls for ten years to pay for it. Other towns used lotteries: Windsor raised £250 in 1762 and Norwich £600 in 1772 for bridge construction.[36]

The correspondent for New London, who wrote in about 1812, reported that to cross the smallest streams, builders set flat stones on abutments also built of stone, and covered them with turf placed grass side down so that continued growth of roots would retain the soil.[37] Builders crossed larger streams with bridges consisting of a deck built on stringer beams with the girts, joists, and floorboards familiar to anyone who had built a barn. Artisans managed to bridge waterways up to forty feet wide with single stringer trestles. They crossed larger streams by placing trestles between timber or stone piers set

Fig. 2. *A narrow, king-post bridge adjacent to the Windham Company's cotton factory carried a town road into the village of Willimantic. From John Warner Barber,* Connecticut Historical Collections *(New Haven: Durrie, Peck and Barber, 1838), p. 446*

on the stream bottom.[38] Lisbon's four large bridges, 140 to 200 feet long, rested on piers.[39] Barber's drawing of Derby (Fig. 1) shows trestles resting on four piers crossing the Housatonic to Huntington (now Shelton).[40] Farmington had four such bridges from a hundred to a hundred and fifty feet long. Bridge builders here drew on the town's abundant supply of easily-quarried sandstone for their abutments and piers.[41]

Westport's bridge over the Saugatuck River used causeways on pilings from each shore leading to pairs of stringer trestles on piers and a draw in the center.[42] Bridges might be much narrower than the roads they served, as in Barber's view of Willimantic (Fig. 2) showing a narrow king-post bridge adjacent to the Windham Company's cotton factory. Piers in a swift stream, such as the Housatonic, were best placed in diamond-shaped boxes filled with stone. Along the Housatonic, ice, trees, or other debris lodged against the piers led to destruction of bridges every seven to ten years.[43] Since the builders of the trestle bridges did not use covers to keep the rain off the timbers, rot destroyed them every ten to fifteen years.[44]

Some builders used causeways made of stone and earth

Fig. 3. *A long trestle bridge supported on multiple piers crossed the head end of Bridgeport harbor. Here shallow water made sinking the piers a relatively easy task. From John Warner Barber,* Connecticut Historical Collections *(New Haven: Durrie, Peck and Barber, 1838), p. 371.*

to reduce the width they had to span with their bridge decks. In Farmington, the flood plain adjacent to the bridges allowed flood waters to spread out and move at low speed, thereby sparing the bridge structures, while in Lebanon the causeways reduced the clear space for the flow of flood waters, leaving them subject to damage from heavy rain.[45]

Bridge builders crossed the shallow water at the upper ends of the harbors at New Haven and Bridgeport by setting a series of stringer trestles on piles driven into the muddy estuary bottom. Builders in Bridgeport crossed 1,320 feet of water with a twenty-four-foot wide bridge in 1791. They built a swing span at the center to allow vessels to pass.[46] (This bridge appears in Barber's drawing of the harbor [Fig. 3].)[47] At the head of the harbor in New Haven, builders in 1798 used stone causeways extending from either shore to cover half the 2,600-foot span of water, and completed their bridge with twenty-seven-foot wide wooden stringer trestles set on piles. Marine worms ate through the piles every five to six years, leaving the proprietors with expensive repairs to make. After an 1807 storm destroyed the structure, they had the causeways extended so as to leave only a 500-foot gap to be covered by the pile-supported trestles.[48]

The Connecticut River was the largest challenge faced by the state's bridge builders. We lack Town Reports describing

the first bridge in the state to cross the Connecticut River, between Enfield and Suffield, or the early bridge at Hartford. The thousand-foot-long Enfield-Suffield bridge, built in 1808 at a cost of $26,000, had trestles resting on six stone piers. Hartford's bridge of comparable length cost over $100,000.[49] The builders of both bridges avoided reliance on sophisticated design principles through their use of numerous piers to support trestles of conventional length.

Bridge Design

Europeans had started writing treatises on bridge engineering in the early eighteenth century. However, the first printed exposition of the basic theory of bridge engineering to reach the United States appeared in the American version of the third edition of the *Encyclopedia Britannica*, published in Philadelphia in 1798. Thomas Pope wrote the first text by an American author, his *Treatise on Bridge Architecture*, in 1811.[50] No one in Connecticut seems to have made much use of these ideas before 1830. The Town Reports describe only one bridge with construction more sophisticated than those built with colonial technique, Col. Ezra Brainerd's wooden arch built before 1819 to carry the Middletown, Durham & New Haven Turnpike over the Pameacha River in Middletown. Brainerd sprung a 160-foot-chord pine-timber arch from bedrock exposed on each bank fifty feet above the stream. The bridge cost $3,000, and the turnpike company contributed an additional $500 for its ironwork.[51] (The site of this bridge is on South Main Street immediately south of Warwick Street.)

Brainerd's bridge in Middletown could not be considered a remarkable engineering achievement since Lewis Wernwag had built a wooden arch-truss bridge with a 340-foot span over the Schuykill in Philadelphia in 1812. Other American bridge designers in the era of the Town Reports include Timothy Palmer, a native of Newburyport, Massachusetts, who built numerous bridges in Pennsylvania, and James Finley, a Pennsylvanian builder of suspension bridges. His 1826 span

Fig. 4. *Towns typically roofed and sheathed their lattice-truss bridges to protect the timber from rot, as here in Windsor. Barber's drawing shows two piers providing extra support for this bridge suggesting, perhaps, a lack of trust in the strength of the newfangled timber truss on the part of Windsor's selectmen. From John Warner Barber,* Connecticut Historical Collections *(New Haven: Durrie, Peck and Barber, 1838), p. 124.*

over the Lehigh River in Palmerton remained in service until 1933.[52]

Ithiel Town is the only Connecticut individual from the days of early republic now likely to be mentioned in histories of bridge building. Town, born to a farm family in 1784 in

Fig. 5. *Removal of the sheathing from the side of this bridge exposed the lattice truss to view. The diagonal braces that gave the trusses transverse stability can be seen under the roof. Carpenters, like those shown here, could build or repair lattice-truss bridges without the aid of specialized tools or equipment. (Photograph by Charles Rufus Harte, courtesy of Fred Chesson.)*

Thompson, Connecticut, had little formal schooling. He learned enough of the elements of architecture through working with carpenters to design New Haven's Center Church in 1812, and supervise its building over the next two years.[53] In his subsequent career as an architect, Town designed many distinguished buildings.

In 1820 Town obtained a patent on the design of the lattice bridge truss later known as the "Town truss." At that time the patent office made little effort to determine originality or prior invention. Vermont carpenters had used the lattice truss design that Town later patented at least as early as 1813 in a bridge over Otter Creek in Pittsford. (This bridge was still in service in 1934.) It was relatively easy for an enterprising, articulate individual to patent something that artisans had developed, and few rural carpenters would have had the resources or connections to challenge Town's patent.

Town promoted use of the lattice truss design, and collected royalties that contributed substantially to his wealth.[54] Even though they had to pay royalties to Town, builders could still save money by replacing old stringer-trestle bridges by lattice trusses. A lattice-truss replacement for the Enfield-Suffield bridge over the Connecticut River in 1832 cost $11,000 less than the original structure.[55] An illustration of a typical Connecticut lattice-truss bridge appears in Barber's drawing for Windsor (Fig. 4).[56] Town corrected the lack of transverse rigidity in the simple lattice truss with the addition of an improved superstructure, which he patented in 1835.[57] He claimed that his truss gave the greatest strength with the least weight. He could not have based this claim on any quantitative analysis because his lattice truss was a highly indeterminate structure (meaning that the forces acting on its various members cannot be determined by the direct calculation from the basic

principles of statics), and no one had an adequate theory of trusses to use for such design work until the mid-nineteenth century.[58] The great practical advantage of the lattice truss was that, built entirely with planks and timbers, fastened with pins only, and free of mortises, it could be built, or repaired, by men lacking specialized skills in joinery (Fig. 5). New Haven historians described the one-hundred-foot span built in 1823 to carry the Hartford Turnpike over the Mill River as the first to be constructed on the lattice truss plan.[59] As previously mentioned, this belief was mistaken.

Colonial Connecticut's road and bridge builders plied their traditional craft methods uninstructed by eighteenth-century improvements in European practice. In the years of the early republic, the French concepts of rationalism embraced by the United States military did not influence the execution of Connecticut civil works as they did its infant arms industry. No institution in the state — certainly not Yale — undertook anything like the instruction offered at France's School of Bridges and Roads. Despite the high value the people of Connecticut put on education, their state remained barren ground for engineering methods and theory. New England bridge builders such as Timothy Palmer did their best work elsewhere.

Only after 1830 was Connecticut's professional elite ready to start applying engineering principles to their civil works projects. In 1833 Horatio Potter, a professor of mathematics at Washington (now Trinity) College and later an Episcopal bishop, designed a 104-foot stone arch to carry Hartford's Main Street over the Little River. Potter's arch stands today as strong as ever, but with its appearance diminished by the construction of the Whitehead Highway over the Little River, and the intrusion of a support structure for the Hartford Public Library.[60]

Ferries

The earliest public ferries were owned by the towns. As early as 1657 the legislature began granting ferry monopolies in exchange for guarantees of service: in that year John Bissel, Jr., received a ferry monopoly at Windsor provided he offered regular crossings at fixed rates. By 1750 Connecticut had four ferries crossing the Thames, twelve over the Connecticut, six on the Housatonic, and one each over the Niantic, Quinnipiac, and Saugatuck. Thereafter, bridges began to replace ferries except on the largest crossings.[61]

By the time the Academy undertook its survey, Connecticut towns had built bridges over most of the rivers that people previously had crossed on ferries. Street names, such as Ferry Street, often survive as indicators of the locations of ferries replaced by bridges. In New Haven, two ferries had provided service across the Quinnipiac River until the town's Proprietors of the Common and Undivided Lands granted a group of entrepreneurs a subsidy in 1798 to build the bridge described above at the head of the harbor.[62] By the time Timothy Dwight wrote his report for the Academy, New Haven had replaced all its ferries by bridges.

Travelers in the early republic had to use ferries to cross the larger rivers, such as the Thames and the lower reaches of and the Connecticut. Pratt's ferry still crossed between

Wethersfield and Glastonbury in 1838.[63] New London used the revenue from its ferry to Groton to support a school.[64] The Connecticut River below Hartford remained a challenge to the builders of wooden bridges. A regular ferry service between Saybrook and Lyme carried travelers over the river near its mouth beginning in 1662. Farther upriver, Chapman's ferry provided service between Haddam and East Haddam after 1694. Thereafter proprietors added additional ferries during prosperous times as travel and trade expanded. The first group of additions included Brockway's in 1724 (Essex to North Lyme), Middletown to Chatham (now Portland) in 1726, and in 1735 the Knowles Landing Ferry from Middletown to Middle Haddam (1735). The period of prosperity just before the Revolution saw the addition of the Upper Houses Ferry between Middletown and Chatham (1759), the Higganum to Middle Haddam (1763), and Warner's in 1769 (Chester to Hadlyme). The final additions came with the East Haddam Ferry (to Haddam) in 1811, and the Haddam Ferry (Haddam to Middle Haddam) in 1814.[65]

As with bridges, Connecticut used both public and private ownership of the ferries. Towns owned two, the Higganum and the Middletown to Chatham; proprietor entrepreneurs ran the rest.

Financing and Maintaining the Road System

Through colonial times and into the period covered by the Town Reports, people in Connecticut used both public and private funding to pay for the their roads, bridges, and ferries. The Town Reports give us only sketchy information about the sources of the money used to build roads. We learn, however, that Guilford residents raised the money for their 1648 bridge over the East River by subscription. Stratfield used a lottery granted in 1791 to raise $7,000 for the bridge it built across the head of Bridgeport harbor. In Kent, the town maintained three of the four bridges over the Housatonic, each of which cost about $1,000, while tolls covered the cost of the fourth.[66]

In 1793 New Haven gave a group of private investors the right to collect tolls for twenty years as an inducement to build the Dragon Bridge (named after an adjoining tavern) to carry Grand Avenue over the Quinnipiac River. The town subsequently raised money by lottery to make this a free bridge.[67] Proprietors issued $60,000 worth of stock to pay for repairs to the bridge at the head of New Haven Harbor after damage caused by a storm in 1807, as described previously. Isaac Tomlinson subscribed over half of the necessary funds, thereby attaching his name to the crossing. It has remained the Tomlinson Bridge through several rebuildings to the present day.[68] In the last third of the nineteenth century the city purchased the Tomlinson Bridge from the private company that owned it, and appropriated funds to modernize it.[69]

The Town Reports have more to say about road maintenance than about construction. Rain runoff, frost heave, fallen trees, and ruts made by carts, wagons, and walking animals all damaged roads. Through the years of the early republic most towns continued the colonial system of road repairs. Selectmen in each town designated districts, each under a supervisor of highways. The supervisors were to call out all able-bodied men to mend roads as needed. In Cornwall, the supervisors issued the call four days a year, or more if necessary. Goshen's selectmen divided the town into twenty districts. Everyone who responded to the supervisor's call received eighty-five cents for a day's work in the spring, but only sixty-five cents in the fall, when both work and road conditions would have been better. Workers could apply the payments toward their taxes.[70] Some supervisors evidently did their work badly: The reporter for Farmington remarked on the "desultory and unsystematic" use of tax money on roads.[71]

The costs of road maintenance reported by the various towns varied substantially (Table I) while the tax rates for roads, where reported, were about the same in most towns (Table II). The data in both tables show the relatively heavy burden roads placed on the towns with small populations. Since these needed road networks nearly as extensive as the more populous towns, the burden necessarily fell more heavily on their citizens.

A mixture of public and private funding had financed Connecticut's roads, bridges, and ferries 170 years with indifferent results. In 1790 the state was about to make a serious commitment to privatization in an effort to improve its internal communications.

Turnpikes

The frustrations and difficulties the General Assembly encountered getting decent roads and bridges built and properly maintained throughout Connecticut led it in 1792 to try privatizing roads. England had shown the way to user support of roads with its 1663 turnpike act, subsequently expanded by the General Turnpike Act of 1767. Virginia created America's first turnpike in 1785 by allowing a group of proprietors to collect tolls to pay for maintenance of a heavily-used road. The 1790s were propitious for privatization in Connecticut. Its citizens disliked taxation, and many did not want to pay for roads that primarily benefited travelers from elsewhere. Merchants who had accumulated wealth from foreign trade were ready to make promising investments. Since the coastal towns lacked water privileges, manufacturers had to set up their factories along the inland rivers, and needed roads to bring in raw materials and ship out products. The existing roads, still in dreadful condition, could not meet their needs.[72]

Connecticut followed the example of England and Virginia in 1792 by issuing charters to proprietors that allowed them to sell stock; build roads; and collect tolls to pay for construction, maintenance, and debt service. They opened the nation's second and third turnpikes, the Mohegan road in New London county and a section of the Old Post Road in Greenwich. By 1803 the General Assembly had chartered fifty turnpike companies. They had completed thirty-nine roads totalling 770 miles, and had already achieved substantial improvements for the travelling public.[73] In their enthusiasm for the new scheme, people thought of turnpike shares as sound investments that would yield a high rate of return. Professional men, merchants, farmers, and manufacturers eagerly bought shares in turnpikes that served their towns, regarding them as local enterprises of civic importance. On some roads shareholders substituted their labor in place of cash for their shares, and took on responsibility for maintenance of sections of the finished road.[74] The minute book of the Killingworth & Haddam Turnpike records, "Voted that each proprietor shall thoroughly repair his share or shares as they fall to him by the 10th day of June in each year." If the repairs were not done, the directors would have them made at the expense of the negligent proprietor.[75]

Connecticut gave turnpike proprietors the right of eminent domain, and made turnpike stock free of taxation. Although the state government invested in banks and other private

the commission's powers to cover all Connecticut turnpikes. Two commissioners were to examine each turnpike annually; they had power to compel the owners to make necessary repairs. Additionally, the state required that turnpikes revert to public ownership once they earned a 12 percent return for their owners. (No turnpike company ever attained this rate of return.)[77]

Connecticut's completed network of turnpike roads interconnected all parts of the state (Fig. 6). Unlike the turnpikes in Massachusetts and Rhode Island, Connecticut's road system neither favored nor excluded any region. The Massachusetts turnpikes radiated from Boston through the eastern half of the state, with none extending beyond the Connecticut River.

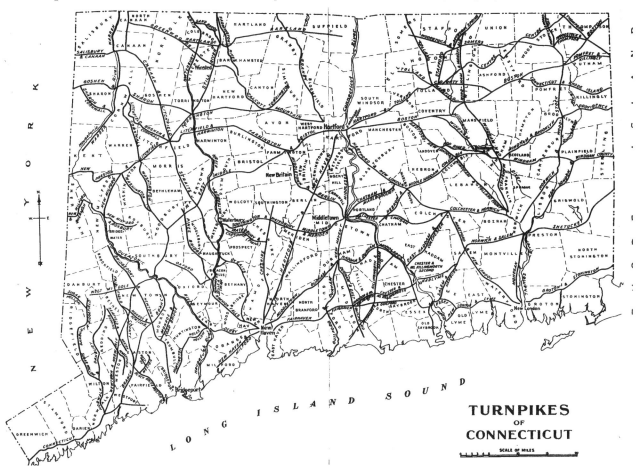

Fig. 6. *Connecticut's turnpikes formed a network that reached every part of the state, thereby serving its widely-dispersed population.* Frederic J. Wood, The Turnpikes of New England *(Boston: Marshall Jones Co., 1919).*

enterprises, it never put public money into turnpike shares. Only two towns, Waterbury and Norwalk, made turnpike investments. Both intended, and failed, to capture trade going elsewhere.[76]

While the turnpikes were truly private enterprises, they operated as regulated public utilities. Each road charter specified the spacing of gates (usually every ten miles) and the toll rates the proprietors could charge. The same year that Connecticut chartered its first turnpike, it appointed a commission to supervise the company, and in 1803 broadened

Three crossed Massachusett's southwest corner, carrying Connecticut roads on toward Albany. All of Rhode Island's turnpike roads radiated from Providence. Six of these joined Connecticut roads at the state line.[78]

Most people in Connecticut favored, or at least accepted, privatization of roads. They liked the idea of roads supported by those who benefited from them, and remembered how ineffective public control of roads had been. The turnpike companies effected large improvements in road standards: all were built wide enough for vehicles to pass whereas most previous roads offered only the occasional passing place. The state-mandated tolls took the most money from those who could afford to pay. Whereas turnpike companies in Pennsylvania charged toll rates that reflected the damage different kinds of vehicles did to their roads,[79] in Connecticut the toll on a four-wheel pleasure carriage was twice that on a loaded wagon, regardless of the load the wagon carried. The proprietors of the Guilford & Durham charged 25 cents for a pleasure carriage, but only 9 cents for an ox cart or wagon drawn by two or more horses, whether loaded or empty. Wealthy visitors were to pay more than the town's industrious farmers. Persons going to gristmills, church, funerals, military duty, town meetings, or to vote travelled free of toll.[80]

Objections often centered on particular gates where a company collected tolls on what had previously been a public road, or on towns' responsibilities for maintenance of the bridges used by the turnpikes. If the residents of a town didn't see any advantage to themselves in a proposed road, they might have their representatives in the General Assembly oppose its authorization. When a group of Norwich merchants petitioned for a road from the East Haddam ferry to New Haven to facilitate their trade in 1810, the Guilford town meeting authorized its representatives to oppose the bill unless it were altered so that there would be no expense to the town.[81]

The Connecticut turnpike network reflected the absence of a dominant city and the uniform distribution of population in the state. It did not concentrate benefits on one city, or benefit particular branches of industry or agriculture. In contrast, farmers in eastern Rhode Island expressed their resistance to the concentration of economic power in Providence and chartered corporations' infringement of their traditional independence by resisting turnpike charters in the legislature, and by threatening violence against company officials.[82]

Local interests organized and financed construction of many of Connecticut's turnpikes. They got them built with no more professional assistance than that of the neighborhood surveyor. Thus, in 1823 Nathaniel Griffing, an entrepreneurial resident of Guilford, thought he and his town could benefit from an improved road to the north. It could induce travelers on boats from New York to disembark at Sachem Head harbor, where Griffing planned to build a hotel, and continue their journeys to Hartford overland rather than by the Connecticut River route, which was liable to be closed by ice in the winter. With fellow townsmen Samuel Eliot and Joel Tuttle, Griffing obtained a charter from the legislature, held the requisite public meeting, and raised the $5,100 capital they needed. After surveyors staked out the road for them, they paid out $1,792 of their capital for land damages, and had their road completed within a year by incorporating existing roads fixed up with minor improvements into their route.[83]

The Middlesex and Guilford reports included data on the cost of turnpike construction (Table III). The costs shown in Table III reflect Connecticut's two types of turnpike franchise, and two standards of road construction. The most common franchise gave a turnpike company an old road in bad repair to rebuild. Less commonly, the franchise required the company to build an entirely new road. In this case the company had to acquire the necessary land for the new road, and build new bridges as specified by its charter. Land damages added significantly to the cost of a turnpike. The Derby Turnpike Company took over an existing road, and had a total cost of $775 per mile. The Hartford & New Haven, a new road, went through valuable land. The company paid $531 per mile for land damages alone.[84]

For the ordinary standard of road construction, the company was expected to reduce the grade over hills, dig drainage ditches along the roadside, and form a convex road surface with the soil at hand. This cost about $500, and rarely more than $1,000, per mile. The higher standard of turnpike construction required the company to build a gravel surface deep enough to withstand frost. Roads made this way were known as "artificial roads" because of the use of brought-in surface material. A well-surfaced road reduced the cost of moving freight from about twenty-five cents to fifteen cents per ton-mile. Such roads might cost as much as $2,500 per mile to build.[85] Connecticut's most expensive turnpike, the New Haven to Hartford, cost $2,280 per mile, which included the cost of planting trees and landscaping along the route.[86] This was far less than the $7,500 per mile cost of the famous Philadelphia to Lancaster Turnpike in Pennsylvania, which had a stone surface for its entire length.[87]

One factor that helped the turnpike companies to keep down their cost was their use of town-owned and maintained bridges. Usually a company had to pay for bridges only at major river crossings. The cost of a major bridge, such as the one that carried the New Preston Turnpike over the Housatonic River (Fig. 7) could be a significant burden on the company.

The guiding principle favored by turnpike builders throughout the United States was to make their roads as nearly straight as possible. This reduced the distance between their end points and so minimized construction costs. Adherence to this principle in hilly Connecticut resulted in steep grades that could have been avoided by more circuitous routes. While a grade of 1/20 was generally accepted as tolerable, many Connecticut turnpikes had steeper grades. Steep grades discouraged the commercial traffic that could have generated much needed revenue to many turnpike companies.[88]

Table III shows that only the Middletown & Meriden and the Middletown & New Haven turnpikes among those covered in the Town Reports had been built to a high standard of construction, while the rest received little more than modest improvement when taken over by turnpike proprietors. A walk over the surviving section of the Cornwall & Washington Turnpike where it crosses the Crooked Esses in Cornwall will show anyone interested just how little some of the turnpike proprietors did in improving their roads. Some of the better turnpikes, such as the Middletown & New Haven, eventually made good routes for state highways that required little re-alignment.

We lack any detailed map of Connecticut's town roads

from the period of the Academy Reports. However, comparison with the Town Reports and with Wood's compilation and map (Fig. 6) shows that the Warren and Gillet map accurately records the turnpikes completed by 1811. By that time the turnpikes gave the entire state a network of through roads. Warren and Gillet include, however, only a few of the non-turnpike roads, and were inconsistent in showing river crossings by bridges. Of the Town Reports, only the one for Willington gives a reasonably complete inventory of the town's bridges: it had three over the Willimantic (there are four today), seven over Fenton's River (eleven today), and three across Roaring Brook (four today). Warren and Gillet showed one each. The comparison with the number of bridges over these streams today suggests that Willington residents were well served by bridges in 1805.

In his description of travel between New London and Montville Barber noted that, since New London was the port of entry for Norwich, that town's merchants had to travel there frequently. Before 1792 few of them tried to make the round trip in a single day, and pleasure carriages never attempted it. "The former road was perfectly fitted to force upon the public mind the utility of turnpike roads... ." After construction of the turnpike between the two cities, the state's first, travelers could easily complete the journey along a smooth and good road in two hours.[89]

Many of the town reporters remarked on the improvement effected by the turnpikes, and the benefits they brought to their communities. Some, such as the reporters for Litchfield and Guilford, thought the turnpikes the only roads worth mentioning. Lebanon reported that the stage road from Norwich to Hartford was a heavy expense until turnpiked, while Wallingford reported that the turnpikes built since 1801 greatly improved the roads through town. Middlesex county had bad roads until its principal roads were turnpiked. By 1819, thirteen turnpikes had opened communications with all parts of the country.[90]

Farmers in Goshen had to ship their exports to the port towns on ox carts or sleds until the turnpikes built by 1811 led them to switch to horse-drawn wagons. In Pennsylvania, the cost of hauling freight per ton mile on turnpikes was half that on ordinary roads, despite the need to pay tolls.[91] Connecticut

shippers probably realized similar savings. The higher standard of quality achieved on the turnpikes relative to that on publicly-financed roads served as an example to the people of Goshen, showing them what could be accomplished and inducing them to improve their local roads. The Guilford selectmen used turnpikes as a standard, as in their 1821 specification that "The highway at East River is to be 18 feet wide and handsomely raised in the middle like a well made turnpike road." Additionally, by taking over the cost of the main roads, the turnpike companies released funds that townspeople could apply to improve their common roads.[92]

Fig.7. *Bulls Bridge carried the New Preston Turnpike over the Housatonic River in the town of Kent. The turnpike company used a lattice truss for the span. The substantial stone abutments kept the bridge above the flood waters that eventually swept away most of the covered bridges that crossed the Housatonic. This early twentieth-century picture shows the bridge little changed from its 1842 construction. To help carry the weight of modern motor vehicles, the state highway department placed steel girders beneath the deck in 1969. (Photograph by Charles Rufus Harte, courtesy of Fred Chesson.)*

Manufacturers may have been the greatest beneficiaries of the turnpike roads. Great loads of baled wool, cotton, and merchandise were to be seen moving along the Hartford & New Haven. The Greenwoods turnpike saw a big increase in traffic as factories were built along its route in the 1820s and 1830s. Additional evidence shows that turnpikes served 88 percent of all inland factories in Connecticut and Massachusetts.[93]

Public Roads in the Turnpike Era

Turnpikes proved valuable to the general welfare, but none ever attained the profitability that would have automatically triggered its conversion to a public road. Only the Derby Turnpike gave its investors a reasonable return, paying an average dividend of 5.1 percent through nearly a century of operation.[94] Owners of poorly planned turnpikes

To
George Griswold
Collector & Surveyor
of Highways for
1816
Sum Total $90..75
11 Cents for a man & } pr ho[ur]
12 Cents for a Team
And you are hereby directed to
Lay out $10 of the above sum
on the Stage Road —
Saml. Fowler Town Cl[erk]

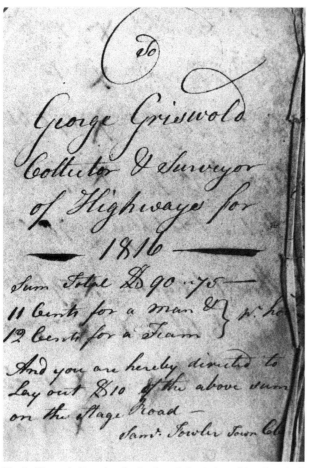

Fig. 8. *Towns built and maintained roads by their traditional methods through the turnpike era. Samuel Fowler, the Guilford town clerk, issued this booklet to George Griswold, one of the town's collectors and surveyors of highways, in 1816. Griswold was to collect the road tax from each property owner in his district, either by involuntary labor at the rate of 11 cents per hour for a man and 12 cents for a team, or in cash. (Courtesy of the Guilford Keeping Society and the Guilford Free Library.)*

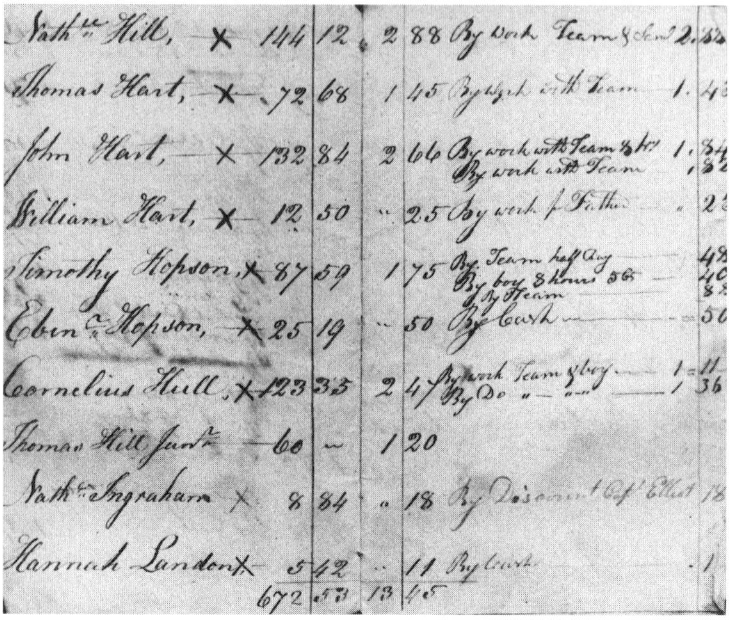

began abandoning their roads as early as 1814. In the face of competition from railroads, turnpike proprietors cut back on maintenance, and accelerated the pace of abandonment in the 1840s. The last turnpike road (the Derby) passed into public ownership in 1895.[95] Most turnpike owners received nothing for their property, thereby losing their initial investments.[96]

Roads not privatized remained firmly in local control throughout the turnpike era. The Guilford town archives show that the selectmen laid out roads as authorized by the town meeting, paid damages to those whose land was taken for these roads, received petitions for repair of roads citizens thought defective or for rerouting roads considered inconvenient. In only two cases among the petitions for the period 1800 to 1845 did townsmen feel sufficiently dissatisfied with the selectmens' decision to carry their requests to the county court.

The selectmen hired townsmen to carry out tasks that would later be entrusted to professionals. Abraham Chittenden received $2.06 for one day's service as Committee to lay out a road to Blackrock on October 7, 1805. Each of the seventeen men designated Collector and Surveyor of Highways had the duty of collecting the road tax, either in labor or cash. In 1816 the rate was 2 cents per dollar of property valuation, and nine out of every ten men paid it by working on the roads. They received 11 cents per hour, and an additional 12 cents per hour if they brought a team (Fig. 8; Fig. 9). These rates remained unchanged over the next decade. By 1836 the town had raised the tax to 3 cents on the dollar, and had reduced the rate it allowed for work to 9 cents, with 11 cents for a team. By then only 10 percent of the townspeople met the road tax by their own labor.[97] Five years later the town had dropped the work option: everyone paid their road tax in cash. Thus, when Connecticut replaced the colonial system of involuntary road labor with the alternative of work or cash payment, citizens (in Guilford, a representative town) gradually opted out of road work in favor of paying cash.[98]

Survivals

While Connecticut has a rich heritage of houses from colonial and early republic times that can show us aspects of domestic life, little physical evidence of its transportation system remains for us to study. Repeated rebuildings have destroyed most traces of the early roads, except where towns have

Nathl Hill, ×	144	12	2 88	By work Team & [illegible]	2.[illegible]
Thomas Hart, ×	72	68	1 45	By work with Team	1.4[illegible]
John Hart, ×	132	84	2 64	By work with Team & [illegible] / By work with Team	1.84 / [illegible]
William Hart, ×	12	50	.. 25	By work of Father	.2[illegible]
Timothy Hopson, ×	87	59	1 75	By Team half day / By boy 8 hours 56 / By Team	48 / 4[illegible] / [illegible]
Eben. Hopson, ×	25	19	.. 50	By Cash	50
Cornelius Hull, ×	123	35	2 47	By work Team & boy / By Do	1.11 / 1 36
Thomas Hill Junr	60	—	1 20		
Nathl Ingraham ×	8	84	.. 18	By Discount [illegible] Elliot	18
Hannah Landon ×	5	42	.. 11	By Cash	.1[illegible]
	672	53	13 45		

Fig. 9. *Guilford's town clerk entered the valuation of each property and the tax each owner had to pay in the collector and surveyor's booklet. The collector then recorded how each person paid, as in the examples here, by work, work with team, by boy and team, by work of father, or by cash. (Courtesy of the Guilford Keeping Society and the Guilford Free Library.)*

abandoned formerly-used routes. The occasional early-nineteenth-century milestone is still to be found.[99] One surviving, unimproved segment that can be walked to get an idea of what early roads were like is the part of County Road in Guilford and Madison now on the land of the Regional Water Authority. A walk down the unaltered, surviving section of the Greenwoods Turnpike in North Canaan (Fig. 10) shows the improvements effected by the better turnpike companies.[100]

No bridge from the period covered in the Town Reports is listed on the National Register, or in the Department of Transportation's historical booklet.[101] However, the brownstone arch and spandrels of the bridge over Allyn's Brook built in 1823 for the Middletown, Durham, and New Haven Turnpike can be seen under the modern Route 17 highway bridge. Silas Bernard built this bridge for the turnpike company at a cost of $1,000 after a flood destroyed the previous structure in February 1822. The 30-foot long, 25-foot wide arch was covered with fill in a 1927 highway reconstruction, and exposed during road reconstruction in 1995.[102] A path allows a visitor to see the old bridge under the modern highway.

Two surviving significant bridges were built just after the 1830 end of the Academy's Town Report period. Farmington built the stone arch Pequabuck Bridge at Meadow Road in 1833 to replace wooden spans that the town had to rebuild in 1801 and 1819. The Bates Avenue Bridge in Putnam, although built about 1840, is representative of the small arch bridges built earlier.[103]

Travellers can still cross the Connecticut River on ferries operated by the state at two long-established sites. One ferry connects Rocky Hill with South Glastonbury. The second runs between Chester and Hadlyme.

Conclusion

Connecticut's early roads reflected Yankee ideas of practicality and individualism. Citizens at town meetings voted for roads barely adequate to meet their immediate needs, and balked at coordinating their efforts with those of their neighbors to create through routes for travelers. Then in the forty years between 1790 to 1830 Connecticut, by embracing privatization with state regulation, passed from dependence on colonial roads as bad as any in North America to a new road system that facilitated travel and served the needs of the state's expanding commerce and manufactures. Bridges crossing all but the lower reaches of the Connecticut River freed travelers from dependence on ferries. Both Timothy Dwight and Benjamin Silliman, vigorous explorers of the state, testified to how much the new turnpikes facilitated their travels. Silliman reported in 1819 that "The fine turnpike on which we commenced our journey, was, but a few years since, a most rugged uncomfortable road; now we passed it with ease and rapidity."[104]

In 1830 Connecticut stood poised to enter an era of new transportation systems. Some of the state's entrepreneurs had already caught the national enthusiasm for canals. As early as 1822 they formulated plans for a Ousatonic Canal that would follow the Housatonic River from the Sound into the northwest's ironmaking district. Potential investors were saved from heavy losses when the proprietors abandoned the project in 1825. Investors in New Haven's Farmington Canal, opened in 1828 and abandoned in 1847, were not so fortunate. Long winters and heavy grades that required numerous locks made canals a poor choice in Connecticut. Additionally, railroads would soon offer cheaper, more reliable, year-round transportation systems. The Academy Reports cover the period when people in Connecticut relied on roads and turnpikes for inland travel. For the next hundred years, railroads would claim most funds for new construction, leaving the roads to languish until the advent of motor vehicles.

Fig. 10. *This section of the Greenwoods Turnpike in North Canaan was never converted to use by motor vehicles. Although trees have intruded along the verge, the original size of the road and its relatively steep grade are evident. Traversing a turnpike by horseback or horse-drawn vehicle brought a traveler into a more intimate relation to the environment than is possible with travel over modern roads by motor vehicle. (Photograph by the author.)*

TABLE I
Annual Cost of Road Maintenance

Bethlehem	$0.45 per person or	$2.95 per household
Farmington	0.36	2.50
Franklin	0.90	5.88
Goshen	0.47	3.34
Preston	0.08	0.58

Notes: These data are calculated from the road costs included in the Town Reports, and town populations and households listed by Pease and Niles. The data for Preston are only the amount raised by tax; the low figure indicates that a substantial amount of the cost was not raised that way. [Pease, John C., and John M. Niles, *A Gazetteer of the States of Connecticut and Rhode Island*, Hartford: Marsh, 1819.]

TABLE II
Tax Rates for Road Work

	Rate	Population
Goshen	1.5 cents	1,631
Lebanon	1.0	2,580
Preston	1.5	1,764
Sharon	1.0	2,606
Union	3.0	750
Wallingford	1.5	2,325

Note: The tax rates in cents per dollar or property valuation are from the Town Reports, and the population data, from Pease and Niles. The dates of the reports range from 1800 (Lebanon) to 1812 (Goshen). [Pease, John C., and John M. Niles, *A Gazetteer of the States of Connecticut and Rhode Island*, Hartford: Marsh, 1819.]

TABLE III
Cost of Turnpike Construction

Name	Date	Length	Cost per Mile
Middlesex Turnpike	1802	32 miles	$291
Hebron & Middle Haddam	1802	13.5	594
Colchester & Chatham	1808	18	505
Middletown & Berlin	1808	20	747
Chatham & Marlborough	1809	10.5	865
East Haddam & Colchester	1809	10.5	599
Middletown & Meriden	1809	7	1,025
Durham & East Guilford	1811	14	714
Middletown & New Haven	1813	23.5	1,702
Killingworth & Haddam	1813	15.5	706
Beaver Meadow	1815	4.25	580
Haddam & Durham	1815	7.75	529
Chester & N. Killingworth	1816	7.15	420
Pautapaug & Madison	1818	16	625
Fair Haven	1824	19.2	391
Guilford & Durham	1824	17.5	291

Note: Data are from the Middlesex and Guilford reports. Taylor's table reports additional data. Philip E. Taylor, "*The Turnpike Era in New England*," Ph.D. diss., Yale University, 1934.

Mines, Minerals, Mineral Fuels, and Quarries: Connecticut, 1800-1832

H. Catherine W. Skinner and Brian J. Skinner

Introduction

Embedded in the information solicited by the Connecticut Academy of Arts and Sciences in 1800 are two rather interesting topics. The fifth and seventh articles of the Solicitation Letter, but mostly the fifth, asked individuals to comment on things that were literally beneath their feet. The fifth article asked about "Mines and Minerals, especially those most useful, as iron, copper, lead, silver, sulphur; also quarries of stone, with the kind and quality of the stone, and its distance from navigable water." The seventh asked about "Fuel of all kinds, as wood, coal, peat, or turf—the quantity and quality—distance from navigable water—increase or decrease of fuel, and price of the several kinds." These questions focused on the environment, on earth materials, on things that were useful—in fact essential—in their daily lives. The inhabitants of Connecticut sought from their sur-roundings the stones needed in constructing their houses, barns, and churches, their dams and wells; fortunately stones were plentiful and easily available in Connecticut. They sought mineral fuels, principally peat and coal, albeit not very successfully, and they scavenged and prospected for the metals they could use in their cookware, farm implements, and weapons. Every landowner would have scouted his territory for water and wood, but he would also have examined the rocks, and looked for any bounty that might be extracted from them. Evidence of those searches is recorded in names that have come down to us; for example, Lead Mines Hill in Union, Silvermine Road in Middletown, Coppermine Road in Oxford, and Isinglass Road in Portland. Iron deposits were eventually found, as were deposits of copper, barium sulfate, and tungsten, but unfortunately the bounty of Connecticut rocks was sparse compared to those in many of the later states to join the Union.

The historian of geology, Arthur Mirsky, pointed out in 1979 that "except for iron and building materials, at the beginning of the American Revolution the original thirteen states were not using their mineral resources to any significant extent." There were two reasons the original states did not develop thriving mining industries. The first reason was political: England discouraged the colonies from developing

Benjamin Silliman, Sr. (1779-1864) President of the Connecticut Academy of Arts and Sciences 1836-1847. Plate II in The First One Hundred Years of American Geology, *By George P. Merrill, Yale University Press (1924).*

any mineral industries that might be competitive with those in the mother country, and this had a dampening effect on investment for mining. Colonists were certainly aware the ores could be valuable but soon learned that deposits were hard to find and harder still to exploit. Challenging the mother country on the issue of minerals was rarely worth the fight. The second, and more important reason was geological: nature did not favor the development of a mining industry because, as Mirsky points out, the original colonies lay along the Atlantic coast where "the nature of the geology...is not especially favorable for significant mineral deposits. Thus the minerals known in the original colonies occurred in relatively small deposits compared to what would be discovered elsewhere beyond the Appalachians during the nineteenth and twentieth centuries."[1]

In 1800 very little was known about the geology of Connecticut. Indeed the whole field of geology was very little known in the new Republic. The first map showing details of mineral occurrences in North America was published in France in 1752 by Jean-Etienne Guettard.[2] A more important and more influential map was published in 1787 by Johann David Schöpf, who was a surgeon to the Hessian troops during the American Revolution, and who, following peace in 1783, made a tour from Canada to Florida.[3] It is hardly surprising that two maps published in Europe should be little known in the young United States of 1800 and that geology and mineralogy were strange names to most people. Dramatic changes for Connecticut geology started in the early 1800s with the appointment in 1802 of Benjamin Silliman, a recent graduate of Yale College, as Professor of Chemistry and Natural History at Yale, and with the first mineral assessment of the State in 1837 by Charles Upham Shepard, one of Silliman's former students.[4] Today the bedrock, the soil cover, and the minerals that make up the different rock types that are present in Connecticut have been carefully studied and described in detail by geologists. What is really surprising about Silliman's appointment is that, as George Merrill remarks in discussing the rise of geology in the United States, until then "none of the sciences were taught in the colleges and other institutions of learning in America or England...The movement, therefore, by President Dwight in 1798 toward the establishment in Yale College of a department for the teaching of these subjects, was of the greatest importance and of far-reaching consequences."[5] Dwight chose Benjamin Silliman for the new post. The authors of the Town Reports collected in Volume 1, many of whom had graduated from Yale, but much before Silliman began teaching geology, could hardly be aware of this new way of focusing on their environment. Silliman's contributions, outlined below, are a benchmark in the history of American science, showing clearly the transfer of a new field of knowledge from European centers to the fledgling United States.[6]

As we recount the portions of the Town Reports related to Articles 5 and 7, the modern reader will recognize that the authors, many of them landowners and farmers, obviously took their environment very seriously. They knew full well that their sustenance, their food and all their domestic comforts, as well as their economic well-being and future, depended on the stones they hauled, the rocks they quarried, the soils they tilled, the fields they pastured and manured, and the metals they could find and mine. Many of their answers were very brief, for example, Samuel Nott responded "Nothing" to Article 5 about mines and minerals.[7] A few respondents ignored one or both questions, but sufficient authors answered to allow a reasonable evaluation of the importance of metals and stone to the economies of the reporting towns. Although a few minor occurrences of peat[8] and coal were mentioned, no occurrence was sufficiently large to justify exploitation, so virtually all of the reporters who answered Article 7 did so in terms of wood. Wood is a renewable resource; once cut it can be re-grown. This essay addresses only mineral substances, metal, and mineral fuel, and does not evaluate wood and other renewable fuels.

The written contributions arrived from towns all over Connecticut, so it is helpful briefly to review the topography and the geology of the state in order to understand whence the reports originated.

The Topography of Connecticut

Connecticut comprises four distinct topographic regions. The Western Upland is all of the hilly, rolling lands lying westward of a line running from approximately West Haven, on the coast, to North Granby on the Massachusetts border. The highest elevation (Bear Mountain, 2,316 feet high), and the steepest terrains of the state, are in the Western Upland; these rugged lands pose major impediments to transport, and as a result the Western Upland was the last part of the state to be settled and developed by European colonists. The Eastern Upland, which includes all of the lands lying to the east of a line that runs approximately north-northeasterly from Lighthouse Point in New Haven through Middletown, north to Somers and into Massachusetts, is hilly but not so high and rugged as the elevated lands of the west.

The two upland regions are separated by a broad lowland, the Central Valley, which contains the Connecticut River within its northern two-thirds of length. The river rises in northern New Hampshire, flows south forming the border between Vermont and New Hampshire, through Massachusetts into Connecticut and then into Long Island Sound. Navigable throughout most of its length in Connecticut, the river and its tributaries, such as the Farmington, provided water access to the interior of the state and into neighboring Massachusetts. Such important towns as Northampton, Holyoke, and Springfield in Massachusetts, and Hartford and Middletown in Connecticut, are located on the banks of the Connecticut River—but the extensive river access of 1800 is now compromised by several dams. The Central Valley is a region of gentle slopes, low elevations and, for the most part, good soils. Productive soils, good pastures, and navigable access determined that the earliest European settlements in the State were in the Central Valley—Windsor, 1633; Wethersfield, 1634; Hartford, 1635; New Haven, 1638.[9] But not all of the Central Valley is flat and low. The steep-sided Metacomet Ridge

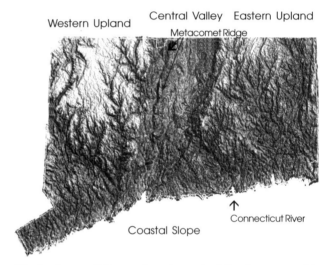

The landscape of Connecticut shows the following topographic divisions: the Eastern and Western Uplands which are separated by the broad Central Valley. Within the valley, the steep-sided Metacomet Ridge is a striking topographic high. Along the coast a region of gently rising topography is known as the Coastal Slope. Center for Earth Observation, courtesy Laurent Bonneau, August 2002.

separates the Central Valley into two parts. The Metacomet Ridge consists of tough, erosion-resistant basaltic layers that originally formed as lava flows. Within the northern half of the Valley the Ridge runs north-south and is close to the western side; south of Middletown the Ridge bends and runs east-west, preventing the further southward flow of the Connecticut River. As a result the river leaves the Central Valley at Middletown and has cut a deep channel through the rocks of the Eastern Uplands on its way to Long Island Sound.

The fourth geographic region is the Coastal Slope, a strip about ten miles wide of gently rising topography. Within the Slope the elevation rises gently inland at an average rate of about 50 feet per mile. The strip is hilly, not smooth, and the increase in elevation away from the coast is noted by a steady increase in the height of the hilltops. Drawing on evidence from the coastline south of New York, it is thought probable that the Coastal Slope in Connecticut was once a smooth surface covered by sediment, similar to that which today covers the coastal plain in New Jersey. Erosion exposed ancient rocks and produced today's topography; on the exposed topography the most recent glaciation deposited rock flour and boulders. Although not as productive as parts of the Central Valley, the glacial soils of the Coastal Slope nevertheless supported intensive farming. The gentle topography of the Coastal Slope, especially in the southern and central portions, makes for easier farming than the more rugged Eastern and Western Uplands. This fact, together with ready access to water transport along the nearby shore, favored agricultural development and therefore the early settlement of the Coastal Slope—the earliest towns of the Slope, almost coeval with those of the Central Valley, are Deep River (formerly Saybrook), 1635; Fairfield,

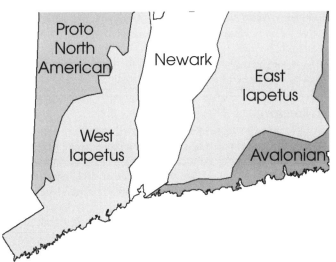

The four geological terranes of Connecticut: Proto North American, Iapetos, Newark and Avalonian. The origins and reasons for the names of the terranes are discussed in the text. Center for Earth Observation, courtesy Larry Bonneau, August 2002.

Guilford, Milford, and Stratford, all 1639.

Of the 49 responses to the Academy's Solicitation Letter presented in Volume I, three were duplicate reports, 21 came from towns and parishes in the Eastern Highlands, and from the Coastal Slope east of the Central Valley. From the Central Valley, there were nine reports, including those from Durham, Farmington, New Haven, and Wallingford. The remaining sixteen reports came from towns in the Western Highlands or towns located in the Coastal Slope to the west of the Central Valley.

By about 1675 arable lands of the Central Valley and the Coastal Slope had been claimed; newcomers were obliged to proceed inland up rivers, such as the Housatonic and Naugatuck, and seek their opportunities in the Uplands. The mostly glacial soils of the Uplands were as good for tillage and pasture as those of the Coastal Slope, but slopes were steeper, and while the Central Valley and Coastal Slope had been cleared by native Americans, dense forests still covered many of the hills of the Uplands. These had to be removed before farming could proceed beyond the narrow river valleys the

colonist had followed to enter the Uplands. Although settlement of the Uplands was slower than settlement of the Coastal Slope and Central Valley, land clearing and the spread of farming and pasturing in the Uplands proceeded rapidly. The first American geographer, Jedidiah Morse, reported in 1789 that the forests of Connecticut had been cleared, and the farms and towns of the Uplands were as populous as those of the Central Valley and Coastal Slope. The total population of the State he placed at 209,150.[10] Morse also reported that the abundant agricultural output of the State was so large that it played a major role in feeding the Revolutionary Army—at that time Connecticut was known as *The Provision State.* Testimony to the productiveness of the soils, and to the hard work of the farmers, can be found in Morse's assessment of the size of Connecticut's farms—they were small, ranging in size from fifty to four hundred acres. A good farmer could produce a bountiful yield from a small acreage.

Connecticut was founded and settled by colonists of mainly English origin. Their livelihood was agrarian, so it is hardly surprising that they went first to the places where soil was both accessible and easy to work. Unlike the later settlement of the western United States, where the search for mineral wealth played a major role in development, the distribution of mineral wealth had little to do with the settlement of Connecticut. However, mineral wealth, especially in iron, clay, brownstone, gravel, traprock, and granite, eventually did have a lot to do with the economy of the State, but except for iron and brownstone, much of the mineral economy postdated the time of the Town Reports.

Before drawing on what the Town Reports actually reported, we briefly discuss the geology so that the provenances of the materials that were mined and used can be more clearly understood and placed in the context of the environment of Connecticut as it was then and is today.

The Geological Terranes of Connecticut

Two centuries of research by geologists has revealed that over the past three billion years the continent of North America has slowly increased in size as it has grown outward from a core of ancient rocks. The ancient core, known as a craton, itself an assemblage of small pieces welded together, can be seen on the surface in Canada and in mid-continent United States near the border with Canada, where rocks ranging in age from 2.0 to 3.5 billion years can be found. Within the United States the core of ancient rocks continues south as far as Texas, but they are mostly covered by younger, flat-lying sedimentary rocks that are less than 500 million years old.[11]

Growth of the continent outward from this ancient core was spasmodic rather than regular. The continent grew larger over 2 billion years by capturing large rock masses from elsewhere—oceanic islands, volcanoes, even bits of other continents—and the attached masses were added to the sides of the craton by a process geologists call *continental accretion.* All of today's continents, we now know, are mixtures of different rock masses, some formed in place, some rafted in from elsewhere. Geologists refer to any large rock mass that is structurally discrete and different from adjacent masses of rock as a *terrane*. If a terrane is captured from elsewhere, the process of capture is called *accretion*, and the captured mass is an *accreted terrane*. In technical terms, geologists refer to a continent as an assemblage of terranes.

Connecticut consists of four terranes, one is part of the ancient continental core, two are accreted, and one is a strip of sedimentary rocks formed in place and layered across the center of the State. The whole concept of terranes and how continents grow by accretion was of course unknown at the time of the Town Reports.

The terranes of Connecticut are shown on the previous page. Read Michael Bell and Chet Raymo and Maureen Raymo for more detailed discussions of their origins.[12] The terranes have very different origins and, except for the Newark terrane, which coincides exactly with the Central Valley, the terrane boundaries do not coincide with pronounced topographic features—one has to look at the rocks themselves to detect the differences between the terranes. The most westerly, and most ancient terrane, was once the edge of North America as it existed a billion years ago. Known as the Proto-North American terrane, this body of ancient rocks occupies the western part of the Western Uplands. Two other terranes, both of them accreted, and called, respectively, the Iapetus and the Avalonian terranes, lie to the east of the Proto-North American terrane and were accreted between 500 and 300 million years ago. These two accreted terranes make up about 60 percent of the state; the Iapetus terrane is found in both the Western and Eastern Uplands, the Avalonian terrane is confined to the Eastern Uplands and the eastern half of the Coastal Slope. The fourth terrane, the Newark terrane, includes all of the rocks in the Central Valley. The Central Valley consists of sedimentary rocks and former lava flows that fill a long trough in the Earth's crust. The Newark terrane was not accreted; it was formed in place in the Late Triassic and Early Jurassic periods, about 200 million years ago, and is so named because its origin, and the rocks it contains, are identical to those of the rocks underlying northern New Jersey, including Newark.

Erosion

With the formation of the Newark terrane, a process that took 50 million years and ended about 150 million years ago, the basic framework of Connecticut was complete, and ever since then erosion has slowly etched and formed the landscape we see today. At some stage or stages the sea probably invaded the state and deposited a thin layer of sediment that is hypothesized to have covered the Coastal Slope, and probably went even farther inland. Today these sediments are gone, but odd clues of their former presence, such as a fossil log of a 100-million year old tree found in the gravels of the Housatonic River during dam construction, are tantalizing evidence of their former existence.[13] From geological evidence we know that at least 20 miles of rock have been eroded from the Iapetus terrane, during 300 million years or more, and also that the land surface of the Newark terrane has been lowered at least several miles over the past 150 million years.

The debris from the extensive erosion of the State has been carried eastward to the ocean by the streams and rivers of the State, and now lies offshore as a blanket of sediment that covers the eastern margin of North America.

Erosion is a slow process involving both chemical and physical changes. Some rocks resist erosion more strongly than others. The most resistant rocks are the metamorphic and igneous rocks of the Eastern and Western Uplands—that is why these are places of elevated topography. The least resistant rocks are the red-brown sandstones of the Central Valley, which is why the Central Valley is today a lowland. Within the Central Valley the difference in resistance to erosion between the tough basalts that once flowed as lavas across the landscape and the relatively soft sandstone is striking—the Metacomet Ridge stands in testimony to the difference. Its elevation is a boon to the quarrymen who quarry the basalt— popularly called traprock from the Germanic word *trappen*, meaning step, alluding to great topographic steps of basalt in southern Sweden. The Ridge is a highland, making for easy access and minimizing water accumulation problems in the quarry openings.

Glaciation

The most recent event in the long period of erosion that has etched and shaped the face of Connecticut is the scouring of the land surface by great continental ice sheets over the past million years. When an ice sheet advances it changes most aspects of the surface—but left in place are the ridge elevations and the drainage basins. As the ice moves it picks up and carries forward all the loose sediment in river valleys, all the soil, and all the loose bits of rock. An advancing ice sheet cleans and polishes, and when the ice sheet melts, it simply deposits its load of rock debris on the glacially modified surface, and leaves an unsorted, disorganized mantle of glacially transported sediment everywhere on the land surface.

The most recent ice sheet had melted away by about 12,000 years ago and in its wake it left the land covered by ice-deposited debris called *till*. Because the till is ground-up rock debris, it makes rich soils, but many of the soils are hard to work because the till also contains boulders too large to be moved by plows. Throughout the Uplands one can find stone walls produced as a result of farmer-cleared fields. But in the valleys of the State, post-glacial reworking of till has occurred. Water from the melting glaciers picked up, transported, and redeposited some of the finer particles of the glacial sediment, leaving the boulders behind. New Haven and Hartford, for example, are both built on sediments deposited by glacial melt waters. Many of today's rivers—the Connecticut, the Farmington, and the Quinnipiac are examples—were partly dammed by glacial debris, and behind the dams temporary lakes of glacial melt water formed. Over time the melt waters deposited layer upon layer of fine, clay-rich sediments in the glacial lakes. These clays were once the feed for Connecticut's great brick-making industry.

Peat forms in closed basins or in slow-draining swamps in many environments; in Connecticut the most common environment was formerly glaciated terrains where acid-loving plants accumulated. Given the geological history of Connecticut, a good deal of the State would potentially have been amenable to the formation of peat. A few of the Town Reports acknowledge that peat does indeed occur within their borders. But without exception they dismiss it as unimportant. For example, Samuel Nott of Franklin comments "A little use has been made of a poor kind of peat," and George Stanley of Wallingford says "Peat is found in various parts of the town, but not used."[14]

Connecticut's Mineral Endowment

Connecticut's endowment of valuable and precious minerals was not rich. It took a century and a half for European settlers to explore and evaluate the State carefully, and although many small and scientifically interesting mineral occurrences were found, no metalliferous bonanzas were located. Deposits of copper, iron, cobalt, lead, and zinc, and even traces of gold were discovered and tested. Several copper mines were opened in the eighteenth century. The ore bodies were small, and the ores difficult to smelt, and all of the mines seem to have been money losers. The best known operation was the Newgate Mine in East Granby, so called because the mine workings were later used as a prison known as Newgate. Following discovery of copper in 1705, the legislature passed an act (1709) legalizing an association to mine the Newgate deposit. According to Charles Rufus Harte "this act constitutes the first mining company charter granted in this country."[15] In the mid-nineteenth century, a copper mine in Bristol was active and briefly was one of the largest copper mines in the country, but poor management led to the collapse of the venture. The iron ores of the northwest corner of the State were the basis of a profitable and historically important iron industry that endured for a century and a half, but not an industry that could compete with the much larger and richer ore deposits that were eventually discovered elsewhere in the country, as in the Mesabi Range of Minnesota. For a brief time in the nineteenth century, the Jinny Hill mine in Cheshire was a leading producer of barite (barium sulfate), an ingredient in paints.

The colonists were practical and industrious. The Town Reports attest to their industry and engineering skills. When local stone had properties suitable for some need, such as making chimneys, house walls, hearths, foundations, or paving, they adapted the best of what was offered, and if near water transport, they developed export industries. The building-stone industry, for example, flourished from the end of the eighteenth century into the early years of the twentieth century; a few small operators continue today.

Clays suitable for making bricks and tiles were, and still are, widespread in small amounts throughout the State. Within the valley of the Connecticut River and its main tributaries, as well as in the valleys of some of the other rivers of the State, huge deposits of glacial-lake clay exist and around them a large industry was developed in the nineteenth and early twentieth century. Today the industry is a shrunken remnant, even though plenty of clay remains. The industry is unlikely to revive because other activities are now carried out on the lands underlain by the remaining un-mined clay.

Sand and gravel are also widely distributed throughout the State—like the clay deposits, sand and gravel are legacies of the waning ice sheet. The sands and gravels have been used extensively for road building and other construction purposes such as concrete making. Sand and gravel deposits are water laid and tend to be deposited in valleys; the sites of deposition tend to be the same places that are ideal for human settlements. Deposits of sand within the state are still large, but accessible deposits are severely limited because towns and roads now sit atop the major undeveloped supplies. Downtown New Haven, for example, is sited on large sand deposits. In response to declining general availability of sand and gravel, the State's crushed rock industry has flourished. Today, crushed rock from the basalts of the Metacomet Ridge is quarried from some of the world's largest traprock quarries.

In the Proto-North American terrane there are huge deposits of marble formed from ancient marine limestones. The marble, which is exposed throughout the drainage basin of the Housatonic River, is of excellent chemical quality and has many practical uses, but it was of only local interest until the railroad made the valley of the Housatonic River accessible. Smaller and less desirable beds of marble are located at a few places in the Iapetus terrane. Some of the soils of New England do need lime to offset acidity, but much of Connecticut's lime was too far removed from water transport for an export industry to develop.

There was however, a small local market for marble as a source of lime in iron smelting and a limited export industry of cut marble for building stone was also developed; Marbledale, near New Milford, was once a minor but important source of such stone. Marble mining for chemical and local fertilizer use continues in a limited way to the present day.

The only metalliferous deposits in the State of any significance were iron ores. The earliest iron ores were bog ores, found in swamps in many parts of the State, and exploited as early as the seventeenth century. The iron industry did not really become important until larger ore bodies of a different kind were found and exploited in the northwestern corner of the State. These ores are unusual in that they were formed by the weathering of Proto-North American terrane rocks. The weathering was ancient—we don't know exactly how ancient, but long before glaciation and possibly as old as 100 million years. Long-continued weathering removed soluble constituents and left an insoluble residue behind, consisting largely of iron hydroxide. It was this material that became the feed for the blast furnaces. Quartz and marble were added to the blast furnace feed as flux, and the furnaces were fired by charcoal made from hardwood trees. The iron mine at Roxbury was different. There, veins of iron carbonate of uncertain geologic age, but at least some hundreds of millions of years, were mined and treated in a blast furnace that has been well preserved and is worth a visit for its historic interest. Unfortunately it was an economic failure. Connecticut's iron ores were not especially rich nor particularly desirable; the success of its iron industry was due to abundant charcoal and readily available water power to pump air into the blast furnaces and to provide power for hammers and rolling mills at iron works.

Data from the Town Reports

We discuss the Reports in groups according to the geological terrane in which a town is situated. For convenience, the largest, the Iapetus terrane, is divided into an Eastern and Western part. The Eastern part of the Iapetus terrane lies to the east of the Central Valley (which is occupied by the Newark terrane). The Western part of the Iapetus terrane lies to the west of the Valley. Table 1 lists the towns in each of the five regions. Not all of the towns provided answers to Articles 5 and 7, and of those that did, only a few provided sufficient information for a clear assessment of the quality and magnitude of the resources. A probable reason for the paucity of information was suggested in 1837 by Charles Shepard, who stated in the preamble to his mineralogical examination of Connecticut that education in geology and mineralogy, and therefore the potential for recognizing mineral resources, was minimal among the largely farming community:

> Without wishing to speak disrespectfully of a community which has never been placed second to any other in the Union for its widely diffused intelligence and general sagacity of character, I may still be permitted to say that information related to the mineral kingdom was almost everywhere found to be singularly deficient.[16]

Shepard's remarks were made three decades after Yale's Benjamin Silliman had started teaching geology and mineralogy to Yale students.[17] As mentioned above, many authors of the Town Reports were graduates of the College, but before Silliman's course was offered.

The Proto-North American Terrane

Towns in the northwestern corner of the State are underlain by rocks of the Proto-North American terrane. We have contributions to the Academy survey from Cornwall, Kent, Litchfield, Sharon, Winchester, and Washington, portions of which also fall into the terrane.

Elijah Allen of Cornwall noted that "in 1800 Messrs. Matthew Paterson and Tryal Tanner Burnt a killn of Lime of Lime Stone taken from their Farms in the South East of the middle of the Town."[18] The burnt lime (CaO) was for sweetening the acid soil. Allen further observed "there are sundry Quarries of a grayish coloured stone which splits well and makes fine stone for Building Chimneys etc."[19] This was apparently some kind of metamorphic rock, probably a gneiss.

Allen remarked on an attempt to mine black lead, which is an old name for the carbon mineral, graphite. Graphite was then, and is today, a commodity of relatively low value. Allen's account is an example of the inexperience of the local citizens. In 1757 a deposit of black lead appears to have been found at what is now known as Mine Mountain. The then proprietors of the town designated Mr. Abraham Raymond and others to dig the ore; when the ore was sold, the proprietors were to get a one-fifth share of the proceeds. Allen then records what is a typical optimistic report by a promoter: "I have found a letter from Michael Judah of Norwalk dated Decr. 3rd, 1767 in which he informs that the Black Lead Ore found in Cornwall would fetch 100 Dollars in Holland per ton; this he knew by a sample he had sent. He thought the Ore would gross better as they descended into the Hill. He wrote he had sent a sample to London but had no return."[20]

A second Cornwall Report written by Oliver Burnham records more details of the venture. The town proprietors had apparently sequestered sixty acres of land on which the ore was discovered. They granted mining options to an outside group that arranged for a ton of material to be sent to London and Amsterdam for testing. Burnham comments: "it appears to be pure and excellent of the kind. In the year 1767 the same company applied for a grant to work the mine further but since some suspicions having arisen respecting the accuracy of the first report they were refused liberty to proceed."[21] Two common mistakes are recorded in this story. First, there is no reason to believe that an ore will "gross better" in depth but promoters are always prone to suggest so. Second, putting the testing of samples in the hands of a promoter is a sure help to the hand of the promoter going into investors' pockets.

Allen recounts another tale that is testimony to the energy and optimism of the populace for making money from their land, *without fully understanding what they were doing*. Allen reports that "Some years past Mr. James Douglass, then in full Life, Dug 130 Feet Perpendicular into a solid Rock, and then about 20 Feet more in an Oblique or sloping descent, in expectation of finding some precious Ore, but without success. Out of which Mine there Issues a large Sulphurous Spring of Water which Waters about 20 Acres of Land and is found by experience to fertilize and enrich the Land much more than Irrigation with a common Brook or Spring water, and is thought in Time will amply repay the Cost of diging the Mine."[22] Probably Mr. Douglas followed a vein containing iron pyrites (FeS$_2$, fool's gold)[23] and it was the oxidized product of the vein that produced the sulphurous water. The water sounds like what we call acid mine drainage today and one has to wonder at the claim for fertilizing qualities.

Barzillai Slosson provides amusing details of a mining swindle in Kent:

> About 3 miles North Eastward from the place is another mine of iron ore which has never been worked to any purpose. This ore is of a bright shining appearance, is quite heavy, and has a great portion of sulphur. Soon after the settlement of the town this mine was discovered, and was then supposed to abound in silver. This conclusion was drawn from the shining appearance of the ore. Five acres of ground, including the precious treasure, was divided into 54 shares which were rapidly sold. A German was employed to refine and purify the metal; a furnace was erected; silver was made in

abundance and the dreams of the proprietors were soon to become realities. At length the German and the silver disappeared together. The proprietors sustained considerable losses, but they charged them all upon the fraud of the German and even to this day our old people, who lived at the time the frenzy prevailed, still believe the basis of the ore to be silver—even when you show them a piece of it hanging to a magnet![24]

The proprietors were swindled because they were unaware of the nature of common minerals, while the German was obviously both knowledgeable and dishonest. The vein that was mined apparently contained iron oxide (magnetite) and fool's gold (iron sulfide). The silver was undoubtedly provided by the German and introduced into the furnace to fool gullible observers. He apparently also knew enough about metallurgy to recover whatever he put into the furnace, so that it looked as if "silver was made in abundance."

Despite the interest in minor minerals and a record of failed ventures, it is iron that made the northwestern towns famous. In his 1801 Cornwall Report Elijah Allen, referring to bog ores, commented that "Some appearance of Iron Ore has been found in different parts of the Town but none has been wrought to any good Account."[25] There were forges in Cornwall but as Michael Gannett has noted, "Cornwall's forges worked pig iron that was produced elsewhere."[26]

Barzillai Slosson writes of Kent: "In the South part of the town—about 3 miles East of the River, and about half a mile North of New Milford is a valuable mine of iron ore...This mine was discovered at an early period and has been constantly worked since the first settlement of the town." Slosson further comments: "The iron made from this ore is generally brittle, & not proper for ship building or for farming utensils. Mixed with ore from Salisbury or Frederickstown it makes iron of an excellent quality for any use. The iron made from this ore without any mixture is generally made into nails, to which purpose it is very well adapted."[27]

Washington, most of which lies in the Western Iapetus terrane, also reported iron ore. Daniel Brinsmade reported: "There has been lately discovered a bed of iron ore of a most excellent quality, two tons and a half of ore producing a ton of iron, and the quantity is supposed to be inexhaustible."[28] The location of this material is uncertain, but presumably it was bog ore and was in the portion of Washington that lies in the Proto-North American terrane.

It should be noted that the Proto-North American terrane yielded iron ore from several sites and in the eighteenth and nineteenth centuries the ore was smelted at many localities. Mine sites were usually different from smelting sites—the smelters were located where waterpower was available and the ore was taken there to be processed. Connecticut iron was well known to the fledgling Republic during its fight for independence. Connecticut supplied metal for the guns of the American Army in the Revolutionary battles, and did so again for the North during the Civil War. It was not until the opening

of the ore from the Lake Superior region in the 1880s, often by workers who moved west after gaining experience in northwest Connecticut, that the United States iron industry grew to world-class dimensions. The early history of iron mining and smelting in Connecticut is a topic covered in two recent Connecticut Academy publications.[29]

The Western Division of the Iapetus Terrane

The Western half of the Iapetus terrane includes the towns of Bethlem (now Bethlehem), Goshen, Litchfield, Milton, Northfield, Ridgefield, Stratfield (now Bridgeport), Watertown, and portions of the town of Washington. Reports from these towns commonly comment on the roughness of the land and consequent farming difficulties. For example, James Morris, the author of the Litchfield County Report, described what was clearly the most meaningful aspect of the geological environment for the people of Northfield: "The surface of this parish is uneven, and in many parts stony, rough and hard for tillage. The soil is generally good and produces good grass and grain. Orchards flourish well."[30] There are few discussions of metals in these reports, but most of them discuss building stones and clays.

Lewis Norton, writing in the Goshen Report of 1812, commented that "The face of the country here, like that of most of the towns in this state is variegated. The hills run chiefly in a northerly and southerly direction." Further on, Norton wrote "There are several places here in which clay suitable for bricks and earthen ware may be obtained. Grey sand is found on the margin of some ponds, and in one meadow supposed to have been once the place of a pond."[31]

When metallic deposits were reported from towns in the Western Iapetus terrane, it was to record lack of success. Samuel Goodrich of Ridgefield wrote:

> There are, in most of the mountains amongst the rocks and stones, appearances of Sulpher and Iron. Tho there has not yet any bed been opened that promiscs to pay thc cxpcnsc of working. There have been several attempts to dig after the precious metals and a considerable quanty of ore has been carried away, but to collect any quantity of metal has proved impracticable.

However, he goes on with more optimism, "There are several beds of lime stone of good qualities and some quarries of a grayish & skyblue stone which is serviceable in building but no free stone."[32] By free stone Goodrich refers to rocks that break easily into useful blocks and slabs. Azel Backus of Bethlem also comments on easily shaped stones: "There are many quarries of Gneiss remarkable for enduring fire, which can be split and broken into any shape."[33] Both Ridgefield and Bethlem, however, were too far from navigable water for a viable quarry-stone industry to develop.

The Ridgefield Report is typical of most reports from towns in the Western division of the Iapetus terrane—townspeople utilized whatever local stone was available, but they lived in a region that lacked mineral commodities that could be exported. Instead, they grazed cattle and sent meat and cheese to market in exchange for other goods.

The Eastern Division of the Iapetus Terrane

The situation with respect to mineral resources in the Eastern Iapetus terrane is notably different from that of the Western division. In part the difference was due to more accessible water transport, but it seems also to reflect a more knowledgeable and possibly wealthier community. Reports for this division were received from the towns of Canterbury, East Haddam, Franklin, Haddam, Killingworth, Lebanon, Lisbon (two parishes), Pomfret, Union, Willington, and part of Chatham. Six of the towns responded in some degree to Articles 5 and 7.

Levi Clark's report from Haddam provides an excellent example of an export industry developed on a local resource: "There are three important sources of wealth from which this town derives her prosperity; viz., Fisheries, Quarries, and Shipbuilding." The author then discusses the quarries as follows:

> About three quarters of a mile below the Court House, two valuable quarries of stone have been opened, one on the East & the other on the West side of Connecticut river. They both belong to the same vein which extends across the bed of the river into the Hills on Each side to an undiscovered distance and in a line nearly North & South. The East quarry has been pursued nearly a hundred rods up the hill & sunk in many places thirty & forty feet deep from the surface of the earth...The stone taken from these quarries (which run obliquely nearly opposite the Court House) are of a mingled blue & white, constituting a dark dappled grey. They are easily split to almost any given thickness, very smooth and are manufactured with very little assistance from the chisel. As they lie near the river they are easily transported by water. They are sent to New York in large quantities, & are used to pave the side walks of that city, & for a variety of other purposes. About 50 laborers are this year employed in the two quarries. [34]

Rocks in the Haddam area are metamorphic, mainly gneisses and schists, and because they are mica-rich—a mineral that breaks readily along flat planes—they split easily and cleanly to provide large, smooth surfaces.

Levi Clark had an interest in minerals but only limited knowledge of what he found. He speculated on some interesting crystals:

> About one and a half miles southwest from the Court House is Long-Hill. On which are found

the crystallizations which accompany this communication. The Hill lies about 150 feet above the surface of the river. It is a dry pasture, yields sweetfern, & the crystals lie a few inches below the surface. They are of various forms & sizes, & of different degrees of transparency. They are found unconnected with each other & scattered in unequal distances. They are generally hexagonal, & the angles often as regularly proportioned to each other, as if measured by the artist. I could not find those of equal size, regularity, or transparency with others which I have seen. I send a variety of them, some of which you will observe to be fluted; another regularly pointed; many seamed; with the manner in which they are often combined. [35]

Those crystals were clearly quartz and of little value at the time, though they may have some value today as items for costume jewelry or good-luck charms.

Still interested in crystals, Clark describes what are almost surely crystals of iron pyrites:

> The ore No. 1 is in the same form as when taken from the bed, except somewhat broken at the edges. Nearly a hundred more were dug out, equally regular in their shape, but generally smaller in size. I concluded they are chiefly or entirely sulphureous. I wish them analyzed by Mr. Professor Silliman, if he will please do me the favor; & should be happy to know their proportions & value. They are perhaps common and valueless; but ignorance & wonder are commonly companions, & to that cause perhaps my curiosity may be ascribed. [36]

Silliman's skills as a mineralogist and chemical analyst had apparently become well known in the few years he had been a Yale professor.

Clark, still focusing on minerals, comments, "A few rods west of the Court Houses is an abrupt rock, rising nearly perpendicularly for several yards. It commands an extensive & pleasant view to the east & south. It is called Isinglass Hill, and large flakes of that fossil are found upon it." [37] Isinglass is an old name for clear, colorless mica, now called muscovite. The term fossil then meant any materials in a rock, not just the buried remains of life.

In the Union Report of 1803, Solomon Wales mentions "a small brook from lead mine pond" and "great bodys of iron oar, & in some ledges their appears to be great quantitys of sulpher..." [38] As with other reporters, Wales seems to be describing iron sulfide.

The Willington respondent Samuel Dunton reported that "Mines and minerals none have been discovered Except iron ore which has been found in Considerable Quantities in the northerly part of the Town but is calculated principally for furnace use there are plenty of Stone for building & fence and Some quarries of an Excellent quallity."[39]

The Killingworth Report mentions an historically interesting experiment in 1761 of producing iron from magnetic particles (magnetite) in beach sand: "A forge was formerly improved on Menunketesuck River, in the south-eastern part of North-Killingworth. In this for a season iron was made from black sand."[40]

Discussing in 1819 the possible re-opening of a mine in the Eastern Iapetus part of Chatham (now Portland), David D. Field wrote:

> About 1762 a cobalt mine was opened at the foot of Great Hill under the direction of Dr. Stephaunes, a German, and improved for a little time. About 1770 he reviewed the improvement of it in connection with two gentlemen by the name of Erkelin and Khool, and continued it for two or three years. Many casks of ore were obtained and shipped to Europe. But as all the persons concerned in the mine, laborers as well as principals, were foreigners, and as the ore was exported, little is known of its character or value. After they left it, it was entirely neglected till last autumn. Since then several men have been employed in searching for cobalt in and near the former openings, and have been so successful as to encourage the hope that the mine will be permanently improved. The scarcity of this mineral, and its uses in porcelain and linen manufactories, render it highly desirable that the contents of this mine should be thoroughly explored."[41]

When John F. Schairer published his account of the minerals of Connecticut in 1931, he reported the presence of several different cobalt minerals at the workings of the old Chatham cobalt mine. Schairer also provides information on what was shipped in the casks referred to by Field: "One thousand pounds of cobalt were shipped to England where it was found to be nickel containing a low percentage of cobalt."[42] The Chatham Mine provides another example of actions inadequately supported by mineralogical knowledge. There seems to be little doubt from Schairer's record that some cobalt minerals were successfully mined and that twenty tons of ore were sent to China. Exactly which minerals were mined out and what happened to the twenty tons is not recorded but presumably it was used to make cobalt blue pigments used in the Chinese ceramics industry. Nor is it clear whether the cobalt mine was ever profitable.

The Avalonian Terrane

The Avalonian terrane is justly famous for its granite quarries—the Stony Creek granite is still successfully mined today. Together with "improvements in agriculture, in which the great body of the inhabitants are still engaged," the town reporter for Madison expressed enthusiasm about its successful granite industry in 1832:

> Six years since some individuals undertook to quarry stone from some of the granite ledges & rocks which are found in Madison parish, & succeeded. The business has increased until about 100 hands are employed in the warm season of the year, in getting out the stone, working them, & carting them to the water-side; whence they are shipped for New York, Philadelphia & various other places. They are used principally for curbing, & are sold from 30 to 60 cents per foot. The greater part of the stone have hitherto been obtained from ledges south of Boston street, tho' considerable quantities have been obtained elsewhere. These different branches of business evince that a spirit of industry & enterprise is awake among the people.[43]

The Saybrook Report records an interesting deposit of steatite, a soft mineral that can be readily carved and worked:

> A quarry of Steatite or Soapstone exists in Pautapoug, half a mile north of the Congregational meeting-house. This appears to have been known to the Indians, as pots and mortars made of this stone have been found in their graves on the Point, and in fields in the neighbourhood. Thirty or forty years since, it was procured by the owners of a furnace in Killingworth, for the purpose of making an oven for baking steel. In 1815, some gentlemen obtained a lease of the quarry for 20 years, got out fifty tons of the stone and sent it to New York; where, on examination, it was declared to possess durable qualities, and be susceptible of a fine polish, but to be too hard to be extensively useful.[44]

Saybrook, like other towns in the Avalonian terrane, was also a source of building stones:

> A quarry of Gneiss stone, resembling the quarries in Haddam, called Deep-river Quarry, because it is in the neighbourhood of that river, was opened in 1812. This is near a cove, navigable for scows, half a mile from Connecticut river. Several hands have been employed in it and it promises to be profitable. Another quarry of similar description was opened some years after on Mitchel's Neck. Some others were opened in the vicinity last year and one two to three years ago near Cedar-swamp.[45]

In Preston, Levi Hart mentioned in 1810 that both clay for bricks and building stones were mined for local use. A stone that had particularly desirable properties for hearths received special comment: "The northeast corner of the parish is a high rocky ground, abounding with stone, which appear for cutting & are applied for hearths & other uses in chimney building, & are excellent to endure the fire." Hart also comments, "Clay is to be found in various places near this stream [Quonabaug] & brick have been made from some of it."[46]

In Pomfret, stone production was especially for gravestones: "There is in this Town, a Quarry, or two, out of which have been dug & letter'd grave Stones; but of late, not much improv'd, since the Death of a Grave Stone maker, here."[47]

On the coast, the New London Report records the use of beach sand: "There is a beach of clean white sand, useful for floors & for mortar. The many boat loads & cartloads that are taken away, are replaced by the influx of the sea."[48]

The Newark Terrane

The only geological terrane in the State with the kind of geology in which coal might be expected is the Newark terrane. Two of the Town Reports from the Newark terrane do indeed report coal, but unfortunately not coal of sufficient quantity and quality to warrant mining. The reporter for Chatham comments: "Coal was discovered at Indian-hill about thirty years ago. But whether it exists there or in any other part of the town in any considerable quantities, must be determined by future researches."[49] A somewhat more detailed report is provided for Middletown, across the river from Chatham: "In some cases the slatestone is from ten to fifteen feet thick so thickly impregnated with bitumen, that it will burn. Here veins of coal are much the largest and most frequent." The reporter then goes on to discuss the search for coal: "The earth has been explored by boring sixty or seventy feet. But although coal has been discovered, it has not been found in sufficient quantities to defray the expense of digging for it."[50] The present authors have not found any record of actual coal production in the State or even further testing of coal resources in the 200 years since the Town Reports.

One of the more detailed accounts of mines and stones in the Newark terrane is given by the Farmington Report. Concerning mines, the reporter writes that "An opinion prevailed in the early part of the settlement of the town that there were mines of different kinds in the east mountain." To confirm this opinion, in 1712 a lease was given to some adventurous citizens:

> Patridge and Belcher made an opening on the mountain in the parish of Northington, 'tis reputed some copper ore was obtained, but not a sufficient quantity to make the business lucrative, and it was discontinued; about the same time a mine was opened on the east side of the mountain in the first society, perhaps one mile

from the southeast corner of Northing society a north east course; the kind of mineral substance taken from this place I am unable to determine but suppose it to be Bismuth or Antimony. The ore runs in small veins through a soft stone joining upon a white hard diamond stone, it is of a bright yellow and when broken lies in thin plates differently disposed, tinged with a dark blue or high copper colour—The veins of soft stone and ore may be seen on the sides but not running through the large junks of diamond stone thrown out in diging. The rock in which this stratum of white stone and ore lay is a blue flint: the earth tumbled into different places formerly dug so that it is impossible to determine whether there is any quantity of ore there at present.[51]

Considering the geology of the Farmington area, it is unlikely that either bismuth or antimony was present in the material discussed. Schairer mentions bismuth in the town of Monroe in the Western part of the Iapetus terrane, but none for Farmington. From the above description it seems possible that the vein was quartz and that barium sulfate, iron sulfide, and goethite, an iron hydroxide, were present. The Farmington mine is apparently another example of misplaced hopes based on inadequate information and insufficient mineral expertise.

An interesting but eventually unsuccessful mining venture is also recorded by the Middletown author:

> A lead mine was opened about forty years ago, near Butler's Creek, as it enters Connecticut river, two miles southeast from the city. The vein runs north-easterly towards the river, and as it approaches it, sinks abruptly into the earth. It is enclosed in a granite rock which renders it difficult to get the ore. It is mineralized with sulphur, and is partly steel-grained and partly cubic lead ore, the former containing the greatest portion of silver, but neither enough to pay the expense of separation: it also contains a portion of zinc."[52]

The writer is describing an ore consisting of galena (lead sulfide), and sphalerite (zinc sulfide). Although the ore was mined, and seized from British hands at the time of the American Revolution, the lead mine was never a profitable venture.

The Middletown reporter comments on several other interesting mineralogical features in that town, for instance: "At the bottom of Prospect-Hill, west of Middlesex Turnpike, is a Chalybeate spring. This has been known, and occasionally visited, for many years. About 1810, a bathing-house was erected near it, and it became a place of considerable resort for people in the vicinity, for one or two seasons; but it is now generally neglected, and the house is removed."[53] A chalybeate spring is an old name for water strongly flavored with iron salts.

Rocks of the Newark terrane provide the well-known brown sandstone—commonly called "brownstone"—that has been widely used for residential buildings in eastern towns and cities of the United States. Three Reports discuss brownstone production in considerable detail for Farmington, Middletown, and Chatham.

Where building stones are concerned, the Farmington author is detailed and rightly enthusiastic:

> Stone proper for buildings, causeys, bridges &c. are found in great quantities; perhaps no town in the State is more abundantly supplied and in a situation to accommodate the inhabitants than this; they are and may be obtained from detached rocks being in part above the surface of the ground and running in some instances to a considerable depth into the [earth]—From a quarry and from the surface of the ground, being flat thin stones turned up by the plough.[54]

The Farmington reporter here describes brownstone of the same kind that is mined in other parts of the Newark terrane. Clearly there were, and no doubt are, abundant supplies in the town, yet no large export industry of Farmington stone was developed. The reason is the cost of transportation: although the Farmington River was available for water transport, the river is not deep enough for large barges. Middletown and Chatham, by contrast, are on the Connecticut River and accessible to large barges, so an export business for brownstone developed there.

The Middletown respondent reports: "Free-stone, or rather dark grey sand-stone, abounds in Middletown. Many of the loose stones on the surface are of this description. It is found not only in sinking wells, but appears more or less in the bed and banks of the various streams."[55]

The town of Chatham, as previously mentioned, is partly in the Newark terrane, partly in the Eastern part of the Iapetus terrane. The Chatham Report discusses the quarrying of brownstone in some detail and provides data not given in the Middletown Report. "At a meeting held in that town [Middletown] in 1665, it was resolved that no one should dig or raise stones on the east side of the river, but an inhabitant of Middletown, and that twelve pence should be paid to the town for every tun of stones taken. As early as this, they were transported in vessels to other places."[56] It seems likely that brownstone from the Middlefield and Chatham quarries was the earliest profitable export of a mined material from Connecticut.

The town of Chatham on the east side of the Connecticut River is today's Portland, and the Portland quarries eventually became the largest and most successful of the State's brownstone producers. After many years of inactivity, a small operation is, at this writing, again producing brownstone at the Portland quarries.

By far the most detailed and explicit of all the Town Reports is that of New Haven (1811), prepared by Timothy Dwight, President of the Academy and President of Yale. Dwight clearly influenced the nature of the Solicitation Letter, and it is equally clear that he had a great interest in Article 5. To answer for New Haven, Dwight turned to his young colleague Benjamin Silliman, whose separate publication on the topic, written in 1806, had finally appeared in 1810 in the first volume published by the Connecticut Academy of Arts and Sciences.[57] Dwight acknowledges his help from Silliman in the New Haven Report—"For the following account of the mineralogy of this township, the Academy is indebted to Professor Silliman"—but has drawn on his own explorations, too.[58]

Dwight next calls attention to ongoing field work: "The mineralogy and geological structure of New-Haven and its vicinity, have been recently examined with much attention. This examination is not yet completed, but the following facts and observations connected with them will be found tolerably correct." The plain of New Haven, he writes,

> is wholly alluvial, and is composed of beds of siliceous sand, and gravel, arranged in strata nearly parallel and extending to a depth greater than any wells have penetrated. The sand is more or less ferruginous, and presents no interesting minerals, except such as appear to have been accidentally deposited, or brought from other situations, viz quartz, flint, jasper, and feldspar, which are considerably abundant, and agate, sappare, and garnets, which have been found in a few instances.[59]

The sands that underlie New Haven are glacial-age sediments that were deposited by streams that emanated from the melting ice. The concept of continental glaciation was thirty years in the future, so neither Dwight nor Silliman understood the glacial origin of the alluvium that underlies New Haven. With few exceptions, however, the kinds of alluvium and rocks in the New Haven area are correctly identified:

> The fine amphitheater of hills, which encircle New Haven in all parts, except those occupied by the water, presents an interesting variety, both as it respects its geological formation, and the individual minerals which have been discovered. On the eastern side of the Harbor, the rocks are chiefly granite, greenstone and sandstone. Only a few rocks of granite occur...The sandstone is extremely coarse and may more properly be called, at least, in many instances, a conglomerate or puddingstone.[60]

The observations and geologic insight of Silliman are obvious in the correct use of geologic terms, although Dwight goes on to describe East and West Rock in his own fashion as follows:

> North-east and northwest of New Haven, at a distance of two miles from the town and from each other, rise two perpendicular eminences,

or bluffs, exhibiting precipices of naked rock, and called the East and West Mountains...There can be no hesitation in pronouncing them to be greenstone rocks called by the popular name of *whin* in Scotland, and *trap* generally throughout Europe. The term *basalt* has been more loosely and inaccurately applied to rocks of this description...There is a striking resemblance between greenstone mountains of New-England among themselves, and the same description of mountains in Scotland, and in many other parts of the world.[61]

Dwight and Silliman were incorrect in dismissing the term basalt—it is indeed the correct term, and greenstone is a nonspecific and incorrect term. However, the noted resemblance between the rocks of New England and Scotland is absolutely correct.

Dwight proceeds in his Report to describe the particular minerals found in the trap rocks. They included chalcocite (Cu_2S), a distinctly radiated kind of quartz, epidote and prehnite—"very beautiful specimens of it (prehnite) are found at East Rock" —and an interesting zeolite mineral that occurs in horizontal veins. He even provides details of mineral identification in the laboratory:

It may not be amiss to remark, that in deciding the character of the...minerals, their specific gravity was ascertained to correspond with that mentioned in the systematical books. The zeolite was found to be soft, to intumesce before the blow-pipe, to fuse into a white enamel, and to gelatinize with acids. The prehnite intumesced before the blow-pipe, and melted into greenish slag. It was so hard as to scratch glass, and give sparks with steel.[62]

Silliman had learned the methods of mineralogy well in the years since his appointment in 1802, and had demonstrated them to Dwight.

Dwight mentions another interesting mineralogical feature of New Haven:

The beach...about a mile below the village of West Haven, presents an interesting phenomenon, the solution which may be found in the rocky strata, which we have been describing. The beach is covered with magnetic iron sand; uncommonly pure, and very sensible to the magnet. It may be obtained in large quantities and is used by the inhabitants of New Haven for sanding paper, and sometimes for an ingredient in a firm and dense mortar.[63]

Dwight's geological excursions are clear as he moves farther afield from the actual town of New Haven, westward from the Newark terrane and entering the Western Iapetus terrane:

Leaving the hills which immediately bound the plain of New Haven, and proceeding westward on the great road leading to New-York, some additional facts may be noticed. Greenstone continues to be the prevailing rock of the country, and for several miles, we cross extensive ridges of this rock and of greenstone slate.

Dwight is here referring to a kind of greenstone different from the previously mentioned greenstones of East and West Rocks. The greenstones of the Western Iapetus terrane are metamorphic rocks and are green because they contain a greenish mica-like mineral called chlorite.

At the distance of five or six miles from New Haven, the strata of greenstone slate become very extensive and regular...The country here is filled with ridges consisting chiefly of greenstone slate, which look generally to the south-east, with considerable chasms or small valleys between them, so as to resemble, very much a series of billows when the sea runs high.. To this general formation, there is one remarkable and striking exception. About 5 miles west of New Haven commences a range of serpentine, both common and noble, and mixed with primitive limestone and bitterspath. As this range proceeds westward, the limestone predominates more and more over the serpentine; and soon the rock becomes primitive stratified limestone... with the strata of limestone remarkably regular.[64]

Bitterspath is an old name for the common carbonate mineral of magnesium and calcium, today called dolomite.

We have extracted heavily from the New Haven Town Report to show how thorough Dwight was in his descriptions but it aids our purpose that he continues:

A quarry has been opened in these calcareous strata for the purpose of obtaining marble, for the limestone which has been mentioned appears properly to deserve that name. The structure of the rock is schistose. Its texture is minutely granular. Its prevailing color is that of the Italian dove marble; but very much variegated by innumerable veins of calcareous spar or bitterspath, of very fine and brilliant white, by an admixture of serpentine forming green spots, and by black spots and clouds which sometimes are magnetic ore, and sometimes appear to be serpentine of a dark hue. Marble also occurs here of a deep black, beautifully illuminated by white cloud. As far as the investigation has gone, the calcareous strata are divided into large distinct tables; so that they can be taken out in many instances, without making any other fracture than what exists naturally.

Pieces of marble have been sawn and polished, and though only weathered pieces have hitherto been tried, the stone exhibits so fine a texture, so high a luster, and such beautiful delineations of color, as to justify the belief that as a marble it will prove a valuable acquisition to the country.[65]

Dwight also mentions the potential use of some rocks in addition to marble; for example, in the case of local serpentine, which he says "admits of a handsome polish and is very beautiful. The noble serpentine which is found in it is of a very deep green mixed with yellow, and is susceptible of so high a polish as to become a perfect mirror." He lists a few minerals specifically: green talc as resembling French chalk, amianthus "as fine as that in Corsica," and other common species such as actynolite, tremolite, chlorite, phosphate of lime, jasper, flint, red and common quartz, puddingstone and pitchstone, and iron pyrites (FeS_2). And he remarks that the lead mineral galena is found in several places.[66] Most of these mineral rock names are accurate and in use today.

Finally Dwight recounts the discovery of a lump of native copper weighing 90 pounds by "Mr. Josiah Todd of North-Haven, when gathering fruit on the Hamden hills ... It was lying on the surface of a flat rock, at some places adhering to it, and even running into its crevices. He with several other persons afterwards sought for more, but as they, by their own confession, had superstitious fears respecting it, they probably did not make a very minute investigation, and no more was found."[67] Copper was a highly prized metal and the citizens of Connecticut were always on the lookout for signs of its presence. Many Town Reports contain references to copper but none details a successful mine. In 1837, however, the Bristol copper mine, as mentioned above, was opened on the boundary between the Newark and Western Iapetus terranes, and was briefly one of the larger copper mines in America.

Closing Remarks

All told, the mineralogical section of the New Haven Report is over three pages in length. Most of the Report is exact, professional, and completely intelligible to a geologist or mineralogist of today. Not so for all of the other Town Reports. There, mineralogical terms are loosely and frequently incorrectly used.

The Town Reports are a striking record of a time of great change in the level of technical and scientific understanding in the United States. With the exception of the New Haven Report, they all attest to a dearth of technical knowledge about geology and/or mineralogy on the part of the writers. But who were the writers? They were ministers, town officers, land holders, and others who had been educated in the classical manner, mostly at Yale. There were, of course, a few people in the country who did have a practical knowledge of mining and smelting, but they were not these writers.

Had the Academy sent out their Solicitation Letter in 1850 instead of 1800, very different responses would have been written. Starting in 1812, all seniors in Yale College were required to take a course in geology and mineralogy—a requirement that lasted for 80 years. It did not take long for an educated body of people to start influencing ideas and to have a positive effect across the United States. Changes in the population at large were much slower; as Shepard noted in his 1837 Report, farmers were still largely uneducated in geology and mineralogy. Silliman's students, however, were carrying his teachings to other institutions, and geological surveys were started.[68] The magnitude of the change being wrought is best demonstrated by the publication of the first edition of *A System of Mineralogy* by James Dwight Dana in 1837, the same year as Shepard's report.[69] Dana was arguably Silliman's best student, and he went on to become one of America's most distinguished scientists. His *System of Mineralogy* quickly became the most important mineralogical reference book in the English language. Now in its eighth edition, and retitled *Dana's New Mineralogy*, Dana's system is still utilized and is still the preeminent mineralogical reference in English.[70]

TABLE 1

Connecticut Towns and their Locations in the Four Terranes

PROTO-NORTH AMERICAN TERRANE
Cornwall
Kent
Sharon
Washington (part in Iapetus Terrane)
[Winchester]

IAPETUS TERRANE - Western
Bethlem
Goshen
Litchfield
Milton
Northfield
Ridgefield
[Stratfield]
Washington
Watertown

IAPETUS TERRANE - Eastern
[Bolton (North)]
Canterbury
[Coventry]
East Haddam
Franklin
Haddam
Killingworth
Lebanon

Lisbon (Hanover)
Lisbon (Newent)
Pomfret
[Tolland]
Union
Willington
[Windham]

AVALONIAN TERRANE
[Guilford]
Madison
New Haven (part in Newark Terrane)
New London
Preston
Saybrook

NEWARK TERRANE
Chatham
Cheshire
Durham
East Windsor
Farmington
Middletown
New Haven
[Wallingford]
[Wintonbury (Bloomfield)]

[ ] indicates the authors did not supply information on questions 5 and 7.

Wild Animals in Connecticut's Changing Landscape

Harvey R. Smith and Tim W. Clark

A "dreary wilderness of savages and wild beasts" was how a nineteenth-century East Windsor resident described the Connecticut landscape that had existed when the first European settlers arrived in the early seventeenth century.[1] Colonial accounts emphasized the abundance of both game and timber. But Connecticut's forests and animal populations had already undergone considerable change by the time colonists began to exert their impacts.[2] Due to natural ecological transition and the effects of Indian uses, the state at that time consisted of a mix of virgin and modified forests, cleared land, wetlands, and meadows. The arriving Europeans, whose survival depended on agriculture, rapidly transformed the land. The forests were chopped down and wild animals were hunted

for food, trapped for fur, or destroyed as pests. Open fields, pastures, hedgerows, scattered woodlots and remnant forests dominated during the eighteenth and nineteenth centuries. These landscape alterations, of course, greatly affected the wild animals. By the time of the Town Reports project of 1800, the state's wildlife populations had experienced dramatic alterations, and the ensuing two hundred years imposed even more changes.

This essay describes the "wild animals" mentioned in the Town Reports and compares them with the present status of wildlife in the state, with a focus on eight species. It also characterizes the landscape of the early nineteenth century and looks at human and contextual factors that have influenced

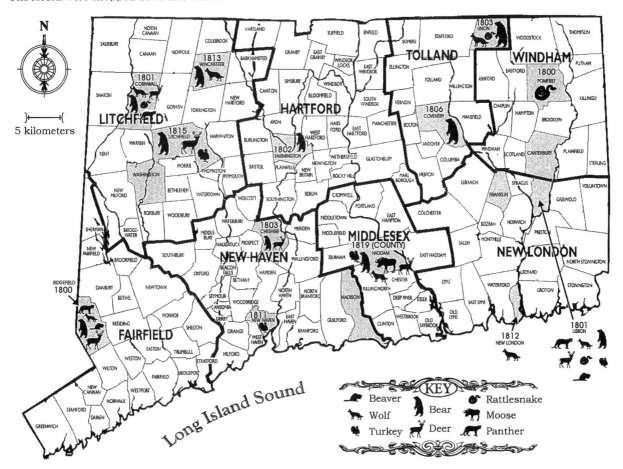

Map of the Connecticut Town Reports, showing the town location of eight of the most frequently mentioned species.

animal populations. The authors analyzed the original Town Reports and other records and literature on Connecticut's landscape and wildlife history. They also researched the context and perspectives of the respondents. Finally, they consulted with specialists Joseph Miller (late professor and librarian at the Yale School of Forestry and Environmental Studies), Noble Proctor (biologist at Southern Connecticut State University), Paul Rego (biologist with the Wildlife Division of the Connecticut Department of Environmental Protection), David M. Smith (professor emeritus of forestry at the Yale School of Forestry and Environmental Studies), and Andrew Lord (attorney specializing in environmental law).

The Connecticut Town Reports

In the questionnaire for its Statistical Account 1800, the Connecticut Academy of Arts and Sciences invited comment on: "wild animals, now or heretofore known; their increase or decrease, and from what causes; new species, migration, and natural history of birds."[3] The reports vary greatly in detail but provide an important look at Connecticut's wildlife. Their value lies as much in what the respondents did not say as what they did say. Three accounts of particular usefulness were those by Elijah Allen, a surveyor in Cornwall; David Hale, a pastor in Lisbon (Newent parish); and Samuel Goodrich, a pastor in Ridgefield—all of which were returned to the Academy in 1800 or 1801.

The solicitation of information through a questionnaire can raise doubts and create difficulty in interpretation depending on the questionnaire itself and the occupation, education, experience, sex, age, and other attributes of the respondents.[4] It was necessary to address those factors to interpret the data and understand Connecticut's wildlife circa 1800, which, in turn, informs our modern understanding of biodiversity, landscape-scale habitat change, and species conservation and recovery.

Respondents in seventeen towns made reference to only twenty-five mammals, eleven birds, eight reptiles, and no amphibians (Tables 1 and 2: Appendix 1). Sixteen respondents did not mention any specific wild animals, and David McClure of East Windsor, in reference to the number of Indians in the town at the time of his report in 1806, remarked that they had "disappeared with the game of the woods."[5]

Only a tiny percentage of the 390 bird species and nearly one-third of the twenty-six reptile species recognized in Connecticut today were reported (Table 2; see Appendix II for scientific names). Mammals, and especially carnivores, dominated the focus of respondents. Nearly half of the fifty-two mammal species found in the state at present were mentioned in the Town Reports, including ten of the twelve carnivores present today. This reflects the settlers' keen attention to "predatory wild beasts." Elk, moose, and deer were reported, although extirpation[6] of elk and moose (except for occasional strays) has left only the white-tailed deer today. "Moles," "bats," "rabbits," and "mice" were generically mentioned. Other rodents appearing in the reports were woodchuck, squirrel (generic as well as grey, black, red, and flying), chipmunk, and beaver.

The predominance of mammals in the reports was not unexpected. "Wild animals" and "wild beasts" often were synonymous with mammals in early historical records. Benjamin Trumbull, for instance, wrote describing Indian dress, "Their ornaments were pendants . . . these were in the form of birds, beasts, and fishes."[7] "For beasts," wrote the Reverend Francis Higginson in 1630, "there are some beares . . . .Also here are severall sorts of Deere . . . . Also Wolves, Foxes, Beavers, Otters, Martins, great wild Cats, and a great Beast called a Molke [moose] as bigge as an oxe."[8] It also was apparent by 1800 that land clearing, population increase, and hunter impact had seriously reduced animal diversity and abundance (see source notes, Table 1).

Changes in the Wild Animals

Wild animals played an important role in the history of Connecticut and affected settlement through various relationships with people. We examine in detail the changing status of eight wild animal species that figured prominently in the Town Reports. William Wood, who produced the earliest comprehensive record of New England's natural resources, mentioned most of these species in his poetic description "Of the Beasts that Live on the Land." Note that his poem ascribes human values to all the animals. "It will not be amiss to inform you of such irrational creatures as are daily bred and continually nourished in this country, which do much conduce to the well-being of the inhabitants, affording not only meat for the belly but clothing for the back. The beasts be as followeth:

> The kingly lion and the strong-armed bear,
> The large-limbed mooses, with the tripping deer,
> Quill-darting porcupines, and racoons be
> Castled in the hollow of an aged tree;
> The skipping squirrel, rabbit, purblind hare.
> Immured in the selfsame castle are,
> Lest red-eyed ferrets, wily foxes should
> Them undermine, if rampired but with mold.
> The grim-faced ounce, and ravenous, howling wolf,
> Whose meagre paunch sucks like a swallowing gulf.
> Black, glistering otters and rich-coated beaver,
> The civet-scented musquash smelling ever. [9]

Black Bear

This is the only bear native to the eastern United States. It ranged throughout Connecticut and probably was common in wooded areas until the middle of the nineteenth century.[10] Wood wrote that "for bears they be common,"[11] and Trumbull spoke of "fat bears"[12] providing food for settlers. Noah Phelps reported that in Simsbury from about 1677 to 1689 "the inhabitants were much annoyed by wild beasts. Bears and wolves were so plenty, as to be particularly troublesome." [13] James Cardoza believed that bears were well distributed in western and central Connecticut during the colonial period, but found few records of their presence in the eastern part of the state from 1751-1850.[14] The Town Reports from Coventry, Lisbon, Union, and Middlesex County provide new records

Beaver pond, Litchfield, Connecticut (photograph by Roger T. Zerillo, U.S. Forest Service).

for eastern Connecticut. Feared and considered a nuisance because of damage to cornfields and attacks on swine, bears were continually persecuted.[15] But it does not appear that the General Assembly ever offered a bounty for their destruction, although in 1666 Fairfield passed a one-year bounty of fifty shillings.[16] After the mid-1700s the killing of bears became a noteworthy event.[17] Following a kill in Goshen in 1840,[18] Cardoza was unable to document another record until 1913. Auren Roys noted that "the timid deer, the bear, the wolf, and the panther, and the wildcat" seem now to be exterminated,[19] and Sherman Adams claimed that "it is safe to say that, perhaps for fifty years, the bear has been extinct in Connecticut."[20] Since 1990 there has been a small resident population.

White-tailed Deer

Well-known for the white underside of the tail, which is raised high when the deer takes flight, this is the only deer remaining in the state except for occasional stray moose. Deer apparently were plentiful at the time of settlement, providing both food and hides for clothing. According to Glover Allen, by 1642 the deer population must have decreased noticeably as the "General Court of Connecticut forbade the trade in articles of iron with the Indians, nor were the whites allowed to buy any venison skins until further liberty be granted."[21] The export trade in deer skins eventually restricted the supply for the colonists themselves, and in May 1677 the court "forbade the shipment of any such skins out of the colony"—the first game law of its kind in the country.[22] In 1698 the three southern states of New England uniformly began to protect deer,[23] but numbers continued to decline through the eighteenth century. By the time of the Academy's questionnaire, deer appeared extirpated from the state. According to the Reverend Samuel Goodrich of Ridgefield in 1800 (Table 1), "there were formerly Deer . . . in the woods . . . but they are now extinct."[24] James Linsley records only one deer killed the previous year (in Waterbury).[25] A deer killed at Lake Saltonstall in 1877 and one in western Connecticut in 1882 were considered most

unusual occurrences.[26] The species still was very rare in the state at the turn of the twentieth century with only an occasional stray crossing the border from Massachusetts.[27] Present deer populations are considerably more abundant than in pre-European times.[28]

Beaver

The beaver, the largest rodent in North America, was no doubt a major agent of landscape change during the presettlement period.[29] In precolonial times beavers were distributed widely in forested Connecticut habitats wherever suitable watercourses permitted the construction of dams and lodges. In 1637 beaver skins were valued at nine shillings per pound by the General Court and were actually used as currency.[30] Beaver pelts also were the mainstay of the early fur trade.[31] But the beaver population of the Connecticut River Valley was depleted seriously by the late 1660's;[32] the animal's low reproductive rate and sedentary habits made it vulnerable to concentrated harvest. Fur trading posts on the Connecticut River in Wethersfield, Hartford, Windsor, and Springfield saw their trade decline seriously by 1650, and by the end of the century the fur trade had lost its economic importance.[33] In his 1842 presentation to the Yale Natural History Society, Linsley reported the beaver to be extinct in the state. Adams wrote, "I do not find that any legislation measures were taken to prevent their extermination, and now, alas! they are gone from Connecticut, and perhaps from New England, forever."[34] Mentioned in the Town Reports from Lisbon and Ridgefield[35] (see Table 1), beaver were remembered as having long ago disappeared.

Wolf

The largest wild canid of North America, the wolf once roamed throughout Connecticut. Wood termed them "the greatest inconveniency the country hath."[36] It was perhaps the wild beast feared most by the settlers and considered one of the most annoying and ubiquitous inhabitants of the forest.[37] Trumbull stated that "wolves were numerous . . . when the settlements commenced, and did great damage to the planters, killing their sheep, calves, and young cattle."[38] Bounties for their destruction were ordered by the General Court in 1647 and paid throughout that century.[39] Edward Jenkins provided the following account regarding a wolf killer employed by the town of Hartford in 1640: "It is ordered yt Learance Woodward shall spend his Time abought killing of wolfes & for his Incoragmentt he shall have 4s 6d a week for his bord in casse he kill not a wolfe or a deare: in ye weake; but if he kill a wolf or a deare he is to pay for his bord himself & if he kill a deare we are to Have it for 2d a pound."[40] In 1695 the townsmen were ordered to give Clement Miner a deed of sale for "8 acors of swampy land near Goodman Houghs which land is for consideration of 8 wolves by him killed"[41] (see Table 1). As late as 1808 a bounty of ten dollars for each adult wolf and five dollars for each whelp was offered by Connecticut law.[42] A notable wolf kill in the state was by Revolutionary War hero General Israel Putnam in Pomfret in the 1750s.[43] Adams described what might have been the last pack of wolves in the state: in 1786 wolves were reported around Norfolk, pursued by nearly eighty men, surrounded, and all four of them captured.[44] The last record we could find was of a large wolf killed by Moses Bulkley near Bridgeport in 1839.[45] Constant persecution, increasing rural and urban development, and reduction of the deer herds, resulted in the steady decline of wolves in Connecticut.[46]

Moose

The moose is the largest of all living deer and has probably always been a straggler into Connecticut from more northern spruce forests. Goodwin stated that as far as he knew there were no records of moose in the state, although he thought it possible that they were present at the beginning of the sixteenth century. Morton described the moose: "I will speake of the Elke, which the Savages call a Mose; it is a very large Deare, with a very faire head and a broade palm,...6 foote wide between the tips...He is of the bigness of a great horse."[47] Because this was near Plymouth, Adams thought it fair to assume that they were sometimes in Connecticut. In fact, Trumbull described the moccasins worn by Connecticut Indians in the 1630s as "shoes without heels...made generally of moose hide."[48] Occasional stragglers from Massachusetts were seen during the seventeenth and eighteenth centuries, and one was killed in 1770 in Middlesex County (see Table 1). But the moose, if ever a native, has long since disappeared from the state and was reported as practically extinct in Massachusetts by the beginning of the nineteenth century.[49]

Mountain Lion

The mountain lion—or catamount, as it was called by the early settlers—is the second largest native cat in North America. This large, shy, unspotted, tawny-colored cat was never common in Connecticut, but in the early days it was not uncommon in suitable places of the northern part of the state, especially in the wooded mountains of Litchfield County.[50] Wood wrote, "Concerning lions, ...Some likewise being lost in woods have heard such terrible roarings as have made them

Eastern mountain lion or "catamount" killed in Barnard, Vermont, November 24, 1881, by Alexander Crowell (photograph courtesy of Vermont Historical Society).

much aghast, which must either be devils or lions."[51] Mountain lions were once destructive enough that in 1694 the legislature provided for a bounty of twenty shillings for each lion killed and as late as 1769 still paid four to five shillings. Decreased prey abundance (mainly deer), large bounties, and civilization contributed to their rapid disappearance. In Windsor in 1767 a mountain lion was tracked by a landowner and shot after it killed nine of his sheep[52] (see Table 1). The species was probably extirpated by about 1800 although individuals may occasionally have strayed from New York.[53] Some remained in Vermont and New Hampshire until 1888.[54] This species has not returned to the state.

Wild Turkey

Native only to this continent, the turkey symbolizes to many the wilderness as the first Connecticut settlers found it. Historical records agree on the abundance and tameness of wild turkeys in the early days of settlement in southern New England. Early colonists were surprised at their abundance. As many as 12,000 are thought to have been present at one time.[55] In 1632, Thomas Morton stated that turkeys were easily shot "because, the one being killed, the other sit fast neverthelesse; and this is no bad commodity."[56] A man could kill a dozen turkeys in half a day. However, in 1672 John Josselyn noted that English and Indian hunters had "now destroyed the breed, so that 'tis very rare to meet a wild turkie in the woods."[57] Turkeys disappeared from large sections of their original range due to the relentless exploitation and elimination of their original forest habitat, particularly in the Northeast. The last recorded observation of a native wild turkey in Connecticut, prior to reintroduction in the 1970s, was at Totoket Mountain, Northford, in 1813.[58]

Rattlesnake

The timber rattlesnake, one of only two poisonous snakes found in Connecticut, was among the most feared inhabitants of the forest. This snake lives in hills or mountains of moderate height, migrating to lower ground to find water during dry seasons. William Wood wrote that "that which is most injurious to the person and life of man is the rattlesnake,...her poison lieth in her teeth, for she hath no sting. When any man is bitten by any of these creatures, the poison spreads so suddenly through the veins it causeth death unless he had the antidote to expel the poison."[59] Rattlesnakes were much more widespread in Connecticut in colonial times as indicated by the historical accounts and by the numerous topographic features named "rattlesnake."[60] Rev. Samuel Goodrich wrote, "There were at the first settlement great numbers of rattlesnakes & snakes equally pisonous but they are almost distroyed—one method for their distruction was the turning the swine among them which devoured them."[61]

Caulkins provided a dramatic description of rattlesnake hunts: "A tremendous host of these baneful reptiles sallied forth every spring from the ravines and clefts of the rocks.... How strong then must have been the nerves of those who went forth to do battle with these coiling monsters...with their venom at its height and all their lithe articulations exalted to the point of furious attack and desperate encounter."[62] The first fifteen days in May appear to have been the season for hunting rattlesnakes, and large numbers of people would turn out for this purpose. The General Court at Hartford approved bounties to encourage the destruction of rattlesnakes. In Norwich in 1720 the bounty was doubled to 4d per head and 76 snakes were killed; records indicate that in 1731 the number claiming the bounty was nearly 300. In 1739 Norwich raised the bounty to ten shillings a head for all rattlesnakes killed provided the killer took an oath that he went for no other

The wild turkey, exterminated in Connecticut during the early 1800s, has once again become a common sight in Connecticut's landscape because of extensive reforestation and the reintroduction of wild birds in the 1970s. (Photograph by Glenn "Tink" Smith).

purpose than to destroy them. Subsequently, the number of bounties paid declined as the rattlesnake population was decimated. By 1866 Caulkins assumed that the rattlesnake was extinct in that area. Twenty years earlier, though, Linsley believed the rattlesnake could still be found in more than half the towns of the state.[63] Interestingly, the Town Reports (see source notes, Table 1) provide accurate testimony of the fate of the rattlesnake in Connecticut. The snake is now confined to two areas—the mountainous terrain of northwestern Litchfield County contains several large dens, and a cluster of smaller dens occur in the central part of the state.[64]

Mammalian Species Gains and Losses

By the time of the Connecticut Town Reports project, the diversity and relative abundance of the state's mammalian fauna had been altered dramatically by the settlement process. Several species that once were common had either disappeared or become extremely rare while others, such as woodchucks, rabbits, and squirrels, experienced large population increases. The Town Report respondents were well aware of the changed landscape, increased civilization, clearing of the land, and hunting pressure and their effects on the disappearance of some large quadrupeds (Table 1, source notes). Assessment of species gains and losses of terrestrial mammals in Connecticut between the turn of the nineteenth and twenty-first centuries is difficult. Many changes had already occurred before records were kept. Early records provided only fragmentary, anecdotal accounts, typically of the larger quadrupeds, and some accounts are contradictory. Competent naturalists were not available until the early 1800s.[65]

In 1842 the Reverend James H. Linsley, member of the Connecticut Academy of Arts and Sciences, catalogued the state's mammals for the Yale Natural History Society. He faced the same problem of assessing changes: "As nothing of the kind (it is believed) has heretofore been attempted in this state, it is difficult to determine how many species, hitherto unknown in the state, I have been able to add to our list."[66] Linsley identified for the first time the less conspicuous and smaller mammals of Connecticut in the mid-nineteenth century, listing twenty-four genera and fifty-five species of terrestrial mammals (excluding domestic livestock). He recognized the white-tailed deer as the only remaining member of the family Cervidae in the state. With the exception of the beaver, which he listed as extirpated, Linsley took a conservative approach as to the status of the bear, lynx, mountain lion, wolf, fisher, and marten by saying or implying that it was still possible that these species occasionally strayed into the state.

In 1896 Sherman Adams published an account of the mammals that existed or had existed in Connecticut since the prehistoric era.[67] He reported that "we would still have about 29 genera and about 50 species in the state besides the bats, and marine mammals." Absent from the state at the time of his account were the beaver, wolf, bear, marten, fisher, lynx, panther, wapiti (elk), caribou, and moose.

Goodwin supposed that elk could have occurred in the state during the sixteenth and seventeenth centuries. Godin stated that "the wapiti was the most widely distributed of our hoofed game animals." Hays reported that the species was found all along the East Coast from Canada to the Gulf of Mexico.[68] Elijah Allen stated that "at the first settlement of this town, Deer, Bear, Wolves & some Panthers was seen, and near 40 years since an Elk was killed here."[69] Goodwin found no conclusive evidence that eastern woodland caribou were ever in Connecticut. As a result, it is not clear whether elk can be considered a loss.[70]

Woodrats were reported by Goodwin on the high hills of Litchfield County; he caught a specimen near Kent.[71] Godin believed that this species was probably an animal of the past and it is not listed on the current checklist of Connecticut's wildlife.[72]

The opossum, the state's only marsupial, extended its natural range to Connecticut sometime early in the twentieth century. Adams was told of one caught in East Granby in the mid-nineteenth century; if that report was accurate it was probably not a resident but either an escaped or released animal.[73] According to Goodwin, "Thirty years ago, the opossum was unheard of in Connecticut, but during the past 20 years it has established itself in considerable numbers in the southeastern part of the state."[74] It was not considered common in the state until 1945.[75]

Godin described forty-three genera and fifty-six species of terrestrial mammals in the state, which is comparable to the current Connecticut Department of Environmental Protection species checklist of forty-one genera and fifty-two species.[76] Despite taxonomic change evidenced by the higher number of genera, the number of species has remained fairly constant since Linsley's 1842 report. In fact, Richard DeGraaf and Ronald Miller reported relatively few extirpations of vertebrate species in New England despite major landscape changes. They attributed this to the apparently resilient nature of the temperate forest community, the continental ranges of most species, and the existence of many refugia in the landscape even during the height of land clearing.[77] Godin listed only six native mammalian species that have been extirpated from New England, representing 9 percent of the total number of native species that bred regularly in the region: eastern timber wolf, wolverine, eastern mountain lion, walrus, elk, and eastern woodland caribou.[78]

Several alien species have been introduced into Connecticut. The house mouse probably was introduced into North America accidentally about the time of first settlement[79] and the Norway rat, believed to have originated in Asia, was introduced about 1775.[80] The European hare was introduced intentionally from Hungary at the end of the nineteenth century; a release in 1893 at Millbrook, New York, was believed to have been the most successful in terms of population increase and spread, and the last importation was in 1910 or 1911.[81]

The Coyote, a Latter-day Immigrant

Through extension from its natural range from its ancient home in the West, the coyote has in recent decades entered the northeastern United States, where it has become a major carnivore in eastern ecosystems.[82] The eastern coyote, a more robust, wolf-like animal than western individuals,[83] mainly inhabits brushy edges of second-growth hardwood forests, fields interspersed with thickets, and marshlands[84]. Unlike the wolf and mountain lion, which were unable to adapt to increasing urban development and landscape change, the coyote is a true opportunistic generalist that has successfully exploited change. Human migration westward created a trail of environmental change that enabled the coyote to occupy this new ecological niche.[85] Without competition from larger predators, the coyote colonized areas where food resources were available. It has been postulated that the elimination of the wolf was the major factor that opened a niche allowing for the range expansion of coyotes.[86]

Wetzel believed the first coyotes in Connecticut arrived from Massachusetts and possibly New York in the early 1950s.[87]

Others believe coyotes did not appear until the late 1950s. Population densities remained low at first, but by 1970, following a period of rapid population expansion, their distribution included the entire state. The coyote population increased until the mid-1980s when it is thought to have stabilized.[88]

The return of a major carnivore to Connecticut's ecosystem after a century (since the wolf disappeared) raises questions on how coyotes will influence the vertebrate community. In northern regions, competition has resulted in an apparent dominance hierarchy among canids.[89] Red fox populations are in decline in Connecticut because of competition from coyotes and reforestation.[90] Coyotes also compete with and dominate all age classes of bobcats. Predation by coyotes on bobcats has been reported; and competition for limited prey may reduce bobcat numbers in areas recently colonized by coyotes.[91] Through the natural processes of ecological adjustment, Connecticut's wildlife community will change in species diversity and abundance. The colonization of coyotes will also require adjustment in human values since this carnivore is almost certain to run into conflicts with the interests of some farmers, pet owners, and others, while at the same time it brings ecological value as a key predator in the state's ecosystems.

Migration of Birds

The migration of birds was addressed only in the Town Reports of Ridgefield (1800), Farmington (c. 1810) and New London (c. 1812), even though inquiry was specifically made by the Academy. The Reverend Samuel Goodrich of Ridgefield provided the following account of his observations of migrating passenger pigeons: "There are at seasons great flights of pigeons, but not so frequent as formerly as they change their course more to the westward as the country becomes cleared & settled..."[92] Interestingly, this is the only reference we found in any of the Town Reports to the enormous flocks of passenger pigeons that were once known to be miles long and

Through natural range extension from the west, the coyote began appearing in Connecticut during the 1950s. (Photograph by Bill Byrne, Massachusetts

would obscure the sun.[93] The curiosity and limited state of knowledge about migration are typical of the time. The following is from the anonymous Farmington respondent: "The migration of these birds is a phenominon in nature hard to account for, in sundry respects; as where or to what place do they move?...That they do migrate into southern states or a warmer climate is not made evident by these facts & experience ...It is more likely they are sheltered in hallow trees or crevises in rocks or in stone walls in barns & in hovils, secure from freezing."[94] The New London respondent, also anonymous, reported that "birds, collecting in flocks, in the fall, probably migrate to other climes—Those that do not so collect, but appear in the spring...have, it is presumed, wintered, in a torpid state, in hollow trees, or cavities of the rocks, or in the water.... Many swallows have been observed, in the month of August, hovering round, or perched, in pensive mood, near bodies of water, & all at once disappearing."[95] These observations support those of early ornithologists who explained the autumn disappearance of many birds by claiming that they become torpid after taking shelter in a reed bed, a hollow tree, or the mud of a stream.[96]

Since ancient times migration has inspired a variety of erroneous explanations. Early observations of amphibians, reptiles, and some mammals in a torpid state logically prompted a theory of hibernation to explain the seasonal disappearance of birds. Even Linnaeus, the most influential naturalist of the eighteenth century, was convinced that swallows hibernated in the mud.[97] In 1703 an anonymous essayist in England asserted that migratory birds flew to the moon to seek refuge in cold weather, a trip taking sixty days. Conflicting theories of migration and hibernation persisted until the second half of the nineteenth century, when migration was universally accepted as the reason for the seasonal absence of large numbers of common birds from their breeding ranges.[98]

Changes in the Landscape

Landscape patterns and disturbance regimes have profound effects on the abundance, distribution, and diversity of wild animals.[99] As habitats change so do animal populations. The respondent for Lisbon (Newent parish) noted: "Catamount, bear, wolf, deer, wildcat, and beaver were formerly found here, but long ago have disappeared."[100]

Pre-settlement to 1700

When the English first became acquainted with Connecticut it seemed a vast wilderness. The dominant feature of the landscape was the forest. "There were no pleasant fields, nor gardens, no public roads, nor cleared plats. Except in places where the timber had been destroyed, and its growth prevented by frequent fires, the groves were thick and lofty."[101] However, William Wood wrote, "Whereas it is generally conceived that the woods grow so thick that there is no more clear ground than is hewed out by the labor of man it is nothing so...in many places diverse acres being clear so that one may ride ahunting in most places of the land if he will venture himself for being lost."[102] Along the southern coast, from the

Changes in the landscape: Top, old growth forest characteristic of Connecticut around 1700; middle, agricultural clearing, which was at its height around 1830; bottom, reforestation of old fields in pine, 1915 (photographs courtesy of Harvard Forest Models, Fisher Museum, Harvard Forest, Petersham, Massachusetts).

Saco River in Maine all the way to the Hudson River, the woods were described as remarkably open, almost park-like at times.[103] Pyguag (the Indian name for Wethersfield, and adjoining areas) was reported to have signified "cleared land."[104]

Inland, much old-growth forest existed, best described as mixed hardwood-hemlock-white pine.[105] A primeval forest in Petersham, Massachusetts, thirty miles north of Connecticut, shows how much of the state might have looked about 1700. Although the early landscape was dominated by forest, it also included natural clearings, open grasslands, wetlands, and tidal marshes. As evidence for open grassland habitat, Gross wrote that "in Connecticut as in Massachusetts the early records though meager indicate that the Heath Hen was present in certain districts of the state."[106]

Cronon described a diverse patchwork of precolonial habitat that resulted from a cumulative sequence of history and ecological processes (e.g., wind, hurricanes, fire, and disease). In addition to lightning-caused fire, selective burning was done by Indians, typically in the spring and fall, to prepare land for cultivation and to enhance hunting. This created a heterogeneous, mosaic environment with forests in varying states of ecological succession.[107] Regular fires promoted what ecologists call "edge effect," which provided good habitat for a diversity of wildlife. Trumbull estimated that there were 16,000 to 20,000 Indians in Connecticut at the time of settlement.[108] They had a mobile lifestyle, shifting their subsistence bases to maximize fishing, hunting, or agriculture. Seasonal mobility reduced the impact on the ecosystem while agricultural practices enabled larger populations to sustain themselves.[109] It is not known how far into the region's interior the Indians modified the landscape, but their impact was dramatic where they practiced agriculture.[110]

Pioneer Subsistence Farming through the 1700s

European settlements differed greatly from mobile Indian communities that took advantage of ecosystem diversity. The English believed in and required permanent settlements.[111] To the settlers the forest was an impediment to the essential task of preparing land for crops[112] and as the population grew, more forest land had to be cleared for cultivation and for lumber, fences, and fuelwood. Once established, cleared fields and pastures became fixed features of the landscape. The Europeans' sedentary way of life had a rapid and dramatic impact on the landscape. According to Harper, the percentage of forest cover in Connecticut declined from nearly 90 percent at the time of settlement to less than 70 percent by 1700[113]. During the same period the state's population increased from about 2,000 to 24,000.[114] Whitney estimated the earliest phases of forest clearance on the East Coast at an annual rate of 0.4 percent; it required one hundred years to clear 50 percent of the land. After 1750, however, the rate increased to 0.8 to 1.3 percent. By 1713 two-thirds of the area of the state was settled, and by 1754 the whole state was occupied.[115] Connecticut's population in 1750 was estimated at 100,000 and had reached

237,635 in 1790, the time of the first U.S. Census. As populations expanded, the average family farm in Connecticut shrank from 486 acres in 1680 to 166 acres in 1750 and to 81 acres in 1790.[116]

According to Jenkins, as late as 1790 it was possible that nine out of every ten breadwinners in the state were engaged in some form of agriculture. A century later the number was three out of ten.[117]

Height of Intensive Agriculture, 1800-1840

By the early nineteenth century, farms had expanded to their fullest. About 65 percent of the state's land was cleared and under some form of agricultural use. Miles of stone walls traversed the landscape, enclosing crop fields or pasture land. The Lisbon reporter for the parish of Hanover, Andrew Lee, wrote in 1800 that "improved lands are fenced with stone walls & chestnut rails. The former increase. By the next age they will probably be the only fence."[118] Daniel N. Brinsmade, writing the Washington Town Report, added confirmation: "Timber for fencing is decreasing; but many farmers have stone on their grounds sufficient to make all their necessary fences."[119] At the time of the Town Reports, the primary concern of Connecticut farmers was still subsistence; commercial farming did not really begin until after 1810.[120]

Although data and analysis of forest utilization during the seventeenth and eighteenth centuries are lacking, the 1796 Connecticut tax returns provide an accurate landscape profile just prior to the time of the Town Reports. Williams reported that "579,847 acres, or 29.1 percent of the state were classed as brush pasture which was cutover land and old fields with forest regrowth used exclusively as pasture. In addition were 425,595 acres, or 21.4 percent of surface area, of clear pasture. There was another 606,573 acres [30.4 percent] of uninhabited woodland, some of which must also have held wild stock."[121] The last figure agrees with the estimate by Harper that by 1790 forest cover was less than 35 percent.[122]

Forest clearing, lumbering, and intensive agriculture all peaked by the mid-nineteenth-century.[123] By then thousands of acres of forest had disappeared, many wetlands had been drained, rivers dammed, and beaver ponds with their associated diversity of wildlife had nearly vanished from the landscape. From a high of 95 percent at the time of European settlement, the state's forests had been reduced to about 30 percent by 1850.[124]

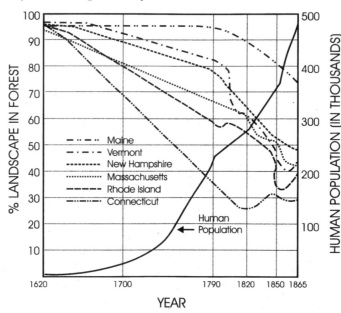

Changes over time in forest cover and human population growth in the six New England states. Native Americans are not included.

Farmland Abandonment and Reforestation

According to Favretti, the beginning of the nineteenth century saw a virtual exodus from Connecticut farms, although farm abandonment for New England as a whole is generally reported later, around 1840.[125] Reasons for abandonment included unprofitable agriculture, lure and accessibility of more fertile midwestern lands, children leaving to work in factories, rural decline, and farm reorganization.[126] As farms were abandoned, trends in land clearing were reversed and agricultural lands gradually reverted to forest. Reforestation continues to the present. Today, Connecticut's landscape is once again dominated by forest, although dramatic changes have occurred.[127] The present area covered by forest is estimated at nearly 65 percent, a level last seen shortly after 1700.

Reforestation initiated a succession of plant communities. For example, around 1910 a crop of old-field white pine might have grown from a nearby seed source, with hardwoods coming in after the pines were cut. In other areas, eastern redcedar fields with brush and shrubs dominated large areas, followed by the volunteer hardwood forests typical of the present landscape.[128] Historic land uses often resulted in even-aged forests. A decline in the abundance and distribution of some forest vertebrates may be explained by "successional" waves.[129] For example, grassland and shrubland birds are specialists that quickly disappear from a site as succession proceeds.[130] The decline of agriculture and reversion to forest have essentially eliminated grassland birds from New England.[131] The white-tailed deer, a subclimax species, thrived during the regrowth of the forest when heavy cutting early in the twentieth century created an abundance of nutritious browse. Regrowth and maturation of the forest put the browse out of reach by 1930,[132] but since then, continued reforestation has created more habitat, thus larger deer populations, which now have become a suburban nuisance.

Vertebrate Recolonization

No forest mammal became extinct during the dramatic habitat changes that took place in the settlement of Connecticut. Some species, such as the wolf and mountain lion, were permanently extirpated while others have successfully recolonized through reintroduction or natural range extension. According to DeGraaf and Miller, relatively mobile species that had wide distributions and survived at low densities in remnant woodlands were able to recolonize former ranges as forests became reestablished.[133] It appears that the key to the recolonization of most species was the rapid rate and extent of reforestation.

Stray moose still wander into the state. The number of moose sightings is expected to increase in the future, and three specimens from Connecticut recently were relocated into New York to reduce potential conflicts with humans and to return them to suitable habitat.[134]

The beaver, virtually extirpated in Connecticut by 1842, was first reintroduced in 1914. Subsequent releases in the 1920s through the 1940s, combined with natural movement into the state in the 1940s from populations in Massachusetts and New York, led to about twenty known colonies in the 1950s. Beavers continued to increase, and in 1961 the first regulated harvest was allowed. Today the beaver population in Connecticut is conservatively estimated at 6,000 individuals.[135] The wildlife manager's challenge is to balance the regulated harvest with the animal's tendency to destroy its limited habitat. Beaver create a mosaic of successional stages as they colonize and then abandon waterways.[136] And their return provides a wealth of new ecological relationships.

The fisher, another extirpated furbearer, was considered absent since the late 1800s until it was reintroduced into the northwestern portion of the state in 1989 and 1990. At the same time, a natural range extension from Massachusetts occurred in the northeastern part of the state; three sightings were made in that area shortly before the northwestern releases.[137] The fisher was listed as a species of special concern on the state's first endangered species list in 1992. It has since been removed from that list because the present population is estimated to be in the hundreds.

The eastern wild turkey was extirpated in the state by 1813, but with reforestation a number of reintroduction efforts were attempted from 1956 to 1970. Although these resulted in only limited establishment, the release program of 1975 was successful, and wild turkeys gradually spread throughout the state. Because of the success of the newly established population, a limited spring harvest was allowed in 1981—Connecticut residents were able to hunt wild turkeys for the first time in 170 years.[138]

The black bear also has recolonized Connecticut by natural range extension. Prior to1990 the black bear was considered only a transient, but since then the state has had a small and growing resident population.

Changes in the People

The respondents in the Town Reports talked about four basic relationships to wild animals: 1) they provided a source of food; 2) they provided furs and hides for leather; 3) they damaged crops, poultry, and livestock; or 4) they were feared or avoided. These represent only three of nine basic values of nature—utilitarian, dominionistic, and negativistic—identified by Stephen Kellert in his book, *The Value of Life: Biological Diversity and Human Society* (see Table 3). Kellert explains that "these nine values, considered biological in origin, signify basic structures of human relationships and adaptation to the natural world developed over the course of human evolution."[139] The limited range of relationships and values expressed in early literature are understandable when we remember that the "wilderness" landscapes the colonists encountered in the New World had disappeared in Europe centuries earlier. Such values were appropriate to a society trying to survive in an alien wilderness. The persistence of English values and customs was an attempt to re-create a familiar society and its accompanying landscape. Whitney noted that most of the beasts of the wilderness at that time could be placed in one of two categories—the noxious or the useful.[140] In fact, the dichotomy evident in the Town Reports is clearly moral—animals were perceived as good or bad. The bounty system, for instance, was imposed to rid the wilderness of bad beasts.

Other values identified by Kellert, although not expressed explicitly in the Town Reports, had been expressed by people of earlier periods. For instance, 170 years prior to the Town Reports, William Wood exhibited naturalistic and aesthetic values when he described the flying squirrel as "not very big, slender of body, with a great deal of loose skin which she spreads when she flies, which the wind gets and so wafts her batlike body from place to place. It is a creature more for sight and wonderment than either pleasure and profit." Of musquashes (muskrats), he wrote: "The male hath two stones which smell as sweet as musk, and being killed in winter and the spring, never lose their sweet smell. . . . One good skin will perfume a whole house full of clothes if it be right and good."[141]

Animal Attacks on Humans

In the Coventry Town Report, Jesse Root provided the only account of an animal injuring a human: "In this town lived & died, the famous

Connecticut homestead, Litchfield, circa late 1790s, and stone walls (photographs by Roger T. Zerillo, U.S. Forest Service).

Jonathan Fowler, who took an enraged old bear which had attacked his father, by the throat, threw her on the ground, upon her back, & slew her, with no other weapons than a pine knot."[142] Unfortunately, the report lacks further detail.

Caras pointed out that animals are not inherently but rather "potentially" dangerous. Cardoza explained this distinction by pointing out that animals attack under provocation when wounded or harassed. For instance, there was an account from Simsbury of a wounded bear turning on its pursuers.[143] Provocation also may be inadvertent, and knowledge of an animal's habits is important to avoid risk of injury. For example, Wood understood a bear's defense of its young: "For bears, they be common, being a great black kind of bear which be most fierce at strawberry time, at which time they have young ones."[144] Although possible, unprovoked attacks by healthy animals are very rare.

Although wolves and rattlesnakes gave the greatest cause for concern to the early settlers, yet, to our knowledge there are no reports of harm to humans from unprovoked attacks. Wood related that "it was never known yet that a wolf ever set upon a man or woman. Neither do they trouble horses or cows; but swine, goats, and red calves...be often destroyed by them."[145] Thomas Morton wrote regarding wolves, "They are fearful curres, and will runne away from a man as fast as any fearful dogge."[146] Of the rattlesnake, feared for its "fatal con-

sequences," Wood wrote of it as "never offering to leap or bite any man if he not be trodden on first."[147] Caulkins similarly concluded that "though the rattlesnake is considered a slow-moving animal that seldom bites unless first trodden upon or struck, he is furious in his charge."[148] The noted herpetologist Raymond Ditmars knew of three rattlesnake bites in the southern Berkshires, one fatal.[149]

Changing Values

The Litchfield farmstead shown in the photograph was built just prior to the time of the Town Reports project. Its stone fences remind us of the dramatic physical changes in the landscape and the equally striking changes in people's attitudes, ideas, and values toward nature and "wild animals." The study of landscapes is a study of the societies that both fashion and reflect those landscapes.[150] "Improved lands" meant cleared lands. Thick stone walls are indicative of land that was formerly tilled, while narrow walls composed of a single row of boulders mark land that was formerly pastured or grazed.[151] Both have now become part of the forest landscape. Connecticut's stone walls always have been utilized heavily by small mammals as nesting, resting, and seed-cache sites, which probably are responsible for the higher incidence of oaks and hickories along these fencerows today.[152] Once considered part of the drudgery of clearing land, stone walls are viewed two centuries later for their aesthetic qualities as part of the landscape, for their symbolism of our historic past, and for the natural, ecological, and scientific values associated with wildlife communities in forest ecosystems.

Benjamin Trumbull wrote that "it was absolutely necessary, that they should turn the wilderness into gardens and fields, that they should plant and cultivate the earth, and obtain some tolerable harvest."[153] "Man gets accustomed to everything," wrote Tocqueville in 1831. "He gets used to every sight. . . . [He] fells the forest and drains the marshes. . . . The wilds become villages, and villages towns. The American, the daily witness of such wonders, does not see anything astounding in all this. This incredible destruction, this even more surprising growth, seem to him the usual progress of things in this world. He gets accustomed to it as to the unalterable order of nature."[154]

As the agricultural-subsistence way of life has changed, so has people's relationship to nature. Consumption, domination, and fear of wild animals—while still with us today—have diminished in prominence, while other values have come to the forefront. Modern American society tends to value wildlife for its naturalistic, aesthetic, symbolic, ecological, and scientific attributes. Except for the writings of William Wood,[155] we found little evidence of these values in early literature, including the Town Reports. On the other hand, few people today relate to white-tailed deer or beavers as sources of meat, leather, or fur. Today the naturalistic value is as important as the utilitarian value was in the seventeenth through the nineteenth centuries. Conflicts among values still exist, though. People in Connecticut, for example, are uneasy about the increasing bear population: they want the animals removed when they come into conflict (dominionistic, negativistic), but do not want the bears harmed (moralistic, naturalistic).

Finally, in focusing on landscape and other changes in Connecticut during the last two hundred years, we have minimized discussion of Native Americans' changing relationships to the landscape and wildlife. A more complete consideration of Indian economic, ecological, and symbolic relationships to nature and wildlife from precolonial times to the present would show even more dramatic transformations in values. For further reading we recommend William Cronon's superb study, *Changes in the Land: Indians, Colonists, and the Ecology of New England.*[156]

Game Laws Reflect Changing Values

The European settlers brought with them not only a preconceived plan for the natural order of the landscape, but also their ideals for the protection and ownership of wild animals as property. Connecticut's wild animals were first protected under English game laws that included only wild turkey, grouse, and related birds, but not deer.[157] However, Bouvier's *Law Dictionary*[158] defined game as "birds and beasts of a wild-nature, obtained by fowling and hunting." Clearly, game was viewed and protected as property and strongly associated with people's utilitarian values. The following quotes from the U.S. Supreme Court Justice's opinion in *Geer v. State of Connecticut* illustrate the principle that wild animals

were property with utilitarian value: "wild animals, belong to those who take them,"[159] and "The preservation of such animals as are adapted to consumption as food or any other useful purpose is a matter of public interest, and it is within the police power of the state. ...to make such laws as will best preserve such game, and secure its beneficial use in the future to the citizens."[160]

The earliest game laws probably were the hunting privileges granted in 1629 by the West India Company to persons planting colonies in the New Netherlands and the provisions for the right of hunting in the Massachusetts Bay Colonial Ordinance of 1647. In 1677 Connecticut prohibited the export of deer, the first law of its kind in American game protection.[161] By the end of the colonial period, twelve colonies had enacted game laws. For example, Connecticut closed hunting seasons for protection of game and even closed hunting for years to allow scarce game species to recover. Bounties on "bad" beasts were enacted to protect game, livestock, and public safety. We are not aware of any protection for non-game species until passage of the first laws protecting insectivorous birds in Connecticut and New Jersey in 1850.[162]

A review of Connecticut wildlife laws and case law suggests a clear shift in attitudes toward non-consumptive use. Conservation did not occur until 1901 when Connecticut prohibited the killing of non-game birds and the destruction of their nests and eggs. Interestingly, great horned owls and hawks, other than ospreys, were not among the birds protected by that act, which has subsequently been revised. The earliest general federal statute, the Lacey Act, was passed in 1900 to regulate the importation of birds and animals and interstate traffic in game. The federal Endangered Species Act was passed in 1973. Connecticut did not pass legislation to protect species that were endangered, threatened, or of special concern until 1989.

Wildlife Challenges in the Next Century

The distribution, abundance, and diversity of Connecticut's wild animals will continue to change because of dynamic, interrelated environmental factors.[163] New environmental problems will challenge natural resource managers throughout the twenty-first century. Yahner identified five factors that will affect the ecological integrity of eastern deciduous forests: 1) biodiversity conservation and ecosystem management; 2) forest fragmentation; 3) education; 4) recreation; and 5) regional and global influences.[164] It was not until the latter part of the twentieth century, as peoples' values toward nature changed, that protection of biodiversity became a major concern. According to Wilcox and Murphy, forest or habitat fragmentation has been described as the most serious threat to biological diversity worldwide.[165] Forest fragmentation results when a large, relatively mature forest is converted into smaller tracts by roads, agriculture, suburbanization, timber harvesting, or other uses. Although forest habitats in Connecticut have increased dramatically in the last century due to farm abandonment, new land uses—specifically, housing developments in rural areas—continue to threaten the state's natural communities and will continue well into the twenty-first century. According to Paul Rego, state wildlife managers are faced with two problems: first, habitat is being removed, and second, opportunities for human interactions with wildlife are increasing (in particular bears and moose).[166]

Extinction and endangerment of several wildlife species in eastern deciduous forests have been attributed partially to forest fragmentation, which reduces habitat to patches too small to supply the species' requirements for food, water, and cover. Isolation of patches also affects movements and dispersal capabilities of some species.[167] Fragmentation of Connecticut's woodlands, coupled with the loss of tropical forest wintering grounds, has contributed to a dramatic population decline in several neotropical migratory bird species.[168]

Conclusion

The Town Reports that responded to the Connecticut Academy of Arts and Sciences survey in 1800 included surprisingly little detail about "wild animals." There are probably several explanations for this. By this period in the state's development, people's attentions were primarily focused on farming. For instance, Timothy Dwight, who did not return New Haven's report until 1811, bluntly stated that everyone was "closely engaged in his own business" and thus unwilling "to write on subjects, unconnected with his personal concerns." Dwight's only mention of wildlife–in what was otherwise one of the most complete Town Reports–was as follows: "On that part of the plain, which is between Mount Pleasant and Milford Hills, the original growth was the shrub oak. Wild turkies abounded on this plain, as late as the year 1695."[169] In addition, so much of the "megafauna" had already disappeared by 1800 that people no longer gained significant utilitarian benefits from wild animals nor did they have much to fear from them. As a result, they may not have paid much attention to wildlife. Respondents also seemed to have a limited notion of what constituted "wild animals" and thus answered the question very narrowly. For example, there was very little mention of small, economically-unimportant vertebrates. Nor was there any apparent attempt by respondents to seek information from more knowledgeable individuals on specialized topics. Although there were some keen observers, even centuries earlier, we found no written material from naturalists in Connecticut for this period.

Nevertheless, the Town Reports do make it clear that Connecticut's residents knew that wildlife populations had changed in abundance and distribution since colonial times. The causes were acknowledged as both direct killing and the clearing of land. There were lamentations later in the century that "now, alas! they are gone . . . perhaps . . . forever."[170] But the agricultural landscape that dominated Connecticut in 1800, that had been so hard won from the "thick and lofty" forests, must have been viewed as a permanent change for the better and the concomitant loss of wildlife a minor sacrifice.

Now, two hundred years later, many animal populations have been restored and people have developed new relationships with wild animals and natural habitats and much more is known about the biology and ecology of Connecticut's wildlife species. Numerous laws at state and federal levels provide for the monitoring, management, and protection of a wide variety of species. People directly enjoy wildlife through birding, fishing, hunting, whale watching, wildlife tourism and art, and visiting zoos.[171] The relationship of people and wildlife is probably more favorable now than it has been for many decades. Yet the return of the state's wildlife, through resiliency, recolonization, reintroduction, or expanded ranges, has depended largely on the return of the forests, which now face renewed threats. Although shifts in perspectives have resulted in practices that conserve and enhance wildlife rather than destroy it, there remain many conflicting values and circumstances that may overshadow or encroach upon our concern for wildlife. Burgeoning human populations, the penchant for "trophy" houses in pristine settings, and the fear of wildlife-borne diseases are only a few of the many dangers that jeopardize the state's forests, wetlands, and other habitats as well as the wild animals.

As we enter the twenty-first century, we must ensure that Connecticut's wildlife heritage is preserved. Although there are attempts to "protect" species and ecosystems by incorporating them into economic market systems, long-term biodiversity protection will come only when more people are animated by what E.O. Wilson termed "biophilia"–our profound need, indeed, craving for personal, direct experience with wild animals and plants and our kinship with all life.[172] We hope that two hundred years from now our descendants will commend our guardianship of Connecticut's rich wildlife legacy.

TABLE I.

Wild animals mentioned in the Connecticut Town Reports, and their relationship to people

Wild Animal (as named in report)	Number of reports	Town Source[1]	Source Notes	Relationship to People[2]
Black bear	10	3, 4, 5, 7, 14, 15, 17, 23, 26, 31	(3) "extinguished by the increase of inhabitants and clearing the land"	food, fur/pelts, damage to crops
			(7) "plentiful 40 years ago"	and livestock, feared/avoided
			(26) "hunters have either killed them or drove them off"	
White-tailed deer	8	3, 4, 14, 15, 17, 23, 26, 31	(15) "many years after settlement were numerous"	food, hides/leather
			(17) "common...till winter of 1763"	
			(23) "they are now extinct"	
Wolf	7	4, 14, 17, 19, 23, 26, 31	(14) "long ago have disappeared"	feared/avoided, damage to livestock, fur/pelts
			(19) "in 1695 the town gave Clement Miner 8 acres of land for wolf killing"	
			(26) "were plenty 50 or 60 years ago but are now not seen as hunters have either killed them or drove them off"	
Fox (red & grey)	6	3, 4, 14, 26, 28, 31	(4) "are still to be found here"	fur/pelts, damage to poultry
			(26) "are very troublesome...destroyed our poultry"	
			(28) "...more numerous in a settled country than in a forest"	
Wildcat (Bobcat)	6	4, 14, 15, 23, 26, 31	(4) "are still to be found here"	fur/pelts, damage to livestock
			(15) "destroy sheep and lambs. Considerable mischief...in the winters of 1811 and 1812."	
			(31) "were common...as settlers increased...diminished as the country became cleared"	
Wild turkey	5	14, 15, 17, 18, 23	(15) "many years after settlement...wild turkies were numerous"	food
			(17) "plenty in 1680 and occasionally seen as late as 1700"	
			(18) "abounded on this plain as late as the year 1695"	
Rattlesnakes	5	4, 14, 21, 23, 26	(4) "fatal consequences...by these deliterious reptiles"	feared/avoided
			(21) "where many of those snakes creep out and are killed"	
			(26) "were very plenty inhabitants destroyed them...." "...rare to hear of one now"	
Mink	4	4, 14, 23, 26	(4) "are still to be found here"	fur/pelts
			(26) "live in Mashepogue pond"	

[1] See Appendix I for town name.

[2] Relationship derived from Connecticut Town Reports and reviewed historical accounts or records.

[3] Species assumed based on description in Town Report.

TABLE I. (cont.)

Wild animals mentioned in the Connecticut Town Reports, and their relationship to people

Wild Animal (as named in report)	Number of reports	Town Source[1]	Source Notes	Relationship to People[2]
Muskrats or Musquashes	4	4, 14, 23, 26	(4) "are still to be found here" (26) "live in Mashepogue pond"	food, fur/pelts
Skunk (striped)	4	4, 8, 23, 28	(8) "an increase of...cause unknown"	fur/pelts, damage to poultry
Woodchuck	4	8, 23, 26, 28	(8) "an increase of...cause unknown" (26) "destroys our corn and grane"	(food) damage to crops
Panther or Catamount	3	4, 14, 23	(4) "these animals leave all cultivated and inhabited places" (14) "formerly found here...but long ago have disappeared" (23) "they are now extinct in our woods"	damage to livestock
Otter	3	14, 23, 26	(14) "some are now rarely seen" "...of an amphibious nature"	fur/pelts
Raccoon	3	4, 14, 23	(4) "are still to be found here" (23) "some few..."	food, fur/pelts damage to poultry
Squirrel (all kinds)	3	7, 26, 28	(7) "havock they make of the Indian corn while it is in the field" (26) "are very troublesome, destroys our corn and grane"	damage to crops
Striped or streaked squirrel (chipmunk)	3	4, 23, 26	(4) "are still to be found here"	damage to crops
Beaver	2	14, 23	(14) "formerly found here but long ago have disappeared" (23) "there were formerly...in our ponds"	food, fur /pelts
Rabbits	2	23, 28	(23) "are very plenty"	food, fur/pelts
Grey squirrel	2	4, 23	See squirrels, this table	damage to crops
Crow	2	7, 26	(26) "we have...which pull up our corn as soon as it gets out of the ground"	damage to crops
Hare	1	28	(28) "large as a small dog & entirely white"	food, fur/pelts
Porpoise	1	16	(16) "Summer of 1792 or 3...fishery set up." "...during the season caught six or seven hundred of this kind of fish. These skins were tanned..."	food, hides/leather
Moose	1	17	(17) "one was killed in 1770"	food, hides/leather
Elk	1	4	(4) "near 40 years since an elk was killed here"	food, hides/leather
Red fox	1	23	(23) "are found there"	fur/pelts
Grey fox	1	23	(23) "are found there"	fur/pelts
Black squirrel	1	4	(4) "are still to be found here"	damage to crops
Red squirrel	1	23	(23) "have multiplied to a very surprising degree"	no information
Flying squirrel	1	4	(4) "are still to be found here"	no information
Weasels	1	23	(23) only mentioned	damage to poultry

TABLE I. (cont.)

Wild animals mentioned in the Connecticut Town Reports, and their relationship to people

Wild Animal (as named in report)	Number of reports	Town Source[1]	Source Notes	Relationship to People[2]
Moles	1	23	(23) "several sorts of..."	no information
Bats	1	23	(23) "several sorts of..."	no information
Mice	1	23	(23) "several sorts of..."	no information
Shark	1	2	(2) "three militia called to New London to help guard the coast were chased by a 9½ foot shark which they were able to kill as they returned from fishing in a canoe."	feared/avoided
Blackbird	1	26	(26) "pull up our corn as soon as it gets out of the ground"	damage to crops
Partridges	1	23	(23) "The birds are chiefly those of passage—but those of which tarry with us thro the winter are..."	
Pigeons	1	23	(23) "The birds are chiefly those of passage—but those of which tarry with us thro the winter are..."	no information
Quails	1	23	(23) "The birds are chiefly those of passage—but those of which tarry with us thro the winter are..."	no information
Snowbirds	1	23	(23) "The birds are chiefly those of passage—but those of which tarry with us thro the winter are..."	no information
Wood cocks	1	23	(23) "The birds are chiefly those of passage—but those of which tarry with us thro the winter are..."	no information
Wood ducks	1	23	(23) "The birds are chiefly those of passage—but those of which tarry with us thro the winter are..."	no information
Woodpeckers	1	23	(23) "The birds are chiefly those of passage—but those of which tarry with us thro the winter are..."	no information
Wrens	1	23	(23) "The birds are chiefly those of passage—but those of which tarry with us thro the winter are..."	no information
Watersnakes	1	2	(2) "...snakes infest the pond"	no information
Adder	1	23	(23) "There are yet a few black snakes,..."	no information
Black snake	1	23	(23) "There are yet a few black snakes,..."	no information
Northern copperhead[3]	1	23	(23) "...& snakes equally poisonous..."	feared/avoided
Milk snake	1	23	(23) "There are yet a few black snakes,..."	no information
Northern redbelly snake[3]	1	23	(23) "...a few very small red and green snakes..."	no information
Striped snake	1	23	(23) "There are yet a few black snakes,..."	no information

TABLE II

Comparison of the number of species of amphibians, reptiles, birds, and terrestrial mammals mentioned in the Connecticut Town Reports with the number of species found at present in the state.

Taxon	Common name	Minimum Number of species (Town Reports)	Number of species (found at present[1])	Percentage of species found at present/ reported in 1800
Class Amphibia	Amphibians	0	22	0
Class Reptilia	Reptiles	8 [8]	26	30.8
Class Aves	Birds	11 [7]	390	2.8 [9]
Class Mammalia	Mammals	25	52	48.1
Order				
Marsupialia	Opossums	0	1	0
Insectivora	Moles & shrews	1 [2]	8	12.5
Chiroptera	Bats	1 [3]	7	14.3
Lagomorpha	Hares & rabbits	2 [4]	4	50
Rodentia	Rodents	8 [5]	19	42.1
Carnivora	Flesh eaters	10 [6]	12	83.3
Artiodactyla	Deer	3	1	300

[1] Sources: State of Connecticut, DEP Wildlife Bureau Publication NHW-3 (1988); DeGraaf, Richard M., and Deborah D. Rudis. "New England Wildlife: Habitat, Natural History, and Distribution. U.S. Department of Agriculture Forest Service," *Northeastern Forest Experiment Station, General Technical Report NE-108.* Broomall, PA; Godin (1977), Goodwin (1935), Klemens (1993), *Connecticut Field List,* compiled by the Connecticut Rare Records Committee of the Connecticut Ornithological Association (1995).

[2-8] The following animals were generically mentioned: [2]moles, [3] bats, [4] rabbits, [5] mice, [6] weasels, [7] blackbird; therefore, one species was added to each group; [8]water snake, adder, black snake, striped snake; four species were added to Reptiles. [9] Includes accidentals

TABLE III

Values of nature and living biodiversity (after Kellert 1996).

Value	Definition
Utilitarian	Gaining material benefit to satisfy human needs
Naturalistic	Satisfaction obtained from the direct experience of nature and wildlife
Ecologistic-scientific	Gaining comprehension and sometimes control through systematic exploration of nature
Symbolic	Using nature to express ideas and emotions
Dominionistic	An urge to suppress nature, subdue and control unruly or threatening elements
Humanistic	Developing emotional attachments, such as with pets
Moralistic	An ethic to minimize harm to other creatures based on the basic kinship of all life
Negativistic	Aversion, fear, or dislike of certain elements

APPENDIX I

Source list of Connecticut Town Reports

Number	Town	Report Date	Number	Town	Report Date
1	Bethlem	1812	18	New Haven	1811
2	Canterbury	1801	19	New London	c. 1812
3	Cheshire	1803	20	North Bolton	1800
4	Cornwall (2 reports)	1800-1801, 1812	21	Pomfret	1800
5	Coventry	1806	22	Preston	1801
6	East Windsor	1806	23	Ridgefield	1800
7	Farmington	1802	24	Stratfield	1800
8	Franklin	1800	25	Tolland	1804
9	Goshen	1812	26	Union	1803
10	Guilford	1832	27	Wallingford	1811-1812
11	Haddam	1808	28	Washington	1800
12	Kent	1812	29	Watertown	1801
13	Lebanon	1800	30	Willington	1805
14	Lisbon (2 reports)	1800, 1801	31	Winchester-Winsted	1813
15	Litchfield (county)	1815	32	Windham	1800
16	Madison	1832	33	Wintonbury	1802
17	Middlesex (county; includes 7 towns)	1819		(Bloomfield)	

APPENDIX II
List of Common and Scientific Names

Common Name	Scientific Name
Reptiles	
Northern redbelly snake	*Storeria o. occipitomaculata*
Eastern milk snake	*Lampropeltis t. triangulum*
Timber Rattlesnake	*Crotalus horridus*
Northern copperhead	*Agkistrodon contortrix mokeson*
Birds	
Wood Duck	*Aix sponsa*
Osprey	*Pandion haliaetus*
Wild Turkey	*Meleagris gallopavo*
Heath Hen	*Tympanuchus c. cupido*
American Woodcock	*Scolopax minor*
Passenger Pigeon	*Ectopistes migratorius*
Great Horned Owl	*Bubo virginianus*
American Crow	*Corvus brachyrhynchos*
Mammals	
Virginia Opossum	*Didelphis virginiana*
Eastern Cottontail	*Sylvilagus floridanus*
Hare, snowshoe	*Lepus americanus*
Hare, European	*Lepus europaeus*
Woodchuck	*Marmota monax*
Squirrel, black or gray	*Sciurus carolinensis*
Squirrel, red	*Tamiasciurus hudsonicus*
Squirrel, flying	*Glaucomys* sp.
Beaver	*Castor canadensis*
Muskrat	*Ondatra zibethicus*
Norway Rat	*Rattus norvegicus*
Allegheny woodrat	*Neotoma magister*
House Mouse	*Mus musculus*
Wolf, gray	*Canis lupus*
Coyote	*Canis latrans*
Fox, red	*Vulpes vulpes*
Fox, gray	*Urocyon cinereoargenteus*
Black Bear	*Ursus americanus*
Raccoon	*Procyon lotor*
Marten	*Martes americana*
Fisher	*Martes pennanti*
Wolverine	*Gulo gulo*
Weasel, long-tailed, and ermine	*Mustela* sp.
Mink	*Mustela vison*
Striped Skunk	*Mephitis mephitis*
River Otter	*Lutra canadensis*
Mountain Lion	*Felis concolor*
Lynx	*Felis lynx*
Bobcat	*Felis rufus*
White-tailed Deer	*Odocoileus virginianus*
Moose	*Alces alces*
Eastern Woodland Caribou	*Rangifer tarandus caribou*
American Elk	*Cervus elaphus*
Walrus	*Odobenus rosmarus*

Connecticut Woodlands 1800-1836

George McLean Milne

The quiet world in which the respondents to the Connecticut Academy's Solicitation Letter lived was one in which the role of the woodlands was far different from what people in the twenty-first century might easily imagine. Throughout this essay's account, there is an oft-repeated theme: "Wood was the only fuel; wood the principal raw material."

One can get a picture of what that world looked like by visiting Old Sturbridge Village in Massachusetts, which attempts to re-create a village of the 1830s. The Village is, quite properly, a museum. The elusive reality is that of a complex, hard-working, passionate community, serious and sometimes contentious. Another visual resource is the now famous Currier and Ives prints of New England homesteads, whose publication began in 1835 and which looked back, sometimes sentimentally, to earlier days.

The great virtue of the Town Reports, which the Academy collected, is that the reporters were present at the times and places where events occurred and historic conditions prevailed. They wrote without sentimentality, occasionally with laconic humor and yet with that deeper appreciation that led Samuel Smith in 1832 to write his patriotic hymn, "My Country, 'tis of Thee" in which are the lines:

> I love thy rocks and rills,
> Thy woods and templed hills.

His words evoke the picture of wooded hillsides with white spired churches on their horizons.

The Ancient Forest

In order to understand the woodlands as they existed at the time of the Academy's enquiry in 1800, one must realize that by that time Connecticut had nearly two hundred years of history behind it—time enough for two successive stands of trees to grow to maturity. For the English colonists, the first necessity was to provide food and shelter for themselves and their animals. To gain this end they had literally to subdue the wilderness. About 96 percent of Connecticut's land was covered by forest.[1]

They set about to clear the land for farming, armed with hand tools and prodigious energy. Their method of clearing was extravagantly wasteful: trees were girdled and burned in the field, with the best logs sawed into boards, and with what must have seemed an infinite supply of cordwood for the huge fireplaces of their dwellings. An 1800s observer in Canterbury reported oak stumps that "appear 8 feet in diameter & perhaps were cut 100 years since."[2]

The clearing of land for farming resulted by 1800 in open fields and pastures covering about 48 percent of the state.[3] This setting of established communities was the Connecticut to whose towns the Academy directed its survey of the woodlands and of a way of life unique in the American epic.

A Rich Diversity

In 1800 as now, Connecticut woodlands supported a rich variety of trees and shrubs. One of the interesting aspects of the Academy's survey is that trees, beyond providing lumber and firewood, were living objects of interest in themselves. It was in 1820 that Henry David Thoreau began keeping a journal of his rambles around the woods and streams of Concord, Massachusetts, accounts that in his lifetime filled twenty volumes with his observations. He had a quick eye for beauty in the pastoral wilderness of Concord and came close to making a religion out of man's spiritual and moral relation with Nature (spelled with a capital "N"). William Wordsworth in England's Lake District likewise propounded a sense of reverence for the woods and the hills. In America, the poet John Greenleaf Whittier (b. 1802) looked back from old age to a childhood memory of a great winter snowstorm with the wind whistling outside, and the family gathered round the big fireplace. The time of the woodlands was thus a time of sentiment and of nascent science which added an incalculable dimension to long days' labor with axe and spade and plow.

The people who responded to the Academy's inquiry knew their trees, and valued and used that knowledge. Fourteen out of approximately forty Reports included lists of known trees. Some of these are noted below. All the trees identified in 1800 exist in Connecticut today. (This does not include exotic species, which have been introduced from abroad, such as Norway maple and spruce.)

A basic tree list was submitted by Azel Backus, minister in Bethlem:

Ash	Cherry (wild)	Pepperidge
Bass wood	Elm	Sassafras
Beach (sic)	Hickory	Poplar
Birch	Maple (sugar)	Sumach
Dogwood	Maple (white)	WhiteSumac
Buttonwood	Hornbeam	Butternut
Chesnut (sic)	The Oaks, Black, White and Rock[4]	

To this list, other respondents added the family of pines, the cedars, Willow, Hemlock, Red Oak and black, yellow, and white Birch. Such lists are suggestive rather than definitive, because a number of the species had local names. Soil and moisture conditions determined which species flourished in different locations. Connecticut woodlands were not a monoculture; they were a rich mixture and this contributed to their vigor and interest. They formed the resource to which the people of Connecticut turned for firewood to heat their homes, and lumber for their manifold enterprises.

Home Fires

"Wood was the only fuel." To all practical purposes this was the situation during the time of the Academy's inquiry. The amount of wood used as fuel was enormous and it was wastefully utilized. The magnitude of this factor is suggested by the provision in early Connecticut towns for their ministers. Their contracts called for a cash salary sometimes paid "in kind" in commodities to which a cash value was assigned, and for an annual allowance of firewood. As an example, the Reverend Hercules Weston in Cornwall received £70, plus 20 cords of wood—a pile 160 feet long and four feet high. Twenty cords seemed an average amount in other parishes. As time went on and a cash economy more prevailed, Eliphaz Alvord in 1813 in Winchester reported that the minister was given thirty dollars with which to buy his own wood.[5] Multiply this factor by the number of houses in a village, and the demand becomes considerable both on the woodland source and upon the time and energy of those who had to cut and split the logs.

Even down to 1830, the fireplace, inefficient though it was, was the source of heat in most homes. The fireplaces were huge, and were used also for cooking. In many cases chimneys were built of fieldstone and were poorly mortared. This made them the frequent cause of house fires—so much so that in the town of Cornwall there was an inspection of chimneys, which found two-thirds of them to be "fourth rate."[6]

Saw Timber

One of the characteristics of the settlers of Connecticut was that from early days they built substantial houses. No log cabins for them! They needed boards for this enterprise, and satisfying that need led to a proliferation of sawmills. Though Connecticut could claim more than thirty species of trees, those most in demand for saw timber were white pine, soft and easily worked, yet strong; hemlock, found in damp and shady woods; hard maple, and chestnut, that most versatile and valuable of trees, and oak, heavy and strong.

Owing to the destructive land clearing practices of the colonial generations, by 1800 high quality saw logs were scarce and expensive in many parts of the state. Pine, the lumber for construction, was being shipped in from Maine.

In the Connecticut Town Reports are descriptions of the logging and sawing process. First, the tree was felled. This was usually done with a two-man cross-cut saw, in an exercise of strength and teamwork. By almost unanimous agreement, felling was done in cold weather—February or "the old of the moon in March."[7] The logic of this timing is the fact that in winter the wood of the tree trunk contained the minimum amount of sap, and was the least subject to decay. The durability of wood was an important consideration in the days before treated lumber. With axe and saw, the log was trimmed of branches and made ready for hauling to the mill by draft animals.

Oxen vs. Horses

There was lively discussion in the records: which was the best source of motive power—oxen or horses? These animals had to work both in the woods and in farm fields. John Cotton Smith of Sharon, writing in 1807, reported that in the preceding fifteen years oxen had steadily grown in favor:

> The horse costs more at first, is more expensive to keep...at the close of life is worth absolutely nothing...while the ox, of less original cost, is less expensive to keep, more hardy and equally powerful; after literally filling his days with usefulness may be turned into beef, and thus give back to his owner more than his first cost.[8]

Lewis Norton of Goshen reported that oxen were better suited to rough ground, "drawing more steadily, and more capable of enduring fatigue than horses."[9] Horses, nevertheless, worked faster on roads and smooth land free of stones.

From the perspective of the mechanized twentieth century, the number of draft animals employed on Connecticut farms and in the woodlands is astonishing. For example, Goshen reported 115 yoke of oxen and 324 horses, and Farmington 155 teams of oxen. These animals and the skilled teamsters who knew and drove them worked together hauling logs to the mill.

Connecticut Sawmills 1800-1830

Reading the Town Reports, one is surprised at the large number of sawmills that were in operation. Almost every rural town had at least one; some had as many as ten and the average had about five. The large number is accounted for by the fact that many of these mills were small operations located near the stands of timber to be cut, and on seasonal streams that could supply waterpower only in winter and spring when water levels were high. The same streams were also shared with gristmills and various textile operations.

On larger rivers there were more substantial and permanent installations. Deep in the woods in Lebanon are the massive stone ruins of such a mill, with its dam and channels, but with its wooden elements long rotted away. Perhaps the largest of all was a giant in East Haddam, with eight blades and a carriage that could accommodate logs up to 70 feet long.[10] In an excellent restoration, one can see at Old Sturbridge Village a water-powered, "up and down" sawmill, which supplies the Village with many of its needs for lumber today.

Upon arrival at a sawmill, the teamster turned the logs over to the sawyer who settled each log in the carriage, and clamped it for the right slab thickness. He would then open the sluices; the rush of water would start the ponderous turning of the great wheel, and the saw cut a fraction of an inch with each powerful stroke along the length of the log.

In conclusion, the observer from Farmington wrote: "The work performed by those mills is in sawing the timber of our own forest into plank board, scantling, & slitwork of every description."[11] He wrote with feeling about a mountainside mill which he saw: "When in motion it serves to delight the eye and imagination by presenting to the beholder from the plain below, a most beautiful and picturesque cascade."[12]

Wooden Pipes for Water Supply

Among the first requirements of the early Connecticut settlers was a supply of water. The Goshen Report mentioned that "wells can be obtained in almost any place."[13] Throughout the state the wells ranged from twelve to over 40 feet in depth. Water was drawn from these either by an oaken bucket, swung down on a well-sweep, or cranked up on a windlass. In many houses there was a cistern which collected rainwater.

In addition there were natural flowing springs. These were of particular interest, because with the hard work and ingenuity of people they led to the building of aqueducts from the water sources to homes and villages. These aqueducts were described by the Winsted report author as:

> ...made of logs, from ten to sixteen inches in diameter, bored by hand and connected, by a tube or thimble of iron, The ends of the logs are not pared down in the manner that is in common use for the purpose of being inserted into each other. A similar aquaduct [sic] was laid twenty-two years ago in a neighbouring town, and required but trifling repairs...[14]

These wooden-pipe aqueducts carried water over remarkable distances, in Sharon 600 rods (nearly 10,000 feet or about a mile and three-quarters) from "a large spring of excellent water" to the village.[15] In Washington a similar aqueduct 300 rods long passed "through a deep valley" and rose "more than one hundred & fifty feet" on the other side.[16]

Logs were bored with a long shafted auger, and the cost installed varied from $1 to $2 per rod of pipe. These feats were examples of the uses to which forest products served the communities in the days before metal pipes were available.

Wooden Ships, Iron Men

The period from 1800 to 1830 made heavy demands on Connecticut for building ships. It included the 1812-1814 war with Great Britain, the last naval war fought with wooden ships under sail. It saw the evolution of the American coast-wise schooner, and the high point of the "tall ships" era.

Ship building was an important business along the Connecticut River from Middletown to Long Island Sound. Oak was the favorite material for the framing and planking of

vessels, and could be obtained "from the back parts of Haddam and from North Killingworth."[17]

The first ship built in Chatham Parish in 1741 was a schooner of 90 tons. Later on, between 1806 and 1816, 12,500 tons of shipping were constructed at one yard, including privateers, coasters and two warships which were never armed because of the "occurrence of peace."[18]

Further downstream at Saybrook Point, there were shipyards producing 1,200 to 2,000 tons of shipping annually.[19] The volume of shipping is suggested by the fact that in 1815 there belonged to the River ports 7 ships, 18 brigs, 19 schooners and 38 sloops, totalling over 9,375 tons.[20]

Other Wood Products

Timber also had to be cut for roads and for the bridges and highways. In lieu of taxes, farmers had the option of contributing labor toward these public works. One farmer fashioned—doubtless primarily of wood—an ox-drawn road scraper for this purpose.[21] White oak was in particular demand for barrel staves and for wooden buckets, tubs, and barrels, the latter being used for storing large quantities of cider, some of which was distilled into brandy. Wagons also were built locally in many towns. So-called "pleasure carriages" were introduced about 1750, a luxury that one respondent from Farmington criticized: "it was with apparent reluctance we have deviated in any respect from the good old beaten track of our ancestors..."[22]

In fact, a myriad of useful things—among them furniture, cabinetry, clocks, tools, and even machines—were made primarily of wood. Yet the forest also provided non-wooden necessities and luxuries of life. One of these was maple sugar. Sugaring was practiced on a number of farms but in small quantity owing to a dearth of trees and the great amount of wood fuel required for boiling: this was the case in Cornwall. Some families would make enough sugar for their own use. Solomon Wales of Union wrote:

> I have 50 or 60 trees...within 60 rods of my house & many of them more than a foot [in diameter] which were not bigger than my finger 40 years ago which I begin to tap...I have made on an average more than a hundred weight [of sugar] in a year & a sufficiency of melases...[23]

Another important product was charcoal. Scattered around Connecticut today in the woods are shallow bowl-shaped pits fifteen feet across, where the logs were stacked, covered with brush and mud and fired. Charring converted wood into carbon, a pure and hot burning fuel. This charcoal was essential to the blacksmith's forge, and the forge was essential to the community for shoeing the horses and making and repairing scythes, axes, and other needed tools.

One of the earliest non-wooden products of the forest, especially during the initial clearing of land for agriculture, was potash, made from wood ashes. It was an ingredient in making soap and glass.[24] By the time of the Town Reports, however, the ashes were more valued as fertilizer than for making potash.[25]

The Cordwood/Timber Crisis

It has been noted heretofore that from the earliest colonial times wood was looked upon as the fuel for both heating and cooking in Connecticut households. Large, inefficient fireplaces and a growing population combined to make increasing demands on what was in many areas a decreasing reserve of cordwood.

"Much wood"—and the records do not say how much—was cut and consumed by local farmers. Most of the farms had woodlots from which trees were the principal crop and from which farmers sold firewood to supply neighbors who did not have their own woodlots. During the period of the 1830s, the cost of woodland rose rapidly and ranged between $50 and $90 per acre, as people sought to protect themselves against future shortages.

Within the state, rural areas sold wood to the cities, carting it 5 to 10 miles in wagonloads. Farmington and Wintonbury sent "hundreds of cords" to Hartford. New Haven was supplied from neighboring towns and, by more economical transport, by boats from across Long Island Sound.

New Haven is an excellent case in point because its report was prepared in meticulous detail by Timothy Dwight, President of Yale College and the Connecticut Academy:

> The use of coal is almost unknown...Wood...in the opinion of the inhabitants [is] a pleasanter and cleaner fire...About one third of the fuel consumed here is imported from Long Island, Guilford, or the borders of the Hooesteanuc [Housatonic], or Stratford river.

Then follows an exercise in statistics:

> ...it appears, that in the year ending June, 1806, the tonnage of vessels bringing wood to the City of New Haven amounted...to 4305. Vessels are supposed to carry half a cord to a ton, which gives 2152 ½ cords...[or] estimated in round numbers at 2500 cords. If one third of the wood consumed in the City of New Haven is imported the whole will ...be 7500 cords, or ten cords to a house, including, however, all that is consumed by Yale College...[26]

Much wood was also exported from Connecticut, more from Haddam than from any other town in the state. "From Higganum Landing 2000 cords were exported in 1807 and probably 1000 from other places, and it may fairly be calculated that...3000 cords are exported annually...principally to New York."[27] Allowing 8 feet to a standard cord, 3,000 cords would make a woodpile 24,000 feet long or a bit over 4 miles.

How did all this cutting of firewood affect the whole of Connecticut's woodlands? A review of the Town Reports yields a variety of answers. In general, the communities farthest out from the major rivers and highways were the most likely to be optimistic about supplies for the future, while those closer in realized more clearly that the resource was a limited and a decreasing one. The consensus for the state as a whole was one of concern, as more and more land was cleared of trees to create fields and pastures. The period of the Town Reports, we now know, was a period of rapid deforestation in Connecticut. This concern found expression in a sense of frugality in the use of wood, and led to practices, which were early beginnings of the science of forestry, though that discipline had not been given a name.

The Challenge: Conserving the Woodlands

In 1830, as today, efforts at conserving vital resources depend upon the vision and diligence of the human beings involved. These elements are not always present, witness the report from Lebanon:

> Where lands have been suffered to be overrun with bushes, the original stock has prevailed mixed...with...creeping briars & sumacs...&... poisonous ivy...timber and fuel are very scarce so that in many places firewood costs as much for family use as bread and corn, and is growing scarcer, cattle being suffered by many to run in their wood lots and destroy the sprouts, but where due care is taken...the stumps and roots of trees will send out a great number of sprouts which grow rapidly.[28]

The Reverend Samuel Nott of Franklin, who preached his last sermon at the age of 96, summed up the scarcity problem in four words, "good land, bad management."[29]

Chestnut Trees and Fencing

Fences enclosing wood lots were the principal method of protecting sprouts and young trees from browsing sheep and cattle. Before commenting on fence building we should remember the materials used, especially since those materials are no longer available today. The fencing industry was built around the chestnut tree. This magnificent species was dealt a sad and untimely blow early in the twentieth century when a virulent fungus disease killed all the American chestnuts, leaving only sprouts, which died before reaching maturity.

In 1800-1830, fences were made chiefly with chestnut rails. Chestnut trees were among the most versatile and valuable in all the Connecticut woodlands. They grew fast and tall and straight. Large trees made excellent saw timber and provided food for mast-eating animals. When cut down, they sent forth vigorous and fast-growing sprouts. One of their most valuable qualities was the fact that chestnut posts, rails, and later railroad ties were more resistant to decay than those from any other deciduous common tree.

Chestnut was less in demand for firewood. It had a disconcerting way of snapping in the fire and sending sparks flying out into the room. This proclivity could somewhat be controlled by felling the trees in winter when the wood contained less sap. A great virtue for the fence-builder was the fact that chestnut split more easily than oak, hickory or maple.

These qualities, along with fence-protected wood lots, led to an early form of tree farming, with posts and rails being harvested on a 25-30 year rotation. In the early nineteenth century wood lots were rich in this invaluable commodity and fencing was big business. In Bethlehem Azel Backus reported that "in a particular string of fence on Doct Bellamy's farm there are more than 1000 rails of chestnut cut in February that are more than 60 years old," while the Reverend Ebenezer Kellogg of Bolton wrote that from his parish many loads of rails were annually transported ten and twelve miles to Hartford and Windsor.[30]

John Treadwell wrote from Farmington describing the different kinds of fence: post and rail, with white oak posts and 4 to 6 rails; stone and wood with a low wall of stone about 2 feet high surmounted by posts and 2 to 3 rails. The latter was deemed the best kind of fence for Farmington. The stone and wood construction explains the present-day mystery of low stone walls running through woods that were once open fields. The stone alone never would have deterred vagrant heifers from wandering once the wooden superstructure had rotted away. Then there were the full height stone walls. Finally, and worst of all, was the brush fence, made by lopping small trees.[31]

George Washington Stanley, a judge and prominent citizen of Wallingford, wrote:

> The enhanced price of Fencing timber of which the quantity is decreasing ought to convince the farmer of the expediency of substituting stone. Duration, security, cheapness of the materials, & improvement of the farm by clearing it of a nuisance, are strong reasons for giving preference to the latter material. Yet as in all cases when old habits are concerned, the progress of conviction is slow, & of reformation scarcely perceptible.[32]

The Advent of Stoves

As mentioned earlier, in 1800 fireplaces were used for both cooking and heating, and they were notoriously wasteful of fuel. Change, however, was in the making, with cast iron and sheet metal becoming more readily available for stoves, while fireplaces were made shallower and more efficient. Judge Stanley commented on the stabilized situation in Wallingford in 1811:

> Timber...& wood are plenty; & within the last 15 years the quantity is supposed not to have decreased—This is attributed to the preservation of sprouts by enclosing wood Lands, and a more strict economy in the consumption of fuel by the use of stoves; and the improved construction of fire places.[33]

Coal and wood burning stoves—the ornate but effective parlor heating stoves, and the massive kitchen ranges that revolutionized cooking—were increasingly common from the 1820s onward and are remembered with nostalgic affection by the present older generation. These fixtures helped conserve wood. They became part of the equipment of typical homes until they were superseded by other means of heating in the early twentieth century.[34]

Emigration and Immigration

The period of the Town Reports saw many broad national changes that accelerated later in the nineteenth century with the rise of steamboat and railroad transportation, the invention of telegraph, telephone, and electric light and power, and the exploitation of petroleum as a fuel. These changes removed constraints of dependence upon wood energy, waterpower, and sheer muscle. The effects upon the woodlands and the rural way of life in Connecticut, though gradual, were profound.

Emigration from Connecticut to westward lands, keenly felt by respondents to the Academy's enquiry in 1800-1830, continued throughout the nineteenth century. For instance, the population of Lebanon was 4,166 in 1790, dropped to 2,194 by 1840, and reached a low point of 1,343 in 1920.[35] Similar declines were noted in many of the outlying towns of the state, while burgeoning industrial cities attracted workers from the countryside. Former farmers let fields, hard won from the woods by their ancestors, revert to woodlands again. Within a century Connecticut became once more two-thirds wooded. The abandoned farmland was of little economic value, a fact that enabled Austin Hawes, the first State Forester, to buy at minimal cost the lands which were the beginning of State Forests and Parks.[36]

The reforestation of Connecticut was followed by yet another change, more fundamental and continuing today. Following World War II, the automobile came into its own as the universal instrument of transportation, with an impact for which the State was scarcely prepared—the commuter culture, suburbanization of the rural towns and fragmentation of the countryside under the euphemistic term of development. Beyond the scope of this essay, the challenge of the future for the woodlands, farms, and open spaces is to preserve them as a fitting habitat, not only for the creatures of earth and woodland and sky, but for people in an environment that is happy and wholesome for body and spirit.

Epilogue

The decade 1800-1830 marked the golden age and the swan song of the craftsmen and the largely self-sufficient towns of the Connecticut countryside—a way of life beyond recapture.

Beyond the labor of field and woodland, perhaps the greatest heritage of those years is the character of those who lived through them. This could hardly be better typified than in the life and words of Solomon Wales, sometime Selectman and Town Clerk of Union, and Captain in the Revolution. He wrote to the Academy, describing how a nearby mill sawed 100,000 board feet of pine boards each year, and how he plowed his stony soil, dressed and watered his garden, and fed well his animals. Then followed these lines, his valedictory:

> As I am now in the 75th year of my age & live on the heights of land & follow farming & no help but a boy of eight years old, have always been chearful & contented & lived happy in my family & scarcely ever knew what it was to want a good appetite & have always practised being up and stirring before the sun, I must beg to be excused from anything further & if any information hear will contribute to the great object I shall think myself well rewarded.[37]

Solomon Wales died March 20, 1805, and is buried in the Old Cemetery in Union.

Connecticut Towns circa 1800

Some Botanical and Ecological Observations

William A. Niering

An exploration into the writings from some Connecticut towns in the early 1800s reveals a myriad of interesting botanical and ecological findings. Obviously, by that time European settlement of southern New England and clearing of fields for agriculture had made widespread changes in the original forest vegetation. Therefore, some of the relevant questions asked by present-day ecologists and historians include: what was the nature of the pre-colonial forest resources and how had they been modified? What were the impacts on the associated wildlife? How did the settlers affect and utilize the aquatic resources, especially the wetlands? This essay will explore these and other interesting ecological and botanical aspects of the Town Reports.

The Changing Forests

Many of the Town Report writers focused on the timber resources of their time, as well as the nature of earlier forest vegetation. They reported that trees "of original growth" included oaks, chestnut, walnuts, hickory, ash, birch, butternut, poplar, beech, soft maple (probably red maple), sugar maple, willow, elm, alder, sassafras and basswood.[1] (It should be noted that common names used in the reports may pose certain problems of interpretation, which this essay will attempt to deal with as accurately as possible.) Second-growth forests were reported to contain oak, chestnut, hickory, butternut, white ash and sassafras.[2] In Union, the hills were reported to be well stocked with pine, probably white pine. Another evergreen, hemlock, was mentioned in only a few of the responding towns.[3] This would appear to reflect its localized occurrence or its early exploitation for timber and widespread use in the tanning industry. In addition, it may also be related to its inability to sprout after cutting or the role of Indian fires, which would have tended to restrict this fire-sensitive species to more mesic[4] ravine sites.

Following cutting of the original oak-dominated forests, chestnut had replaced the oak as the important forest tree. In Canterbury, Hezekiah Frost reports that

Chestnut trees in America were destroyed by chestnut blight early in the twentieth century. This pressed specimen of American Castanea vesca or Castanea dentata chestnut leaves and catkins is a rare example from a century earlier. Horatio N. Fenn, A Collection of Plants of New-Haven and its Environs Arranged According to the Natural Orders of Jussieu, 1822, Vol. 4, p. 185. Courtesy of the Yale Herbarium, Peabody Museum of Natural History, Yale University, New Haven, Connecticut.

the original forest growth included white, black and yellow oak (probably chinquapin oak)[5], but in the 1800s chestnut was much more important:

This may be proved by a number of observations. In searching the woods for ancient stumps no chestnut is to be found, but most are oak. Some appear 8 feet in diameter and perhaps were cut 100 years since. Our chestnut is outstripping all our other timber, where chestnut is in the same grove with oak it bids fair to entirely over shade the oak in a few years. And yet oak is 10 times as plenty as chestnut; which could not have been the case if chestnut bore any proportion to oak at first.[6]

These observations not only indicate the impressive size of the trees in the pre-colonial forest but also the role of forest disturbance in favoring the vigorous, stump-sprouting chestnut. It was capable of very rapid growth and was considered an extremely valuable tree. Thus the abundance of chestnut later (circa 1900), when the chestnut blight struck, appears to be anthropogenically related. Extensively used for construction of the well-known Virginia split rail fences, chestnut was becoming scarcer in some towns by the 1800s, necessitating the use of stone walls or a combination of stone and wood for fencing.[7] Its eventual demise in the first quarter of the twentieth century, due to the chestnut blight, resulted in the loss of an important timber tree as well as food for wildlife. Although oak and hickory filled the gap left by the chestnut, research is currently underway to re-establish this important tree by using hypovirulent strains of the fungus to counter the disease.[8]

Soon after their arrival, the colonists recognized the role of Indian burning in the forests. The effect of Indian burning, as described by a Dr. Hildreth in the Pomperaug Valley of western Connecticut around 1675, is most illuminating:

While the red men possessed the country, and every autumn set fire to the fallen leaves, the forests presented a most noble and enchanting appearance. The annual firings prevented the growth of shrubs and underbrush, and destroying the lower branches of the trees, the eye roved with delight from ridge to ridge, and from hill to hill; which like the divisions of an immense temple, were crowded with innumerable pillars, the branches of whose shafts interlocking, formed the arch-work of support to that leafy roof, which covered and crowned the whole. But since the white man took possession, the annual fires have been checked, and the woodlands are now filled with shrubs and young trees, obstructing the vision on every side, and converting these once beautiful forests into a rude and tasteless wilderness.[9]

The settlers had also used fire to improve their pastures and attract wildlife.[10] In the Ridgefield Report, Samuel Goodrich mentions that the higher rough land had been burned in the past, but that such burning had now ceased and new forest growth was developing.[11] The reintroduction of fire in the form of prescribed burning to simulate certain effects of Indian burning, from a research perspective, has been underway at the Connecticut College Arboretum since the late 1960s.[12] Such forest burning has resulted in the creation of open park-like forests somewhat like those mentioned by Dr. Hildreth in the seventeenth century. Post-agricultural old-field sites have also been burned to favor the native prairie grass little bluestem (*Schizachyrium scoparium*).[13] Such open meadows were also part of the early vegetation pattern in southern New England.[14] The Connecticut Department of Environmental Protection (DEP) has used prescribed burning in forests and meadows for the past decade. Thus, prescribed burning is now recognized as a sound vegetation management technique for favoring oak seedling reproduction and perpetuating oak-dominated forests of the various types recognized by Braun in the eastern deciduous forest.[15]

First Regional Flora

Among early botanical studies, an impressive flora[16] of "vegetable productions" for the town of New Haven was compiled by Dr. Eli Ives and published as part of the *Statistical Account of the City of New Haven* in 1811. It comprised some 324 taxa including trees, shrubs, and herbaceous plants, and may well represent the first such regional flora in the State. It is reproduced in its entirety within the New Haven Town Report in Volume One of this book.[17] The author of this list, Dr. Ives, lectured on botany to Yale University medical students for many years and encouraged students to collect the local flora. He also started the botanical garden for medicinal plants. The Yale University Herbarium has recently restored four volumes dating from 1822 that contain pressed specimens of the New Haven flora.[18]

Ives's floristic list is interesting in terms of native versus introduced species and the diversity of various habitats represented. For example, there are over twenty introduced herbaceous species listed such as ox-eye daisy (*Chrysanthemum leucanthemum*), wild carrot (*Daucus carota*) and butter and eggs (*Linaria vulgaris*). Woodland wildflowers were also well represented, probably associated with the adjacent trap rock ridges. The two bog species mentioned, pitcher plant (*Sarracenia purpurea*) and cranberry (*Vaccinium macrocarpon*) may well have been associated with the now severely altered kettleholes along Crescent Street. Finally, several salt marsh forbs[19] were included, but no grasses, in particular not the *Phragmites australis* so conspicuously associated with tidal wetlands today. This may lend support to the hypothesis that the aggressive strain of *phragmites* that currently dominates many of our tidal wetlands has been introduced or evolved since then.[20]

Leaves and flowers of Rhus vernix, *poison sumac gathered and pressed by a student of Dr. Eli Ives at the Yale College Medical Institute in 1822. Horatio N. Fenn, A Collection of Plants of New-Haven and its Environs Arranged According to the Natural Orders of Jussieu, 1822, Vol. 4, p. 97. Courtesy of the Yale Herbarium, Peabody Museum of Natural History, Yale University, New Haven, Connecticut.*

Timothy Dwight also included in the New Haven report a comprehensive list of the thirty-one trees of "our forests" and the twenty-five shrubs that were "natives of this Township."[21] All of these species are still present in the flora of Connecticut.

The Town Reports pointed out plants that were particularly harmful or beneficial. Among poisonous plants, they identified poison ivy on the dry uplands, and poison sumac, also referred to as poison elder tree, in the swamps. "Mercury vine," also referred to as the red sumach shrub (another name for poison ivy), was also recognized as poisonous.[22] St. Johnswort (*Hypericum perforatum*), found in open fields and introduced from Europe, was used for medicinal purposes.[23] In fact, in the last decade, it has appeared in our pharmacies as an herbal remedy to counter depression. In the town of Bethlem, this plant was recognized as a pasture weed that was increasing and considered hazardous to sheep.[24] To control its spread, it was recommended that plaster of Paris be applied to the fields for one or two years. A plant that was frequently destroyed was the European introduced common barberry (*Berberis vulgaris*), since it was the alternate host to wheat rust.[25] A veterinarian remedy involving specific plants is revealed in the following: "For Horse distemper and cutaneous complaints, a Rowel in the breast, with a piece of the root of Phytolau or Pokeweed [*Phytolacca*]; of Arum or wake robin [*Trillium*]; inserted within the skin of the Rowel is the best external application."[26]

Changing Wildlife Patterns

In most towns, one of the most striking patterns was the decrease in wildlife. With forest clearing and hunting pressure, deer, bear, wildcats, mountain lions and moose had declined, whereas foxes, hares (snowshoe rabbits), raccoons, minks, muskrats, cottontail rabbits, skunks and several different squirrels (probably red, gray, and flying squirrel), had increased.[27] Because of increasing human population and forest clearing, Cheshire's deer and bear, formerly important, were now extinct and Farmington's wildlife had decreased in the past forty years.[28] However, in the northwest part of the State, the wildcat was still present and occasionally destroyed sheep.[29] Two mammals favored by agricultural clearing were the fox, which raided the chicken coops, and squirrels, which tended to feed on stored corn.

Snakes, especially rattlers, had been frequent in Cornwall, where their dens were numerous. A bounty of 6 pence paid by the Town in 1741 for each dead rattlesnake tail went up each year, reaching three shillings in 1747.[30] In Ridgefield, they were also reported to have been present in great numbers before they were almost completely destroyed by turning the swine loose on them.[31] Black snakes, striped snakes (probably garter snake), milk snakes, and a few red and green snakes were also reported as well as water snakes in brooks and ponds.

Among the bird life, wild turkey, which were originally important, had decreased in numbers by 1800. A few were reportedly seen in the Town of Ridgefield. Partridge (probably ruffed grouse), and quail (probably bobwhite quail), were plentiful in some years, and meadow birds (possibly meadow larks), woodcock, woodpeckers, wrens and snowbirds (possibly juncos), were also observed as well as some ducks in season.[32] The passenger pigeon was still observed in great numbers. "There are at seasons great flights of pigeons, but not so frequent as formerly as they change their course more to the westward as the country becomes cleared and settled."[33] There were also occasional insect outbreaks on the agricultural lands.

With the removal of extensive forested areas it was to be expected that dramatic changes would occur in the region's fauna, marked by a decline in the larger mammals, whereas those more adaptable to human habitation, like the fox, persisted or increased. Today most of the same species of the 1800s persist. Of course deer, which had declined during the colonial period, have since increased with protection and suburbanization, which has created a favorable "edge" habitat that they prefer. Wild turkeys have been reintroduced and are thriving. There has also been an increase in certain predators, including the coyote. The demise of the passenger pigeon was in progress in the 1800s, continuing with forest removal and the slaughter of vast numbers of these birds to their eventual extinction in the early part of the twentieth century. The extermination of rattlesnakes is a practice that continued into the twentieth century in Pennsylvania.[34] Such intentional killing may have contributed to the present highly localized distribution of these reptiles.

Wetlands and Water-Related Resources

Water and wetlands were resources of considerable interest and importance to the early settlers, since their water was derived primarily from shallow wells 10-25 feet in depth. In addition, watercourses provided the main source of waterpower. Long Island Sound and fresh water streams also provided an invaluable source of aquatic resources. In Coventry, streams were reported as pure and supporting such fish as "streaked perch, succors, roach, bullheads and eells."[35] During the shad runs in Canterbury, 900-1,000 fish were taken in a day.[36] In Haddam, thirty seines were annually employed in the shad fishery, which extended from March to the end of June. Here, more than 30,000 shad were taken in a season— more than 2,000 at a draft.[37] Along the Sound in Stratfield, large quantities of herring or alewives were barreled for market, and sea perch, crabs and oysters were also caught.[38]

Timothy Dwight gives an extensive account of the fish taken from the New Haven harbor and streams. Shad were also taken in considerable numbers in season (2,400 at a single draft). He says "Of such importance was the fishery esteemed, that a considerable number of law suits were carried on for the purpose of acquiring, and defending titles to the fishing places."[39] Other marine animals, which were not eaten, included shark (rare), porpoise and sturgeon (neither common) as well as dogfish and toadfish. Whitefish (a kind of herring) was used as a fertilizer in many places and considered superior to any other. The fish came in large schools in the month of June. One needed 10,000-12,000 fish to dress an acre of cropland.[40]

Shellfish reported in the New Haven estuary included oysters, long clams and round clams, the muscle (mussel), the escallop (scallop), lobster, crab, periwinkle, and shrimp. Tortoise (possibly the diamond-backed terrapin) were also present. Long and round clams were taken in considerable quantities. In prime oyster beds in the Quinnipiac between 4,000-5,000 bushels were taken annually; they were "small but well-flavoured." New Haven harbor had important oyster grounds until the storm of 1770 overwhelmed the beds with masses of mud.[41] Commercial development of the estuarine shellfish resources was also underway. The Madison Channel Company seeded areas with oyster as early as 1828 and thereafter took 200 bushels with 1,000 bushels anticipated.[42]

In New Haven harbor, the accumulating sediments were considered the precursor to salt marsh formation, which is precisely how marsh development has been documented to occur.[43]

While seaweed was commonly gathered for fertilizer, the fringing salt marshes were used for hay. In Madison, the inhabitants had formerly depended on the extensive salt marshes along the Neck and East Rivers to support their stock. The blackgrass (*Juncus gerardii*) cut from the meadows was good for the cattle, whereas the salt hay (*Spartina patens*) alone "will barely preserve cattle" but was useful together with other kinds of fodder. The blackgrass yielded 2¼- 2½ tons per acre while the salt hay yielded ¾ to 2 tons per acre.[44]

Some marshes were diked and tidally restricted. This occurred in 1769 on the West River in New Haven, where a tide gate prevented full tidal flushing, and resulted in the demise of the salt water species. By the first year, after the grasses died, the salt marsh grasses were succeeded first by white grass (*Agrostis alba*) and afterwards, on about half the tract, by speargrass (*Triglochin*) and clover.[45] One is not sure of the particular species being referred to by common names only in this account; however, there is no mention of common reed grass (*Phragmites australis*), which currently takes over most salt marshes that are diked or otherwise altered. This omission lends further support to the hypothesis that this grass, although probably present around 1800, since it is native, was not abundant, as is the present form which has evolved or been introduced since 1800.[46]

The Reports reveal much purposeful alteration of fresh-water wetlands. This included damming, draining, and removal of organic matter as a soil amendment, although the last was not widely practiced. Although many wetlands were drained to increase the agricultural land, current research in Lebanon has documented that there was actually an increase in wetlands in the eighteenth century due to stream course modifications.[47] Apparently, both draining and damming were associated with farming and with obtaining waterpower for the many mills throughout the State in the eighteenth and nineteenth centuries.

In fresh water wetlands, forest clearing probably occurred in the winter when they were frozen and more accessible. Cutting of pine and cedar (probably southern or Atlantic white cedar), can actually favor their re-establishment, as has been documented by current forestry practices. Such wetlands, however, often contain red maple as an associated tree. The red maple is a more shade-tolerant tree, which may account for the change in Franklin of "a pine and cedar swamp into a maple one" and also its dominance today in coastal forested wetlands.[48]

Extreme Climatic Events
and Local Climatic Change

Extreme but natural climatic events had a marked effect on the vegetation and associated biota 200 years ago. In New Haven numerous drought years were reported before and around 1800 (1762, 1763, 1782, 1796, 1800 and 1805). In 1782, drought conditions were so severe that roots of grasses were killed in many places even where the soil was rich. In 1805 "gardens extensively perished." In contrast, 1795 was one of the wettest summers when it rained thirty-five days (whole or part) in a ten-week period. Everything molded. Plants in gardens "perished by dissolution, in every stage of their germination to

maturity. The seeds of hollyhock, the peas and beans sprang in the pod; and grew in many instances several inches."[49] The years 1807, 1808, 1809 also were very wet.

Along the Connecticut River major flooding was reported in 1801 and earlier floods were noted in 1642 and 1703 that continually added to the floodplain sediments. Ice scouring and water were also damaging.[50] Of special interest is a major flood in Winsted, Connecticut. "On the 31st day of January 1807, the Earth being then frozen to an uncommon depth; a storm of rain commenced, and increased so rapidly, that in a short time streams were swelled so that Mills and Bridges were swept off by the violence of the floods."[51] This was repeated in 1955, when another major flood sent the Mad River rampaging down the Main Street of Winsted, wreaking havoc, and provoking construction of a flood control dam by the U.S. Army Corps of Engineers to prevent another such disaster. In 1796 a tornado passed over New Haven and Ridgefield and the devastation was great. In July 1799, hail seven inches in circumference was reported in Franklin to have broken windows and destroyed all fruits, while in Goshen, hailstones two inches in diameter did considerable damage to young timber.[52]

A most interesting hypothesis is presented by John Treadwell concerning local climatic change due to extensive deforestation of the State by the 1800s. He indicates "that the extremes of hot and cold are less now than formerly" and "the total quantum of cold in a year is considerably diminished." He further reported that people used to depend upon travelling on snow, on distant journeys, especially to the Northwest; but now this mode of travel was precarious. "Frequent thaws take place in situations far inland as they have been known to do on the coast." Forest clearing of the West and Northwest "gives extension to the South winds, which prevail over the Northwest winds;" this "produces rain instead of snow....Formerly, the immense regions of North and West were a grand reservoir of snow defended by the forests from the South winds and the sun, during the winter." In addition, Treadwell further postulates that "the myriads of culinary fires...render it [the air] more temperate."[53] When the cold in the country was very piercing there was a change as one approached a populated town and more mildness in the air. This argument sounds highly plausible in light of current data concerning the effects of deforestation on local climate.

In conclusion, it is obvious that there is a great wealth of interesting ecological and botanical information reported by the learned civic leaders around the 1800s. What has been revealed in this paper is a mere snapshot of this rich historical record documented by our ancestors.

The Physical Environment of Connecticut Towns: Processes, Attitudes and Perceptions Then and Now

Robert M. Thorson

Introduction

The year was 1799. The place was a meeting room somewhere at Yale College in New Haven, Connecticut. Members of the newly organized Connecticut Academy of Arts and Sciences (CAAS) were assembled to draft a questionnaire soliciting, among other Articles or topics, "every species of information...relative to the...Natural...history...of the State." On the agenda was geology, the science of the earth's physical, chemical, and biological processes, a discipline yet to be invented. There was, however, no mistaking the members' interest in the subject, for many of their questions dealt with the origin of the landscape, climate change, hydrology, mining and soil genesis.[1] So important was geology to the questionnaire that nineteen of its thirty-two "Heads of Inquiry" dealt with such earthly matters as minerals, moisture, and manure.

Within the year, carriages were rumbling along recently improved, but still dusty, roads of Connecticut carrying a circular letter written by Simeon Baldwin, Recording Secretary for the Academy. A copy of the letter was posted to some informed gentleman who, more often than not, was a minister with an undergraduate degree from Yale, and whose job it was to return the completed questionnaire as soon as possible. Several of the responses came in quickly, but most trickled in over a dozen years or so. Altogether, forty-two separate individuals concerning forty-seven towns returned fifty responses. They encompassed the full geographic diversity of the state, extending from: the western highlands of Cornwall; across the broad interior lowlands of East Windsor to the eastern highlands of Union and Pomfret; south to the rock-guarded salt marshes at New London; then, finally west to the sand plains of Stratford. Collectively, their responses beautifully describe the physical environment of the state in the first decade of the nineteenth century, a time when stone walls and gristmills dominated the built environment.[2]

Across the Atlantic a revolution in geology was brewing.[3] The Scottish physician-turned-farmer-turned-geologist James Hutton, widely regarded as the "father of geology" published his cumbersome and nearly intractable *Theory of the Earth, With Proofs and Illustrations*, in 1795, only a few years before the questionnaire was being constructed. It was not until 1802, well after the Solicitation letter had been sent, that his friend at the Royal Society, John Playfair, promulgated Hutton's ideas using prose that would reach a wider audience. Then in 1807 the Geological Society was established in Kingsway, London. So primitive was the American understanding of geology at this time that the glacial till on which Connecticut farmers labored was still thought to be "drift," a chaos of sediment that settled in the wake of Noah's deluge; Louis Agassiz's glacial theory had yet to be invoked to account for these odd sediments, which were often referred to as "hardpan" or "boulder clay." Only Benjamin Silliman of Yale College, whose comments were included in the response by Timothy Dwight for New Haven, seems to have been aware that a new science was being conceived on opposite Atlantic shores. (Note: Silliman's contribution is elaborated upon in the Discussion section that follows.)

In this context, the responses to the CAAS Solicitation letter contain first-hand, eyewitness observations of earthly processes at a critical time in the history of science and technology. Most of the responses offered up a largely biblical, essentially Aristotelian, view of the world at a time when intellectual innocence was fading; a time when geological ideas were creeping in to consciousness of the clergy; a time of growing doubt among the intelligentsia regarding the age of the earth and about who (or what) was in charge of it. Being well educated, few of the same ministers would, two centuries later, have disputed the origin of the earth from cold dust, the abyss of time, the plain facts of evolution, and the notion that continents wander aimlessly about the face of the earth.[4] Two centuries later, the purpose of this essay is to convey what learned men understood about their physical environment and expressed in the Connecticut Town Reports.

Only upon writing this essay did I realize what had changed most about the landscape of southern New England during the last 200 years was neither the terrain nor our technical understanding of it, but, rather, our perception of the land itself.[5] This interpretation is relegated to the end of my essay. My more immediate and important task of reviewing the responses to the questionnaire dealing with the physical aspects of the post-Colonial world occupies the bulk of my text. Using the numerical list of the original Solicitation letter as my guide, this essay is organized by subject into the following headings:

Archaeology	Agriculture
Terrain	Transportation
Hydrology	Climatology
Non-renewable Resources	Remarkable
	Occurrences

Following the factual, or "text" portion of the assignment under the heading "Responses," the text moves on to the "context and interpretation" component, under the heading "Discussion."

Responses

Most of the responses are incomplete, even mundane. Several, however, stand out for either their exhaustive detail and (or) scientific astuteness. Elijah Allen of Cornwall provides us with our only eyewitness account of a meteorite explosion, raising the question "Why was such a dramatic event witnessed by only one respondent?" David Field of East Haddam, an amateur seismologist nearly two centuries ahead of his time, provides what may be the most important longitudinal study of Connecticut's most earthquake-prone area, near Moodus. David McClure, of East Windsor, was a keen observer of the Connecticut River, a fluvial geomorphologist on par with many specialists today. John Smith's report from Sharon reveals that he understood, from empirical observations, the linkages between groundwater hydrology and surface runoff. John Treadwell, from Farmington dealt with the thoroughly modern subject of climate change, and the contemporary human influences upon it. Timothy Dwight's late (1811) report for New Haven was unusually systematic and thorough, perhaps owing to the contribution of Professor Silliman, and also because he had a chance to read the shortcomings of those arriving on time.

Throughout the collection of responses, especially those quoted in this essay, you will find a general terseness to the phrasing, a lexicon of unusual words, and some truly unorthodox ways of spelling, capitalization, and punctuation. Streams pay tribute to rivers, rather than merely join them. Mills take their "seats" on streams. Wheat is wheet. Peat is peet. Loam is loom. Water is sweet. Mephitic, salubrious, chalybeate, and freestone, all undefined in the text, are now largely archaic, and seldom used.[6] As you read this essay, and encounter what look like typographical errors in quotes, please keep in mind that these CAAS reports predate Noah Webster's dictionary, whose success at bringing consistency to American English took its toll on the individuality of written expression.

Archaeology

Article 2d:...Indian names of places...traces of their settlement...

Every respondent was well aware that "Indians" formerly occupied the land. In only one case was the land described as having been taken by conquest. Instead, the "transfer of land" to the European colonists was almost always by way of purchase, although few of our respondents knew from whom, and under what circumstances. David Field, of Haddam, an exception to this rule, wrote that the lands were purchased of four Indian kings, Sachusquatevemapid, Keawaytahue, Turramuggus, and Nabahuett, and two Indian queens, Sepunnemo-pampcossame and Towkishe. These names are included here simply because they are so interesting, linguistically.

By the time the Town Reports were written, the Indians had become a marginalized minority element within each Connecticut town. To judge by these second-hand descriptions of their vocations and activities, most Indians seem to have lost contact with their own spiritual traditions. Although most of the respondents were aware of Indian names for rivers, coves, and hills, few of them knew the oral traditions surrounding the names, and fewer, still, were able to describe *physical* traces of the Native American past, which is the task of this essay.

Several points are interesting in this regard: First, only a few respondents described burning of the woods by Indians, possibly suggesting that this phenomenon has been exaggerated, at least by revisionist historians.[7] A reduced ecological impact for Indian burning would be consistent with the apparent conflict between a few widely quoted anecdotal descriptions for woodland burning when compared with the actual dearth of tangible evidence for the phenomenon preserved today in sediment cores (charcoal, pollen, carbon isotopes).[8] Secondly, most of the discoveries of the Indian past were made during the normal everyday business of plowing or clearing the land, usually with arrowheads, pots, hatchets, and other items providing clues to former settlement. Accidental discoveries of actual burial grounds, many with skeletons *in situ*, were given in a half dozen responses. Systematic excavations were not noted, although "pot-hunting" for material remains of the "savages" must have been going on at the time. Archaeology was yet to be a formalized discipline.

Finally, the following anecdote is of interest, especially for its symbolism:

> A stone with a human head & neck, roughly carved, now lying in a fence half a mile northeast of Madison meeting-house is supposed to have been used by them as an idol. If so, they were idolaters.[9]

This story of an Indian religious idol finding its way into a stone wall can be seen as an especially evocative physical tale in which the material culture of Native America is assimilated into the stony residue of European farming.[10]

This tale – one literally written in stone – recapitulates and reinforces the sweeping ideological changes that were taking place at the time. The archaeological and documentary evidence converge.

Terrain
Landscape

Article 3a: ...the face of the country, in regard to mountains, hills, valleys and plains, rocks, stones, clay, sand...

Responses here ranged from terse statements such as "... the land is uneven..." to detailed descriptions of mountains, valleys, hills, and plains, and the relative portions taken up by each of them in a town. Because there was no systematic way of summarizing the responses,[11] this essay provides a few representative examples: Ebenezer Kellogg writes of Bolton: "The land on the east part of the Society is mountainous; interspersed with vallies. Some ledges of rocks—considerably stony. The west part... is level & not too much incumbered with stone."[12] Lewis Norton writes of Goshen: "The face of the country, like that of most of the towns...is variegated."[13] From these Reports, we get the impression that variety in the landscape was appreciated for its own sake, and that the familiar words we still use to describe the landscape had slightly different, more imprecise meanings. For example, the word "mountain" was used interchangeably for any large hill, with examples cited from every region in the state, including the lowlands of the southeast. Few would use the word today to describe anything east of the Connecticut River, suggesting that the transformation of the word "mountain" mirrors the transformation, by enlargement, of our own world view.

On the whole, the respondents' view of the landscape was strictly utilitarian; the earth was there to serve its master, the "husbandman," who, in turn, was there to fertilize, and thereby enhance, the anticipant womb of the soil. Approximately half of the Reports included romantic sentiments about the landscape, feelings that preachers may have been more prone to express than the swarthy farmers of their town. Six respondents couldn't restrain themselves: John Foot, looking westward from Cheshire, saw a "chain of mountains extending from New Haven to Montreal, affording a most beautiful landscape with its romantic tops."[14] Elijah Allen, on contemplating Cornwall: "...the first View of the Town of Cornwal to a Stranger is some what Romantick, as being intersperced with Hills and Dales."[15] John Treadwell, contemplating the base of a basalt ridge in Farmington: "An east view of the town from the west side of the meadow is delightful, the prospect shews the ruged wildness of nature in the mountain that stands in the rear, & the mild and prolific eveness of the meadow in front."[16] Barzillai Slosson described the Housatonic River in Kent: "...[the] Ousantonic...rushes with great violence down a rocky steep for the considerable distance. In times of high water it forms a scene truly sublime."[17] James Morris of Litchfield described a most "...enchanting view." Timothy Dwight, perhaps not to be outdone, described part of New Haven this way: "An observer placed at the foot of the West mountain [West Rock]...is forcibly struck with the grandeur, and sublimity, of the numerous and lofty columns which there form an extended front."[18]

Soils

Article 3b: The face of the country, in regard to...rocks, stones, clay, sand, nature of the soil...

It is on this topic that the respondents commented most, in particular about the physical landscape. Here are some examples, none of which are sufficiently detailed for comparisons with soils today, for the purposes of evaluating soil change: Azel Backus of Bethlem reported: "The soil is good with diversities; black and red loom with a hard pan at about 3 feet from the surface are prevailing soils."[19] Ebenezer Kellogg writes of Bolton: "The soil...in the eastern part is generally a blackish dirt intermixed with gravel & stone—some spots a little clay...it is natural for grass and good for pasture and mowing—The western...is a loomy soil—intermixed...with gravel or sand."[20] James Morris of Litchfield noted that "The soil of the township, generally, is black and red loam, and clay. From the variety of the soil, there is a corresponding variety of forest trees."[21] It seems as though everyone described soil in a different way.

Time and time again the respondents wrote about how the terrain and its soil were closely coupled; such a close relationship underlies an informal soil taxonomy based not on how the soil actually looked, but on how it could be put to use. This, again, reflects their utilitarian view. These are the categories of soils I was able to glean from their descriptions.

Interval Lands

These were flat lands immediately adjacent to small and large rivers, some of which were probably natural meadows at the time of settlement. Most farmers understood that the "slime" deposited by the "retiring" of the annual floods was the agent responsible for creating the flat interval lands adjacent to rivers which were universally recognized as having deep, black soils that were productive for tillage and mowing. These areas were also valued for being stone free, for being readily accessible from town streets, which were often laid out on terraces just above the intervals.

Pasture Land

Most of the land was neither mountainous, nor flat. Although generally hilly and stony, such terrain was exceptionally good for growing grass because it was most often underlain by glacial till (hardpan), which is the compacted sediment that was smeared onto the landscape at the base of the moving ice sheets. Till holds water well because it is so fine grained and compacted, and retains nutrients well because it is loaded with finely ground rock fragments. Material this fine grained, if on level land or in a closed depression, will lead to poor drainage and swampy conditions. But when this material occurs on gentle slopes of glacially streamlined hills, the combination of uniform slope, water retention, and nutrient availability led to exceptionally good soils for pasture.

Sandy soils

The terrain above the reach of the annual floods was often underlain by gravelly or sandy soils above flat river terraces and shorelines associated with meltwater rivers and lakes. These were recognized as being lighter drier soils more suitable for grain crops and easier to clear owing to limited root depth and to smaller, fewer stones. They were, however, less "strong" in terms of nutrients and less able to hold "manure" because they lacked the fine-grained, silt- and clay-sized fragments characteristic of till and alluvium.[22]

Woodlot soils

These were found in rough, inaccessible, often rocky places where cultivation was impossible, and where even pasture was difficult. These soils included bedrock ledges, as well as areas littered with boulders where trees could flourish. Most of these areas were cut over for firewood, and many lent themselves well to orchards.

Swamp soils

These were places where wood could be easily cut, especially in winter, and where, if the land were drained, tillage could be practiced with great benefit. Swamp soils also supplied black muck for "manure," and, in a few cases, peat for fuel.

Curiosities

Article 3c:...curiosities, natural...

Curiously, our respondents did <u>not</u> seem to be very curious about natural history. Only eleven responded to this question, four in the negative, stating explicitly that there were no natural curiosities. When one was mentioned, it was usually a rock of some kind, perhaps exceptionally large, composed of some unusual substance, or alleged to be inscribed. There were, however, several notable cases. David McClure from East Windsor called attention to the fact that the *in situ* roots and trunks of trees exposed in the bank of the Connecticut River existed at a level so deep as to suggest that the river has been rising.[23] We now know that he was correct because sea level has been rising since deglaciation, which commenced about 20,000 years ago. Samuel Nott described the "Dragon's Hole" in Franklin, a cavern created by the collapse of a part of what he called "Ayers Mountain," which is now, and was then, a ridge no more than several hundred feet high.[24]

Hydrology

Today, hydrology is a unified science linking precipitation, groundwater movements, river flow, channel form, and human consumption; geology lays claim to the integrative aspects of the field. In the CAAS Town Reports, information concerning hydrology was solicited under a variety of separate questions, and responses were scattered throughout each text. Their responses regarding hydrology are gathered under the following six sub-categories: river processes, stream flow, water supply, springs, damps, and changes.

River Processes

Article 4a: Rivers...

The first sub-category deals with the physical river processes such as deposition, scouring, or changes in navigation.[25] Responses were intensely local, idiosyncratic and often stimulated by personal curiosity. In addition to his observations already mentioned regarding sea level rise, David McClure of East Windsor understood the downstream effects of piers on nucleating sand bars, the flood regime with two seasonal freshets, and the way in which meandering rivers build one bank while simultaneously cutting the other. McClure describes not only the mechanism of sand bar movement but its long-term migration as well:

> A flat or sand bar, containing about fifty acres, is gradually moving down, and goes about forty rods, annually. It is bare in the summer...It moves only when covered with water. The stream then washes along the surface successively, until the whole mass is turned over.[26]

David Field, in his report on Middlesex County, also describes observable systematic changes in the river channel of the Lower Connecticut River estuary and speculated on its man-made cause. Specifically, he described how the depth of the main channel was apparently related to the number of sandbars observed at low flow.[27]

Stream flow

Article 4a: Rivers...streams...lakes and ponds, their sources and used as to mills, navigation...

The second aspect of hydrology in the Town Reports dealt with water supply as an industrial commodity. Here the flow of a river was measured not in cubic feet per second, but rather by the number of mills that could be powered by its flow. Most of the responses were generalized, with statements such as "there is plenty of water," or there are "many mill seats." From Cornwall, Oliver Burnham provides this example: "There are almost innumerable other Streams some of which are sufficient for Mills a considerable part of the Year."[28] The general view was that there was sufficient water most of the year for hydropower, then a vital part of the local economy. A separate part of this question concerns "cataracts or falls," some of which were mentioned, the largest being a fall of seventy feet in Kent, over a distance of about 20 rods.[29] Most often, the respondents simply said they existed, without describing them.

Water Supply

Article 4f...plenty or scarcity of water for domestic uses....Wells, their depth on different grounds...

The final concern dealt with water supply for human consumption. Here, there was a concern for water quality, as well as quantity. Some of the best quantitative data in the Town Reports are to be found in the answer to this question, which includes the depth of wells. Overall, the Reports are fairly consistent. The water table was almost always found at a depth ranging from a minimum of 10-15 feet to a maximum of 30-40 feet. Four towns differentiated the depth of wells in uplands from that of lowlands. Three towns (Cornwall, Kent, Watertown) reported that the water table was shallower in hill country than in the valleys. Two reasons are involved.

The first explanation for the lower water tables in the lowland has to do with river incision. Most of the large valleys are south-draining, and are deeply incised into the glacial sand and gravel that once filled them. By cutting so deeply, they lowered the water table where it was connected to the river by aquifers. In contrast, the smaller streams in the uplands had less opportunity to cut deeply into their glacial sediment, allowing water tables to remain much nearer the surface. There is a second reason for this as well. In the uplands the rock and lodgment till prevent the infiltration of water, keeping the level of the water high. In contrast, many of the lowlands are filled with sand and gravel (today called stratified drift aquifers), materials that are too permeable to hold up the water, but which are able to store and yield tremendous quantities of water. Only the town of Ridgefield reported the opposite to be true, where the water table is shallower in the valleys. This unusual Report probably results from a local deficiency in sand and gravel near the base of the valley, or, alternatively, the main valley may not have been deeply cut.

Most respondents were well aware that the depth below the surface to water did not track that of the surface very closely and that the depth to the water table was quite constant, except in drought years. It is clear that they understood that subterranean waters behaved independently from surface waters.

In terms of water quality, the word excellent or "sweet for use" crops up time and time again. Unlike today, access to fresh water was not taken for granted. Most of the respondents downplayed the importance of aqueducts—by which they meant pipes, usually wooden ones—because access to groundwater was so ubiquitous.

A functional taxonomy was applied to water based on four criteria: Hardness; water could be either sweet or hard. Potability; drinkable or not drinkable. Utility for washing; fit or not fit. Medicinal qualities; yes or no. This classification is broadly similar to those in use today.

Changes in water quality, both in space and time, were also noted. In some parts of the state, particularly in the northwest, the respondents noted a change in the quality of water as one moved from a region of crystalline rock to one of calcareous rock, where the water was "harder" owing to the abundance of dissolved solids. In two cases it was noted that the quality changed over time as a result of the 1755 earthquake, whose epicenter was over a hundred miles away. This topic will be addressed later.

Springs

Article 4b:...springs (if remarkable) especially mineral and medicinal springs...

The respondents answered this question in an erratic fashion. Many discussed springs under the questions dealing with natural water, saying simply that the "ground was springy," or that "springs and streams were abundant." Members of the CAAS already knew this; they were interested only in springs that were remarkable, "...especially mineral and medicinal springs." Ten respondents noted the presence of mineral springs in their town, using the term chalybeate to describe its waters, a term meaning iron-rich, that has since become practically extinct. Of these, seven indicated that the spring was of medicinal value, whereas three indicated it was not. Curiously, there was no regional pattern to the responses, even though the northwestern and central portions of the state often have alkaline waters with high dissolved solids.

Damps

Article 4h:...Accidents by damps or mephitic air in wells or other places.

Most of the respondents ignored this question, although four respondents took the trouble to report none. In only one case was there such an accident. It happened as Solomon Wales of Union watched his own son turn pale and almost faint when he went down into a well to "stone" its foundation; they drew the boy up quickly, otherwise he might have perished.[30] Such a singular occurrence was likely due to the release of a gas that was heavier than air, probably carbon dioxide, one that may have been trapped below a layer of fine-grained sediment cut by the well excavation.

Changes

Article 4g:...changes of [water] quality within the present age—failure of streams in consequence of clearing the land, increase or decrease of water...

On this point the Academy members were soliciting information to test a prevailing hypothesis that too much forest clearing was jeopardizing their water supply. Indeed, there was a concurrence of opinion among the respondents that forest clearing had caused a few wells to go dry that might not have otherwise, and a few streams to dry up earlier than normal during the summer season. But, all in all, such changes, when noted, were felt to be minor, at least in the year 1800. The town of Coventry, in the eastern highlands provides a notable exception. There, Jesse Root describes:

> ...[a] great lake, called by the natives Wongumbcoog; it is fed by springs, its waters are pure; the bottom principally stoney & sandy; and within about thirty years passd the water has fallen many feet, owing, it is supposed, to the clearing up the country.[31]

In this case, the groundwater table was probably strongly influenced by forest clearing, although natural climatic variability cannot be ruled out. It would not be long before this lake, and nearly every other natural body of standing water throughout southern New England, would be raised and regulated by means of a dam, eliminating forever the possibility of using ponds as hydrologic barometers, so to speak.

Most of the concern about hydrological changes, however, dealt with reductions in flow of medium-sized streams during the summer-autumn milling season. What happened was this: Forest clearing diminished the base flow to streams by reducing the recharge to aquifers, which is responsible for maintaining stream flow between storms. Cleared soils, especially if eroded and compacted by livestock, froze deeper, preventing infiltration by snowmelt and spring rain. Reduced infiltration meant that the water table—whose gradual summer-long decline contributes to stream baseflow—would not be able to rise as high. It is for this reason that the effects of forest clearing were felt primarily in reduced streamflow rather than in the supply of water to wells.[32]

The relatively greater effect of clearing on the flood hydrograph of streams is curiously not mentioned, perhaps because this hydrologic effect is not as predictable as the low-water one. Recognizing human effects amidst the normal noise of the flood signal would have been difficult. Only later would the effect of forest clearing be noticed on large rivers.[33]

Non-renewable Resources

Although three separate Articles dealt with the use of non-renewable resources, the responses were often combined.

Mines and Minerals

Article 5a:...Mines and Minerals, especially those most useful as iron, copper, lead, silver, sulphur...

The overall impression is that mining was a much more common and much more local activity than at present. This is due to the high cost of transporting ore on poor roads without the use of fossil fuels. Descriptions of mining are generally not very sophisticated.[34] Here is an example from Ridgefield by Samuel Goodrich: "There are, in most of the mountains amongst the rocks and stones appearances of Sulpher and Iron...There are several beds of lime stone of good qualities."[35] Iron was the most commonly mentioned ore. Nearly every town claimed some sort of vein where iron minerals could be found, but only in the northwestern part of the state were they exploited with considerable success. Two other sources of iron—namely bog iron and black sand—were used, but not significantly.

Other metallic minerals such as copper, lead, silver, cobalt, were mentioned in several of the Town Reports, but more so as curiosities, partly because they were harder to refine. Benjamin Silliman, in Timothy Dwight's report for New Haven, mentioned a ninety-pound boulder of copper that was discovered, then "put to use."[36] No respondent mentioned the presence of gold, which we now know was available in a few areas. The respondents may have felt that there were many minerals out there to be exploited, but that they had to await the technical, essentially European, technology for exploiting them.

Non-metallic minerals were more important. Lime was reported in a variety of towns of the northwest, where marble outcrops were common, but not elsewhere in the state. Clay for brick was present in most of the towns. Many respondents described the mining of brick clay, but not its manufacture. The respondents, in my opinion, felt that there was an inexhaustible supply of clay, whose economic value was limited chiefly by other factors.

Quarries

Article 5b:...also, quarries of stone, with the kind and quality of the stone, and its distance from navigable water...

Almost every town had a quarry from which it obtained stone for building curbs, doorsills, building foundations, and chimneys. Levi Hart describes his native Preston as a land "...abounding with stone, which appear for cutting & are applied for hearths & other uses...& are excellent to endure the fire."[37] The kinds of stone quarried included:

• Native rock, which is now known to be high-grade metamorphic rock
• Freestone, which was the term used for the grayish and reddish sandstone of the Connecticut River Valley
• Soapstone, or steatite, which was reported only in Saybrook

• Marble, which was clearly restricted to the northwestern towns
• Slate, which was locally obtained and carved for gravestone markers.[38]

Of these, only the first, typically a gneiss or a schist, was widely quarried in every town.

Fuel

Article 7:...Fuel of all kinds, as wood, coal, peat, or turf, the quantity and quality...

Organic fuels were of three kinds: coal, peat, and wood.

Coal

Two of the reports from the Connecticut River Valley, where the rocks are sedimentary, mentioned the presence of coal that could be mined and burned, often from small seams of sub-bituminous coal and organic shale that never figured prominently in the mining industry. In Middletown the shale was "...so impregnated with bitumen that it burned."[39] There was already a good supply of so called hard coal (imported Pennsylvania anthracite) at market—even an oversupply—so there was little reason to mine the limited quantities of coal discovered in the hills of the central valley.

Interestingly, one of the Reports indicated that most of the coal burned was made from maple wood.[40] In this case they were obviously referring to charcoal, a mistake that would not likely be made today.

Peat

This organic fuel was widely present in every town, and would have also been visible and available as a consequence of wetland draining and ditching. Although the Solicitation letter specifically asked for the use of peat as fuel, only one report confirmed its limited use, although several others mentioned its presence in an offhand way. Wood was clearly the fuel of choice. The best discussion of peat as a fuel comes from John Treadwell's Farmington report: "...the only fuel... is wood....There being no coal, peat or turf yet discovered. It is believed, however, peat and turf might be found...in ditching near those swamps or morasses, a species of peat has been thrown up, much resembling that found in Ireland."[41]

Wood

Inclusion of wood in this category provides an insight as to how wood was viewed. Curiously, it was treated as a non-renewable commodity, one to be shipped away like ore, rather than harvested like a crop. It is quite clear that wood was a source of great revenue for rural people, especially those from towns bordering navigable water. Such farmers were mining the land of trees, rather than maintaining a woodlot, and, as such, participating in an export economy, rather than subsistence farming. At this scale, the industries of mining and forestry were effectively one in the same.

Agriculture
Manuring

Article 10a:.....Manures...lime, limestone, shells, ashes, salt, marl, swamp, creek and sea mud, plaister of paris, sea weed...

Manure did not mean solid dung, which is a modern connotation. Instead, manure was often liquid, and could include anything that, when added to the soil, enhanced the growth of crops. In addition to stable dung, the word manure encompassed irrigation water, as well as shells, sea weed, decaying fish, wood ash, muck from swamps, and, curiously, the wash from roads.[42] It seems that everyone had an opinion on this subject, because it was so vital to the farm economy. Manuring, when correctly done, was clearly the most important thing that a farmer could do to keep his land productive. Their view of manure, however, was not technical one. Most of the respondents agreed that stable manure, especially when enhanced with vegetable compost, ash and a little lime was an elixir for crop growth. Farmers from shoreline towns had access to materials that those of inland towns did not; they were astonished at the effects of decaying fish on grain crops.

"Plaister of paris," was specifically mentioned in the questionnaire. This was then a common word for the mineral gypsum, a slightly soluble form of calcium sulphate. It had the simultaneous advantage of "sweetening" or reducing the acidity of New England soils, which are notably deficient in alkaline salts, as well as providing the sulphur required for many plant proteins. Such field "lime" was used sparingly owing to its cost. Lewis Norton of Goshen provides the usual response to this question: "On suitable lands...the crop is much increased...by the use of plaister of Paris." Other farmers reported the opposite effect.

Ditching and Draining

Article 9b: Agriculture...improvements by draining and diking marshes, meadows and ponds...

Draining and diking marshes, meadows, and ponds was common practice, although only twelve respondents bothered to note this activity in their town. Their reports encouraged more diking and ditching because the organic soils of swamps were known to be fertile and stone free. David Field gives us an example from Durham regarding the use of swamp land for agriculture and suggests its potential: "The tract of low land was called by the Indians Coginchaug, or the long swamp... [which]...is generally cleared, and yields a large quantity of coarse grass. The tract might be rendered valuable by more effectual draining."[43] The coarse grass may not be grass at all, but a mixture of sedges and reeds, one of which (Phragmites) has recently become a serious invasive threat to New England wetlands.

Irrigation

Article 10b:...Manures...the effects of irrigation or watering lands...

Irrigation was widely recommended. Those who tried it were rewarded with enhanced crops at limited expense, especially on south-facing slopes, which, by being warmer, would also have been drier. The widely reported practice of irrigation contrasts with our retrospective view that New England was, and remains, a well-watered country. This apparent paradox can be explained by the fact that New England is, indeed, exceptionally well watered just below the surface, but that its sunny soils, especially sandy ones, dry out as quickly here as anywhere.

A curious report on irrigation is found in the response of Elijah Allen, of Cornwall: "James Douglass...dug 130 feet perpendicular into solid rock....Out of which Mine there Issues a large Sulphurous Spring of Water, which Waters about 20 acres of Land and is found to Fertilize and enrich the Land much more than Irrigation with common spring water."[44] This water probably contained alkaline metals like calcium, potassium, and magnesium derived from the calcareous shales and marbles that drained out onto soils developed on a different kind of rock.

Fencing

Article 12: Fences; the materials and mode of erecting them, kinds most used—increase or decrease of timber for fencing—the best kinds of...hedges...

A variety of materials—rail, brush, pole, board, hedge, stone, and stumps—were used for fencing on pioneering farms. Azel Backus provides an example of a typical fencing report from Bethlem: "Although there are stones enough on the Surface of the Town to fence it into convenient lots there are not the usual number of Ledges...Fence is generally of the Virginia Construction with Chesnut rails. But walls of stone with posts and two or three rails on the top are succeeding decayed fences of wood."[45]

The Town Reports make it clear that, out of the constellation of fencing types, only three categories of fencing were predominant in settled New England by the turn of the nineteenth century:

- Virginia rail fencing in which the rails rested on the ground (or on a few stones)
- Post-and-rail fence in which a hole was dug to receive the post
- A hybrid fence of stone and wood, in which a low accumulation of crudely stacked stone was brought to the legal height of a fence using wooden posts and rails. With the wood now rotted away, these fences are most often referred to simply as stone walls.

Most of the fences mentioned were made of wood, specifically American chestnut. Fences on rougher terrain were more apt to use the Virginia rail type of construction, which required no digging of post holes. Curiously, the height of a wooden fence was seldom mentioned. Only two of the reports listed the number of rails required for an adequate fence: Farmington had five, and Winchester had six.

Hybrid fences, those with stone at the bottom and wooden rails on top, were becoming quite common by the beginning of the nineteenth century. Timothy Dwight made it clear that the hybrid fence was a wooden fence with "the space between the lower rail and the ground being filled up with a wall of stone."[46] Most respondents, however, considered the hybrid fence a stone wall, even when wooden rails achieved most of the height. Given the rarity of post and rail fencing in the absence of stone, and its abundance with stone, it is reasonable to speculate the dry microclimate of the raised pile of stone played a role in the ubiquity of the hybrid fence. Erecting a post by moving a few stones was not only easier than digging a hole in the ground, but the post would last longer as well.

The geography of stone versus wooden fencing is also clearly indicated in the Town Reports. For example the town of East Windsor, lacking hard metamorphic fieldstone and having abundant lowlands covered with fine grained lake sediments, reports no stone walls. Towns such as Stratfield, Canterbury, and Farmington, which have approximately equal portions of sandy and non-sandy land, mention areas with stone fencing and areas without.

Hedges were the most common means by which enclosures in Britain were regulated or "fenced." Their absence in New England is highlighted by the fact that only one respondent (Goshen) bothered mentioning them. The availability of other materials for fencing that prevented the widespread adoption of this well-known technology, although other factors such as plant pathogens and cultural forces were clearly at work. Hedging was an inconsequential part of the farming business in America.

Transportation Infrastructure
Roads
Article 20a:...Roads...present state of them...

The condition of roads was noted in nearly all of the Town Reports. Most likely, the respondents felt that roads were recently greatly improved through the use of turnpike companies. Most of the respondents understood that drainage was the key to the success of a road; thus, the best roads were often those on the well-drained gravel terraces paralleling many small valleys above the floodplains. The anonymous report from New London provides a good example of this sentiment: "Much more art is required to preserve, than to make, a good road. Could every drop of water, that falls from the sky, or rises out of the ground, be turned off the road by itself, little else would be necessary."[47]

Bridges
Article 20b:...Bridges...recent state of them...

Few of the towns were large enough to finance bridges worthy of note. Most respondents noted their presence, then said they were not worth discussing, being simple wooden affairs with stone abutments. "These bridges are not infrequently swept away by large floods" is how they were described in Farmington,[48] giving us the impression that bridges were temporary. River ice, logjams, and scouring were the main culprits in taking a bridge down. Aaron Putnam provides

a sample description from Pomfret: "as to Bridges,...others among us have often suffer'd much, by Floods, & Freshets; to secure against Injury People have tho't it necessary...[that]... Buttments be made sure; & to prevent Damage by cakes of Ice, to have breakers..."[49]

Modern bridges across the Thames at New London, the Connecticut south of Springfield, and the lower Housatonic Rivers would have greatly astonished the respondents, several of whom specifically ruled out the possibility that such bridges could ever be built.

Climatology
Discussions of climate fall under four separate Heads of Inquiry—climate, health, meteorology, and remarkable occurrences.

General
Article 29a:...Climate....

Descriptions of the climate were often written in plain statements like that of Franklin's Samuel Nott: "the climate is ...good."[50] Sometimes they are more elaborate, such as the one provided by Elkanah Tisdale of Lebanon: "The town lying high and being hilley appears colder in winter & enjoys a freer breeze in summer than flat low, level tracts."[51] Or Ridgefield: "The land...being so elevated & descending to the North, occassions a very cold tho healthy air and we have an abundance of snow..."[52] Whether they mentioned it or not, these authors understood that climate has a distinct geography.

Health
Article 29b:...the diseases most prevalent in high and low situations, near streams of running water, or marsh and stagnant water, on the north and south sides of hills and mountains, and on different soils....

Respondents were much more specific about the effects on health. High, cold air was considered "salubrious" whereas low ground was universally considered to be unhealthful, with dysentery, fevers, ague mentioned in ten of the reports as having been associated with stagnant waters and low ground. Mr. Robbins writes of Norfolk: "Situated on high ground, and enjoying a salubrious atmosphere and pure water, the inhabitants have been blessed with a greater share of health, than has generally prevailed in most other parts of the state."[53]

Conversely, low areas were known to be unhealthy places, as Lewis Norton of Goshen informs us: "The town...[has]... few or no marshes, stagnant waters, or low and unhealthy situations."[54] Thus, draining of lowland swamps was considered as an important way to enhance the health of towns. Such actions were often justified based on actual correlation between lowland flooding and disease. Andrew Lee of Lisbon was a witness:

> ...about AD 1725 a disease, which was termed the burning ague, broke out...near a large pond, which had been dammed (I suppose with a view

to help in distroying the trees & bushes) and spread for five or six miles around. It proved very mortal, carrying off one-third part of the adult inhabitants...[Shortly] after the pond was drained the disorder ceased.[55]

One of the least scientific interpretations made throughout the reports was the erroneous, epidemiological, view that the health of the town can be measured by the age of its oldest inhabitants. We now know that genetics and lifestyle play important roles as well.

Meteorology

Article 29c:...Meteorological observations.

This was one of the least appreciated categories in the Solicitation letter. Many respondents ignored it completely. Others simply commented on the path of storms, or the date at which snow melted, or the time when the rivers rose. Only John Treadwell, of Farmington was specific and precise. For example, he considered the cobbles in the soil as climatic buffers that should be left in the soil because they "keep the land loose, retain evaporation in times of drought, accelerate vegetation in the spring & by retaining the heat... longer than common earth, they moderate the cold of the succeeding night, and either prevent or lessen...frosts."[56] He also noted prophetically that "another cause of the decrease of cold air in the Atlantic Settlements,...is the myriads of culinary fires... [and]...the great increase in animal life,"[57] both of which yield heat to the atmosphere, especially during winter temperature inversions. Modern climatologists refer to this as the "heat island" effect, one that has confounded the global assessment of anthropomorphic climatic change.

Extremes

Article 30: Remarkable seasons or occurrences in the natural world; as tempest, rain, hail, snow, and innundations [add drought]...

Most of the events mentioned under the question "remarkable occurrence" were climatic in nature, in which case the respondent described those years with deepest snow, largest floods, coldest winters, latest frosts, largest hail, wettest summers, and years of drought. Hurricanes and tornadoes were also mentioned. David Field from Middlesex County writes: "On the 17th of February, 1717, the greatest snow fall every known in this country, attended by a dreadful tempest...[the winters of 1737-8, 1740-1, 1779-80 were uncommonly cold...the wettest season...was in the summer and fall of 1795..."[58]

Although one might expect to find a pattern in the responses, none was apparent, other than two nearby towns mentioning the same storm, or the same wet year. In fact, many of the towns appeared to contradict each other. Only the drought of 1762 came through strongly enough to be defined as pattern. The lack of coincidence for nearby towns may not be due to sloppy or incorrect weather keeping. Rather it might be due to the local nature of tempests and deep snows.

Remarkable...occurrences

Earthquakes

Article 30: Remarkable.. occurrences in the natural world....

The Reports contain important documentary evidence for three seismic phenomena.

1755 Cape Anne, Massachusetts: Most important is the documentation of the geographic extent of the 1755 earthquake, New England's largest known historic earthquake, which took place near Cape Anne Massachusetts.[59] Noises as large as "explosions" caused by fracturing of crustal rock took place in the extreme northwestern corner of the state, in Cornwall. In Farmington, ground accelerations were strong enough to topple chimneys. Water wells in Lisbon, Farmington, and Union were changed significantly, suggesting that subsurface movements— either consolidation of unconsolidated material, or the movement of blocks along bedrock fractures—were taking place. Importantly, there is no apparent geographic gradient to the reported effects of the 1755 earthquake across Connecticut.

Moodus Noises: The report of David Field provides important documentary history for what are known as Moodus noises, audible seismic phenomena that have long been known to characterize Moodus, the site of the most intense seismicity in southern New England. Importantly, Rev. Field describes their pattern as having the "noises like those of small arms... hundreds in twenty years, some terrible,...sometimes every day, great numbers in the space of a year, often coming down from the north, imitating slow thunder then breaking like cannon shot which shakes houses."[60] This is a surprisingly precise and depictive description of the Moodus noises; recent ones, though more accurate, concern fewer and smaller events.

Mr. Field also describes their historical pattern. The history begins with observations by Native Americans who called the place Mackimoodus, or the place of noises. David Field understood that these noises were associated with earthquakes "for which [the area] has ben famed from time immemorial."[61] Based on a letter, he describes how a minor earthquake in 1727 caused the noises to cease for ten or twenty years, after which time they again became rather violent. Apparently, this pattern repeated itself after the 1791 earthquake, at which time the noises ceased again. Field's report provides suggestive evidence for a long-term pattern in which a large earthquake can release the local ambient stress beneath Moodus.

Finally, Field's report contains a speculation on the triggering causes of the Moodus noises, one that is consistent with our current understanding of shallow seismicity: "A gentleman...observed that for twenty six years they have occurred almost uniformly in a dull and heavy state of the atmosphere."[62]

1791 East Haddam, Connecticut: David Field described a locally significant earthquake on May 16, 1791, at about 10 a.m. strong enough to knock down chimneys, open up rifts in the earth, and trigger rockfalls near Moodus River falls.[63] He also noted that this event was felt (presumably by his correspondents) in New York, Boston, and Northhampton. He reported that it consisted of many violent shocks, rather than simply one, indicating rupture along a fault at depth followed by aftershocks.

Meteorite

Article 30: Remarkable...occurrences in the natural world...

The Article on "Remarkable Occurrences" did not request any astronomical phenomenon. Yet Elijah Allen in Cornwall recorded one. His comment is quoted here in full because it is one of the earliest to be noted and because it may be the only eighteenth century account of a "fireball" to make use of the speed of sound.

> Between 6 and 7 o'Clock in the Evening on the 17th of October A.D. 1788 a Meteor was seen here, passing from North East towards the Southwest, which burst in the Air, and about 5 Minutes after (it was Judged) a Report was heard. Computing sound to be conveyed in the air at the Rate of 1142 feet in a Second of Time, and that it was 5 Minutes after the Explosion before the Report was heard, the Meteor must be 64 Miles & 7/8ths Distant from us when it Burst and disappeared.[64]

Discussion

Regionalism

Four separate regions of the state can be identified by the way respondents described their physical environment: the northwest, inland towns elsewhere, shoreline towns, and the lower Connecticut River estuary.

In the *northwest*, the focus of the respondents was on hard-rock mining—especially iron ore and marble—in addition to the standby of livestock husbandry. Only in the northwest does mining rise above the level of a curiosity and do materials other than local ledge become important. Accordingly, there seems to be less attention paid to soil description, possibly suggesting that grazing, rather than tillage or mowing, was the main agricultural activity in this region. *Inland towns elsewhere* in the state derived their incomes almost exclusively from livestock farming. Each valley had its own intervals, hillsides, ledges, and marshlands. It is in these descriptions that we find the best differentiation of the landscape in terms of soil type and performance. *Shoreline towns* of Long Island Sound focused on the state of their navigation channels and the change in the fisheries, many of which were altered by the construction of dams across rivers. Their descriptions of farming are rather ordinary, and clearly secondary.

Of all descriptions, those of the *Connecticut River estuary* were most diversified, at least economically. Tillage farming and hay production were enhanced by the access to productive interval lands flooded annually by New England's largest river. The particular geological history of the Connecticut River, with its abundant Pleistocene glacial lake beds, Mesozoic sedimentary rocks (which include coal and fossils), and glacially deepened valleys allowed navigation to proceed up as far as Windsor, giving large ships access to brick factories, trap rock, and freestone quarries. The export of fuel wood was also enhanced by proximity to navigable water.

Empirical Geology

The word geological was mentioned only by Professor Silliman of Yale College, whose detailed account of the geology and mineralogy of the New Haven area was wholly contained within the 1811 response by his colleague, Timothy Dwight. Other than Silliman, who traveled to Scotland to learn geology in 1805, and who concentrated almost exclusively on mineralogy and bedrock stratigraphy of the New Haven area, no other respondent could be considered a scientist.[65] Yet many of the respondents saw and understood what would only later be formally investigated as geology. Collectively, the respondents were:

- Classifying topography based on its geologic origin,
- Interpreting ancient plateaus as ancient erosional surfaces uplifted by tectonic forces,
- Mapping bedrock for both utilitarian and natural history purposes, which included recognition of the great Triassic border fault,
- Recognizing and interpreting the origin of postglacial deposits and landforms by observing their formation; sand dunes; river interval lands; peat from swamps,
- Using the estuarine circulation of the Connecticut River estuary to account for the distribution of islands and submerged sand bars, and to explain how effects were coupled,
- Acknowledging the effects of rising sea level, and interpreting the origin of salt marshes and bay mud,
- Recognizing and describing a variety of distinctive landforms produced by glaciation,
- Differentiating groundwater from surface water hydrology,
- Evaluating how the transmission of groundwater through different aquifers affected their chemistry,
- Recognizing that soil pH regulates the uptake of nutrients by plants,
- Accurately dating and explaining not only the effects of local earthquakes, produced near Moodus, but in characterizing the effects of the 1755 Cape Ann Earthquake.
- Knowledgeable about how floods can be enhanced and mitigated by reservoir attenuation, natural channel constrictions, and deforestation.

Source of Data

Initially, I had hoped that the Town Reports would contain measurable environmental data—depth of channels, size of rivers, years of drought, quantities of river flow, etc.—that could be used as a 200-year-old baseline for comparisons with the modern environment. Similarly, I had also hoped that the respondents were witnessing environmental phenomenon—soil erosion processes, change in hydrology, systematic changes in the river morphology—which would be impossible today, owing to "development" during the last two centuries. Finally,

I was curious about the spatial reliability of reported phenomenon.

With the few notable exceptions, I was disappointed to find little of value in this regard. For example, only Elijah Allen reported the visual and sonic effects of the powerful meteorite explosion in 1788, one that was witnessed all over southern New England by colleagues interviewed by Ezra Stiles.[66] How was such an event missed by the others? What does this say about their responses to solicited information? With respect to quantitative measurement, there are only a few examples, and no datum horizons listed that would allow continued measurement of changes taking place 200 years ago. Exceptions to the limited use of the information are these:

River Migration

David McClure provided us with a migration rate for the banks of the Connecticut River in East Windsor. He noted that the river has increased in width and decreased in depth by its undermining of the banks: "Seventy and eighty years ago corn grew where the middle of the river now runs."[67] Since the river was described at 100 rods wide, it had moved 50 rods in 75 years, giving us a rate of 10.7 feet per year. Such a rate is important because this report came at a time just before the river began to be manipulated by wharves and riprap. Perhaps this is the natural rate of bank migration, at least in this one spot.

Salt Marsh Accumulation

Timothy Dwight provides us with the rate at which the New Haven harbor was changing possibly as a consequence of mud draining down the Quinnipiac River. He reported that "The northwestern side of the harbour has undergone great changes since the settlement of the town...forty six years since, there was more water...from thirty rods to three-fourths of a mile...owing to the influx of earth...conveyed into it by rains and streams; and partly, and indeed almost entirely, to the continual accumulation of what is called harbor or Creek mud; believed...to be principally a marine vegetable....The mud... seems not unlikely to convert a considerable part of the [harbor] into a tract of salt marsh."[68]

Historic Sedimentation

David Field reported that a sand bar near the mouth of the Connecticut River was changing its configuration during settlement.[69] Three shallow channels were now giving way to a single deeper one, possibly as a consequence of increasing runoff, which in turn, may have been caused by land use changes in the watershed upstream.

Selected Attitudes
Wetlands

Swamps were called many things (morass, slackwaters, defiles, stagnant, marshes) and were viewed in contradictory terms. Clearly, they were resources from which:

• Cedar and pine timber were cut,
• Peat was taken for fuel,
• Muck was extracted for manure,
• Game animals were hunted,
• Bog iron was taken for forges, and
• Tillage fields could be made by draining and agricultural improvements.

But just as surely, swamps were universally loathed as a source of disease and poisonous water. Every attempt was made either to drain swamps or to avoid them. Today, in an age when we treasure our wetland resources, this view is historically significant.

Soil Erosion

Topsoil loss is a "hot-button" environmental topic today. Thus, I found it surprising that soil erosion (i.e., surface losses from overland flow and gully propagation) was mentioned only once, and then only in a positive sense. This was by John Treadwell, from Farmington: "Water running from the highways is...of great benefit, as it brings a rich manure with it, and is worthy of attention, as it saves what would otherwise be lost by running to the rivers, and from thence to the sea..."[70] My colleagues and I have demonstrated that erosion and topsoil loss was a common and ubiquitous phenomenon in small valleys throughout southern New England,[71] as is the now the case globally where the hooves of livestock meet loamy soils in well-watered regions.[72] So why was topsoil loss so invisible to the Yankee farmers? Quite clearly, the modern perception that colonists fretted about soil erosion is erroneous. Instead, they were concerned with soil fertility.

Stone Walls

The collective response to the Solicitation letter provides an attitudinal survey for the subject of stone walls at a time when the conversion from wooden fencing to stone was underway. The respondents make it clear that stone walls were an American phenomenon rather than just a colonial one; that stone walls were most often associated with well-established farms, rather than with pioneering homesteads; and that farmers remained ambivalent about fieldstone, even in the year 1800. Stone was clearly seen as a resource for fencing, though it was primarily an encumbrance to cultivation.

Eight of the Town Reports speculated on the transformation to stone walls from wooden fencing. In Bethlem, stone walls with posts and two or three rails are "succeeding decayed fences of wood" implying a gradual transformation toward the permanent solution requiring less maintenance.[73] Lisbon reported that stone walls increased at the expense of chestnut rails and that "by the next age they will be the only fence." Litchfield, Wallingford, Winchester and Willington reported that a diminishing supply of chestnut was at least partly responsible for the transformation to stone walls. Washington simply stated that the transition was happening, but did not attribute its cause to the shortage of wood for fencing.[74]

Perceptions

The gentlemen who were asked to characterize the geological and hydrological resources in 1800 had no alternative but to do so in a qualitative, descriptive, and anecdotal manner. Hard data, which were already available for the social, economic, and ecclesiastical conditions at that time, were simply not available for natural phenomenon such as the measured heights of hills or the discharges of streams. This dearth of data on the natural environment forced respondents to rely on their own personal experience. Two respondents felt so strongly about the primacy of personal experience that they refused to answer questions for which they had only hearsay evidence. All in all, the responses yield a collection of personal impressions regarding the terrain, soils and water at the scale of small villages.

Two centuries later, the responses to a similar questionnaire could be prepared without leaving a climate-controlled office, and could be returned without experiencing the dust and dung of early turnpikes. A modern respondent—more likely a professional civil servant in a town planning and zoning department than a parish deacon—could download a variety of high-resolution thematic maps to a workstation via the Internet. Hard data on environmental parameters of interest (stream flow, depth to the water table, and the alkalinity of the soil) could be obtained with a few clicks of a "mouse," then rendered seamlessly into digital, end-user products using GIS (geographic information system) software programmed with numerical optimization algorithms.

The first approach was intensely local, qualitative, individualistic, and conceptually integrated. The second is global, quantitative, abstract, and thematic. Such a comparison begs the question "Which characterization of the Connecticut landscape is the best one? The answer to this question, at least the one given to us by the history of technology, is that the modern approach is better than the old-fashioned one, because the latter replaced the former. In modern times, however, we are often misled to believe that the quality of environmental management is limited by access to high-quality hard data. Could it be, however, that our contemporary, data-rich approach has, instead of improving things, actually made them worse? Could it be that gains in our technical proficiency have been offset by the plethora of environmental regulations and the vast bureaucracies required to implement them?[75]

Indeed, knowledge is power. Digital information has become the coin of the realm. But we must not mistake one for the other, knowledge for data. Sadly, many of us now spend more time litigating the environment than examining it. The majority of contemporary New Englanders understand "how the earth works" in a way that is inferior to that of the original respondents, at least in practical terms. For example, how many priests, ministers, rabbis spreading God's word today know the depth to the groundwater table below their own homes, much less the average and extreme values for their towns? How many of them can recall which of the last several decades were those of drought or heavy rain? Do they know why crushed lime works on some soils, but not others?

Where to find a vein of coal? What the last earthquake did to their town? The speed of sound in the atmosphere? Good answers to these, and many more, questions were freely given, often from memory, by the respondents, most of whom probably never had a science course in college.

Thus, from my perspective as an earth science educator, it seems as though we have traded data for detachment. The transition from coalesced farmsteads to coalesced suburbs has removed us—physically—from daily interaction with the earth. Ironically, the poor, those who were most closely connected with the physical environment in 1800, are now those most alienated from it, because open, uninhabited land has become a luxury to be afforded, rather than an obstacle to be overcome. Given our physical and psychological remove from earthly matters, we have, without knowing it, entrusted the decision-making authority for environmental affairs to regulators, each of whom has expertise and control over a progressively shrinking piece of the pie. Separate people, even separate agencies, now monitor the pH of soils, the oxygen content of wetlands, the rate of snowmelt, and the release of fish. Turtles carry transmitters. Transducers experience what a farmers' toes once did. Processes are simulated instead of experienced. Fewer and fewer of us comprehend how nature works.

These "regulators" about whom I write are my friends, some of whom are ex-students. They, too, commute home to gardens, backyard hammocks, picnic sites, and shoreline retreats, where they continue to experience nature up close, as did the Connecticut Academy's respondents. Thoreau's *Walden* and Aldo Leopold's *Sand County Almanac*—arguably the salient environmental critiques of their respective centuries—derive their strength not from the abstraction of quantitative information but from the subjective intimacy of real places. Local places. Personal places. Out-of-the-way places. Cold and hot ones. Seasonal places. Places like a farm in Willington or a tidal marsh in Bridgeport. Thus, in many respects, each collection of responses to the Solicitation letter, at least in terms of the physical environment, was not wholly unlike the much more famous collections of essays by Thoreau and Leopold.

Environmental intimacy can still be achieved in our favorite places, but surrender cannot, for we now hold too much power over Nature. This was not the case two centuries ago, when the first generation of Americans—among them the authors of the Town Reports—were busy regulating streams, draining swamps, shooting wildlife, and quarrying ledges. When their crops were destroyed by hail the size of "Hen's Eggs,"[76] however, no one was there to declare the storm's swath a federal disaster area. Life went on. When bridges were destroyed by freshets, they were quickly replaced by those who used them, knowing that it was only a matter of time before nature claimed them once again. When a shoreline wharf was built, its negative consequences for navigation were taken in stride. For these examples—each of which today would precipitate a decade of litigation—there seems to be little blame...no sense of embarrassment...no sense of "...Oh well, we'll get it right the next time." Nor is there a hint of futility. Rather, there is a sense of reasoned surrender to those things beyond human control.

A good example of such surrender comes from David Field's report for the coastal town of Madison on Long Island Sound.[77] It was here that a Newport company set up a porpoise fishery in 1792-93, which managed to catch "during the season, six or seven hundred of this kind of fish: in one instance 75 at a draught" in order to convert them to good use; their skins for the fine leather needed for the bellows of blacksmith's forges; their oil (six gallons each) for lighting; their carcasses for manure. Two centuries later, in an age when "whale watching" generates millions of tourist dollars, this description is appalling, even arrogant. Yet the porpoises, in the end, won out. Apparently, they quickly learned not to approach "...the spot where these depredations were made upon their numbers." The fishing company submitted to its loss, pulled anchor, and moved away. The porpoises survived just fine.

In the final analysis, the letters returned to the CAAS office contain the words of well-educated rural people, words laid down on rag paper with a quill pen, words that evoke the smells, sights, and sounds of local experience. Nowhere among them will you find laser-printed executive summaries of electronically transmitted, remotely obtained data. In some small way, each of the Town Reports—even when filtered over the gulf of two centuries—bespeaks a love of their state that few of us could capture today. Their soils "answer" to applications of manure, rather than merely respond to them. Their swamps "answer" to drainage. These people were conversing with their environment, not just occupying it.

The Ups and Downs of the Connecticut Town

in the Preindustrial Era

Christopher Collier

Introduction

The New England town is an American original. There was nothing like it in the old England whence the New Englanders came. Though there were variations in the legal relations of town to colony, the organization and substance of town life was pretty much the same in Massachusetts, Connecticut, Rhode Island, and New Hampshire.

A full discussion of the establishment and development of the Connecticut town calls for detailed attention to geography, politics, and religion. The geographic considerations include the acquisition of the land from Indians, the assignment of land by the colony government to proprietors, and the division of town lands among proprietors. They also include questions of population dispersal and density in relation to community control and support and in relation to economic viability in a largely agricultural society. I deal only most cursorily with these matters. The focus of this essay is on the political and religious aspects of town development in the seventeenth and eighteenth centuries and the towns' demographic and economic collapse in the nineteenth century. It traces the ebb and flow of two tides of rural town rise and fall; a third, the suburban movement of the post World War II era, is outside of our focus here.

Lands and Bounds

No one knew, of course, what Connecticut was in 1634. The original settlers, in their Fundamental Orders, merely called themselves "the Inhabitants and Residents of Windsor, Hartford and Wethersfield now cohabiting and dwelling in and up on the River of Connectecotte and the Lands thereunto adjoyneing." The settlement was sanctioned by Massachusetts Bay and given a cloak of questionable legality by the Warwick Patent of 1631. But the settlers, claims Connecticut's most authoritative historian, "all were legally trespassers."[1]

The bounds of the Warwick Patent if successfully prosecuted would have made Connecticut a strip of land about seventy miles deep north from Long Island Sound extending from the Narragansett Bay, all the way to the Pacific Ocean. The Patent described Connecticut as including "all the lands and grounds, place and places, soil, wood, and woods, grounds, havens, ports, creeks and rivers, waters, fishings, and hereditaments whatsoever...from the western ocean to the south [Pacific] sea."[2] Such inclusiveness over so vast an area is amazing to contemplate, and long, arduous, and often acrimonious, even bloody, efforts were made to fulfill parts of these claims. The Charter of 1662 reaffirmed these bounds in

a general way, but conflicts with neighboring colonies, and judicial action under the Articles of Confederation in 1786 narrowed the limits to roughly what they are today. Though not finally settled in detail until 1881, eighteenth-century boundaries enclosed an area close enough to Connecticut's present 5,009 square miles to treat it as that size. It is likely that the Warwick Patent did not receive the ultimate sanction of the King's signature, but the Connecticut settlers bought it in 1644 as it remained their best claim to legitimacy. In any event, the settlements upon the "River of Connectecotte" were remote enough from His Majesty to feel secure for the present against even the longest arm of royal law, and besides, in the vast "lands and grounds, place and places...havens, ports, creeks and rivers..." they needed concern themselves only with their immediate surroundings.

And their immediate surroundings concerned them very much, indeed. Historians agree that religious differences played little, if any, part in the decision to leave Massachusetts. The motives may have been partly political, especially in the case of the leaders, but the principal moving force was the desire for land sufficient for a good living. The intent of the first emigrants from Massachusetts, it was reported to Governor Bradford of Plymouth upon whose land they were trespassing, was "to be a great town and have commodious dwellings for many together."[3] And the land was there for taking. It had been wrested from the River Indians by the Pequots, squatted on by the Dutch, bought from the Pequots by some Plymouth adventurers, and now the acquisitive Massachusetts Bay people would crowd in and overwhelm them all. The organization of the land, then, was taken up simultaneously with the organization of political and ecclesiastical life.

The English Heritage

The vast acres of howling wilderness, wrested from Indians who were greatly depleted by European diseases and soon conquered or co-opted by military might, needed organization in the English manner. But New England was not old England and frontier conditions required major adaptation of traditional forms. Those forms were the medieval town and parish.

In the British tradition, the distinction between parishes and townships was not always clear. The parish was the most ubiquitous administrative unit in England throughout the seventeenth and eighteenth centuries. In an area of about 50,500 square miles, there were 15,635 "parishes or townships levying their own rates, by their own officials, as distinct units of local administration," or about one for every 3.25 square miles. They differed greatly in size, however, from just a few acres in urban settlements to vast areas that themselves included two, three, and even fifteen or twenty townships. On the other hand, some areas called townships included several parishes.[4]

The term town and township are found frequently in medieval and early modern British records, but they were applied to numerous sorts of local administrative bodies, and sometimes merely to groups of buildings, in much the same way that seventeenth-century Connecticuters used the term village. It was the parish in England that administered work-houses, pumps, pounds, whipping posts and stocks, watchhouses, and weights and measures. "The financial importance of the parish was equally overwhelming....Measured by the amount of its taxation alone, the parish outweighed all other governing authorities....Very frequently the Parish was nothing but the Township in its ecclesiastical aspect,..." and as the manors decayed, the parishes became "civil parishes" and were established as such by English law in 1834.[5]

It was the parish model that seventeenth-century New Englanders brought with them from England. At its origin, Massachusetts Bay founders referred to the several settlements as plantations and towns, and assigned to them authorities and administrative functions carried out in England by the parish. The church, or ecclesiastical body politic which had traveled intact from England was joined by the town, or civil body politic, both subservient to the General Court. As one modern scholar has pointed out, "The New England town originated as an organization to cope with the temporal problems of a Puritan church congregation on the frontier."[6]

The varied nature of towns and townships in England gave those terms an understandable vagueness when used by early New Englanders. Town was used synonymously with plantation, settlement, village, and even people, that is, "with the utmost looseness of meaning," through the early 1630s.[7] In Connecticut, the colony preexisted the towns, authorized them, and eventually in Connecticut, articulated their functions.[8] Indeed, the settlements along the Connecticut River, quite unambiguously, called themselves towns, and the term appears in the second entry of the public record in June, 1636.[9] What follows is a description of the development of the Connecticut town in its legal, institutional, and tangible elements. A look at it at the end of the eighteenth century when it reached full development is a good way to start.

Descriptions and Definitions

The Marquis de Chastellux, crossing Connecticut in 1780 wrote in his diary as he viewed Plainfield, "what is called in America a 'town' or 'township' is only a certain number of houses dispersed over a great space, but which belong to the same corporation and send deputies to the General Assembly of the state. The center or headquarters of these towns is the 'meeting-house' or church. This church sometimes stands alone, and is sometimes surrounded by four or five houses only; whence it happens that when a traveler asks the question, 'How far is it to town?' he is answered, 'You are already

there.'; but if he happens to specify the place he wishes to be at, either the 'meetinghouse,' or such and such a tavern, he is not unfrequently told, 'It is seven or eight miles away.'"[10] A few years later his countryman, Brissot de Warville wrote, "As you may know my friend, in the interior of America the word 'town' designates a territory of eight or ten miles over which are scattered 50, 100, or 200 houses. This division into towns is necessary to permit the people, who are spread over a vast area, to come together for elections. Otherwise, the inhabitants would go sometimes to one town meeting and sometimes to another, and this would lead to great confusion. Besides, it would be impossible to determine the population of each township, and population must be considered as the only true basis for the division of the state. Thus the precise establishment of boundaries must be a necessary consequence of a free constitution. No people have given this point as much attention as have Americans."[11]

Connecticut's most intimate eighteenth-century observer, Timothy Dwight, provides his definition, too: "A town," he wrote in 1796, "....denotes a collection of houses in the first parish, if the township contains more than one, constituting the principal, and ordinarily the original, settlement in that parish....Town is also used sometimes to denote a township,.... In legal language it intends the inhabitants of a township assembled in lawful town meeting." Noah Webster, in the early nineteenth-century, defined town as "a collection of houses, a district of certain limits, the inhabitants or the legal voters...."[12]

The Legal and Constitutional Context

Dwight and Webster describe the town primarily as a legal rather than a geographic or social entity. In important respects they are right to give this constitutional matter primacy, for all the things that Connecticut towns do or are forbidden to do are defined by the colony/state government. Towns in Connecticut have no rights, no "original autonomy," but only mandates and privileges authorized by the colony/state government.[13] This is so because of the English charter system of incorporation under which—in its broadest sense so as to include royal and proprietary grants—all English colonies in America were established.

But ancient English legal traditions required reconfiguration in the New World if settlers there were to safeguard their property and political rights. The legal traditions had to be twisted, warped, and even broken under the stress of land hunger, economic survival, Indian prior occupancy, and the ideological requirements of covenanted godly communities.

The principal legal problem encountered by the breakaway groups that settled along the Connecticut River between 1634 and 1636 was that they were outside the Massachusetts bounds, but needed her official sanction to legitimate their local government. It was well known to all the leading individuals that corporations could not incorporate sub-units.[14]

The General Assembly, however, routinely established towns with all the legal appurtenances of corporations. They could elect officers, levy taxes, dispose of property, compel labor on highways, sue and be sued, etc.[15] Sometimes towns were "incorporated"; sometimes "erected, constituted, made and embodied into a town"; sometimes merely granted "the same privileges of other towns."[16] Town status was complete when the freemen began to send deputies to the Assembly and pay colony taxes—sometimes many years after the town was named, bounded, and granted the usual administrative authorities.

By the revolutionary era, the legal status of towns was fully rationalized. In 1795 Zephaniah Swift in his *System of the Laws of the State of Connecticut* could confidently state that "Connecticut is divided into a number of small corporations, called towns." They were, he said, in a legal sense "an important branch of the state executive, and are calculated to regulate those minute and subordinate concerns of the people, which cannot be reached in very large corporations."[17] In this post-revolutionary era, Connecticut's sovereign authority was taken for granted, but Swift also implied that the state is a large corporation and the towns are small corporations; thus corporations did in fact incorporate inferior corporations. Towns, said the Connecticut Supreme court in 1887, citing among other precedents, Swift's definition, "differ from trading companies, and even from municipal corporations elsewhere. They are territorial corporations, into which the State is divided by the legislature,...for political purposes and the convenient administration of government; they have those powers only which have been expressly conferred upon them by statute, or which are necessary for conducting municipal affairs; and all the inhabitants of towns are members of the quasi corporation."[18]

Internally, then, Connecticut town government had developed full articulation during the seventeenth century. Towns had a residential center—or several of them—an ecclesiastical polity, a company or more of militia, a full grown civil government, and representation in the General Assembly. They had authority to elect their own officers, divide out lands, and levy local taxes, and responsibility to keep records, maintain the militia, a church and school, to keep up highways and bridges, to collect the colony taxes, and to report mischiefs and misdemeanors occurring within their bounds. The development of the Connecticut towns from their primitive organization in the mid-1630s to the incorporation of five cities in 1784 is a story of ebb and flow as the focus of social and municipal activity shifted to other entities.

In Connecticut the functions of social organization, at first concentrated in the town meeting, were shortly divided into three local governing bodies. The proprietors' meeting was to administer the land; the church meeting was to establish ecclesiastical policy; and the town meeting was to legislate and administer the civil affairs of the unit. For a short while this worked well enough at most places, but soon both the church and proprietary bodies adopted exclusivist policies and separated themselves from the town. The proprietories eventually atrophied as their landholdings were distributed. But the secular arm of the church—the ecclesiastical society—by the early eighteenth century came to dominate.

The Rise of the Parish

In Connecticut, government was practical. There was concern that all inhabitants have relatively easy access to ministerial services, and that no family live too far from a parish center to escape social control. The dominating ideal was to collect enough people to support an ecclesiastical society within a reasonable distance of a church. Thus division into parishes rather than breaking up towns was favored. In this way, intraparish, and later intratown controversy was abated by dividing off discontented parishioners, and the practice of the communitarian ideal was promoted. In cases of settlement beyond the reach of either local civil or ecclesiastical control, the ideal was abandoned. The colony government failed to curb land sales and distribution, and the population became dispersed. The centrifugal pull of vacant land was too strong for the centralization of community.

The New England ideal in the seventeenth century was a coincidence of citizens of the town and members of the church. But admission to the church was greatly restricted, so the ideal was not approached. However, religious affairs were organized not only within the church, but also within the ecclesiastical society, a body consisting of all the town voters who lived within the bounds of the parish. At first, town bounds and parish bounds were the same, so that town and society voters were the same men, and the town determined ecclesiastical as well as secular affairs. The relation between town and church became complicated when, beginning in Hartford in 1670, one body of town voters was divided into two or more parishes; or as in other cases, parish bounds crossed town lines to include parts of two or three towns. What developed was a tripartite hierarchy of meetings: church, society, and town, along with the rapidly disappearing proprietors' meetings.

The church was limited to those men and women who had in some special way achieved baptism as adults or whose parents had; or by other criteria established variously by individual churches with increasing liberality in the eighteenth century. This body was limited to such concerns as determining its own membership, the rules governing baptism, eligibility for election to the office of deacon or elder, the phrasing of its articles of faith and association, and procuring communion plate and wine. The church per se did not quite atrophy, but the most important ecclesiastical functions were under the control of the society.

In scattered settlements, the General Court noted in 1677, "the posterity of such, most them, are endangered to degenerate to heathenish ignorance and barbarism."[19] Thus colony policy was to break towns into parishes rather than to establish whole new civil governments as was the Massachusetts practice. The people seemed to prefer it this way for the ecclesiastical society came to fulfill all their social needs. Political matters concerned them less.

As more churches were built in the outlying regions of the towns, convenience dictated that the closer centers of social focus assume additional administrative functions. Thus, for perhaps the whole middle half of the eighteenth century, the parish became the focus of community for most Connecticut families. The town did not atrophy to the extent that the church did, but it did lose its primacy as the administrative and psychological center of the community. Parishes took on most of the functions of both the church and the town. It was not until the politicizing events of the revolutionary era that Connecticut yeomen demanded as easy access to political centers as they had long since gained to ecclesiastical centers.

The effort was to maintain community—or rather to reestablish it—in the face of a population that was not only separated geographically, but had also become divided on theological grounds. Traditionally, the General Assembly had accepted diversity of opinion and practice *among* the parishes in order to maintain harmony *within* towns and throughout the colony as well. The religious battles associated with the Great Awakening left many towns fragmented into numerous parishes. That the vast majority of these new parishes also constituted separate geographic areas made possible the reestablishment of units in which harmony prevailed. In virtually every case in which two congregations were established within the same parish bounds, they had coalesced again by the late eighteenth century; but those established with their own geographic identity not only continued to exist, but in scores of cases became full-fledged towns. Perhaps it is to be expected that groups of parishioners living close to each other might adopt the same deviant theological position and petition for separate parish status. But it seems likely that rapid expansion into the northwest and northeast highlands brought about such long compulsory trips to church that just plain inconvenience of travel underlay the surface squabbling over baptism and church membership. In other words, perhaps the theological and liturgical differences were only covers for shortening distances from the church and enhancing local real estate values.

The General Assembly readily granted requests for separate parishes if the petitioners fulfilled five conditions. They should have the explicit acquiescence of the mother parish or town—which they often did not; their numbers should be significant; their tax list should be large enough to support the ministry; there should be some hardship involved in getting to their present legal meetinghouse; and the proposed new parish should consist of a compact area not exceeding a radius from the center of three or four miles.

Of 196 petitions for separate society status entered between 1680 and 1780, forty-eight were granted in the same year; twenty-eight the next year; and thirty-six more within the next three years. Twenty-one groups of petitioners had to wait six to ten years, and nineteen waited eleven to twenty years. Five settlements patiently renewed their petitions for periods ranging from two to three decades, but they were luckier than the fourteen groups who were refused outright. A number of those whose petitions were rejected reapplied after combining with other groups, and were successful in that capacity; some were granted winter privileges which satisfied them at least temporarily. It is quite clear, however, that by the middle of the eighteenth century the Assembly wanted to bring ministerial, school, and other parish services within easy walking distance of every Connecticut citizen.

In any concrete sense community must have a spacial dimension, and proximity is the essential cement. Though "community" has come to be viewed more and more as a psychological attribute, rather than a defined place with administrative and social connections, in preindustrial societies it has an essential face-to-face core. Face-to-face societies require geographic proximity. In New England towns there was one point at which administrative functions and social interactions came together, and that also happened to be the ceremonial center—the meetinghouse. As long as most people could gather at the meetinghouse at least weekly without undue hardship, church and the much less frequent town meetings could function as the center for geographic and psychological community. When, however, too many families lived too distant from the meetinghouse, they built one closer to home.

At first the new meetinghouse was to be the "ceremonial center" only, but very quickly it also became the center of administration for the activities of greatest concern to eighteenth-century New England families. Thus the parish meetinghouse rather than the town meetinghouse—soon to be called merely the "town house"—became the center of community for all families for which it held the closest religious services. The parish, then, became not only the prime unit of social administration, but also the focus for feelings of community.

As the differentiation between town and parish became more fully articulated, men in the outlying parishes began to transfer to their ecclesiastical society various authorities assumed from the town and from the church.

Taxes to pay for the construction of the meetinghouse and for the support of the minister were levied by the society and this control over the purse strings gave that body, rather than the much more limited church membership, the ability to determine the selection and dismissal of ministers. The location of the meetinghouse was the secular matter of greatest concern to parishioners, and this too, was decided by the society membership. In many cases, especially during early stages of organization, society rates exceeded town rates. When building meetinghouses, settling ministers, or hiring new ones, society rates could run as much as five times those of the mother town. Society committees also held and managed lands and funds designated for religious purposes. In this capacity society officers signed deeds, negotiated sales, kept accounts and entered suits at law. In 1712 and 1717 legislation was passed shifting responsibility for schools from the towns to the parishes, and in 1727 towns were authorized to delegate their obligation to maintain pounds to "any particular parish, hamlet, vicinity or part of any town."[20] It became customary to divide militia companies to conform to parish bounds. Outlying parishes petitioned the General Assembly to compel mother towns to lay out highways providing access between town center and society center. Parishes were even known to administer shepherds and gristmills.

Many societies were complete villages, sometimes exercising almost all the authorities of towns; the exceptions being that the three men annually chosen to order their meetings and affairs were called "the committee" instead of "selectmen"; societies were not allowed deputies to the General Assembly, and they still paid town and country rates to the collector of the town wherein they resided. But they elected an executive committee, moderators, clerks, collectors, and constables; established schools and taxed for their support; were authorized to distrain property of delinquents; and could sue and be sued. They often nominated town officers, and even deputies to the General Assembly, who were then rubber-stamped at town and freemen's meetings. Hamlets, indeed, took on such responsibilities even before they were set off as societies. Thus Canada parish (Hampton) in Windham already had its own burying ground, fenceviewers, and pound which the society took on when established in 1716. When it also organized its own militia company, the voters there "needed only to repair to Windham Green for town-meetings."[21]

Societies preempted so many aspects of town administration in the mid-eighteenth century that in some cases as in Stamford, "there was little for the local government to do." In that town there were ten or eleven town meetings annually during the years of active land division. When the land was all divided out, and especially when society meeting was separated from town meeting, the average fell to two per year for the whole period 1703 to 1773. The Stamford pattern was general throughout the colony during the pre-revolutionary eighteenth century.[22]

The parish meetinghouse with its associated schools and a neighborhood tavern served as sufficient geographic focus for any sense of community the secularized puritan still held on the eve of the Revolution. The upshot of this transfer of secular function from town to parish was that colonial Connecticut yeomen came to focus their communal sentiment upon the more local institution. Colonial Connecticut was not divided up into towns so much as into parishes. Parishes became the unit of prime concern to pre-revolutionary eighteenth-century Connecticut citizens. The town as a focus for communitarian sentiment and activity, and for most administrative matters, had been displaced. But it would rise again.

The Revival of the Town

It was the American Revolution that revivified the long dormant town spirit in Connecticut. A revival of political concern hit Connecticut's yeomen with the imperial crisis of the 1760s and 1770s. The one public function still denied to parishes was representation in the General Assembly. Discussion, articulation, and implementation of resistance to Parliamentary policy were colony-level matters, and to play a part in that, freemen had to have close and easy access to the General Assembly through locally elected deputies. Thus many parishes began to ask for full town status. And many got it. In the eleven years, 1779 to 1789, twenty-eight new towns were incorporated.

In that great period of town division two counties, five cities, and twenty-eight new towns were incorporated. Yet it had taken sixty years previous to 1779 to incorporate twenty-eight towns, and would take forty years after 1789 to incorporate a similar number. Between 1710 and 1784, 153 parishes had been set off.[23] Of the twenty-eight towns incorporated in the 1780s, two were areas that had no civil government

(Barkhamsted and Colebrook); two were river divisions (Brookfield and East Hartford). The remaining were of two very similar classes. Eight were split off when their commercial centers were incorporated as Connecticut's first cities. New Haven's rural outposts were reconstituted as Woodbridge, Hamden, North Haven, and East Haven; and Norwich's farmlands as Bozrah, Franklin and Lisbon; New London shed Montville. Sixteen township petitions were granted specifically and exclusively on pleas of non-accessibility of civil government and deprivation of voting rights. But, of course, these complaints were voiced by most of the towns resulting from city incorporations and river problems, also.

This sudden burst of town divisions merits explanation. A good measure of that explanation lies in the ideological impulses generated by the rhetoric of revolution and the rights of man that so permeated the reading of Connecticut's unusually literate yeomen in the years between the Stamp Act crisis of 1765 and the close of the war in the early 1780s.

Logistical problems were always stressed in these petitions for town incorporation. Most of them in the years before the Revolution, faced almost always with hostility from the mother town, were unsuccessful. What opened the floodgates that caused a sea change in Assembly sentiment was an ideological transformation—one that changed subjects into citizens. Petitions presented before the imperial crisis stressed the inability to fulfill obligations to town, colony, and His Majesty; with the new rhetoric of liberty and equality, petitioners emphasized the denial of rights brought about by their residence distant from the town meetings.

Redding, the last of the old particular plantations still unincorporated (though enjoying parish privileges since 1729 and attached to Fairfield for purposes of civil government) was the first to find the key that would unlock the Assembly's reluctance to incorporate new towns out of old ones. In 1754 the inhabitants had petitioned for town status because they were "obliged to travil to the Town & Freemans meetings and to carry all Such thing (sic) to Record, as are to be Recorded, & to pay the Town & Country Reats, & to Transport such things as are taken by Executions to be Sold at the Signpost &c." Further, they desired the right to tax the people for the purpose of building roads, "a very Great & Necessary Previledge, Injoyed in Common by the Rest of his Majesties Subjects." This petition was turned down by the General Assembly, but in 1767, just after the Stamp Act excitement another and different approach proved successful. The plea that because of great distances to the Fairfield town house "We (tho there are many Freemen among us,) never can enjoye the Priviledges common to the Rest of our fellow subjects of haveing our Voices in the Choice of our publick Government officers or Town officers we are also for the same Reason under a Necessity of being taxed in all Town Rate that are from Year to Year laid without ever haveing a Voice in the Matter and are also oblidged to submit to all Town Acts and Votes without ever being active in them, whether beneficial or prejudicial to us...."[24]

Perhaps the most striking instance of this altered approach is that of Hampton. In a 1768 petition her citizens claimed they lived too far from Windham—their town—"for Negociating of

Town affairs & Business & other Occasionall & Juridential affairs which by Law is Required & Directed to be Transact'd in Each Town In this Colony..." That petition unsuccessful, they tried again in 1785. This time they held that distance brings "a total deprivation of those just Rights Liberties and Privlidges which God and nature hath given to us, especially of choosing our own Rulers & Representatives."[25] A town charter was granted.

Benjamin Trumbull universalized: "There are certain periods," he wrote in North Haven parish's petition for town incorporation, "when it is expedient for smaller Parts of great communities to separate and become distinct towns by themselves. It is what not only the happiness of individuals, the public emolument, (but also) the interests of liberty and religion as well as general convenience require....We have the same natural right with you to a distinct representation and other town privileges."[26]

Thus, incorporation of new towns must have been a factor working towards "steady habits" rather than against them. Simeon Baldwin pointed out in 1786 that steady habits result from real self-government, a prerequisite of which is proximity to town meeting places. This perhaps explains the willingness to divide towns, contrary to the usual tendency, in a time, 1786, when as one deputy said, "All men are on Tiptoe, the waters are troubled and the people are just ready to jump in and be healed." Noah Webster recognized the close relationship of the people to the legislature when he remarked at the time of Shays' Rebellion that there was no disturbance in Connecticut "because the Legislature wear the complexion of the people."[27]

Geographically, the effect of these town divisions was to bring civil government within no more than six miles of virtually every voter by the beginning of the Federal Era. Thus it was, then, that the rhetoric of the American Revolution provided the justification, if not, indeed, the very impulse, for the wider distribution of town government which brought government and the center of community close to every Connecticut citizen.

Additionally, since it was those towns that were largest in population as well as area that were divided, a relative uniformity in numbers was maintained even as the overall population increased, so that representation in the General Assembly remained relatively proportionate. The number of towns with populations of 1,000 to 4,000 increased from 73 percent to 85 percent of the whole between 1774 and 1790, and the average and median populations actually diminished. In 1774 there were seventy-five towns with a median population of 2,229; in 1800 there were 107 towns with a median population of 2,177. In the same period, the average area of a town had decreased from 65.7 square miles to 46.7 square miles. Population density had gone from 39.6 people per square mile to 50.2. By 1840 when the move to the cities that depopulated the country towns began to be apparent, there were 139 towns with a median population of 2,018 each spread over thirty-six square miles, giving a density of sixty-two people. That is the optimum figure for a mixed agriculture/artisanal economy. But from there on the country town began a steep decline that saw populations cut to halves, thirds, and even less than their maxima in the pre-industrial era.

As the rhetoric of the Revolution provided the justification for dividing towns in the late eighteenth century, industrial densities brought on the divisions of the nineteenth century— of which there were twenty-nine after 1840. But that was in the unknowable future when the reporters to the Academy of Arts and Sciences surveyed their towns.

From a Hollow Maturity to an Empty Old Age

Thus it came about that by 1800 there were 107 towns in Connecticut. Their internal structures—government, churches, schools, highway supervision, pounds, and all the other accoutrements of preindustrial community life—were well established, the tracks of tradition well worn, soon to become rutted routines. Indeed, except perhaps for the naturally exuberant young, by the mid-nineteenth century life in these little villages had become a crashing bore. They were largely self-contained little fortresses, moated against invading innovation and self-satisfied in their tightly circumscribed provincialism.[28]

The preindustrial era, the days before the railroad shattered their quiet isolation, was the heyday of the Connecticut towns. The schools were, after 1795, run by separate school societies which in turn delegated authority to tiny school districts. The churches, strictly defined, were still run by the church membership; the militia companies had decayed into social clubs of young men principally concerned with the twice a year training day bash, a drunken orgy of horse races and turkey shoots; the eight counties administered the courts, licensed taverns and supervised some highways.

But the towns still elected three to seven selectmen, one or two deputies to the General Assembly, and a score or more local officials, some with nominal and some with real duties. Justices of the peace administered justice. Ministers mediated neighborhood squabbles. Town constables kept relative order. But nobody else did much of anything but work all day long six days a week and socialize between services on Sundays. The towns drifted along on their sleepy way, untouched by the affairs of governments or great corporations thirty or three hundred miles away. They administered themselves lightly and badly, but apparently happily. Their isolation was bliss.

"Few of us can adequately conceive of the seclusion of the great majority of New England villages two generations ago," wrote President Noah Porter of Yale in 1882. "Even those which were on the great roads and rivers and harbors were shut up to themselves and their own resources. They were singularly self-dependent and self-sufficing. They were in an unusual degree self-contained...." Porter claimed that such a community, which has few books, letters, or newspapers and rarely even visitors, "will make the most of that which is within itself."[29] Romantic retrospection by elderly fugitives who hadn't visited their childhood neighborhoods in decades colored these drab villages with the hues of their happy yesteryears.

Harriet Beecher Stowe, half a century after she left Litchfield as a thirteen-year-old, described the villages of her childhood as, "each a separate little democracy shut off by rough roads and forests from the rest of the world, organized round the church and the school as a common center." New England in those days before the railroad, she recalled, "was a sort of half Hebrew theocracy, half ultra-democratic republic of little villages...." Gideon Hollister, author of a mid nineteenth-century history of Connecticut, wrote as a novelist years later that each village was content to drift "remote from the great struggles of life as if it had been a world by itself." Connecticut towns of the nineteenth century, wrote Donald G. Mitchell, a trained observer of rural life, "were as quiet as a sheepfold...."[30]

The romantic novelists had their supporters among journalists, too. Writing in 1889, a most knowledgeable reporter highlighted the excitement rather than the tedium of these old agricultural villages. "In the old days the town was a far more symmetrical community than it is now. The interests and the emotions of rural society focused more perfectly within the town limits. At an epoch before railroads, telegraphs, telephones and daily newspapers, and when a journey to the nearest city by the clumsy stagecoach was the red-letter event of a human life, each town, with its villages, had to create its own social orbit. Hence the township life was more localized, more centripetal, more intense. It expressed itself both in personal feelings and in social or civic forms from which Yankee communities are now fast drifting away: in a keener neighborly spirit; in more eager interest in the contentious but educational town meetings; in more frequent occasions of intercourse, such as the village lyceums, the sewing societies, singing schools and ordinary social gatherings. The theocratic church alone, with its pastor invested with well-nigh pontifical dignity, was an immense factor in centering and vitalizing the town idea which permeated the whole life of the rural citizen." And, indeed, the scientific perspective of Benjamin Silliman informed his description of Kent as "seeming to be dropped in among the mountains, and almost secluded from the rest of the world." [31]

These accounts are not convincing. Even as one reads the novels of Stowe, Hollister, and others, it is difficult to share their excitement in the cornhusking and quilting bees, the village "illuminations," and the daily arrival of the passing stage. Well before the nineteenth century, westward migration brought demographic stasis to many Connecticut towns. Connecticuters were leaving the state in droves. In 1800 the Academy's reporter from Lebanon claimed that if, over the previous thirty years, all those who had pioneered to Vermont, New York, and points west with their progeny had stayed, the town's population would be three times its 3,652 residents. Westward migration continued apace until the rise of the mill village and manufacturing city after 1830.

And the numbers tell us that the farmers' children were leaving the fields as fast as they could to cluster in the cities where there were always lots of good company, better educational and cultural opportunities, vastly more diverse occupational choice, and more money for easier work. Their flight

puts the lie to the rosy scenarios sketched by the astigmatic romantics of the day.

Canterbury, for instance, had a population of 1881 in 1790 and ninety fewer fifty years later. The population of Cheshire was 2,288 in 1800, the same in 1810, and then in a demographic shift of tectonic dimensions lost nine people in the next ten years. East Haddam lost 129 residents in the half century after 1790. Indeed, most towns lost population throughout the nineteenth century and did not reachieve their peaks until the suburban movement after World War II. By 1920, 30 percent of the state's people lived in three of its 168 municipalities. The real transforming migration was not that which made western pioneers out of farmers' children, but rather that which drew the coming generation to the burgeoning cities. Bridgeport, a mere borough of Stratford in 1801, with a population in 1830 of 2,800, boasted 143,555 residents in 1920. One of its suburbs, Trumbull, had 1,291 residents in 1800 and 1,642 in 1910; and another, Monroe, fell from 1,522 in 1830 to 1,002 in 1910. It happened all over Connecticut.[32] By the 1890s more people were dying in the decaying country towns than were being born there.[33] The country towns would not be reborn again, until incarnated after World War II as the suburbs we know today.

The Academy's reporters, then, were describing towns that had recovered from the eclipse caused by the rise of the parish, but had reached a kind of stasis. In the years between the end of the Revolution in 1783 and the great migration into the cities beginning about 1830, the Connecticut town reached beyond maturity. The senile sterility of the late nineteenth century saw another collapse of the country town, an atrophying like that again of the age of the parish, a time when the steam engine rather than the meetinghouse was the dynamic center of Connecticut society.

The era of maturity, then, was not one of growth, demographic, economic, or cultural. It was an era of stability, one that called forth from the aging denizens of the old-time village the poignant pangs of childhood life: recess at the one-room schoolhouse, the Saturday church supper, the bundled hayride in the dry snows, the strawberry festival and the shoreside clambake.

In 1800 or thereabouts, when the Academy's reporters were making their surveys, the towns still seemed vital: They weren't, as it turned out, it just seemed that way. In fact, they were motionless. As the sharp-eyed Harriet Beecher Stowe noted about the early nineteenth-century meetinghouses, the Connecticut towns of that era had become "a sort of museum of antiquities—a general muster-ground for past and present."[34]

The ample supply of water power, the well-developed system of toll roads and harbors, the practicality of small-capital industrial ventures, and the near universal literacy of an energetic and materialist workforce, and agricultural competition from the west, would soon power the collapse of these little republics. It is good that the Academy's reporters gave us these descriptions at the moment they did, for the Connecticut town would never be the same again.

The Remarkable Complexity of the Simple New England Town

Bruce Daniels

Poets, Professors, and Towns

The word "*simplicity*" settles comfortably around the public memory of the New England town. The town center evokes images of a village green, meetinghouse, one-room school, and general store. The outlying countryside is dotted with clapboard farmhouses, weathered barns, stone walls, and meandering dirt roads. Along the coast a handful of masted schooners and a flotilla of rowboats are tied up at wharves stretching out from rickety wood stairs. The citizens of a town know and like each other. They dress alike, marry close to home, and pitch in to help when trouble strikes. We see these citizens working in the fields and sitting down to large family dinners. Collectively they come together to worship at church, deliberate at town meetings, drill with the militia, and quilt trousseaus. The earliest New Englanders—those plain-speaking Puritans—may have been a mite sour, but by and large they were a God-fearing, sturdy lot of decent pilgrims. By the Revolution, they had loosened up a bit. Flinty yankees emerged from the dour Puritans but the two personalities shared an essence.[1]

This then is the poetic history that the nineteenth century crafted for the eighteenth and seventeenth. Even the shadow of Puritan sanctimony could not cast much shade on the simple, pristine town which gave New England its regional identity and which also served as a model of democracy and decency to the new American nation. Nathaniel Hawthorne dominated the nineteenth century's views of Puritanism. His vision was dark and complex. Hawthorne's genius, his friend Herman Melville wrote, lay in his capacity to see meanings in man's black recesses. But Hawthorne did not dominate the nineteenth century's views of the Puritan village—that literary distinction fell to Henry Wadsworth Longfellow, Hawthorne's classmate in the Bowdoin College class of 1823. Longfellow was the poet of the New England town. Hawthorne probed the depths of Puritanism to find the New England soul; Longfellow celebrated the simplicity and purity of the New England town "*under a spreading chestnut tree.*" Hawthorne's saintly Hester Prynne, introspective Reverend Arthur Dimmesdale, and vengeful Dr. Roger Chillingworth all provide tortured testimony to the complexity and ambiguity of the Puritan ethos. But Longfellow's village smith—"*a mighty man is he*"—gave equally strong historical witness to the crystalline virtues of work, family, piety, and duty embedded in the New England town. Longfellow's smith—the literary ideal of the New England freeman— "*earns whate'er he can,*

and looks the whole world in the face, for he owes not any man.*"[2]

As the writing of history moved from poets to professors in the late nineteenth century, the new academic scholars embraced a paradigm of New England that at first blush seems to be logically untenable: their historical picture of the region fused the contradictory visions of both Hawthorne and Longfellow. Let me be puckish and use the writings of three men bearing New England's most famous surname, Brooks Adams, James Truslow Adams, and Herbert Baxter Adams (no close family relationship among them) to illustrate this seemingly impossible feat. In *The Emancipation of Massachusetts* (1887), Brooks described a New England that was forced to escape the darkness of Puritan tyranny in order to prepare itself for the democratic light of the American Revolution. Other muckraking historians such as Vernon Parrington and Charles Beard echoed this view in several influential overviews of early America. It was James Truslow Adams, however, in *The Founding of New England* (1921), who brought this attack on Puritanism to a shrill apotheosis. Under his pen, New England's founders were cruel, abusive, greedy, and antithetical to the most basic requirement of democracy—respect for the opinion of others. The Adamses spoke for a generation of scholars and the students they taught who learned this new "*progressive*" interpretation of America's origins. For over fifty years, *The Scarlet Letter's* image of the repressive Puritan—shorn of Hawthorne's subtlety—coursed through the writing of New England's most respected historians.[3]

But at the same time, Longfellow's image of the democratic town remained vibrant. Herbert Baxter Adams, the first distinguished scholar of local institutions, opened his famous book, *The Germanic Origins of New England Towns* (1881) with the following quotation from Lewis Morgan's inaugural presidential address to the American Association for the Advancement of Science:

> In early New England we reach the birthplace of American institutions. Here was developed the township with its local self-government, the basis and central element of our political system. Upon the township was formed the county, composed of several towns similarly organized; the state composed of several counties; and finally the United States composed of several

states; each organization a body politic, with definite governing powers in subordinate series. But the greatest of all, in intrinsic importance, was the township, because it was and is the unit of organization and embodies the great principles of local self-government. It is at once the greatest and the most important of American institutions, because it determines the character of the state and national government.[4]

The question of how New Englanders could simultaneously be dictatorial Puritans and democratic townsmen did not unduly trouble historians or their public. Herbert Baxter Adams ascribed town government to ancient Germanic traditions that obviated the more transitory Puritan influence. Others agreed. A colleague of Adams's at Johns Hopkins University, Woodrow Wilson, in volume one of his *History of the American People* (1901), extolled the simplicity and democracy of the New England town, and then noted tartly, "*the colony as a whole was by no means so democratic.*"[5]

This coupling of tyrannical Puritans with democratic towns came under attack in the 1930s as scholars such as Samuel Eliot Morison and Perry Miller rescued Puritanism from its harshest critics. In his *Builders of the Bay Colony* (1930), Morison softened Puritanism considerably by weaving individual men and women into the everyday fabric of the New England village. Miller subjected the Puritan mind to a profound and sympathetic analysis that recast all of American intellectual history and raised it leagues above the diatribes of Brooks and James Truslow Adams. After World War II, the Morison-Miller view of Puritanism made it relatively easy to believe that the religious beliefs of New England's founders could coexist comfortably with a modicum of local self-government.[6]

Ironically, just as this view of a more humane, less bigoted Puritanism began to gain sway, the simplicity and democracy of the New England town came under attack by a new generation of social-scientific historians in the 1960s and 1970s. Attacks on the Longfellow image of the town now joined the Morison-Miller attacks on the Hawthorne image of Puritanism. New Left historians, who identified great defects in the democracy of Cold-War America, also raised doubts about the reality of democracy in the colonial New England town. The town might appear on the surface to be a simple vehicle for expressing the will of the people but these scholars argued, if one probed beneath the charm of the placid village green, a hidden web of wealth, social status, family networks, and elitist intellectual assumptions inevitably placed local power in the hands of a ruling clique. The fathers of the town were well-to-do, educated gentlemen who controlled the town meeting and passed leadership on to their sons. Thus, social complexities obviated institutional simplicity.[7]

A quarter century later, historians have grown weary of debates over the meaning of democracy in the New England town and have largely abandoned them. Studies of gender roles, consumerism, health, deviance, literacy, and communications have become more popular than analyses of officeholding, wealth distribution, and voting patterns. The fruits of the hundreds of articles and books that probed the social and political underpinnings of the New England town, however, have led to at least one inescapable conclusion: the colonial New England town permitted a substantial diversity of experience. From physical size to political practice to social customs, New England towns differed—occasionally dramatically—among themselves. The range might not have been as great as that which existed in the Middle Colonies, which were known for their diversity, but nevertheless, local life in New England was more heterogeneous than Brooks, James Truslow, and Herbert Baxter Adams ever imagined. The *concept* of the town meeting was certainly simple and every town held them, but that may be where the simplicity and uniformity of New England's local regional identity ended.

Members of the Connecticut Academy of Arts and Sciences were obviously aware of some of this diversity when they sent their Solicitation letter to the towns in 1800 for local historical and statistical information. The articles—or topics—they posed seemed to be based substantially on the same assumptions held by modern historians: physical, material circumstances underlay many of the political and social differences. Like all good social scientists, of course, the Academy's members must have had some thoughts about what they were likely to learn, but they did not prejudge the results. They were trying to collect data in an honest attempt to find out what they did not know—to give some precision to preconceived general patterns or to find out that their preconceptions may have been wrong. The answers to their survey took so long to be assembled and came in so many different forms that little use of them has been made until this present project. And squeezing any significance out of them still will be difficult. They testify to diversity and complexity in Connecticut, which was surely New England's most homogeneous colony—but they do not lend themselves easily to analysis. They need to be processed with rigor and they need to be placed in the context of what we already know about New England and Connecticut towns at the end of the eighteenth century.

New England Towns in 1790

The Federal Census of 1790 considerably sharpened our statistical knowledge of New England. Formal and informal censuses had been taken periodically in all of the New England colonies and they are invaluable for assessing the growth of English civilization in the region and the impact of European peoples on native culture and the environment. All of these colonial censuses, however, suffered serious deficiencies. One of the most oft used, the Connecticut Census of 1730, underestimated the colony's population by 40 percent. All parishes that were forgiven taxes because of economic hardship were left out; faulty multipliers were used to convert militia rolls to population data; and, inexplicably, a few entire towns were not enumerated. Forward and backward projections from other censuses confirm just how wrong the 1730 census was. Most colonial Massachusetts' censuses relied on estimates derived from applying a multiplier to the number of rateable polls which were turned in for each town—a crude method at best. During the Revolution, each of the new states did conduct better censuses but the exigencies of civil war distorted reality. Boston, for example, became a relatively small town after being shut as a port and occupied by the British in 1775. The Federal Census of 1790, thus, took the first relatively accurate count of New England's data at the end of its period of political apprenticeship and on the eve of the Connecticut Academy's survey of towns. The first federal census had some mistakes also—most notably in Connecticut's Litchfield County—but, in general, it provided a good measure of the new nation at peace. It is the American Domesday Book.[8]

Vermont joined the American confederation in 1791 but was enumerated as if it were a state in 1790; and, although Maine was not officially set off from Massachusetts until 1820, it was regarded as a distinct political entity by 1790 and counted apart from Massachusetts. Thus, all six of the New England states appear as separate units within the regional identity that has persisted to the present.

The 1790 census provides us with our first snapshot of New England as the region that we know today. The census lists 878 towns in New England. Massachusetts with 243 had the most, Rhode Island with 30 the fewest. At first blush, Connecticut's total of 101 towns seems too few when compared to New Hampshire's 190, Vermont's 186, and Maine's 128. New Hampshire, Vermont, and Maine, however, all had much of their land on the northern frontier of New England that was still in the process of being surveyed and populated by white settlers. Hence, many of the towns in the White and Green Mountains or in the Maine interior

were in reality embryonic political creations with populations of less than one hundred residents.[9]

Differing states of frontier development, however, do not explain all the regional variations. Topography accounted for as much. Connecticut and Rhode Island had a less rugged physical surface than northern New England or parts of western Massachusetts. The granite and marshes of northern New England meant that many of its towns would always be more lightly populated than those of southern New England. Few parts of Connecticut or Rhode Island could not sustain some type of farming activity or were completely unfit for building homes. Thus, Connecticut and Rhode Island towns averaged 2,356 and 2,294 persons respectively, making them approximately 50 percent larger than Massachusetts' towns, which averaged 1,559 persons. Maine, New Hampshire, and Vermont towns, with average populations of 754, 746, and 459 respectively, were small by comparison.

In addition to frontier conditions and topography, political decisions also affected both the population and physical size of New England's towns. Most of the towns laid out in the first three quarters of the seventeenth century consisted of huge tracts of land, much of which remained uncultivated and unsettled for at least two generations. In Connecticut, the largest, Farmington, had 224 square miles; the next, Simsbury, had 184. Providence, Rhode Island, contained all the land of present-day Providence County, at least one-third of the entire colony. Dedham and Andover, Massachusetts, each had about 200 square miles at their founding. All of these early large towns became sub-divided into several towns by 1790. Providence, for example, spawned eight other towns; Farmington gave rise to three by 1790 but four more would follow in the nineteenth century. The process usually followed a pattern determined by geography. Often these large towns

TABLE I

New England Population Data by Town/State in 1790

State	Population	Towns	Persons Per Town	Square Miles	Persons Per Square Mile
Connecticut	238,127	101	2,356	5,009	47.5
Massachusetts*	378,787	243	1,559	8,257	45.9
New Hampshire	141,885	190	746	9,304	15.2
Rhode Island	68,825	30	2,294	1,214	56.7
Maine**	96,540	128	754	—	—
Vermont	85,539	186	459	9,614	8.9

* Does not include any data from Maine.

**Data on Maine's physical size would be irrelevant in 1790; most of the state's borders were disputed and its territory unsettled by Americans.

were settled on both sides of a river. As land transportation developed, the river became perceived more as a barrier to everyday travel and less as the highway it had been when water travel had been the dominant mode. Eventually residents of the village on each side of the river would aspire to town status. Similarly, if a town stretched from the coastline far into the interior, farmers and traders might develop differing political interests that would provoke the backcountry residents to seek a town government to reflect their own needs. Sometimes one part of a town was just too distant from the town center to allow its residents to take part comfortably in the town's political or economic business.[10]

In all of the New England colonies, when a group of settlers aspired to town status, they had to present a petition to the colony government requesting an act of incorporation. Usually, the original town resisted the efforts of a group of its inhabitants to hive off. Political units of any sort seldom like to give up territory and New England towns were no exception: the hiving-off process engendered division and bitterness. For most of the colonial period, Connecticut resisted the division of towns more so than Massachusetts did. By 1760, only seven towns in Connecticut had been carved out of old ones, compared to sixty-one of them in Massachusetts. During the Revolutionary era, dissenting parts of Connecticut towns became emboldened by the fiery political rhetoric of the time and were more assertive and successful in their petitions to the General Assembly. In the 1780s, Connecticut incorporated twenty-four new towns from within its old ones. Massachusetts also picked up the pace of town creation, however, and by 1790 a total of 102 new towns had been carved out of existing ones. Thus, Massachusetts's towns were physically smaller than Connecticut's primarily because of Massachusetts's greater willingness to indulge the aspirations of local dissenters. Connecticut successfully maintained more of the founding Puritan commitment to unity than did the rest of New England and thus it maintained larger and more populous towns.[11]

Salt water affected town development as much or more so than political culture or land quality. Instead of dividing New England's towns by colony or topography, one could just as easily divide the region into ports and landlocked towns. The salt-water and major river ports of Connecticut, Massachusetts, New Hampshire, and Rhode Island shared a set of characteristics that transcended colony governments and institutional arrangements. Port towns tended to have a greater ethnic diversity and higher population density, more criminality and poverty, and a more skewed distribution of wealth than landlocked towns. Ports also tended to be physically smaller than inland towns. In short, port towns were more urban than their inland counterparts and manifested greater class distinctions. Rhode Island, which today calls itself "the ocean state," was also the ocean colony. Twenty of Rhode Island's thirty towns had salt-water harbors. Approximately one of four Connecticut towns were ports and one of six Massachusetts towns were. Well over half of Maine's population lived in ports but three-fourths of its towns were landlocked. New Hampshire had merely eighteen miles of coastline but the meandering estuaries of Piscataqua Harbor provided at least one hundred miles of salt-water shoreline. Given the shallow draft requirements of eighteenth-century ships perhaps twenty of New Hampshire's towns still functioned as ports in 1790. Vermont, of course, was not a maritime state.[12]

The difference between ports and inland towns was growing more, not less, pronounced at the end of the eighteenth century. As New England developed its backcountry, the region's agriculture became more specialized, commercial, and dependent on distant markets. Ports became gateway communities and retail centers of merchants, laborers, and artisans who moved goods and provided services. The lives of both inland farmers and the coastal commercial class became increasingly sensitized to fluctuations in the Atlantic trading cycles and to political events; but port residents more directly felt the sting of economic and imperial crises. Farmers could use local markets more readily to buffer the impact of distant forces. They tightened their belts during downswings and increased production during good times. Boom cycles in ports attracted entrepreneurs and laborers; bust cycles plunged them into business failures and unemployment. The urban landscape of ports also looked increasingly different from that of the inland towns. Urban wealth became more ostentatiously displayed in mansions, stores, carriages, and clothes; so, too, urban poverty become more visible. The American Revolution added even more instability to life in port towns since they were more vulnerable to military attack and economic blockade. After the Revolution many roared back with the resumption of peacetime trade; others such as Newport, Rhode Island, or Portsmouth, New Hampshire, never recovered their colonial positions of preeminence.[13]

Thus, the New England town, which Herbert Baxter Adams extolled as the birthplace of American democratic institutions, took many forms in 1790. The thirty-six square mile township of historical fame was not too far from the New England average in 1790, but this number was only a statistical convenience. Some towns were as small as ten square miles; others still were over one hundred. Although small towns in which everyone did indeed know each other still existed in southern New England, most of Connecticut's, Massachusetts's, and Rhode Island's were populous enough to make many townspeople strangers to one another. New Hampshire, Maine, and Vermont tended to be home to the intimate small town by 1790 and, even in those states, the small towns tended to be the newest ones: hence their local societies did not embrace generations of stable relationships. New England in 1790 was more diverse and dynamic—a region of more variety and change—than Longfellow's poetic history would suggest.

New England's Gift to American Democracy

And yet, Herbert Baxter Adams could easily brush aside much of the above analysis as irrelevant to his fundamental argument. Demographic, geographical, physical, economic distinctions be damned; all colonial New England towns shared the same political institution—the town meeting—regardless of their social makeup. Town meetings governed every inch of New England soil and this, he felt, was New England's gift to the United States and to American democracy.

Puritans invented the town meeting—of this there should be no doubt. From time to time scholars have conducted amazingly fanciful searches for the town meeting's origins. Herbert Baxter Adams, for example, wandered in the Black Forest of Germany and found the town meeting in the Saxon *Tun* of Teutonic tribes. George Bancroft looked to even more ancient impulses coming out of Athenian democracy. Historians of local government in England such as Beatrice and Sydney Webb appropriately saw links between the English parish and New England town government.[14] In truth, of course, some concept of a community meeting plays an important role in local government in much of the world from ancient India to North American native tribes. Specifically, however, the town meeting that emerged in New England derived directly from Puritanism. It was the secular, political equivalent of the Congregational church meeting. Puritan reformers believed that a meeting of all the regenerate men in a parish constituted the ultimate authority for that religious society. Fearful both of state interference in religion and of clerical meddling in government, the Puritan settlers of New England consciously separated the institutions of church and state even though both existed to promote a Godly way of life. The two spheres should cooperate closely, be mutually supportive, and turn to each other for advice but they should not become entangled. The town meeting was the central agency of one of the two spheres—a Congregational political meeting to govern parallel to the Congregational church meeting.

New Englanders remained attached to the town meeting as a true and pure form of local government long after religious dissent ended Puritan hegemony and made the Congregational church meeting just one of several forms of local religious government. No cities were incorporated in colonial New England and when urban reformers tried to bring municipal government to the region, town meeting zealots vehemently resisted it. Municipal incorporation would have substituted representative governments—aldermen meeting as a town council in closed sessions—for the direct democracy of the town meeting open to all freemen. Yet, the sheer number of people in many towns militated against continuing town-meeting government. So, too, did the clashing economic interests of merchants and farmers who found it increasingly difficult to maintain a sense of shared community. Nevertheless, Boston remained under town government until 1822 when it belatedly received a municipal charter. Rhode Island incorporated its largest town, Newport, in 1784 but rescinded the order in 1787 when opponents argued before the General Assembly that city government was "*novel, arbitrary, and altogether unfit for free republicans...a derogation of those rights and immunities which freemen are indisputably entitled to.*" Not until 1853 could city proponents overcome town-meeting die-hards and get the act reissued. Providence became Rhode Island's first city in 1837 and

Portsmouth became New Hampshire's first one in 1849. Only Connecticut successfully incorporated cities in the late eighteenth century. In 1784, Hartford, Middletown, New Haven, New London, and Norwich received acts of municipal incorporation for portions of their central districts. Merchants in the business districts of these five towns had fought for the acts because they had been stymied by outlying, parsimonious farmers in their efforts to promote trade and commercial development. But Connecticut's exception is the proverbial one that proves the rule of New England's fierce attachment to the town meeting. The General Assembly required the new city governments to hold an annual city meeting and any person who was a freeman—a registered voter—could attend and vote on all matters of policy. So the city meeting acted much like a town meeting for the commercial district. Even more importantly, each of the five cities still remained part of the parent town. "*Always provided, that anything in this act notwithstanding,*" Hartford's charter read, "*the inhabitants living within the limits of said city...remain a part of said town of Hartford.*" In reality, incorporation as cities gave residents in the central district of the town a special jurisdiction to raise taxes for commercial development and to hold courts to regulate business transactions. These city residents still remained subject to and a part of town meeting government.[15]

The Complexity of Town Government: The Connecticut Example

If the origins and principles of town-meeting government were simple and straightforward, the actual operations proved more complex. One can imagine difficulties arising from what today would be the anomaly of having a city remain part of a town. From the beginning of New England in the 1620s and onwards, implementing the concept of a town meeting provoked discussion and dispute much as implementing the concept of a pure church did. Questions inevitably arose: Who should be allowed to vote? Who did vote? How often should town meetings be held? How much power should the meeting delegate to its officers? How many officers should be elected? Should officeholding be confined to an elite few?

Let us consider briefly the answers Connecticut's towns gave to these questions. This will leave us with a sense of the state of Connecticut town government at the time when the Connecticut Academy of Arts and Science conducted its survey. It will also leave us with some idea of the conditions of town government on the eve of the settlement of the West.

Who should be allowed to vote?

The answer to this question changed substantially over the colonial period. Under the Fundamental Orders of Connecticut of 1639 and then under the Connecticut Charter of 1662, authorities distinguished between "freemen" who could vote in colony and local elections and "inhabitants" who could vote only in town meetings. To be a freeman one had to have a sizeable estate and be admitted by the General Court. This necessitated a trip to Hartford, the capital. To be an inhabitant one had only to be a local resident or property owner and be of "honest conversation." Neither status required church membership although few dissenters were admitted to freemanship in the seventeenth century or thought to be of honest conversation by the local town meeting. In 1669, when relatively good data are available, the percentage of freemen in a town correlated significantly with the town's proximity to Hartford, the capital. In the river towns of Hartford, Wethersfield, and Windsor approximately 63 percent of adult white males were admitted freemen and 75 percent of heads of households were. Further down the river at Middletown, 50 percent of adult white males were admitted freemen and in distant Norwich only 25 percent were. Obviously, many prospective freemen did not think that the status was worth a time-consuming trip. Probably most white adult males in all these towns assumed the status of inhabitant and felt free to take part in town meetings.[16]

In 1678 the General Court rescinded its requirement that local voters personally travel to Hartford to be admitted as freemen, and in 1729 the General Assembly (as the General Court was known after 1698) transferred the formal power to admit freemen to the towns. A specified amount of property was still required for admission to freemanship but it was minimal and almost any farmer or tradesman could satisfy the criterion. After 1729 no clear distinction between freemen and inhabitants seemed to exist. Town selectmen met a few hours before town meetings to examine men who wished to be registered. If satisfied after a perfunctory questioning, the selectmen instructed the town clerk to enroll the individual as a freeman in the minutes of the town meeting. Hence, neither a lack of money nor institutional roadblocks prevented most adult white men from voting. Nor did religious dissent: Anglicans, Baptists, and Separatists experienced little trouble registering. Women and blacks could not be freemen; neither could an indigent person on poor relief or a chronic troublemaker.[17]

Who did vote?

The percentage of adult white males enrolled as freemen in various towns of the late eighteenth century ranged from a high of 80 percent to a low of 25 percent. Apathy played a greater role in voting than did law. Many men simply did not bother to become enrolled. Town meeting minutes show registration patterns were erratic. Young men often did not bother to enroll until a controversial issue jolted them out of lethargy. Then they enrolled in droves to be able to express their opinions. Two clear correlations can also be established for participating in elections. Neither is surprising. First, the closer a man lived to the meetinghouse, the more likely he was to register as a freeman; and second, the most populous towns had the lowest percentage of freemen. Smallness in a given electorate gave added value to each man's vote.[18]

How often were town meetings held?

For much of the colonial period, the frequency of meetings remained unregulated by colony statutes. But, during the second quarter of the eighteenth century, the three colonies of southern New England imposed minimum requirements on their towns. Massachusetts required all towns to meet twice a year; Rhode Island required four meetings annually. Connecticut required towns to meet once a year in an annual election meeting although most towns met more frequently. Towns met sometimes as often as twenty times a year or as infrequently as the one meeting mandated by law. But, amidst this range, patterns did exist. In general seventeenth-century towns met more often than eighteenth-century ones; new towns met more often than old ones; and small towns met more than large ones. Explanations for these patterns are not hard to find. The more a town was based on a shared sense of community, the more often it met; the more a town was simply a political unit of government, the less often it met. In the seventeenth century, the Puritan ethos brought towns to meeting often as much as ten or fifteen times a year. People attended church more often than they would later in the eighteenth century and they also were more attentive to their civic duties. New towns—even those founded in Litchfield County in the 1740s—also met often to hammer out the absorbing details of setting up a new community. And the residents of small towns seemed more anxious to maintain personal involvement in government than their more anonymous and mobile counterparts in urban towns.

In general the frequency of town meetings in all types of towns declined in the 1730s and 1740s. In the second half of the eighteenth century, Connecticut's well-established towns tended to meet only once or twice annually. The meeting elected officers, passed by-laws presented by the selectmen, and ratified a budget and tax rate drawn up in advance by town officers. Lack of attendance could present problems. One might think that the meeting was becoming irrelevant — a perfunctory gathering to satisfy colony law and ratify decisions made by elected officers. This it could be. But one extraordinary set of data suggests that Connecticuters did not believe that town meeting democracy was irrelevant or perfunctory. They took the town meeting for granted during times of tranquillity and consensus but in times of crisis or disagreement they demanded meetings to express their views. In almost every town that lapsed into a period of meeting only once or twice a year, some traumatic event politicized the citizenry and prompted a flurry of town meetings to deal with the problem. Not uncommonly towns would jump from an average of one or two meetings to ten or fifteen for a year and then subside to the previous low number. Thus, even during their periods of least activity, town meetings retained their potential as latent democratic institutions capable of being instantly transformed into a forum for dissent, debate, and rebuke.[19]

How many officers did the town meeting elect?

From a few officers in the seventeenth century, elected officials increased to substantial numbers—approximately averaging 50 in 1725, 65 in 1750, and 80 in the 1780s. The General Assembly required each town to elect men to specific officers but did not stipulate the numbers. Two principles shaped the size of the town bureaucracy. First, any person who received pay from the town services had to be chosen by the voters. Thus, many towns elected "a man to sweep the meetinghouse" or "to dig the graves" or even to be "the hog watcher." The more tasks a town needed done, the more people it chose to office even though many of these elected officials were clearly somewhat less than political leaders. Second, towns made efforts to spread officers throughout their various neighborhoods or sections. Physically large towns therefore usually elected more officers than more populous but physically smaller ones. Farmington, the only Connecticut town with an area greater than 200 square miles, elected the most officers, 206 in one year, most of whom performed perfunctory duties such as maintaining highways or fences in Farmington's many outlying parishes.[20]

How much power was delegated to town meeting officers?

In Connecticut, as in Massachusetts and New Hampshire, the town executives were called selectmen. Connecticut law specified that each town should elect three, five, or seven selectmen: the odd number prevented tie votes. By the Revolution, the twenty or so most populous towns elected seven and smaller ones elected three or five. Seventeenth-century selectmen had a myriad of duties ranging from being the major keepers of morality to making sure that parents taught their children "an honest lawful calling." Selectmen were patriarchs who took on the characteristics of village elders—magesterial, figures of informal as well as formal authority. Selectmen kept a watchful eye on their communities.

In the eighteenth century, as the intensity of Puritan piety waned and as towns grew in size and diversity, selectmen became more political leaders and less village elders. One should not overstate this: a stern look from a selectman might still rebuke an unruly boy in 1790, but, in general, eighteenth-century selectmen lost some of their informal authority as patriarchs and replaced it with a new authority as overseers of the burgeoning town-meeting bureaucracy. Many mid-range offices were created by towns in the eighteenth century: listers, who assessed people's estates for tax purposes; raters, who calculated the taxes needed to sustain budgets; and commercial officers to inspect weights and measures and maintain fair practices in markets and stores. These joined constables, a clerk, treasurer, tax collector, fence viewers, and highway surveyors who were all increasingly directed to report to the selectmen who became the town's local political supervisors.[21]

Several factors combined to enhance the power of local officeholders. First, towns themselves gained a greater degree of autonomy as the seventeenth-century Connecticut community of Puritan saints metamorphosed into an eighteenth-century state of economically aggressive, politically assertive citizens who worshipped at competing churches. A fundamentally religious society gave way to a political one. The prevailing ethos of the eighteenth century did not allow for the same degree of central control over the towns as the

Puritan moral-magistrates had exercised in the early and mid-seventeenth. Nor was central control within the administrative capacity of the General Assembly: with 101 towns and a population of nearly a quarter of a million people in 1790, the technology was inadequate for a unitary political state. Additionally, on the local level, as we have seen, in times of harmony and prosperity, the town meeting was pleased to allow its elected officers to shoulder the burden of everyday governance. Yankee farmers and merchants learned that political apathy gave them more time to compete in the marketplace.

Whom did the towns elect?

If the General Assembly and the local citizenry tended to abdicate decision-making to town officers, whom did the freemen choose to trust with power? Who ran town government? The answer is not surprising. The very same legislators, farmers, merchants, who were too busy making laws or making a living were the people who served as officers of the town meeting. The vast majority of respectable, adult white males served as an officer of the town meeting at some time in their life and most served in several capacities. A substantial degree of elitism characterized each town's election of deputies to the General Assembly but only a slight degree of elitism—beyond that of gender and race—characterized town-meeting officeholding. Certainly, prestigious families were over-represented on boards of selectmen, but, in general, the meeting rotated local offices among those able to perform the required duties. Public virtue and fair play required that many men accept the burden of serving their town for a time. Young men often served in lesser offices that were more functionary than discretionary and then moved on to higher-level jobs if they showed ability. Some towns deliberately rotated the office of selectman among a large cadre of officeholders; Norwich and Saybrook, for example, had turnover rates in the eighteenth century of over 90 percent. Other towns might keep one particularly effective and willing selectman in office for twenty years but surround him with many other men moving in and out of the office. Population growth, of course, did reduce statistically the likelihood of any man serving in a major office, but comparative numbers notwithstanding, Connecticut towns were awash with the possibility of participatory, political democracy.[22]

The New England Town and the New American Nation

Massachusetts, New Hampshire, and Rhode Island provided somewhat different answers to the above questions I have posed to Connecticut; but none of their responses deviated significantly from what became the accepted New England norms. Rhode Island, of course, would be expected to be the farthest afield. Most—but not all—of Rhode Island's towns developed outside of the Puritan fold; nevertheless, this dissenting colony of exiles and misfits— "Rogue's Island"— embraced a Congregational meeting form of town government. Rhode Island towns called their local executives councilors instead of selectmen; and Rhode Island towns exercised some powers over schools and vital statistics that were left to the church parish in Connecticut and Massachusetts, but by and large, the institutional differences between the dissenters on Narragansett Bay and the rest of New England were as much cosmetic as real. When imperial authorities placed five towns from the old Plymouth Colony under Rhode Island's jurisdiction in 1746, the five formerly Puritan communities made the transition with little fuss. Partly this was possible because, by the mid-eighteenth century, Puritan New England had been forced to accept religious dissenters in their midst. Most Puritan New England towns had Anglicans, Baptists, or even Quakers by the end of the colonial era. As often as not, these disrupters of Zion were not outside radicals but brothers and sisters, sons and daughters, cousins and friends, of members of the establishment. Thus socially and religiously the rest of New England began to resemble Rhode Island. And partly, Rhode Island towns adhered to the eighteenth-century New England norm because Rhode Island's original settlers and a majority of its subsequent migrants were devout Protestants with close personal and religious ties to their Puritan neighbors. The early antagonisms between the radicals who followed Roger Williams, Anne Hutchinson, Samuel Gorton, and William Coddington to Providence Plantation and Aquidneck Island should not obscure the very real community of interests shared by all the reform Protestants of New England.

The common political culture of Connecticut, Massachusetts, New Hampshire, and Rhode Island towns needs no identification to a nation and world that often confuses the borders and geography of these little states crammed into what appears to be a tiny region. To a Texan, Mexican, or Canadian, New England seems to be a homogeneous, tightly knit society. Most of the country and world seem to be quite willing to admit that New England has produced a disproportionate amount of American history. Hawthorne and Longfellow may have espoused dramatically different views of the early New England town—one dark and brooding, one light and airy—but the two literary giants agree that American history owes a special debt to Puritanism and to the New England town. And the poets as well as the professors have done their jobs well—perhaps too well—of convincing their fellow citizens of these special debts. Of course, by the beginning of the nineteenth century, the Puritan town did not exist. Religion no longer united New England; history, economics, and political bonds tied the secular towns of 1800 together. It is our job as historians to convince people who may be tired of hearing about the Puritan New England town that we need to know more about the towns of the early republic. New complexities emerged to be discovered as the simple New England town continued on its charmed role in American history.

MAPS

BIOGRAPHICAL SKETCHES

NOTES

SELECTED BIBLIOGRAPHY

INDEX

Index Map 1812

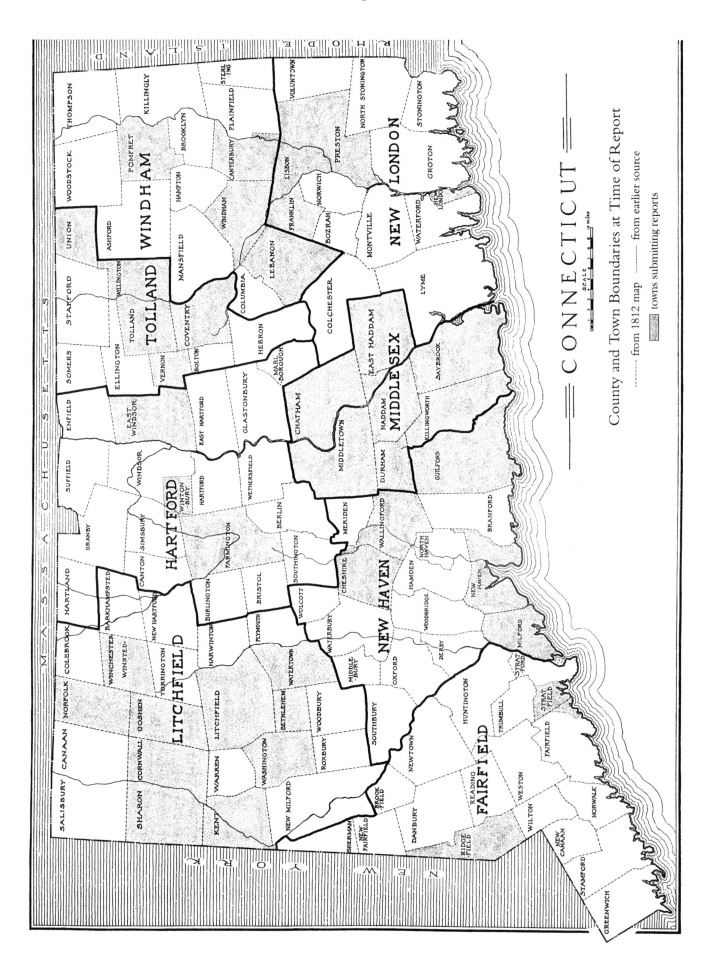

Index Map 2002

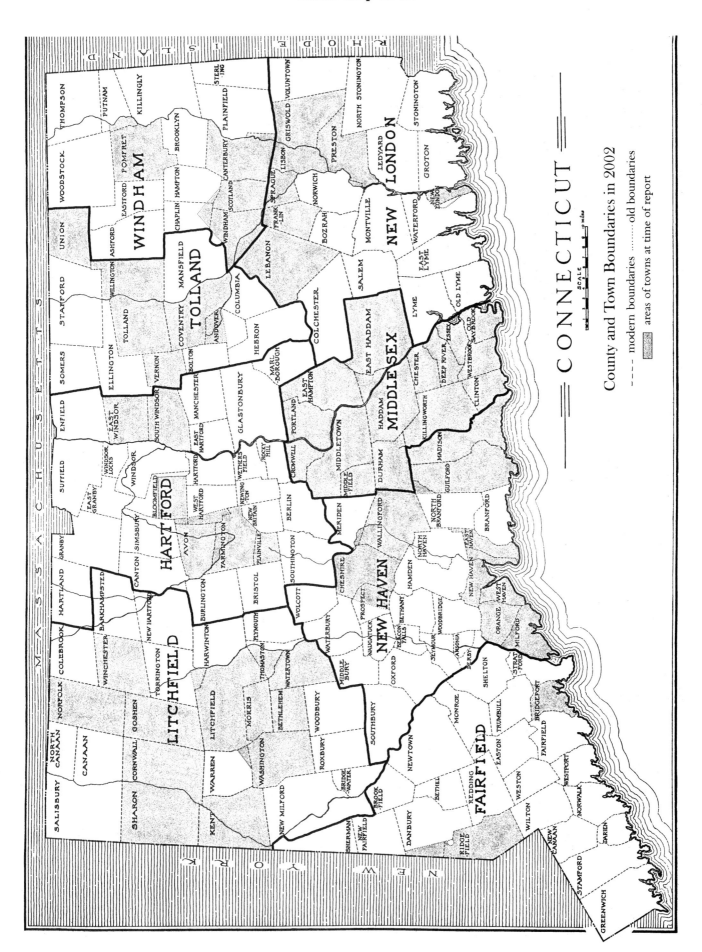

CONNECTICUT

County and Town Boundaries in 2002

- - - - modern boundaries .... old boundaries

areas of towns at time of report

SCALE

0 5 10 miles

Turnpike Map

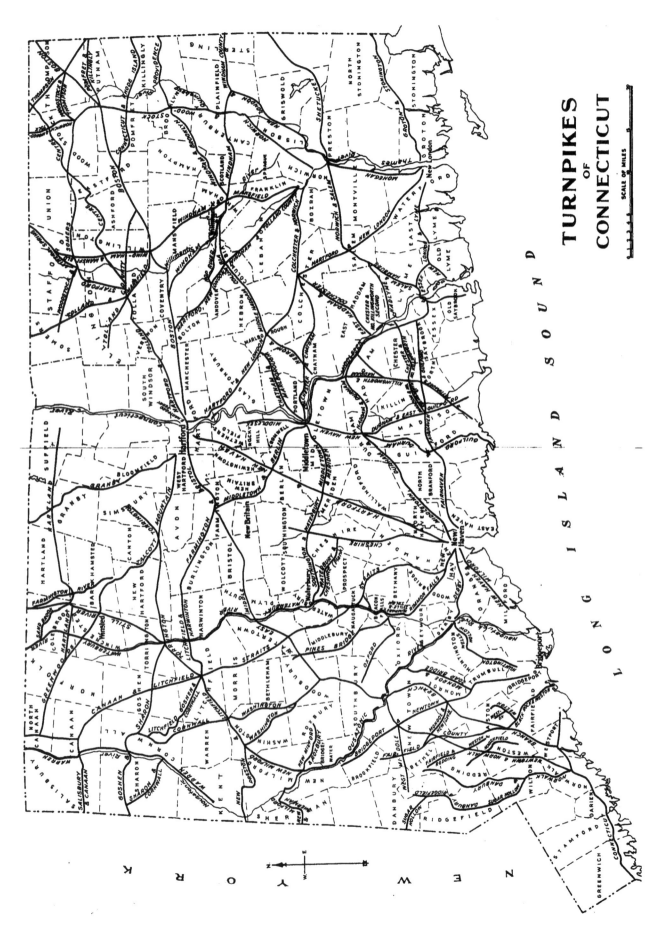

TURNPIKES
OF
CONNECTICUT

Connecticut's turnpikes formed a network that reached every part of the state, thereby serving its widely-dispersed population.
Frederic J. Wood, The Turnpikes of New England (Boston: Marshall Jones Co., 1919).

Topographical Map

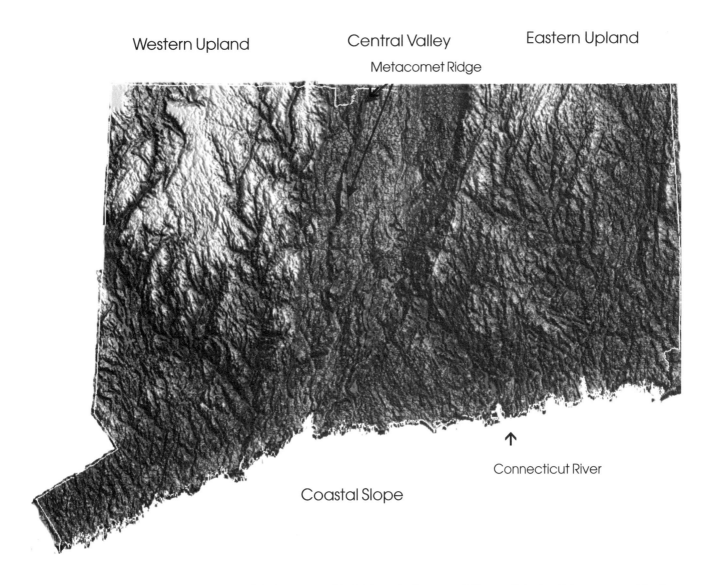

The landscape of Connecticut shows the following topographic divisions: the Eastern and Western Uplands which are separated by the broad Central Valley. Within the valley, the steep-sided Metacomet Ridge is a striking topographic high. Along the coast a region of gently rising topography is known as the Coastal Slope. Center for Earth Observation, courtesy Laurent Bonneau, August 2002.

Distribution of Wild Animals

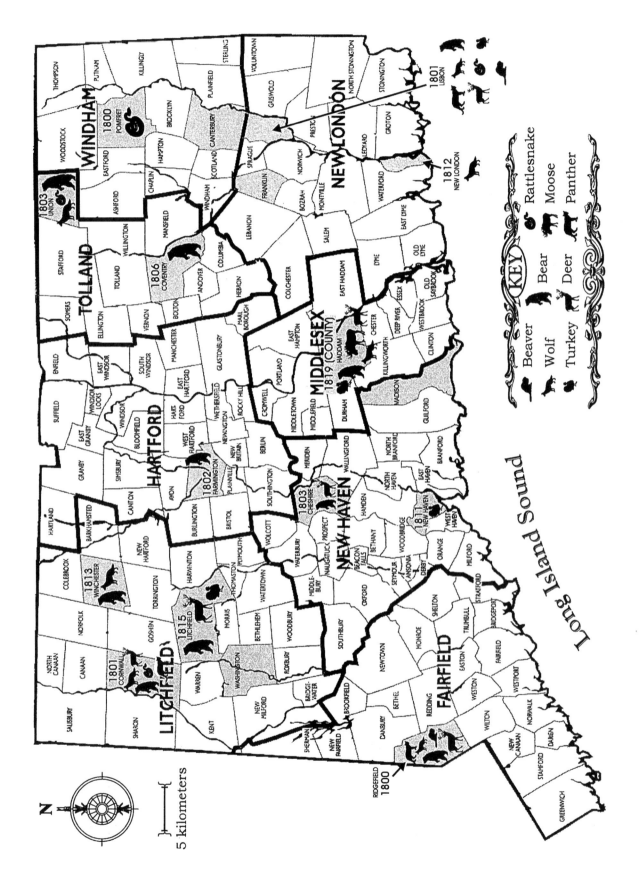

Map of the Connecticut Town Reports, showing the town location of eight of the most frequently mentioned species.

Legend for Warren & Gillet 1812 Map

EXPLANATION.

House of Public Worship .... 🏛

Court House .... 🏛

Academy .... 🏛

Town House .... 🏛

Woollen Manufactory .... W

Cotton   do. .... ✳

Gun & Pistol do. .... ⊙

Cutlers   do. .... S

Clock   do. 2

Button   do. 4

Wire   do. .... O

Grist Mill .... ✧

Saw Mill .... ✳

Paper Mill .... ✺

Fulling Mill .... ✛

Oil Mill .... ⊖

Powder Mill .... ✳

Slitting Mill .... ⧻

Distillery .... ⊠

Glass Works .... ▲

Furnace ..... ■   Iron Works ... ⊡

Light House .... ⌂

Rock on the Coast .... +

Buoy .... ⚲

Spindle .... ⚲

Mountain ....

Ore Bed .... ◉

Shoal ....

City ....

Borough ....

County Line ....

Town Line ....

Turnpike Road ....

Common Road ....

Biographical Sketches of Essayists

TOBY A. APPEL is Historical Librarian at the Cushing/Whitney Medical Library, Yale University, and a research affiliate in the Section of History of Medicine, Yale University. She holds a Ph.D. in history of science from Princeton University and a M.L.S. from the University of Maryland. Before coming to Yale, she taught history of science and history of medicine at New York University, University of Maryland, and University of Florida. Her writings include, besides numerous contributions to edited books and journals, *The Cuvier-Geoffroy Debate: French Biology in the Decades Before Darwin* (New York: Oxford Univ. Press, 1987) and *Shaping Biology: The National Science Foundation and American Biological Research, 1945-1975* (Baltimore: Johns Hopkins Univ. Press, 2000). She is currently researching medical sects, societies, and the state in nineteenth-century Connecticut.

RICHARD BUEL is Professor of History Emeritus at Wesleyan University, where he taught for 40 years. He is the author of *Securing the Revolution* (1972); of *Dear Liberty* (1980); with Joy D. Buel, of *The Way of Duty (1984)*; and of *In Irons: Britain's Naval Supremacy and the American Revolutionary Economy* (1998). He was educated at Amherst College and Harvard University and has been the recipient of several fellowships, including one from the Guggenheim Foundation, two from the American Council of Learned Societies, and two from the National Endowment for the Humanities. He is currently a member of the Connecticut State Historical Commission and the Connecticut Humanities Council.

GRETCHEN TOWNSEND BUGGELN is Director of the Research Fellowship Program, Winterthur Museum, Garden & Library, and Associate Professor in the Winterthur Program in Early American Culture. She is interested in the material culture of Americans past and present, particularly those artifacts that reflect and shape religious belief and practice. Her 1995 Yale Ph.D. dissertation was a study of the religious architecture of Connecticut's Protestant in the early national period. Revised, it will be published by the University Press of New England in 2003 as *Temples of Grace: the Material Transformation of Connecticut's Churches, 1790-1840.*

TIM W. CLARK is a Professor Adjunct in the School of Forestry and Environmental Studies (FES) and a Fellow in the Institution for Social and Policy Studies, Yale University. He is also Board President of the Northern Rockies Conservation Cooperative in Jackson, Wyoming. His major interests are in applied conservation, analysis and organizational behavior in the natural resources arena, and analysis and development of policies and programs for conservation of species and ecosystems. He has investigated more than thirty mammal species (marsupials, insectivores, rodents, carnivores, ungulates, primates) in ten states and three foreign countries, mostly with a "single species" approach, and mostly with threatened and endangered species in recent years. His 1997 book, *Averting Extinction: Reconstructing Endangered Species Recovery,* uses as a case study his experiences with the endangered black-footed ferret recovery program.

CHRISTOPHER COLLIER, Professor of History Emeritus at the University of Connecticut at Storrs, is Connecticut State Historian. He has written extensively about the history of Connecticut for both scholarly and popular readers. Among his works are *Roger Sherman's Connecticut: Yankee Politics and the American Revolution* and *The Literature of Connecticut History,* an annotated bibliography of some four thousand published works. More recently he has published scholarly articles on the Connecticut town in *The New England Quarterly,* "Sleeping with Ghosts: Myth and Public Policy in Connecticut, 1634-1992;" and in the *Bulletin* of the Connecticut Historical Society, "New England Specter: Town and State in Connecticut History, Law, and Myth." Collier earned a B.A. at Clark University and a Ph. D at Columbia.

EDWARD S. COOKE, JR., the Charles F. Montgomery Professor of American Decorative Arts and Chair of Yale University's Department of the History of Art, received his B.A. from Yale College (1977), his M.A. from the Winterthur Program in Early American Culture at the University of Delaware (1979) and his Ph.D. in 1983 from Boston University. His research interest is American material culture, especially furniture and its makers. His book *Making Furniture in Pre-industrial America: The Social Economy of Newtown and Woodbury, Connecticut* received the Charles F. Montgomery Prize when it was published in 1996. He has curated collections, fostered museum exhibits and spoken from coast to coast on varied manifestations of craftsmanship. He has contributed dozens of articles to books and journals in the two decades between writing "Domestic Space in the Federal-Period Inventories of Salem Merchants," in 1980 and "From Manual Training to Freewheeling Craft: The Transformation of Wood Turning, 1900-1976" in 2001.

KATHY J. COOKE received her Ph.D. from the University of Chicago, and currently is a member of the History Department of Quinnipiac University. She was a Fellow in the Program in Agrarian Studies at Yale University 1998-99. Her research speciality is the history of breeding in the United States in the late nineteenth and early twentieth centuries. She is completing projects on American eugenics and feminism, and on the history of agricultural breed associations.

CAROLYN C. COOPER, research affiliate in Yale University's Economics Department, is an historian of technology. Her doctoral dissertation (Yale 1985) won the Allan Nevins Prize of the Economic History Association in 1986. Her book, *Shaping Invention: Thomas Blanchard's Machinery and Patent Management in 19th-Century America* appeared in 1991. She has enjoyed fellowships at the National Museum of American History in Washington D.C. and at the Philadelphia Center for Early American Studies, University of Pennsylvania. She studies the historical relation of patenting to invention and has guest-edited a special issue (Oct. 1991) of *Technology and Culture* on that topic. Her shorter works pertinent to the early American republic include contributions to *Windows on the Works: Industry on the Eli Whitney Site 1798-1979* (1984); to *Early American Technology: Making and Doing Things from, the Colonial Era to 1850* (1994); and to a special issue (1988) of *IA, the Journal of the*

Society for Industrial Archeology on the Springfield Armory. She currently collaborates in a forthcoming book about the industrial heritage of New Haven.

BRUCE C. DANIELS, Professor and Chair, Department of History, Texas Tech University, is author of several books including: *The Connecticut Town: Growth and Development, 1635-1790* (1979) and *Puritans at Play: Leisure and Recreation in Colonial New England* (1995, 1996). A former Peace Corps volunteer (Bihar, India, 1964-65) and Fulbright scholar (Duke University, 1993-94), Daniels also served as editor of the *Canadian Review of American Studies* (1978-86) and president of the Canadian Association for American Studies (1991-93). In 1996, Daniels was a candidate for the Democratic Party's presidential nomination in the New Hampshire Primary where he finished 7th in a field of 22 Democratic Party candidates.

ROBERT B. GORDON, Professor of Geophysics and Applied Mechanics at Yale University, received his undergraduate and doctoral degrees from Yale. He taught at Columbia University before joining the Yale faculty in 1957. Gordon's research is published in 129 papers in refereed journals, including 54 in archaeometallurgy and the history of technology. He is the author or co-author of eight books, the most recent being *The Texture of Industry, an Archaeological View of the Industrialization of North America* (with Patrick M. Malone, 1994); and *American Iron 1607-1990* (1996); *Industrial Heritage in Northwest Connecticut, a Guide to History and Archaeology* (with Michael Raber, 2000); and *A Landscape Transformed* (2001). He was a fellow at the Philadelphia Center for Early American Studies, University of Pennsylvania, in 1988-99, and Regents' Fellow at the National Museum of American History, Smithsonian Institution, in 1991. He received the Abbott Payson Usher Prize from the Society for the History of Technology in 1991, and the Norton Prize from the Society for Industrial Archeology in 1984 (shared), 1986 (shared), and 1997.

PETER P. HINKS is Assistant Professor of American History at Hamilton College in Clinton, New York. He is also the Associate Editor of the Frederick Douglass Papers. He is the author of *To Awaken My Afflicted Brethren: David Walker and the Problem of Antebellum Slave Resistance,* which in 1998 received the Gustavus Myers Center Award for the Study of Human Rights in North America. Currently, Professor Hinks is researching and writing on slavery, emancipation, and race in Connecticut between 1750 and 1850.

HOLLY V. IZARD is research historian at Worcester Historical Museum and formerly a research historian at Old Sturbridge Village. She holds a Ph.D. in American and New England Studies from Boston University (1996), and for many years has been studying New England society, economy, culture, and material life in the eighteenth and early nineteenth centuries on the microanalysis level of individuals and their communities. Articles of which she is author or co-author, about early nineteenth-century New England farming and farming households, have appeared in *The Proceedings of the American Antiquarian Society* 103 (1993), *Agricultural History* 65 (Summer 1991), and *Annual Proceedings of the Dublin Seminar for New England Folklife,* 1986 (1988).

DAVID W. KLING (Ph.D., University of Chicago, 1985) is Associate Professor of Religious Studies at the University of Miami. He is the author of *A Field of Divine Wonders: The New Divinity and Village Revivals in Northwestern Connecticut, 1792-1822* (1993), which was awarded the Kenneth Scott Latourette Prize in Religion and Modern History. He has published articles in the *Journal of*

Men's Studies, Religion and American Culture, and the *History of Education Quarterly.* His book, *The Bible in History: How the Texts Have Shaped the Times* will be published by Oxford University Press.

HOWARD R. LAMAR received his doctorate from Yale University in 1951. He taught at Yale from 1949, serving as William Robertson Coe Professor of American History and Sterling Professor of American History until his retirement in 1994. He is the author of *Dakota Territory, 1861-1889* (1956, reprinted 1997), and *The Far Southwest, 1846-1912* (1966, revised and reprinted 2000). Among his many editing credits is *The Reader's Encyclopedia of the American West* (1977), which has been revised and published as the *New Encyclopedia of the American West* (1998). Although his special fields are frontier and western American history, he has long maintained an interest in Connecticut history, having served as Alderman of the City of New Haven, 1951-1953. He has taught courses on nineteenth-century New Haven history and given papers on the role of the Dutch in Connecticut history. He was a member of the Connecticut Humanities Council, 1987-1992, and organized a three-day symposium on the history of Grove Street Cemetery on the occasion of its two-hundredth anniversary (1998).

JILL E. MARTIN, Professor of Legal Studies and Chair of the Legal Studies Department at Quinnipiac University, received her B.A. at Keuka College in 1977, J.D. at Albany Law School, Union University in 1980, and M.A. at Yale University in 1990. Her professional specialties are paralegal education and the history of Native Americans' legal status. Her articles on these subjects have appeared in the *Journal of Paralegal Education and Practice* (1987), *Journal of the West* (1990, 2000), *Western Legal History* (1990, 1995), *Connecticut Lawyer* (1992), and *American Indian Law Review* (1998). Her 1990 article "'Neither Fish, Flesh, Fowl, nor Good Red Herring': The Citizenship Status of American Indians, 1830-1924" has been chosen for reprinting in *American Indians and U.S. Politics: A Companion Reader,* edited by John Meyer (2002).

GEORGE McLEAN MILNE, retired minister in the United Church of Christ, studied at St. Andrews University in Scotland, received a B.S. from University of Massachusetts in 1937 and B.D. and M.Div. from Yale Divinity School in 1940. He served in the U.S. Navy 1943-1946. With interests bridging religion, history, and environmental conservation, he has extended his pastorate from parishes in Hebron/Gilead, (1940-1952) and Woodbridge (1952-1979) to the forests of Connecticut, as member and past president of the Connecticut Forest and Park Association. He is the author of *Ongoing Pilgrimage* (1972), *Twenty-Five Years in Woodbridge* (1977), *A Year of Parish Prayers* (1979), *Lebanon: Three Centuries in a Connecticut Hilltop Town* (1986), and *Connecticut Woodlands* (1995).

RUTH BARNES MOYNIHAN is an historian and writer on American and women's history. She studied at Smith College and later earned her B.A. at the University of Connecticut, and her Ph.D. in 1979 from Yale University. Her work includes a biography of Oregon's Abigail Scott Duniway, *Rebel for Rights* (1983), and a museum exhibition essay, *Coming of Age: Four Centuries of Connecticut Women* (1989). She also co-edited *So Much to Be Done: Women Settlers on the Mining and Ranching Frontier* (2nd edition, 1998) and the two-volume *Second to None: A Documentary History of American Women from 1540 to 1993* (1993). Mother of seven children, and a lifelong resident of Connecticut, she is currently working on a multi-generational history of a Connecticut family.

WILLIAM A. NIERING died August 30, 1999, having completed writing his essay for this volume. He was Lucretia L. Allyn Professor of Botany at Connecticut College, Director of the Connecticut Arboretum 1965-1988 and Research Director of the Connecticut College Arboretum 1988-1999. He studied biology and botany at Pennsylvania State College (B.S.1948 and M.S. 1950) and at Rutgers University earned his Ph.D. in botany and plant ecology in 1952. A member of the Ecological Society of America, the Botanical Society of America and of Connecticut, the Society of Wetland Scientists, the Explorers Club, the Connecticut Forest and Park Association and other professional societies, he wrote many reviews and articles on botany and ecology in his almost fifty-year scientific career. He is also author of *The Life of the Marsh: the North American Wetlands* (1966), *A Book of Wildflowers* (1984), and the Audubon Society Nature Guide, *Wetlands* (1985); and co-author of *The Audubon Society Field Guide to North American Wildflowers—Eastern Region* (1979) and *Wetlands of North America* (1991).

WILLIAM N. PETERSON, the Senior Curator at Mystic Seaport Museum, earned his B.A. in history at Eastern Connecticut State College and has done graduate work at the University of Rhode Island. He has lectured and written extensively about the Connecticut maritime experience including articles detailing the history of the southeastern Connecticut menhaden fishery, the ship carvers at Mystic, Connecticut, and the New London Jibboom Club, a nineteenth century seamen's fraternal organization. His *Mystic Built: Ships and Shipyards of the Mystic River, Connecticut 1784-1919* received the prestigious John Lyman Book Award from the North American Society of Oceanic Historians (NASOH), for the best book published in American maritime history in 1989. He co-authored the book *Historic Buildings at Mystic Seaport Museum,* published in 1996, which received an Award of Merit from the Connecticut League of Historical Organizations. He contributed to *Boats: A Manual for Their Documentation*, published by the American Association for State and Local History, and to the highly acclaimed book *America and the Sea: A Maritime History*, published in 1998. He was the Historical Advisor and contributing writer for Connecticut Public Television and the Connecticut Humanities Councils collaborative documentary entitled "Connecticut and the Sea," which received the Wilbur Cross Award in1990.

BRIAN J. SKINNER has conducted geological research and teaching at Yale University since 1966, and was named Higgins Professor of Geology and Geophysics in 1972. He received his B.Sc. (Hon.) at the University of Adelaide in Australia in 1950, and Ph.D. at Harvard University in 1955. Before coming to Yale he taught at the University of Adelaide and did research in geology, geochemistry and mineralogy at the U.S. Geological Survey in Washington, D.C. He was editor of the journal *Economic Geology* from 1969 to 1995 and editor or co-editor of six books, including *The Oxford Companion to the Earth* (2000). Author or co-author of over ninety articles in scientific journals and books, he also wrote *Earth Resources,* which appeared in six languages in three editions from 1969 to 1986, and collaborated in writing a dozen other books, including *Geology Today: Understanding our Planet* (1999, second edition in press) and *The Dynamic Earth* (first edition 1989, fourth 2000), which has provided the basis for six audio-visual presentations in the "Great Teachers Series" of the Association of Yale Alumni.

H. CATHERINE W. SKINNER is research affiliate and lecturer at Yale University in the Department of Geology and Geophysics and in orthopaedics and rehabilitation at the Medical School. Following college at Mt. Holyoke (B.A. 1952), she pursued graduate education at Radcliffe/Harvard (M.A. 1954) and the University of Adelaide in Australia (Ph.D. 1959). Her research and teaching specialty is minerals and mineralization as found in biological systems and related to normal growth, development, and disease in human beings. She has been appointed visiting professor at Harvard, Cornell, University of Adelaide and Stanford, and has served as president and publications chairman of the Connecticut Academy of Arts and Sciences. In addition to over sixty published papers, her writings include co-authorship of *Asbestos and other Fibrous Material: Mineralogy, Crystal Chemistry and Health Effects* (New York: Oxford Univ. Press, 1988) and of *Dana's New Mineralogy*, 8th edition (New York: John Wiley & Sons, 1997) and co-editorship of three collected works in her field, the most recent being *Geology and Health: Closing the Gap* (New York: Oxford Univ. Press, 2002).

CAROLINE FULLER SLOAT graduated from Mount Holyoke College and immediately went on to take a M.A. in history at the University of Connecticut. For the next twenty-five years, she was employed by Old Sturbridge Village as a research historian and in progressively more responsible positions in connection with the museum's publications and interpretation to the visiting public. As historian, she researched and wrote about many topics in early nineteenth-century rural life: storekeeping and rural economics, household furnishings and domestic life, to suggest the broad areas of the museum's demonstrations and interpretations. She served as editor of the members' magazine, *Old Sturbridge Visitor* from 1980 to 1993, researched and produced *the Old Sturbridge Village Cookbook* (1884, second edition 1994), and also edited and contributed to *Meet Your Neighbors—New England Portraits, Painters, and Society, 1790-1850* (1992), and *Clockmaking in New England, 1750-1850* (1993), two Old Sturbridge Village publications. Since 1993, Caroline Sloat has been employed at the American Antiquarian Society, where she is currently director of scholarly programs.

HARVEY R. SMITH, a wildlife biologist with over thirty years of research experience, began his career with the U.S. Forest Service in 1966 studying predators of the gypsy moth. He received a M.F.S. degree in wildlife biology from the Yale University School of Forestry and Environmental Studies in 1972. He is recognized internationally for his biotelemetry research on the effects of intraperitoneal transmitter implantation on small mammal behavior and somatic growth, effects of exploitation on the population dynamics of muskrats, and the role of predation in forest pest dynamics. He has served as a member of three scientific delegations that visited the former Soviet Union between 1986 and 1990 to study the role of vertebrates as predators of pest insects and their role in forest protection management. Prior to his retirement in 2001, his major research focus was on small mammal habitat associations.

ROBERT M. THORSON holds a joint appointment in the Department of Geology and Geophysics and the Department of Anthropology at the University of Connecticut, where he has taught since his arrival from Alaska in 1984. Within the geosciences, his current interests lie in the tectonic geomorphology and paleoseismology of glaciated regions, and in the environmental impacts of development in Latin America. His current archaeological interest in the historical landscapes of New England, which lie hidden beneath retransported soils and second growth forest, and whose salient manifestations are stone walls, has prompted him to write a scientific summary of this work, *Stone By Stone,* (New York, Walker & Company, 2002). It reached the hardcover, regional bestseller list for September, 2002, but he considers his greatest honor to be a letter received from the

Washington State Geological Survey in February, 2000, which requested a better copy of his dissertation, because the old one had become worn out. As a Fulbright Scholar during the 1998-1999 academic year, he lectured widely in Chile while working with their national geological survey. Other visiting academic appointments have been in Civil Engineering (Universidad Tecnica de Federico Santa Maria, Valparaiso; 1999), Geography (Dartmouth College; 1992), and History (Yale University, 1991). He lives with his family in Storrs, Connecticut. He is a member of the American Association for the Advancement of Science, the American Geophysical Union, the Geological Society of America, and the Connecticut Academy of Arts and Sciences.

DANIEL VICKERS, Professor in the Department of History at the University of California in San Diego, received his B.A. at the University of Toronto in 1975 and his Ph.D. at Princeton University in 1981. He formerly taught at the University of Wyoming (1983-84) and the Memorial University of Newfoundland (1984-99). A member of the Omohundro Institute of Early American History and Culture, he studies work, especially farming and fishing, in the colonial and early national periods of American social history. He has contributed articles on these subjects to the *Journal of American History* (1985), the *William and Mary Quarterly* (1983, 1990, 1993) and to essay collections edited by others: *Seventeenth Century New England* (1984), and *Work and Labor in Early America* (1988). His book *Farmers and Fishermen: Two Centuries of Work in Essex County, Massachusetts, 1630-1850* appeared in 1994.

PAUL EDWARD WAGGONER was born and educated in Iowa, a descendent of people who had farmed in that state from its early days. In 1951 he began work at the Connecticut Agricultural Experiment Station in Haven, researching plants and their pests, soil and water. From 1972 to1987 he directed the Station, which is a child of Yale and first in the Western hemisphere. Directing the Station during its Centennial in 1975 gave him an affinity for history, and working on Connecticut farms and forests more than 40 years taught him the character of its stones and soils.

NOTES*

Buel
The Connecticut Academy

1. John A. Krout and Dixon R. Fox, *The Completion of Independence* (New York, 1944), p. 332; Rollin G. Osterweis, *The Sesquicentennial History of the Connecticut Academy of Arts and Sciences*, Connecticut Academy of Arts and Sciences *Transactions* 38 (1949): 105; Charles E. Cuningham, *Timothy Dwight 1752-1817: A Biography* (New York, 1942), p. 344; Edmund S. Morgan, *The Gentle Puritan: A Life of Ezra Stiles 1727-1785* (New Haven, 1962), pp. 159-162.

2. Richard Buel Jr., *Dear Liberty: Connecticut's Mobilization for the Revolutionary War* (Middletown, Conn., 1980), chapter 2.

3. Buel, chapters 3-6.

4. Buel, pp. 197, 222, 260.

5. Buel, pp. 121ff, 189-90, 215ff, 324.

6. Buel, pp. 307ff.

7. Buel, pp. 5-6.

8. Buel, pp. 16, 311-13.

9. For the Connecticut Wits, see Henry A. Beers, *The Connecticut Wits and Other Essays* (New Haven, 1920), chapter 1; Leon Howard, *The Connecticut Wits* (Chicago, 1943), Part II; Victor E. Gimmestad, *John Trumbull* (New York, 1974), especially chapter 5. For the collaboration of David Humphreys, Joel Barlow, John Trumbull, and Lemuel Hopkins in *The Anarchiad*, see *The Anarchiad: A New England Poem (1786-1787)*, ed. Luther G. Riggs (1861; reprinted ed., Gainsville, Fla., 1967).

10. Buel, *Dear Liberty*, pp. 331-32.

11. E. James Ferguson, *The Power of the Purse* (Chapel Hill, 1963) chaps. 13-15.

12. Buel, pp. 333. For British seizures in 1793-1794, see Richard Buel Jr., *Securing the Revolution: Ideology in American Politics 1789-1815* (Ithaca, N.Y., 1972), p. 55.

13. Buel, *Dear Liberty*, p. 332.

14. Harlan Hatcher, *The Western Reserve: The Story of New Connecticut in Ohio* (Indianapolis, 1949), p. 25; Helen M. Carpenter, "The Origin and Location of the Firelands in the Western Reserve," *The Ohio State Archeological and Historical Society Quarterly* 44 (1935): 165-174.

15. Hatcher, p. 66ff; Carpenter: 192-193.

16. Accounts of the protection British naval vessels offered American vessels appear in *Connecticut Journal* (New Haven), February 2, June 13, July 25, 1798.

17. Richard Purcell, *Connecticut in Transition* (Middletown, Ct., 1963), p. 47.

18. Purcell, p. 38; Carl Bridenbaugh, *Mitre and Sceptre; Transatlantic Faiths, Ideas, Personalities and Politics, 689-1775* (New York, 1962), passim; Patricia Bonomi, *Under the Cope of Heaven* (New York, 1986), pp. 199-209.

19. Bonomi, pp. 210-216; and Charles Royster, *A Revolutionary People at War* (Chapel Hill, 1979), chapters 1-4 emphasize the clergy's role in the revolutionary mobilization. For examples of the part played by Connecticut's Congregational clerics, see Levi Hart, *Liberty Described and Recommended; a sermon, preached to the corporation of freemen in Farmington, at their meeting on Tuesday, September 20, 1774* (Hartford, 1775); Enoch Huntington, *A Sermon, delivered at Middletown, July 20th. A.D. 1775* (Hartford, 1775; and Huntington, *The Happy Effects of Union, and the fatal tendency of division. Shewn in a sermon preached before the freemen of the town of Middletown, at their annual meeting, April 8, 1776* (Hartford, 1776); Abiel Leonard, *A Prayer Composed for the Benefit of the Soldiery* (Cambridge, 1775); Moses Mather, *America's Appeal to the Impartial World* (Hartford, 1775); Nathan Perkins, *A Sermon, Preached June 2, 1775* (Hartford, 1775); Ebenezer Baldwin, *The Duty of Rejoicing under Calamities* (New York, 1776); Judah Champion, *Christian and Civil Liberty and Freedom Considered and Recommended* (Hartford, 1776). Published sermons constitute only the tip of the iceberg.

20. Middlesex County, p. 184.

21. Stephen E. Berk, *Calvinism versus Democracy: Timothy Dwight and the Origins of American Evangelical Orthodoxy* (Hamden, Conn., 1974), pp. 28-32; Stephen A. Marini, *Radical Sects of Revolutionary New England* (Cambridge, Mass., 1982).

22. Timothy Dwight, *The Duty of Americans at the Present Crisis Illustrated in a Discourse Preached on the Fourth of July, 1798* (New Haven, 1798), passim; John C. Smith, *An Oration, pronounced at Sharon* (Litchfield, 1798), p. 7ff.

23. Buel, *Securing the Revolution*, pp. 138, 187, 206.

24. Osterweis, pp. 106-107; Kenneth Silverman, *Timothy Dwight* (New York, 1969), chap. 3, esp. pp. 82, 89.

25. C.J. Hoadley et al. eds. *Public Records of the State of Connecticut* (Hartford, 1894-), IX, p. 404.

26. Silverman, p. 114ff; Cuningham, p. 294ff; Berk, *Dwight*, argues that the poem, "Greenfield Hill," was a verse version of the same strategy as does Christopher Grasso in his *A Speaking Aristocracy: Transforming Public Discourse in Eighteenth-Century Connecticut* (Chapel Hill, 1999), pp. 336-38. Grasso credits Dwight with developing a "rhetoric of redemptive provincialism" (p. 374) to which the Town Reports lent authority.

27. Buel, *Securing the Revolution*, chapter X, esp. pp. 240 and 243.

28. Cf. Gordon S. Wood, *The Radicalism of the American Revolution* (New York, 1992), pp. 271-75 with Bishop's address.

29. Purcell, p. 153.

30. Purcell, p. 139.

31. Middlesex County, pp. 188-189.

32. Norman L. Stamps, "Political Parties in Connecticut 1789-1819" Ph.D. diss., Yale, 1950, p. 49.

33. See for instance George W. Stanley, *An Oration Delivered at Wallingford, August 8, 1805. In Commemoration of the Independence of the United States* (New Haven, 1805), passim, esp. pp. 3-5, 7, 12, 17.

34. Lynn W. Turner, *William Plummer of New Hampshire* (Chapel Hill, 1962), chapter VIII is the best treatment of the conspiracy.

35. Burton Spivak, *Jefferson's English Crisis: Commerce, Embargo, and the Republican Revolution* (Charlottesville, Va., 1979), chap. 4.

36. Purcell, p. 178; Spivak, *Jefferson's English Crisis*, pp. 141-44; Hoadley, et al., IX, 123-25; 187-93; *Middlesex Gazette* (Middletown), March 2 and 9, 1809.

37. Buel, *Securing*, pp. 277-79; Hoadley et al., IX, p. 188; Charles Warren, *Jacobin and Junto* (Cambridge, Mass., 1931), 216ff.

38. William Bentley, *The Diary of William Bentley* (Salem, Mass., 1905-14), III, pp. 405, 408-09, 412-13, 415, 430; Warren, p. 245ff.

39. Purcell, p. 179; *The Debates and Proceedings in the Congress of the United States* (Washington, D.C., 1834-1856), 10th Congress, 2nd session, 1525; *Niles' Weekly Register* (Baltimore), II, 208; J.C.A. Stagg, *Mr. Madison's War* (Princeton, N.J., 1983), p. 24.

40. This publication is Volume I, No. 1 of *The Statistical Account of the Towns and Parishes in the State of Connecticut*, the first of the Town Reports published by the Academy.

41. The *Connecticut Journal* (New Haven), March 9, 1809 condoned the destruction of the sloop as an "act of feeling and resentment" that was "managed with so much adroitness and secrecy, that the citizens were undisturbed." Republicans had a different view, see Warren, p. 233.

42. Buel, *Securing*, pp. 279-80; Stagg, chap. 2.

43. Joseph A. Goldenburg, "Blue Lights and Infernal Machines: the Blockade of New London," *Mariner's Mirror* 61 (1975): 385-97; Rankine G. Hinman, "Connecticut and the Federal System during the War of 1812: Conflicts of Sovereignty and Vital Interests," M.A. Thesis, Trinity College, 1957, see p. 43ff.

44. Harrison G. Otis, *Otis' Letters in Defence of the Hartford Convention* (Boston, 1824), p. 52; Buel, *Securing*, p. 285; Stagg, pp. 472-73.

45. Enlistments remained low in Connecticut, though. See Irene H. Mix, *Connecticut Activities in the Wars of the Country; a Summary* (Washington, D.C., 1932), 43; Warren, pp. 249, 251-52, 259, 279.

46. Otis, *Letters*, pp. 59, 78; *Niles' Weekly Register* (Baltimore), III, 306-07. For Franco-American diplomacy before the war, see Clifford L. Egan,

---

*Note: References to the individual Town Reports are found in *Voices of the New Republic: Connecticut Towns 1800-1832, Volume I: What They Said*

Neither Peace nor War: Franco-American Relations, 1803-1812 (Baton Rouge, La., 1983), chap. 7.

47. Hinman, pp. 29-41.

48. Purcell, pp. 43, 179-186.

49. Warren, pp. 266-68; [Matthew Carey], *The Olive Branch; or Faults on Both Sides*, 7th ed. (Philadelphia, 1815), pp. 308-15; also *Niles' Weekly Register* (Baltimore), V, p. 380; VI, p. 119; VII, pp. 194-196; Hinman, p. 157.

50. *Niles' Weekly Register* (Baltimore), IX, pp. 2-3; Buel, *Securing*, pp. 289-91.

51. Purcell, chaps. 8-9; also William C. Dennis, "A Federalist Persuasion: the American Ideal and the Connecticut Federalists," Ph.D. diss., Yale, 1971, chapter 8. Jarvis M. Morse, *A Neglected Period of Connecticut's History* (New Haven, 1933), p. 5ff emphasizes the degree to which the new constitution preserved some of the unprogressive features of the colonial government.

52. Silverman, *Dwight*, pp. 149-51; Cuningham, *Dwight*, p. 335ff.

53. Reprinted in Barbara M. Solomon, ed., *Travels in New England and New York* (Cambridge, Mass., 1969).

Kling
A View From Above

1. "AN ACT To incorporate the Connecticut Academy of Arts and Sciences," passed by Connecticut Legislature in October 1799, reprinted in CAAS *Memoirs*, Vol. 1, no. 1 (1810).

2. See Charles Roy Keller, *The Second Great Awakening in Connecticut* (New Haven, 1942); David W. Kling, *A Field of Divine Wonders: The New Divinity and Village Revivals in Northwestern Connecticut, 1792-1822* (University Park: Penn., 1993); and James R. Rohrer, *Keepers of the Covenant: Frontier Missions and the Decline of Congregationalism, 1774-1818* (New York, 1995).

3. Roland Berthoff, "Writing a History of Things Left Out," *Reviews in American History* 14 (1986): 1-16, cited in Nathan O. Hatch, *The Democratization of American Christianity* (New Haven, 1989), p. 7.

4. Such valuable sources include church records housed at the Connecticut State Library (Hartford); *Contributions to the Ecclesiastical History of Connecticut* (New Haven, 1861); Frederick Lewis Weis, *The Colonial Clergy and the Colonial Churches of New England* (Boston, 1936); and Albert Bates, *List of Congregational Ecclesiastical Societies* (Hartford, Conn., 1913).

5. See Keller, chaps. 5-7; and Rohrer.

6. See M. Louise Greene, *The Development of Religious Liberty in Connecticut* (1905; repr., Freeport, N.Y., 1970); and William G. McLoughlin, *New England Dissent, 1630-1883: The Baptists and the Separation of Church and State* (Cambridge, Mass., 1971), Vol. 2, pp. 915-1062.

7. See Hatch; and Roger Finke and Rodney Stark, *The Churching of America, 1776-1990: Winners and Losers in Our Religious Economy* (New Brunswick, N.J., 1992), chap. 3.

8. For statistics and location of these minorities, see Richard J. Purcell, *Connecticut in Transition: 1775-1818* (1918; new ed., Middletown, Conn., 1963), chap. 2; Keller, chap. 8; and Bruce C. Daniels, *The Connecticut Town: Growth and Development, 1635-1790* (Middletown, Conn., 1979), chap. 4.

9. Daniels, p. 104.

10. Farmington, p. 66.

11. For a bibliographical essay on these newer approaches, see Charles L. Cohen, "The Post-Puritan Paradigm of Early American Religious History," *William and Mary Quarterly*, 3rd ser. (October 1997): 695-722.

12. Farmington, p. 66.

13. Middlesex County, p. 180.

14. For the text of the Cambridge Platform and other key documents illustrating the faith and practice of the Congregational churches, see Williston Walker, *The Creeds and Platforms of Congregationalism* (1893; repr., Philadelphia, 1960).

15. Walker, p. 499.

16. David D. Hall, *The Faithful Shepherd: A History of the New England Ministry in the Seventeenth Century* (New York, 1974).

17. For the initial reception or rejection of the Platform, see Richard Bushman, *From Puritan to Yankee: Character and Social Order in Connecticut, 1690-1765* (New York, 1970), pp. 150-155.

18. See Haddam (1808), p. 169; Kent, p. 125; Middlesex County, p. 180; New Haven, p. 320; Pomfret, p. 408; Stratfield, p. 32; Wallingford, pp. 339, 341; Watertown, p. 155; Winchester-Winsted, p. 160.

19. Cited in Matthew Spinka, *A History of the First Church of Christ Congregational, West Hartford, Connecticut* (West Hartford, Conn., 1962), p. 66.

20. Middlesex County, p. 180.

21. Farmington, p. 65.

22. For an extensive treatment of this subject, see Robert G. Pope, *The Half-Way Covenant: Church Membership in Puritan New England* (Princeton, N. J., 1969).

23. Some historians, such as Edmund Morgan, viewed the covenant differently, arguing that its passage evidenced increased piety. That is, the clergy were responding not to those who were derelict about religion but to those whose heightened religious sensibilities kept them from applying for full church membership. Declension set in, but not until the early eighteenth century. See Edmund S. Morgan, *Visible Saints: The History of a Puritan Idea* (New York, 1963).

24. James P. Walsh, "The Pure Church in Eighteenth Century Connecticut" (Ph.D. diss., Columbia University, 1967), p. 218.

25. Michael Zuckerman, *Peaceable Kingdoms: New England Towns in the Eighteenth Century* (New York, 1970); but see chap. 4 for a discussion of division.

26. Paul R. Lucas, *Valley of Discord: Church and Society along the Connecticut River, 1636-1725* (Hanover, N.H., 1976).

27. Ridgefield, p. 27; Tolland, p. 383.

28. See Kling, chap. 5.

29. Canterbury, p. 396.

30. See Clarence C. Goen, *Revivalism and Separatism in New England: Strict Congregationalists and Separate Baptists in the Great Awakening* (New Haven, Conn., 1962), pp. 302-09.

31. On itinerancy, see Timothy D. Hall, *Contested Boundaries: Itinerancy and the Reshaping of the Colonial American Religious World* (Durham, N.C., 1994).

32. Goen, p. 70.

33. Wallingford, p. 341.

34. Edwin Scott Gaustad, *The Great Awakening in New England* (1957; Chicago, 1968), p. 111.

35. For a discussion of this controversy, see Gaustad, p. 111; and Bushman, pp. 216-20. For Dana's theology, see Allen C. Guelzo, *Edwards on the Will: A Century of American Theological Debate* (Middletown, Conn., 1989), pp. 155-164.

36. Cornwall (1800-1801), pp. 99-100.

37. Stephen Foster, "A Connecticut Separate Church: Strict Congregationalism in Cornwall, 1780-1809," *New England Quarterly* 39 (Sept. 1966): 309-33.

38. Donald M. Scott, *From Office to Profession: The New England Ministry, 1750-1850* (Philadelphia, 1978), p. 8.

39. Longitudinal studies spanning the early seventeenth to mid-nineteenth centuries conclude that the late 1790s and early 1800s mark a turning point in clerical mobility patterns, for during this period ministerial terms began to decline dramatically. See Daniel H. Calhoun, *Professional Lives in America* (Cambridge, Mass., 1965), chap. 4; Scott, chap. 4; John A. Andrew III, *Rebuilding the Christian Commonwealth: New England Congregationalists and Foreign Missions, 1800-1830* (Lexington, Ky., 1976), chap. 3; and Kling, chap.1.

40. Scott; Andrew, p. 39.

41. Scott, p. xi.

42. James W. Schmotter, "Ministerial Careers in Eighteenth-Century New England: The Social Context, 1700-1760," *Journal of Social History* 9 (Winter 1975): 257.

43. Clifford K. Shipton, "The New England Clergy of the 'Glacial Age,'" *Publications of the Colonial Society of Massachusetts*, XXXII (1937), p. 50, cited in Bushman, p. 157.

44. Canterbury, p. 396.

45. Keller, p. 197. If the itinerant had a wife, his allowance was doubled. If he had a family, each child below age seven was allotted $16, and between ages 7 and 14, $24.

46. Litchfield County, p. 138; Lyman Matthews, *Memoir of the Life and Character of Ebenezer Porter, D.D.* (Boston, 1837), pp. 55-56.

47. Ebenezer Porter to Asahel Hooker, 14 November 1805, Edward Hooker Letter Collection, no. 11, Congregational Library, Boston.

48. Bushman, pp. 156-58.

49. Ezra Stiles, *The Literary Diary of Ezra Stiles*, ed. Franklin B. Dexter (New York, 1901), 3:374. See also Farmington, pp. 68-69; Kling, chap. 5.

50. Lebanon, p. 401.

51. Guilford & Madison, p. 262.

52. Middlesex County, p. 196.

53. Middlesex County, p. 217.

54. Litchfield County, p. 138.

55. Middlesex County, p. 204.

56. Guilford & Madison, p. 262.

57. New Haven, pp. 320-321.

58. Schmotter argues for a decline in clerical status, whereas Jackson Turner Main, *Society and Economy in Colonial Connecticut* (Princeton, N. J., 1985), p. 318, "perceives no deterioration in the situation or status of ministers."

59. Madison, pp. 271-272.

60. Madison, p. 272.

61. For example, on the Great Awakening in Connecticut see Gerald F. Moran, "The Puritan Saint: Religious Experience, Church Membership, and Piety in Connecticut, 1636-1776" (Ph.D. diss., Rutgers University, 1974); Gerald F. Moran, "'Sinners Are Turned into Saints in Numbers': Puritanism and Revivalism in Colonial Connecticut," in *Belief and Behavior: Essays in the New Religious History*, ed. Philip R. Vandermeer and Robert P. Swierenga (New Brunswick, N.J., 1991), pp. 38-62; James P. Walsh, "The Great Awakening in the First Congregational Church of Woodbury, Connecticut," *William and Mary Quarterly*, 3rd ser., 28 (October 1971): 543-62; Peter Onuf, "New Lights in New London: A Group Portrait of the Separatists," *William and Mary Quarterly*, 3rd ser., 37 (October 1980): 627-43. On the Second Great Awakening, see Kling, chap. 6. For a study spanning both awakenings, see Stephen R. Grossbart, "Seeking the Divine Favor: Conversion and Church Admission in Eastern Connecticut, 1711-1832," *William and Mary Quarterly*, 3rd ser., 46 (1989): 696-740.

62. Litchfield County, p. 139.

63. Middlesex County, pp. 227, 232.

64. Moran, "'Sinners Are Turned into Saints,'" p. 55.

65. On the "feminization" of Protestant religion in the late eighteenth and early nineteenth centuries, see Ann Douglas, *The Feminization of American Culture* (New York, 1977); Richard D. Shiels, "The Feminization of American Congregationalism, 1730-1835," *American Quarterly* 33 (Spring 1981): 46-62; Barbara Welter, "The Feminization of Religion in Nineteenth-Century America," in *Clio's Consciousness Raised*, ed. Lois Banner and Mary Hartman (New York, 1973), pp. 137-57; David Schuyler, "Inventing a Feminist Past," *New England Quarterly* 51 (September 1978): 291-308; David S. Reynolds, "The Feminization Controversy: Sexual Stereotypes and the Paradoxes of Piety in Nineteenth Century America," *New England Quarterly* 53 (March 1980): 96-106.

66. See Kling, pp. 205-207.

67. Daniels, p. 104.

68. Purcell, pp. 39-59; Keller, pp. 193-200.

69. *Contributions to the Ecclesiastical History of Connecticut*, pp. 262-268.

70. On circumstances in the life of Johnson leading up to the Yale defection, see Joseph J. Ellis, *The New England Mind in Transition: Samuel Johnson of Connecticut, 1696-1772* (New Haven, Conn., 1973), esp. chap. 4.

71. Middlesex County, p. 179.

72. Cornwall (1800-1801), p. 101.

73. Billy Hibbard, *Memoirs of the Life and travels of B. Hibbard*, 2nd ed. (New York, 1843), p. 175. See also Purcell, p. 76.

74. Finke and Stark, p. 283.

75. Finke and Stark, p. 55.

76. See Preston, p. 368; Stratfield, p. 32. Anabaptists originated within the sixteenth-century Continental Reformation, Baptists within seventeenth-century English Puritanism.

77. Ridgefield, p. 27.

78. Purcell entitled his first chapter, "The Rise of Infidelity to 1801," while Keller took up the subject in chapter two, "The Challenge to Orthodoxy." Keller cited a 1798 pronouncement by the Presbyterian General Association that decried the "general dereliction of religious principle and practice among our fellow citizens" (pp. 1-2).

79. Martin E. Marty, *The Infidel: Freethought and American Religion* (Cleveland, Ohio, 1961), p. 21.

80. For an extended discussion of this issue, see Kling, pp. 48-54.

81. Asahel Hooker, "The Moral Tendency of Man's Accountableness to God . . . A Sermon, preached on the day of the general election at Hartford, . . . May 9, 1805" (Hartford, Conn., 1805), p. 32.

Buggeln
The Religious Landscape

1. Excellent treatments of this period's religious history are found in Jon Butler, *Awash in a Sea of Faith: Christianizing the American People* (Cambridge: Harvard University Press, 1990) and Nathan O. Hatch, *The Democratization of American Christianity* (New Haven: Yale University Press, 1989). The best accounts of Connecticut's particular religious character are found in David W. Kling, *A Field of Divine Wonders: The New Divinity and Village Revivals in Northwestern Connecticut, 1792-1822* (University Park, Pennsylvania: Pennsylvania State University Press, 1993) and in the classic Richard Purcell, *Connecticut in Transition, 1775-1818* (1918. Reprint, Middletown, Connecticut: Wesleyan University Press, 1963).

2. Purcell, pp. 12, 48.

3. Bruce Daniels, *The Connecticut Town: Growth and Development 1635-1790* (Middletown, Conn.: Wesleyan University Press, 1979), p. 104.

4. Daniels, p. 101.

5. See Kevin M. Sweeney, "Meetinghouses, Town Houses, and Churches: Changing Perceptions of Sacred and Secular Space in Southern New England, 1720-1850," *Winterthur Portfolio* 28 (Spring 1993): 59-93.

6. For more about the relationship between religion and refinement, see Richard L. Bushman, *The Refinement of America: Persons, Houses, Cities* (New York: Knopf, 1992).

7. Sharon, p. 149.

8. East Windsor, p. 42.

9. Middlesex County, pp. 238-239.

10. At this time there were no general incorporation laws and no private corporations. See Gordon S. Wood, *The Radicalism of the American Revolution* (New York: Vintage Books, 1991), pp. 321-22; Oscar and Mary P. Handlin, *Commonwealth: A Study of the Role of Government in the American Economy: Massachusetts, 1774-1861* (1947. Revised edition. Cambridge, Mass.: Belknap Press of Harvard University Press, 1969), pp. 87-105.

11. Middlesex County, p. 180.

12. Lisbon (Hanover), p. 353.

13. New Haven, p. 321.

14. Kling, note 122, p. 70.

15. Middlesex County, p. 181.

16. *Report of the Committee on the Claims of Connecticut Against the United States* (Hartford, 1817).

17. Cheshire, p. 250.

18. Christopher Collier, ed., *Public Records of the State of Connecticut*, May 1802-October 1803, Vol. XI (Hartford: Connecticut State Library, 1967), pp. 223-4.

19. See John Samuel Ezell, *Fortune's Merry Wheel: The Lottery in America* (Cambridge: Harvard University Press, 1960).

20. Sharon First Congregational Church Records, October 5, 1807, Connecticut State Library.

21 See Robert Dinkin, "Seating the Meetinghouse in Early Massachusetts," *New England Quarterly* 43 (1970): 450-464.

22. New Haven, Trinity Episcopal Society Records, MS Group B85, New Haven Colony Historical Society.

23. Hartford, First Congregational Society Records, 11 January 1811 (microfilm, Connecticut State Library).

24. New Haven, p. 309.

25. Litchfield County, p. 132.

26. *Litchfield County Post*, August 29, 1826.

27. Benjamin Silliman, "Sketches of a tour in the counties of New-Haven and Litchfield in Connecticut ...," *American Journal of Science, and Arts*, Vol. II, no. 2 (November 1820): 230.

28. See, for example, Edmund Ware Sinnott, *Meeting House and Church in Early New England* (New York: McGraw-Hill, 1963).

29. Middlesex County, pp. 226, 234.

30. New London, p. 361.

31. Cornwall (1800-1801), p. 99.

32. See Glenn M. Andres, "Lavius Fillmore and the Federal Style Meeting House" in Peter Benes, ed., *New England Meeting House and Church: 1630-1850* (Boston: Boston University, 1980): 30-42.

33. Middlesex County, p. 179.

34. David D. Field, *A History of the Towns of Haddam and East-Haddam* (Middletown, 1814), p. 33.

35. J. Frederick Kelly, *Early Connecticut Meetinghouses*, Vol. 2 (New York: Columbia University Press, 1948), pp. 111-117.

36. Field, *A History*, pp. 99-100.

37. Goshen, p. 117; Watertown, p. 155.

38. Preston, p. 368.

39. Preston, p. 368.

40. Coventry, p. 379.

41. Preston, p. 368.

42. Wintonbury, pp. 78-79.

43. Litchfield County, p. 136.
44. Cornwall (1800-1801), p. 100.
45. Goshen, p. 120.
46. Farmington, p. 66.
47. Ridgefield, p. 27.
48. Cornwall (1800-1801), p. 101.
49. New Haven, p. 324.

K. Cooke
Art and Science in Crop and Livestock Improvement

1. Franklin, p. 348; Watertown, p. 155; Willington, p. 391; Wallingford, p. 343; Cheshire, p. 249; Killingworth, p. 215; Durham, p. 218; Preston, p. 369.
2. Ridgefield, p. 24; Canterbury, p. 398; East Windsor, p. 40.
3. Winchester, p. 160; New Haven, p. 310.
4. Winchester, p. 160; New Haven, p. 309.
5. Middlesex County, p. 177-178; Bolton (N.), p. 374.
6. Canterbury, p. 398; Washington (1800), p. 152; Franklin, p. 348.
7. Middlesex County, p. 177; Goshen, p. 115; Bolton (N.), p. 374.
8. Union, p. 386; Ridgefield, pp. 25-26; Goshen, p. 116.
9. Canterbury, p. 395; Lisbon (Hanover), p. 353.
10. Franklin, p. 350.
11. Margaret Rossiter, *The Emergence of Agricultural Science: Justus Liebig and the Americans, 1840-1880* (New Haven, 1975), p. 6. See also C. Langdon White, Edwin J. Foscue, and Tom L. McKnight, *Regional Geography of Anglo-America* (3rd ed., Englewood Cliffs, N. J., 1964), pp. 72-76.
12. Bolton (N.), p. 374; Goshen p. 114; Bethlem, p. 85; Litchfield County, p. 131.
13. Stratfield, p. 31.
14. Middlesex County, p. 178; Sharon, p. 147; Litchfield County, p. 131; Cheshire, p. 249.
15. Middlesex County, p. 178; New Haven, p. 310.
16. Middlesex County, p. 179.
17. Middletown, p. 188; Goshen, p. 116; Cheshire, p. 249.
18. Sharon, pp. 145, 147.
19. Cheshire, p. 249; Winchester, p. 160.
20. Wallingford, p. 343; Sharon, p. 148; Bethlem, p. 85.
21. Canterbury, p. 395.
22. Farmington, p. 57.
23. Farmington, p. 61.
24. Winchester, p. 159.
25. James H. Shideler, "Agricultural History Studies: A Retrospective View," in Frederick V. Carstensen, Morton Rothstein, and Joseph A. Swanson, eds. *Outstanding in His Field: Perspectives on American Agriculture in Honor of Wayne D. Rasmussen* (Ames, 1993), pp. 3-4.
26. Timothy Pickering, *An Address from the Philadelphia Society for Promoting Agriculture, with a Summary of Its Laws* (Philadelphia, 1785), excerpts reprinted in *Readings in the History of American Agriculture,* Wayne D. Rasmussen, ed. (Urbana, 1960), pp. 42-44.
27. *Memoirs of the Pennsylvania Agricultural Society,* 1824, pp. 110-111, 138-141.
28. William S. King in *Transactions of the Agricultural Societies in the State of Massachusetts for 1852* (Boston, 1853), p. 408.
29. Goshen, p. 116.
30. Lisbon (Newent), p. 358; Canterbury, p. 395; Cornwall (1812), p. 110; Farmington, p. 59.
31. Seth Sprague, "Neat Cattle," printed in *Transactions of the Agricultural Societies in the State of Massachusetts for 1852* (Boston, 1853), pp. 726-731.
32. James L. Lush, *Animal Breeding Plans* (Ames, Iowa, 1938), pp. 20-21; see also Hilton M. Briggs, *Modern Breeds of Livestock* (New York, 1949), pp. 19-20.
33. Edward D. Eddy, *Colleges for Our Land and Times: The Land-Grant Idea in American Education* (New York, 1956), p. 77. See also Margaret W. Rossiter, "The Organization of the Agricultural Sciences," in Alexandra Oleson and John Voss, eds. *The Organization of Knowledge in America, 1860-1920* (Baltimore, 1979), p. 214.
34. Preston, p. 369.
35. Kent, p. 125; New Haven, p. 309; Winchester, p. 159.
36. Middletown, p. 190; Killingworth, pp. 216-217; Farmington, p. 49. See also Jared Eliot, *Essays upon Field Husbandry in New England* (New London: T. Green, 1748).
37. Rasmussen, p. 54; Rodney H. True also mentions Custis and Watson in "The Early Development of Agricultural Societies in the United States," *Annual Report of the American Historical Association for 1920* (Washington, 1925), p. 300.
38. Elkanah Watson, *History of the Rise, Progress, and Existing Conditions of the Western Canals in the State of New York from September 1788 to 1819. Together with the Rise, Progress, and Existing State of Modern Agricultural Societies, on the Berkshire System, from 1807 to the Establishment of the Board of Agriculture in the State of New York, January 10, 1820* (Albany, 1820), p. 115.
39. Watson, pp. 116-118. Lush also discusses the importance of fairs for disseminating information about breeding animals. Lush, pp. 178 and 183. True also concluded that the agricultural society "through its effect on great numbers of farmers hastened very greatly the dissemination of new information, awakened the spirit of improvement and made concrete the work of intellectual leaders." True, pp. 304, 306.
40. Wallingford, p. 342.
41. Harriet Ritvo, *The Animal Estate: The English and Other Creatures in the Victorian Age* (Cambridge, Mass., 1987), p. 49. Jeremy Rifkin restates Ritvo's argument in *Beyond Beef: The Rise and Fall of the Cattle Culture* (New York, 1992), pp. 60-63.
42. True, p. 299.
43. Rasmussen, p. 41.
44. Pickering, pp. 42-44.

Waggoner
Fertile Farms Among the Stones

1. Warren and Pearson's index of farm prices, the U.S. Bureau of the Census, *Historical Statistics of the United States, Colonial Times to 1970* (Washington, D.C., 1975), Series E 53. Their goal was an index corresponding to that of the Bureau of Labor Statistics for later years. Their foundation was mainly prices in New York City. Although Rothenberg's index of prices received by farmers in Massachusetts fluctuated synchronously with the New York index, it fluctuated less, showing some insulation between farmers throughout a state and a port city. Winifred B. Rothenberg, *From Market-places to a Market Economy* (Chicago, 1992), p. 111.
2. Cornwall (1800-1801), p. 96. In Franklin, p. 347, Samuel Nott confirmed the affliction of stones was general by quoting, "Nature having spent all her store—Heap'd up rocks, she could no more."
3. Michael M. Bell, *The Face of Connecticut: People, Geology, and the Land.* Hartford: State Geological and Natural History Survey of Connecticut, *Bulletin* 110: 196 pp., pp. 146-157.
4. Bell, p. 113.
5. Jared Eliot, *Essays Upon Field Husbandry in New England, and Other Papers, 1748-1762,* Harry J. Carman and Rexford G. Tugwell, eds. (New York, 1934), p. 29. A map shows that almost all New England colonies sought the hay of natural grasslands on marshes, Howard S. Russell, *A Long, Deep Furrow: Three Centuries of Farming in New England* (Hanover, NH, 1976), p. 55.
6. Timothy Dwight, *Travels in New England and New York,* Barbara M. Solomon and P.M. King, eds. (Cambridge MA, 1969), Vol. 1 p. 155.
7. Farmington, p. 50.
8. Dwight, Vol. 2, p. 366.
9. Marion F. Morgan, "Soils of Connecticut," *The Connecticut Agricultural Experiment Station Bulletin* 320 (September 1930): 911.
10. Cornwall (1800-1801), p. 97.
11. Litchfield County, p. 129.
12. Farmington, p. 56.
13. Cornwall (1800-1801), p. 95.
14. Guilford, p. 257.
15. Percy W. Bidwell, "Rural Economy in New England at the Beginning of the Nineteenth Century," *Transactions* of the Connecticut Academy of Arts and Sciences, Vol. 20, no. 5 (New Haven, 1916), pp. 241-399. p. 335 describes woodpiles.
16. Rodney H. True, "Jared Eliot, Minister Physician, Farmer" in Eliot, *Essays Upon Field Husbandry,* p. xxviii. Cornwall (1800-1801), p. 105.
17. New Haven, p. 308. R.V. Reynolds and Albert H. Pierson, *Fuel Wood Used in the United States, 1630-1930.* United States Department of Agriculture Circular 641. (Washington, DC, 1942), p. 10.
18. John F. O'Keefe, Harvard Forest, Petersham MA 01366. Private communication.

19. J. Ritchie Garrison, *Landscape and Material Life in Franklin County, Massachusetts. 1770-1860* (Knoxville, TN, 1991), p. 51.

20. New Haven, p. 308.

21. A reasonable growth on Connecticut forests is 1/2 cord per acre. Multiplying 7,500 cords by two for a half cord per acre, a two for half forested and a two for a semicircle on New Haven's landward side brings the estimate to 60,000 acres. The radius of that area of 94 square miles is 10 miles.

22. Guilford, p. 258.

23. East Windsor, p. 39; Goshen, p. 115; Wallingford, p. 340.

24. Dwight, Vol. 3, p. 366 and Vol. 4, p. 363.

25. Cornwall (1800-1801), p. 96; Canterbury, p. 398.

26. Cornwall (1800-1801), p. 103; Farmington, p. 62.

27. John Warner Barber, *Connecticut Historical Collections* (New Haven, 1836), p. 88 and p. 465. Bell made good use of Barber's accurate wood cuts to show Connecticut, including its fences, in the early nineteenth century: Michael M. Bell, "Stone Age New England: a Geology of Morals" in *Creating the Countryside: the Politics of Rural and Environmental Discourse*, E. Melanie DuPuis and Peter Vandergeest, eds. (Philadelphia, 1996), pp. 29-64.

28. U.S. Department of Agriculture, *Agricultural Statistics* (Washington DC, 1990), p. 454.

29. Bethlem, p. 84.

30. Litchfield County, p. 133.

31. Lee wrote of a humble farmer whose only aspiration was town drummer of Lebanon. Sometimes, beating the drum carried him in imagination to a world much more exciting than routine plowing, planting and harvesting. As he hoed in his field one morning, his neighbor Captain Clark astride a horse and in an outfit meant to be a uniform greeted him with "I am getting up a company to join Prescott and Putnam; I want you as drummer." Without a word, the humble farmer left his hoe standing in the row. He was bored by isolation. William Storrs Lee, *Yankees of Connecticut* (New York, 1957), p. 54.

32. "Subsistence farming, a type of farm in which both commercial crops and personal needs are provided by the land being cultivated. From colonial times until the mid-1850s family farms were self sufficient units growing commodities for sale as well as for personal consumption." Edward L. Schapsmeier and Frederick H. Schapsmeier, *Encyclopedia of American Agriculture* (Westport CT, 1975), p. 334.

33. Bidwell, pp. 331, 355, 375.

34. Eliot, p. 143.

35. Dwight, Vol. 1, p. 293

36. Dwight, Vol. 2, p. 89.

37. Ridgefield, p. 24.

38. Rothenberg, p. 85.

39. Bidwell, p. 284.

40. Doris B. Townshend, *Journal of a Gentleman Farmer 1829-1832* (East Haven, Conn., 1985), p. 85.

41. Dwight, Vol. 1, p. 139.

42. Bidwell, p. 313.

43. Madison, p. 272.

44. Bidwell, p. 312, quoting from the U.S. Commissioner of Agriculture, 1866.

45. Rothenberg, p. 92.

46. Washington, p. 152.

47. Dwight, Vol. 1, p. 137.

48. Bidwell, pp. 294, 299-303.

49. Bidwell, p. 303.

50. Bidwell, p. 304.

51. Cornwall (1800-1801), p. 102.

52. For a cogent presentation of von Thünen's theory see David Horsfall, "David Horsfall on von Thünen's Model," *Geographical Magazine* 64 (October 1992):53.

53. Wallingford, p. 343, and Wintonbury (Bloomfield), p. 77.

54. Dwight, Vol. 3, p. 366 and Barber's woodcut, p. 357.

55. Guilford, p. 258. Since the Sachems Head Yacht Club recently celebrated its centennial and its harbor is filled only with yachts, it is hard to imagine bellowing cattle there. Other New England examples of the working of von Thünen's law abound. E.g., "Crop specialization was determined by distance and transportation to markets: urban towns and their adjacent areas concentrated on cordwood, market crops and milk, more distant towns shipped butter, cheese and hay." David R. Foster, "Land-Use History and Four Hundred Years of Vegetation Change in New England" in *Global Land Use Change. A Perspective from the Columbian Encounter*, B. L. Turner, A. Gomez Sal, F. Gonzalez Bernaldez, and F. diCastri, eds. (Madrid, 1995), pp. 273-274.

56. Bidwell, p. 316.

57. Goshen, p. 117 and Dwight, Vol. 3, p. 330.

58. New London, p. 365.

59. Bidwell, p. 338.

60. Bidwell, p. 304, Goshen, p. 116 and Litchfield County, p. 142.

61. Dwight, vol. 2, p. 259.

62. Emergency Relief Commission, *The Connecticut Guide* (Hartford, 1935), p. 97. Lewis Norton, who invented pineapple cheese shaped like that fruit, wrote the Goshen Report. On page 116 he told how to make cheese, including varnishing it with the yellowish-red pulp of Caribbean annatto seeds. On the same page he reported that wagons hauled Goshen produce to New Haven for shipment to South and West Indies. When Barber drew his picture of Goshen, he featured cows and a youthful drover, p. 468.

63. "About 1830 it was estimated that a New England milch cow of medium quality would give 1,500 quarts of milk in a year, which would make 166 pounds of butter or 375 pound of cheese." Percy W. Bidwell and John I. Falconer, *History of Agriculture in the Northern United States, 1620-1860* (Washington, 1925), p. 229.

64. Goshen, p. 116.

65. Bidwell and Falconer, p. 427.

66. Stratfield, p. 32.

67. Dwight, Vol. 3, p. 11.

68. David Humphreys (1752-1818), a graduate of Yale 1771, was Timothy Dwight's friend from college days and became a lieutenant colonel in the Revolution and a close friend of Washington. Humphreys represented the United States in Portugal and Spain. Recalled in 1801 by Jefferson, he experimented with merino sheep and the manufacture of cloth and paper. Dwight enthusiastically described Humphreys' model factory and community near Derby. Dwight, Vol. 3, pp. 275.

69. After a peak in 1814, wool prices fell to about one-sixth in a decade. U.S. Bureau of the Census, *Historical Statistics* series E 127.

70. Guilford, p. 256.

71. U.S. Bureau of the Census, *Historical Statistics* series A195 and Z8.

72. Ridgefield, p. 28.

73. Ridgefield, p. 28.

74. The 1973 dollars calculated as $37.86 per pound sterling were in turn converted to 1990 dollars by the producer price index for crude materials. U.S. Bureau of the Census, *Historical Statistics* series Z169-191.

75. Richard J. Purcell, *Connecticut in Transition: 1775-1818* (Middletown CT, 1918 reprinted in 1963), p. 187.

76. Dwight, Vol. 1, p. 136.

77. Ridgefield, pp. 23 and 25.

78. Lebanon, p. 403.

79. Preston, pp. 367-368.

80. Litchfield County, p. 139.

81. Bidwell, p. 385. The U.S. Bureau of the Census, *Historical Statistics* series A2, reported it rose from about 3,929,000 in 1790 to about 7,240,000 in 1810, an 84 percent rise.

82. Bidwell, p. 387 gives populations of these six counties in 1790, 1800, and 1810.

83. Dwight, Vol. 3, p. 372 and Vol. 2, pp. 321-324.

84. Oliver Wolcott, quoted in Purcell, p. 224.

85. In 1800, Connecticut's rural population was 238 thousand, and in the first half of the eighteenth century Massachusetts militia rations were about 3,000 calories per day according to U.S. Bureau of the Census, *Historical Statistics*, series A203 and Z195. The statistics in series K502-597 report nineteenth-century corn and wheat yields of about 25 and 12 bushels per acre, which are about the same as estimated for New England near 1800 by Bidwell and Falconer, p. 101.

86. Sharon, pp. 145, 147.

87. Michael M. Bell, "Did New England Go Downhill? *Geographical Review* (1989) 79:450-466. For a sample of the opinion that soils were depleted, see Russell, pp. 235, 237, 313, 391, 524-525, or Bell, p. 451.

88. U.S. Census Office, *Statistics of Agriculture* (Washington DC, 1895), p. 355.

89. U.S. Department of Agriculture, *Agricultural Statistics* (Washington DC, 1993), p. 31.

90. For cropland see U.S. Department of Agriculture, p. 348. For expenditure on fertilizers, see U.S. Bureau of the Census, *Statistical Abstract*, p. 667 and U.S. Bureau of the Census, *Census of Agriculture*,

Connecticut State and County Data (Washington, DC, 1994), p. 8. For value of crops, see U.S. Department of Agriculture, p. 379.

91. Glenn Motzkin, David R. Foster, Arthur Allen, Jonathon Harrod, and Richard Boone, "Controlling Site to Evaluate History: Vegetation Patterns of a New England Sand Plain," *Ecological Monographs* 66 (1966):345-365.

92. David R. Foster, Tad M. Zeybryk, Peter K. Schoonmaker and Ann L. Lezberg, "Post-Settlement History of Human Land-Use and Vegetation Dynamics of a Tsuga Canadensis (Hemlock) Woodlot in Central New England," *Journal of Ecology* 80 (1992):773-786.

93. Canterbury, p. 397; Kent, p. 125.

94. Bidwell, pp. 245 and 248.

95. Bidwell, pp. 368 and 372.

96. Horace Bushnell, *Work and Play; or Literary Varieties* (New York, 1864) cited by Bidwell, p. 368.

97. Bethlem, p. 83.

98. See the Solicitation Letter of 1800 in the front of this volume.

99. Cheshire, p. 249.

100. Cornwall (1800-1801), p. 98.

101. East Windsor, p. 39.

102. Goshen, p. 115.

103. Dwight, Vol. 2, p. 321.

104. For arguments that dense population encourages invention, see Ester Boserup, *Population and Technological Change,* (Chicago, 1981), p. 76 et. seq.

105. John Adams, quoted in Purcell, p. x.

106. Coincidentally, Dwight's Republican enemies who edited the *Mercury* in Hartford frequently quoted the discoverer of oxygen, Joseph Priestley, who fled England because of his sympathy with the French Revolution (Purcell, p. 17). In America, Priestley befriended Jefferson, which would have displeased Federalist Dwight.

107. Barbara M. Solomon in the Introduction to Dwight, Vol. 1, p. xviii; Fisher 1866 cited by Purcell 1918, p. 21; and Rollin G. Osterweis, *Three Centuries of New Haven, 1638-1938* (New Haven, 1953), p. 22.

108. Daniel Yergin, *The Prize: the Epic Quest for Oil, Money, and Power* (New York, 1991), pp. 19-34.

109. Harold C. Knoblauch, Ernest M. Law and W.P. Meyer, "State Agricultural Experiment Stations," *U.S. Department of Agriculture Miscellaneous Publication* 904 (Washington, D.C., 1962): pp. 8-25. Margaret W. Rossiter, *Emergence of Agricultural Science. Justus Liebig and the Americans, 1840-1880* (New Haven, 1975), pp. 10-176. Rossiter relates the success of agricultural chemistry at Yale and The Connecticut Agricultural Experiment Station and its failure at Harvard. Paul E. Waggoner, "Research and education in American Agriculture," *Agricultural History* 50 (1976): 230-247.

110. Eliot, pp. 5, 15 and 27. Eliot stands alone in the eighteenth century at the USDA web site for history of research,

http://www.usda.gov/history2/text10.htm.

111. C.A. Browne, "Liebig and the Law of the Minimum," in *Liebig and after Liebig,* F.R. Moulton, ed. (Washington,DC, 1942), pp. 71-82.

112. Dwight, Vol. 1, p. 276.

113. Pomfret, pp. 407-408.

114. Benjamin Silliman, quoted in Rossiter, p. 10.

115. Farmington, p. 60.

116. Farmington, p. 59.

117. Dwight, Vol. 2, p. 359, Madison, p. 268 and New Haven, p. 310.

118. New Haven, pp. 310, 312.

119. Garrison, p. 36.

120. Bidwell, p. 248.

121. Union, pp. 388, 387.

Izard
The State of Connecticut Agriculture in 1800

1. Timothy Dwight, *Travels in New England and New York* (Cambridge: The Belknap Press of Harvard University Press, 1969), introductory essay by editor Barbara Miller Solomon with the assistance of Patricia M. King, Vol. I, p. xlv.

2. New Haven, p. 303.

3. Only one respondent was identified as an ordinary farmer, seventy-five-year-old Solomon Wales who reported on Union in 1803 after men of letters declined the assignment. He concluded his report with: "Sir, I believe your Honour will think that I have answered as many and more of the questions, considering my age, education and ability, as is prudent for

me to attempt . . . . I have appointed several days for some of the principal inhabitants to meet and assist me but never one met." Union, p. 388.

4. As the editor to his volumes explained, "Timothy Dwight's *Travels in New England and New York* is now acknowledged as a work of intrinsic merit: it is invaluable as a contemporary record and interpretation of New England at the beginning of the nineteenth century. Timothy Dwight was no ordinary Connecticut Yankee. At the turn of the nineteenth century he was the most prominent minister of the established Congregational clergy in New England; eloquent preacher, recognized author, and distinguished educator, he acquired knowledge and skill in farming, gardening, literature, and music with equal zest." Dwight, *Travels,* Vol. I, pp. ix-x.

5. See Timothy Dwight's preface to *Travels,* Vol. I.

6. Henry Glassie, "The Practice and Purpose of History," *The Journal of American History,* 81 (December 1994): 961-968. Also, see Henry Glassie, "Meaningful Things and Appropriate Myths: The Artifact's Place in American Studies," in Robert Blair St. George, ed., *Material Life in America* (Boston: Northeastern University Press, 1988), pp. 63-92.

7. Quote, David M. Roth, *Connecticut: A Bicentennial History* (New York: W.W. Norton & Company, Inc., 1979), p. 21. For general information on agriculture and farming practices in Connecticut agriculture also see Albert E. Van Dusen, *Connecticut* (New York: Random House, 1961); Bruce Fraser, *The Land of Steady Habits: A Brief History of Connecticut* (Hartford: Connecticut Historical Commission, 1988); Malcolm L. Johnson, *Yesterday's Connecticut* (Miami, Florida: E.A. Seeman Publishing, Inc., 1976); Rudy J. Favretti, *Highlights of Connecticut Agriculture* (College of Agriculture and Natural Resources of the University of Connecticut, 1976); and Richard L. Bushman, *From Puritan to Yankee: Character and the Social Order in Connecticut, 1690 to 1765* (New York: W.W. Norton & Company, Inc., 1967).

8. Dwight, *Travels,* Vol. I, p. 123.

9. Favretti, *Highlights,* pp. 14, 18.

10. Kevin M. Sweeney, "From Wilderness to Arcadian Vale: Material Life in the Connecticut River Valley, 1635-1760," in *The Great River: Art & Society of the Connecticut Valley, 1635-1820* (Hartford: Wadsworth Atheneum, 1985), pp. 17-28. Also see Robert Blair St. George, "Artifacts of Regional Consciousness in the Connecticut River Valley, 1700-1780," *The Great River,* pp. 29-40, and Richard D. Brown, "Regional Culture in a Revolutionary Era: The Connecticut Valley, 1760-1820," *The Great River,* pp. 41-62.

11. Farmers and merchants in Massachusetts' coastal and River Valley towns were early attuned to the marketplace, but towns in the interior remained more focused on household needs until the nineteenth century. See, for example, Andrew H. Baker and Holly V. Izard, "New England Farmers and the Marketplace, 1780-1865: A Case Study," *Agricultural History* 65 (Summer 1991): 29-52, and "Farmers' Adaptations to Markets in Early Nineteenth-Century Massachusetts," in Peter Benes, ed., *The Farm: The Dublin Seminar for New England Folklife Annual Proceedings 1986* (Boston: Boston University, 1988), pp. 95-108.

12. Farmington, p. 64.

13. Middlesex County, p. 178.

14. Goshen, p. 116.

15. Middletown, in Middlesex County Report, p. 187.

16. New Haven, p. 317.

17. New Haven, p. 317.

18. Haddam, in Middlesex County Report, p. 199.

19. Winsted, pp. 163, 164.

20. Farmington, p. 64.

21. Middlesex County, p. 178.

22. Wallingford, p. 340.

23. Lebanon, p. 402.

24. Union, p. 387.

25. Bethlem, p. 85; Goshen, p. 116.

26. Kent, p. 125.

27. Preston, p. 369.

28. Franklin, p. 349.

29. Dwight, *Travels,* Vol. III, p. 11. After lengthy discussion he noted: "I have mentioned this subject thus particularly because it is in a great measure particular to this spot."

30. Wintonbury (Bloomfield), p. 77.

31. Middlesex County, p. 177.

32. Wallingford, p. 343.

33. Ridgefield, p. 24.

34. Stratfield, p. 31. The manuscript reads "1,000$ per acre."

35. Franklin, p. 348; Lisbon (Newent), p. 358; Lisbon (Hanover), p. 353.

36. Lebanon, p. 402.

37. Union, p. 386.
38. Cornwall (1800-1801), p. 98.
39. Middlesex County, p. 177.
40. Farmington, p. 57.
41. New Haven, p. 308.
42. New London, p. 362.
43. New London, p. 362.
44. Watertown, p. 155.
45. Farmington, p. 62.
46. Bethlem, p. 85.
47. Lisbon (Hanover), p. 353.
48. Lisbon (Newent), p. 358.
49. Goshen, p. 116.
50. Farmington, p. 62.
51. Sharon, p. 147.
52. The Sharon respondent on p. 147 noted in his discussion of manuring that: "The use of oxen, which has now become universal in this town, was the cause of agricultural prosperity." Timothy Dwight noted a significant Dutch population in the southern Fairfield County town of Greenfield whose ways "resemble not a little the people of the neighboring county of Westchester" in New York. Dwight, *Travels*, Vol. III, p. 346.
53. Farmington, pp. 57-62.
54. Cornwall (1800-1801), p. 97.
55. Middlesex County, p. 178.
56. Dwight, *Travels*, Vol. II, p. 362.
57. Lisbon (Newent), p. 358.
58. Middlesex County, p. 178.
59. Cornwall (1800-1801), p. 103.
60. Middlesex County, p. 178.
61. Canterbury, p. 398.
62. Washington, p. 152.
63. See Richard L. Bushman, *The Refinement of America: Persons, Houses, Cities* (New York: Alfred A. Knopf, 1992), and Cary Carson, Ronald Hoffman, and Peter J. Albert, eds., *Of Consuming Interests: The Style of Life in the Eighteenth Century* (Charlottesville: Published for the United States Capital Historical Society by the University of Virginia, 1994).
64. Dwight, *Travels*, Vol. I, p. 162-219.
65. Farmington, pp. 51-53.
66. Wintonbury (Bloomfield), p. 77.
67. Wintonbury (Bloomfield), p. 77.
68. East Windsor, p. 40.
69. Wintonbury (Bloomfield), p. 78.
70. Farmington, pp. 50-51.
71. Middlesex County, p. 177.
72. Middlesex County, pp. 177, 179.
73. East Haddam, in Middlesex County Report, p. 203.
74. East Haddam, in Middlesex County Report, p. 203.
75. Durham, in Middlesex County Report, p. 218.
76. Durham, in Middlesex County Report, p. 218.
77. Dwight, *Travels*, Vol I, pp. 156-158.
78. Middletown, in Middlesex County Report, p. 188.
79. Interestingly, the Guilford and Madison Reports are written by the Reverend David D. Field, formerly of Middlesex County. [Madison was his home town; he lived in N.Y. State when he wrote the Guilford and Madison Reports. Editor's note]
80. Cheshire, p. 249.
81. Cheshire, p. 249.
82. Wallingford, p. 343.
83. New Haven, p. 304.
84. New Haven, p. 309.
85. New Haven, p. 309.
86. Dwight, *Travels*, Vol. II, p. 359.
87. Dwight, *Travels*, Vol. III, pp. 365-366.
88. Dwight, *Travels*, Vol. III, pp. 346-359.
89. Ridgefield, p. 23.
90. Ridgefield, p. 24. Elsewhere he noted there was a good tan works in town with fifty vats, a small hatting manufactory, two shoe and boot manufactories sending abroad 5,000 pairs of shoes and boots annually, and at least one cabinetmaker furnishing goods for Ridgefield and neighboring towns. (p. 26.)
91. Ridgefield, p. 24.
92. Ridgefield, p. 25.
93. Ridgefield, p. 25.
94. Stratfield, p. 32.

95. Stratfield, p. 31.
96. Dwight, *Travels*, Vol. III, pp. 363-364.
97. Dwight, *Travels*, Vol. II, p. 367.
98. Dwight, *Travels*, Vol. II, pp. 24-25.
99. New London submitted a report, but it is too slim to be of any use on agriculture.
100. Franklin, pp. 348-349.
101. Dwight, *Travels*, Vol. II, p. 23.
102. Lisbon (Hanover), p. 353.
103. Lisbon (Hanover), p. 353.
104. Lisbon (Newent), p. 358.
105. Lisbon (Newent), p. 358.
106. Lisbon (Hanover), p. 354.
107. Pomfret, p. 407.
108. Lebanon, p. 402.
109. Canterbury, p. 395.
110. Canterbury, p. 398.
111. Lebanon, p. 403.
112. North Bolton (Vernon), p. 374.
113. North Bolton (Vernon), p. 374.
114. Union, p. 386.
115. Union, p. 387.
116. North Bolton (Vernon), p. 374.
117. Cornwall (1800-1801), p. 107.
118. Goshen, p. 116.
119. Sharon, p. 147.
120. Goshen, p. 116.
121. Goshen, p. 116.
122. For Colonial Connecticut, Jackson Turner Main has studied property values and sizes from probate records. See chapter six, "The Farmers" in his *Society and Economy in Colonial Connecticut* (Princeton, N.J.: Princeton Univ. Press, 1985).

Sloat
Connecticut's Home Dairies

1. See Article 15, Connecticut Academy's Letter of Solicitation of 1800, which can be found at the beginning of this volume. The title of the article is taken from the Cornwall Report, p. 98.
2. Two scholars who have devoted considerable effort to the study of dairying by women are Joan M. Jensen and Sally McMurry. Jensen focuses on the mid-Atlantic from 1750 to 1850. McMurry has published studies of Oneida County, New York, between 1820 and 1885 in which she documents the transition of butter making and then cheese making from the family farm dairy to a commercial creamery or cheese factory and, by the end of the period, to the sale of fluid milk from the farm. Evaluating women's work on family farms posed a "methodological and theoretical problem of major proportions," Jensen has written in "Butter Making and Economic Development in Mid-Atlantic America from 1750 to 1850," *Signs*, Vol. 13 (1988): 813-29, quote on p. 813. See also, Joan M. Jensen, *Loosening the Bonds: Mid-Atlantic Farm Women, 1750-1850* (New Haven: Yale University Press, 1988), and Sally McMurry, *Transforming Rural Life: Dairying Families and Agricultural Change, 1820-1885* (Baltimore: Johns Hopkins University Press, 1995).
3. Edward S. Cooke, Jr., notes the role of the woodworkers in his comments about the coopers of New Milford, Roxbury, Woodbury, and Bethlehem, *Making Furniture in Pre-Industrial America* (Baltimore: Johns Hopkins University Press, 1996), p.12. Cooke doesn't get the seasons of the produce that will fill the staved containers or the variety of forms quite right, but the point is well taken. The Academy's respondent for Wintonbury (Bloomfield) stated that "About fifteen hundred meal casks, consisting of hogsheads, barrels and tierces were made and marketed in 1801." (p. 77) In addition, many barrels would have been needed for the transportation and storage of cider (a product named in another of the Academy's questions).
4. See, for example, the diaries of Samantha Barrett and Zeloda Barrett of New Hartford, Connecticut. Connecticut Historical Society.
5. Lebanon, p. 403.
6. New Haven, p. 328.
7. Elijah Allen's Cornwall Report, p. 98 and Lewis Mills Norton's for Goshen, p. 116 are the only ones to give commodity prices for butter (Cornwall) and cheese. Allen suggests separate prices for butter in the fall and in the summer, but the average of $.17 and $.14 is $.155, a half cent

more than the price given in Goshen. In Goshen cheese was worth 6d or $.083 per pound and these figures were used to calculate values for quantities described elsewhere. A firkin holds 56 pounds.

8. Goshen, p. 116.

9. Timothy Dwight, *Travels in New England and New York*, ed. Barbara Miller Solomon (Cambridge, Mass.: Harvard University Press, 1969), Vol. 2, p. 259.

10. Goshen, pp. 115, 116.

11. "The cheese made here and designated for market is usually painted. This is best done by boiling the annetto [sic] in quick lye, in which to a certain degree it will dissolve, and mixing a sufficient quantity of the preparation with the milk. This preparation may be kept any time, and it is not known that the taste of the cheese is affected by it." Goshen, p. 116.

12. Litchfield, p. 142.

13. Cornwall (1800-1801), pp. 98-99.

14. The Cornwall Report (1800-1801), p. 98 is the only one to allude to the seasonal divergence in the price of butter. The early summer was the optimal time for butter making when the reports were made. Then, taking advantage of the richer, cream-laden milk and cooler weather, there was time for the cream to rise over forty-eight hours so that it could be skimmed and churned into butter. During the summer, it was more practical to make cheese every day before the milk soured. By fall, the amount of cream in a day's milking declined, and cream could be held longer until enough was available for churning.

15. Cornwall (1800-1801), p. 99.

16. This process is detailed "in the course of daily events" in the diaries of Samantha and Zeloda Barrett of New Hartford. The reason for the seasonal range in the value of work is that in an agricultural society, there was abundant field work for men and dairying and such household work as feeding the farmhands for women that could only be done in the summertime.

17. Cornwall (1800-1801), pp. 98, 107.

18. Washington (1800), p. 152.

19. Sharon, p. 147.

20. Winchester, p. 160; Winsted, pp. 163-164.

21. Ridgefield, p. 25.

22. Despite the economy that this might have represented, a British manual reprinted in the United States noted that "turnips give butter a disagreeable taste." The recommended procedure for removing this taste was to "warm the cream and pour it into a tub or pail of cold water, then skim the cream off the water." The "foul taste" would be left behind in the water. Josiah Twamley, *Dairying Exemplified, or The Business of Cheese-making: Laid Down from Approved Rules, Collected from the Most Experienced Dairy-women, of Several Counties*. First American ed. from the second British. Providence, R.I., 1796, pp. 65-66.

23. Stratfield, p. 32.

24. Dwight, *Travels,* Vol 3, p. 359.

25. Entering Cheshire in 1998 from the major highways, this driver was greeted by signs proclaiming this the bedding plants capital of Connecticut.

26. Wallingford, pp. 343, 340. Although dairying was not considered to be an important occupation, textile production was. The presence of carding and fulling mills and a reported 145 looms in families on which woolen and linen-and-cotton cloths worth $21,510.81 were manufactured yielded a figure far outstripping any other figures for manufacturing reported to the Secretary of State on the "last census."

27. Guilford, pp. 256, 257.

28. Middlesex County, p. 203.

29. Dwight, *Travels,* Vol. I, p. 162.

30. Dwight, *Travels,* Vol. I, pp. 170-71.

31. Farmington, pp. 66-67.

32. Wintonbury, p. 78.

33. In the rich river valley 100,000 bushels of grain (wheat, rye, corn, and barley), 7,000 barrels of cider, and 1,700 swine were raised annually. No numbers are given for sheep nor is there an account of a flax crop as there was in the river-edge towns to the south, yet it was reported (Article 16) that "tow cloth and flannels are manufactured in families, and some it sent by the merchants to Albany and the northward." East Windsor, p. 39, 40.

34. Dwight, *Travels,* Vol. I, p. 162, describing his ride from Middletown to Hartford.

35. Bolton, p. 374.

36. Union, pp. 386-387.

37. Tolland, p. 383.

38. Bolton, p. 374, Union p. 386; cf. Dwight *Travels,* Vol. III, p. 94 on Mansfield; and Vol. II, p. 136 on Vernon and Stafford.

39. Dwight, *Travels*, Vol. III, p. 93.

40. Canterbury, p. 395.

41. Ellen D. Larned, *History of Windham County, Connecticut* (Worcester, Mass., 1880), Vol. II, p. 365.

42. Ellen D. Larned, *Historic Gleanings in Windham County, Connecticut* (Providence, 1899), pp. 143-44

43. Lebanon, pp. 402-403.

44. Larned, *History of Windham County*, Vol. II, p. 252. Citing Dwight, Larned also notes that Daniel Putnam was proprietor of the "largest dairy in town" and purveyor of "cheese not excelled by any this side of the Atlantic" at the end of the century through having purchased "much of the Malbone estate." Godfrey Malbone (1724-1785), had retreated to 3,000 acres in Pomfret and Brooklyn from Newport, R.I., in financial embarrassment in 1766. There, he settled into agriculture assisted by twenty-seven slaves, working with a complement of livestock willed to Godfrey and his brother John, that included 80 cows, 45 oxen, 30 steers, 40 two-year-olds, 20 yearlings, 39 calves, 6 horses, 600 sheep, 150 goats, and 150 hogs. Larned, *History of Windham*, Vol. II, pp. 6, 258.

45. Dwight, *Travels*, Vol. III, p. 93; Joseph Mathewson, father of Darius, purchased Colonel Israel Putnam's farm in 1795, neighboring, if not adjoining the Malbone-Putnam property. There Darius lived with his wife and they continued the tradition of making prize-winning cheese. Larned, *History of Windham County*, Vol. II, p. 262.

46. Larned, *History of Windham County*, Vol. II, pp. 388-97, passim.

47. Canterbury, pp. 398.

48. New London, p. 365.

49. Preston, p. 369.

50. Lisbon, p. 354.

51. Franklin, p. 349.

52. Main is discussing farms of 80 acres, which yielded "an average standard of living," to 120 acres. Jackson Turner Main, *Society and Economy in Colonial Connecticut* (Princeton, N.J.: Princeton University Press, 1985), pp. 214-15.

53. Other studies noting the same phenomenon include Sally McMurry, "Women and the Expansion of Dairying: The Cheesemaking Industry in Oneida County, New York, 1830-1860," unpublished paper presented at the Berkshire Conference, June 1987; unpublished training papers for the interpretation of the Emerson Bixby House at Old Sturbridge Village.

54. Main, *Society and Economy*, pp. 214-17.

55. Barbara E. Lacey, "The World of Hannah Heaton: The Autobiography of an Eighteenth-Century Connecticut Farm Woman," *William and Mary Quarterly*, 3d ser. vol. 65 (1988): 280-304, especially 287, 295-98.

56. Sarah Anna Emery, *Reminiscences of a Nonagenarian* (Newburyport, Mass., 1879), pp. 7-8.

57. Stephen Walkley Jr. (1832-1919), Southington, Conn., quoted in Abbott Lowell Cummings, "Notes on Furnishing a Small New England Farmhouse," *Old-Time New England*, 48 (1958): 83.

58. McMurry, *Transforming Rural Life*, 72-99. Quotes on p. 78 and 83.

59. Editions of *The Art of Cheesemaking* appear to have been published in Concord, N.H., by George Hough in 1793 (Evans microfiche series 25123), in Boston by Benjamin Edes in 1797 (not in Evans), and in 1798 in Windham (Evans 33315, but only 8 pages survive), and Litchfield, Connecticut (at AAS). Joshua Johnson's *The Art of Cheesemaking...was* published for the help of dairywomen in Albany at the press of Charles R. and George Webster in 1801 (Shaw-Shoemaker 739, 12 pp.). Reproducing an edition published in the previous year by Benjamin Edes of Boston, Evans 33315 is the eight extant pages of the American Antiquarian Society's Byrne imprint, not the Collier as it appears in the Short-Title Evans; 33316 is not in the Readex microfiche series.

60. "Butter Churns on a New Principle," *The Connecticut Magazine*, 1 (April 1801): 128-30.

61. *The Art of Cheesemaking, Taught From Actual Experiments, by which More and Better Cheese May be Made From the Same Quantity of Milk* (Windham, Conn.: John Byrne, 1798), p. 5.

62. Twamley, *Dairying Exemplified*, p. 7.

63. Twamley, *Dairying Exemplified*, p. 68.

64. "Butter Churns on a New Principle," pp. 128-30. The barrel churn and standard vertical churn were improved by the addition of a fly wheel and crank, as shown in an engraving by Amos Doolittle.

65. *Art of Cheesemaking*, p. 16.

66. See for example, on rennet: Maria Rundell, *A New System of Domestic Cookery* (New York, 1815), p. 254; *The Cook's Own Book* (Boston, 1832), p. 173, evidently intended to be used in making cheese cream and cheesecakes. Making and preserving hard cheese: Rundell, pp.

255-56; Mrs. Glasse, *The Art of Cookery Made Plain and Easy*, new. ed. (Alexandria, Va., 1805), p. 281.
67. Rundell, *Domestic Cookery*, p. 8.
68. Rundell, *Domestic Cookery*, pp. 255-56.
69. Twamley, *Dairying Exemplified*, pp. 64, 66.
70. Mary Ann Meredith, "The Dairymaid's Challenge," *Old Sturbridge Visitor*, 26 (Summer 1986): 9.
71. Laurel Thatcher Ulrich, "Wheels, Looms, and the Gender Division of Labor in Eighteenth-Century New England," *William and Mary Quarterly*, 3d Series, LV (January 1998): 3-38, quote on p. 35.

Moynihan
With "Unshaken Heroism and Fortitude"

1. Lebanon, p. 403. All quotations from Town Reports retain original spelling and punctuation, without the use of *sic*.
2. For an example of women weavers bartering their labor in the nearby town of Colchester, see "*Diaries of Abigail and Elizabeth Foote*," 1775, Mss., Connecticut Historical Society (CHS), excerpts in Ruth B. Moynihan, Cynthia Russett and Laurie Crumpacker, eds., *Second to None*, Vol. I (Lincoln: U. of Nebraska Press, 1993), p. 118-121, and Ruth B. Moynihan, *Coming of Age: Four Centuries of Connecticut Women* (Hartford: CHS, 1989, 1991), pp. *55-56*.
3. Lebanon, p. 403.
4. Cornwall (1800-1801), p. 98.
5. Cornwall (1800-1801), p. 99.
6. Cornwall (1800-1801), p. 107; Bethlem, p. 87.
7. Wallingford, p. 340; Winchester-Winsted, p. 164.
8. Sharon, p. 148.
9. Farmington, p. 65.
10. Lisbon (Hanover), p. 354; Ridgefield, p. 24; Pomfret, pp. 408, 407.
11. Bolton (N.), p. 374. England forbade the export of its industrial technology, but men who could learn and reproduce it by memory (like the more famous Samuel Slater of Rhode Island) were quick to make use of their skills in post-Revolutionary America. Mr. Warburton's "uncommon mechanical genius," learned in England where industrialization had begun in the mid-eighteenth century, must have given him great entrepreneurial advantages. Incidentally, an 1819 report about Vernon described "2 Cotton Factories, one of which, it is believed, was the first establishment in the State. . . " See John C. Pease and John M. Niles, *A Gazetteer of the States of Connecticut and Rhode Island* (Hartford: William S. Marsh, 1819), p. 302. Today these same mills sit empty and news reports tell of the town's continuing efforts to figure out what to do with them.
12. Timothy Dwight pointed out that "with the aid of this machine [the cotton gin], one person will cleanse a thousand pounds" of cotton in a day, whereas it had formerly been one pound a day per person. In 1811 New Haven had "one cotton manufactory, containing all the usual machinery for spinning and twisting cotton." New Haven, p. 318, 308.
13. Pomfret, p. 407. Pictures of some much later machines are in Harvey Green, *The Light of the Home: An Intimate View of the Lives of Women in Victorian America* (N.Y.: Pantheon, 1983), pp. 73-74. Green says, "The washing machine was an innovation of the post Civil-War era." Susan Strasser, in *Never Done: A History of American Housework* (N.Y.: Pantheon, 1982), p. 116, says, "The earliest clothes-washing machines imitated the motion of the human hand on the washboard, using a lever to move one curved surface over another, rubbing clothes between the two surfaces, each ribbed like a washboard." This washer was "Based on longstanding British precedents and first patented in the United States in 1846." She too says that, "home machines began to appear immediately following the Civil War." See also Ruth Schwartz Cowan, *More Work for Mother: The Ironies of Household Technology from the Open Hearth to the Microwave* (N.Y.: Basic Books, 1983), picture essay following p. 150.
14. Goshen, p. 116.
15. Watertown, p. 156; Franklin, p. 349; Litchfield County, p. 142; Stratfield, p. 32. *Webster's Third New International Dictionary* gives 56 pounds as the weight of a firkin of butter.
16. Goshen, pp. 115, 116.
17. Bethlem, pp. 86, 87. See Moynihan, *Coming of Age*, p. 56, for other hat-makers and also early silk-makers in Mansfield, Conn. See also Nancy F. Cott, *The Bonds of Womanhood: "Woman's Sphere" in New England, 1780-1835* (New Haven: Yale U. Press, 1977), pp. 39-40.
18. Ridgefield, p. 25; New Haven, p. 329.
19. New London, p. 364; Middlesex County, p. 188.

20. See Moynihan, *Coming of Age*, pp. 53-54, for two prescriptions found in a young woman's 1830s "friendship book," for the cure of "stricture" and "inward fever." They involved careful home preparation of mixed ingredients (several of which can be found in the list given by Dr. Eli Ives to New Haven's Timothy Dwight; New Haven, pp. 313-317). The handwritten notes and the "Friendship Book" of Lydia Amourette Kneeland (my great-great grandmother) are now in Connecticut Historical Society Collections.
21. Farmington, pp. 62-63; Cornwall (1800-1801), p. 104; Ridgefield, p. 25; New Haven, p. 311, see also pp. 313-317.
22. Goshen, p. 120.
23. Among the Town Reports, there appear to be only "one or two" refined flour mills, located in the prosperous town of East Windsor, which also had six grist mills—see East Windsor 1806, p. 40. See Cowan, "Milling Flour and Making Bread," in *More Work for Mother*, pp. 46-53, for analysis of changes involved when new refining mills replaced gristmills. Amelia Simmons' *American Cookery* (Hartford, 1796), the first cookbook printed in America, also deplored the use of garlic except for medicine. See Moynihan, *Coming of Age*, p. 53.
24. Lebanon, p. 403; Canterbury, p. 397.
25. Litchfield County, p. 141.
26. New Haven, p. 333; East Windsor, p. 41.
27. Guilford & Madison, pp. 256, 269; Cornwall, p. 101; Ridgefield, p. 28.
28. Litchfield, pp. 135, 132. This particular epidemic devastated the whole northeast during the Revolution. Abigail Adams, wife of statesman John Adams, wrote him eloquent, heart-breaking letters describing the care required under such circumstances, in which she nursed her niece and her mother and his brother, all of whom died. See Lyman Butterfield, ed., *The Adams Family Correspondence*, Vol. 1 (Cambridge: The Belknap Press of Harvard University Press, 1950), letters of Aug. 10, Sept. - Nov. 27, 1775; or see Butterfield, et al., *The Book of Abigail and John: Selected Letters of the Adams Family, 1762-1784* (Cambridge: Harvard Univ. Press, 1975), pp. 106-08, 112.
29. Union, pp. 385-386.
30. Wintonbury, p. 78.
31. New Haven, p. 327.
32. Middlesex County, p. 182.
33. New London, p. 364; Middlesex County, p. 182.
34. Pomfret, p. 408; Lisbon (Hanover), p. 354.
35. Farmington, pp. 73-74; Goshen, p. 118.
36. See Laurel Thatcher Ulrich, *A Midwife's Tale: The Life of Martha Ballard, Based on Her Diary, 1785-1812* (N.Y.: Knopf, 1990), pp 254-61; Richard W. and Dorothy C. Wertz, *Lying-In: A History of Childbirth in America* (N.Y.: Schocken, 1979), Chaps. 1, 2.
37. Wallingford, p. 342.
38. Canterbury, p. 399; Farmington, p. 72. Costume design for stylish young women in the 1820s featured low-cut gowns in flimsy materials.
39. Farmington, p. 51.
40. Farmington, p. 50.
41. Farmington, p. 50; Guilford and Madison, p. 270.
42. Farmington, p. 51.
43. Ridgefield, p. 28; Litchfield County, p. 133.
44. Middlesex County, pp. 227, 232. See Ann Lane Douglas, *The Feminization of American Culture* (N.Y.: Knopf, 1977).
45. Middlesex County, p. 193.
46. See Moynihan, *Coming of Age*, pp. 88-91. Stewart's speeches appear in Marilyn Richardson, ed., *America's First Black Women Political Writers* (Bloomington: U. of Indiana, 1987).
47. New Haven, p. 332.
48. Coventry, p. 379; Goshen, p. 120. Interestingly, it was Jesse Root's daughters who founded the "Female Friendly Society" in Coventry in 1812, for "the improvement of the female character . . . and the promotion of Christian knowledge and piety." See Betty Brook Messier and Janet Sutherland Aronson, *The Roots of Coventry, Connecticut* (Coventry: The 275th Anniversary Committee, 1987), pp. 155, 157. See also Cott, Chap. 4. The five Smith sisters and their mother of Glastonbury were notable for their activism, rooted in the social milieu of the time. See Kathleen L. Housley, *The Letter Kills But the Spirit Gives Life: The Smiths—Abolitionists, Suffragists, Bible Translators* (Glastonbury: Historical Society of Glastonbury, 1993).
49. Middlesex County, p. 187; Lebanon, p. 403; Wallingford, p. 340.
50. Preston, pp. 367-368.
51. Franklin, p. 349; Pomfret, p. 408; Cheshire, p. 249; Canterbury, p. 398; East Windsor, p. 40; Middlesex County, pp. 219, 187, 178—Whitestown had been founded by Hugh White, Esq. of Middletown in 1784 who was

followed by many families from the Middletown vicinity. It included "the whole western portion of New York; a tract which did not then contain 200 English inhabitants" but by 1812 had 280,000 people, "including the large and flourishing village of Utica, and the fine villages of Whitesborough and New Hartford."

52. Sharon, p. 145; Cornwall (1800-1801), p. 95. For a poignant account of what this meant in the life of one Connecticut woman, see Joy Day Buel & Richard Buel, Jr., *The Way of Duty: A Woman and Her Family in Revolutionary America* (N.Y.: W.W. Norton, 1984), pp. 235-45.

53. Farmington, p. 64. Peter Dobkin Hall, in *The Organization of American Culture, 1700-1900: Private Institutions, Elites, and the Origins of American Nationality* (N.Y.: N.Y.U. Press, 1982), has discussed Connecticut influence through migration and trade relationships. Cott, *Bonds of Womanhood*, p. 10, notes that "migrants...consciously contributed to the making of a nation (the Northern part of it, at least) in their image."

54. Historian Linda Kerber first coined the phrase "Republican Motherhood" to define this phenomenon, in *Women of the Republic: Intellect & Ideology in Revolutionary America* (Chapel Hill: U. of No. Carolina, 1980), p. 235 and Chaps 7-9. Also, Mary Beth Norton, *Liberty's Daughters: The Revolutionary Experience of American Women, 1750-1800* (Boston: Little, Brown and Co., 1980), pp. 228ff.

55. See Housley, *The Letter Kills But the Spirit Gives Life*, esp. Chaps. 1, 3, 4.

56. Middlesex County, pp. 181, 240-241.

57. Wallingford, p. 341; Goshen, p. 118; Union, p. 387; Winchester-Winsted, pp. 161, 164.

58. Cornwall (1800-1801), pp. 107, 101.

59. Farmington, p. 49.

60. Lebanon, p. 401.

61. Middlesex, p. 181; New Haven, pp. 321, 323-324.

62. New Haven, p. 324; New London, p. 364.

63. Winchester-Winsted, p. 164; Wallingford, p. 341; Cornwall (1800-1801), p. 107.

64. Litchfield, pp. 131, 135-136. For an excellent description of Litchfield in 1809, and of Miss Pierce's school, see Kathryn Kish Sklar, *Catharine Beecher: A Study in American Domesticity* (New Haven: Yale U. Press, 1973), Chap. 2. On July 4, 1839, nine years before the now famous Seneca Falls "Declaration of Sentiments," Miss Pierce's students issued a satirical "Ladies' Declaration of Independence"—see Moynihan, *Coming of Age*, pp. 97-98. The original is in Litchfield Historical Society Library.

65. Wallingford, p. 342. Both Kerber, *Women of the Republic*, and Norton, *Liberty's Daughters*, describe women's Revolutionary War activities. Barbara Lacey, "Women in the Era of the American Revolution," *New England Quarterly* 53 (Dec. 1980), cites numerous newspaper reports from Norwich, Ct. about women's activities.

66. *Hartford Courant*, Nov. 6, 1786, reprinted in Moynihan, *Coming of Age*, Fig. 31, p. 104, and Moynihan, et al., *Second to None*, Vol. I, pp. 193-94.

67. See Moynihan, *Coming of Age*, p. 96. Brewster, "An Acrostick for my Only Daughter," in *Poems on Divers Subjects* (New London, 1757). The "Female Advocate" is cited in Linda Kerber, *Women of the Republic*, p. 198.

68. Moynihan, *Coming of Age*, p. 88; the quote appears in Lacey, "Women in the Era of the American Revolution," p. 541, from "Minutes of the Ladies' Society, 1800-1805," Vol. l, Connecticut Historical Society.

69. Haddam, p. 170.

70. Middlesex County, p. 183.

71. Goshen, p. 118.

72. East Windsor, p. 42. See Moynihan, *Coming of Age*, p. 87, for an admiring description of Esther Stoddard Edwards by Theodore Dwight, quoted in Sereno Dwight, *Life of President Edwards* (N.Y., 1829), p. 18.

73. Cornwall (1800-1801), p. 102.

Appel
Disease and Medicine in Connecticut

1. Noah Webster, *A Brief History of Epidemic and Pestilential Diseases; with the Principal Phenomena of the Physical Word, Which Precede and Accompany Them, and Observations Deduced from the Facts Stated* (Hartford: Hudson & Goodwin, 1799); George Rosen, "Noah Webster—Historical Epidemiologist," *Journal of the History of Medicine and Allied Sciences* 20 (1965): 97-114.

2. Webster, *Brief History*, p. xi.

3. Elijah Munson, "On the Origin, Symptoms, & c. of the Yellow Fever, in New-Haven," pp. 174-184, and Eneas Munson, "On the Treatment Most Successful in the Cure of the Yellow Fever, in New-Haven, in 1794, &c. &c.," pp. 184-193, in Noah Webster, comp., *Collection of Papers on the Subject of Bilious Fevers, Prevalent in the United States for a Few Years Past* (New York: Hopkins, Webb and Co., 1796).

4. Webster, *Collection of Papers*, p. iv. In the face of epidemics, Connecticut towns took both types of measures; they instituted quarantines and passed local public health legislation. On public health in Connecticut at this time, see Ira Hiscock, "The Background of Public Health in Connecticut," in *The Heritage of Connecticut Medicine* ed. Herbert Thoms (New Haven: Whaples Bullis Company, 1942), pp. 137-150, 216-217; and Elizabeth A. Hodapp, "Public Health in Colonial New Haven," *Journal of the History of Medicine and Allied Sciences* 27 (1972): 54-64.

5. Webster, *Brief History*, p. viii; Webster, *Collection of Papers*, p. iv. On the debate over the origin of yellow fever in Philadelphia, see Martin S. Pernick, "Politics, Parties, and Pestilence: Epidemic Yellow Fever in Philadelphia and the Rise of the First Party System," in *A Melancholy State of Devastation: The Public Response to the 1793 Philadelphia Yellow Fever Epidemic*, ed. J. Worth Estes and Billy G. Smith (New York, Science History Publications, 1997), pp. 119-146.

6. Webster, *Collection of Papers*, pp. vi-x. See also *Noah Webster: Letters on Yellow Fever Addressed to Dr. William Currie* (Baltimore: Johns Hopkins University Press, 1947). This volume reprints letters addressed by Webster to the eminent Philadelphia physician, William Currie, who espoused a contagionist view of yellow fever, and published in the (New York) *Commercial Advertiser* in 1797.

7. Noah Webster, "To the Clergymen or other well-informed Gentlemen in the several Towns in Connecticut," New Haven, May 7, 1798, circular reprinted in *Medical Repository* 2 (1799): 112-114, quote on p. 113.

8. James H. Cassedy, *Demography in Early America: Beginnings of the Statistical Mind, 1600-1800* (Cambridge, Mass.: Harvard University Press, 1969), esp. pp. 274-304.

9. The Academy's plan to collect such medically-related data was reported in "Plan for Observations on the Weather, Seasons, and Physical Phenomena," *Medical Repository* 3 (1800): 299-300.

10. Tolland, p. 383. On the healthiness of the local environment, see also Goshen, p. 118; Wallingford, p. 342; Union, p. 387; Willington, p. 392; Litchfield County, pp. 132, 140. On swamps and marshes, see Farmington, p. 72; Union, p. 386; Wintonbury (Bloomfield), p. 78; Lebanon, p. 402; Lisbon (Hanover), p. 354; Ridgefield, p. 28; and Goshen, p. 118.

11. Bethlem, p. 84.

12. On the various diseases in Connecticut around 1800, see Linda Ann McKee, "Health and Medicine in Connecticut, 1785-1810," Ph.D. dissertation, University of New Mexico, 1971. On the belief in the transmutability of diseases and their regional distinctiveness, see John Harley Warner, *The Therapeutic Perspective: Medical Practice, Knowledge, and Identity in America, 1820-1885* (Princeton, N.J.: Princeton University Press, 1997). For an example of diseases assuming varied forms, see Elisha North's discussion of an unusual "epidemic fever" in Goshen in 1795. Goshen, p. 118.

13. The Sharon Report recalled that about the time of the settlement of the town, a Moravian minister took a large number of Native Americans to Pennsylvania "where they took the small pox and all except three died." Sharon, p. 145.

14. Ernest Caulfield, *A True History of the Terrible Epidemic Vulgarly called the Throat Distemper*. (New Haven: Published for the Beaumont Medical Club by the Yale Journal of Biology and Medicine, 1939), esp. pp. 78-92; Bethlem, pp. 83, 87; Farmington, pp. 71-72; Goshen, p. 118; Guilford, p. 257; New Haven, p. 327; Pomfret, p. 408; Ridgefield, p. 28; McKee, pp. 74-80.

15. Wallingford, p. 342.

16. On smallpox in America, see Donald R. Hopkins, *Princes and Peasants: Smallpox in History* (Chicago: University of Chicago Press, 1983), pp. 234-294.

17. McKee, pp. 49-62, esp. pp. 52-53.

18. Ridgefield, p. 28.

19. Guilford, p. 257.

20. Goshen, p. 118; Sebastian R. Italia, "Elisha North: Experimentalist, Epidemiologist, Physician, 1771-1843," *Bulletin of the History of Medicine* 31 (1957): 505-536.

21. As reported by McKee, p. 58.

22. Bethlem, pp. 83, 84; Farmington, pp. 71-72; Goshen, 118; Lebanon, p.

403; Litchfield County, p. 139; New Haven, p. 327. Typhoid fever is a bacterial disease that is often spread by polluted water. Typhus epidemics, caused by rickettsia and transmitted by insect vectors, are associated with filth and overcrowding and were prevalent in places such as military camps. Although no definitive diagnosis can be made of the "typhus" described in the Town Reports, the disease was much more likely to have been typhoid fever than typhus. The two conditions were not clearly distinguished until the mid-nineteenth century.

23. Farmington, p. 72; Guilford, p. 257; Lebanon, p. 403; Lisbon (Hanover), p. 354; Litchfield County, p. 132 (see also p. 139); New Haven, p. 327; Stratfield, p. 33; Wintonbury (Bloomfield), p. 78; McKee, pp. 70-74. The term dysentery now refers to several infections, some of which are caused by a bacillus and some by a plasmodium.

24. Lisbon (Hanover), p. 354. On malaria, see also McKee, pp. 95-100.

25. Lebanon, p. 403.

26. New Haven, p. 327; Elijah Munson, esp. pp. 177, 182, and Eneas Munson, esp. p. 192. See also McKee, pp. 62-69; and Frederick H. Hoadley, "A Review of the History of the Epidemic of Yellow Fever in New Haven, Conn. in the Year 1794." *Papers of the New Haven Colony Historical Society* 6 (1900): 223-261.

27. New London, p. 364. "An Account of the Pestilential Disease which prevailed at New-London (Connecticut), in the Summer and Autumn of 1798; communicated in a Letter from the Rev. Henry Channing to Dr. Mitchill," *Medical Repository* 2 (1799): 402-44; Thomas Coit, "Additional Account of the Pestilential Fever which prevailed at New-London (Connecticut); communicated in a Letter from Dr. Coit to Dr. Mitchill, dated New-London, January 11, 1799." *Medical Repository* 2 (1799): 407-408; Alfred Labensky, "Samuel Holden Parsons Lee and Yellow Fever in New London," in Thoms, *Heritage of Connecticut Medicine,* pp. 114-120. Labensky states that there were 350 cases and 81 deaths from August through October 1798, although he does not cite sources.

28. Farmington, pp. 73-74, esp. p. 73. Spinal meningitis is an inflammation, usually bacterial, of the membranes covering the spinal cord.

29. Goshen, p. 118; Elisha North, *A Treatise on a Malignant Epidemic, Commonly Called Spotted Fever; Interspersed with Remarks on the Nature of Fever in General, &c.* (New York: T. and J. Swords, 1811), esp. p. 7; Italia, p. 514; McKee, pp.81-88.

30. See McKee, pp. 92-94 (measles), pp. 94-95 (influenza), pp. 118-120 (worms), and pp. 132-135 (pneumonia and pleurisy).

31. Farmington, p. 72; Lisbon (Hanover), p. 354; and Preston, p. 369. See also North, *Treatise on a Malignant Epidemic,* p. 37. On the classification of fevers, see Lester S. King, *Transformations in American Medicine: From Benjamin Rush to William Osler* (Baltimore: Johns Hopkins University Press, 1991), pp. 36-65.

32. Bethlem, p. 87. On the *Medical Repository,* see Richard J. Kahn and Patricia G. Kahn, "The Medical Repository – The First U.S. Medical Journal (1797-1824)," *New England Journal of Medicine* 337 (December 25, 1977): 1926-1930. Over a quarter of the original subscribers were not physicians. On Smith, see *The Diary of Elihu Hubbard Smith (1771-1798),* ed. James A. Cronin (Philadelphia: American Philosophical Society, 1973).

33. Cassedy, *Demography in Early America,* 23-40; James H. Cassedy, "Church Record-Keeping and Public Health in Early New England," in *Medicine in Colonial Massachusetts, 1620-1820,* eds. Philip Cash, Eric H. Christianson, and J. Worth Estes (Boston: The Colonial Society of Massachusetts, 1980), pp. 249-262.

34. The Rev. Azel Backus, "Some Account of the Epidemics which Have Occurred in the Town of Bethlem, Connecticut; from its Settlement to the Present Time, Extracted from a Letter to Mr. Smith," *Medical Repository* 1 (1798): 523-525, quote on p. 523. For the full text of Backus's "Account" see note #12 for the Bethlem Town Report in the present publication.

35. Bethlem, p. 86. Similar data were given for 1810 in which 17 "persons not taxed" were not part of the breakdown. See Bethlem, p. 87.

36. New Haven, p. 333.

37. Litchfield County, p. 141. There were 703 other members of the population left out of the age breakdown, either because they were not taxed or slave. Data were also provided for the town of Litchfield in 1810.

38. See T.H. Hollingsworth, *Historical Demography* (Ithaca, NY: Cornell University Press, 1969), pp. 139-147. I thank James Hanley for this reference and for assistance in interpreting the statistical data in the reports.

39. Guilford, p. 257.

40. Guilford, p. 257.

41. Bethlem, p. 87.

42. Litchfield County, p. 135.

43. Litchfield County, p. 140.

44. Wintonbury, p. 78; Lisbon (Hanover), p. 354.

45. New Haven, p. 333. See also data for 1752-1785 for the First Society of Farmington. Farmington, p. 72.

46. Litchfield County, p. 139.

47. Bethlem, p. 87; Litchfield County, p. 139; Lisbon (Hanover), p. 354.

48. Bethlem, p. 87; Litchfield County, pp. 139; Lisbon (Hanover), p. 354; New Haven, p. 333.

49. Farmington, p. 72.

50. Farmington, p. 69.

51. See, for example, Farmington, pp. 64, 70; Litchfield County, p. 133; New Haven, pp. 318, 325.

52. On mental illness, see Gerald N. Grob, *The Mad among Us: A History of the Care of America's Mentally Ill* (Cambridge, MA: Harvard University Press, 1994).

53. Litchfield County, p. 136.

54. Ridgefield, p. 28.

55. On theories of disease, see King, pp. 36-65. On therapeutics, see Charles E. Rosenberg, "The Therapeutic Revolution: Medicine, Meaning, and Social Change in Nineteenth-Century America," in *The Therapeutic Revolution: Essays in the Social History of American Medicine,* ed. Morris J. Vogel and Charles E. Rosenberg (Philadelphia: University of Pennsylvania Press, 1979), pp. 3-25; J. Worth Estes, "Medical Skills in Colonial New England," *New England Historical and Genealogical Register* 134 (1980): 259-275; and J. Worth Estes, "Therapeutic Practice in Colonial New England," in Cash, et al., *Medicine in Colonial Massachusetts, 1620-1820,* pp. 289-379.

56. Farmington, p. 73; North, *Treatise on a Malignant Epidemic.*

57. New Haven, pp. 313-317. The Town Reports blamed the barberry bush and St. John's wort, originally introduced for medicinal purposes, for significant agricultural damage. See Ridgefield, p. 26; and Preston, p. 369.

58. Estes, "Medical Skills in Colonial New England"; Estes, "Therapeutic Practice in Colonial New England."

59. On medicinal springs, see Kent, p. 124; Litchfield County, pp. 130, 137; New London, p. 362; Preston, p. 368; and Union, p. 385. On Stafford Springs, see Estrellita Karsh, "Taking the Waters at Stafford Springs: The Role of the Willard Family of Boston in America's First Health Spa," *Harvard Library Bulletin* 28 (1980): 264-281.

60. On minister/physicians in New England in the seventeenth and eighteenth centuries, see Patricia A. Watson, *The Angelical Conjunction: The Preacher-Physicians of Colonial New England* (Knoxville: University of Tennessee Press, 1991). Watson (pp. 147-151) identifies some 33 minister/physicians who began ministerial careers between 1630 and 1770 and who died in Connecticut. On Eliot, see Herbert Thoms, *The Doctors of Yale College 1702-1815 and The Founding of the Medical Institution* (Hamden, Conn., Shoe String Press, 1960), pp. 17-23. On Collins, who was also a graduate of Yale College, see Litchfield County, p. 132.

61. For general discussions of New England physicians in the eighteenth and early nineteenth centuries, see Richard D. Brown, "The Healing Arts in Colonial and Revolutionary Massachusetts: The Context for Scientific Medicine," in *Medicine in Colonial Massachusetts, 1620-1820,* pp. 35-47; and Eric H. Christianson, "Medicine in New England," in *Medicine in the New World: New Spain, New France, and New England,* ed. Ronald L. Numbers. (Knoxville, Tenn.: University of Tennessee Press, 1987), pp. 101-153. Nineteenth-century minister/physicians were likely to be medical missionaries.

62. New Haven, p. 319. See also Goshen, p. 117; Litchfield, p. 130; and Tolland, p. 383.

63. McKee, pp. 69, 206-222.

64. On popular medicine, see Charles E. Rosenberg and William Helfand eds.,*"Every Man His Own Doctor": Popular Medicine in Early America* (Philadelphia: The Library Company of Philadelphia, 1998) which contains essays by Charles Rosenberg and William Helfand. On American editions of Buchan and other popular titles, see Robert B. Austin, *Early American Medical Imprints, 1668-1820* (Washington, D.C.: National Library of Medicine, 1961).

65. Rebecca J. Tannenbaum, "'What is Best to Be Done for These Fevers': Elizabeth Davenport's Medical Practice in New Haven Colony," *New England Quarterly* 70 (1997): 265-284; Rebecca J. Tannenbaum, *The Healer's Calling: Women and Medicine in Early New England* (Ithaca, N. Y.: Cornell Univ. Press, 2002). Elizabeth Davenport, wife of the first minister of New Haven, treated members of her community, albeit not for pay. Some early women healers in New England were called "doctresses" and charged for their services. On Ballard, see Laurel Thatcher Ulrich, *A Midwife's Tale: The Life of Martha Ballard, Based on Her Diary, 1785-*

1812 (New York: Knopf, 1990).

66. Rebecca Rogers Hobart, b. 1732, Record book, 1765-1801, MANUS 44902, Connecticut Historical Society; Philena Smith Hickox, Record book, 1791-1813, MANUS 93838, Connecticut Historical Society. See also Jennet Boardman (1765-1849), Record books, 1815-1849, MANUS 79112, Connecticut Historical Society. Boardman, who practiced in Hartford, attended a total of 1053 births.

67. The Farmington Report noted the importance of alert "nurses & tenders" to the outcome of treatment for spotted fever, and also the need for the town to hire nurses to care for the sick in the alms house. Farmington, pp. 70, 74.

68. A list Yale graduates, 1702-1815, who practiced medicine is found in Thoms, pp. 177-182. One of the few Connecticut physicians in the 1790s to have a medical degree was Samuel Willard, manager of the spa at Stafford Springs, who graduated from Harvard Medical School in 1787 and returned to Connecticut in 1795. See Karsh, "Taking the Waters at Stafford Springs."

69. Barnes Riznik, "The Professional Lives of Early Nineteenth-Century New England Doctors," *Journal of the History of Medicine and Allied Sciences* 19 (1964): 1-16, esp. pp. 14-15. On institutional development in Massachusetts, see Philip Cash, "The Professionalization of Boston Medicine, 1760-1803," in Cash, et al., *Medicine in Colonial Massachusetts*, pp. 69-100.

70. Gert M.K. Wallach "Background of the Litchfield County Medical Association of 1767," *Connecticut Medicine* 31 (April 1967): 270-271; Byron Stookey "A Medical Society for the Massachusetts, New York and Connecticut Physicians, 1779-1790," *Connecticut Medicine* 30 (March 1966): 189-192.

71. The petition is reprinted in *Reprint of the Proceedings of the Connecticut Medical Society from 1792 to 1829 Inclusive* (Hartford: The Case, Lockwood & Brainard Company, 1884) [henceforth, Proc. CMS], p. iii.

72. Creighton Barker, "The Origin of the Connecticut State Medical Society," in Thoms, *The Heritage of Connecticut Medicine*, 1-9; New Haven County Medical Society, *Cases and Observations; by the Medical Society of New Haven County, in the State of Connecticut, Instituted in the Year 1784* (New Haven: Printed by J. Meigs, 1788); George Blumer, "*Some Remarks on 'Cases and Observations; by the Medical Society of New Haven County,'*" in *The Heritage of Connecticut Medicine*, pp. 10-23, 213-214. In the 1780s the proposed state society was to have a membership limited to seventy, similar to the early Massachusetts Medical Society.

73. Proc. CMS, pp. vi-viii.

74. The members are listed in Proc. CMS, May 15, 1793, pp. 12-16. Population data are from U.S. Bureau of the Census, *Historical Statistics of the United States Colonial Times to 1957* (Washington D.C., Bureau of the Census, 1969), p. 13.

75. Proc. CMS, pp. ix, May 1800, p. 77.

76. Proc. CMS, May 17, 1796, p. 40; Proc. CMS, May 1797, p. 50. On Perkins, see Jacques M. Quen, "Elisha Perkins, Physician, Nostrum-Vendor, or Charlatan?" *Bulletin of the History of Medicine* 37 (1963): 159-166.

77. Proc. CMS, October 19, 1804, pp. 113-114; Proc. CMS, October 16-17, 1805, pp. 117-119.

78. New Haven, p. 323.

79. On the founding and early years of the Medical Institution of Yale College, see Whitfield Bell, "The Medical Institution of Yale College, 1810 1885," *Yale Journal of Biology and Medicine* 33 (Dec. 1960): 169-183; Herbert Thoms, "Ezra Stiles and the Plan of a University," and "Timothy Dwight and the Medical Institution of Yale College," in Thoms, *The Doctors of Yale College*, 101-109, 111-121; Harold S. Burr, "The Connecticut State Medical Society and the Medical Institution of Yale College," in Thoms, *Heritage of Connecticut Medicine*, pp. 24-30; and Gerard N. Burrow, *A History of Yale's School of Medicine: Passing Torches to Others* (New Haven: Yale University Press, 2002).

80. Cash, p. 91.

81. *General Hospital Society of Connecticut Centenary, 1826-1926* (New Haven: The Society, 1926), p. 5. On the nineteenth-century hospital, see Charles E. Rosenberg, *The Care of Strangers: The Rise of America's Hospital System* (New York: Basic Books, 1987).

82. This was the third such mental asylum in the United States, after Philadelphia and Boston. See Gerald N. Grob, pp. 33-34; Thoms, *Doctors of Yale College*, pp. 65-69.

Hinks
The Connecticut Academy
and Black Emancipation

The author wishes to express his appreciation to the following individuals for their thoughtful comments on this essay: Carolyn Cooper, Doug Egerton, Robert Forbes, Howard Lamar, Donna Pintek, James B. Stewart, and David Waldstreicher.

1. "An Act to Incorporate the Connecticut Academy of Arts & Sciences," 1799, Connecticut Academy of Arts & Sciences Archives, Manuscripts & Archives, Yale University Library.

2. See the Connecticut Town Reports Solicitation Letter of 1800 in the front of this volume.

3. The following works treat emancipation in the North in the late eighteenth and early nineteenth centuries: Arthur Zilversmit, *The First Emancipation: The Abolition of Slavery in the North* (Chicago: University of Chicago Press, 1967); Graham Hodges, *Slavery and Freedom in the Rural North: African Americans in Monmouth County, New Jersey, 1665-1865* (Madison, Wisc. Madison House, 1997); Graham Hodges, *Root & Branch: African Americans in New York & East Jersey, 1613-1863* (Chapel Hill: University of North Carolina Press, 1999); Gary Nash, *Freedom by Degrees: Emancipation in Pennsylvania and Its Aftermath* (New York: Oxford University Press, 1991); Gary Nash, *Forging Freedom: The Formation of Philadelphia's Black Community, 1720-1840* (Cambridge: Harvard University Press, 1988); Shane White, *Somewhat More Independent: The End of Slavery in New York City, 1770-1810* (Athens, GA: University of Georgia Press, 1991); Joanne Pope Melish, *Disowning Slavery: Gradual Emancipation and "Race" in New England, 1780-1860* (Ithaca: Cornell University Press, 1998); Richard Newman, "The Transformation of American Abolition: Tactics, Strategies and the Changing Meanings of Activism, 1780s-1830s," Ph.D Diss.: State University of New York at Buffalo, 1998.

4. Jonathan Edwards, Jr., "The Injustice and Impolicy of the Slave-Trade, and of Slavery of the Africans" (Providence, 1792), p. 30.

5. Simeon Baldwin, "Address to the Connecticut Society for the Abolition of Slavery," pp. 29, 10 May 1792, Series IV, box #69, folder #831, Baldwin Family Papers, Manuscripts & Archives, Yale University Library.

6. Joseph Bloomfield, President of the American Convention of Abolition Societies, to the Connecticut Society for Promoting the Abolition of Slavery, 7 January 1794, Series I, box #5, folder #82, Baldwin Family Papers, Manuscripts & Archives, Yale University Library.

7. While Federalist rule in Connecticut was secure throughout the 1790s, early opposition to the ancient balloting system and to state support for the Congregational church was growing. The opposition leader then was Abraham Bishop who, unlike most Republicans, was vehemently opposed to slavery, sanctioned the slave revolt in St. Domingue, ridiculed the Federalist's "Liberating Societies" as he called them, and vituperated their state-supported church. He helped forge a far more vigorous opposition after the turn of the century. See Tim Matthewson, "Abraham Bishop, 'The Rights of Black Men,' and the American Reaction to the Haitian Revolution," *Journal of Negro History*, 67 (Summer 1982): 148-53.

8. Thomas Jefferson, *Notes on the State of Virginia*, ed. William Peden (New York: W.W. Norton & Co., 1972), p. 143.

9. Jefferson, *Notes on the State of Virginia*, p. 143.

10. See "Letters and Documents Relating to Slavery in Massachusetts," Massachusetts Historical Society, *Collections*, Fifth Series, 3 (1877), pp. 373-431 & "Queries Respecting the Slavery and Emancipation of Negroes in Massachusetts, Proposed by the Hon. Judge Tucker of Virginia, and Answered by the Rev. Dr. Belknap," Massachusetts Historical Society, *Collections*, First Series, 4 (1795), pp. 191-211.

11. "Queries Respecting the Emancipation of Negroes," p. 380.

12. St. George Tucker, "A Dissertation on Slavery: With a Proposal for the Gradual Abolition of It, in the State of Virginia" (Philadelphia, 1796). See also Winthrop Jordan, *White Over Black: American Attitudes Toward the Negro, 1550-1812* (Chapel Hill, N.C., Univ. of North Carolina Press, 1968), pp. 555-61.

13. The following works treat slavery in Connecticut and New England: Lorenzo Greene, *The Negro in Colonial New England* (New York: Atheneum, 1968); William D. Piersen, *Black Yankees: The Development of an Afro-American Subculture in Eighteenth-Century New England* (Amherst: University of Massachusetts Press, 1988); Bruce Stark, "Slavery in Connecticut: A Re-Examination," *The Connecticut Review* 9 (November

1975): 75-81; Bernard C. Steiner, *History of Slavery in Connecticut* (Baltimore, 1893); William C. Fowler, "The Historical Status of the Negro, in Connecticut" in William C. Fowler, *Local Law in Massachusetts and Connecticut Historically Considered* (Albany, 1872), pp. 113-48; Frederick Calvin Norton, "Negro Slavery in Connecticut," *The Connecticut Magazine* 5 (June 1899): 320-28; Ralph Foster Weld, *Slavery in Connecticut* (Hartford: Tercentenary Commission of the State of Connecticut, 1935); Mary H. Mitchell, "Slavery in Connecticut and Especially in New Haven," *Papers of the New Haven Colony Historical Society* 10 (New Haven, 1951): 286-312; Jane DeForest Shelton, "The New England Negro. A Remnant," *Harper's New Monthly Magazine* 88 (December 1893-May 1894): 533-38.

14. William Leete, quoted in J. Hammond Trumbull and Charles J. Hoadley, eds., *The Public Records of the Colony of Connecticut*; herein after *Public Records of the Colony of Connecticut* (Hartford, 1859-1890), Vol. 3, p. 298.

15. Bernard Steiner grossly overestimates the number of slaves in Connecticut in 1715 at 1,500. See Steiner, *History of Slavery in Connecticut*, p. 84. Lorenzo Greene's figure for 1730—700 slaves—which is drawn from British Board of Trade estimates is more accurate. Greene, *The Negro in Colonial New England*, p. 90.

16. *Public Records of the Colony of Connecticut*, Vol. 5, pp. 52-53. For further slave regulations, see *Public Records of the Colony of Connecticut*, Vol. 6, pp. 390-91; and *Public Records of the Colony of Connecticut*, Vol. 7, p. 290.

17. *Public Records of the Colony of Connecticut*, Vol. 7, p. 584, and *Public Records of the Colony of Connecticut*, Vol. 9, p. 596.

18. *Public Records of the Colony of Connecticut*, Vol. 10, pp. 618, 623. Bruce Stark's invaluable calculations indicate that the latter figure is probably the more accurate one although not for the reasons indicated in the original report to the Board of Trade. See Stark, "Slavery in Connecticut," pp. 75-81.

19. *Public Records of the Colony of Connecticut*, Vol. 11, p. 630.

20. *Public Records of the Colony of Connecticut*, Vol. 13, pp. 485-92, 499. There is a very significant error in census calculations for blacks in 1774 which ripples through the work of the great scholar of New England slavery, Lorenzo Greene, and the less meticulous Bernard Steiner. The final tabulation of total blacks in the colony on p. 491—6,464—actually includes the total number of Indians in the colony as well. The correct figure is the one cited in the text and that is drawn from the total number of blacks listed as living in each of the counties listed on pp. 485-90. See also Stark, "Slavery in Connecticut," pp. 75-81.

21. Joanne Melish in her book on emancipation and its aftermath in New England makes an interesting argument for the greater impact of slave labor on the growth of the New England economy in the eighteenth century than determined by several other contemporary economic historians who have confined the impact of that labor to non-productive, marginal, household work that had little impact on economic growth. In part, Melish suggests that the slaves' household labors well may have freed numerous white males to engage in more expansive commercial activities. Melish, *Disowning Slavery*, pp. 12-23.

22. For an illustration of this dispersal, see the map (Figure 1) in Piersen, *Black Yankees*, pp. 16-17. For more exact figures of their population in numerous Connecticut towns, see *Public Records of the Colony of Connecticut*, Vol. 10, pp. 78-79, and especially *Public Records of the Colony of Connecticut*, Vol. 13, pp. 485-92.

23. Greene, *The Negro in Colonial New England*, pp. 107-08; Mary E. Perkins, *Chronicles of a Connecticut Farm* (Boston, 1905), pp. 61-63; Howard W. Preston, "Godfrey Malbone's Connecticut Investment," *Collections* of the Rhode Island Historical Society, 16 (October 1923), pp. 115-19. For a fascinating story of the slaves on the Browne estate during and after the Revolution, see Alfred M. Bingham, "Squatter Settlements of Freed Slaves in New England," *Bulletin* of the Connecticut Historical Society, 41 (July 1976), pp. 65-80.

24. Melish, *Disowning Slavery*, p. 16.

25. For the most thorough treatment of the slavery of New England as "family slavery," see Piersen, *Black Yankees*, pp. 25-48, 93-95.

26. Regarding the annual ritual of electing black governors in New England, see Piersen, *Black Yankees*, pp. 117-40.

27. While however focusing on the plantations of the Narragansett region and their larger numbers of slaves, Robert K. Fitts has significantly challenged this conventional understanding of New England slavery in *Inventing New England's Slave Paradise: Master/Slave Relations in Eighteenth-Century Narragansett, Rhode Island* (New York: Garland Publishing, 1998).

28. "A Customer," *The Connecticut Journal, and the New-Haven Post-Boy*, 31 December 1771.

29. Samuel Sewall, "The Selling of Joseph: A Memorial" (Boston, 1701); Elihu Coleman, "A Testimony Against That Anti-Christian Practice of Making Slaves of Men" (Boston, 1733).

30. *The Public Records of the Colony of Connecticut*, Vol. 4, p. 40.

31. *The Connecticut Journal; and New-Haven Post-Boy*, 18 December 1767 and 1, 8 January 1768.

32. *The Connecticut Journal; and the New Haven Post-Boy*, 21 December 1774.

33. Levi Hart, "Some Thoughts on the Subject of Freeing the Negro Slaves in the Colony of Connecticut, Humbly Offered to the Consideration of All Friends to Liberty and Justice" (1775), Connecticut Historical Society.

34. Hart, "Some Thoughts," p. 4.

35. Hart, "Some Thoughts," p. 4.

36. Hart, "Some Thoughts," pp. 6-7.

37. Hart, "Some Thoughts," p. 4. Joanne Melish significantly fails to recognize this expansion of civic liberty, which Hart anticipated for freed blacks as the process of gradual emancipation unfolded over the years. Instead, she claims Hart expected that the emancipated would continue largely without individual agency and that their direction would be passed from private individuals to the community at large through extended apprenticeship programs and stern penalties for any black malefactors. Melish, *Disowning Slavery*, pp. 57-64.

38. Jonathan Edwards, Jr., vividly summarizes these positions in Edwards, "The Injustice and Impolicy of the Slave Trade, and of the Slavery of the Africans: Illustrated in a Sermon Preached before the Connecticut Society for the Promotion of Freedom, and for the Relief of Persons Unlawfully Holden in Bondage, at Their Annual Meeting in New Haven, Sept. 15, 1791" (Boston: Wells and Lily, 1822), p. 33.

39. Joanne Melish either ignores or is unaware of the spectrum of white opinion regarding and hopes for black freedom in 1780s-90s. She incorrectly argues that whites exclusively sought to evade "the emerging necessity of creating a new set of relations with free people of color and, instead, [to transfer] to them their old assumptions about slaves as publicly available commodities in permanent need of direction and control. The effect was to undermine any possibility of a shared entitlement between people of color and whites to real freedom and its fruits which might otherwise have taken root as slavery withered." Melish, *Disowning Slavery*, p. 107.

40. Hart, "Some Thoughts," p. 4; Noah Webster, "Effects of Slavery on Morals and Industry" (Hartford, 1793), p. 40.

41. Webster, "Effects of Slavery on Morals and Industry," p. 37.

42. See, for example, Vincent Rosivach, "Three Petitions by Connecticut Negroes for the Abolition of Slavery in Connecticut," *Connecticut Review* (Fall 1995), pp. 79-92, David O. White, *Connecticut's Black Soldiers, 1775-1783* (Chester, Conn: Pequot Press, 1973); and Venture Smith, *A Narrative of the Life and Adventures of Venture, a Native of Africa, but Resident Sixty_Years in the United States of America* (New London, Conn, 1798).

43. Webster noted deleterious effects of centuries of subjugation upon the character of the Irish and of Jews: "Effects of Slavery on Morals and Industry," pp. 9-10.

44. See, for example, Webster, "Effects of Slavery on Morals and Industry," pp. 13, 37; and Zephaniah Swift, "An Oration on Domestic Slavery" (Hartford, 1791), pp. 18-19.

45. Noah Webster thought slavery could be extirpated in the South over the course of two centuries: "Effects of Slavery on Morals and Industry," pp. 37-38. See also Swift, "An Oration on Domestic Slavery," p. 19; and Edwards, "The Injustice and Impolicy of the Slave Trade," p. 38.

46. Henry Channing to Simeon Baldwin, 22 November 1790, Baldwin Family Papers, Series I, Box #4, Folder #66, Manuscripts and Archives, Yale University Library.

47. *Connecticut Journal* 28 January 1796.

48. Union, p. 387.

49. Willington, p. 392.

50. Pomfret, p. 407; Winchester, p. 161; Ridgefield, p. 27.

51. New London, p. 364.

52. Cheshire, p. 250; East Windsor, p. 40; Lebanon, p. 403; Lisbon (Hanover), p. 355; Farmington, p. 70; Sharon, p. 149; New Haven, p. 325.

53. Farmington, p. 70; Sharon, p. 149; Lebanon, p. 403; Cheshire, p. 250; New Haven, p. 325; New London, p. 364; Willington, p. 392; Winchester, p. 161.

54. Sharon, p. 149; New London, p. 364; Stratfield, p. 33.

55. Lebanon, p. 403.

56. Ulrich Bonnell Phillips, *American Negro Slavery: A Survey of the Supply, Employment and Control of Negro Labor as Determined by the*

Plantation Regime (Baton Rouge: Louisiana State University Press, 1969), pp. 342-43. (First published in 1918.)

57. Wallingford, pp. 341-342.

58. Dwight, "The Charitable Blessed: A Sermon Preached in the First Church in New Haven" (New Haven: Sidney's Press, 1810), pp. 20-21.

59. Dwight, "The Charitable Blessed," pp. 20-21.

60. Dwight, "The Charitable Blessed," p. 22.

61. Dwight, "The Charitable Blessed," pp. 20-21.

62. Dwight, "The Charitable Blessed," p. 20.

63. Re-enfranchisement did not occur until 1869!

64. James Truslow Adams, "Disfranchisement of Negroes in New England," *American Historical Review* 30 (April 1925): 545.

65. "Letter from Genl. Robert Goodloe Harper" in *First Annual Report of the American Society for Colonizing the Free People of Colour of the United States* (Washington, DC, 1818), pp.15, 16. See also Philip J. Staudenraus, *The African Colonization Movement, 1816-1865* (New York: Columbia University Press, 1961).

66. Information on officers in the New Haven auxiliary of the American Colonization Society can be found in *The Third Annual Report of the American Society for Colonizing the Free People of Colour of the United States* (Washington, 1820), p. 139.

67. See, for example, William Law & Elnathan Beech to Simeon Baldwin, David Daggett, & Elizur Goodrich, 26 April 1792; Theodore Dwight to Elizur Goodrich, David Daggett, & Simeon Baldwin, 14 June 1792; and David Daggett to Simeon Baldwin, 20 January 1793, in Baldwin Family Papers, Series I, Box #5, folders #74 & #76, Manuscripts & Archives, Yale University Library.

68. Leonard Bacon, "A Plea for Africa; Delivered in New Haven, July 4th, 1825" (New Haven: T. G. Woodward &Co., 1825), pp. 12-13.

69. [Leonard Bacon], "Review of the Reports of the American Colonization Society" (New Haven, 1823?), p. 11.

70. Bacon, "Review of the Reports," p. 20.

71. Leonard Bacon, "Review on African Colonization," *Quarterly Christian Spectator* 2 (September 1830), p. 472.

72. Bacon, "Review of the Reports," p. 17.

73. Bacon, "Review of the Reports," pp. 14, 17.

74. Bacon, "Review of the Reports," p. 13.

75. This is only the barest treatment of this important early nineteenth-century theological transformation and its relationship to contemporary racial trends. The following works offer a much more thorough review: Joseph A. Conforti, *Samuel Hopkins and the New Divinity Movement: Calvinism, the Congregational Ministry, and Reform in New England Between the Great Awakenings* (Grand Rapids, Mich.: Christian University Press, 1981); Hugh Davis, *Leonard Bacon: New England Reformer and Antislavery Moderate* (Baton Rouge: Louisiana State University Press, 1998), pp. 42-64; Hugh Davis, "Northern Colonizationists and Free Blacks, 1823-1837: A Case Study of Leonard Bacon," *Journal of the Early Republic*, 17 (Winter 1997), pp. 651-75.

76. Wallingford, pp. 341-342.

77. See note 6.

78. In a pathbreaking synthesis of a remarkable range of contemporary research on race, antislavery, and society in the early national and antebellum North, Prof. James Brewer Stewart illuminates the deep discouragement black activists of the 1830s encountered when continuing to promote moral improvement as the principal strategy for achieving black advance and inclusion in American society while anti-black Jacksonians and working-class whites increasingly defined blacks as irremediably inferior morally and biologically to white Euro-Americans. James Brewer Stewart, "The Emergence of Racial Modernity and the Rise of the White North, 1790-1840," *Journal of the Early Republic* 18 (Summer 1998), pp. 181-217.

Martin
Invisible Indians

1. See, at the beginning of this volume, the Academy's Letter of Solicitation of 1800, articles 1st and 2nd.

2. Farmington, p. 64; Litchfield, p. 133; Middlesex, p. 179; Saybrook, p. 209; New Haven, p. 318; New London, p. 362.

3. Bethlem, p. 84; Bolton, p. 373; Farmington, p. 56; Kent, p. 125; Litchfield, p. 129.

4. Colin G. Calloway, ed., *After King Philip's War: Presence and Persistence in Indian New England* (Hanover: University Press of New England, 1997), p. 18.

5. Sharon, p. 145.

6. *Johnson v. McIntosh*, 21 U.S. (8 Wheat.) 543, 5 L.Ed. 681 (1823).

7. *Johnson*, p. 588.

8. *Johnson*, p. 588.

9. *Worcester v. Georgia*, 31 U.S. (6 Pet.) 515, 8 L. Ed. 483 (1832).

10. *Worcester*, p. 543.

11. Bethlem, p. 83; Haddam (1808), p. 170; Haddam (in Middlesex County Report), p. 197; New Haven, p. 303; Preston, p. 367; Guilford, p. 253-254.

12. East Windsor, p. 37; Farmington, p. 63; Haddam (1808), p. 170; Middlesex, p. 173; Killingworth, p. 215; New Haven, p. 303.

13. William Cronon, *Changes in the Land: Indians, Colonists, and the Ecology of New England* (New York: Hill and Wang, 1983), p. 65.

14. Henry W. Bowden and James P. Ronda, eds., *John Eliot's Indian Dialogues: A Study in Cultural Interaction* (Westport: Greenwood Press 1980), pp. 12-13.

15. Canterbury, p. 395; Guilford, p. 254; Lebanon, p. 401; Killingworth, p. 215; Saybrook, p. 208; Pomfret, p. 407; Preston, p. 367; Windham, p. 411.

16. Saybrook, p. 207.

17. Saybrook, pp. 206-207. See also, John Mason, *A Brief History of the Pequot War* (Boston: S. Kneeland & T. Green, 1736) (Ann Arbor: University Microfilms, Inc., 1966); Laurence M. Hauptman, "The Pequot War and Its Legacies," in Laurence M. Hauptman and James D. Wherry, eds., *The Pequots in Southern New England: The Fall and Rise of an American Indian Nation* (Norman, Okla.: Univ.of Oklahoma Press, 1990), pp. 71-76; John W. DeForest, *History of the Indians of Connecticut from the Earliest Known Period to 1850* (Hartford: Wm. Jas. Hamersley, 1852) (Scholarly Press, 1970), Chapter IV; Mary E. Guillette, *American Indians in Connecticut: Past to Present* (State of Connecticut, 1979), pp. 4-6.

18. Guilford, p. 258.

19. Saybrook, p. 208.

20. Middletown, p. 185.

21. Hauptman, p. 76; Guillette, pp. 6-7.

22. New London, p. 361.

23. East Windsor, pp. 43-44.

24. East Windsor, p. 37; Haddam (1808), p. 169; Cornwall (1800-1801), p. 103; Kent, p. 123; Lisbon (Newent), p. 357; Middlesex, p. 174; New Haven, p. 304; Pomfret, p. 407; Preston, p. 369; Ridgefield, p. 23; Lisbon (Hanover), p. 353; Stratfield, p. 31; Union, p. 387; Washington (1800), p. 151; Willington, p. 391.

25. DeForest, p. 1.

26. DeForest, p. 43.

27. DeForest, p. 44.

28. DeForest, p. 44.

29. William A. Starna, "The Pequots in the Early Seventeenth Century," in Hauptman and Wherry, *The Pequots in Southern New England*, p. 46.

30. Starna, p. 46.

31. Cronon, p. 89.

32. Russell Bourne, *The Red King's Rebellion: Racial Politics in New England 1675-1678* (New York: Atheneum, 1990); Francis Jennings, *The Invasion of America: Indians, Colonialism and the Cant of Conquest* (New York: W.W. Norton & Co., 1975), Chapter 17; Douglas Edward Leach, *The Northern Colonial Frontier 1607-1763* (New York: Holt, Rinehart and Winston, 1966), Chapter 4; Alden T. Vaughan, *New England Frontier; Puritans and Indians 1620-1675* (Boston: Little, Brown and Co., 1965), Chapter XII; DeForest, pp. 279-288.

33. DeForest, p. 280.

34. Guilford, p. 258.

35. Wallingford, p. 338.

36. East Windsor, p. 38.

37. Bourne, p. 201.

38. Vaughan, p. 320.

39. Jill Lepore, *The Name of War: King Philip's War and the Origins of American Identity* (New York: Alfred A. Knopf, 1998), p. 153.

40. Lepore, p. 153.

41. Lepore, p. 153; see also DeForest, p. 287.

42. Charles M. Segal and David C. Stineback, *Puritans, Indians, and Manifest Destiny* (New York: G.P. Putnam's Sons, 1977), p. 28.

43. See Jennings, p. 135; Cronon, p. 56; Segal and Stineback, p. 75.

44. See Jennings, p. 135; Cronon, p. 56; Segal and Stineback, p. 75.

45. Guillette, p. WP10.

46. Guillette, p. WP11.

47. J. Hammond Trumbull and Charles J. Hoadley, *Public records of the Colony of Connecticut*, (Hartford, 1859-1890), Vol. I, p. 402, cited in

DeForest, p. 203.

48. 1 Stat. 137; see also 1 Stat. 139, 1 Stat. 469, 1 Stat. 743, 2 Stat. 139.

49. Kent, p. 124.

50. Stratfield, p. 31.

51. Segal and Stineback, p. 28.

52. Donna Keith Baron, J. Edward Hood, and Holly V. Izard, "They Were Here All Along: The Native American Presence in Lower-Central New England in the Eighteenth and Nineteenth Centuries" in *William and Mary Quarterly*, 3d Series, Vol. LIII, No, 3, July 1996, p. 564.

53. Baron, Hood and Izard, pp. 565-6.

54. Lepore, p. 185.

55. Calloway, p. 14.

56. Lisbon (Newent), p. 357; Lisbon (Hanover), p. 353; Farmington, p. 55; Kent, p. 124.

57. Guilford, pp. 261-262.

58. Haddam (in Middlesex County Report), p. 201.

59. Bowden and Ronda, p. 23.

60. Segal and Stineback, p. 17.

61. DeForest, p. 303-4.

62. Lepore, p. xiii.

63. Lepore, p. 47; see Barry O'Connell, ed., *On Our Own Ground: The Complete Writings of William Apess, A Pequot* (Amherst: University of Massachusetts Press, 1992).

64. DeForest, p. 1.

65. DeForest, p. 446.

66. East Windsor, p. 38.

67. Letter of President Jefferson to William Henry Harrison, February 27, 1803, in Francis Paul Prucha, ed., *Documents of United States Indian Policy*, Second Edition (Lincoln, Nebr.: Univ. of Nebraska Press, 1990). p. 22.

68. 4 Stat. 411-12 (Ch. 148) (1830).

69. Francis Paul Prucha, *American Indian Policy in the Formative Years: Indian Trade and Intercourse Acts, 1790-1834* (Cambridge: Harvard University Press, 1962), p. 224.

70. See *Elk v. Wilkins*, 11 U.S. 94 (1884). See also, Jill E. Martin, "'Neither Fish, Flesh, Fowl, nor Good Red Herring:' The Citizenship Status of American Indians, 1830-1924," in *Journal of the West*, Vol. XXIX, No. 3, July 1990, p. 75.

71. *Cherokee Nation v. Georgia*, 30 U.S. (5 Pet.) 1, 8 L.Ed. 25 (1831).

72. *Cherokee Nation*, p. 17.

Vickers
Fisheries

1. For the purposes of this essay, fisheries are defined broadly to include fresh and salt-water fisheries, as well as the whale and sea fisheries.

2. Mackerel was cod's only competitor of consequence in the colonial period—salted wet, put down in barrels and shipped to the West Indies.

3. I found not one reference to fisheries in any of the following: Bruce C. Daniels, "Economic Development in Colonial and Revolutionary Connecticut: An Overview," *William and Mary Quarterly*, 3d Ser., 37 (1980), pp. 429-450; Toby L. Ditz, *Property and Kinship: Inheritance in Early Connecticut* (Princeton, N.J., 1986); Bruce H. Mann, *Neighbors and Strangers: Law and Community in Early Connecticut* (Chapel Hill, N.C., 1987). Extremely brief references to river fisheries exist in Richard L. Bushman, *From Puritan to Yankee: Character and the Social Order in Connecticut, 1690-1765* (Cambridge, Mass., 1970), p.108; Robert J. Taylor, *Colonial Connecticut: A History* (Millwood, N.Y., 1979), p. 96.

4. Charles J. Hoadley, ed., *Records of the Colony and Plantation of New Haven, 1638-1665*, (Hartford, Ct., 1857-1858).

5. J. Hammond Trumbull and Charles J. Hoadley, eds., *Public Records of the Colony of Connecticut, 1636-1776*, (Hartford, Ct., 1859-1896), Vol. III, pp. 417, 424-425. Here in after *Public Records of the Colony of Connecticut*. These two acts seem to have been inspired by similar pieces of legislation passed somewhat earlier in Massachusetts, for the language is quite similar. See Nathaniel B. Shurtleff, ed., *Records of the Governor and Company of the Massachusetts Bay in New England*, (Boston, 1853-54), Vol. III, pp. 223, 265-266, Vol. IV, p. 450.

6. See Taylor, p. 96, for an unreferenced claim that Connecticut merchants were exporting merchantable cod to the Mediterranean during the eighteenth century.

7. Naval Officer Shipping Lists for Barbados, 1680-1689, C.O. 132 / 13, 14, Public Record Office.

8. Hoadley, *Records of New Haven Colony,* Vol. I, p. 311.

9. *Public Records of the Colony of Connecticut*, Vol. III, p. 193; Vol. V, pp. 177-178; Vol. VII, p. 308; Vol. IX, p. 494; Vol. XII, p. 528.

10. *Public Records of the Colony of Connecticut*, Vol. V, p. 506. Originally the act applied just to the Quinebaug, Shetucket, and Windsor Ferry Rivers. It was later extended to their tributaries (1719), Fishing Cove in Lyme (1722), Sumner Creek in Middletown (1726), Eight-Mile Creek in Lyme (1755), and the Housatonic River (1764). *Public Records of the Colony of Connecticut*, Vol. VI, pp. 115-116; Vol. VI, p. 324; Vol. VII, p. 14; Vol. X, p. 412; Vol. XII, p. 248.

11. *Public Records of the Colony of Connecticut*, Vol. XII, pp. 498-499. This act was replaced by a new and more restrictive one that applied, however, to the Shetucket and Quinibaug Rivers only. See *Public Records of the Colony of Connecticut*, Vol. XIV, p. 83.

12. *Public Records of the Colony of Connecticut*, Vol. XII, p. 639; Vol. XIII, pp. 48, 118, 126-127, 258-259, 271, 401-402, 616, 626; Vol. XIV, pp. 42-43, 117, 128, 233-234.

13. Marshall MacDonald, "The Connecticut and Housatonic Rivers and Minor Tributaries of Long Island Sound," in George Brown Goode, ed., *The History and Methods of the Fisheries*, (section V of Goode, ed., *The Fisheries and Fishery Industries of the United States*, (Washington, D.C., 1884-1887), Vol. I, pp. 660-663. This paragraph draws most of its evidence from the upper reaches of the Connecticut River as it flows through Massachusetts. For some suggestion that these same practices were followed in Connecticut, see the sources cited above in notes 6-9. See also Middlesex County, p. 176.

14. MacDonald, pp. 660-661; Robert Greenhalgh Albion, *The Rise of New York Port, 1815-1860* (New York, 1939, reprint ed., Hamden, Conn., 1961), p. 281.

15. Haddam (1808), p. 169; East Windsor, p. 39; Middlesex County, pp. 175-176; New Haven, p. 319.

16. Timothy Dwight, *Travels in New England and New York*, ed. Barbara Miller Solomon, with the assistance of Patricia M. King, (Cambridge, Mass., 1969), Vol. I, p. 164.

17. For an argument that distinguishes between the pre-capitalist culture of farmer/fishermen and the capitalist culture of New England industrialists of the early national period, see Gary Kulik, "Dams, Fish, and Farmers: Defence of Public Rights in Eighteenth-Century Rhode Island," in Steven Hahn and Jonathan Prude, eds., *The Countryside in the Age of Capitalist Transformation: Essays in the Social History of Rural America* (Chapel Hill, N.C., 1985), pp. 25-50. For a more realistic view of colonial New Englanders and their relationship to the environment, see William Cronon, *Changes in the Land: Indians, Colonists, and the Ecology of New England* (New York, 1983); and on the capability of pre-industrial fishing practices to make measurable impact on marine environments, see Peter Pope, "Early Estimates: Assessment of Catches in the Newfoundland Cod Fishery,1660-1690," in Daniel Vickers, ed., *Papers Presented at the Conference Entitled "Marine Resources and Human Societies in the North Atlantic Since 1500,"* (St. John's, Nfld., 1997), pp. 7-40; also in this publication see Jeffrey A. Hutchings, "Spatial and Temporal Variation in the Exploitation of Northern Cod, Gadus morhua: A Historical Perspective from 1500 to Present," pp. 41-68; Laurier Turgeon, "Fluctuations in Cod and Whale Stocks in the North Atlantic During the Eighteenth Century," pp. 87-120; Sean Cadigan, "Marine Resource Exploitation and Development: Historical Antecedents in the Debate Over Technology and Ecology in the Newfoundland Fishery, 1815-1855," pp. 331-384.

18. There are no substantial references to fisheries in colonial New York in *Documents Relative to the Colonial History of the State of New York*, ed. and trans., E.B. O'Callaghan and Berthold Fernow, 15 vols. (New York, 1865-1887); Virginia Harrington, *The New York Merchant on the Eve of the Revolution* (New York, 1935); Cathy Matson, *Merchants and Empire: Trading in Colonial New York* (Baltimore, 1997).

19. H. Scott Gordon, "The Economic Theory of a Common Property Resource: The Fishery," *Journal of Political Economy* 42 (1954), pp. 124-142.

20. On New England's fisheries, see Daniel Vickers, *Farmers and Fishermen: Two Centuries of Work in Essex County, Massachusetts, 1630-1850* (Chapel Hill, N.C., 1994), pp. 263-289. On the social structure of work in seventeenth and eighteenth-century Connecticut, see Jackson Turner Main, *Society and Economy in Colonial Connecticut* (Princeton, N.J., 1985), pp. 174-196, 286-287; Jackson Turner Main, *Connecticut Society in the Era of the American Revolution* (Hartford, 1977), pp. 17-22; Daniel Vickers, "Nantucket Whalemen in the Deep-Sea Fishery: The Changing

Anatomy of an Early American Labor Force," *Journal of American History* 72 (1985), pp. 277-296.

21. Between 1793-96, the U.S. Customs District of New London reported an average of only 15 licensed fishing vessels over 20 tons. By 1797-1802, that figure had climbed to 26, and in 1814-1820, it reached 63. See Licenses of Vessels Above 20 Tons to Carry on the Fishing Trade, 1793-1802, 1814-1875, in Records of the U.S. Customs District of New London, Connecticut, RG 36, Federal Records Center, Waltham, Mass., microform edition at G.W. Blunt Library, Mystic Seaport, Mystic, Conn. I am indebted for this reference to Andrew W. German.

22. New London, p. 363.

23. Dwight, Vol. II, p. 368.

24. A. Howard Clark, "The Coast of Connecticut and its Fisheries," in G. Browne Goode, ed., *A Geographical Review of the Fisheries Industries and Fishing Communities for the Year, 1880* (section II of Goode, ed., *Fisheries and Fishery Industries*), p. 317.

25. Edward Ackerman, *New England's Fishing Industry* (Chicago, 1941), pp. 47-50; Ernest Ingersoll, "The Oyster, Scallop, Clam, Mussel, and Abalone Industries," in Goode, ed., *History and Methods*, II, pp. 507-512; *Public Records of the Colony of Connecticut*, Vol. XII, p. 500; New Haven, p. 320.

26. New Haven, pp. 319-320; Guilford and Madison, p. 258; Dwight, Vol. II, p. 358; Ingersoll, p. 516.

27. Governor Montgomerie to the Lords of Trade, Dec. 21, 1730, in O'Callaghan and Fernow, V, p. 905; Ingersoll, pp. 554-557.

28. Dwight, Vol. III, p. 214.

29. Ingersoll, pp 520-539. Again I am indebted for information on oyster-cultivation to Andrew W. German.

30. In early nineteenth-century Connecticut, menhaden was termed "whitefish." See sources in notes 30-33.

31. New Haven, p. 310, Madison, p. 268; Middlesex County, p. 177. Unreferenced sources claim that the menhaden fishery began on Long Island a little earlier, during the 1780s and 1790s. See G. Brown Goode and A. Howard Clark, "The Menhaden Fishery," in Goode ed., *History and Methods*, Vol. I, pp. 370-371.

32. New Haven, p. 310; Dwight, Vol. II, pp. 361-362; Vol. III, pp. 213.

33. Madison, p. 268.

34. Middlesex County, p. 178.

35. Dwight, Vol. II, pp. 213, 361-362.

36. Goode and Clark, pp. 371-372.

37. Goode and Clark, p. 330.

38. Goode and Clark, p. 330.

39. Goode and Clark, p. 334; Ackerman, p. 46; William N. Peterson, "'Bony-Fish': The Menhaden Fishery at Mystic, Connecticut," *Log of Mystic Seaport* 33 (1981), pp. 23-36; John Frye, *The Men All Singing: The Story of Menhaden Fishing* (Virginia Beach, Va., 1978). The tentative nature of these conclusions reflects the fact that the history of this important fishery remains relatively ill-charted.

40. Richard M. Jones, "Sealing and Stonington: A Short-Lived Bonanza," *Log of Mystic Seaport* 28 (1977), pp. 119-126. This article was based on Jones, "Stonington Borough: A Connecticut Seaport in the Nineteenth Century" (Ph.D. diss., City University of New York, 1976). See also Briton Cooper Busch, *The War Against the Seals: A History of the North American Seal Fishery* (Kingston, Ont. and Montreal, Que., 1985), pp. 3-37. The New England sealing industry is a fascinating and reasonably well-documented topic that deserves more attention.

41. On the early history of the industry in New London, see Barnard L. Colby, *For Oil and Buggy Whips: Whaling Captains of New London County, Connecticut* (Mystic, Ct., 1990), pp. 2-4.

42. Robert Owen Decker, *The Whaling City: A History of New London* (Chester, Conn., 1976), pp. 74-93, 110-123.

43. Compare the catches recorded for Connecticut ports in 1935 in Ackerman, p. 219, with the totals for 1880 in Clark, p. 314.

Peterson
Ships and Shipping

1. Richard J. Purcell, *Connecticut in Transition 1775 -1818* (Washington, D.C., 1918), pp. 1-4.

2. Stephen P. Skinner, "The Maritime Economy of Fairfield, Connecticut 1793-1820," n.p. This paper was delivered at the Spring 1997 meeting of the North American Society of Oceanic Historians in Newport, Rhode Island. As the presenter stated, much of this paper relied upon the research and records of Elsie N. Danenberg.

3. Skinner, n.p.

4. Tonnage in this case does not refer to the weight of the vessel but rather to its registered carrying capacity.

5. Skinner, n.p.

6. Thomas A. Stevens, "Connecticut River Navigation," in James W. Miller, ed. *As We Were on the Valley Shore* (Guilford, Conn. 1976), p. 104.

7. Roger M. Griswold, "First Sailing Vessels and Merchant Mariners on the Connecticut River," *The Connecticut Magazine*, Vol. 10, No. 3, 1906, p. 464.

8. Eric Roorda, "Our Position is a Most Commanding One," *The Log of Mystic Seaport*, (Winter 1993; Spring 1994): 66.

9. Roorda, Winter 1993, p. 69.

10. William N. Peterson, *Mystic Built: Ships and Shipyards of the Mystic River 1884-1919* (Mystic, Conn, 1989), p. 2. Country produce, particularly from eastern Connecticut, usually referred to commodities such as "potatoes," oats, white beans, cider, cheese and pressed hay.

11. Peter D. Hall, "Pieces of a Puzzle: The West Indies Trade and the Culture of the Connecticut Valley" in *A Grand Reliance: The West Indies Trade in the Connecticut River Valley, 1630-1830*, p. 6. see also the essay by Thomas R. Lewis. This catalog was printed in conjunction with an exhibition of the same title curated by Brenda Milkofsky and held at the Connecticut River Museum, Essex, Connecticut in 1992. See also *Naval Officer Shipping Lists for Barbados 1680 - 1689*, Public Record Office.

12. See also F. Lee Benns, *The American Struggle for the British Carrying Trade, 1815-1830* (Bloomington,Ind., 1923).

13. Robert G. Albion, *The Rise of New York Port* (New York, 1967 [reprint]), p. 125.

14. Albion, p. 125.

15. Albion, p. 244.

16. Richard C. McKay, *South Street: A Maritime History of New York* (Riverside, Conn, 1969 [revised reprint]), pp. 91-94. See also John G.B. Hutchins, *The American Maritime Industries and Public Policy, 1789-1914* (Cambridge, Mass., 1941).

17. Albion, p. 249.

18. Stevens, p. 105.

19. Harry J. Carmen, ed., *American Husbandry* (New York, 1939), pp. 44-45. See also Gaddis Smith, "The Agricultural Roots of Maritime History," *American Neptune*, Vol. 44 (1984).

20. See Roorda, "Our Position..." and Richard Pares, *Yankees and Creoles: The Trade between North America and the West Indies before the American Revolution* (Cambridge, 1956). For a good description of sugar cane production see Richard S. Dunn, *Sugar and Slaves: The Rise of the Planter Class in the English West Indies* (New York, 1973).

21. Stevens, p. 108.

22. Frances Manwaring Caulkins, *History of New London* (New London, Conn., 1852), p. 574.

23. *Connecticut Gazette*, May 30, 1804.

24. Gaddis Smith, "Agricultural Roots of Maritime History," *American Neptune*, Vol. 44, 1984, p. 6.

25. *Connecticut Gazette*, February 27, 1784.

26. *Connecticut Gazette*, January 7, 1801.

27. Frances M. Caulkins, *History of Norwich* (Hartford, Conn., 1866), p. 499.

28. *Connecticut Gazette*, January 14, 1791.

29. *Connecticut Gazette*, November 11, 1801. Also reported in the same paper on September 2, 1801, was the schooner *Winthrop* under Captain Thomas Randall which was "...struck by a waterspout off Abaco and sank in five minutes. No lives were lost."

30. *Connecticut Gazette*, February 20, 1811.

31. Caulkins, *History of Norwich*, p. 275.

32. Caulkins, *History of Norwich*, p. 478.

33. Linda Maloney, *The Captain From Connecticut: Life and Times of Isaac Hull* (Boston, 1986), p. 8.

34. Maloney, p. 9.

35. Caulkins, *History of Norwich*, p. 428.

36. Lewis, *Grand Reliance*, p. 2.

37. Caulkins, *History of Norwich*, p. 479.

38. Cornelia Penfield Lathrop, *Black Rock Seaport of Old Fairfield Connecticut 1644-1870* (Fairfield,Conn., 1930), p. 11.

39. Timothy Dwight, quoted in Charles Brilvich, *Walking Through History, The Seaports of Black Rock and Southport* (Fairfield, Conn., 1977), p. 5.

40. Charles R. Stark, *Groton, Conn. 1705 - 1905* (Stonington, Conn., 1922), p. 386.

41. Lewis, p. 3.

42. Lewis, p. 3.

43. Lewis, p. 2.

44. Connecticut newspapers from the late eighteenth and early nineteenth century give a clear indication that a dozen or more vessels were sometimes coming and going from Connecticut to the West Indies each week. See, for example, the *Connecticut Gazette* for December 31, 1795 which lists 14 vessel departures at New London.

45. Caulkins, *History of New London*, p. 581.

46. *Connecticut Gazette*, January 29, 1806.

47. *Connecticut Gazette*, December 31, 1795.

48. *Connecticut Gazette*, June 25, 1806.

49. Benjamin W. Labaree, et. al, *New England and the Sea* (Middletown, Conn., 1972), pp. 37-43.

50. For an insight into the allure of privateering see the *Connecticut Gazette*, July 22, 1812.

51. *Connecticut Gazette*, May 20, 1807.

52. *Connecticut Gazette*, July 27, 1808.

53. *Connecticut Gazette*, December 28, 1808.

54. *Connecticut Gazette*, September 25, 1811. See also Purcell, pp. 1-4.

55. Peterson, p. 212. *Mary* was a new vessel launched in 1811 by Christopher Leeds at the "Head of the River" at Mystic. After the war, she was raised and made at least one voyage to Ireland with a cargo of tobacco.

56. *General Shipping & Commercial List* (New York), February 21, 1815.

57. Benjamin W. Labaree, et. al, *America and the Sea* (Mystic, Conn., 1998), p. 285.

58. New London, p. 363.

59. Peterson, p. 127.

60. Peterson, p. 127.

61. *Connecticut Gazette*, September 5, 1804.

62. *The Yankee*, a Stonington, Connecticut newspaper, reported on October 13, 1824 that no fewer than nine vessels were engaged from that town in the "Straights fishery," referring to the Straight of Belle Isle, north of New Foundland. See George Brown Goode, *The Fisheries and Fishery Industries in the United States*, (Washington, D.C., 1884). See also the "Fisheries" essay in this volume by Daniel Vickers for an overall understanding of Connecticut fisheries during this period.

63. Robert Owen Decker, *The Whaling Industry of New London* (York, Penn., 1973). Decker's valuable research lists all known whaling vessels and their departures and arrivals from 1718 to 1908. He credits the Sloop *Society* with a voyage in 1718, but this is a clear anomaly and is not indicative a pattern.

64. Isabel MacBeth Calder, *The New Haven Colony* (New Haven,Conn., 1934), p. 160.

65. R. B. Wall, "New London Shipbuilding Boomed," *The Day*, Feb. 13, 1926.

66. Stevens, p. 104.

67. Middlesex County, Note F, pp. 224-225.

68. Haddam, pp. 169-170.

69. Middlesex County, p. 188.

70. Robert O. Decker, *Cromwell, Connecticut, 1650 - 1990: The History of a River Port Town* (West Kennebunk, Me., 1991), p. 66.

71. Peterson, pp. 31-32.

72. Peterson, pp. 119-125.

E. Cooke
The Embedded Nature of Artisanal Activity

1. The quotations are taken from "AN ACT To incorporate the Connecticut Academy of Arts and Sciences," passed by the Connecticut Legislature in October, 1799, reprinted in *Memoirs* of The Connecticut Academy of Arts and Sciences, Vol. 1, part 1 (1810), p. v.

2. Farmington, p. 57. See also the essays in this volume by Kathy Cooke, Holly Izard, and Paul Waggoner.

3. For example, see D. F. Sotzmann's map of 1796 (Hamburg: Carl Ernst Bohn) or Moses Warren and George Gillet's map of 1811 (Hartford: Hudson & Goodwin). The key for the former map included designations for distilleries, grist mills, oil mills, paper mills, fulling mills, powder mills, saw mills, potash works, furnaces, and iron works; while that of the latter map included the same as well as slitting mills, glass works, woolen manufactories, cotton manufactories, gun and pistol manufactories, cutlers manufactories, clock manufactories, button manufactories, and wire manufactories.

4. For more details on these manufacturers, see the essays in this volume by Carolyn Cooper, Ruth Moynihan, and Caroline Sloat. The same sort of focus can be found in the responses to the 1820 Census of Manufactures, in which cotton and woolen mills, iron forges, arms manufacturers, distilleries, and other large or highly capitalized operations predominate in the manuscript responses and the published summary: *Records of the 1820 Census of Manufactures: Schedules for Connecticut* (National Archives Microfilm Publications #279, Roll 4).

5. Farmington Report, pp. 64-65, refers to "useful" and "common" articles.

6. Bolton, p. 374; Nancy Evans, *American Windsor Chairs* (New York: Hudson Hills, 1996), p. 346; Farmington, pp. 64-65; Phyllis Kihn, "Connecticut Cabinetmakers Part II," *The Connecticut Historical Society Bulletin* 33, no. 1 (January 1968), p. 14; and Peter Bohan and Philip Hammerslough, *Early Connecticut Silver, 1700-1840* (Middletown, Conn.: Wesleyan Univ. Press, 1970), pp. 226 and 231.

7. On Gold and Ritter, see Meredith Williams and Gray Williams, Jr., "'MD. by Thos. Gold': The Gravestones of a New Haven Carver," *Markers 5* (1988), pp. 1-59; on Chapin and Williams, see William Hosley and Gerald Ward, eds., *The Great River: Art & Society of the Connecticut Valley, 1635-1820* (Hartford: Wadsworth Atheneum, 1985), pp. 188-91, 228-32, and Joseph Lionetti and Robert Trent, "New Information on Chapin Chairs," *Antiques* 129, no. 5 (May 1986), pp. 1082-1095; on Burnap, see Penrose Hoopes, *Shop Records of Daniel Burnap* (Hartford: Connecticut Historical Society, 1958), and Hosley and Ward, pp. 342-43 and 356-62.

8. On Danforth, see John Carl Thomas, *Connecticut Pewter and Pewterers* (Hartford: Connecticut Historical Society, 1976), pp. 96-102; on Tracy, see Evans, *American Windsor Chairs*, pp. 285-302; and on Walden, see James Slater, *The Colonial Burial Grounds of Eastern Connecticut & the Men Who Made Them. Memoirs* of the Connecticut Academy of Arts and Sciences, Vol. 21 (1987).

9. Lebanon, p. 403; and Goshen, p. 117. Carolyn Cooper and Christopher Bickford kindly provided biographical information on the correspondents.

10. For example, see Jackson Turner Main, *Society and Economy in Colonial Connecticut* (Princeton, N.J.: Princeton Univ. Press, 1985), pp. 241-56. For an in-depth study of artisanal composition in the Chesapeake, see Jean Russo, "Self-Sufficiency and Local Exchange: Free Craftsmen in the Rural Chesapeake Economy," in Lois Carr, Philip Morgan, and Jean Russo, eds., *Colonial Chesapeake Society* (Chapel Hill: Univ. of North Carolina Press, 1988), pp. 389-432.

11. Although I read through all forty-five of the known surviving Town Reports, I closely examined for the purpose of this analysis the thirty reports filed by the end of 1812 (another fifteen were submitted between 1813 and 1832). Of the thirty towns with early reports, I could find tax assessments with specified faculty assessments, or taxes on craftsmen's shops, from the late eighteenth century for eighteen. The Connecticut Historical Society has a good number of the assessments, particularly those of 1797 and 1798. These lists tabulate numbers of polls and animals, provide the total number of acres in town broken down by types or uses of those holdings, summarize the number of fireplaces of different quality thereby suggesting the general quality of housing in town, enumerate certain consumer goods, such as watches, silver, or chaises, and list all inhabitants who owned a faculty, or shop. The latter includes professionals such as lawyers or doctors, merchants, tavern keepers, saw and grist mill owners, and craftsmen. In regard to the craftsmen, only those who owned their own shop were listed. Renters, journeymen, apprentices, and other non-propertied artisans did not appear on these assessment lists, which makes it impossible to determine the overall number of craftsmen in a town. Nevertheless faculty assessments do help reveal the number of full shops in a town. Another archival source is the Connecticut Valley Archive at the Wadsworth Atheneum. This compilation of photographs of objects made and owned in the Valley and citations to craftsmen was gathered during the research phase for the exhibition "The Great River."

12. The classification of the towns is adapted from Bruce Daniels, *The Connecticut Town: Growth and Development, 1635-1790* (Middletown, Conn: Wesleyan Univ. Press, 1979), pp. 140-70.

13. The two port towns' silversmiths made more than spoons, which constituted the bread and butter work of the silversmiths in the country towns: Bohan and Hammerslough, *Early Connecticut Silver*, pp.130-33, 179-95, 235, 243-44, and 255.

14. On the importance of East Windsor, see Hosley and Ward, *The Great River*; Thomas and Alice Kugelman, "The Hartford Case Furniture Survey," *Maine Antique Digest* 21, no. 3 (March 1993), Section A, pp. 36-38; and Alice Kugelman, Thomas Kugelman, and Robert Lionetti, "The

Chapin School of East Windsor, Connecticut," *Maine Antique Digest* 22, no 1 (January 1994), Section D, pp. 12-14.

15. Farmington, pp. 50-51, 64-65, and 67; Bohan and Hammerslough, *Early Connecticut Silver*, pp. 226 and 231; and Shirley DeVoe, *The Tinsmiths of Connecticut* (Middletown, Conn.: Wesleyan University Press, 1968), p. 25.

16. Edward Cooke, Jr., *Making Furniture in Preindustrial Connecticut: The Social Economy of Newtown and Woodbury, Connecticut* (Baltimore: Johns Hopkins Univ. Press, 1996), esp. pp. 190-99; and Gregory Nobles, "The Rise of Merchants in Rural Market Towns: A Case Study of Eighteenth-Century Northampton, Massachusetts," *Journal of Social History* 24, no. 1 (Fall 1990), pp. 5-23.

17. Wallingford, pp. 340 and 343.

18. Lebanon, p. 403; Robert Trent and Nancy Lee Nelson, "New London County Joined Chairs 1720-1790," *The Connecticut Historical Society Bulletin* 50, no. 4 (Fall 1985); and Cooke, *Making Furniture in Preindustrial Connecticut*, esp. pp. 14-15 and 82-90.

19. Preston, p. 369; and Edgar Mayhew and Minor Myers, *New London County Furniture 1640-1840* (New London, Conn.: Lyman Allyn Museum, 1974), pp. 56-61, 118, and 120.

20. Cornwall (1800-1801), pp. 98 and 101; Robert Gordon, "Materials for Manufacturing: The Response of the Connecticut Iron Industry to Technological Change and Limited Resources," *Technology and Culture* 24, no. 4 (October 1983): 602-34; Goshen, p. 117; Lura Woodside Watkins, *Early New England Potters and Their Wares* (Cambridge, Mass.: Harvard University Press, 1950), pp. 173-75; and John Worrell, "Ceramic Production in the Exchange Network of an Agricultural Neighborhood," in Sarah Turnbaugh, ed., *Domestic Pottery of the Northeastern United States, 1625-1850* (New York: Academic Press, 1985), pp. 153-69.

21. Cooke, *Making Furniture in Preindustrial Connecticut*, esp. pp. 190-99.

22. When dealing with historiographic prejudices and hierarchies, it is important to understand who wrote the standard interpretation and what shaped their point(s) of view. My discussion of craftsmen in Connecticut has been informed by the literature on gender and artists, particularly the invisibility of women artists. For a good discussion of these issues, see Griselda Pollock, *Vision and Difference: Femininity, Feminism, and the Histories of Art* (New York: Routledge, 1988).

23. Jean Pierre Brissot de Warville, *New Travels in the United States of America* (1788; reprint ed., Durand Echeverria, ed., Cambridge, Mass.: Belknap Press of the Harvard University Press, 1964), p. 117. On the issues of agriculture reform, see Robert Gross, "Culture and Cultivation: Agriculture and Society in Thoreau's Concord," *Journal of American History* 69, no. 1 (June 1982), pp. 42-61; and Peter Benes, ed., *The Farm* (Boston: Boston University, 1988).

24. The clearest presentation of Hamilton's ideas are his 1791 "Report on Manufactures," compiled with the help of Tench Coxe, which has been reprinted in Harold Syrett et al, eds., *Papers of Alexander Hamilton*, 26 vols. (New York, 1961-78), vol. 10, pp. 230-340. For more on Hamilton's great influence on an entire generation of American economists, see Jacob Cooke, "Tench Coxe, Alexander Hamilton, and the Encouragement of American Manufactures," *William and Mary Quarterly* 32 (1975), pp. 369-92.

25. James Walsh, "'Mechanics and Citizens': The Connecticut Artisan Protest of 1792," *William and Mary Quarterly* 42, no. 1 (January 1985): 66-89; and the *Connecticut Courant*, April 23, 1792, p. 2.

26. *Records of the 1820 Census of Manufactures: Schedules for Connecticut*, pp. 79 and 83.

27. On the context of preindustrial craft in Connecticut, see Cooke, *Making Furniture in Preindustrial Connecticut*.

28. Richard Candee, "John Langdon's Unusual Census of 'Mechanical Labor': The 1820 Artisans of Wiscasset, Jefferson, Alna, Edgecomb, and Whitefield, Maine," *Maine Historical Society Quarterly* 27, no. 1 (Summer 1987): 24-37. The questions for the Census were:

RAW MATERIALS EMPLOYED
1. The kind?
2. The quantity annually consumed?
3. The cost of the annual consumption?
NUMBER OF PERSONS EMPLOYED
4. Men?
5. Women?
6. Boys and Girls?
MACHINERY
7. Whole quantity and kind of Machinery?
8. Quantity of Machinery in operation?
EXPENDITURES

9. Amount of capital invested?
10. Amount paid annually for wages?
11. Amount of Contingent Expenses?
PRODUCTION
12. The nature and names of Articles Manufactured?
13. Market value of the Articles which are annually manufactured?
14. General Remarks concerning the Establishment, as to its actual and past condition, the demand for, and sale of, its Manufactures.

29. For a good discussion of the intensification of production rooted in mixed agricultural practices, see Christopher Clark, *The Roots of Rural Capitalism: Western Massachusetts, 1780-1860* (Ithaca, NY: Cornell Univ. Press, 1990). The changes in consumption and material life are discussed in Jack Larkin, *The Reshaping of Everyday Life, 1790-1840* (New York: Harper and Row, 1988), and Philip Zea, *Pursuing Refinement in Rural New England 1750-1850* (Deerfield, Mass.: Historic Deerfield, Inc., 1998).

30. A very useful discussion of the complexities of skilled work in a modern society is Douglas Harper, *Working Knowledge: Skill and Community in a Small Shop* (Chicago: Univ. of Chicago Press, 1987). On the confusion over handcraft and workmanship and the necessity of understanding skilled workmanship, see David Pye, *The Nature and Art of Workmanship* (NewYork: Cambridge University Press, 1968).

Cooper
Technology in Transition

I thank Robert Gordon for his photography, drawings, and explanations of iron metallurgy (but absolve him from errors that may remain in my rendition of it), Sandra Rux for insights into textile handcraft, and Pat Malone for helpful comments on an early draft of this essay.

1. "Technology" is both knowledge and practice of ways to make and do useful things. In mankind's prehistory and history, technology preceded science, and it continues to include more than applied science. We can distinguish different combinations of information, skills, and equipment as different "technologies" belonging to different industries, places, or times.

2. This essay examines answers to these Articles in the Academy's Solicitation Letter of 1800: 4th, "streams...lakes and ponds, their sources and uses as to mills;" 8th, "Furnaces, forges, and mills...curious machinery...mechanical powers...applied to useful purposes;" and 16th, "Manufactures...in families and in manufactories..."

3. Terry S. Reynolds, *Stronger Than a Hundred Men: A History of the Vertical Water Wheel* (Baltimore, 1981), Chapter 5.

4. Robert B. Gordon, "Hydrological Science and the Development of Water Power for Manufacturing," *Technology and Culture* 26 (1985): 204-235.

5. Louis C. Hunter, "Waterpower in the Century of the Steam Engine" in Brooke Hindle, ed., *America's Wooden Age: Aspects of its Early Technology* (Tarrytown, N.Y., 1975), pp. 160-192.

6. Hunter, pp. 170, 172.

7. Middletown, p. 188.

8. Hunter, p. 191. See also Carroll W. Pursell, Jr., *Early Stationary Steam Engines in America* (Washington, D.C, 1969), p. 73.

9. Table I omits reports by towns and parishes (Coventry 1806, Haddam 1808, Lisbon [Newent], Lisbon [Hanover], Northfield parish, South Farms parish, and Windham) that did not report any industrial sites of the ten kinds shown, which are the kinds most frequently mentioned overall.

10. Bethlem, p. 84; Farmington, p. 72; Lisbon (Hanover), p. 354. See the essay in this volume by Toby Appel on the understanding of disease and medicine in the Town Reports.

11. For a contrary situation in Rhode Island, see Gary Kulik, "Dams, Fish, and Farmers: Defense of Public Rights in Eighteenth-Century Rhode Island," in Steven Hahn and Jonathan Prude, *The Countryside in the Age of Capitalist Transformation, Essays in the Social History of Rural America* (Chapel Hill, N.C., 1985).

12. For an excellent single source, see Robert B. Gordon and Patrick M. Malone, *The Texture of Industry: An Archaeological View of the Industrialization of North America* (New York, 1994).

13. Victor S. Clark, *History of Manufactures in the United States: Volume 1, 1607-1860* (New York, 1929), p. 63. Referring to a wider geographic and chronological span, Louis C. Hunter says tolls varied from 1/12 to as much as 1/4. *Waterpower in the Century of the Steam Engine*, Vol. 1 of *A History of Industrial Power in the United States, 1780-1930* (Charlottesville, Va., 1979), p. 4.

14. Wallingford, p. 340. Hunter, *Waterpower*, p. 12 ff. cites numerous heroic feats of endurance by frontier farmers to get to and from a gristmill.

15. Cornwall, 1801, p. 108. "Bolting" was for screening and sifting meal and flour.

16. Evans had to relinquish patents he held from a few states before the federal patent system began in 1790. Greville Bathe and Dorothy Bathe, *Oliver Evans, a Chronicle of Early American Engineering* (Philadelphia, 1935), p. 23.

17. Farmington, pp. 56-57; Franklin, p. 348.

18. The first timber cutting sawmill known to historians of technology was one in Normandy in 1204. Bradford Blaine, "The Application of Waterpower to Industry During the Middle Ages," (PhD dissertation, University of California at Los Angeles, 1966), p. 155.

19. See Charles E. Peterson, "Early Lumbering: A Pictorial Essay," in Hindle, ed., *America's Wooden Age*, pp. 63-64.

20. Richard Candee, "Merchant and Millwright: The Waterpowered Sawmills of the Piscataqua"; Benno M. Forman, "Mill Sawing in Seventeenth Century Massachusetts," both in *Old Time New England*, LX #4 (April-June, 1970).

21. Charles F. Carroll, *The Timber Economy of Puritan New England* (Providence, 1973), p. 110. Another writer estimates the sawmill's output at "3,000 feet of lumber in a working day...20 to 25 times the output of two men working in a pit." Michael Williams, *Americans & Their Forests: A Historical Geography* (Cambridge, England, 1989) p. 96. Yet another estimate was 4,000 feet in 24 hours. J. Leander Bishop, *A History of American Manufactures from 1608 to 1860* (Philadelphia, 1864) Vol. 1, p. 104.

22. Massachusetts Historical Society, *Winthrop Papers* (Boston, Mass., 1929-) Vol. VI: New London town grant to John Winthrop Jr., Feb. 14, 1652, p. 249; letter from Emmanuel Downing to John Winthrop Jr. Dec. 14, 1652, p. 247. These documents, as well as fragments of saw blades and saw-tooth waste scraps from the archaeological excavations of the Saugus Iron Works, support interpretation of Jenks's "new Invented Saw Mill," patented in 1646 along with "divers other Engines for making of edge tooles," as a mill for making saws instead of a mill for sawing boards. I am indebted to Curtis McKay White of the Saugus Iron Works National Historic Site for these references.

23. See Table I. The town of Litchfield had eighteen sawmills serving its population of over 4,500.

24. Farmington, p. 57.

25. Cornwall (1800), pp. 103-104; Union, p. 386; Farmington, p. 56.

26. Sawmill Park is about two miles east of Ledyard Center on Route 214 (Iron Street). The sawmill operates when water flow is adequate, in spring and autumn.

27. P. d'A. Jones and E. N. Simon, *Story of the Saw* (Manchester, 1961), p. 44, p. 50. See also Nathan Rosenberg, "America's Rise to Woodworking Leadership," in Hindle, ed., *America's Wooden Age*, pp. 37-62.

28. By 1875, of the 2,148 saws in Massachusetts mills, 83 percent were circular saws, eleven percent were "still the old up-and-down type," but only about one percent were band saws. Williams, p. 168.

29. Use of sulfurous coal fuel made wrought iron "hot short" or brittle at high temperatures.

30. Coppicing left roots and stubs of trees, from each of which many new trees sprouted upward. Harvesting these just when they were big enough for charcoaling saved effort splitting larger branches and trunks, and meant that a new crop would be ready sooner than if the trees were intended for timber.

31. Absorption of different small amounts of carbon during smelting produced completely different qualities in the iron. Carbon's role was not understood scientifically until the late eighteenth century, but its effects were obvious early on. Bloomery iron and finery iron, lacking carbon, could be hammered, bent, and welded. Cast iron, containing as much as 3 to 4.5% carbon, was hard and strong, but brittle and not weldable. See Cyril Stanley Smith, "The Discovery of Carbon in Steel," *Technology and Culture 5* (1964): 149-175.

32. Mary Stetson Clarke, *Pioneer Iron Works* (Philadelphia, 1968), p. 29. Later blast furnaces grew more efficient, requiring less charcoal and flux per ton of ore. Higher quality ore also yielded more iron per ton of ore.

33. "Saugus Iron Works: Official Map and Guide," National Park Service, U.S.G.P.O., 2000. A reconstruction of the Saugus iron works is a National Historic Site near Lynn, Massachusetts.

34. The site, near present-day Lake Saltonstall, is now covered with highway fill, which prevents archaeological excavation. Robert B. Gordon, *American Iron 1607-1900* (Baltimore, 1996), pp. 55-57.

35. The following discussion of the northwest Connecticut iron industry is based on that by Robert B. Gordon in *American Iron*. See also Robert B. Gordon and Michael S. Raber, *Industrial Heritage in Northwest Connecticut: A Guide to History and Archaeology* (New Haven, 2000).

36. The first two were Russia and Sweden. James A. Mulholland, *A History of Metals in Colonial America* (Tuscaloosa, Ala., 1981) p. 116.

37. Robert B. Gordon, "Materials for Manufacturing: The Response of the Connecticut Iron Industry to Technological Change and Limited Resources," *Technology and Culture* 24 (1983): 602-634.

38. Kenneth T. Howell and Einar W. Carlson, *Men of Iron: Forbes and Adam* (Lakeville, Conn., 1980), p. 88.

39. I am indebted to Robert B. Gordon for his table of 21 blast furnaces built in the Salisbury district from 1762 to 1918, showing their opening and closing dates. For histories of individual blast furnaces, see Gordon and Raber, Kenneth T. Howell & Einar W. Carlson, *Empire Over the Dam* (Chester, Conn., 1974) and Edward Kirby, *Echoes of Iron* (Sharon, Conn., 1998).

40. Sharon, p. 146; Kent, p. 125. Both of these towns acquired blast furnaces years later, in 1825. Chatham, p. 195. Ore for the forge at Chatham "was formerly brought from West Point" N.Y., presumably by water.

41. Kent, p. 125. Rolling and slitting mills flattened iron and sliced it into bars or rods.

42. Washington (in Litchfield Co.), p. 137-138; Washington (1800), p. 151.

43. Winsted, p. 164.

44. Tench Coxe reported 410 naileries in the United States in 1810, whose total annual output of nails was 15,727,914 pounds, or on average 19 tons each. He didn't distinguish between naileries producing nails wrought from nail rod and those producing cut nails. Tench Coxe, *A Statement of the Arts and Manufactures of the United States of America for the Year 1810* (Philadelphia, 1814), p. 11.

45. Ezekiel Reed of Bridgewater and Jacob Perkins of Newburyport, both in Massachusetts, invented nail-cutting machines by 1790; 120 patents for nail manufacture were granted from 1790 to September 1825. Bishop, pp. 488, 492, 498.

46. Cornwall (1800) p. 103; Sharon, p. 148; New Haven, p. 308 (The report also listed "1 nailer," p. 319); Winsted, p. 164.

47. Litchfield Co., pp. 130, 137. Middlesex Co., pp. 189, 203. The terms "factory" and "manufactory" are ambiguous, for they both might still make wrought iron nails by hand. The Washington report also mentions eight blacksmiths. East Haddam's factory "was erected in 1809, but...lately has not been much used."

48. Cornwall (1800), p. 101. Cornwall's output was far below the national average in 1810 of nineteen tons (see Tench Coxe, cited above).

49. Amos J. Loveday, Jr., *The Rise and Decline of the American Cut Nail Industry* (Westport, Conn., 1983), Chapter 1, "The Technology and the Market" pp. 1-36 includes useful bibliographical notes. At Wareham, Massachusetts, the Tremont Nail Company preserves and uses nineteenth-century machines to make cut nails.

50. Between cast and wrought iron in carbon content, a steel blade keeps a sharp edge longer than wrought iron and springs back if bent. Wrought iron is stronger in tension than cast iron, and cast iron is stronger in compression than wrought iron, but a steel rod or beam is stronger in tension than both, and equal or better in compression than cast iron. Like wrought iron but unlike cast iron, steel is malleable, ductile, and weldable.

51. The carbon content of steel ranges from .08% to 1.7% but is usually less than 1%. Cyril Stanley Smith and R.J. Forbes, "Metallurgy and Assaying" in Charles Singer, E.J. Holmyard, A.R. Hall, and Trevor I. Williams, *A History of Technology*, (London: Oxford University Press, 1957), Vol. 3, pp. 27-71, p. 35. See also Gordon, *American Iron*, pp. 174-76 for a description of making blister steel.

52. Saybrook, in Middlesex Co., p. 208.

53. The Eliots sent specimens of iron and of steel to the Society of Arts in London; the iron won the gold medal. Bishop, ...*American Manufactures...*,Vol. 1, p. 515. Killingworth, in Middlesex Co., p. 217. Richard S. Allen, "Connecticut Iron and Steel from Black Sea Sands," *IA, the Journal of the Society for Industrial Archeology*, 18 (1992): 129-132.

54. Benjamin Huntsman, a watchmaker in England who wanted high-quality steel for watch springs, developed the crucible steel process in 1740-42. In Collinsville, Connecticut, the Collins ax factory established a crucible steel operation in the mid-1860s. Gordon, *American Iron*, pp. 176,178.

55. For the Bessemer process, see Gordon, *American Iron*, Fig. 10-1, p. 223. Modern decorative "wrought iron" items are in fact made of mild steel. The only source of real wrought iron since its production ceased is scrap from antique wrought iron objects. Gordon, p. 263.

56. Coke is to coal as charcoal is to wood, namely the carbon matrix surviving a smoldering fire in which impurities are burned off.

57. Blast furnace remains are easily visible at the Sloane-Stanley State Museum in Kent, and at Beckley Furnace State Industrial Monument in East Canaan. Useful field guides to these and other Northwest Connecticut iron-making sites are found in Kirby, *Echoes of Iron* and in Gordon and Raber, *Industrial Heritage*.

58. Among others, People's State Forest near Winsted incorporates former

furnace woodlots, as does Mine Hill Forest Preserve, privately owned but open to the public, near Roxbury. In eastern Connecticut, see Old Furnace State Park, near Brooklyn.

59. For the history of tanning, see John W. Waterer, "Leather," in Singer, *et al*, Vol. II, pp. 147-57.

60. Ridgefield, p. 26; Litchfield, p. 130; (barkmills) Cornwall (1800), p. 97, New Haven, p. 308; (output) Farmington, p. 64, Stratfield, p. 32, Wallingford, p. 340, and Winsted, p. 164; (prices) Wallingford, p. 340.

61. New Haven, p. 329; Stratfield, p. 32.

62. Shoemakers in Milton and Washington, whose reports do not mention tanneries, would have little trouble finding leather nearby at tanneries in the borough of Litchfield and the town of Bethlem, respectively. The seven other shoemaking towns were: Farmington, Goshen, Guilford, Lebanon, Madison, New Haven, and Ridgefield, which all had tanneries.

63. Bethlem, New Haven, and Washington produced saddles and harness; New Haven produced leather gloves and bellows.

64. The classic description of the evolution of shoemaking methods in America is Blanche Hazard, *The Organization of the Boot and Shoe Industry in Massachusetts Before 1875* (Cambridge, Mass., 1921). See also Paul G. Faler, *Mechanics and Manufacturers in the Early Industrial Revolution; Lynn Massachusetts, 1780-1860* (Albany, N.Y., 1981) and Alan Dawley, *Class and Community, the Industrial Revolution in Lynn* (Cambridge, Mass., 1976).

65. For making shoes by hand, see D.A. Saguto, "The 'Mysterie' of a Cordwainer," *Chronicle of the Early American Industries Association* 34 (March, 1981): 1-7.

66. Lebanon, p. 403; New Haven, p. 319.

67. Guilford, p. 256; Madison, p. 268.

68. Ridgefield, p. 26.

69. Middletown (in Middlesex Co.), p. 188; New Haven, p. 319; note from William Daggett to Timothy Dwight, February 24, 1807, in Yale University Library, Manuscripts and Archives, Record Group 1373 (CAAS Archives) Box 20, folder 280.

70. For details of shoemaking mechanization, see Ross Thomson, *The Path to Mechanized Shoe Production in the United States* (Chapel Hill, N.C., 1989).

71. New Haven, p. 319; New London, p. 362; Middlesex Co., p. 179.

72. New Haven, p. 329; Ridgefield, p. 26.

73. For further details on cider-making in that era, see the entry "cider" in Samuel Deane, *The New-England Farmer; or Georgical Dictionary...*(Boston, 1822), pp. 84-86. For history and techniques of home cider-making up to modern times, see Vrest Orton, *The American Cider Book*, (New York: Farrar, Straus and Giroux, 1973 or North Press reprint 1995).

74. Canterbury, p. 395; Sharon, p. 148.

75. Cornwall (1800), Franklin, Lisbon (Hanover), Litchfield, New Haven, New London, Preston, and Union reported making cider without mentioning distilleries, but Cornwall (1812) reported "much [cider] is distilled," p. 110. Seven towns reported an annual figure for the town's total cider production. Of those, the three without distilleries—Cornwall (1800), Franklin, and Preston—averaged 2,338 barrels per annum, while the four with distilleries—North Bolton, Cheshire, East Windsor, and Wintonbury—averaged 4,150 barrels per annum. If we average the high and low annual figures that Bethlem reported and add that (3,807.5) to the latter calculation, it makes an average of 4,081.5 barrels for those five towns.

76. Bethlem, p. 85. Since Bethlem had a population of 1,118 men, women, and children, an annual home consumption of 5,000 gallons of cider brandy implies nearly 4.5 gallons each.

77. Wallingford, p. 340; Canterbury, p. 398; Sharon, p. 148; Bolton, p. 374.

78. Assuming 31.5 gallons to a $1.00 barrel of cider and 50 cents per gallon of apple brandy, as in Bethlem and Wallingford.

79. New Haven, p. 312, 329; Stratfield, p. 32. The standard barrel contains 31.5 gallons.

80. Haddam had two cider distilleries besides its gin distillery. Within the other distilleries listed in Table I, Bethlem had one non-cider distillery implied (for potato gin), Bolton one (for rye gin), Chatham one (for rum), East Windsor two (for gin), Middletown one (for rum), and Wintonbury one (for rum).

81. Bethlem, p. 85. This gin earned a profit of 20 cents per bushel of potatoes. Besides the inferred potato distillery, Bethlem had "7 Distilleries of Cyder," p. 85.

82. Bolton, p. 374. None of the reports used the term "whiskey."

83. New Haven, p. 329; in the New London Report, see the table showing "Schedule of Exports from, & Imports into, the District of New London." It shows no export of brandy, gin, or rum. Between 1800 and 1811, however, the amount of molasses imported through New London was usually between 100,000 and 200,000 gallons, but hit a low of 35,318 gallons in 1803 and a high of 441,059 gallons (despite the Embargo) in 1808.

84. Middlesex Co., pp. 188, 195. A hogshead contains 63 gallons, twice as much as a barrel.

85. See the New London import-export table. "Spirits" imported through New London averaged 161,165 gallons annually from 1790 through 1811, far outstripping the exports of cider brandy and country gin from New Haven or Stratfield mentioned above. But this figure includes a sharp decline from 161,741 in 1807 to 24,630 in 1810 before rebounding to 190,439 in 1811.

86. Cornwall (1812), p. 110.

87. Calculated from data in "Letter from the Secretary of the Treasury transmitting a Report in Pursuance of the House of Representatives Resolution March 9, 1816," January 13, 1817. (Washington, D.C.: William A. Davis, 1817), p. 5. Early American Imprints, Second Series #42630. The ad in 1809 appeared in the *Connecticut Mirror* on July 10, quoted by Viggo E. Bird in "Early Beginnings of Connecticut Industry," *A Newcomen Address* (Princeton, 1937), p. 18.

88. Haddam (1819), p. 199. It hadn't yet been run at full capacity.

89. John C. Pease and John M. Niles, *A Gazetteer of the States of Connecticut and Rhode-Island* (Hartford: William S. Marsh, 1819), p. 16.

90. Pease and Niles, p. 36.

91. In those towns that had reported or implied to the Connecticut Academy they had 28 cider and ten non-cider distilleries, Pease and Niles reported 50 distilleries in 1819, only ten of which were cider distilleries. Pease and Niles described the scale of one of the six distilleries in Chatham as "considerable" and four of the six in East Windsor as "extensive." p. 65, p. 280.

92. Pease and Niles judged that the product is "essentially deleterious, destructive to health, to morals, and social order and happiness." However, they added, "it is by no means an established theorem, that its local manufacture increases its local consumption" and "That the manufacture of grain-spirits...has had a favourable influence upon...agricultural interests, cannot be doubted." p. 37.

93. Goshen, p. 116, 120.

94. The heading "Spinning" in Table I refers to establishments called factories or manufactories for cotton or wool. The carding machines and fulling mills in this table are assumed to be separate entities, independent of the spinning mills, which I also assume included, besides spinning machines, unenumerated carding machines, and (in woolen factories) fulling mills. See for instance the equipment of the Humphreysville woolen mill listed in Cole, Vol. I, p. 254.

95. Table II omits reports by towns and parishes (Cheshire, Coventry 1806, Haddam 1808, Kent, Lisbon [Newent], Lisbon [Hanover], Madison, Northfield parish, South Farms parish, Stratfield, Winchester, Winsted, and Windham) that did not report any textile production or processing sites.

96. Peter M. Molloy, *et al, Homespun to Factory Made: Woolen Textiles in America 1776-1876* (North Andover, Mass., 1977), pp. 4-16; Martha Coons, *et al, All Sorts of Good Sufficient Cloth: Linen-Making in New England 1640-1860* (North Andover, Mass., 1980), pp. 34-48. These well-illustrated publications excellently cover all stages of linen and woolen cloth production in the indicated time-periods.

97. I thank handloom weaver Sandra Rux for her information about weaving on hand looms.

98. Gail Fowler Mohanty, "Experimentation in Textile Technology, 1788-1790, and its Impact on Handloom Weaving and Weavers in Rhode Island," *Technology and Culture* 29 (1988): 30.

99. The account book of part-time turner Shadrach Steere suggests two spinning wheels—for wool and for linen—per family would be common. Carolyn C. Cooper and Patrick M. Malone, "The Mechanical Woodworker in Early 19th-Century New England as a Spin-off from Textile Industrialization," paper for conference at Old Sturbridge Village, spring 1990.

100. Bethlem, p. 87. Bethlem's population was 1,118 in 1810, the year in which 80 looms were counted there. The estimate of six persons per family implies about 186 families. 186/80 = 2.325 families per loom. For the "common estimate of six to a family," see Litchfield County report, p. 139.

101. Using 1810 population figures and the conventional estimate for that time of six persons per "family" or household, we can calculate that in 1812 Wallingford had about 387 families (2,325/6) to be served by its 145 looms and Washington (1815) had about 262 families (1,575/6) relying on its 50 looms. Wallingford, p. 340; Washington (1815), p. 137.

102. If we assume that virtually every family had at least one spinning wheel and at least one woman who used it, we must conclude that 106 of Bethlem's 186 families either sent their yarn for weaving to the 80 loom-possessing families, or borrowed (or rented) the use of the looms. If the former, the loom possessors had to specialize in weaving to a greater extent than the non-possessors. If on the contrary, we assume (less realistically, given the fact that

several spinners are needed to supply one weaver) that loom-possessing families were the only ones with spinning wheels, then those families would need to have several spinning wheels (and spinners) per loom-and-weaver, specialize highly in cloth production, and have little time left for other activities like farming.

103. Lebanon, p. 403.

104. Bethlem, p. 86. "Dutch" spinning wheels were for spinning flax. The existence in Bethlem of a "mill for dressing flax" fibers (p. 85) suggests that much of the reported cloth production (p. 87) was linen, or that Bethlem was exporting dressed flax. The 4,000 yards of "Cloth dressed" would be woolen.

105. Bethlem's population in 1810 was 1,118. The Farmington report (p. 64) estimated that "The manufactures in familys [of woolens and linens]...chiefly for family consumption, may be estimated upon an average at about 20 yard for each [family]..." At an estimated 6 persons per family, this works out at less than 4 yards for each person's new clothes per year. If this consumption rate per family applied in Bethlem, too, then there was a 10 yard surplus produced per person.

106. Wallingford, 1812 addendum, p. 13.

107. Cornwall (1800), p. 107. Cornwall's population in 1800 was 1,614.

108. Cornwall (1800), p. 98; East Windsor, p. 40; Watertown, p. 156.

109. Ridgefield, p. 36. Money values in this period were frequently, as here, expressed in terms of English currency. One shilling equalled one-twentieth of a pound. It was worth about 17 cents.

110. New Haven, p. 329; Stratfield, p. 32.

111. Farmington, p. 64.

112. John Treadwell, to judge by his handwriting, wrote this section.

113. Farmington, p. 64. Treadwell counts the 15,000 yards of Stephen Brownson's "manufactory" separately from his estimate of 10,000 yards made "in familys."

114. Ridgefield, p. 26. See also discussion in Coons, *...Linen-Making...*pp. 22-28.

115. Arthur H. Cole, *The American Wool Manufacture* (Cambridge, Mass,1926), Vol. 1, pp. 4, 11.

116. Guilford, p. 256. Cole, p. 11, lists it as the third fulling mill after ones in East Hartford and Stamford.

117. See Cole, Vol. 1, pp. 128-132. In addition to his discussion of "gig-mills" for raising nap and of shearing machines, see other mentions: New Yorker Samuel Dorr patented a shearing machine in 1792 that ran woolen cloth past a rotating "cylinder wrapped with knives," Molloy *et al*, p. 96; Eleazar Hovey of Canaan, N.Y. received a patent May 20, 1812 for a shearing machine which he said would shear a yard of cloth per minute, Bishop, Vol. I, p. 176; and Isaac Sanford, co-owner of the steam-powered Middletown woolen mill, had received a patent March 27, 1799 for a "machine for dressing cloth," Pursell, p. 91-92.

118. Chatham (in Middlesex Co. Report), p. 195.

119. Table II shows that of the factories or manufactories enumerated under "Spinning" in Table I, seven were for wool-spinning, less than half the number (19+) for independent carding machines. Similarly, by 1810, the year of the census of manufactures, there were about 32 woolen mills reported for the entire country by the census and by other sources, far outnumbered by the 1,776 carding machines that it reported. Even if all the woolen mills had as many as ten carding machines each, which is quite unlikely, the remainder outside the woolen mills would be more than four times as numerous. See Cole, Vol. 1, p. 95; Vol. 2, Appendix B, "List of Factories Started Between 1800 and 1815" pp. 281-282.

120. Cole, Vol. 1, p. 88.

121. Molloy, *et al*, pp. 66. For an excellent account of carding machine technology and its spread, see Laurence Gross, "Wool Carding: A Study of Skills and Technology," *Technology and Culture* 28 (1987): 804-827.

122. Such a carding machine can be viewed in operation at Old Sturbridge Village in Massachusetts and at the American Textile History Museum in Lowell, Massachusetts.

123. Cole, Vol. 1, p. 97.

124. See David J. Jeremy, *Transatlantic Industrial Revolution: The Diffusion of Textile Technologies Between Britain and America, 1790-1830s* (Cambridge, Mass., 1981), pp. 78-79, 82.

125. See Barbara M. Tucker, *Samuel Slater and the Origins of the American Textile Industry, 1790-1860*, (Ithaca, N.Y. 1984), especially Chapter 2. Like Eli Whitney, Samuel Slater has become a legendary figure in American history. For a revisionist view of his contribution to textile mechanization in this country, see James L. Conrad, Jr. "The Making of a Hero: Samuel Slater and the Arkwright Frames," *Rhode Island History* 45 (February 1986): 3-13.

126. Tucker, pp. 51-52. The Slater Mill Historic Site in Pawtucket is today a museum in which old machines run to demonstrate textile technology history.

127. For an account of mill villages in Dudley, Oxford, and Webster in

Massachusetts, see Jonathan Prude, *The Coming of Industrial Order; Town and Factory Life in Rural Massachusetts 1810-1860* (New York, 1983), as well as Tucker, *...Slater and the Origins...*, Chapters 5-7.

128. Pomfret 1800, p. 408. For the history of the Pomfret Manufacturing Company, see William R. Bagnall, *The Textile Industries of the United States* (1893), pp. 416-423, reprinted in Gary Kulik, Roger Parks, and Theodore Z. Penn, *The New England Mill Village, 1790-1860* (Cambridge Mass., 1982) pp. 191-198, and a reconstructed map of the site as of 1835, pp. 200-201.

129. [Albert Gallatin], *Report from the Secretary of the Treasury, on the Subject of American manufactures, prepared in obedience to a resolution of the House of Representatives, April 19, 1810...*(Boston, 1810), reprinted in Kulik *et al*, *...Mill Village...*, p. 156.

130. Albert Gallatin, *Report....1810* in Kulik *et al*, p. 156, Table B, p. 162. The Pomfret Manufacturing Company owned the mill in Stirling also; two more were already built in Killingly and Plainfield but not yet in operation. More mills escaped notice by the 1810 census: nineteenth-century textile historian William R. Bagnall indicates that preceding the Pomfret company "There were five cotton factories in operation in the State of Connecticut in 1805"–in New Haven, East Hartford, Suffield, North Bolton, and Middletown–and that they continued in operation throughout the period of the Connecticut Town Reports. Bagnall, p. 419, reprinted in Kulik *et al*, *...Mill Village...* p. 194.

131. Pease and Niles, *Gazetteer*, p. 16.

132. Of the cotton factories reported as currently operating, only one, in Bolton (N.), began before the Embargo of 1807. Except for New Haven, which we know from other sources had a cotton mill before 1800 and whose report is dated 1811, the others are dated after the War of 1812: those in Litchfield County, published 1815 or towns in Middlesex County, published 1819. The terms "factory," "manufactory," and "mill" seem not to have different meanings when referring to textile production in the Town Reports.

133. Bolton (N.) p. 374. This date of "a few years" before the Report in 1801 should correct the date of 1802 for Warburton's mill given by Bagnall, writing many decades later, p. 419.

134. Middletown, p. 189; East Haddam, p. 203; New Haven, p. 308; Litchfield, p. 130.

135. Timothy Dwight, *Travels in New England and New York*, Barbara Solomon, ed. (Cambridge, Mass., 1969), Vol. 3, p. 275.

136. Lebanon, p. 403; Bethlem, p. 86.

137. Ellsworth S. Grant, *The Miracle of Connecticut* (Hartford: Connecticut Historical Society, n.d.), pp. 54-55.

138. Timothy Dwight, *Travels*, Vol. 3, p. 275, as summarized in Cole, Vol. 1, p. 254. A "picker" loosened and removed debris from wool before it was washed, dried, and carded. A "billy" took in strips of carded wool and lightly twisted them together end-to-end to produce roving, to be wound on a bobbin and fed into the spinning jenny. Stocking frames were hand-operated knitting machines, whose history dates back to invention in 1589 in England by Rev. William Lee.

139. For more about the Hartford Woolen Manufactory, see Cole, Vol. 1, pp. 64-69, and Grant, pp. 55-57.

140. Sharon, p. 148.

141. Gallatin in Kulik *et al*, p. 159, p. 164.

142. Pease and Niles, p. 17. Only one Town Report, Guilford and Madison, was published later than 1819, and it mentions no textile mills.

143. Goshen p. 117; Norfolk, in Litchfield Co., p. 142.

144. Middletown, p. 188. This was one of ten engines that Oliver Evans had put in operation in the United States by 1812, ranging from ten to 25 horsepower. Bishop, Vol. 2, p. 180.

145. Middletown, p. 188. Bishop, Vol. 1, p. 180 says the Middletown Woolen Manufacturing Company broadcloth "sold at nine and ten dollars a yard by the piece."

146. James Mease, M.D., *Archives of Useful Knowledge, A Work Devoted to Commerce, Manufacturers, Rural and Domestic Economy, Agriculture, and the Useful Arts* (Philadelphia, 1812), Vol. 2, pp. 364, 368.

147. Middletown, pp. 188-189.

148. East Haddam, p. 203. The fire had also consumed a "clothier's works and dressing shop" at the site.

149. Killingworth, p. 216; Chatham, p. 195.

150. A wool factory in Northampton, Massachusetts was said in 1812 to "move by water...150 spindles" as well as "by hand 410 spindles," but Arthur Cole doubted it and wrote "For this purpose the jenny was not really suitable, and there are no authenticated cases of this apparatus being adapted to power work." Cole, Vol. 1, p. 112.

151. Spinning jacks were similar to the cotton-spinning "mules," invented by Samuel Crompton in England c. 1779, contained one to two hundred spindles, and were operated by men. Molloy *et al*, p. 74. The earliest spinning jack that Arthur Cole found reference for was set up in 1802 at North

Andover, Massachusetts by James Scholfield. He had immigrated to America to join his brothers John and Arthur, who were active in establishing wool carding mills. See Cole. Vol. 1, pp. 112-114.

152. Molloy *et al*, p. 82, 88; Cole, Vol. 1, p. 123, finds power looms beginning in use for satinets in the late 18-teens and 1820s, and notes that the Census of 1820 recorded "eight power looms in a mill of Middlesex County, Connecticut."

153. Deane, ...*Georgical Dictionary*..., p. 142. Deane's entry "Flax" pp. 138-146, gives much information and international comparisons on flax growing and preparation for textile production.

154. "one mill for dressing flax," Bethlem, p. 85; "one flax dressing machine," Goshen, p. 114; "1 flax-mill," Washington, in Litchfield Co., p. 137.

155. Coons, ... *Linen-Making in New England*... p. 26-27, citing *The New England Farmer*, November 18, 1835 p. 148 and February 9, 1831, p. 233.

156. New Haven, p. 329; Stratfield , p. 32. A bushel of flax seed weighed about 56 pounds.

157. For use of store account books in this way, see Thomas Dublin, "Women and Outwork in a Nineteenth-Century New England Town..." in Steven Hahn and Jonathan Prude, *The Countryside in the Age of Capitalist Transformation* (Chapel Hill, N.C., 1985), p. 52, Table 2.1, p. 56.

158. For use of factory account books, see Gail Fowler Mohanty, "Experimentation in Textile Technology" cited above in note 98.

159. Edwin Sutermeister, *The Story of Papermaking* (Boston, Mass., 1954), pp. 12-14.

160. Bishop, ...*Manufactures*... Vol. 1, p. 200.

161. John Bach McMaster, *A History of the People of the United States, from the Revolution to the Civil War,* (New York: D. Appleton & Co., 1885), Vol. 2, p. 63.

162. Sutermeister, p. 14. A ream is 480 or 500 sheets. At nearly four dollars, a ream of paper was expensive—worth several days' wages for most workers at that time.

163. Middletown, p. 189. This was in the part of Middletown known as Middlefield.

164. New Haven, p. 329.

165. Judith A. McGaw, *Most Wonderful Machine; Mechanization and Social Change in Berkshire Paper Making, 1801-1885* (Princeton, 1987).

166. The Hollander was a large elliptical tub of water in which a power-driven cylinder studded with about thirty knives rotated closely above a stone or metal bedplate. Sutermeister, p. 130. As its name suggests, the Hollander originated in the Netherlands, around 1680.

167. This assumes a scene not much different from that in Berkshire County paper mills of the 1820s. McGaw, Table 3.3, p. 77 shows labor costs per ream produced 1821-1830 in Zenas Crane's mill in Dalton, Mass.

168. McGaw, p. 164. The "cylinder" machine, patented in England in 1809 and the United States in 1816, began making paper at Gilpin Mill, near Wilmington, Delaware in 1817. Joan Evans, *The Endless Web, John Dickinson & Co., Ltd 1804-1954,* (London: Jonathan Cape, 1955) calls the American patent a "plagiary," p. 10.

169. The Fourdrinier machine, invented in 1799 in France and improved in England, was first imported in 1827 from England and installed at Saugerties, N.Y. Sutermeister, p. 149-152.

170. Over the nineteenth century, use of Fourdrinier machines outstripped that of the cylinder machines. McGaw, Fig. 6.2 p. 160, p. 102.

171. McGaw, pp. 27-28, 40, 191-96; New Haven, p. 329; Stratfield, p. 32.

172. William D. Ennis, *Linseed Oil and Other Seed Oils* (New York, 1909), p. 262; University of California, *Berkeley Wellness Letter*, Vol, 15, issue 9 (June, 1999), p. 5.

173. Clark, p. 82.

174. Howard S. Russell, *A Long, Deep Furrow: Three Centuries of Farming in New England* (Hanover, N.H., 1976), p. 141.

175. Ennis, p. 198; Russell, p. 297. Guilford reported none in 1832.

176. Uncooked meal yielded a smaller quantity of higher quality oil.

177. Carter Litchfield, et. al, *The Bethlehem Oil Mill 1745-1934...German Technology in Early Pennsylvania* (Kemblesville, Pa.,1984), pp. 48-51. The technology used by the Bethlehem Moravian community was that of eastern Germany, whence they had immigrated in 1741. The oil mill proper was part of several milling activities at the same waterpower site on Monocacy Creek.

178. Ennis, p. 1.

179. Ennis, p. 17, p. 197.

180. Whitney Eastman, *The History of the Linseed Oil Industry in the United States* (Minneapolis, 1968), pp. 124-127.

181. See Article 32, "Distinguished characters, who have been natives or residents in the town." The "arts" in those days included mechanical arts.

182. In addition to the inventions discussed here, the Town Reports mention invention of a submarine (Saybrook, p. 214), a cheese press (Goshen, p. 115), a

washing machine (Pomfret, p. 407), a threshing machine (Sharon, p. 147), and a carriage odometer/speedometer (Wallingford, p. 340).

183. New Haven, p. 308; Guilford, p. 273.

184. John Warner Barber, *Connecticut Historical Collections* (New Haven and Hartford, 1836) p.228. "Some person" is possibly an allusion to Amos Whittemore, an American who is credited with inventing in 1797 a more complete machine discussed below.

185. Henry Howe, *Memoirs of the Most Eminent American Mechanics*... (New York, 1858), p. 149.

186. Winsted, p. 164. To draw wire, Samuel and Luther Hodley and James Boyd set up a wire factory in 1812, using waterpower available at the Winsted clock factory. There bar iron from Salisbury was hammered down to ½ inch square, then swaged to round rods and drawn by self-acting pincers, eighteen inches at a time, through a succession of steel dies to make wire of any thickness down to a "hair's diameter in size." *History of Litchfield County, Connecticut*, (Philadelphia, 1881) p. 201. I thank Robert Gordon for this reference.

187. Winsted, p. 164. Samuel and Luther Hoadley, whose wire factory is noted above, and Coe, Miller & Co. began making cards in 1812. The children inserting the wire teeth worked at home. The *History of Litchfield County, Connecticut* published in 1881 says these businesses closed down after 1815 when cheaper cards were imported from England, and Levi Lincoln invented a machine that made the entire card, p. 203. I thank Robert Gordon for this reference.

188. Howe, pp. 147, 149-50. The New York Manufacturing Company was incorporated "with a capital of about $800,000, of which $300,000 was [for]...manufacturing cotton and wool cards, and building the necessary machinery and factories...," p. 153.

189. Whitney quoted in Jeannette Mirsky & Allan Nevins, *The World of Eli Whitney* (New York, 1952), pp. 108, 138. The manufactory was at the corner of Wooster and Chestnut streets.

190. Whitney, quoted in Mirsky and Nevins, p. 138.

191. New Haven, pp. 318-319.

192. David D. Field, *A History of the Towns of Haddam and East-Haddam* (Middletown, Conn., 1814), p. 12. Hezekiah Scoville of Haddam furnished gun barrels to Whitney; see Felicia Johnson Deyrup, *Arms Makers of the Connecticut Valley...1798-1870* (Northampton, Mass., 1948) p. 44.

193. Deyrup, p. 43.

194. Middletown, p. 189. "Rifles" should be "muskets" if they were produced on contract for the United States Ordnance Office. Sharp-shooting rifles were not issued to soldiers until many decades later than this report.

195. Merritt Roe Smith, *Harpers Ferry Armory and the New Technology* (Ithaca, N.Y., 1977), p. 212.

196. A substantial literature exists on this subject; in addition to Deyrup and Smith, see Nathan Rosenberg, ed., *The American System of Manufactures* (Edinburgh, 1969), Otto Mayr and Robert C. Post, eds., *Yankee Enterprise* (Washington, D.C., 1981), David Hounshell, *From the American System to Mass Production, 1800-1932* (Baltimore, 1984).

197. New Haven, p. 319.

198. However, John Hall (1781-1841), an inventive gunsmith in Maine, designed and patented a breech-loading rifle in 1811 and won Ordnance Department support in 1819 for its experimental production in a separate factory near the Harpers Ferry Armory. Designed for ease of machine production, it achieved interchangeability of parts by 1828, but never replaced the muzzle-loading musket as a standard-issue weapon. Merritt Roe Smith, Chapters 7 and 8.

199. See, for instance, Thomas R. Navin, *The Whitin Machine Works Since 1831* (Cambridge, Mass., 1950), and George Sweet Gibb, *The Saco-Lowell Shops...* (Cambridge, Mass., 1950).

200. See Merritt Roe Smith, "John H. Hall, Simeon North, and the Milling Machine: The Nature of Innovation among Antebellum Arms Makers," *Technology and Culture*, 14 (1973): 573-591. For later examples of anonymous innovation, see Patrick M. Malone, "Little Kinks and Devices at Springfield Armory, 1892-1918," *IA, Journal of the Society for Industrial Archeology* 14 (1988): 58-76.

201. Edwin Battison, "A New Look at the 'Whitney' Milling Machine," *Technology and Culture* 14 (1973): 592-598.

202. A working replica of the milling machine, made for the Smithsonian Institution, is now displayed at the Eli Whitney Museum in Hamden, Connecticut, at the site of Whitney's Armory.

203. Joseph Wickham Roe, *English and American Tool Builders* (New Haven, 1916), p. 165-66.

204. Saybrook, (in Middlesex Co.) p. 209. "Pods" and "bowls" in this account refer to the curved pod-shaped cutting blade of the tool, which was superseded by the helically-twisted "screw" blade of such tools nowadays.

205. Under other ownership from 1830, when the brothers L'Hommedieu moved their operation upstream, their old factory continued making augers and bits, becoming in 1879 the site of the Russell Jennings Co., which by 1890 grew to be "one of the largest bit manufacturing establishments in the world." Thelma Clark, editor, *Kate Silliman's Chester Scrapbook* (Chester, Conn., 1986), pp. 108, 147, 148.

206. E. L'Hommedieu, at various times of Norwich, Saybrook, or Chester, Connecticut, obtained patents for a "double podded center-screw" auger on July 31, 1809; for a "screw" auger on July 17, 1816; for a "single-twist" auger on October 1, 1830; for an "auger or bit" on February 11 1835; and Patent #627 for a gimlet on March 10, 1838. Morton D. Leggett, compiler, *Subject Matter Index of Patents for Invention, 1790-1873* (Washington, D.C., 1874), Vol. 1, pp. 24-26, 606. (Patents began having numbers on July 4, 1836, when the modern Patent Office was established.)

207. Ellsworth S. Grant, *Yankee Dreamers and Doers* (Chester, Conn., 1973), p. 205. For more about the early patent system, see the special issue of *Technology and Culture* on inventions and patents, Vol. 32 # 4 (October 1991).

208. See answers in the Town Reports to Article 14 about tenant farming, and Article 26 about poor relief—not a big item in the town budgets.

209. Union, p. 387.

Gordon
Travel on Connecticut's Roads, etc.

I thank Carolyn Cooper and Michael Raber for helpful discussions on transportation issues in early Connecticut, and Darwin Stapleton and Roger Parks for their review of the first draft of this paper. David Dudley, Joel Helander, Nona Bloomer, and Edith Nettleton helped me find documents relating to roads in Guilford town archives.

1. Farmington farmers lived in town and had to travel a mile or more to their fields or pastures, often in several directions (Farmington, p. 50).

2. Philip E. Taylor, "The Turnpike Era in New England," Ph.D. diss., Yale University, 1934, pp. 23-24. For a general introduction to early Connecticut roads, see Isabel S. Mitchell, *Roads and Road Making in Colonial Connecticut* (New Haven: Yale University Press, 1933).

3. The traveler grasped the tail of the horse as it swam across the stream.

4. Llewellyn N. Edwards, *A Record of History and Evolution of Early American Bridges* (Orono: Univ. of Maine Press, 1959), pp. 20-22.

5. Bernard C. Steiner, *A History of the Plantation of Menunkatuck*, (Baltimore: Steiner, 1897), p. 216.

6. Rollin G. Osterweis, *Three Centuries of New Haven, 1638-1938* (New Haven: Yale Univ. Press), p. 34.

7. Steiner, p. 211.

8. Taylor, p. 38.

9. Steiner, p. 211.

10. Osterweis, p. 101.

11. R.B. Gordon, and M.S. Raber, *Industrial Heritage in Northwest Connecticut, a Guide to History and Archaeology* (New Haven: Connecticut Academy of Arts and Sciences, 2000); R.B. Gordon, "Choice of Method for Making Wrought Iron in the Salisbury District of Connecticut," *Journal of the Historical Metallurgy Society* 31 (1997): 25-31.

12. Taylor, p. 8.

13. Taylor, p. 38.

14. Percy W. Bidwell, *Rural Economy in New England at the Beginning of the Nineteenth Century, Transactions* of the Connecticut Academy of Arts and Sciences 20 (New Haven, 1916), pp. 241-399; see p. 313.

15. Stewart H. Holbrook, *The Old Post Road* (New York: McGraw-Hill, 1962), p. 20; Frederic J. Wood, *The Turnpikes of New England* (Boston: Marshall Jones, 1919), p. 29.

16. Edwards, pp. 24, 45; David B. Steinman and Sara R. Watson, *Bridges and Their Builders* (New York: Dover, 1957), p. 115.

17. Taylor, p. 73.

18. Richard J. Purcell, *Connecticut in Transition*, 1918 ed. republished, Middletown: Wesleyan University Press, 1963, pp. 65-67.

19. Lebanon, p. 403.

20. Middlesex County, p. 179.

21. Farmington, p. 64.

22. East Windsor, p. 41.

23. Farmington, p. 48.

24. Canterbury, p. 397; Cornwall (1800-1801), p. 98; Goshen, p. 116.

25. Cornwall (1800-1801), p. 98; Guilford p. 258.

26. Cornwall (1800-1801), p. 103; Goshen, p. 117; Lebanon, p. 403; Lisbon

27. Bidwell, pp. 314-315.

28. Osterweis, p. 161.

29. Madison, p. 272.

30. Holbrook, pp. 1-7.

31. Osterweis, p. 161.

32. Middlesex County, p. 225.

33. Guilford, p. 256; Steiner, p. 211.

34. Christopher Colles, *A Survey of the Roads of the United States of America, 1789*, ed. W.W. Ristow (Cambridge: Harvard University Press, 1961).

35. Edwards, pp. 20-33.

36. Taylor, pp. 59, 65.

37. New London, p. 364.

38. Robert Fletcher and J.P. Snow, "A History of the Development of Wooden Bridges," *Transactions of the American Society of Civil Engineers* 99 (1934): 314-408, see p 339.

39. Lisbon (Newent), p. 358.

40. John W. Barber, *Connecticut Historical Collections* (New Haven: Durrie, Peck and Barber, 1838), p. 197.

41. Farmington, pp. 55, 67-68.

42. Barber, drawing on p. 411.

43. Cornwall (1800-1801), p. 104; Kent, p. 125.

44. Farmington, p. 68.

45. Farmington, p. 67; Lebanon, p. 403.

46. Stratfield, p. 32.

47. Barber, p. 371.

48. New Haven, p. 320.

49. Barber, p. 32.

50. Steinman and Watson, p. 114.

51. Middlesex County, p. 179.

52. Eda Kranakis, *Constructing A Bridge* (Cambridge: MIT Press, 1997), pp. 17-96.

53. Joseph W. Roe, "Early New Haven Inventors," in *Inventors and Engineers of Old New Haven* (New Haven: New Haven Colony Historical Society, 1939), pp. 12-14.

54. Fletcher and Snow, p. 403.

55. Barber, p. 32.

56. Barber, p. 124.

57. Edwards, pp. 56, 60.

58. Steinman and Watson, p. 112.

59. See for example W.P. Trowbridge, "Town's Truss," *Columbia School of Mines Quarterly*, July 1888, p. 13. This bridge had diagonals made of three-inch planks crossing at 80° spaced on four-foot centers and connected with trenails two and a quarter inches in diameter. A replica of this bridge stands on the grounds of the Eli Whitney Museum in Hamden, Conn.

60. Bruce Clouette and Matthew Roth, *Connecticut's Historic Highway Bridges* (Hartford: Connecticut Department of Transportation, 1991), p. 26.

61. Taylor, p. 55.

62. Edward E. Atwater, *History of the City of New Haven* (New York: Munsell, 1887), p. 350.

63. Barber, p. 113.

64. New London, p. 363.

65. Middlesex County, note H, p. 226.

66. Steiner (quoting Field), p. 216; Stratfield, p. 32; Kent, p. 125.

67. Atwater, p. 350.

68. New Haven, p. 320.

69. Osterweis, p. 275.

70. Cornwall (1800-1801), p. 99; Goshen, p. 117.

71. Farmington, p. 67. Bidwell, p. 311, quotes a scathingly humorous account of the ineffectiveness of town road maintenance by called-out citizens. It was, however, written by someone making a case for increased state spending.

72. Taylor, pp. 71-98.

73. Wood, p. 14.

74. Wood, p. 7; Taylor, pp. 99-100, 161.

75. J.W. Miller, ed., *As We Were on the Valley Shore*, Guilford: Shore Line Times Publishing Co., 1976, p. 139.

76. Taylor, pp. 102, 108.

77. Wood, p. 34; Taylor, pp. 105, 111.

78. I thank Roger Parks for bringing the differences in the New England turnpike networks to my attention.

79. Donald C. Jackson, "Roads Most Travelled: Turnpikes in Southeastern Pennsylvania in the Early Republic," in *Early American Technology*, ed. J.A. McGaw (Chapel Hill: University of North Carolina Press, 1994), p. 230.

80. Joel E. Helander, *Oxpasture to Summer Colony* (Guilford: Helander,

1976), p. 217.

81. Miller, p. 139.

82. Taylor, pp. 113-114, 119, 140-142, 165; Daniel P. Jones, *The Economic and Social Transformation of Rhode Island, 1780-1850* (Boston: Northeastern Univ. Press, 1992), pp. 46-57, 68-81.

83. Helander, pp. 214-217.

84. Taylor, p. 185.

85. The first Virginia turnpike to be made with a stone surface was built in 1824, and cost $3,294 per mile; Robert F. Hunter, "Turnpike Construction in Antebellum Virginia," *Technology and Culture* 4-2 (1963): 177-200.

86. Wood, pp. 14-15, 33, 35; Taylor, p. 182; Hunter, pp. 177-200.

87. Jackson, pp. 197-239.

88. The method of determining grade was from the angle of repose of a wagon, the slope at which the vehicle once placed in motion would just continue to roll. For the best roads this grade was 1/35. On a good American road the grade was 1/20, and often steeper. (Hunter, p. 188.) On the effect of steep grades on revenue, see Taylor, p. 286.

89. Barber, p. 334.

90. Middlesex County, p. 179.

91. Wood, p. 36.

92. Goshen, p. 117; Guilford Town Archives, Box 50, Guilford Free Library.

93. Taylor, pp. 228-230; H.C. Warren, "Thoroughfares in Early Republic Controlled by Corporations," *Connecticut Magazine* 8 (1903): 721-729.

94. Taylor, p. 279.

95. As revenue declined and turnpike proprietors ignored repair orders, towns were notified so they could take over, as in this notice from Andrew Griswold and David Fowler in November 1863: "We the undersigned commissioners of the Fair Haven Turnpike road do hereby certify that we have performed the duty assigned us under Sections 3rd and 4th of the act of May 1863 (and approved June 19th 1863) and have ordered the necessary repairs upon said road and given notice required by law which said order has not been complied with. We therefore give notice as by Sect. 5th of said act required, to the town clerk of Guilford that said notice and order have not been complied with." Guilford Town Archives, Box 50.

96. Taylor, pp. 280, 348.

97. Between 1816 and 1820 the cost of living dropped by 30 percent, and over the next two decades changed relatively little. *Historical Statistics of the United States*, Washington: GPO, 1960, p. 115. Thus, the change in the road tax from 2 to 3 cents per dollar was a real increase at the same time that the town diminished the value it placed on citizen's labor.

98. Documents in the Guilford town archives, Box 50, Guilford Free Library.

99. Henry P. Sage, "Ye Mylestones of Connecticut," *New Haven Colony Historical Society Papers* 10 (1951): 1-101.

100. Gordon and Raber.

101. Clouette and Roth.

102. New England Chapters, Society for Industrial Archeology *Newsletter*, 16-1 (1996): 8.

103. Clouette and Roth, pp. 25, 27; Barber, p. 32.

104. Quoted in Jarvis M. Morse, *A Neglected Period in Connecticut's History 1818-1850*, (New Haven: Yale University Press, 1933, reprint, 1978, NY: Octagon Books), p. 257.

Skinner
Mines, Minerals, Quarries, and Fuels

1. Arthur Mirsky, "Geology Resources of the Original Thirteen United States (summary)," in Cecil J. Schneer, ed., *Two Hundred Years of Geology in America* (Hanover, N.H.: University of New Hampshire Press, 1979), pp. 39-41.

2. Jean-Etienne Guettard, Plate VII in *Mémoires de l'Académie Royale de Sciences*, Paris, 1752.

3. Johann David Schöpf, *Beyträge zur Mineralogischen Kenntniss des Oestlichen Theils von Nord Amerika und seiner Gebürge* (Erlangen: J.J. Palm, 1787).

4. Charles U. Shepard, *A Report on the Geological Survey of Connecticut* (New Haven, Conn.: State of Conn., 1837).

5. George P. Merrill, *The First One Hundred Years of American Geology* (New Haven, Conn., Yale Univ. Press, 1924), pp. 23-24.

6. For Silliman's life, see John F. Fulton and Elizabeth H. Thomson, *Benjamin Silliman 1779-1864: Pathfinder in American Science* (New York: Henry Schuman, 1947); Chandos Michael Brown, *Benjamin Silliman: A Life in the Young Republic* (Princeton: Princeton University Press, 1989).

7. Franklin, p. 348.

8. Many different spellings, such as peat, peet, and peete, appear in the Reports, or tun, tonne, ton. We use modern spelling, except in quoting an original document.

9. *State of Connecticut Register and Manual* (Hartford, Conn.: State of Conn., 2001).

10. Jedidiah Morse, *The American Universal Geography* (Elizabethtown, [N. J.]: Shepard Kollock), 1789), pp. 217-218.

11. For information on the concepts of cratons and continental growth, refer to any standard text on physical geology, such as Brian J. Skinner and Stephen C. Porter, *The Dynamic Earth: An Introduction to Physical Geology* (New York: John Wiley and Sons, 2000).

12. Michael Bell, *The Face of Connecticut: People, Geology, and the Land* (State Geological and Natural History Survey of Connecticut, Bulletin 110, 1985); Chet Raymo and Maureen E. Raymo, *Written in Stone: A Geological and Natural History of the Northeastern United States* (Chester, Conn.: Globe-Pequot Press, 1989).

13. Personal communication, Professor Leo Hickey. This fossil is now in the collections of Yale University's Department of Geology and Geophysics.

14. Franklin, p. 348; Wallingford, p. 340.

15. Charles Rufus Harte, "Connecticut's Iron and Copper," Connecticut Society of Civil Engineers, *Annual Report* #60, 1944, pp. 131-166.

16. Shepard, pp. 10-11.

17. Brian J. Skinner and Barbara L. Narendra, "Rummaging Through the Attic; a Brief History of the Geological Sciences at Yale," in Ellen T. Drake and William M. Jordan, eds., *Geologists and Ideas: A History of North American Geology* (Boulder, Colo.: Geological Society of America, 1985), Centennial Special Vol. 1, pp. 355-376.

18. Cornwall, 1801, p. 103.

19. Cornwall, 1801, p. 103.

20. Cornwall, 1801, p. 108.

21. Cornwall, 1812, pp. 109-110

22. Cornwall, 1801, p. 105.

23. For information on pyrites or any other mineral mentioned in this paper refer to a standard mineralogy text, such as Cornelis Klein and Cornelius S. Hurlburt, Jr., *Manual of Mineralogy*, 21st ed. (New York: John Wiley and Sons, 1999).

24. Kent, p. 125.

25. Cornwall, 1801, p. 96.

26. Michael Gannett, ed., *Cornwall in 1801 by Elijah Allen* (Cornwall, Conn.: Cornwall Historical Society, 1985) p. 39, note 41.

27. Kent, pp. 124-125.

28. Washington, 1800, p. 151.

29. Gregory Galer, Robert Gordon, and Frances Kemmish, *Connecticut's Ames Iron Works: Family, Community, Nature, and Innovation in An Enterprise of the Early American Republic* (New Haven: Connecticut Academy of Arts and Sciences, 1998); Robert Gordon and Michael Raber, *Industrial Heritage in Northwest Connecticut: A Guide to History and Archaeology"* (New Haven: Connecticut Academy of Arts and Sciences, 2000).

30. Litchfield County, Northfield parish, p. 136.

31. Goshen, p. 114.

32. Ridgefield, p. 24.

33. Bethlem, p. 84.

34. Haddam, 1808, p. 169.

35. Haddam, 1808, p. 170.

36. Haddam, 1808, p. 170.

37. Haddam, 1808, p. 170.

38. Union, pp. 385-386.

39. Willington, p. 391.

40. Killingworth, in Middlesex Co., p. 216. See *Essay on the Invention, or Art of Making Very Good, if Not the Best Iron, from Black Sea Sand*, by Jared Eliot, M.A., of Killingworth (New York: John Holt, 1762).

41. Chatham, in Middlesex Co. p. 195.

42. John Frank Schairer, *Minerals of Connecticut* (Hartford, Conn.: The State Geological and Natural History Survey, 1931) Bulletin 51, p. 108.

43. Madison, p. 268.

44. Saybrook, in Middlesex Co., p. 208.

45. Saybrook, p. 208.

46. Preston, p. 368.

47. Pomfret, p. 407.

48. New London, p. 362.

49. Chatham, in Middlesex Co., p. 195.

50. Middletown, in Middlesex Co., pp. 187.

51. Farmington, p. 55.

52. Middletown, p. 187.
53. Middletown, pp. 186-187.
54. Farmington, p. 55.
55. Middletown, p. 187.
56. Chatham, p. 195.
57. Benjamin Silliman, "Sketch of the Mineralogy of the Town of New Haven," *Memoirs* of the Connecticut Academy of Arts and Sciences (New Haven, 1810), Vol. 1, pp. 83-96.
58. New Haven, p. 305. Between 1796 and 1811, Timothy Dwight made thirteen journeys, the journals of which his family published in 1821 and 1822 as *Travels in New England and New York*. They have been reprinted in a new edition by Barbara M. Solomon, ed. (Cambridge, Mass.: The Belknap Press of Harvard Univ. Press, 1969).
59. New Haven, p. 305.
60. New Haven, p. 305.
61. New Haven, p. 305.
62. New Haven, p. 306.
63. New Haven, p. 306.
64. New Haven pp. 306-307.
65. New Haven p. 307.
66. New Haven, p. 307.
67. New Haven, pp. 307-308.
68. See Leonard G. Wilson, ed., *Benjamin Silliman and His Circle: Studies on the Influence of Benjamin Silliman on Science in America* (New York: Science History Publications, 1979).
69. James Dwight Dana, *A System of Mineralogy* (New Haven: Durrie & Peck and Henrick & Noyes, 1837).
70. Richard V. Gaines, H. Catherine W. Skinner, Eugene E. Foord, Brian H. Mason, and A. Rosenzweig, *Dana's New Mineralogy*, 8th ed. (New York: John Wiley and Sons, 1997).

Smith & Clark
Wild Animals

We would like to thank the following individuals for their valuable contributions to the manuscript through our consultations: Denise Casey (writing and editing), Andrew Lord (legal), Joseph Miller (historical and procurement of historical literature), Noble Proctor (ornithology), Paul Rego (wildlife), and David Smith (forestry). We also thank Vicki Bomba-Lewandoski, Erin Keller, Heidi Schoenfeldt, and Diane Smith for technical assistance and search through historical records. We are very grateful to Vince D'Amico for the graphics, Roger Zerillo for photography, and Richard DeGraaf, Roland Clement, Noble Proctor, and Charles Remington for their helpful reviews of the manuscript. We are especially appreciative of Katherine McManus for the preparation of the manuscript. Her assistance through all phases of the project contributed greatly to the manuscript.
1. East Windsor, p. 38.

2. William Cronon, *Changes in the Land: Indians, Colonists, and the Ecology of New England* (New York, 1983), Gordon G. Whitney, *From Coastal Wilderness to Fruited Plain: A History of Environmental Change in Temperate North America, 1500 to the Present* (Cambridge, England, 1994).
3. Article 22 of the Connecticut Academy of Arts and Sciences Solicitation letter. See the complete questionnaire in this volume and the responses and the introductory essay in Volume I, *What They Said*, for background on the project.
4. Stephen R. Kellert, *The Value of Life: Biological Diversity and Human Society* (Washington, D.C., 1996).
5. East Windsor, p. 38.
6. Extirpation: The extinction of a species within a particular geographic region, as for example North America or New England, but not from its total worldwide distribution. Extinction: The complete and irrevocable disappearance of all individuals constituting a taxon throughout the worldwide range of that taxon.
7. Benjamin Trumbull, *A Complete History of Connecticut, Civil and Ecclesiastical, from the Emigration of its First Planters from England, in the year MDCXXX, to the year MDCCXIII*, Vol. I (Hartford, 1797); ...to the year 1764, Vol. II (New Haven, 1818), Vol. 1, p. 46.
8. Higginson, quoted in Cronon, p. 23.
9. William Wood, *New England's Prospect* (Amherst, 1634), pp. 41-42.
10. George G. Goodwin, *The Mammals of Connecticut* (Hartford, 1935).
11. Wood, p. 42.
12. Trumbull, *History of Connecticut*, Vol. I, p. 25.
13. Noah A. Phelps, *History of Simsbury, Granby, and Canton from 1642-1845* (Hartford, 1845), p. 76.
14. James E. Cardoza, "The history and status of the black bear in Massachusetts and adjacent New England states", *Research Bulletin* No. 18 (Westborough, Mass., 1976), p. 52.
15. Whitney, 1994.
16. Elizabeth H. Schenck, *The History of Fairfield, Fairfield County, Connecticut* (New York, 1889).
17. Cardoza, p. 53
18. Augustine G. Hibbard, *History of the town of Goshen, Connecticut* (Hartford, 1897).
19. Auren Roys, *A brief history of the town of Norfolk from 1738 to 1844* (New York, 1847), p. 59.
20. Sherman Adams, *The native and wild mammals of Connecticut* (Hartford, 1896), p. 11.
21. Glover M. Allen, *Fauna of New England* (Boston, 1904).
22. T.S. Palmer, "Chronology and Index of the More Important Events in American Game Protection, 1776-1911" (Washington, DC, 1912), p. 13.
23. Allen, 1904.
24. Ridgefield, p. 26.
25. James H. Linsley, "A Catalogue of the Mammals of Connecticut, Arranged According to their Natural Families," *American Journal of Science and Arts* 43 (1842): 352.
26. Goodwin, 1935.
27. Adams, p. 15.
28. Richard H. Yahner, *Eastern Deciduous Forest Ecology and Wildlife Conservation* (Minneapolis, 1995), pp. 29-30.
29. Brian G. Slough, and R.M.F.S. Sadlier, "A Land Capability Classification System for Beaver (Castor canadensis Kuhl.)," *Canadian Journal of Zoology* 55 (1977): 1324-1335.
30. Adams, p. 12.
31. Whitney.
32. Stephen Innes, *Labor in a New Land: Economy and Society in Seventeenth-century Springfield* (Princeton, 1983).
33. Cronon.
34. Adams, p. 12.
35. Lisbon (Newent), p. 358; Ridgefield, p. 26.
36. Wood, p. 46.
37. Whitney.
38. Trumbull, *History of Connecticut*, Vol. 1, p. 39.
39. Adams, p. 8.
40. Edward H. Jenkins, "Connecticut Agriculture," in Norris G. Osborn, ed., *History of Connecticut, in Monographic Form* (New York, 1925), Vol. II, p. 315.
41. Frances M. Caulkins, *History of New London, Connecticut: From the first survey of the coast in 1612, to 1860* (New London, 1895), p. 142.
42. Adams, p. 8.
43. David Humphreys, *The Life and Heroic Exploits of Israel Putnam, Major-General in the Revolutionary War* (New York, 1835).
44. Adams, p. 9.
45. Linsley, p. 348.
46. Glover M. Allen, "History of the Virginia Deer in New England" in *Proceedings* of the New England Game Conference (1929), pp. 19-38.
47. Goodwin, p. 175; Thomas Morton, *New English Canaan* [1632], ed. Charles F. Adams (Boston, 1885).
48. Adams, p. 14; Trumbull, *History of Connecticut*, Vol. 1, p. 45.
49. Middlesex County, p. 179; Goodwin, p.176; Jocelyn Crane, "Mammals of Hampshire County, Massachusetts," *Journal of Mammalogy* 12 (1931): 267-273.
50. Alfred J. Godin, *Wild Mammals of New England* (Baltimore, 1977), Goodwin, p. 84.
51. Wood, p. 42.
52. Adams, p. 7; Glover M. Allen, Extinct and Vanishing mammals of the Western Hemisphere with Marine Species of All the Oceans, (n. p., American Committee on International Wildlife Protection, Special Bulletin, 1942).
53. Linsley; Adams, p. 7.
54. Carolyn Merchant, *Ecological Revolutions—Nature, Gender, and Science in New England* (Chapel Hill, 1989), p. 67.
55. Steven N. Jackson, "Wild Turkey Hunting Season Report, Spring 1981 Report" (Hartford, 1981), p 1.
56. Morton, p. 193.
57. John Josselyn, quoted in Cronon, p. 100.
58. John W. Aldrich, "Historical Background," in Oliver H. Hewitt, ed., *The Wild Turkey and Its Management* (Washington, D.C., 1967), pp. 3-16; C. Hart Merriam, *A Review of the Birds of Connecticut* (New Haven,

1877); Stephen N. Jackson, "Connecticut Wild Turkey Program" (Hartford, 1980), p. 1.

59. Wood, p. 35.

60. Michael W. Klemens, *Amphibians and Reptiles of Connecticut and Adjacent Regions*" (Hartford, 1993).

61. Ridgefield, p. 26.

62. Frances M. Caulkins, *History of Norwich, Connecticut* (Hartford, 1866), p. 298.

63. James H. Linsley, "*A Catalogue of the Reptiles of Connecticut arranged according to their Families*," *American Journal of Science and Arts* (1844) 46: 37-51.

64. Klemens, 1993.

65. Ludlow Griscom, *The Birds of Concord* (Cambridge, 1949).

66. Linsley, p. 346.

67. Adams, p. 4.

68. Goodwin, p. 169; Godin, p. 288; W.J. Hays, "Notes on the Range of Some of the Animals in America at the Time of the Arrival of the White men," *American Naturalist 5* (1871): 387-392.

69. Cornwall (1800-1801), p. 104.

70. Goodwin, p. 178

71. Goodwin, p. 124.

72. Godin; Connecticut Department of Environmental Protection, "Connecticut's Wildlife: a Checklist of Birds, Mammals, Reptiles, and Amphibians" (Hartford, 1988).

73. Adams, p. 12.

74. Goodwin, p. 23.

75. Ralph Wetzel, "The Invasion of Connecticut" (Univ. of Conn. at Storrs, unpublished paper, 1979), p. 2.

76. Godin; Connecticut DEP, "Connecticut's Wildlife."

77. Richard M. DeGraaf and Ronald I. Miller, "The Importance of Disturbance and Land-use History in England: Implications for Forested Landscapes and Wildlife Conservation," in R.M. DeGraaf and R.I. Miller, eds., *Conservation of Faunal Diversity in Forested Landscapes* (London 1996), p. 14.

78. Godin.

79. Godin.

80. Adams, p. 13.

81. Goodwin, p. 161.

82. Harvey R. Smith and Charles L. Remington, "Food Specificity in Interspecies Competition: Comparisons between Terrestrial Vertebrates and Arthropods," *BioScience* 46 (1996): 444.

83. R.K. Wayne and N. Lehman, "Mitochondrial DNA Analysis of the Eastern Coyote: Origins and Hybridization," in A.H. Boer, ed., *Ecology and Management of the Eastern Coyote* (Fredericton, Canada, 1992), pp. 9-22; Gary R. Goff, et al., *Eastern Coyote* (*Canis Latrans*) (Ithaca, 1984).

84. Godin.

85. Gary C. Moore and Gerry R. Parker, "Colonization by the Eastern Coyote (*Canis latrans*)," in A.H. Boer, p. 33.

86. L. David Mech, *The Wolf: the Ecology and Behavior of an Endangered Species* (Garden City, 1970).

87. Wetzel, p. 2.

88. Laurence P. Pringle, "Notes on Coyotes in Southern New England," *Journal of Mammalogy* 41 (1960): 278; Paul Rego, pers. comm.

89. John A. Litvaitis, "Niche Relations between Coyotes and Sympatric Carnivora," in A.H. Boer, p. 73.

90. Paul Rego, pers. comm.

91. Litvaitis, p. 77; Litvaitis and Daniel J. Harrison, "Bobcat-coyote Niche Relationships during a Period of Coyote Population Increase," *Canadian Journal of Zoology* 67 (1989): 1180-1188.

92. Ridgefield, p. 26.

93. Trumbull, *History of Connecticut*, Vol. I, p. 39.

94. Farmington, p. 68.

95. New London, pp. 363-364.

96. Jean Dorst, *The Migration of Birds* (Boston, 1962).

97. Linnaeus, as cited in Roger F. Pasquier, *Watching Birds: an Introduction to Ornithology* (Boston, 1977), p. 192.

98. Dorst, 1962.

99. Robert L. Burgess and David M. Sharpe, *Forest Island Dynamics in Man-dominated Landscapes* (New York, 1981); Edward O. Wilson, *Biophilia* (Cambridge, 1984).

100. Lisbon (Newent), p. 358.

101. Trumbull, *History of Connecticut*, Vol. 1, p. 37.

102. Wood, p. 38.

103. Cronon; Merchant.

104. Howard S. Russell, *Indian New England before the Mayflower* (Hanover, 1980), p. 14.

105. D. Smith, pers. comm.

106. Alfred O. Gross, "The Heath Hen," *Memoirs* of the Boston Society of Natural History, 6, no. 4 (1928): 497.

107. Cronon; Whitney.

108. Trumbull, *History of Connecticut*, Vol. 1, p. 40.

109. Cronon.

110. DeGraaf and Miller, p. 10.

111. Whitney.

112. Michael Williams, *Americans and Their Forests, a Historical Geography* (Cambridge, 1989), p. 55.

113. Roland M. Harper, "Changes in the Forest Area of New England in Three Centuries," *Journal of Forestry* 16 (1918): 447.

114. Jenkins, p. 323.

115. Whitney; Jenkins, p. 323.

116. Merchant, p. 185.

117. Jenkins, p. 323.

118. Lisbon (Hanover), p. 353.

119. Washington, p. 152.

120. Jenkins, p. 346.

121. Williams, pp. 68-69.

122. Harper, p. 447.

123. Jenkins; Merchant, p. 195.

124. Harper, p. 447.

125. Rudy J. Favretti, *Highlights of Connecticut Agriculture*, (Storrs, 1976), p. 18; Whitney; Williams.

126. Whitney.

127. Whitney.

128. D. Smith, pers. comm.

129. John A. Litvaitis, "Response of Early Successional Vertebrates to Historic Changes in Land Use," *Conservation Biology* 7 (1993): 870.

130. DeGraaf and Miller, p. 17.

131. Robert A. Askins, "Population Trends in Grassland, Shrubland, and Forest Birds in Eastern North America," *Current Ornithology* 11 (1993): 1-34.

132. Whitney.

133. DeGraaf and Miller, p. 19.

134. Paul Rego, pers. comm.

135. Paul Rego, pers. comm.

136. DeGraaf and Miller, p. 16; Whitney, 1994.

137. Paul Rego, pers. comm.

138. Jackson.

139. Kellert, p. 26.

140. Whitney, 1994.

141. Wood, p. 45.

142. Coventry, 1809, p. 380.

143. Roger A. Caras, *Dangerous to Man* (Philadelphia, 1964); Cardoza, p. 69; Phelps, p. 76.

144. Wood, p. 42.

145. Wood, p. 45.

146. Thomas Morton, quoted in Godin, p. 281.

147. Wood, p. 66.

148. Caulkins, p. 298.

149. Raymond Ditmars as cited in George H. Lamson, "The Reptiles of Connecticut," *Research Bulletin 54* (Hartford, 1935).

150. Whitney.

151. Stephen H. Spurr, "Forest Associations in the Harvard Forest," *Ecological Monographs* 26 (1956): 245-262.

152. Lowell Sinclair et al., "Influence of Stone Walls on the Local Distribution of Small Mammals," *University of Connecticut Biological Sciences Series* 1 (1967): 43-62; Whitney.

153. Trumbull, *History of Connecticut*, Vol. I, p. 67.

154. Alexis de Tocqueville, quoted in Williams, p. 5.

155. Wood.

156. Cronon.

157. Palmer, p. 8.

158. John Bouvier, *A Law Dictionary Adapted to the Constitution and Laws of the United States of America and of the Several States of the American Union, with References to the Civil and Other Systems of Foreign Law* (Philadelphia, 1856).

159. 161 U.S. 795 at 523 (1896).

160. 161 U.S. 796 at 533 (1896).

161. Palmer, pp. 9, 13.

162. Palmer, p. 10.

163. DeGraaf and Miller, 1996.

164. Yahner, p. 170.

165. Bruce A. Wilcox and Dennis D. Murphy, "Conservation Strategy: The Effects of Fragmentation on Extinction," *American Naturalist* 125 (1985): 879-887.

166. Paul Rego, pers. comm.

167. Yahner, p. 100.

168. Harvey R. Smith and Nobel S. Proctor, "No home to Return to," *Discovery* 21 (1989), p. 6.

169. New Haven, p. 303.

170. Adams, p. 12.

171. Kellert, p. 12.

172. Stephen R. Kellert and E.O Wilson, eds., *The Biophilia Hypothesis* (Washington, DC, 1993).

Milne
Connecticut Woodlands

1. Lloyd C. Irland, *Wildlands and Woodlots, The Story of New England's Forests* (Hanover, N.H.: University Press of New England, 1982), p. 56.

2. Canterbury, p. 397.

3. Irland says forest cover in Connecticut was 52 percent in 1800, p. 56.

4. Bethlem, p. 84.

5. Cornwall (1800-1801), p. 105; Winchester, p. 161.

6. Cornwall (1800-1801), p. 96, quoting tax list for 1798. [All towns used this nomenclature for fireplaces; the majority of those in surviving tax records appear to be taxed as 3rd or 4th rate. The classification had more to do with tax rate than with condition. Editor's note.]

7. Cornwall (1800-1801), p. 104; East Windsor, p. 39; Pomfret, p. 407.

8. Sharon, p. 147.

9. Goshen, p. 116.

10. East Haddam, in Middlesex Co., p. 203.

11. Farmington, p. 57.

12. Farmington, p. 57.

13. Goshen, p. 115.

14. Winsted, p. 163.

15. Sharon, p. 146.

16. Washington 1800, p. 151.

17. Haddam, Middlesex Co., p. 199.

18. Chatham, Middlesex Co., p. 195.

19. Saybrook, Middlesex Co., p. 209.

20. Middlesex County, Note C, p. 224.

21. Goshen, p. 117.

22. Farmington, p. 64.

23. Union, p. 386.

24. Robert P. Multhauf, "Potash," in Brooke Hindle, ed., *Material Culture of the Wooden Age* (Tarrytown, N.Y.: Sleepy Hollow Press, 1981), pp. 227-240.

25. Farmington, p. 64.

26. New Haven, p. 308.

27. Haddam, Middlesex Co., p. 199.

28. Lebanon, p. 402.

29. Franklin, p. 348.

30. Bethlem, p. 85; Bolton (N.), p. 373.

31. Farmington, p. 62.

32. Wallingford, p. 343.

33. Wallingford, p. 340.

34. For a history of heating and cooking stoves in America, see Priscilla J. Brewer, *From Fireplace to Cookstove: Technology and the Domestic Ideal in America* (Syracuse, N.Y.: Syracuse Univ. Press, 2000).

35. U.S. Census figures reported in *Connecticut State Register and Manual*, 1971, p. 596.

36. See George McLean Milne, *Connecticut Woodlands: A Century's Story of the Connecticut Forest and Park Association* (Rockfall, Conn.: Connecticut Forest and Park Association, 1995).

37. Union, p. 387.

Niering
Connecticut Towns c. 1800

I wish to thank Drs. Joseph Hickey, Mary Helen M. Goldsmith and one anonymous reviewer for their invaluable comments in improving this manuscript. Information concerning Dr. Ives was provided by Dr. Goldsmith.
The assistance of Dr. Carolyn C. Cooper was also greatly appreciated.

1. Washington 1800, p. 151; Wintonbury, p. 77.

2. Washington, 1800, p. 151.

3. Union, p. 386; Canterbury, p. 397; Goshen, p. 115; New Haven, p. 308; and Winchester, p. 159.

4. Mesic refers to an area that is moderate in moisture.

5. Black oak was also sometimes called "yellow" for the color of its inner bark.

6. Canterbury, p. 397.

7. Winchester, p. 160.

8. S.L. Anagnostakis, "Improved Chestnut Tree Condition Maintained in Two Connecticut Plots after Treatments with Hypovirulent Strains of the Chestnut Blight Fungus." *Forest Science* 36 (1990): 113-124.

9. Quoted in H.W. Hicock, "Connecticut Forests ... Asset or Liability." *Northeastern Logger* November (1956): 20-33.

10. Litchfield County, p. 129; Bethlem, p. 84.

11. Ridgefield, p. 24.

12. W.A. Niering, R.H. Goodwin, and S. Taylor. "Prescribed Burning in Southern New England: Introduction to Long-range Studies. In *Proceedings*, 10th Annual Tall Timbers Fire Ecology Conference, Tallahassee, Fla., 1970, pp. 267-286.

13. W.A. Niering and G.D. Dreyer. "Effects of Prescribed Burning on *Andropogon scoparius* in Postagricultural Grassland." *American Midland Naturalist* 122 (1989): 88-102.

14. R.A. Askins, "History of Grasslands in the Northeastern United States: Implications for Bird Conservation." In P.D. Vickery and P.W. Dunwiddie, eds. *Grasslands of Northeastern North America*. Lincoln, MA: Massachusetts Audubon Society, 1998, pp. 119-136.

15. E.L. Braun, *Deciduous Forests of Eastern North America*. Philadelphia, PA: Blakeston Co., 1950; p. 11 defines associations of trees in forest regions; Chapters 6, 7, and 8 discuss the Oak-Hickory, Oak-Chestnut, and Oak-Pine Forest Regions.

16. A "flora" is a listing of plants growing in a certain locality.

17. New Haven, pp. 313-317.

18. The specimens in these four volumes were collected by Horatio Nelson Fenn, a student of Dr. Eli Ives, while studying at the Yale College Medical Institute. The title page of the work reads "*A Collection of Plants of New-Haven and Its Environs Arranged According to the Natural Orders of Jussieu. By Horatio N. Fenn. 1822.*" Known locally as "the Fenn Flora," it is the earliest known collection of flora from Connecticut and is in the keeping of the Paleobotany Division of the Peabody Museum at Yale University.

19. Forbs: broad-leafed plants, as distinct from grasses.

20. M.A.R. Besitka, "An Ecological and Historical Study of *Phragmites australis* along the Atlantic Coast" (unpublished Masters thesis, Drexel University, 1996).

21. New Haven, p. 308.

22. Ridgefield, p. 26.

23. Preston, p. 369.

24. Bethlem, p. 88.

25. New Haven, p. 327; Pomfret, p. 408; Ridgefield, p. 26.

26. Bethlem, p. 88. A rowel is the sharp-toothed wheel in the shank of a spur.

27. Willington, p. 392.

28. Cheshire, p. 249; Farmington, p. 68.

29. Litchfield, p. 130.

30. Cornwall (1800-1801), p. 102.

31. Ridgefield, p. 26.

32. Ridgefield, p. 26.

33. Ridgefield, p. 26.

34. Personal observation.

35. Coventry 1806, p. 377.

36. Canterbury, p. 398.

37. Haddam 1808, p. 169. Seines are large fishing nets with floats along the top edge and weights along the bottom.

38. Stratfield, p. 31.

39. New Haven, p. 319.

40. New Haven, p. 310.

41. New Haven, pp. 319-320.

42. Madison, p. 267.

43. New Haven, p. 309; W.A. Niering and R.S. Warren. "Vegetation Patterns and Processes in New England Salt Marshes." *BioScience* 30(5): 301-307.

44. Madison, p. 269.

45. New Haven, pp. 309-310.
46. Besitka.
47. R.M. Thorson, A.G. Harris, S.L. Harris, R. Gradie III, and M.W. Lefor. "Colonial Impacts to Wetlands in Lebanon, Connecticut," In C. Welby and M.E. Gowan, eds., *A Paradox of Power: Voices of Warning and Reason in the Geosciences* (Boulder, Colorado, Geological Society of America Reviews in Engineering Geology, 1998), Vol. XII, pp. 23-42.
48. Franklin, p. 348.
49. New Haven, p. 325.
50. Middlesex County, p. 175.
51. Winchester, p. 161.
52. Franklin, p. 350; Goshen, p. 119.
53. Farmington, p. 71.

Thorson
Physical Environment of Connecticut Towns

1. The Connecticut Academy of Arts and Sciences (CAAS) Solicitation letter and its purposes are discussed in the companion volume, *What They Said.*
2. Refer to D. Worster, "Transformations of the Earth; Toward an Agroecological Perspective in History," *Journal of American History* 76 (1990): 1087-1106, for a review of how historians, rather than geologists, have examined such changes.
3. Henry Faul and Carol Faul, *It Began with a Stone* (New York: John Wiley & Sons, 1983), provides a good review of the early history of geology.
4. I include here the following thumbnail sketch of the geology of the state, drawn from the following sources: (1) Chet Raymo and Maureen E. Raymo, *Written in Stone: a Geological and Natural History of the Northeastern United States* (Chester, Conn.: The Globe Pequot Press, 1989). (2) John Rodgers, Bedrock Geology Map of Connecticut. Connecticut State Department of Environmental Protection / U.S. Geological Survey: Scale 1:125,000 (1985). (3) Allan P. Bennison, compiler, Geological Highway Map of the Northeastern Region: American Association of Petroleum Geologists, Tulsa, Oklahoma (no date). Connecticut can be divided into four general terranes: craton, Avalonian, Iapetos, and Rift Valley. The craton refers to that part of North America already in existence before the creation of the Appalachian Mountains between about 200-500 million years ago, which took place during a protracted continental collision. These rocks, principally the marbles, slates, and schists of northwestern Connecticut, have been slivered up by younger thrust faults into the high, elongate ridges of the northwestern highlands. Avalonian rocks, the crystalline, largely granitic rocks of easternmost Connecticut and the southeast coast, originated as a separate continental block that was attached to North America during mountain building. The softer rocks of the Iapetos terrane underlie much of the state, which were originally muds and volcanic sandstones from an ancient ocean that was closed as Pangea was assembled. As this super-continent was later rifted apart, small basins were formed that filled with red sandstone and basalt; the central lowland of Connecticut from New Haven to Holyoke is the largest of these Rift Valleys, each of which holds soft sedimentary rock. Following millions of years of erosion, most of the region was gently uplifted, causing the rivers to downcut deeply into the older, more gentle topography, and in the process, creating a series of valleys, each with the cataracts and bedrock gorges that would later be responsible for numerous hydropower sites, as well as a broad uplifted plateau, which would later be inundated by glacial ice and plastered with a stony till, then called "hardpan."
5. Samuel Deane, *The New England Farmer or Georgical Dictionary* (Worcester: Isaiah Thomas, 1790), provides an excellent baseline for documenting agricultural technology, including waterworks and fencing. William Cronon, *Changes in the Land: Indians, Colonists, and the Ecology of New England* (New York: Hill and Wang, 1983), provides a review of how perceptions of the landscape had changed, at least ecologically.
6. These terms are defined by older editions of Webster's *New World Dictionary* accordingly: *Mephitis*, a harmful, bad-smelling vapor coming out of the earth...; *Salubrious*, healthful...; *Chalybeate*, tasting like iron...; *Freestone*, a stone, especially sandstone or limestone, which can be cut easily without splitting.
7. Cronon, p. 49. It must be noted that most of the eyewitness accounts of "burned-over" land were near the coast. This bias is difficult to eradicate from early accounts. By the time settlers moved significantly inland, Indian burning had largely ceased.
8. See J.H. McAndrews, "Human Disturbance of North American Forests and Grasslands: the Fossil Pollen Record," in B. Huntley, and T. Webb, III, eds., *Vegetation History* (Dordrecht, Netherlands: Kluwer Academic Publishers, 1988), pp. 673-697, who documents the case for little vegetation change associated with Indian burning in eastern North America.
9. Madison, p. 254.
10. See Robert M. Thorson, *Stone by Stone: The Magnificent History in New England's Stone Walls* (New York: Walker & Co., 2000).
11. C.S. Denny, "Geomorphology of New England," U.S. Geological Survey Professional Paper 1208 (1982), provides a thorough review of the history of landscape thought in New England.
12. Bolton, p. 373.
13. Goshen, p. 114.
14. Cheshire, p. 249.
15. Cornwall (1800-1801), p. 96.
16. Farmington, p. 51.
17. Kent, p. 124.
18. New Haven, p. 305. The columns to which Dwight refers were caused by contraction of molten rock upon cooling. In particular, West Rock is a resistant sill of diabase (similar to basalt) that was intruded into the host sedimentary rock.
19. Bethlem, p. 84.
20. Bolton, pp. 373-374.
21. Litchfield, p. 130. See also R.G. Bailey, *Ecoregions of the United States* (Ogden, Utah: U.S. Forest Service Intermountain Region, 1978), for a review of forest regions and a review of their history.
22. In the late eighteenth and early nineteenth century, the term "manure" was used in a very general sense for anything added to the soil that would make plants grow better, regardless of whether it was liquid, solid, or gas. Even irrigation water was sometimes referred to as manure.
23. East Windsor, p. 39.
24. Franklin, p. 347.
25. R.H. Meade, "Sources, Sinks, and Storage of River Sediment in the Atlantic Drainage of the United States," *Journal of Geology* 90 (1982): 235-252, and R.B. Gordon, "Denudation Rate of Central New England Determined from Estuarine Sedimentation," *American Journal of Science* 279 (1979): 632-642, discuss the hydrologic impacts of river change and sedimentation caused by European influences.
26. East Windsor, p. 39.
27. Middlesex County, p. 175.
28. Cornwall (1812), p. 109.
29. Kent, p. 124.
30. Union, pp. 385-386.
31. Coventry (1809), p. 379.
32. F.H. Boorman, G.E. Likens, T.G. Siccama, R.S. Pierce, and J.S. Eaton, "The Export of Nutrients and Recovery of Stable Conditions Following Deforestation at Hubbard Brook," *Ecological Monographs* 44 (1974): 255-277 describes how deforestation affected hydrology in a modern experimental watershed.
33. P.C. Patton, "Geomorphic Response of Streams to Floods in the Glaciated Terrain of Southern New England," in V.R. Baker, R.C. Kochel, and P.C. Patton, eds., *Flood geomorphology* (New York: John Wiley & Sons, 1988), pp. 261-277, provides a review of historic flooding for this part of New England.
34. Robert Altumura, *Map of Connecticut Showing Historical Mines and Quarries*, Connecticut Geology and Natural History Survey, Scale 1:125,000.
35. Ridgefield, p. 24.
36. New Haven, pp. 307-308.
37. Preston, p. 368.
38. Respondents used the term "slate" rather generally for any rock with a pronounced, non-sedimentary "cleavage." Technically, there is very little true slate in Connecticut because most of its upland rocks are too high in metamorphic grade.
39. Middletown, p. 187.
40. New London, p. 362.
41. Farmington, p. 56.
42. Refer to Deane (1790), cited earlier, for these and other agricultural terms.
43. Middlesex County, p. 219.
44. Cornwall (1800-1801), p. 105.
45. Bethlem, pp. 84, 85.
46. New Haven, p. 310.

47. New London, p. 364.
48. Farmington, p. 67.
49. Pomfret, p. 408.
50. Franklin, p. 349. A more specific discussion of these climatic phenomena can be found in J.A. Ruffner, "Climate of Connecticut," in *Climate of the States*, Vol. I (Alabama; New Mexico; Detroit, Mich.: Gale Research Company, 1985), pp. 165-176.
51. Lebanon, p. 403.
52. Ridgefield, p. 25.
53. Litchfield County, p. 140.
54. Goshen, p. 118.
55. Lisbon (Hanover), p. 354.
56. Farmington, p. 53.
57. Farmington, p. 71.
58. Middlesex County, p. 183.
59. There are many catalogs of historic earthquakes for New England for different time periods. A widely available example can be found from Ebel, J.E., Seismological Research Letters, Vol. 67, No. 3, 1996, p. 51-68, which cites other catalogs.
60. Middlesex County, p. 202.
61. Middlesex County, p. 202.
62. Middlesex County, p. 203.
63. Middlesex County, p. 202.
64. Cornwall (1800-1801), p. 105.
65. John Greene's book *American Science in the Age of Jefferson* (Ames Iowa, The Iowa State University Press, 1984) illustrates that "organized science" at the time took place in city universities. The fact that our rural respondents knew so much indicates how carefully they watched their environment.
66. Barbara Narendra who helps oversee the Peabody Museum collection of meterorites reported to me that this event was widely seen.
67. East Windsor, p. 39.
68. New Haven, p. 309.
69. Middlesex County, p. 175.
70. Farmington, p. 59.
71. R.M. Thorson, A.G. Harris, S.L. Harris, R. Gradie, III, and M.W. Lefor, "Colonial Impacts to Wetlands in Lebanon, Connecticut," in C.W. Welby and M.E. Gowan, eds., *A Paradox of Power: Voices of Warning and Reason in the Geosciences* (Boulder, Colorado: Geological Society of America Reviews in Engineering Geology, Vol. XII, 1998), provides a summary of erosional impacts based on stratigraphic work in wetlands.
72. R. LeB. Hooke, "On the Efficacy of Humans as Geomorphic Agents," *GSA Today* 4 (1994): 217-225. This paper substantiates the claim that humans are collectively comparable to that of ice ages in terms of their impact on the earth. I agree.
73. Bethlem, p. 85.
74. Lisbon (Hanover), p. 353; Litchfield, p. 131; Wallingford, 343; Winchester, p. 160; Willington, p. 391; Washington, p. 152.
75. See A. Chase, *In a Dark Wood: The Fight over Forests and the Tyranny of Ecology* (New York: Houghton-Mifflin Company, 1995), for a summary of this controversy.
76. Cornwall (1800-1801), p. 105.
77. Madison, pp. 268-269.

Collier
The Ups and Downs of the Connecticut Town

1. The text of the Fundamental Orders is reprinted annually in the *Connecticut Register and Manual*. Charles M. Andrews, *The River Towns of Connecticut* (Baltimore: Johns Hopkins University Studies in History and Political Science), Seventh Series, vols. VII, VIII, IX, 1889. See Vol. VII, p. 20.
2. The most accessible source of the text of the Warwick Patent is Mary Jeanne Anderson Jones, *Congregational Commonwealth: Connecticut, 1636-1662* (Middletown: Wesleyan University Press, 1968), Appendix I.
3. William Bradford, *Of Plymouth Plantation, 1620-1647*, Samuel E. Morison, ed. (New York: Alfred A. Knopf, 1953), p. 281.
4. Sidney and Beatrice Webb, *Manor and the Borough* (New York: Longmans, Green and Co., 1908.), Vol. II, pp. 134-48 and passim. Sidney and Beatrice Webb, *The Parish and the County*. New York: Longmans, Green and Co., 1906, pp. 3-6.
5. Ibid. See also, John Fairfield Sly, *Town Government in Massachusetts, 1620-1660* (Cambridge: Harvard University Press, 1930), Ch. III.
6. Sly, pp. 13-14, 19-20. William Haller, *The Puritan Frontier: Town*

Planting in New England Colonial Development, 1630-1660 (New York: Columbia Univ. Press, 1951), p. 108.
7. Charles M. Andrews, "The Beginnings of the Connecticut Towns," *Annals* of the American Academy of Political and Social Science. I (October, 1890): 170.
8. This point is developed in Christopher Collier, "New England Specter: Town and State in Connecticut History, Law and Myth," *Bulletin* of the Connecticut Historical Society, p. 60. (Summer/Fall, 1995). [Published in 1998].
9. *Public Records of the Colony of Connecticut*. J. Hammond Trumbull, ed., 15 vols. (Hartford: Brown and Parsons, 1850-94), Hereafter *CR*. I, 2. In the first entry they referred to themselves as plantations.
10. Marquis de Chastellux, *Travels in North America in the Years 1780, 1781, 1782*. Howard C. Rice, trans. 2 vols. (Chapel Hill: University of North Carolina Press, 1963), I, 70.
11. J.P. Brissot de Warville, *New Travels in the United States of America, 1788*. Mara Soceanu Vamos and Durand Echeverria, trans. Durand Echeverria, ed. (Cambridge: Harvard University Press, 1964), p. 113.
12. Timothy Dwight, *Travels in New England and New York*, Barbara Solomon, ed. (Cambridge, Harvard University, 1969), Vol. I, 156; Noah Webster, *A Compendius Dictionary of the English Language*. [A facsimile of the first (1808) edition] (New York: Crown Publishers, 1970), p. 314.
13. Collier, p. 60.
14. 1635: "We must distinguish between corporations within England and corporations of but not within England....though plantations be bodies corporate,...yet they are also above the rank of an ordinary corporation." Winthrop's definition fits what today we call municipal corporations. John Winthrop, *Winthrop's Journal: "History of New England,"* James Kendall Hosmer, ed. (New York: Charles Scribner's Sons, 1946), Vol. II, 304. Within the English legal context, however, the standing of Connecticut towns was strictly extra legal. John Palmer a royalist lawyer with no brief for Connecticut having once attempted to force its juncture with New York, wrote in 1689, "For you generally call that a *Town* in America where a number of people have seated themselves together, yet 'tis very well known 'tis so in Name only, not in [legal] Fact; "for a town must have been incorporated and "One Corporation cannot make another." Quoted in Sly, p. 72, n. 1.
15. For the legal scope of town authorities as of 1705, see *CR*. IV:500.
16. *Public Records of the State of Connecticut*, J. Hammond Trumbull, et al., eds. (Hartford: various publishers, 1894-1990). Hereafter *SR*. Vol. II, p. 207; *CR*. Vol. VIII, p. 42, 267; Vol. VII, p. 111. As a legal entity, the town consisted of town meeting voters, called "inhabitants." Freemen constituted a separate body. From 1662 to 1818 it was the freemen, not the inhabitants who elected deputies.
17. Zephaniah Swift, *A System of the Laws of the State of Connecticut* (Windham: the Author, 1795), Vol. I, pp. 116, 61.
18. *Bloomfield v. Charter Oak National Bank*. 121 U.S. 121 (1887). The Connecticut Supreme Court reached this conclusion in 1864 in *Webster Addision v. Harwinton*. 32 Conn. 132.
19. *CR*. Vol. II, p. 328.
20. *CR*. Vol. V, p. 353; Vol. VI, p. 34; Vol. VII, p. 21. See also Bruce Hartling Mann, *Neighbors of Strangers: Law and Community in Early Connecticut* (Chapel Hill: University of North Carolina Press, 1987), Ch. 6.
21. Ellen D. Larned, *History of Windham County, Connecticut*, (Worcester: the Author, 1874), Vol. I, pp. 95, 101.
22. Estelle F. Feinstein, *Stamford from Puritan to Patriot: The Shaping of a Connecticut Community, 1641-1774* (Stamford: Stamford Bicentennial Corporation, 1976), pp. 174-175. Bruce C. Daniels. "Connecticut's Villages Become Mature Towns: The Complexity of Local Institutions," *William and Mary Quarterly*, 3rd series, 34 (January, 1977): 94. Bruce Daniels insists on the continuous primacy of the towns and suggests that the parishes were more like "apprentice towns." Letter to author, June 10, 1999.
23. Hillel Schwartz, "Admissions to Full Communion in the Congregational Churches of Connecticut, 1635-1799." Typescript at the Connecticut Historical Society.
24. Connecticut State Library (Hereafter CSL), Archives, "Towns and Lands." Series 1. Vol. VIII, pp. 222-225, Vol. IX, p. 69.
25. CSL Archives, Vol. X, pp. 88, 95. Series 2, Vol. II, pp. 68, 69.
26. CSL Archives, Series 2, Vol. IX, p. 285.
27. Simeon Baldwin to James Kent (March 8, 1788), "Baldwin Family Collection," Manuscripts and Archives , Yale Universit Library; Gideon Granger in the *Middlesex Gazette*, November 13, 1786; *The Letters of Noah Webster*, Harry R. Warfel, ed. (New York: Library Publishers, 1953), p. 64.

28. A good discussion of the decline of the New England village as a social entity and the profound provincialism exhibited by its residents is Chapter 9 of Perry D. Westbrook, *The New England Town in Fact and Fiction* (Rutherford, N.J., Fairleigh Dickinson Univ. Press, 1982).

29. Noah Porter quoted in Odell Shepard, *Connecticut Past and Present* (New York: Alfred A. Knopf, 1939), p. 178.

30. Harriet Beecher Stowe, *Old Town Folks* (New York: The Library of America, 1982. [1869]), pp. 1288, 885; Gideon H. Hollister, *Kinley Hollow* (New York: H. Holt, 1882), p. 1; Donald G. Mitchell, *Dr. Johns* (New York: Charles Scribner and Company, 1866), p. 21.

31. Clarence Deming, "Town Rule in Connecticut," *Political Science Quarterly* 4 (1889): 425-26; Silliman quoted in the *American Journal of Science* 2 (November, 1820): 215. I have dealt with the decline of the country towns in the post Civil War era in "New England Specter." See note 8.

32. The population figures are drawn from the *Register and Manual* for 1935.

33. Harold J. Bingham, *History of Connecticut*. 4 vols. (New York: Lewis Historical Publishing Company, 1962), Vol. 2, p. 718.

34. Harriet Beecher Stowe, "The Mayflower" quoted in *The Autobiography of Lyman Beecher*, Barbara M. Cross, ed. 2 vols. (Cambridge, Mass.: Harvard University Press, 1961), Vol. 1, p. 152.

Daniels
The Remarkable Complexity of the Simple New England Town

1. For two recent insightful discussions of the New England town as romantic icon see Dona Brown, *Inventing New England: Regional Tourism in The Nineteenth Century* (Washington and London: Smithsonian Institution Press, 1995), pp. 1-13, *passim*; and Joseph S. Wood, *The New England Village* (Baltimore and London: The Johns Hopkins Univ. Press, 1997), pp. 1-8.

2. See Herman Melville's essay "Hawthorne and His Mosses," *Literary World*, No. 185-86 (1850), reprinted in Stanley Bank (ed.), *American Romanticism* (New York: Capricorn Books, 1969), pp. 292-301. Henry Wadsworth Longfellow's "The Village Blacksmith" was first published in 1841 as part of a volume entitled *Ballads and Other Poems*. It has often been set to solo music and in 1890 was arranged for a mixed chorus. "The Village Blacksmith" is one of the most popular English poems in the world. See Charles Welsh (ed.), *The Works of Henry Wadsworth Longfellow*, (Cambridge, Ma. and New York: Wadsworth House, 1909), Vol. IV, p. 215.

3. Brooks Adams, *The Emancipation of Massachusetts* (Boston and New York: Houghton, Mifflin and Co., 1887) especially Chaps. II, IV and V on the Puritans' treatment of dissent.
See Allan Nevins, *James Truslow Adams: Historian of The American Dream* (Urbana, Chicago, and London: Univ. of Illinois Press, 1968), pp. 35-36.

4. Herbert B. Adams, *The Germanic Origins of New England Towns* (Baltimore: The Johns Hopkins Univ. Press, 1881), pp. 5-6. Morgan had given his talk the previous year and the *Boston Journal* (August 26, 1880) had published it.

5. Woodrow Wilson, *A History of the American People*, (New York: Harper and Brothers, 1901, 1902), Vol. I, p. 121.

6. Samuel Eliot Morison, *Builders of the Bay Colony* (Boston: Houghton Mifflin, 1930). Perry Miller wrote much, but his most penetrating and influential analysis of Puritanism is *The New England Mind in the Seventeenth Century* (Cambridge, Mass.: Harvard Univ. Press, 1939).

7. This literature is too voluminous and well known to most scholars to require extensive citations in this essay. The subject is discussed at length in Bruce Daniels (ed.), *Power and Status: Essays on Officeholding in Colonial America* (Middletown, Conn.: Wesleyan Univ. Press, 1986), pp. 3-11.

8. See Daniels, *The Connecticut Town: Growth and Development, 1635-1790* (Middletown, Conn.: Wesleyan Univ. Press, 1979), pp. 46-50, for the analysis of the 1730 census. The Federal Census of 1790 is readily available in most urban and university libraries. *Return of the Whole Number of Persons within The Several Districts of The United States* (Philadelphia: Childs and Swain, 1791: reprint New York: Norman Ross, 1990).

9. These numbers could be adjusted slightly upwards depending on how towns are defined. They do not include approximately twenty towns that

were legally incorporated but had not yet been inhabited.

10. Daniels, *The Connecticut Town*, pp. 34-43, discusses the hiving-off process in general and in specific Connecticut towns. See also Daniels, *Dissent and Conformity on Narragansett Bay: The Colonial Rhode Island Town* (Middletown, Conn.: Wesleyan Univ. Press, 1983), 26-28, 32-33; Christopher P. Bickford, *Farmington in Connecticut* (Canaan, N.H.: The Farmington Historical Society, 1982), pp. 200-205; and Kenneth Lockridge, *A New England Town: The First Hundred Years* (New York: W.W. Norton, 1970), p. 4. Edward M. Cook, *The Fathers of the Towns: Leadership and Community Structure in Eighteenth-Century New England* (Baltimore: The Johns Hopkins Univ. Press, 1976), p. 203, provides the square mileage for most of New England towns settled in the seventeenth century.

11. This is based on work I have previously published. See Daniels, *The Connecticut Town*, pp. 34-43.

12. See Daniels, *Dissent and Conformity*, pp. 113-114, for the influence of a saltwater location. See Charles E. Clark, *The Eastern Frontier: The Settlement of Northern New England, 1610-1763* (New York: Alfred E. Knopf, 1970), pp. 6-7, for the surprisingly generous access to the sea that residents of southern New Hampshire had.

13. John J. McCusker and Russell R. Menard, *The Economy of British America, 1607-1789* (Chapel Hill, N.C., and London: Univ. of North Carolina Press, 1985), pp. 360-367; Lynne Withey, *Urban Growth in Rhode Island: Newport and Providence in the Eighteenth Century* (Albany: State Univ. of New York Press, 1984), pp. 84-89; and Daniels, "Economic Development in Colonial and Revolutionary Connecticut: An Overview," *William and Mary Quarterly* 37, no. 3 (July, 1980): 445-450.

14. Adams, *The Germanic Origins*, pp. 10-24; Edward Channing, *Town and County Government in the English Colonies of North America* (Baltimore: The Johns Hopkins Univ. Press, 1884), pp. 5-57; David Grayson Allen, *In English Ways: The Movement of Societies and the Transferal of English Local Law and Custom to Massachusetts Bay in the Seventeenth Century* (Chapel Hill, N.C.: Univ. of North Carolina Press, 1981), pp. 131-145; David Konig, "English Legal Change and The Origins of Local Government in Northern Massachusetts," *Town and County: Essays on the Structure of Local Government in the American Colonies*, ed. Bruce C. Daniels (Middletown, Conn.: Wesleyan Univ. Press, 1978), pp. 12-37; and Charles Andrews, *The River Towns of Connecticut* (Baltimore: The Johns Hopkins Univ. Press, 1889) pp. 27-28 all discuss various theories of the origins of town government.

15. *Records of the State of Rhode Island and Providence Plantations in New England*, ed. John Russell Bartlett (Providence: Providence Press Co., 1865), Vol. X (1784-1792), pp. 30, 217, 233-234; *The Public Records of the State of Connecticut for the Years 1783 and 1784*, ed. Leonard Woods Labaree (Hartford: The State of Connecticut, 1943), Vol. 5, pp. 343-373; and *State of New Hampshire Manual for The General Court* (Concord, N.H.: N.H. Department of State, 1975), p. 140.

16. Albert McKinley, *The Suffrage Requirements In The Thirteen English Colonies in America* (Philadelphia: The Univ. of Penns. Press, 1905) lists all the suffrage laws in colonial America. See pages 382-406 for Connecticut's. See also Robert J. Dinkin, *Voting in Provincial America: A Study of Elections in The Thirteen Colonies, 1689-1776* (Westport, Conn.: Greenwood Press, 1977), Chaps. III and IV; and Dinkin, "The Suffrage," *Encyclopedia of The North American Colonies*, ed. Jacob Cooke (New York: Charles Scribner's Sons, 1993), pp. 363-372. David Fowler, "Connecticut's Freemen: The First Forty Years," *William and Mary Quarterly* 15 (July, 1958): 312-320.

17. Fowler, "Connecticut's Freemen," pp. 312-333; Bruce Stark, "Freemanship in Lebanon, Connecticut: A Case Study," *Connecticut History* 2 (Jan., 1975): 27-48; Bruce E. Steiner, "Anglican Officeholding in Pre-Revolutionary Connecticut: The Parameters of New England Community," *William and Mary Quarterly* 31 (July, 1974): 403; and Daniels, *The Connecticut Town*, pp. 127-231.

18. Stark, "Freemanship," pp. 27-40 discusses the crucial role of distance and Daniels, *The Connecticut Town*, 130 and appendix VII assembles data from twenty towns to illustrate the sporadic nature of voter registration.

19. This paragraph and several subsequent ones are based on data I have presented previously. See Daniels, *The Connecticut Town*, Tables 7, 8, 9 and 10 on pages 81-84.

20. Daniels, *The Connecticut Town*, p. 191 has data for twenty towns on the correlation between the number of officers and a town's size and population. The Spearman's Rank Correlation Coefficient — 0 = No Correlation; 1 = Perfect Correlation (significant at the .39 Level) — is .80 for officers to land size and .84 for officers to population.

21. Daniels, "Connecticut's Villages Become Mature Towns: The

Complexity of Local Institutions, 1676 to 1776," *William and Mary Quarterly 34* (Jan., 1997): 100-103; and Daniels, "Local Government," *Encyclopedia of the North American Colonies*, ed. Jacob E. Cook, Vol. I, pp. 359-360.

22. Daniels, "Diversity and Democracy: Officeholding Patterns among Selectmen in Eighteenth-Century Connecticut," in *Power and Status*, ed. Daniels, pp. 37-52; Daniels, "Democracy and Oligarchy in Connecticut Towns: General Assembly Officeholding, 1701-1790," *Social Science Quarterly 56* (Dec., 1975): 460-475; William Willingham, "Deference Democracy and Town Government in Windham, Connecticut, 1755 to 1786," *William and Mary Quarterly 30* (July, 1973): 401-421; and Joy B. Gilsdorf and Robert B. Gilsdorf, "Elites and Electorates: Some Plain Truths for Historians of Colonial America," in *Saints and Revolutionaries: Essays in Early American History*, eds. David D. Hall, John Murrin, and Thad Tate (New York: W.W. Norton, 1984).

Selected Bibliography

Ackerman, Edward. *New England's Fishing Industry.* Chicago: Univ. of Chicago Press, 1941.

Adams, Brooks. *The Emancipation of Massachusetts.* Boston and New York: Houghton Mifflin and Co., 1887.

Adams, Herbert Baxter. *The Germanic Origins of New England Towns.* Baltimore: The Johns Hopkins Univ. Press, 1881.

Adams, James Truslow. "Disfranchisement of Negroes in New England." *American Historical Review* 30 (April 1925): 543-547.

Adams, Sherman W. *The Native and Wild Mammals of Connecticut.* Hartford: Case, Lockwood & Brainard Co., 1896.

Albion, Robert G. *The Rise of New York Port, 1815-1860.* New York: C. Scribner's Sons, 1939. Reprinted, Hamden, Conn.: Archon Books, 1961.

Albion, Robert G., William A. Baker, and Benjamin W. Labaree. *New England and the Sea.* Middletown, Conn.: Wesleyan Univ. Press, 1972.

Aldrich, John W. "Historical Background." In *The Wild Turkey and its Management,* edited by Oliver H. Hewitt, 3-16. Washington, DC: The Wildlife Society, 1967.

Allen, David Grayson. *In English Ways: The Movement of Societies and the Transferal of English Local Law and Custom to Massachusetts Bay in the Seventeenth Century.* Chapel Hill, N.C.: Univ. of North Carolina Press, 1981.

Allen, Glover M. *Extinct and Vanishing Mammals of the Western Hemisphere with Marine Species of All the Oceans.* American Committee for International Wildlife Protection, Special Publication 11 (1942).

———. *Fauna of New England.* Vol. 7. Boston: Boston Society of Natural History, 1904.

———. "History of the Virginia Deer in New England." The *Proceedings of the New England Game Conference,* 1929: 19-38.

Allen, Richard S. "Connecticut Iron and Steel from Black Sea Sands." *IA,* the Journal of the Society for Industrial Archeology 18 (1992): 129-132.

Anagnostakis, S.L. "Improved Chestnut Tree Condition Maintained in Two Connecticut Plots after Treatments with Hypovirulent Strains of the Chestnut Blight Fungus." *Forest Science* 36 (1990): 113-124.

Andres, Glenn M. "Lavius Fillmore and the Federal Style Meeting House." In *New England Meeting House and Church: 1630-1850,* edited by Peter Benes. Boston, Mass.: Boston Univ., 1980.

Andrews, Charles M. "The Beginnings of the Connecticut Towns." *Annals of the American Academy of Political and Social Science* 1 (October 4, 1890).

———. *The River Towns of Connecticut.* Johns Hopkins University Studies in Historical and Political Science 7th ser. nos. 7-9. Baltimore: The Johns Hopkins Univ. Press, 1889.

Askins, Robert A. "History of Grasslands in the Northeastern United States: Implications for Bird Conservation." In *Grasslands of Northeastern North America,* edited by P.D. Vickery and P.W. Dunwiddie, 119-136. Lincoln, Mass.: Massachusetts Audubon Society, 1998.

———. "Population Trends in Grassland, Shrubland, and Forest Birds in Eastern North America." *Current Ornithology* 11 (1993): 1-34.

Atwater, Edward E. *History of the City of New Haven.* New York: W.W. Munsell, 1887.

Austin, Robert B. *Early American Medical Imprints, 1668-1820.* Washington, DC: National Library of Medicine, 1961.

Backus, Azel. "Some Account of the Epidemics Which Have Occurred in the Town of Bethlem, Connecticut; from Its Settlement to the Present Time, Extracted from a Letter to Mr. Smith." *Medical Repository* 1 (1798): 523-525.

Bacon, Leonard. "A Plea for Africa; Delivered in New Haven, July 4th, 1825." New Haven, Conn.: T.G. Woodward and Co., 1825.

———. "Review on African Colonization." *Quarterly Christian Spectator* 2 (September 1830): 472.

Bailey, R.G. *Ecoregions of the United States.* Ogden, Utah: U.S. Forest Service Intermountain Region, 1978.

Bailyn, Bernard. *The Peopling of British North America, An Introduction.* New York: Vintage Books, 1986.

Baker, Andrew H., and Holly Izard Paterson. "Farmers' Adaptations to Markets in Early Nineteenth-Century Massachusetts." In *The Farm: The Dublin Seminar for New England Folklife Annual Proceedings 1986,* edited by Peter Benes, 95-108. Boston: Boston Univ., 1988.

Baker, Andrew H., and Holly V. Izard. "New England Farmers and the Marketplace, 1780-1865: A Case Study." *Agricultural History* 65 (Summer 1991): 29-52.

Baldwin, Ebenezer. "The Duty of Rejoicing under Calamities and Afflictions, Considered and Improved in a Sermon, Preached at Danbury, November 16, 1775." New York: Hugh Gaine, 1776.

Baldwin, Simeon. "Address to the Connecticut Society for the Abolition of Slavery." Baldwin Family Papers. Manuscripts & Archives. Yale University Library. Series IV, box #69, folder #831, 29.

Barber, John W. *Connecticut Historical Collections,* New Haven, Conn.: Durrie, Peck and Barber, 1838.

Baron, Donna Keith, J. Edward Hood, and Holly V. Izard. "They Were Here All Along: The Native American Presence in Lower-Central New England in the Eighteenth and Nineteenth Centuries." *William and Mary Quarterly,* 3d ser., Vol LIII, No. 3 (July 1996): 561-586.

Bartlett, John Russell, ed. *Records of the State of Rhode Island and Providence Plantations in New England.* Vol. X. Providence: Providence Press Co., 1865.

Bathe, Greville, and Dorothy Bathe. *Oliver Evans, a Chronicle of Early American Engineering.* Philadelphia: Historical Society of Pennsylvania, 1935.

Battison, Edwin. "A New Look at the 'Whitney' Milling Machine." *Technology and Culture* 14 (1973): 592-598.

Beers, Henry A. *The Connecticut Wits and Other Essays.* New Haven, Conn.: Yale Univ. Press, 1920.

Bell, Michael M. "Did New England Go Downhill?" *Geographical Review* 79 (1989): 450-466.

———. "The Face of Connecticut: People, Geology, and the Land." *State Geological and Natural History Survey of Connecticut,* Bulletin 110 (1985).

———. "Stone Age New England: A Geology of Morals." In *Creating the Countryside: The Politics of Rural and Environmental Discourse,* edited by E. Melanie DuPuis and Peter Vandergeest. Philadelphia: Temple Univ. Press, 1996.

Bell, Whitfield. "The Medical Institution of Yale College, 1810-1885." *Yale Journal of Biology and Medicine* 33 (3) (Dec 1960): 169-183.

Bennison, Allan P., compiler. *Geological Highway Map of the Northeastern Region:* American Association of Petroleum Geologists, Tulsa, Oklahoma (n.d.).

Benns, F. Lee. *The American Struggle for the British West India Carrying Trade, 1815-1830.* Bloomington, Ind. 1923.

Bentley, William. *The Diary of William Bentley, Pastor of the East Church, Salem, Massachusetts.* Salem, Mass.: The Essex Institute, 1905-14.

Berk, Stephen E. *Calvinism versus Democracy: Timothy Dwight and the Origins of American Evangelical Orthodoxy.* Hamden. Conn.: Archon, 1974.

Besitka, M.A.R. "An Ecological and Historical Study of *Phragmites australis* along the Atlantic Coast." Master's thesis, Philadelphia: Drexel Univ., 1996.

Bickford, Christopher. *Farmington in Connecticut.* Canaan, N.H.: The Farmington Historical Society, 1982.

Bidwell, Percy W. "Rural Economy in New England at the Beginning of the Nineteenth Century." *Transactions of the Connecticut Academy of Arts and Sciences.* Vol. 20, no. 5 (1916): 243-399.

Bidwell, Percy W., and John I. Falconer. *History of Agriculture in the Northern United States, 1620-1860.* Washington, DC: Carnegie Institution of Washington, 1925.

Bingham, Alfred M. "Squatter Settlements of Freed Slaves in New England." *Bulletin* of the Connecticut Historical Society 41 (July 1976).

Bingham, Harold J. *History of Connecticut.* 4 vols. New York: Lewis Historical Publishing Company, 1962.

Bishop, Abraham. *Connecticut Republicanism: An Oration of the Extent and Power of Political Delusion.* New Haven, Conn.?, n.p., 1800.

Bishop, J. Leander. *A History of American Manufactures from 1608 to 1860.* 2 vols. Philadelphia: Edward Young & Co., 1864.

Blaine, Bradford. "The Application of Waterpower to Industry During the Middle Ages." Ph.D. diss., Univ. of California at Los Angeles, 1966.

Boardman, Jennet. Record books, 1815-1849, MANUS 79112, Connecticut Historical Society.

Bohan, Peter, and Philip Hammerslough. *Early Connecticut Silver, 1700-1840.* Middletown, Conn.: Wesleyan Univ. Press, 1970.

Bonomi, Patricia. *Under the Cope of Heaven.* New York: Oxford Univ. Press, 1986.

Boorman, F.H., G.E. Likens, T.G. Siccama, R.S. Pierce, and J.S. Eaton. "The Export of Nutrients and Recovery of Stable Conditions Following Deforestation at Hubbard Brook." *Ecological Monographs* 44 (1974).

Boserup, Ester. *Population and Technological Change.* Chicago: Univ. of Chicago Press, 1981.

Bourne, Russell. *The Red King's Rebellion: Racial Politics in New England 1675-1678.* New York: Atheneum, 1990.

Bouvier, John. *A Law Dictionary Adapted to the Constitution and Laws of the United States of America and of the Several States of the American Union, with References to the Civil and Other Systems of Foreign Law.* 6th ed. Philadelphia: Child & Peterson, 1856.

Bowden, Henry W., and James P. Ronda, eds. *John Eliot's Indian Dialogues: A Study in Cultural Interaction.* Westport, Conn.: Greenwood Press, 1980.

Bradford, William. *Of Plymouth Plantation, 1620-1647,* edited by Samuel E. Morison. New York: Alfred A. Knopf, 1953.

Braun, E.L. *Deciduous Forests of Eastern North America.* Philadelphia: Blakeston Co., 1950.

Brewer, Priscilla J. *From Fireplace to Cookstove: Technology and the Domestic Ideal in America.* Syracuse: Syracuse Univ. Press, 2000.

Brewster, Martha. *Poems on Divers Subjects.* New London: 1757.

Bridenbaugh, Carl. *Mitre and Sceptre; Transatlantic Faiths, Ideas, Personalities and Politics, 1689-1775.* New York: Oxford Univ. Press, 1962.

Briggs, Hilton M. *Modern Breeds of Livestock.* New York: Macmillan, 1949.

Brilvich, Charles. *Walking Through History, The Seaports of Black Rock and Southport.* Fairfield, Conn., 1977.

Brissot de Warville, Jacques-Pierre. *New Travels in the United States of America, 1788.* Translated by Mara Soceanu Vamos and Durand Echeverria. Edited by Durand Echeverria. Cambridge, Mass.: Harvard Univ. Press, 1964.

Brown, Chandos Michael. *Benjamin Silliman: A Life in the Young Republic.* Princeton: Princeton Univ. Press, 1989.

Brown, Dona. *Inventing New England: Regional Tourism in the Nineteenth Century.* Washington and London: Smithsonian Institution Press, 1995.

Brown, Richard D. "Regional Culture in a Revolutionary Era: The Connecticut Valley, 1760-1820." In *The Great River: Art & Society in the Connecticut River Valley, 1635-1820.* Hartford: Wadsworth Atheneum, 1985.

Browne, C.A. "Liebig and the Law of the Minimum." In *Liebig and after Liebig,* edited by F.R. Moulton. Washington, DC: American Association for the Advancement of Science, 1942.

Buel, Joy Day, and Richard Buel, Jr. *The Way of Duty: A Woman and Her Family in Revolutionary America.* New York: W.W. Norton, 1984.

Buel, Richard Jr. *Dear Liberty: Connecticut's Mobilization for the Revolutionary War.* Middletown, Conn.: Wesleyan Univ. Press, 1980.

_____. *Securing the Revolution: Ideology in American Politics 1789-1815.* Ithaca: Cornell Univ. Press, 1972.

Burgess, Robert L., and David M. Sharpe. *Forest Island Dynamics in Man-Dominated Landscapes.* New York: Springer-Verlag, 1981.

Burrow, Gerard N. *History of Yale's School of Medicine: Passing Torches to Others.* New Haven, Conn.: Yale Univ. Press, 2002.

Busch, Briton Cooper. *The War Against the Seals: A History of the North American Seal Fishery.* Kingston, Ont. and Montreal, Que.: McGill-

Queens Univ. Press, 1985.

Bushman, Richard L. *From Puritan to Yankee: Character and Social Order in Connecticut, 1690-1765.* New York: W.W. Norton, 1970.

_____. *The Refinement of America: Persons, Houses, Cities.* New York: Alfred A. Knopf, 1992.

Butler, Jon. *Awash in a Sea of Faith: Christianizing the American People.* Cambridge, Mass.: Harvard Univ. Press, 1990.

"Butter Churns on a New Principle." *The Connecticut Magazine* 1 (April 1801): 128-30.

Cadigan, Sean. "Marine Resource Exploitation and Development: Historical Antecedents in the Debate over Technology and Ecology in the Newfoundland Fishery, 1815-1855." In *Papers Presented at the Conference Entitled "Marine Resources and Human Societies in the North Atlantic Since 1500,"* edited by Daniel Vickers, 331-384. St. John's, Nfld.: Institute of Social and Economic Research, 1997.

Calder, Isabel MacBeath. *The New Haven Colony.* New Haven, Conn.: Yale Univ. Press, 1934.

Calloway, Colin G., ed. *After King Philip's War: Presence and Persistence in Indian New England.* Hanover: Univ. Press of New England, 1997.

Candee, Richard. "John Langdon's Unusual Census of 'Mechanical Labor': The 1820 Artisans of Wiscasset, Jefferson, Alna, Edgecomb, and Whitefield, Maine." *Maine Historical Society Quarterly* 27, no. 1 (Summer 1987): 24-37.

_____. "Merchant and Millwright: The Waterpowered Sawmills of the Piscataqua." *Old Time New England,* LX #4 (April-June 1970): 131-49.

Caras, Roger A. *Dangerous to Man.* Philadelphia: Chilton Books, 1964.

Cardoza, James E. "The History and Status of the Black Bear in Massachusetts and Adjacent New England States." *Research Bulletin* 18. Westborough, Mass.: Massachusetts Division of Fish and Wildlife, 1976.

Carey, Matthew. *The Olive Branch: or Faults on Both Sides.* 7th ed. Philadelphia: Matthew Carey, 1815.

Carmen, Harry J., ed., *American Husbandry,* New York, 1939.

Carpenter, Helen M. "The Origin and Location of the Firelands in the Western Reserve." *The Ohio State Archaeological and Historical Society Quarterly.* Vol. 44 (1935): 165-203.

Carroll, Charles F. *The Timber Economy of Puritan New England.* Providence, R.I.: Brown Univ. Press, 1973.

Carson, Cary, Ronald Hoffman, and Peter J. Albert, eds. *Of Consuming Interests: The Style of Life in the Eighteenth Century.* Charlottesville and London: Published for the United States Capitol Historical Society by the Univ. Press of Virginia, 1994.

Cash, Philip, Eric H. Christianson, and J. Worth Estes, eds. *Medicine in Colonial Massachusetts, 1620-1820,* Boston: The Colonial Society of Massachusetts, 1980.

Cassedy, James H. *Demography in Early America: Beginnings of the Statistical Mind, 1600-1800.* Cambridge, Mass.: Harvard Univ. Press, 1969.

Caulfield, Ernest. *A True History of the Terrible Epidemic Vulgarly Called the Throat Distemper.* New Haven, Conn.: Published for the Beaumont Medical Club by the Yale Journal of Biology and Medicine, 1939.

Caulkins, Frances M. *History of New London, Connecticut: From the First Survey of the Coast in 1612, to 1860.* New London: H.D. Utley, 1895.

_____. *History of Norwich, Connecticut: From its Possession by the Indians, to the Year 1866.* Published by the author, Hartford, Conn., 1866.

Champion, Judah. *Christian and Civil Liberty and Freedom Considered and Recommended.* Hartford: Ebenezer Watson, 1776.

Channing, Edward. *Town and County Government in the English Colonies of North America.* Baltimore: The Johns Hopkins Univ. Press, 1884.

[Channing, Henry] "An Account of the Pestilential Disease Which Prevailed at New-London (Connecticut), in the Summer and Autumn of 1798; Communicated in a Letter from the Rev. Henry Channing to Dr. Mitchill." *Medical Repository* 2 (1799): 402-44.

Chase, A. *In a Dark Wood: The Fight over Forests and the Tyranny of Ecology.* New York: Houghton-Mifflin Company, 1995.

Chastellux, François Jean, Marquis de. *Travels in North America in the Years 1780, 1781, 1782.* Translated by Howard C. Rice. Chapel Hill: Univ. of North Carolina Press, 1963.

Christianson, Eric H. "Medicine in New England." In *Medicine in the New World: New Spain, New France, and New England,* edited by

Ronald L. Numbers, 101-153. Knoxville, Tenn.: Univ. of Tennessee Press, 1987.

Clark, A. Howard. "The Coast of Connecticut and its Fisheries." In *A Geographical Review of the Fisheries Industries and Fishing Communities for the Year, 1880.* Section II of *The Fisheries and Fishery Industries of the United States,* edited by George Brown Goode, 311-340. Washington, DC, 1884-1887.

Clark, Charles E. *The Eastern Frontier: The Settlement of Northern New England, 1610-1763.* New York: Alfred A. Knopf, 1970.

Clark, Christopher. *The Roots of Rural Capitalism: Western Massachusetts, 1780-1860.* Ithaca: Cornell Univ. Press, 1990.

Clark, Thelma, ed. *Kate Silliman's Chester Scrapbook.* Chester, Conn.: Chester Historical Society, 1986.

Clark, Victor S. *History of Manufactures in the United States: Volume 1, 1607-1860.* New York: McGraw-Hill, 1929.

Clarke, Mary Stetson. *Pioneer Iron Works.* Philadelphia: Chilton Book Co., 1968.

Clouette, Bruce, and Matthew Roth. *Connecticut's Historic Highway Bridges,* Hartford: Connecticut Department of Transportation, 1991.

Coit, Thomas. "Additional Account of the Pestilential Fever Which Prevailed at New-London (Connecticut); Communicated in a Letter from Dr. Coit to Dr. Mitchill, dated New-London, January 11, 1799." *Medical Repository* 2 (1799): 407-408.

Colby, Barnard L. *For Oil and Buggy Whips: Whaling Captains of New London County, Connecticut.* Mystic, Conn.: Mystic Seaport Museum, 1990.

Cole, Arthur H. *The American Wool Manufacture.* 2 vols. Cambridge, Mass: Harvard Univ. Press, 1926.

Coleman, Elihu. "A Testimony Against That Anti-Christian Practice of Making Slaves of Men." Boston, 1733.

Colles, Christopher. *A Survey of the Roads of the United States of America, 1789,* edited by W.W. Ristow. Cambridge, Mass.: Harvard Univ. Press, 1961.

Collier, Christopher. "New England Specter: Town and State in Connecticut History, Law and Myth." *Bulletin* of the Connecticut Historical Society 60. (Summer/Fall, 1995). [Published in 1998].

Conforti, Joseph A. *Samuel Hopkins and the New Divinity Movement: Calvinism, the Congregational Ministry, and Reform in New England Between the Great Awakenings.* Grand Rapids, Mich.: Christian Univ. Press, 1981.

Connecticut Department of Environmental Protection. "Connecticut's Wildlife: A Checklist of Birds, Mammals, Reptiles, and Amphibians." Hartford: Wildlife Bureau Publication NHW-3, 1988.

Connecticut Emergency Relief Commission. *The Connecticut Guide.* Meriden: Curtiss-Way Co. 1935.

Connecticut Geology and Natural History Survey. *Map of Connecticut Showing Historical Mines and Quarries.* Scale 1:125,000.

Connecticut Medical Society. *Reprint of the Proceedings of the Connecticut Medical Society from 1792 to 1829 Inclusive.* Hartford: The Case, Lockwood & Brainard Company, 1884.

Connecticut State Library, Archives, "Towns and Lands." Ser. 1, Ser. 2, Ser. IX.

Conrad, James L., Jr. "The Making of a Hero: Samuel Slater and the Arkwright Frames." *Rhode Island History* 45 (February 1986): 3-13.

Cook, Edward M. *The Fathers of the Towns: Leadership and Community Structure in Eighteenth-Century New England.* Baltimore: The Johns Hopkins Univ. Press, 1976.

Cooke, Edward S. Jr. *Making Furniture in Preindustrial Connecticut: The Social Economy of Newtown and Woodbury, Connecticut.* Baltimore: The Johns Hopkins Univ. Press, 1996.

Cooke, Jacob. "Tench Coxe, Alexander Hamilton, and the Encouragement of American Manufactures." *William and Mary Quarterly* 32 (1975): 369-92.

Coons, Martha, et al. *All Sorts of Good Sufficient Cloth: Linen-Making in New England 1640-1860.* North Andover, Mass.: Merrimack Valley Textile Museum, 1980.

Cott, Nancy. *The Bonds of Womanhood: "Woman's Sphere" in New England, 1780-1835.* New Haven, Conn.: Yale Univ. Press, 1977.

Cowan, Ruth Schwartz. *More Work for Mother: The Ironies of Household Technology from the Open Hearth to the Microwave.* New York: Basic Books, 1983.

Coxe, Tench. *A Statement of the Arts and Manufactures of the United States of America for the Year 1810.* Philadelphia: A. Cornman, 1814.

Crane, Jocelyn. "Mammals of Hampshire County, Massachusetts." *Journal of Mammalogy* 12 (1931): 267-273.

Cronon, William. *Changes in the Land: Indians, Colonists, and the Ecology of New England.* New York: Hill and Wang, 1983.

Cuningham, Charles E. *Timothy Dwight 1752-1817: A Biography.* New York: Macmillan, 1942.

Dana, James Dwight. *A System of Mineralogy.* New Haven, Conn.: Durrie & Peck and Henrick & Noyes, 1837.

Daniels, Bruce C. *The Connecticut Town: Growth and Development 1635-1790.* Middletown, Conn.: Wesleyan Univ. Press, 1979.

_____. "Connecticut's Villages Become Mature Towns: The Complexity of Local Institutions." *William and Mary Quarterly* 3rd ser., 34 (Jan. 1977): 83-103.

_____. "Democracy and Oligarchy in Connecticut Towns: General Assembly Officeholding, 1701-1790." *Social Science Quarterly 56* (Dec. 1975): 460-475.

_____. *Dissent and Conformity on Narragansett Bay: The Colonial Rhode Island Town.* Middletown, Conn.: Wesleyan Univ. Press, 1983.

_____. "Economic Development in Colonial and Revolutionary Connecticut: An Overview." *William and Mary Quarterly* 37 (July 1980): 429-450.

_____. "Local Government." In *Encyclopedia of the North American Colonies,* edited by Jacob Cooke. Vol. I, 341-362. New York: Charles Scribner's Sons, 1993.

_____. ed. *Power and Status: Officeholding in the American Colonies.* Middletown, Conn.: Wesleyan Univ. Press, 1988.

_____. ed. *Town and County: Essays on the Structure of Local Government in the American Colonies.* Middletown, Conn.: Wesleyan Univ. Press, 1978.

Davis, Hugh. *Leonard Bacon: New England Reformer and Antislavery Moderate.* Baton Rouge: Louisiana State Univ. Press, 1998.

_____. "Northern Colonizationists and Free Blacks, 1823-1837: A Case Study of Leonard Bacon." *Journal of the Early Republic* 17 (Winter 1997).

Dawley, Alan. *Class and Community, the Industrial Revolution in Lynn.* Cambridge, Mass.: Harvard Univ. Press, 1976.

Dayton, Cornelia. *Women Before the Bar: Gender, Law, and Society in Connecticut, 1639-1789.* Chapel Hill: Univ. of North Carolina Press, 1995.

Deane, Samuel. *The New-England Farmer; or Georgical Dictionary.* Worcester: Isaiah Thomas, 1790. 3d ed. Boston: Wells and Lilly, 1822.

Decker, Robert O. *Cromwell, Connecticut, 1650-1990: The History of a River Port Town,* West Kennebunk, Me., 1991.

_____. *The Whaling City: A History of New London.* Chester, Conn.: New London County Historical Society, 1976.

_____. *The Whaling Industry of New London,* York, Pa., 1973.

DeForest, John W. *History of the Indians of Connecticut from the Earliest Known Period to 1850.* Hartford: Wm. Jas. Hamersley, 1852; Scholarly Press, 1970.

DeGraaf, Richard M., and Ronald I. Miller. "The Importance of Disturbance and Land-Use History in England: Implications for Forested Landscapes and Wildlife Conservation." In *Conservation of Faunal Diversity in Forested Landscapes,* edited by R.M. DeGraaf and R.I. Miller. London: Chapman-Hall, 1996.

Deming, Clarence. "Town Rule in Connecticut." *Political Science Quarterly* 4 (1889): 425-26.

Dennis, William C. "A Federalist Persuasion: the American Ideal and the Connecticut Federalists." Ph.D. diss., Yale Univ., 1971.

Denny, C.S. "Geomorphology of New England." U.S. Geological Survey Professional Paper 1208 (1982).

DeVoe, Shirley. *The Tinsmiths of Connecticut.* Middletown, Conn.: Wesleyan Univ. Press, 1968.

Deyrup, Felicia Johnson. *Arms Makers of the Connecticut Valley...1798-1870.* Vol. 33. Northampton, Mass.: Smith College Studies in History, 1948.

Dinkin, Robert J. "Seating the Meetinghouse in Early Massachusetts." *New England Quarterly* 43 (1970): 450-464.

_____. "The Suffrage." In *Encyclopedia of the North American Colonies,* edited by Jacob Cooke. Vol. I, 363-372. New York: Charles Scribner's Sons, 1993.

_____. *Voting in Provincial America: A Study of Elections in the Thirteen Colonies, 1689-1776.* Westport, Conn.: Greenwood Press, 1977.

Ditz, Toby L. *Property and Kinship: Inheritance in Early Connecticut.* Princeton, N.J.: Princeton Univ. Press, 1986.

Dorst, Jean. *The Migration of Birds.* Boston: Houghton-Mifflin, 1962.

Drake, Ellen T., and William M. Jordan, eds. *Geologists and Ideas: A History of North American Geology.* Centennial Special Volume 1. Geological Society of America, 1985.

Dublin, Thomas. "Women and Outwork in a Nineteenth-Century New England Town...." In *The Countryside in the Age of Capitalist Transformation,* edited by Steven Hahn and Jonathan Prude. Chapel Hill: Univ. of North Carolina Press, 1985.

Dunn, Richard S. *Sugar and Slaves: The Rise of the Planter Class in the English West Indies.* Chapel Hill, N.C.: Univ. of North Carolina Press, 1972.

Dwight, Timothy. "The Charitable Blessed: A Sermon Preached in the First Church in New Haven." New Haven, Conn.: Sidney's Press, 1810.

_____. "The Duty of Americans at the Present Crisis Illustrated in a Discourse Preached on the Fourth of July 1798." New Haven, Conn.: Thos. and Sam. Green, 1798.

_____. *Travels in New England and New York.* Edited by Barbara M. Solomon and P.M. King. 4 vols. Cambridge, Mass.: Belknap Press of Harvard Univ. Press, 1969.

Eastman, Whitney. *The History of the Linseed Oil Industry in the United States.* Minneapolis: T.S. Denison & Co., 1968.

Ebel, J.E. *Seismological Research Letters,* Vol. 67, No. 3 (1996): 51-68.

Eddy, Edward D. *Colleges for Our Land and Time: The Land-Grant Idea in American Education.* New York: Harper, 1957.

Edwards, Jonathan Jr. The Injustice and Impolicy of the Slave Trade, and of the Slavery of the Africans: Illustrated in a Sermon Preached before the Connecticut Society for the Promotion of Freedom, and for the Relief of Persons Unlawfully Holden in Bondage, at Their Annual Meeting in New Haven, Sept. 15, 1791." Boston: Wells and Lilly, 1822.

Edwards, Llewellyn N. *A Record of History and Evolution of Early American Bridges,* Orono: Univ. of Maine Press, 1959.

Egan, Clifford L. *Neither Peace nor War: Franco-American Relations, 1803-1812.* Baton Rouge: Louisiana State Univ. Press, 1983.

Eliot, Jared. *Essays Upon Field Husbandry in New England.* New London: T. Green, 1748.

_____. *Essays Upon Field Husbandry in New England, and Other Papers, 1748-1762.* Edited by Harry J. Carman and Rexford G. Tugwell. New York: Columbia Univ. Press, 1934.

Ellis, Joseph J. *The New England Mind in Transition: Samuel Johnson of Connecticut, 1696-1772.* New Haven, Conn.: Yale Univ. Press, 1973.

Emery, Sarah Anna. *Reminiscences of a Nonagenarian.* Newburyport, Mass.: W.H. Huse & Co.,1879; repr. Bowie, Md.: Heritage Books, 1978.

Ennis, William D. *Linseed Oil and Other Seed Oils.* New York: Van Nostrand, 1909.

Estes, J. Worth. "Medical Skills in Colonial New England." *New England Historical and Genealogical Register* 134 (1980): 259-275.

Evans, Nancy. *American Windsor Chairs.* New York: Hudson Hills, 1996.

Ezell, John Samuel. *Fortune's Merry Wheel: The Lottery in America.* Cambridge, Mass.: Harvard Univ. Press, 1960.

Faler, Paul G. *Mechanics and Manufacturers in the Early Industrial Revolution: Lynn Massachusetts, 1780-1860.* Albany: State Univ. of New York Press, 1981.

Faul, Henry, and Carol Faul. *It Began with a Stone.* New York: John Wiley & Sons, 1983.

Favretti, Rudy J. *Highlights of Connecticut Agriculture.* Storrs: College of Agriculture and Natural Resources of the Univ. of Connecticut, 1976.

[Federal Records Center] Licenses of Vessels Above 20 Tons to Carry on the Fishing Trade, 1793-1802, 1814-1875. In Records of the U.S. Customs District of New London, Connecticut. RG 36. Federal Records Center, Waltham, Mass. Microform edition at G.W. Blunt Library, Mystic Seaport, Mystic, Conn.

Feinstein, Estelle F. *Stamford from Puritan to Patriot: The Shaping of a Connecticut Community, 1641-1774.* Stamford, Conn.: Stamford Bicentennial Corporation, 1976.

Ferguson, E. James. *The Power of the Purse.* Chapel Hill, N.C.: Univ. of North Carolina Press, 1963.

Field, David D. *A History, of the Towns of Haddam and East-Haddam.* Middletown, Conn.: Loomis and Richards, 1814.

Fitts, Robert K. *Inventing New England's Slave Paradise: Master/Slave Relations in Eighteenth-Century Narragansett, Rhode Island.* New York: Garland Publishing, 1998.

Fletcher, Robert, and J. P. Snow. "A History of the Development of Wooden Bridges." *Transactions of the American Society of Civil Engineers* 99 (1934): 314-408.

Forman, Benno M. "Mill Sawing in Seventeenth-Century Massachusetts." *Old Time New England,* LX #4 (April-June 1970): 110-130 ff.

Foster, David R. "Land-Use History and Four Hundred Years of Vegetation Change in New England." In *Global Land Use Change. A Perspective from the Columbian Encounter,* edited by B.L. Turner, A. Gomez Sal, F. Gonzalez Bernadaldez and F. di Castri. Madrid: Consejo Superior de Investigaciones Cientificas, 1995.

Foster, David R., Tad M. Zeybryk, Peter K. Schoonmaker and Ann L. Lezberg. "Post-Settlement History of Human Land-Use and Vegetation Dynamics of a *Tsuga Canadensis* (Hemlock) Woodlot in Central New England." *Journal of Ecology* 80 (1992): 773-786.

Fowler, David. "Connecticut's Freemen: The First Forty Years." *William and Mary Quarterly* 15 (July 1958): 312-331.

Fowler, William. "The Historical Status of the Negro, in Connecticut." In *Local Law in Massachusetts and Connecticut Historically Considered.* Albany, N.Y.: J. Munsell, 1872.

Fraser, Bruce. *The Land of Steady Habits: A Brief History of Connecticut.* Hartford: Connecticut Historical Commission, 1988.

Frye, John. *The Men All Singing: The Story of Menhaden Fishing.* Virginia Beach, Va.: Donning, 1978.

Fulton, John F., and Elizabeth H. Thomson. *Benjamin Silliman 1779-1864: Pathfinder in American Science.* New York: Henry Schuman, 1947.

Gaines, Richard V., H. Catherine W. Skinner, Eugene E. Foord, Brian H. Mason, and A. Rosenzweig. *Dana's New Mineralogy,* 8th ed. New York: John Wiley and Sons, 1997.

Galer, Gregory, Robert Gordon, and Frances Kemmish. *Connecticut's Ames Iron Works: Family, Community, Nature, and Innovation in an Enterprise of the Early American Republic.* New Haven, Conn.: Connecticut Academy of Arts and Sciences, 1998.

Gannett, Michael, ed. *Cornwall in 1801 by Elijah Allen.* Cornwall, Conn.: Cornwall Historical Society, 1985.

Garrison, J. Ritchie. *Landscape and Material Life in Franklin County, Massachusetts. 1770-1860.* Knoxville: Univ. of Tennessee Press, 1991.

Gaustad, Edwin Scott. *The Great Awakening in New England.* New York: Harper & Row, 1957.

General Hospital Society of Connecticut. *General Hospital Society of Connecticut Centenary, 1826-1926.* New Haven, Conn.: The Society, 1926.

General Shipping & Commercial List (New York), February 21, 1815.

Geological and Natural History Survey of Connecticut, 1935.

Gibb, George Sweet. *The Saco-Lowell Shops...Cambridge, Mass.:* Harvard Univ. Press, 1950.

Gilsdorf, Joy B., and Robert B. Gilsdorf. "Elites and Electorates: Some Plain Truths for Historians of Colonial America." In *Saints and Revolutionaries: Essays in Early American History,* edited by David D. Hall, John Murrin, and Thad Tate. New York: W.W. Norton, 1984.

Glassie, Henry. "Meaningful Things and Appropriate Myths: The Artifact's Place in American Studies." In *Material Life in America 1600-1860,* edited by Robert Blair St. George, 63-92. Boston: Northeastern Univ. Press, 1988.

_____. "The Practice and Purpose of History." *The Journal of American History* 81 (December 1994): 961-968.

Godin, Alfred J. *Wild Mammals of New England.* Baltimore: The Johns Hopkins Univ. Press, 1977.

Goen, Clarence C. *Revivalism and Separatism in New England: Strict Congregationalism and Separate Baptists in the Great Awakening.* New Haven, Conn.: Yale Univ. Press, 1962.

Goff, Gary R., Joseph C. Okoniewski, Shari L. McCarty, and Daniel J. Decker. "The Eastern Coyote (*Canis iatrans*)." In *New York's Wildlife Resources Services,* No. 16. Department of Natural Resources, College of Agriculture and Life Sciences, Cornell University. Ithaca, N.Y.: Cornell University, 1984.

Goldenburg, Joseph A. "Blue Lights and Infernal Machines: the Blockade of New London." *Mariner's Mirror.* Vol. 61 (1975): 385-97.

Goode, George Brown, ed. *The History and Methods of the Fisheries.* Section V of *The Fisheries and Fishery Industries of the United States,* edited by George Brown Goode. Washington, DC, 1884-1887.

Goodwin, George G. *The Mammals of Connecticut.* Hartford: State Geological and Natural History Survey of Connecticut, Research Bulletin No. 53, 1935.

Gordon, H. Scott. "The Economic Theory of a Common Property Resource: The Fishery." *Journal of Political Economy* 42 (1954): 124-142.

Gordon, Robert B. *American Iron 1607-1900*. Baltimore: The Johns Hopkins Univ. Press, 1996.

_____. "Choice of Method for Making Wrought Iron in the Salisbury District of Connecticut." *Journal of the Historical Metallurgy Society* 31 (1997).

_____. "Denudation Rate of Central New England Determined from Estuarine Sedimentation." *American Journal of Science* 279 (1979).

_____."Materials for Manufacturing: The Response of the Connecticut Iron Industry to Technological Change and Limited Resources." *Technology and Culture* 24 (1983): 602-634.

Gordon, Robert B. and Patrick M. Malone, *The Texture of Industry: An Archaeological View of the Industrialization of North America*. New York: Oxford Univ. Press, 1994.

Gordon, Robert B., and Michael S. Raber. *Industrial Heritage in Northwest Connecticut: A Guide to History and Archaeology*. New Haven, Conn.: Connecticut Academy of Arts and Sciences, 2000.

Grant, Ellsworth S. *The Miracle of Connecticut*. Hartford: Connecticut Historical Society, n.d..

_____.*Yankee Dreamers and Doers*. Chester, Conn.: Pequot Press, 1973.

Grasso, Christopher. *A Speaking Aristocracy: Transforming Public Discourse in Eighteenth-Century Connecticut*. Chapel Hill: Univ. of North Carolina Press, 1999.

Greene, John. *American Science in the Age of Jefferson*. Ames, Iowa: Iowa State Univ. Press, 1984.

Greene, Lorenzo. *The Negro in Colonial New England*. New York: Atheneum, 1968.

Griscom, Ludlow. *The Birds of Concord*. Cambridge, Mass.: Harvard Univ. Press, 1949.

Griswold, Roger M. "First Sailing Vessels and Merchant Mariners on the Connecticut River." *The Connecticut Magazine*, Vol. 10, No. 3 (1906).

Grob, Gerald N. *The Mad Among Us: A History of the Care of America's Mentally Ill*. Cambridge, Mass.: Harvard Univ. Press, 1994.

Gross, Alfred O. "The Heath Hen." *Memoirs* of the Boston Society of Natural History, Vol. 6, No. 4 (1928).

Gross, Laurence. "Wool Carding: A Study of Skills and Technology." *Technology and Culture* 28 (1987): 804-827.

Guillette, Mary E. *American Indians in Connecticut: Past to Present*. State of Connecticut, 1979.

Hahn, Steven and Jonathan Prude, *The Countryside in the Age of Capitalist Transformation, Essays in the Social History of Rural America*. Chapel Hill: Univ. of North Carolina Press, 1985.

Hall, Peter D. "Pieces of a Puzzle: The West Indies Trade and the Culture of the Connecticut Valley." In *A Grand Reliance: The West Indies Trade in the Connecticut River Valley, 1830-1830*. Essex, Conn.: Connecticut River Museum, 1992.

Haller, William. *The Puritan Frontier: Town Planting in New England Colonial Development, 1630-1660*. New York: Columbia Univ., Press, 1951.

Handlin, Oscar, and Mary P. Handlin. *Commonwealth: A Study of the Role of Government in the American Economy: Massachusetts, 1774-1861*. (1947). Rev. ed. Cambridge, Mass.: Belknap Press of Harvard Univ. Press, 1969.

Harper, Douglas. *Working Knowledge: Skill and Community in a Small Shop*. Chicago: Univ. of Chicago Press, 1987.

[Harper, Robert Goodloe] "Letter from Genl. Robert Goodloe Harper." In *First Annual Report of the American Society for Colonizing the Free People of Colour of the United States*. Washington, DC: D. Rapine, 1818.

Harper, Roland M. "Changes in the Forest Area of New England in Three Centuries." *Journal of Forestry* 16 (1918): 442-452.

Harrington, Virginia D. *The New York Merchant on the Eve of the Revolution*. New York: Columbia Univ. Press, 1935.

Hart, Levi. "Liberty Described and Recommended; A Sermon Preached to the Corporation of Freemen in Farmington, at their Meeting on Tuesday, September 20, 1774." Hartford: Ebenezer Watson, 1775.

_____. Some Thoughts on the Subject of Freeing the Negro Slaves in the Colony of Connecticut, Humbly Offered to the Consideration of All Friends to Liberty and Justice. (1775) Connecticut Historical Society.

Hatch, Nathan O. *The Democratization of American Christianity*. New Haven, Conn.: Yale Univ. Press, 1989.

Hatcher, Harlan. *The Western Reserve: The Story of New Connecticut in Ohio*. Indianapolis: Bobbs-Merrill Company, 1949.

Hauptman, Laurence M., and James D. Wherry, eds. *The Pequots in Southern New England: The Fall and Rise of an American Indian Nation*. Norman: Univ. of Oklahoma Press, 1990.

Hays, W.J. "Notes on the Range of Some of the Animals in America at the Time of the Arrival of the White Men." *American Naturalist* 5 (1871): 387-392.

Hazard, Blanche. *The Organization of the Boot and Shoe Industry in Massachusetts Before 1875*. Cambridge, Mass.: Harvard Univ. Press, 1921.

Heimert, Alan F. *Religion and the American Mind, from the Great Awakening to the Revolution*. Cambridge, Mass.: Harvard Univ. Press, 1966.

Helander, Joel E. *Oxpasture to Summer Colony*, Guilford: Helander, 1976.

Henretta, James. "Families and Farms: Mentalité in Pre-Industrial America." *William and Mary Quarterly 35* (January 1978): 3-32.

Hibbard, Augustine G. *History of the Town of Goshen, Connecticut*. Hartford: Case, Lockwood & Brainard Co., 1897.

Hickox, Philena Smith. Record book, 1791-1813, MANUS 93838, Connecticut Historical Society.

Hicock, H.W. "Connecticut Forests ... Asset or Liability." *Northeastern Logger* November (1956): 20-33.

Hindle, Brooke, ed. *America's Wooden Age: Aspects of its Early Technology*. Tarrytown, New York: Sleepy Hollow Restorations, 1975.

Hinman, Rankine Gallien. "Connecticut and the Federal System during the War of 1812: Conflicts in Sovereignty and Vital Interests." Master's thesis, Trinity College, 1957.

History of Litchfield County, Connecticut. Philadelphia: J.W. Lewis & Co., 1881.

Hoadley, Charles J., ed. *Records of the Colony and Plantation of New Haven, 1638-1665*. 2 vols. Hartford, Conn., 1857-1858.

Hoadley, Charles J., et al., eds. *Public Records of the State of Connecticut*. 16 vols. to date. Hartford: Case, Lockwood and Brainard, 1894-.

Hoadley, Frederick H. "A Review of the History of the Epidemic of Yellow Fever in New Haven, Conn. in the Year 1794." *Papers of the New Haven Colony Historical Society*, 6 (1900): 223-261.

Hobart, Rebecca Rogers, Record book, 1765-1801, MANUS 44902, Connecticut Historical Society.

Hodapp, Elizabeth A. "Public Health in Colonial New Haven." *Journal of the History of Medicine and Allied Sciences* 27 (1972): 54-64.

Hodges, Graham. *Root & Branch: African Americans in New York & East Jersey, 1613-1863*. Chapel Hill: Univ. of North Carolina Press, 1999.

_____. *Slavery and Freedom in the Rural North: African Americans in Monmouth County, New Jersey, 1665-1865*. Madison, Wisc.: Madison House, 1997.

Holbrook, Stewart H. *The Old Post Road*, New York: McGraw-Hill, 1962.

Hollingsworth, Thomas Henry. *Historical Demography*. Ithaca: Cornell Univ. Press, 1969.

Hollister, Gideon H.. *Kinley Hollow*. New York: H. Holt, 1882.

Hooke, R. LeB. "On the Efficacy of Humans as Geomorphic Agents." *GSA Today* 4 (1994).

Hoopes, Penrose. *Shop Records of Daniel Burnap*. Hartford, Conn.: Connecticut Historical Society, 1958.

Hopkins, Donald R. *Princes and Peasants: Smallpox in History*. Chicago: Univ. of Chicago Press, 1983.

Horsfall, David. "On von Thünen's Model." *Geographical Magazine* 64 (October 1992): 53.

Hosley, William, and Gerald Ward, eds. *The Great River: Art & Society of the Connecticut Valley, 1635-1820*. Hartford, Conn.: Wadsworth Atheneum, 1985.

Hounshell, David. *From the American System to Mass Production, 1800-1932*. Baltimore: The Johns Hopkins Univ. Press, 1984.

Housley, Kathleen L. *The Letter Kills But the Spirit Gives Life: The Smiths—Abolitionists, Suffragists, Bible Translators*. Glastonbury, Conn.: Historical Society of Glastonbury, 1993.

Howard, Leon. *The Connecticut Wits*. Chicago: Univ. of Chicago Press, 1943.

Howe, Henry. *Memoirs of the Most Eminent American Mechanics: Also, Lives of Distinguished European Mechanics; Together with a Collection of Anecdotes, Descriptions, &c. &c. Relating to the Mechanics Arts*. New York, Harper & Brothers, 1846.

Howell, Kenneth T., and Einar W. Carlson. *Empire over the Dam*. Chester, Conn.: Pequot Press, 1974.

_____. *Men of Iron: Forbes and Adam*. Lakeville, Conn.: privately printed, 1980.

Humphreys, David. *The Life and Heroic Exploits of Israel Putnam, Major-General in the Revolutionary War.* New York: Ezra Strong, 1835.

Hunter, Louis C. *Waterpower in the Century of the Steam Engine.* Vol. 1 of *A History of Industrial Power in the United States, 1780-1930.* Charlottesville: Univ. Press of Virginia, 1979.

Hunter, Robert F. "Turnpike Construction in Antebellum Virginia." *Technology and Culture* 4 (1963):177-200.

Huntington, Enoch. "A Sermon, Delivered at Middletown, July 20th. A.D. 1775." Hartford: Ebenezer Baldwin, 1775.

_____. "The Happy Effects of Union, and the Fatal Tendency of Division. Shewn in a Sermon Preached before the Freemen of the town of Middletown, at their Annual Meeting, April 8, 1776." Hartford: Ebenezer Baldwin, 1776.

Hutchins, John G.B. *The American Maritime Industries and Public Policy, 1789-1914.* Cambridge, Mass., 1941.

Innes, Stephen. *Labor in a New Land: Economy and Society in Seventeenth-Century Springfield.* Princeton: Princeton Univ. Press, 1983.

Irland, Lloyd C. *Wildlands and Woodlots, The Story of New England's Forests.* Hanover, N.H.: Univ. Press of New England, 1982.

Isham, Norman M., and Albert F. Brown. *Early Connecticut Houses: An Historical and Architectural Study.* New York: Dover Publications, 1965; first published by the Preston and Rounds Company in 1900.

Italia, Sebastian R. "Elisha North: Experimentalist, Epidemiologist, Physician, 1771-1843." *Bulletin of the History of Medicine* 31 (1957): 505-536.

Jackson, Donald C. "Roads Most Travelled: Turnpikes in Southeastern Pennsylvania in the Early Republic." In *Early American Technology,* edited by Judith A. McGaw. Chapel Hill: Univ. of North Carolina Press, 1994.

Jackson, Steven N. "The Connecticut Wild Turkey Program." Hartford: Connecticut Department of Environmental Protection, Wildlife Unit Project Report WH 1272, 1980.

_____. "Wild Turkey Hunting Season Report, Spring 1981 Report." Hartford: Connecticut Department of Environmental Protection, 1981.

Jefferson, Thomas. *Notes on the State of Virginia.* Edited by William Peden. New York: W.W. Norton, 1972.

Jenkins, Edward H. "Connecticut Agriculture." In *History of Connecticut in Monographic Form,* edited by Norris G. Osborn. Vol. 2, 289-425. New York: The States History Co., 1925.

Jennings, Francis. *The Invasion of America: Indians, Colonialism, and the Cant of Conquest.* New York: W.W. Norton, 1975.

Jensen, Joan M. "Butter Making and Economic Development in Mid-Atlantic America from 1750-1850." *Signs* 13 (1988): 813-29.

_____. *Loosening the Bonds: Mid-Atlantic Farm Women, 1750-1850.* New Haven, Conn.: Yale Univ. Press, 1988.

Jeremy, David J. *Transatlantic Industrial Revolution: The Diffusion of Textile Technologies between Britain and America, 1790-1830s.* Cambridge, Mass.: M.I.T. Press, 1981.

Johnson, Malcolm L. *Yesterday's Connecticut.* Miami, Florida: E.A. Seeman Publishing, Inc., 1976.

Jones, Daniel P. *The Economic and Social Transformation of Rhode Island, 1780-1850.* Boston: Northeastern Univ. Press, 1992.

Jones, Mary Jeanne Anderson. *Congregational Commonwealth: Connecticut, 1636-1662.* Middletown, Conn.: Wesleyan Univ. Press, 1968.

Jones, P. d'A., and E. N. Simon. *Story of the Saw.* Manchester: Spear & Jackson, 1961.

Jones, Richard M. "Sealing and Stonington: A Short-Lived Bonanza." *Log of Mystic Seaport* 28 (1977): 119-126.

_____. "Stonington Borough: A Connecticut Seaport in the Nineteenth Century." Ph.D. diss., City Univ. of New York, 1976.

Jordan, Winthrop. *White Over Black: American Attitudes Toward the Negro, 1550-1812.* New York: Oxford Univ. Press, 1974.

Kahn, Richard J., and Patricia G. Kahn, "The Medical Repository—The First U.S. Medical Journal (1797-1824)." *New England Journal of Medicine* 337 (December 1977): 1926-1930.

Karsh, Estrellita. "Taking the Waters at Stafford Springs: The Role of the Willard Family of Boston in America's First Health Spa." *Harvard Library Bulletin* 28 (1980): 264-281.

Kaufman, Polly. "Diary of Arozina Perkins," in *Women Teachers on the Frontier.* New Haven, Conn.: Yale Univ. Press, 1984.

Keller, Charles Roy. *The Second Great Awakening in Connecticut.* New Haven, Conn.: Yale Univ. Press, 1942.

Kellert, Stephen R. *The Value of Life: Biological Diversity and Human Society.* Washington, DC: Island Press, 1996.

Kellert, Stephen R., and Edward O. Wilson, eds. *The Biophilia Hypothesis.* Washington, DC: Island Press, 1993.

Kelly, J. Frederick. *Early Connecticut Meetinghouses.* Vol. 2. New York: Columbia Univ. Press, 1948.

_____. *Early Domestic Architecture of Connecticut.* New Haven, Conn.: Yale Univ. Press, 1924.

Kerber, Linda. *Women of the Republic: Intellect & Ideology in Revolutionary America.* Chapel Hill: Univ. of North Carolina Press, 1980.

Kihn, Phyllis. "Connecticut Cabinetmakers Part I." *The Connecticut Historical Society Bulletin* 32, no. 4 (October 1967): 98-144

_____. "Connecticut Cabinetmakers Part II." *The Connecticut Historical Society Bulletin* 33, no. 1 (January 1968): 1-40.

King, Lester S. *Transformations in American Medicine: From Benjamin Rush to William Osler.* Baltimore: The Johns Hopkins Univ. Press, 1991.

Kirby, Edward. *Echoes of Iron.* Sharon, Conn.: Sharon Historical Society, 1998.

Klein, Cornelis, and Cornelius S. Hurlburt, Jr. *Manual of Mineralogy,* 21st ed. New York: John Wiley and Sons, 1999.

Klemens, Michael W. "Amphibians and Reptiles of Connecticut and Adjacent Regions." *Research Bulletin* No. 112. Hartford: State Geological and Natural History Survey of Connecticut, 1993.

Kling, David W. *A Field of Divine Wonders: The New Divinity and Village Revivals in Northwestern Connecticut, 1792-1822.* University Park, Penn.: Pennsylvania State Univ. Press, 1993.

Knoblauch, Harold C., Ernest M. Law, and W.P. Meyer. "State Agricultural Experiment Stations." *U.S. Department of Agriculture Miscellaneous Publication 904.* Washington, DC: Government Printing Office, 1962.

Konig, David. "English Legal Change and the Origins of Local Government in Northern Massachusetts." In *Town and County: Essays on the Structure of Local Government in the American Colonies,* edited by Bruce C. Daniels, 12-37. Middletown, Conn.: Wesleyan Univ. Press, 1978.

Kranakis, Eda. *Constructing A Bridge,* Cambridge, Mass.: M.I.T. Press, 1997.

Krout, Jon A., and Dixon R. Fox. *The Completion of Independence.* New York: Macmillan, 1944.

Kugelman, Alice, Thomas Kugelman, and Robert Lionetti." The Chapin School of East Windsor, Connecticut." *Maine Antique Digest* 22, no 1 (January 1994): 12-14.

Kugelman, Thomas, and Alice Kugelman. "The Hartford Case Furniture Survey." *Maine Antique Digest* 21, no. 3 (March 1993): Section A, 36-38.

Kulik, Gary. "Dams, Fish, and Farmers: Defence of Public Rights in Eighteenth-Century Rhode Island." In *The Countryside in the Age of Capitalist Transformation: Essays in the Social History of Rural America,* edited by Steven Hahn, and Jonathan Prude, 25-50. Chapel Hill, N.C.: Univ. of North Carolina Press, 1985.

Kulik, Gary, Roger Parks, and Theodore Z. Penn. *The New England Mill Village, 1790-1860.* Cambridge, Mass.: M.I.T. Press, 1982.

Labaree, Benjamin W., et. al. *America and the Sea.* Mystic, Conn.: Mystic Seaport, 1998.

Labaree, Leonard Woods, ed. *The Public Records of the State of Connecticut.* Vol. 5 (for 1783 and 1784).Hartford: The State of Connecticut, 1943.

Lacey, Barbara E. "Women in the Era of the American Revolution: The Case of Norwich, Connecticut." *New England Quarterly* 53 (December 1980): 527-543.

_____. "The World of Hannah Heaton: The Autobiography of an Eighteenth-Century Connecticut Farm Woman." *William and Mary Quarterly,* 3d ser. 65 (1988): 280-304.

Lamson, George H. "The Reptiles of Connecticut." *Research Bulletin* 54. Hartford: State Geological and Natural History Survey of Connecticut, 1935.

Larkin, Jack. *The Reshaping of Everyday Life, 1790-1840.* New York: Harper and Row, 1988.

Larned, Ellen D. *Historic Gleanings in Windham County, Connecticut.* Providence: Preston and Rounds, 1899.

_____. *History of Windham County, Connecticut.* 2 vols. Worcester, Mass.: Charles Hamilton, 1880.

Lathrop, Cornelia Penfield. *Black Rock Seaport of Old Fairfield Connecticut 1644-1870.* New Haven, Conn.: Tuttle, Morehouse & Taylor, 1930.

Leach, Douglas Edward. *The Northern Colonial Frontier 1607-1763.* New York: Holt, Rinehart and Winston, 1966.

Lee, William Storrs. *Yankees of Connecticut.* New York: Henry Holt, 1957.

Leggett, Morton D. compiler, *Subject Matter Index of Patents for Invention, 1790-1873.* Washington, DC: U.S. Government Printing Office, 1874.

Leonard, Abiel. *A Prayer Composed for the Benefit of the Soldiery.* Cambridge, Mass.: S. and E. Hall, 1775.

Lepore, Jill. The Name of War: King Philip's War and the Origins of American Identity. New York: Alfred A. Knopf, 1998.

Linsley, James H. "A Catalogue of the Mammals of Connecticut, Arranged According to their Natural Families." *American Journal of Science and Arts* 43 (1842): 345-354.

_____. "A Catalogue of the Reptiles of Connecticut Arranged According to their Families." *American Journal of Science and Arts* 46 (1844): 37-51.

Lionetti, Joseph, and Robert Trent. "New Information on Chapin Chairs." *Antiques* 129, no. 5 (May 1986): 1082-1095.

Litchfield, Carter, et. al, *The Bethlehem Oil Mill 1745-1934... German Technology in Early Pennsylvania.* Kemblesville, Penn.: Olearius Editions, 1984.

Litvaitis, John A. "Niche Relations between Coyotes and Sympatric Carnivora." In *Ecology and Management of the Eastern Coyote,* edited by A.H. Boer, 73-85. Fredericton: Wildlife Research Unit, 1992.

_____. "Response of Early Successional Vertebrates to Historic Changes in Land Use." *Conservation Biology* 7 (1993): 866-873.

Litvaitis, John A., and Daniel J. Harrison. "Bobcat-Coyote Niche Relationships during a Period of Coyote Population Increase." *Canadian Journal of Zoology* 67 (1989): 1180-1188.

Lockridge, Kenneth. *A New England Town: The First Hundred Years.* New York: W.W. Norton, 1970.

Loveday, Amos J. Jr. *The Rise and Decline of the American Cut Nail Industry.* Westport, Conn.: Greenwood Press, 1983.

Lush, James L. *Animal Breeding Plans.* Ames: Iowa State College Press, 1938.

MacDonald, Marshall. "The Connecticut and Housatonic Rivers and Minor Tributaries of Long Island Sound." In *History and Methods of the Fisheries.* Vol. 1. Section V of *The Fisheries and Fishery Industries of the United States,* edited by George Brown Goode, 659-667. Washington, DC: 1884-1887.

Main, Jackson Turner. *Connecticut Society in the Era of the American Revolution.* Hartford, Conn.: American Revolution Bicentennial Commission of Connecticut, 1977.

_____. *Society and Economy in Colonial Connecticut.* Princeton, N.J.: Princeton Univ. Press, 1985.

Maloney, Linda. *The Captain From Connecticut: Life and Times of Isaac Hull.* Boston: Northeastern Univ. Press, 1986.

Mann, Bruce H. *Neighbors and Strangers: Law and Community in Early Connecticut.* Chapel Hill, N.C.: Univ. of North Carolina Press, 1987.

Marini, Stephen A. *Radical Sects of Revolutionary New England.* Cambridge, Mass.: Harvard Univ. Press, 1982.

Martin, Jill E. "'Neither Fish, Flesh, Fowl, nor Good Red Herring:' The Citizenship Status of American Indians, 1830-1924." *Journal of the West,* Vol. XXIX, No. 3 (July 1990): 75-87.

Mason, John. *A Brief History of the Pequot War.* Boston, 1736; Ann Arbor: Univ. Microfilms, Inc., 1966.

[Massachusetts Historical Society] "Letters and Documents Relating to Slavery in Massachusetts." Massachusetts Historical Society, *Collections,* 5th ser., 3 (1877).

_____. "Queries Respecting the Slavery and Emancipation of Negroes in Massachusetts, Proposed by the Hon. Judge Tucker of Virginia, and Answered by the Rev. Dr. Belknap." Massachusetts Historical Society, *Collections,* 1st ser., 4 (1795).

Massachusetts Society for the Promotion of Agriculture. *Transactions.* Boston, 1853.

Mather, Moses. *America's Appeal to the Impartial World.* Hartford, Conn.: Ebenezer Watson, 1775.

Matson, Cathy. *Merchants and Empire: Trading in Colonial New York.* Baltimore: The Johns Hopkins Univ. Press, 1997.

Matthewson, Tim. "Abraham Bishop, 'The Rights of Black Men,' and the American Reaction to the Haitian Revolution." *Journal of Negro History* 67 (Summer 1982).

Mayhew, Edgar, and Minor Myers. *New London County Furniture 1640-1840.* New London, Conn.: Lyman Allyn Museum, 1974.

Mayr, Otto, and Robert C. Post, eds. *Yankee Enterprise.* Washington, DC: Smithsonian Institution Press, 1981.

McAndrews, J.H. "Human Disturbance of North American Forests and Grasslands: the Fossil Pollen Record." In *Vegetation History,* edited by B. Huntley, and T. Webb, III. Dordrecht, Netherlands: Kluwer Academic Publishers, 1988.

McCusker, John J., and Russell R. Menard. *The Economy of British America, 1607-1789.* Chapel Hill, N.C. and London: Univ. of North Carolina Press, 1985.

McGaw, Judith A. *Most Wonderful Machine; Mechanization and Social Change in Berkshire Paper Making, 1801-1885.* Princeton: Princeton Univ. Press, 1987.

McKay, Richard C. *South Street: A Maritime History of New York.* 1934. Revised reprint. Riverside, Conn.: 7 C's Press, 1969.

McKee, Linda Ann. "Health and Medicine in Connecticut, 1785-1810." Ph.D. diss., Univ. of New Mexico, 1971.

McKinley, Albert. *The Suffrage Requirements in the Thirteen English Colonies in America.* Philadelphia: The Univ. of Penn. Press, 1905.

McMurry, Sally. *Transforming Rural Life: Dairying Families and Agricultural Change, 1820-1885.* Baltimore: The Johns Hopkins Univ. Press, 1995.

Meade, R.H. "Sources, Sinks, and Storage of River Sediment in the Atlantic Drainage of the United States." *Journal of Geology* 90 (1982).

Mease, James, M.D. *Archives of Useful Knowledge, A Work Devoted to Commerce, Manufactures, Rural and Domestic Economy, Agriculture, and the Useful Arts.* Philadelphia: David Hogan, 1812.

Mech, L. David. *The Wolf: The Ecology and Behavior of an Endangered Species.* Garden City, N.J.: Natural History Press, 1970.

[*Medical Repository*] "Plan for Observations on the Weather, Seasons, and Physical Phenomena." *Medical Repository* 3 (1800): 299-300.

Melish, Joanne Pope. *Disowning Slavery: Gradual Emancipation and "Race" in New England, 1780-1860.* Ithaca: Cornell Univ. Press, 1998.

Melville, Herman. "Hawthorne and His Mosses." In *American Romanticism,* edited by Stanley Bank, 292-301. New York: Capricorn Books, 1969.

Memoirs of the Pennsylvania Agricultural Society. Philadelphia: J.S. Skinner, 1824.

Merchant, Carolyn. *Ecological Revolutions—Nature, Gender, and Science in New England.* Chapel Hill: Univ. of North Carolina Press, 1989.

Merriam, C. Hart. *A Review of the Birds of Connecticut.* New Haven, Conn.: Tuttle, Morehouse, and Taylor, 1877.

Merrill, George P. *The First One Hundred Years of American Geology.* New Haven, Conn.: Yale Univ. Press, 1924.

Messier, Betty Brook, and Janet Sutherland Aronson. *The Roots of Coventry, Connecticut.* Coventry, Conn.: The 275th Anniversary Committee, 1987.

Miller, Amelia F. *Connecticut River Valley Doorways: An Eighteenth-Century Flowering.* The Dublin Seminar for New England Folklife Occasional Publications. Boston: Boston Univ., 1993.

Miller, J.W., ed. *As We Were on the Valley Shore,* Guilford, Conn.: Shore Line Times Publishing Co., 1976.

Miller, Perry. *The New England Mind in the Seventeenth Century.* Cambridge, Mass.: Harvard Univ. Press, 1939.

Milne, George McLean. *Connecticut Woodlands: A Century's Story of the Connecticut Forest and Park Association.* Rockfall, Conn.: Connecticut Forest and Park Association, 1995.

Mirsky, Jeannette, and Allan Nevins. *The World of Eli Whitney.* New York: Macmillan, 1952.

Mitchell, Donald G. *Dr. Johns.* New York: Charles Scribner, 1866.

Mitchell, Isabel S. *Roads and Road Making in Colonial Connecticut,* New Haven, Conn.: Yale Univ. Press, 1933.

Mitchell, Mary H. "Slavery in Connecticut and Especially in New Haven." *Papers of the New Haven Colony Historical Society,* Vol. 10. New Haven, Conn.: The Society, 1951.

Mix, Irene H. *Connecticut Activities in the Wars of the Country; A Summary.* Washington, DC: Government Printing Office, 1932.

Mohanty, Gail Fowler. "Experimentation in Textile Technology, 1788-1790, and Its Impact on Handloom Weaving and Weavers in Rhode

Island." *Technology and Culture* 29 (1988): 1-31.

Molloy, Peter M., et al. *Homespun to Factory Made: Woolen Textiles in America 1776-1876*. North Andover, Mass., Merrimack Valley Textile Museum, 1977.

Moore, Gary C., and Gerry R. Parker. "Colonization by the Eastern Coyote (Canis latrans)." In *Ecology and Management of the Eastern Coyote*, edited by A.H. Boer, 23-37. Fredericton: Wildlife Research Unit, 1992.

Morgan, Edmund S. *The Gentle Puritan: A Life of Ezra Stiles 1727-1785*. New Haven, Conn.: Yale Univ. Press, 1962.

Morgan, Marion F. "Soils of Connecticut." *The Connecticut Agricultural Experiment Station Bulletin* 320 (September 1930): 911.

Morison, Samuel Eliot. *Builders of the Bay Colony*. Boston: Houghton Mifflin and Co., 1930.

Morse, Jarvis M. *A Neglected Period in Connecticut's History 1818-1850*, New Haven, Conn.: Yale Univ. Press, 1933 (reprint, 1978, New York: Octagon Books).

Morse, Jedidiah. *The American Geography*. Elizabeth Town [N.J.]: Shepard Kollock for the Author, 1789.

Morton, Thomas. *New English Canaan*. Edited by Charles F. Adams. Boston: Publications of the Prince Society, XIV, [1632] 1883.

Motzkin, Glenn, David R. Foster, Arthur Allen, Jonathon Harrod, and Richard Boone. "Controlling Site to Evaluate History: Vegetation Patterns of a New England Sand Plain." *Ecological Monographs* 66 (1996): 345-365.

Moynihan, Ruth B. *Coming of Age: Four Centuries of Connecticut Women*. Hartford, Conn.: Connecticut Historical Society for Connecticut Women's History Project, 1989, 1991.

Moynihan, Ruth B., Cynthia Russett, and Laurie Crumpacker, eds. *Second to None, A Documentary History of American Women, Vol. I: From the 16th Century to 1865*. Lincoln: Univ. of Nebraska Press, 1993.

Mulholland, James A. *A History of Metals in Colonial America*. Tuscaloosa: Univ. of Alabama Press, 1981.

Multhauf, Robert P. "Potash." In *Material Culture of the Wooden Age*, edited by Brooke Hindle. Tarrytown, New York: Sleepy Hollow Press, 1981.

Nash, Gary. *Forging Freedom: The Formation of Philadelphia's Black Community, 1720-1840*. Cambridge, Mass.: Harvard Univ. Press, 1988.

_____. *Freedom by Degrees: Emancipation in Pennsylvania and Its Aftermath*. New York: Oxford Univ. Press, 1991.

Navin, Thomas R. *The Whitin Machine Works Since 1831*. Cambridge, Mass.: Harvard Univ. Press, 1950.

Nevins, Allan. *James Truslow Adams: Historian of the American Dream*. Urbana, Chicago, and London: Univ. of Illinois Press, 1968.

New Haven County Medical Society, *Cases and Observations; by the Medical Society of New Haven County, in the State of Connecticut, Instituted in the Year 1784*. New Haven, Conn.: Printed by J. Meigs, 1788.

Newman, Richard. "The Transformation of American Abolition: Tactics, Strategies and the Changing Meanings of Activism, 1780s-1830s." Ph.D. diss., State Univ. of New York at Buffalo, 1998.

Niering, W.A., and G.D. Dreyer. "Effects of Prescribed Burning on Andropogon scoparius in Postagricultural Grassland." *American Midland Naturalist* 122 (1989): 88-102.

Niering, W.A., and R.S. Warren. "Vegetation Patterns and Processes in New England Salt Marshes." *BioScience* 30 (5): 301-307.

Niering, W.A., R.H. Goodwin, and S. Taylor. "Prescribed Burning in Southern New England: Introduction to Long-range Studies." In *Proceedings* 10th Annual Tall Timbers Fire Ecology Conference, 267-286. Tallahassee, Fl., 1970.

Norton, Frederick Calvin. "Negro Slavery in Connecticut." *The Connecticut Magazine* 5 (June 1899).

Norton, Mary Beth. *Liberty's Daughters: The Revolutionary Experience of American Women, 1750-1800*. Boston: Little, Brown and Co., 1980.

Nylander, Jane. *Our Own Snug Fireside: Images of the New England Home, 1760-1860*. New York: Alfred A. Knopf, 1993.

O'Callaghan, E.B., and Berthold Fernow, ed. and trans. *Documents Relative to the Colonial History of the State of New York*. 15 vols. New York, 1865-1887.

O'Connell, Barry, ed. *On Our Own Ground: The Complete Writings of William Apess, A Pequot*. Amherst: Univ. of Massachusetts Press, 1992.

Osterweis, Rollin G. "The Sesquicentennial History of the Connecticut Academy of Arts and Sciences." *Transactions* of the Connecticut Academy of Arts and Sciences. Vol. 38 (1949): 105-149.

_____. *Three Centuries of New Haven, 1638-1938*. New Haven, Conn.: Yale Univ. Press, 1953.

Otis, Harrison G. *Otis' Letters in Defence of the Hartford Convention and the People of Massachusetts*. Boston: Simon Gardner, 1824.

Palmer, T.S. "Chronology and Index of the More Important Events in American Game Protection, 1776-1911." *Bulletin* No. 41. Washington, DC: USDA Biological Survey, 1912.

Pares, Richard. *Yankees and Creoles: The Trade between North America and the West Indies before the American Revolution*. Cambridge, Mass.: Harvard Univ. Press, 1956.

Pasquier, Roger F. *Watching Birds: An Introduction to Ornithology*. Boston: Houghton-Mifflin Co., 1977.

Patton, P.C. "Geomorphic Response of Streams to Floods in the Glaciated Terrain of Southern New England." In *Flood Geomorphology*, edited by V.R. Baker, R.C. Kochel, and P.C. Patton. New York: John Wiley & Sons, 1988.

Pease, John C. and John M. Niles. *A Gazetteer of the States of Connecticut and Rhode- Island*. Hartford, Conn.: William S. Marsh, 1819.

Perkins, Mary E. *Chronicles of a Connecticut Farm*. Boston, 1905.

Perkins, Nathan. "A Sermon, Preached June 2, 1775." Hartford: Ebenezer Watson, 1775.

Pernick, Martin S. "Politics, Parties, and Pestilence: Epidemic Yellow Fever in Philadelphia and the Rise of the First Party System." In *A Melancholy State of Devastation: The Public Response to the 1793 Philadelphia Yellow Fever Epidemic*, edited by J. Worth Estes and Billy G. Smith, 119-146. New York: Science History Publications, 1997.

Peterson, William N. "'Bony-Fish': The Menhaden Fishery at Mystic, Connecticut." *Log of Mystic Seaport* 33 (1981): 23-36.

_____. *Mystic Built: Ships and Shipyards of the Mystic River 1784-1919*. Mystic, Conn.: Mystic Seaport Museum, 1989.

Phelps, Noah A. *History of Simsbury, Granby, and Canton from 1642-1845*. Hartford, Conn.: Case, Tiffany & Burnham, 1845.

Phillips, Ulrich Bonnell. *American Negro Slavery: A Survey of the Supply, Employment and Control of Negro Labor as Determined by the Plantation Regime*. Baton Rouge: Louisiana State Univ. Press, 1969. (First published in 1918.)

Pickering, Timothy. "An Address from the Philadelphia Society for Promoting Agriculture, with a Summary of Its Laws." Philadelphia, 1785, excerpts reprinted in *Readings in the History of American Agriculture*, edited by Wayne D. Rasmussen, 42-44. Urbana: Univ. of Illinois Press 1960.

Piersen, William D. *Black Yankees: The Development of an Afro-American Subculture in Eighteenth-Century New England*. Amherst, Mass.: Univ. of Massachusetts Press, 1988.

Preston, Howard W. "Godfrey Malbone's Connecticut Investment." *Collections* of the Rhode Island Historical Society, 16 (October 1923).

Pringle, Laurence P. "Notes on Coyotes in Southern New England." *Journal of Mammalogy* 41 (1960): 278.

Prucha, Francis Paul. *American Indian Policy in the Formative Years: Indian Trade and Intercourse Acts, 1790-1834*. Cambridge, Mass.: Harvard Univ. Press, 1962.

_____, ed. *Documents of United States Indian Policy*. 2d ed. Lincoln: Univ. of Nebraska Press, 1990.

Prude, Jonathan. *The Coming of Industrial Order; Town and Factory Life in Rural Massachusetts 1810-1860*. New York: Cambridge Univ. Press, 1983.

Public Records. *Public Records of the Colony of Connecticut, 1636-1776*. Edited by J. Hammond Trumbull and Charles J. Hoadley. 15 vols. Hartford, Conn.: Case, Lockwood & Brainard Co., 1850-1890.

_____. *Records of the Colony and Plantation of New Haven, 1638-1665*. Edited by Charles J. Hoadley. 2 vols. Hartford, Conn., 1857-1858.

_____. *Public Records of the State of Connecticut*. Edited by Charles J. Hoadley, et al. 16 vols. to date. Hartford: Case, Lockwood and Brainard, 1894.

Purcell, Richard J. *Connecticut in Transition, 1775-1818*. Middletown, Conn.: Wesleyan Univ. Press, 1963. (First published in 1918.)

Pursell, Carroll W., Jr. *Early Stationary Steam Engines in America*. Washington, DC: Smithsonian Institution Press, 1969.

Quen, Jacques M. "Elisha Perkins, Physician, Nostrum-Vendor, or Charlatan?" *Bulletin of the History of Medicine* 37 (1963): 159-166.

Rasmussen, Wayne D., ed. *Readings in the History of American Agriculture*. Urbana: Univ. of Illinois Press, 1960.

Raymo, Chet, and Maureen E. Raymo. *Written in Stone: A Geological and Natural History of the Northeastern United States*. Chester,

Conn.: Globe Pequot Press, 1989.

Records of the 1820 Census of Manufactures: Schedules for Connecticut. National Archives Microfilm Publications #279, Roll 4.

Reynolds, R.V., and Albert H. Pierson. *Fuel Wood Used in the United States, 1630-1930.* United States Department of Agriculture Circular 641. Washington, DC: Government Printing Office, 1942.

Reynolds, Terry S. *Stronger Than a Hundred Men: A History of the Vertical Water Wheel.* Baltimore: The Johns Hopkins Univ. Press, 1981.

Rifkin, Jeremy. *Beyond Beef: The Rise and Fall of the Cattle Culture.* New York: Dutton, 1992.

Ritvo, Harriet. *The Animal Estate: The English and Other Creatures in the Victorian Age.* Cambridge, Mass.: Harvard Univ. Press, 1987.

Riznik, Barnes. "The Professional Lives of Early Nineteenth-Century New England Doctors." *Journal of the History of Medicine and Allied Sciences* 19 (1964): 1-16.

Rodgers, John. *Bedrock Geology Map of Connecticut.* Connecticut State Department of Environmental Protection / U.S. Geological Survey: Scale 1:125,000 (1985).

Roe, Joseph W. "Early New Haven Inventors." In *Inventors and Engineers of Old New Haven,* edited by Richard Shelton Kirby. New Haven, Conn.: New Haven Colony Historical Society, 1939.

———. *English and American Tool Builders.* New Haven, Conn.: Yale Univ. Press, 1916.

Roorda, Eric. "Our Position is a Most Commanding One." *The Log of Mystic Seaport,* Winter 1993; Spring 1994.

Rosen, George "Noah Webster—Historical Epidemiologist." *Journal of the History of Medicine and Allied Sciences* 20 (1965): 97-114.

Rosenberg, Charles E. *The Care of Strangers: The Rise of America's Hospital System.* New York: Basic Books, 1987.

———. "The Therapeutic Revolution: Medicine, Meaning, and Social Change in Nineteenth-Century America." In *The Therapeutic Revolution: Essays in the Social History of American Medicine,* edited by Morris J. Vogel and Charles H. Rosenberg, 3-25. Philadelphia: Univ. of Pennsylvania Press, 1979.

Rosenberg, Charles E., and William Helfand. *"Every Man His Own Doctor": Popular Medicine in Early America.* Philadelphia: The Library Company of Philadelphia, 1998.

Rosenberg, Nathan. "America's Rise to Woodworking Leadership." In *America's Wooden Age: Aspects of its Early Technology,* edited by Brooke Hindle, 37-62. Tarrytown, New York: Sleepy Hollow Restorations, 1975.

———, ed. *The American System of Manufactures.* Edinburgh: Edinburgh Univ. Press, 1969.

Rosivach, Vincent. "Three Petitions by Connecticut Negroes for the Abolition of Slavery in Connecticut." *Connecticut Review* (Fall 1995).

Rossiter, Margaret W. *Emergence of Agricultural Science. Justus Liebig and the Americans, 1840-1880.* New Haven, Conn.: Yale Univ. Press, 1975.

———. "The Organization of the Agricultural Sciences." In *The Organization of Knowledge in America, 1860-1920,* edited by Alexandra Oleson and John Voss. Baltimore: The Johns Hopkins Univ. Press, 1979.

Roth, David M. *Connecticut: A Bicentennial History.* New York: W.W. Norton, 1979.

Rothenberg, Winifred B. *From Market-places to a Market Economy.* Chicago: Univ. of Chicago Press, 1992.

Roys, A. *A Brief History of the Town of Norfolk from 1738 to 1844.* New York: Henry Ludwig, 1847.

Royster, Charles. *A Revolutionary People at War.* Chapel Hill: Univ. of North Carolina Press, 1979.

Ruffner, J.A. "Climate of Connecticut." In *Climate of the States.* Vol. I. Alabama; New Mexico; Detroit, Michigan: Gale Research Company, 1985.

Russell, Howard S. *A Long, Deep Furrow: Three Centuries of Farming in New England.* Hanover, N.H.: Univ. Press of New England, 1976.

———. *Indian New England before the Mayflower.* Hanover, N.H.: Univ. Press of New England, 1980.

Russo, Jean. "Self-Sufficiency and Local Exchange: Free Craftsmen in the Rural Chesapeake Economy." In *Colonial Chesapeake Society,* edited by Lois Carr, Philip Morgan, and Jean Russo, 389-432. Chapel Hill: Univ. of North Carolina Press, 1988.

Sage, Henry P. "Ye Mylestones of Connecticut." *Papers of the New Haven Colony Historical Society,* Vol. 10. New Haven, Conn.: The Society, 1951.

Schairer, John Frank. *Minerals of Connecticut.* Hartford, Conn.: The State Geological and Natural History Survey (1931): Bulletin 51.

Schapsmeier, Edward L., and Frederick H. Schapsmeier. *Encyclopedia of American Agriculture.* Westport, Conn.: Greenwood Press, 1975.

Schenck, Elizabeth H. *The History of Fairfield, Fairfield County, Connecticut.* New York: J.J. Little & Co., 1889.

Schneer, Cecil J., ed. *Two Hundred Years of Geology in America.* Hanover, N.H.: Univ. of New Hampshire Press, 1979.

Schwartz, Hillel. "Admissions to Full Communion in the Congregational Churches of Connecticut, 1635-1799." Typescript at the Connecticut Historical Society.

Segal, Charles M., and David C. Stineback. *Puritans, Indians, and Manifest Destiny.* New York: G.P. Putnam's Sons, 1977.

Sewall, Samuel. "The Selling of Joseph: A Memorial." Boston: Bartholomew Green and John Allen,1700.

Shelton, Jane DeForest. "The New England Negro. A Remnant." *Harper's New Monthly Magazine* 88 (December 1893-May 1894): 533-538.

Shepard, Charles U. *A Report on the Geological Survey of Connecticut.* New Haven, Conn.: published by the State, 1837.

Shepard, Odell. *Connecticut Past and Present.* New York: Alfred A. Knopf, 1939.

Sherrow, Doris. "Murder in Middletown: Lower-Class Life in Connecticut in 1815." In *House and Home: The Dublin Seminar for New England Folklife Annual Proceedings 1988,* edited by Peter Benes, 89-100. Boston: Boston Univ. Press, 1990.

Shideler, James H. "Agricultural History Studies: A Retrospective View." In *Outstanding in His Field: Perspectives on American Agriculture in Honor of Wayne D. Rasmussen,* edited by Frederick V. Carstensen, Morton Rothstein, and Joseph A. Swanson. Ames, Iowa: Iowa State Univ. Press, 1993.

Shurtleff, Nathaniel B., ed. *Records of the Governor and Company of the Massachusetts Bay in New England.* 6 vols. in 5 parts. Boston, 1853-54.

Silliman, Benjamin. "Sketch of the Mineralogy of the Town of New Haven." In *Memoirs.* Vol. 1, 83-96. New Haven, Conn.: Connecticut Academy of Arts and Sciences, 1810.

———. "Sketches of a Tour in the Counties of New-Haven and Litchfield in Connecticut..." *American Journal of Science, and Arts,* Vol. 2, no. 2 (November 1820): 230.

Silverman, Kenneth. *Timothy Dwight.* New York: Twayne Publishers, 1969.

Simmons, Amelia. *American Cookery.* Hartford, Conn.: Hudson & Goodwin, 1796.

Sinclair, Lowell R., L.L. Getz, and F.S. Bock. "Influence of Stone Walls on the Local Distribution of Small Mammals." Storrs: Univ. of Connecticut Occasional Papers, Biological Sciences Series 1 (1967): 43-62.

Sinnott, Edmund Ware. *Meetinghouse and Church in Early New England.* New York: McGraw-Hill, 1963.

Skinner, Brian J., and Barbara L. Narendra. "Rummaging Through the Attic: A Brief History of the Geological Sciences at Yale." In *Geologists and Ideas: A History of North American Geology,* edited by E.T. Drake, and W.M. Jordan. Centennial Special Volume 1, 355-376. Geological Society of America, 1985.

Skinner, Brian. J., and Stephen C. Porter. *The Dynamic Earth: An Introduction to Physical Geology.* New York: John Wiley and Sons, 2000.

Skinner, Stephen P. "The Maritime Economy of Fairfield, Connecticut 1793-1820." n.p. Paper delivered at the Spring 1997 meeting of the North American Society of Oceanic Historians in Newport, Rhode Island.

Sklar, Kathryn Kish. *Catharine Beecher: A Study in American Domesticity.* New Haven, Conn.: Yale Univ. Press, 1973.

Slater, James. *The Colonial Burial Grounds of Eastern Connecticut and the Men Who Made Them. Memoirs* of the Connecticut Academy of Arts and Sciences, Vol. 21, 1987.

Slough, Brian G., and R.M.F. S. Sadlier. "A Land Capability Classification System for Beaver (Castor canadensis Kuhl.)." *Canadian Journal of Zoology* 55 (1977): 1324-1335.

Sly, John Fairfield. *Town Government in Massachusetts, 1620-1660.* Chap. III. Cambridge, Mass.: Harvard Univ. Press, 1930.

Smith, Cyril Stanley. "The Discovery of Carbon in Steel." *Technology and Culture* 5 (1964): 149-175.

Smith, Elihu Hubbard. *The Diary of Elihu Hubbard Smith* (1771-1798). Edited by James A. Cronin. Philadelphia: American Philosophical Society, 1973.

Smith, Gaddis. "Agricultural Roots of Maritime History." *American Neptune*, Vol. 44 (1984).

Smith, Harvey R., and Charles L. Remington. "Food Specificity in Interspecies Competition: Comparisons between Terrestrial Vertebrates and Arthropods." *BioScience* 46 (1996): 436-447.

Smith, Harvey R., and Noble S. Proctor. "No Home to Return to." *Discovery* 21 (Feb 1989): 2-7.

Smith, John Cotton. "An Oration, Pronounced at Sharon, on the Anniversary of American Independence, 4th of July 1798." Litchfield, Conn.: T. Collier, 1798.

Smith, Merritt Roe. *Harpers Ferry Armory and the New Technology.* Ithaca: Cornell Univ. Press, 1977.

Smith, Venture. *A Narrative of the Life and Adventures of Venture, a Native of Africa, but Resident Sixty Years in the United States of America.* New London, Conn.: C. Holt, 1798.

Spivak, Burton. *Jefferson's English Crisis: Commerce, Embargo, and the Republican Revolution.* Charlottesville, Va.: Univ. Press of Virginia, 1979.

Sprague, Seth. "Neat Cattle." *Transactions of the Agricultural Societies in the State of Massachusetts for 1852,* 726-731. Boston: Dutton and Wentworth, 1853.

Spurr, Stephen H. "Forest Associations in the Harvard Forest." *Ecological Monographs* 26 (1956): 245-262.

St. George, Robert Blair. "Artifacts of Regional Consciousness in the Connecticut River Valley, 1700-1780." In *The Great River: Art & Society of the Connecticut River Valley, 1635-1820,* edited by William Hosley and Gerald Ward. Hartford: Wadsworth Atheneum, 1985.

Stagg, J.C.A. *Mr. Madison's War: Politics, Diplomacy, and Warfare in the Early American Republic, 1783-1830.* Princeton: Princeton Univ. Press, 1983.

Stamps, Norman L. "Political Parties in Connecticut 1789-1819." Ph.D. diss., Yale Univ., 1950.

Stanley, George W. "An Oration Delivered at Wallingford, August 8, 1805. In Commemoration of the Independence of the United States." New Haven, Conn.: Sidney's Press, 1805.

Stark, Bruce P. "Freemanship in Lebanon, Connecticut: A Case Study." *Connecticut History 2* (Jan. 1975): 27-48.

_____. "Slavery in Connecticut: A Re-Examination." *The Connecticut Review* 9 (Nov. 1975): 75-81.

Stark, Charles R. *Groton, Conn. 1705-1905.* Stonington, Conn.: Palmer Press, 1922.

State of New Hampshire Manual for The General Court. Concord, N.H.: Department of State, 1975.

Staudenraus, Philip J. *The African Colonization Movement, 1816-1865.* New York: Columbia Univ. Press, 1961.

Steiner, Bernard C. *A History of the Plantation of Menunkatuck.* Baltimore: Steiner, 1897.

_____. *History of Slavery in Connecticut.* Baltimore: Johns Hopkins Press, 1893.

Steiner, Bruce E., "Anglican Officeholding in Pre-Revolutionary Connecticut: The Parameters of New England Community." *William and Mary Quarterly 31* (July 1974): 369-406.

Steinman David B., and Sara R. Watson. *Bridges and Their Builders.* New York: Dover, 1957.

Stevens, Thomas A. "Connecticut River Navigation." In *As We Were on the Valley Shore,* edited by James W. Miller. Guilford, Conn., 1976.

Stewart, James Brewer. "The Emergence of Racial Modernity and the Rise of the White North, 1790-1840." *Journal of the Early Republic* 18 (Summer 1998): 181-217.

Stookey, Byron. "A Medical Society for the Massachusetts, York and Connecticut Physicians, 1779-1790." *Connecticut Medicine* 30 (3) (March 1966): 189-192.

Stout, Harry S. *The New England Soul: Preaching and Religious Culture in Colonial New England.* New York: Oxford Univ. Press, 1986.

Stowe, Harriet Beecher. "The Mayflower." Quoted in *The Autobiography of Lyman Beecher,* edited by Barbara M. Cross. Cambridge, Mass.: Harvard Univ. Press, 1961.

_____. *Old Town Folks.* New York: The Library of America, 1982. [1869].

Strane, Susan. *A Whole-Souled Woman: Prudence Crandall and the Education of Black Women.* New York: W.W. Norton, 1990.

Strasser, Susan. *Never Done: A History of American Housework.* New York: Pantheon, 1982.

Sutermeister, Edwin. *The Story of Papermaking.* Boston: S.D. Warren Co., 1954.

Sweeney, Kevin M. "From Wilderness to Arcadian Vale: Material Life in the Connecticut River Valley, 1735-1820." In *The Great River: Art & Society of the Connecticut River Valley, 1635-1820,* edited by William Hosley and Gerald Ward. Hartford: Wadsworth Atheneum, 1985.

_____. "Meetinghouses, Town Houses, and Churches: Changing Perceptions of Sacred and Secular Space in Southern New England, 1720-1850." *Winterthur Portfolio* 28 (Spring 1993): 59-93.

Swift, Zephaniah. "An Oration on Domestic Slavery." Hartford, Hudson and Goodwin 1791.

_____. *A System of the Laws of the State of Connecticut.* 2 vols. Windham: the Author, 1795.

Tannenbaum, Rebecca J. "'What is Best to Be Done for These Fevers': Elizabeth Davenport's Medical Practice in New Haven Colony." *New England Quarterly* 70 (1997): 265-284.

_____. "A Woman's Calling: Woman's Medical Practice in New England, 1650-1750." Ph.D. diss., Yale Univ., 1996.

Taylor, Philip E. "The Turnpike Era in New England." Ph.D. diss., Yale University, 1934.

Taylor, Robert J. *Colonial Connecticut: A History.* Millwood, New York: KTO Press, 1979.

Thomas, John Carl. *Connecticut Pewter and Pewterers.* Hartford, Conn.: Connecticut Historical Society, 1976.

Thoms, Herbert. *The Doctors of Yale College 1702-1815 and The Founding of the Medical Institution.* Hamden, Conn.: Shoe String Press, 1960.

_____. ed. *The Heritage of Connecticut Medicine.* New Haven, Conn.: Whaples-Bullis Co., 1942.

Thomson, Ross. *The Path to Mechanized Shoe Production in the United States.* Chapel Hill: Univ. of North Carolina Press, 1989.

Thorson, R.M., A.G. Harris, S.L. Harris, R. Gradie III, and M.W. Lefor. "Colonial Impacts to Wetlands in Lebanon, Connecticut." In *A Paradox of Power: Voices of Warning and Reason in the Geosciences,* edited by C. Welby and M.E. Gowan. *Reviews in Engineering Geology,* Vol. XII, 23-42. Boulder, Colo.: Geological Society of America, 1998.

Townshend, Doris B. *Journal of a Gentleman Farmer 1829-1832.* East Haven, Conn.: East Haven Historical Society, 1985.

Trent, Robert, and Nancy Lee Nelson. "New London County Joined Chairs 1720-1790." *The Connecticut Historical Society Bulletin 50,* no. 4 (Fall 1985).

Trowbridge, W.P. "Town's Truss." *Columbia School of Mines Quarterly* (July 1888): 13.

True, Rodney H. "The Early Development of Agricultural Societies in the United States." *Annual Report of the American Historical Association for 1920.* Washington, DC: Government Printing Office, 1925.

Trumbull, Benjamin. *A Complete History of Connecticut, Civil and Ecclesiastical, from the Emigration of Its First Planters from England in 1630 to 1713.* Hartford, Conn.: Hudson and Goodwin, 1797.

_____. *A Complete History of Connecticut from the Emigration of Its First Planters from England, in the Year 1630, to the Year 1764; and to the Close of the Indian Wars.* New Haven, Conn.: Maltby, Goldsmith & Co., and Samuel Wadsworth, 1818.

Trumbull, J. Hammond, and Charles J. Hoadley, eds. *Public Records of the Colony of Connecticut, 1636-1776.* 15 vols. Hartford, Conn.: Case, Lockwood & Brainard Co., 1850-1894.

Tucker, Barbara M. *Samuel Slater and the Origins of the American Textile Industry, 1790-1860.* Ithaca: Cornell Univ. Press, 1984.

Tucker, St. George. "A Dissertation on Slavery: With a Proposal for the Gradual Abolition of It, in the State of Virginia." Philadelphia: Matthew Carey, 1796.

Turner, Lynn W. *William Plummer of New Hampshire.* Chapel Hill: Univ. of North Carolina Press, 1962.

Tuttle, Sam. *Sam Tuttle's Picture Book of Old Connecticut.* Scotia, New York: Americana Review, 1979.

Twamley, Josiah. *Dairying Exemplified, or The Business of Cheesemaking: Laid Down from Approved Rules, Collected from the Most Experienced Dairy-women, of Several Counties.* First American ed. from the second British ed. Providence, R.I.: Carter and Wilkinson, 1796.

Ulrich, Laurel Thatcher. *A Midwife's Tale: The Life of Martha Ballard, Based on Her Diary, 1785-1812.* New York: Alfred A. Knopf, 1990.

U.S. Bureau of the Census. *1992 Census of Agriculture, Connecticut State and County Data.* Washington, DC: Government Printing Office, 1994.

_____. *Historical Statistics of the U.S., Colonial Times to 1970.* Washington, DC: Government Printing Office, 1975.

_____. *Statistical Abstract of the U.S.* Washington, DC: Government Printing Office, 1996.

U.S. Census Office. *Statistics of Agriculture.* Washington, DC: Government Printing Office, 1895.

U.S. Department of Agriculture. *Agricultural Statistics.* Washington, DC: Government Printing Office,1993.

Van Dusen, Albert E. *Connecticut.* New York: Random House, 1961.

Vaughan, Alden T. *New England Frontier: Puritans and Indians 1620-1675.* Boston: Little, Brown and Company, 1965.

Vickers, Daniel. *Farmers and Fishermen: Two Centuries of Work in Essex County, Massachusetts, 1630-1850.* Chapel Hill: Univ. of North Carolina Press, 1994.

_____. "Nantucket Whalemen in the Deep-Sea Fishery: The Changing Anatomy of an Early American Labor Force." *Journal of American History* 72, (1985): 277-296.

Waggoner, Paul E. "Research and Education in American Agriculture." *Agricultural History* 50 (1976): 230-247.

Wall, R.B. "New London Shipbuilding Boomed." *The Day,* Feb. 13, 1926.

Wallach, Gert M.K., M.D. "Background of the Litchfield County Medical Association of 1767." *Connecticut Medicine* 31 (4) (April 1967): 270-271.

Walsh, James. "'Mechanics and Citizens': The Connecticut Artisan Protest of 1792." *William and Mary Quarterly* 42, no. 1 (January 1985): 66-89.

Warner, John Harley. *The Therapeutic Perspective: Medical Practice, Knowledge, and Identity in America, 1820-1885.* Princeton: Princeton Univ. Press, 1997.

Warren, Charles. *Jacobin and Junto; or, Early American Politics as Viewed in the Diary of Dr. Nathaniel Ames, 1758-1822.* Cambridge, Mass.: Harvard Univ. Press, 1931.

Warren, H.C. "Thoroughfares in Early Republic Controlled by Corporations." *Connecticut Magazine* 8 (1903): 721-729.

Watkins, Lura Woodside. *Early New England Potters and Their Wares.* Cambridge, Mass.: Harvard Univ. Press, 1950.

Watson, Elkanah. *History of the Rise, Progress, and Existing Conditions of the Western Canals in the State of New York from September 1788 to 1819. Together with the Rise, Progress, and Existing State of Modern Agricultural Societies, on the Berkshire System, from 1807 to the Establishment of the Board of Agriculture in the State of New York, January 10, 1820.* Albany: D. Steele, 1820.

Watson, Patricia A. *The Angelical Conjunction: The Preacher-Physicians of Colonial New England.* Knoxville: Univ. of Tennessee Press, 1991.

Wayne, Robert K., and Niles Lehman. "Mitochondrial DNA Analysis of the Eastern Coyote: Origins and Hybridization." In *Ecology and Management of the Eastern Coyote,* edited by A.H. Boer, 9-22. Fredericton: Wildlife Research Unit, 1992.

Webb, Sidney, and Beatrice Webb. *Manor and the Borough.* 2 vols. New York: Longmans, Green and Co., 1908.

_____. *The Parish and the County.* New York: Longmans, Green and Co., 1906.

Webster, Noah. *A Brief History of Epidemic and Pestilential Diseases; with the Principal Phenomena of the Physical World, Which Precede and Accompany Them, and Observations Deduced from the Facts Stated.* Hartford: Hudson & Goodwin, 1799.

_____. *Collection of Papers on the Subject of Bilious Fevers, Prevalent in the United States for a Few Years Past.* New York: Hopkins, Webb and Co., 1796.

_____. *A Compendious Dictionary of the English Language.* [A facsimile of the first (1806) edition]. New York: Crown Publishers, 1970.

_____. *Effects of Slavery on Morals and Industry.* Hartford: Hudson and Goodwin, 1793.

_____. *Noah Webster: Letters on Yellow Fever Addressed to Dr. William Currie.* Baltimore: The Johns Hopkins Univ. Press, 1947.

_____. "To the Clergymen or Other Well-Informed Gentlemen in the Several Towns in Connecticut." New Haven, Conn., May 7, 1798, circular reprinted in *Medical Repository* 2 (1799): 112-114.

Welch, Marvis Olive. *Prudence Crandall: A Biography.* Manchester, Conn.: Jason Publishers, 1983.

Weld, Ralph Foster. *Slavery in Connecticut.* Hartford, Conn.: Tercentenary Commission of the State of Connecticut, 1935.

Welsh, Charles, ed. *The Works of Henry Wadsworth Longfellow.* 6 vols. Cambridge, Mass., and New York: Wadsworth House, 1909.

Westbrook, Perry D. *The New England Town in Fact and Fiction.* Rutherford, N.J., Fairleigh Dickinson Univ. Press, 1982.

Wetzel, Ralph. "The Invasion of Connecticut." University of Connecticut at Storrs, 1979. (unpublished).

White, C. Langdon, Edwin J. Foscue, and Tom L. McKnight. *Regional Geography of Anglo-America* 3d ed. Englewood Cliffs, NJ: Prentice-Hall, 1964.

White, David O. *Connecticut's Black Soldiers, 1775-1783.* Chester, Conn.: Pequot Press, 1973.

White, Shane. *Somewhat More Independent: The End of Slavery in New York City, 1770-1810.* Athens, Ga.: Univ. of Georgia Press, 1991.

Whitney, Gordon G. *From Coastal Wilderness to Fruited Plain: a History of Environmental Change in Temperate North America, 1500 to the Present.* Cambridge, England: Cambridge Univ. Press, 1994.

Wilcox, Bruce A., and Dennis D. Murphy. "Conservation Strategy: The Effects of Fragmentation on Extinction." *American Naturalist* 125 (1985): 879-887.

Williams, Meredith, and Gray Williams, Jr. "'MD. by Thos. Gold': The Gravestones of a New Haven Carver." *Markers* 5 (1988): 1-59.

Williams, Michael. *Americans and their Forests, a Historical Geography.* Cambridge: Cambridge Univ. Press, 1989.

Willingham, William. "Deference Democracy and Town Government in Windham, Connecticut, 1755 to 1786." *William and Mary Quarterly* 30 (July 1973).

Wilson, Edward O. *Biophilia.* Cambridge, Mass.: Harvard Univ. Press, 1984.

Wilson, Leonard G., ed. *Benjamin Silliman and His Circle: Studies on the Influence of Benjamin Silliman on Science in America.* New York: Science History Publications, 1979.

Wilson, Woodrow. *A History of the American People.* New York: Harper and Brothers, 1901.

Winthrop Family. *Winthrop Papers.* Vol. VI. Boston, Mass.: Massachusetts Historical Society, 1929-.

Winthrop, John. *Winthrop's Journal: "History of New England."* Edited by James Kendall Hosmer. 2 vols. New York: Charles Scribner's Sons, 1946.

Withey, Lynne. *Urban Growth in Rhode Island: Newport and Providence in the Eighteenth Century.* Albany: State Univ. of New York Press, 1984.

Wood, Frederic J. *The Turnpikes of New England,* Boston: Marshall Jones Co., 1919.

Wood, Gordon S. *The Radicalism of the American Revolution.* New York: Alfred A. Knopf, 1992.

Wood, Joseph S. *The New England Village.* Baltimore and London: The Johns Hopkins Univ. Press, 1997.

Wood, William. *New England's Prospect.* Edited by Alden T. Vaughan. Amherst, Mass.: Univ. of Massachusetts Press, [1634] 1977.

Worrell, John. "Ceramic Production in the Exchange Network of an Agricultural Neighborhood." In *Domestic Pottery of the Northeastern United States, 1625-1850,* edited by Sarah Turnbaugh. New York: Academic Press, 1985.

Worster, D. "Transformations of the Earth; Toward an Agroecological Perspective in History." *Journal of American History* 76 (1990): 1087-1106.

Yahner, Richard H. *Eastern Deciduous Forest Ecology and Wildlife Conservation.* Minneapolis: Univ. of Minnesota Press, 1995.

Yergin, Daniel. *The Prize: The Epic Quest for Oil, Money, and Power.* New York: Simon & Schuster, 1991.

Youngs, J. William T. *The Congregationalists.* New York: Greenwood Press, 1990.

_____. *God's Messengers: Religious Leadership in Colonial New England, 1700-1750.* Baltimore: The Johns Hopkins Univ. Press, 1976.

Zea, Philip. *Pursuing Refinement in Rural New England 1750-1850.* Deerfield, Mass.: Historic Deerfield, Inc., 1998.

Zilversmit, Arthur. *The First Emancipation: The Abolition of Slavery in the North.* Chicago: Univ. of Chicago Press, 1967.

Index

Illustrations, photographs, and tables are indicated by **boldface** page numbers. An italicized *f* before a number denotes a figure number, and a *t* indicates a table number. For specific information not listed under towns and counties, see under topics (questions) such as agriculture, religion and churches, Indians, etc.